Pro BizTalk 2006

George Dunphy and
Ahmed Metwally

Apress®

Pro BizTalk 2006

ISBN-13 (pbk): 978-1-59059-699-9

ISBN-10 (pbk): 1-59059-699-4

Printed and bound in the United States of America 9 8 7 6 5 4 3 2

Lead Editor: Jonathan Gennick
Technical Reviewer: Stephen Kaufman, David Stucki
Editorial Board: Steve Anglin, Ewan Buckingham, Gary Cornell, Jason Gilmore, Jonathan Gennick, Jonathan Hassell, James Huddleston, Chris Mills, Matthew Moodie, Dominic Shakeshaft, Jim Sumser, Keir Thomas, Matt Wade
Project Manager: Beth Christmas
Copy Edit Manager: Nicole Flores
Copy Editor: Ami Knox
Assistant Production Director: Kari Brooks-Copony
Senior Production Editor: Laura Cheu
Compositor: Linda Weidemann, Wolf Creek Press
Proofreader: April Eddy
Indexer: John Collin
Artist: Kinetic Publishing Services, LLC
Cover Designer: Kurt Krames
Manufacturing Director: Tom Debolski

Distributed to the book trade worldwide by Springer-Verlag New York, Inc., 233 Spring Street, 6th Floor, New York, NY 10013. Phone 1-800-SPRINGER, fax 201-348-4505, e-mail `orders-ny@springer-sbm.com`, or visit `http://www.springeronline.com`.

For information on translations, please contact Apress directly at 2560 Ninth Street, Suite 219, Berkeley, CA 94710. Phone 510-549-5930, fax 510-549-5939, e-mail `info@apress.com`, or visit `http://www.apress.com`.

The source code for this book is available to readers at `http://www.apress.com` in the Source Code/Download section. You will need to answer questions pertaining to this book in order to successfully download the code.

For my wife and best friend, Keressa—the one who keeps me going;
to my son, Ben—master of LEGO blocks and future hockey-playing,
race-car-driving, rock star astronaut; to my parents, who taught me that
you can do anything you want in life if you strive to be the best.
—George Dunphy

Dedicated to my family: my late grandmother, who taught and raised me;
dad, my role model in Life and my good friend;
mom, who always drove me hard to be one of the best;
my wife and inspiration, Lamia, who supports and helps me every step of the way.
—Ahmed Metwally

To my beautiful wife, Ally, and daughters, Amanda and Anna,
who bring so much joy to my life.
—Rob Cameron

Contents at a Glance

Contents

PART 3 ■ ■ ■ You Mean You Aren't a Developer?

Foreword

When I was first asked to write the foreword for George's book, I thought to myself, "Where do I start?" A fair question, really. When I think about the work that George and his fellow contributing authors have put into this book, well, it's nothing short of a labor of love. I consider it a privilege that I was asked. Although I can't possibly match their contributions, I'll do my best to convey the magnitude of their work, the passion in which they approached it, and why everyone interested in BizTalk development should be reading this book!

I've been working at Microsoft for roughly 5 years now, first as a BizTalk technical specialist, now as the regional program manager for the BizTalk Product team (now part of the greater Connected Systems Division). During my entire tenure, I've worked closely with the BizTalk Product team and, more importantly, with our customers around building BizTalk-based solutions.

I sometimes stand amazed at what I see our customers accomplish with our technology. In some cases, I see BizTalk used for common integration scenarios; in others, I see it driving sophisticated initiatives like Service-Oriented Architecture (SOA), Enterprise Service Bus (ESB), or Business Process Management. We really do have many smart, innovative, and forward-thinking customers!

The fact that BizTalk is used in so many varied solutions and initiatives infers a very real thing: the solutions are possible because BizTalk has reached a commensurate level of maturity and sophistication that make it so.

However, my experience has also taught me that there's no magic bullet to solving the complexity of problems our customers face. The product enables success because it offers the features, architecture, and infrastructure to build successful projects. However, it does not negate the need to have a deeper understanding of the technology so that the correct architecture can be employed. In some cases, a much deeper understanding is required than what one would need with most other technologies offered by Microsoft today. Why is that?

A good friend of mine once told me that integration projects are quite possibly the most difficult work (I would argue the most rewarding) that any consultant will face in the course of their career. This isn't because of the long hours and tedious documentation requirements. No, it's due to the simple truth that integration, as well maturing initiatives like SOA and ESB, often involve a number of products and technologies; security, engineering, and networking constraints; as well as sophisticated interaction patterns with systems, processes, and people.

Think about it for a moment. What I've just described is hardly the typical venue visited by most developer's content in slinging C# code around. Historically, this has been the exclusive domain of integration architects and engineers. Regardless of the technology employed to solve it, integration is a difficult and multifaceted problem that requires smart people. BizTalk just happens to be the technology that's proven over time to be flexible and sophisticated enough to solve it.

Over the years, the BizTalk product team did an amazing job at keeping pace with the evolution of our customers and, more importantly, the issues they face. I've always been extremely proud of the team. Of all the product teams within Microsoft, this is certainly the team that's the most passionate about solving their customer's problems. They first introduced BizTalk Server 2000, which provided fairly simple XML messaging solutions. Though few connectivity options were offered, BizTalk provided a solid foundation for the adoption of XML as a messaging protocol.

The introduction of BizTalk Server 2002 empowered us to significantly expand the problem space for which BizTalk could be leveraged. An incremental version to be sure, but with it we released new connectivity options via Web Services, SQL, and MQSeries adapters. This opened the door for rapid customer adoption!

Since then connectivity options grew quickly to include more vertical-based solution offerings around HL7, HIPAA, Supply Chain, SWIFT, UCCNET, and EDI. BizTalk evolved from laying the foundation for XML messaging to being used to build hubs that managed, translated, and brokered secure messaging through various technologies and protocols in the enterprise. All this, with little or no code required!

In early 2004, a new day dawned with the release of BizTalk Server 2004. The BizTalk product team almost completely rewrote the BizTalk Server technology, introducing new features including the Business Rule Engine, Business Activity Monitoring, pub/sub, and a true orchestration engine. It was these "Enterprise" features that enabled customers to embrace a greater breadth of solutions targeted for BizTalk Server. I don't know how many times customers stared at me in shock when I told them that Microsoft had actually developed a real, forward chaining, RETE rule engine. I now had customers talking seriously to us about SOA, building composite applications in a distributed environment, and managing that environment. Finally!

This year (2006), we released the fourth version of BizTalk, BizTalk Server 2006. We listened to our customers. They told us that managing and administrating solutions across the enterprise was costly and painful. Long-term ROI tends to reside in those pain points. We heard them and invested heavily into solving those problems for them. It's astonishing how enhancing management, administration, and deployment functionality could spur such an uptake in our technology. It seemed as though overnight we grew to having over 6,000 customers!

What an amazing evolution of a product! As you can tell by now, BizTalk solves a lot of real-world problems. It does so by offering up a fairly sophisticated set of technologies and infrastructure . . . perhaps even a "development platform"? We've also learned, when armed with the right skills, an integration consultant can do remarkable work with BizTalk, from reducing development cycles to eliminating manual code dependencies. Simultaneously the consultant can decouple the solution architecture while achieving the separation of interface and logic.

Now, allow me to indulge for a moment and put on my developer's hat. When I think back, I can truthfully say that I probably found doing BizTalk 2000 development, though productive, a little boring and not too exciting. BizTalk 2002 grew it a notch to interesting.

Once we released BizTalk 2004, a new paradigm was introduced. The work became really interesting, challenging, and, dare I say it, even rewarding! It forced me to exercise new development and architecture disciplines, embrace patterns, and exercise creative thought. Though deployments were still a little tedious, I found the work enjoyable. Then we released BizTalk 2006. Now I'm just having fun! I found that the product really takes the development and architecture experience to new heights. What an exciting time to be a BizTalk architect or developer!

Now you can see why I am so excited that George and his fellow authors embarked on writing this book. I've worked with most of them for years. I know they've approached this project with the sincerest passion. It's how they've approached every project with Microsoft. Collectively, they've put their experience in context hoping that you too can do remarkable work with BizTalk Server.

It really is an exciting time to be a BizTalk developer. We've come a long way, and yet the future seems brighter than ever!

Marty Wasznicky
Program Manager
Connected Systems Division

About the Authors

GEORGE DUNPHY is a senior consultant with Microsoft Consulting Services specializing in web technologies and enterprise application development and management. He has 9 years' experience as a consultant and architect with several different companies and has worked with a variety of organizations ranging from Fortune 500 companies to Internet startups.

George is a Microsoft Certified Systems Engineer and a Certified Solutions Developer. He focuses on technologies such as the Microsoft .NET Framework, BizTalk Server, Visual Basic and Visual Basic .NET, Active Server Pages, COM, SQL Server, XML, SOAP and WSDL, TSQL, and web development. He is proficient on multiple platforms including Windows, Linux, and Solaris.

In addition to technical skills, he focuses on managing development teams for large enterprise application development projects. He also has project management experience both as a technical project manager and as an overall project manager and is presently completing the Project Management Professional designation through PMI.

AHMED METWALLY is a senior enterprise strategy consultant with Microsoft and has worked in the IT industry for 12+ years in the areas of systems development, consulting, and engagement management for large federal government departments and Fortune 500 firms. Ahmed is a subject matter expert in the areas of application/system architecture, systems development, and enterprise business automation. He has worked with and managed large strategic accounts including the Canadian Federal Government, Sony Electronics, GE, United Technologies, Hamilton Sundstrand, and OTIS Elevators.

Ahmed has extensive experience architecting and developing enterprise business automation solutions based on Business Process Management engines, Enterprise Application Integration engines (specifically Microsoft BizTalk), web services, and enterprise portals. Ahmed is also the co-owner of multiple patents in the field of application layer technologies. He currently sits on the boards and the technical advisory boards of several technology companies in Canada and the U.S.

Ahmed holds a bachelor of science degree in computer science from the American University in Cairo as well as a master's certificate in project management from the University of Quebec.

With contributions from the following:

ROB CAMERON is employed with Microsoft Corporation in Atlanta, Georgia. He has been with Microsoft since 2000, working as a development consultant providing developer advisory services and escalation management to Fortune 500 enterprise development teams. Prior to his employment at Microsoft, he worked as an independent consultant developing software on the Microsoft platform for over 5 years. He has a master's degree in information technology management and a bachelor's degree in computer science. A former U.S. Navy officer and Naval Academy graduate, he enjoys spending his free time with his wife and two daughters.

CARMAI CONSTANT is a senior software architect with Fey Solutions in Ottawa, Canada. He has 7 years of experience designing and developing software and systems. He focuses on technologies such as the Microsoft .NET Framework, BizTalk Server, COM, SQL Server, and T-SQL. Carmai has a bachelor's degree in software engineering from the University of Ottawa.

SERGEI MOUKHNITSKI is a senior software architect with Sanoraya Consulting in Ottawa, Canada. He has 11 years of experience developing software and systems. Currently Sergei is consulting for the Canadian Government and outsourcing projects.

His area or professional interest is Microsoft business process and data integration technologies. Sergei has a master's degree in computer science from the State Technical University, St. Petersburg, Russia.

About the Technical Reviewers

STEPHEN KAUFMAN is a principal consultant with Microsoft Consulting Services and has been working with BizTalk since the original BizTalk CTP in 1999. In addition, he is an author, trainer, and speaker. He has written Microsoft Knowledgebase articles, a BizTalk tools white paper, as well as a number of other articles. He was a contributing author for the BizTalk Certification Exam 74-135. He also writes a blog focused on integration technologies (http://blogs.msdn.com/skaufman). Stephen has also spoken nationally at events such as Microsoft's Developer Days, TechEd, as well as a number of other conferences.

DAVID STUCKI is a Washington native with a bachelor's degree from the University of Washington. He is also a Microsoft Certified Professional in VC++ and C#. David worked for 2 years in Microsoft Windows Developer Support where he was on the ADSI (Active Directory) and COM support teams. He joined the BizTalk team in 2003 as a software development engineer in test and now works on the BizTalk Messaging Engine team as a software development engineer.

David lives in Duvall, Washington, with his wife, Larissa, and 3-year-old daughter, Abby. His hobbies include camping, hiking, skiing, wakeboarding, mountain biking, playing the trombone, and spending time with family.

ERIK LEASEBURG is an application development consultant with the Microsoft US Enterprise Services ISV practice. He has worked with over a hundred BizTalk Server partners to provide training, support, consulting, and architectural guidance. Erik's technical focus areas include .NET and COM+ development, architecture, and .NET/BizTalk migration, as well as BizTalk Server and SQL Server development and administration. His Microsoft certifications include MCSD, MCAD.NET, MCSD.NET, and MCDBA. Erik has been a consultant for over 12 years (7 with Microsoft) developing applications, web sites, and EAI architectures that span multiple operating systems and environments. Erik lives in Texas and enjoys spending time with his wife and three children.

Acknowledgments

I first will have to thank my wife, Keressa, for putting up with my mood swings and late-night writing sessions while completing this project. She convinced me to keep going, and this would not have been a reality without her. I also would like to thank my son, Ben, for constantly reminding me about what is important in life and for teaching me to build LEGO towers that have no equal.

I will be eternally indebted to Marty Wasznicky for all his work, late nights, and wonderful contributions to the book. We simply could not have done it without his experience, knowledge, and endless supply of resources and support. From myself and Ahmed, Marty, we thank you.

Second, I would like to thank the legal team at Microsoft for all their hard work in allowing us to provide the most relevant and up-to-date content we can. I also would like to thank Gregor Holpe, creator of EnterpriseIntegrationPatterns.com and author of *Enterprise Integration Patterns* (Addison-Wesley Professional, 2003). Gregor's resources are excellent and a treasure to the integration community.

Dave Stucki's and Stephen Kaufman's advice and comments have been worth their weight in gold. The quality of the content has increased tenfold because of their expertise. Last of all, I would like to thank the entire team at Apress—Jonathan Gennick, Beth Christmas, Ami Knox, and Laura Cheu—for the countless amount of work they put into making this book become reality.

George Dunphy

Special thanks to my loving wife, Lamia, for all her support. You are my love, best friend, and partner in life. Thank you for always supporting me and driving me to achieve my dreams. Thank you mom and dad for your continuous support, even though I chose computer science over medicine. Thanks to Youssri Helmy, my mentor, who is continuously driving me to achieve more in life.

Stephen Kaufman and Dave Stucki, thank you for constantly keeping us on our toes and ensuring the completeness of our material. Thanks Jonathan Gennick, Beth Christmas, and Ami Knox for editing and herding all these chapters into this thing called a book.

Special thanks to Marty Wasznicky for his continuous help and all the amazing material that he provided us with.

Ahmed Metwally

Introduction

A Tale of Two Products

When BizTalk was still in its infancy, there were two teams within Microsoft—the Commerce Server team and the COM+ team. The Commerce Server team was implementing technology they called "Commerce Server Messaging Pipelines," essentially software that allowed an application to move messages from one system to another system using the commerce server framework. The goal was to abstract the sending and receiving of messages away from the transports that they used. For example, using this framework, a developer would not care about the physical implementation of how the messages were sent; that information would be abstracted away into another construct called a port. The port would talk to an adapter, which handled the communication to and from the medium in question, whether it was a file system, an FTP server, or a web server.

At the same time, the COM+ team was implementing a new graphical workflow representation system they called XLANG. XLANG schedules, as they were called, would compile down to a binary format and run within the XLANG engine inside of COM+. Each schedule would be **drawn**, not coded, to model a business process that the developer was trying to automate. This schedule could also access existing components that were present within the organization assuming they used the principles of n-tiered architecture and had implemented a well-defined Business Object Library.

The rumor was that when Bill Gates saw these two technologies, he immediately sought to find a way to combine them. His vision was to allow the developer to graphically draw workflow that modelled a business process and allow information needed by that process to be received and sent freely within or outside an organization. He envisioned a "next-generation programming language" type of tool that allowed even nonprogrammer types to model a business process, interact with already defined business objects, and send and receive messages without having to worry about the details of how to physically implement this transport. With that, BizTalk 2000 was born.

The Platform Today

Please note that in the preceding paragraphs, the words ".NET" and "web services" are nowhere to be seen. These concepts were afterthoughts and were implemented after the original shipping product was released. Of course, these concepts have been addressed with version 2004 and again with BizTalk 2006. The product has come a long way in 6 years.

In its early versions, the tool was powerful but not complete. The first two editions of BizTalk laid the groundwork for implementing real business process automation within many organizations, but they lacked the robustness of a real development environment, proper administration tools, an application release management service, and several other features. With the introduction of BizTalk 2004, many of these issues have been addressed. With BizTalk

2006, the platform is a mature and robust application services platform with a feature set that is a rival to any other in the industry. This, coupled with BizTalk ease of use and deep .NET and Windows integration, makes it a natural choice for many of the EAI and BPI projects that organizations are now undertaking.

This book is targeted towards the architect. This is the person who, at the end of the day, wears either the success or failure of any software project. Our hope is that this book will give that person the tools and know-how to successfully implement a BizTalk solution and feel comfortable that he has designed the best application possible.

PART 1

Readme.1st

The first two chapters of this book are designed to help architects and team leaders perform the most important tasks of any BizTalk project starting in its infancy. In these chapters, we cover the following:

- What BizTalk is and is not designed for
- An overview of BizTalk Server's key features
- Resource and estimated budget requirements
- Answers to the most common questions concerning implementing BizTalk in a new project scenario

CHAPTER 1

BizTalk in the Enterprise

The BizTalk Server 2006 product is a group of application services that facilitate the rapid creation of integration solutions. BizTalk Server is designed specifically to integrate disparate systems in a loosely coupled way. BizTalk Server is a toolkit, and within this toolkit you will find tools to help you build your application. The trick, like the wise Scottish man said, is "using the right tool for the right job."

The art of creating a BizTalk solution is exactly that, using the right tool from the BizTalk toolkit to accomplish the task at hand. If you were to look at two BizTalk projects that address identical problems, designed by two architects, you would, most likely, see two completely different-looking solutions. Both solutions would probably work; however, generally one solution would be more correct because it would properly use BizTalk's tools as they were designed. This book will attempt to address how to properly use each of the tools within BizTalk in the manner in which they were intended. The other thing the book will do is show how each of the tools can be used to solve integration problems in an efficient way. In reality though, most of the features within BizTalk are flexible enough that you can generally solve most problems using only one piece of the BizTalk puzzle.

Since BizTalk allows you to address a problem in dozens of different ways, there is no one answer as to how to implement a BizTalk solution. To help address this issue of how best to implement a given solution, Microsoft will be releasing several enterprise application guidelines for BizTalk 2006 that should alleviate some of this confusion, but this problem will never go away. This book will build upon those patterns as well as provide some advanced concepts, examples, and patterns to allow software architects to properly build complex solutions using BizTalk Server.

What Is in the Toolkit

Inside BizTalk Server, you will find tools, each of which address a specific type of problem. Before learning about those tools, it is important to know what the architecture is for a "typical" BizTalk solution. Figure 1-1 illustrates the typical architecture for a BizTalk-based solution.

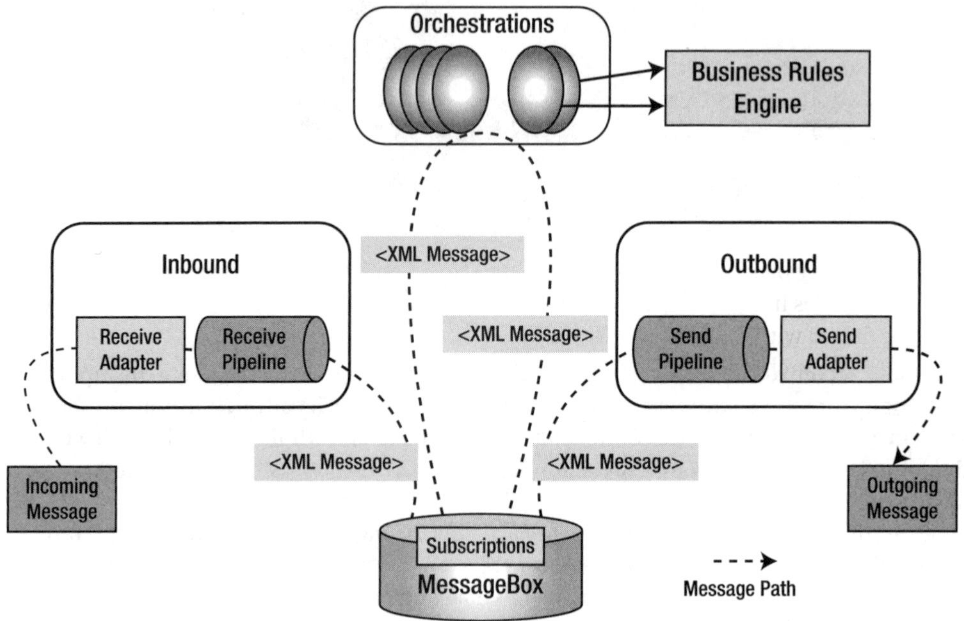

Figure 1-1. *Typical BizTalk scenario*

At its most basic, BizTalk is designed to receive inbound messages, pass them through some form of logical processing, and then deliver the result of that processing to an outbound location or subsystem. The art of architecting a BizTalk project begins with how to solve these three simple yet all-important tasks. Each of the tools in the following list is dissected throughout various sections of the book, but a simple explanation of each is provided here after the list.

- Ports and adapters
- Business Activity Monitoring and Business Activity Services
- Pipelines
- Pipeline components
- Orchestrations
- Transformations
- Messaging Engine
- Business Rule Engine
- EDI Services

Ports and **adapters** provide the logical abstraction for sending and receiving messages to and from BizTalk. They allow you to code your application in a generic fashion and not worry about the implementation details of how these messages will be consumed and delivered. A **port** is a logical construct that can receive and send messages to/from the BizTalk

Messagebox. The port must be married to a specific receive location to accept the message. The receive location then is tied to a specific **adapter**, which provides the details of how the message will be transported. These two constructs along with the BizTalk Messagebox provide the basis for the messaging infrastructure within the product.

BizTalk provides several adapters out of the box including those for FTP, File Access, SOAP, HTTP, SMTP, POP3, MSMQ, and MQSeries, all examples of transport-specific adapters. Transport adapters are usually tied to a specific wire protocol, providing the means by which to send the message. BizTalk also includes application adapters, which are used to integrate with specific third-party products such as Oracle's Database Server and ERP (Enterprise Resource Planning) packages like SAP and PeopleSoft. The complete list of transport and application adapters included within BizTalk can be found at www.microsoft.com/biztalk. Additional adapters can be purchased from third-party vendors or custom developed within Visual Studio 2005 using the BizTalk Adapter Framework.

Business Activity Monitoring (**BAM**) and **Business Activity Services** (**BAS**) provide the infrastructure to perform application instrumentation and metric reporting. BAM provides the ability to instrument your application to provide business-level data that is much more relevant than the default system-level information that is available in the base product. Examples of this would be

- How many purchase orders were processed?
- How many transactions failed last week? Last month?
- What was the total volume of messages received from a supplier?

BAS, on the other hand, provides a simple yet powerful way to display metric data from BAM and other system-level subservices using Microsoft SharePoint Portal Services. Most organizations will integrate the BAS portal into an existing SharePoint infrastructure rather than build an entire SharePoint site around BAS itself.

Pipelines provide a way to examine, verify, and potentially modify messages as they are received from and sent to BizTalk. They allow you to deconstruct messages that contain multiple documents and/or header information into a format that is more logical to the application or business user. Pipelines are applied to ports and are either a **send pipeline** or a **receive pipeline** depending on the directional flow of the message. Pipelines provide the necessary infrastructure for pipeline components (which we'll discuss in more detail a little later) or components that are executed within the various stages of a pipeline. Pipelines and pipeline components are unique constructs that only exist within the context of a BizTalk solution, and as such are generally unique to solutions that use BizTalk. Pipelines and pipeline components are created within the Visual Studio development environment using C# or VB .NET.

Pipelines function according to the concept of **assembly and disassembly**. Pipelines, which can assemble or disassemble, contain pipeline components, which are responsible for preparing the message to be sent. These components convert the internal BizTalk XML message to the appropriate XML or non-XML outbound format of the message, based on the type of assembler and properties set in the schema. For example, the assembling component of the pipeline may dictate that the message is to be sent in a flat-file text format and not XML format. BizTalk ships with default assemblers that allow you to assemble XML or flat-file messages by default with the option of writing custom assembling components. In addition, pipelines that contain assembling components assemble and wrap the message in an envelope or add a header or trailer (or both) to the message. During assembly, some properties are moved from the message context to the body of the document or to the envelope. The message context is the internal BizTalk representation of the metadata about the message such as the inbound transport type, the message type, and any special properties to be included that describe the message.

The opposite of assembling components are disassembling components, which execute on the receiving side of a message flow. Disassembling components prepare a message to be broken down into separate message documents according to the envelope and document schemas defined within BizTalk. Like assembling components, disassembling components may convert non-XML messages into their XML representation, to be processed by BizTalk. The message is then disassembled into individual messages that can be consumed by separate orchestrations or send ports. The message is disassembled by stripping the envelope information, breaking the message up into individual documents, and then copying envelope or message body property information to the individual message **contexts**. The message context is metadata about the message that is tied to the message data when it is processed by BizTalk. Exactly which properties are copied to the context is determined by the schema of the document and what properties it has defined for **promotion**, a term used to describe the way BizTalk copies properties from the message body to the message context.

Pipelines have various **stages** in which components can be executed. Stages are much like events in that they have a set order in which they execute and can be used to ensure that pipeline component logic executes in the correct order. Each stage can potentially execute more than one pipeline component depending on where it is located. This is explored in detail in Chapter 4. The pipeline is coded within the Visual Studio 2005 environment as shown in Figure 1-2. The stages for the two types of pipeline are as follows:

- Send pipeline stages:
  - Pre-Assemble
  - Assemble
  - Encode
- Receive pipeline stages:
  - Decode
  - Disassemble
  - Validate
  - Resolve Party

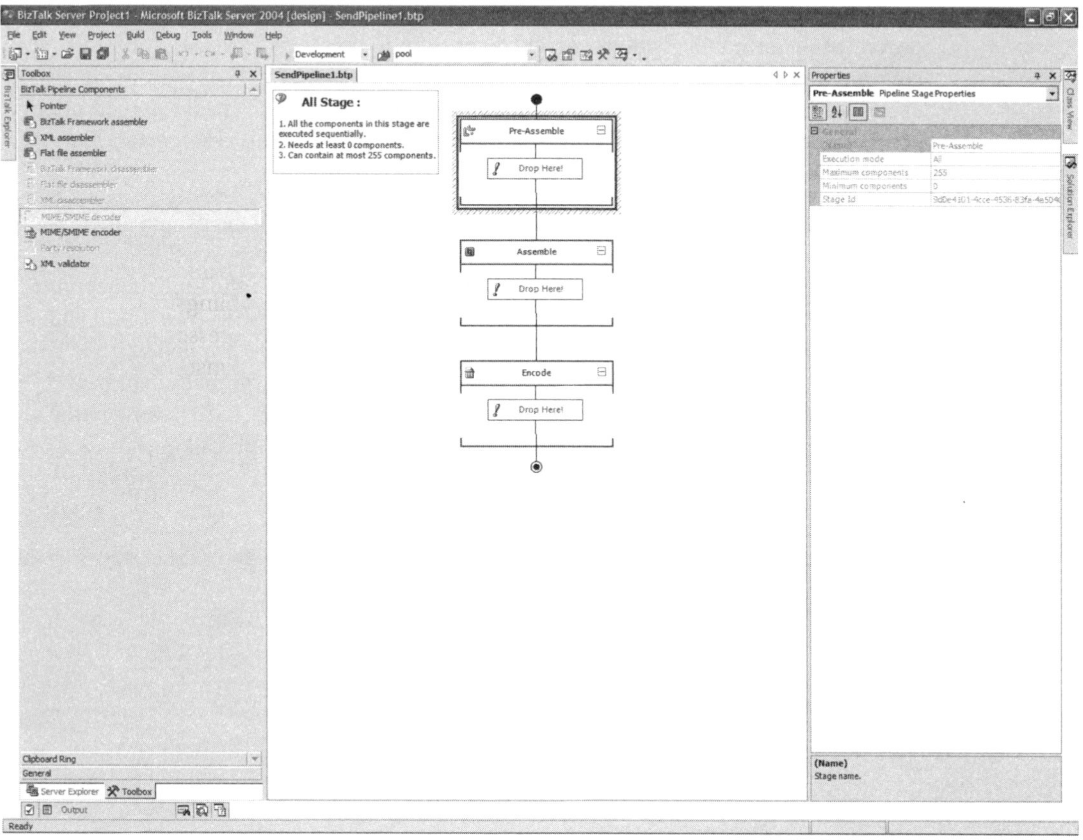

Figure 1-2. *BizTalk Send Pipeline Designer*

Pipeline components are classes that are executed within the various stages of a BizTalk server pipeline. Custom pipeline components implement a specific set of application interfaces required by the BizTalk framework. Several default pipeline components are shipped with the product that provide standard functionality that most pipelines require, examples of which are as follows:

- **Disassemblers and assemblers**: Components that allow a pipeline to examine an inbound document and separate it into logical parts, or likewise take several separate documents and assemble them into one document. In most projects, the inbound or outbound document is a container or an **envelope** document that may contain several other distinct but related document types, each with their own schema.
- **Validators**: These allow for the pipeline to validate the document according to a default specification. The default validators allow the pipeline to verify that the document is valid XML. Custom validators can be written to perform solution-specific validation.

- **Encoders and decoders**: As the name suggests, these allow the pipeline to either decode an inbound message or encode an outbound message. The default BizTalk components allow you to encode or decode S/MIME messages. Most custom encoder/decoder components perform either custom security routines or specialized cryptographic operations. (See Chapter 5 for a pipeline component implementation that performs cryptographic operations.)

Orchestrations are used to graphically model workflow and provide the primary mechanism to implement business process automation within the product. Orchestrations are by far the most powerful tool within the BizTalk Server toolbox as they allow for the rapid development and deployment of complex processes that in many circumstances can be implemented with little to no coding. Orchestrations are created within Visual Studio and are compiled into .NET assemblies that are installed into the BizTalk Management Database. Assemblies deployed to this database must also be installed into the Global Assembly Cache and have a strong name. The Orchestration Designer is a primarily visual tool. It allows you to graphically see the workflow you are creating, as Figure 1-3 demonstrates.

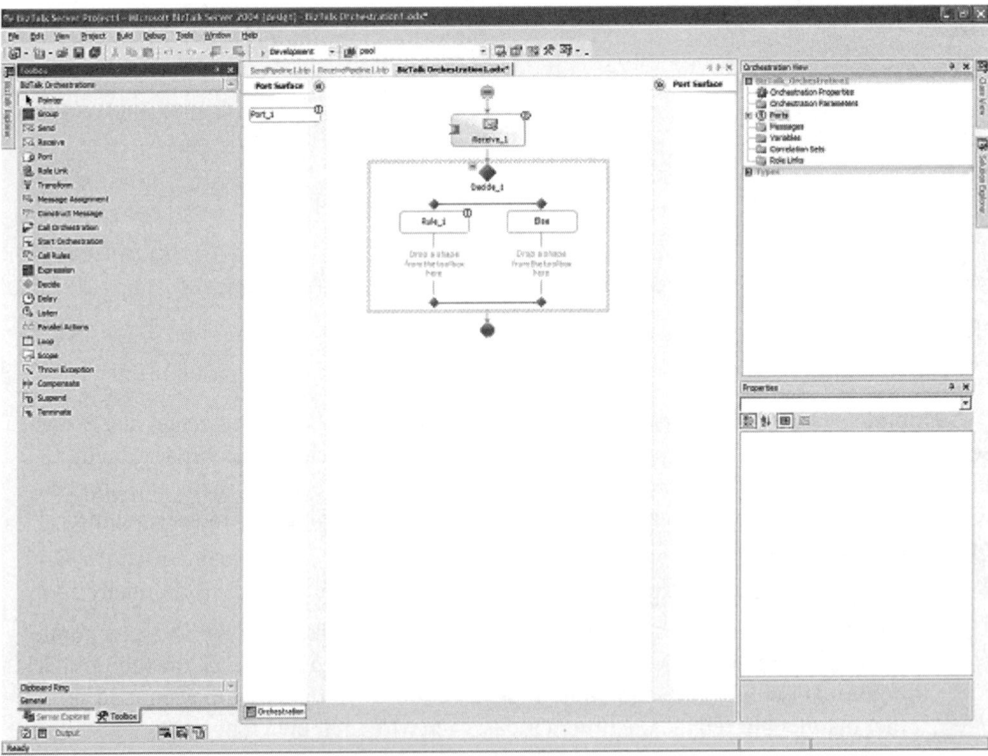

Figure 1-3. *BizTalk Orchestration Designer*

Transformations allow the application to map one message specification to another and transform data as it is processed. BizTalk messages are XML documents within the system, and as such, transformations are created from XSL (eXtensible Stylesheet Language) stylesheets. Transformations in BizTalk 2004 used the Microsoft XML Document Object Model (XML DOM) as their primary transformation engine. Starting in BizTalk 2006, the transformation engine is a custom solution developed by the BizTalk Server team. This new transformation engine is designed to increase the performance of transforming complex and especially large messages while preserving fault tolerance. Transforming large messages (greater than 10MB) proved to be problematic in BizTalk 2004 due to issues with out-of-memory conditions that occurred within the transformation engine, which was the main reason for this features' redesign.

Transformations can be applied in two places within a BizTalk solution—on a port when a message is sent or received or from within an orchestration. Each design pattern has its own pros and cons, which are discussed later in Chapter 6.

The **Messaging Engine** is the heart of BizTalk. The engine is responsible for ensuring that messages are received and routed to the proper location, that transaction isolation and consistency occurs, and that errors are reported. In reality, the Messaging Engine is the "Server" component of BizTalk Server. The Messaging Engine uses several BizTalk databases to store message information and metadata as well as system-level parameters. The Messaging Engine uses Microsoft SQL Server as its data storage facility. The central database for messages within BizTalk is called the **Messagebox**. SQL Server is not required to be physically installed on the same machine as BizTalk Server, and we recommend it be installed in its own environment for high-transaction and fault-tolerant solutions. A SQL Server license is required for BizTalk and is not included in the price of the product.

Typically, organizations will invest in separate and robust SQL Server development, testing, and production environments. Each BizTalk solution within the organization would use the appropriate SQL Server environment depending on the requirements of the application and its phase of implementation.

The **Business Rule Engine** (**BRE**) is a facility where business rules can be modeled using a simple GUI and called from within the BizTalk Server environment. The BRE is designed to allow for versioning and modification of implemented business rules without having to change the processes within BizTalk that use them. Most solutions use the BRE to implement things that require frequent updates such as a discount policy percentage or calculations that are updated frequently as a result of legal or government regulations.

Electronic Data Interchange (**EDI**) **Services** is a documented and accepted set of standards for exchanging electronic documents between organizations. EDI is traditionally used within legacy applications that have been implemented prior to the XML standard from the W3C. EDI documents are text based in nature and have a variety of document specifications depending on the data to be exchanged and the industry that uses them. BizTalk Server provides mechanisms for parsing these EDI documents into XML as well as connectivity to legacy data sources such as Value Added Networks and proprietary dial-up services.

Common Enterprise Usage

Most enterprises are looking for BizTalk to solve a particular problem. In many scenarios, this problem is related to having unrelated and disconnected systems exchange data in a standard, consistent, and reliable way. Often enterprises need to automate and streamline manual or inefficient processes in order to achieve a competitive advantage. Whether you are implementing an integration solution or a workflow automation solution, the tools that BizTalk provides allow an architect to design reliable and robust solutions faster than is often achievable by custom coding a solution from scratch using standard development languages and tools. With this in mind, it is important to understand what BizTalk achieves well and what is does not in order to fully realize any efficiency that a BizTalk solution can bring.

In other scenarios, organizations are using BizTalk orchestrations to connect and route messages to services within SOA environments. Often, the web services within the organization may be managed within different groups or even external parties. In these cases, orchestrations provide an excellent way to expose higher-level business functionality by calling, transforming, and routing messages between decoupled web services.

New BizTalk Solution Checklist

One of the key decisions that most new BizTalk application architects have to make is whether to use BizTalk or build their solution completely from scratch. The choice can only come from experience and an understanding of what BizTalk does well. The following sections explore some questions that need answering before starting any major BizTalk initiative.

What Are the Teams' Current Core Skill Sets? What Skill Sets Will the Team Need to Attain?

BizTalk projects require many skills to varying degrees depending on the size and complexity of the solution being implemented. These skills along with knowledge of the Microsoft Windows Server operating system represent a base of knowledge to start planning a BizTalk development and support team.

.NET Development

BizTalk is designed to be extended in several ways: the most common being through the custom development of .NET code, the second being through the implementation of custom business logic within orchestrations. If your project will require a significant amount of customization and business logic code, it is imperative that your team's core skill set be in .NET development.

Most teams underestimate the amount of custom code that they will need to write. It is extremely rare that a solution will have its entire business logic exclusively written within orchestrations or BizTalk transformations. If custom pipeline or adapter coding is required, a solid understanding of application programming interfaces (APIs) and object inheritance is a necessity.

The native BizTalk APIs are exposed exclusively to Windows applications usually running managed code; however, it is possible to access the BizTalk assemblies using COM but not as efficiently. All samples that are shipped with the product are written in Managed Code.

XML

People often overlook the fact that BizTalk is built entirely using XML as the data representation mechanism. Everything that passes through BizTalk is represented as an XML document at one point or another. If the solution requires the use of BizTalk schemas, knowledge of XML Schema Definition (XSD) language and XML document manipulation is a must-have. One of the great features of the product is that it exposes nearly all of its internal data structures and properties and allows you to examine, search, and modify most of the metadata that is stored for a BizTalk artifact, whether it is a message in the system or a system object such as a port. To take advantage of this, however, you must understand how XSD schemas are coded, and how to examine and manipulate them using the Microsoft XML Document Object Model.

Windows Management Instrumentation

Windows Management Instrumentation, or WMI, is one of the most underused and potentially least understood features of the Windows operating system. WMI is a management technology that allows scripts to monitor and control managed resources throughout the network. Resources include hard drives, file systems, operating system settings, processes, services, shares, registry settings, networking components, event logs, users, and groups. WMI is built into clients with Windows 2000 or above, and can be installed on any other 32-bit Windows client.

Thorough understanding of WMI is not required for a small to medium-sized BizTalk implementation, but it certainly helps. BizTalk has numerous WMI events that can be subscribed to and monitored to help give detailed information as to the overall health of a BizTalk solution. Additionally, custom WMI events can be coded and inserted into your BizTalk application to allow for custom instrumentation code that will be available to most enterprise server monitoring tools such as Microsoft Operations Manager. This is something that is often overlooked. Teams will generally implement instrumentation in the forms of performance logging, text files, debug output, etc., but this data is rarely available to system administrators who can most benefit from it. Implementing custom application instrumentation using WMI can help facilitate transitions for an application into a production environment scenario.

Microsoft Operations Manager (MOM) is Microsoft's enterprise system management tool and is able to listen to WMI events. MOM can be used to notify administrators in the case of a system failure and provide information as to the overall health of a system. BizTalk 2006 has a management pack for MOM that is used for this purpose. Additionally, custom management packs can be created to provide additional counters and information to MOM.

SQL Server

BizTalk uses Microsoft SQL Server as its primary data storage mechanism. SQL Server provides BizTalk with the ability to cluster database installations to achieve fault tolerance and high availability, as well as providing a supported and reliable way to ensure transaction stability and overall performance.

Deep SQL Server knowledge is not required for low-volume application designs; however, for systems that will have large volumes of messages being processed (in the order of greater than 20 messages per second), SQL Server knowledge on the team is a definite must-have. In high-volume scenarios, it becomes increasing important to understand how to properly distribute the BizTalk Server databases to achieve maximum performance as well as maintain reliability and scalability options. SQL Server also includes several performance-tuning tools such as the SQL Profiler, Tracing, and the SQL Server Enterprise Management Console, which allow DBAs to tune and monitor traffic within the database. This performance-tuning knowledge becomes increasingly more important as the volume of transactions a system is designed to accommodate increases.

What Are the Project Timelines? Will the Team Be Using BizTalk Exclusively to Decrease Development Time?

If the only reason you are looking at BizTalk is because you hope it will allow you to hit a project milestone or decrease overall project risk, then you need make sure you are using BizTalk for the right reasons. BizTalk is not a cure-all solution. Projects that are running behind schedule do not just have "BizTalk thrown in there" to make the unrealistic deadline go away. Most project managers want to find the "magic bullet" that can solve all their projects' problems. BizTalk has a place in these types of scenarios, but it is a means to an end, and not the end in and of itself.

Implementing BizTalk within any project carries with it a certain level of risk and challenges. In the end, what may happen is that you trade one risk for another. In order to be successful in this type of scenario, the solution must have features or subsystems on the projects' critical path that can be easily inserted and replaced with the appropriate BizTalk tool while at the same time not increasing the overall project risk.

If your project is in danger of not meeting a deadline, and you think that BizTalk may be just the tool for implementing some of the project requirements, the easiest way to evaluate whether BizTalk will work is to implement a series of simple proof of concepts. In most situations, software does not need to be purchased for this, and a 120-day demo copy of the product can be downloaded from www.microsoft.com/biztalk/evaluation/trial/default.mspx for free. During this proof-of-concept phase, Microsoft field staff can be engaged to help ensure the prototypes are successful and address any technical issues that may arise. Involving Microsoft field staff in these types of situations is generally the easiest way to help alleviate the risk of taking on the creation and success of any proof-of-concept or prototype activities while engaged in an already risky project.

Is There Enough in the Budget to Implement BizTalk?

Whether you have the budget to implement BizTalk will depend on the size and complexity of the solution. Typical implementations cost anywhere from $15,000 on the low end and upwards of $500,000+ on the high end for hardware and software costs. These are exclusive of any custom development, support, or hosting costs.

BizTalk Server Editions

BizTalk as a solution provides many options for configuring the product to help ensure the right mix of hardware and software is purchased. The product is available in the following editions:

- **Standard Edition**: BizTalk Server 2006 Standard Edition is designed for small and medium-sized organizations. It enables you to integrate up to 10 internal applications with up to 20 external trading partners. This edition supports only one- or two-processor machines and does not support clustered deployments. If the product is installed on a multiprocessor machine, it will only use up to two of the available processors. Since Standard Edition does not support scaling-out solutions using multimachine BizTalk Server group processing or scaling to multiple processor machines, it is generally intended for stand-alone applications with moderate transaction volumes. Standard Edition still allows for scaling out the SQL Server that BizTalk Server uses. For example, it is possible to install BizTalk Standard Edition on a single-processor machine but have it access SQL Server Enterprise Edition on a multiprocessor, clustered environment.
- **Enterprise Edition**: BizTalk Server Enterprise Edition is the full-featured version of the product. It is able to use multiprocessor machines and supports BizTalk Server application clustering via BizTalk Server Groups.
- **Developer Edition**: BizTalk Server Developer Edition is the enterprise edition of the product licensed to run in development and testing environments only. This is ideal for installation on development team members' workstations and for installation in staging or quality assurance environments for application testing purposes only; it cannot be used in any production scenarios. Developer Edition is available as part of a Microsoft Developer Network (MSDN) subscription.

SQL Server Editions

Like BizTalk, SQL Server also has separate editions to meet the varying needs of customer requirements and installation situations. The two main versions of SQL Server are **Standard Edition** and **Enterprise Edition**. The key difference between the two versions in the context of a BizTalk Server environment is their support for database clustering. Only SQL Server Enterprise Edition supports database clustering, and it requires Microsoft Windows Server Enterprise Edition as its installed operating system to install the cluster server software.

Required BizTalk Server and SQL Server Hardware

The minimum hardware requirements for BizTalk Server as published by Microsoft are as follows:

- Minimum configuration:
  - 900 megahertz (MHz) or higher Intel Pentium–compatible CPU
  - 1024 megabytes (MB) of RAM
  - 6 gigabyte (GB) hard disk
  - CD-ROM or DVD-ROM drive

Please note that this is a minimum configuration to allow the product to run. In actuality, a typical BizTalk Server machine will have some variant of the following hardware:

- Common configuration:
  - 2.6 GHz or higher Pentium IV
  - 1536MB of RAM
  - RAID 5 hard disk array for application data
  - RAID 0+1 hard disk array for operating system
  - CD-ROM or DVD-ROM drive

As stated before, every BizTalk installation needs a SQL Server instance. In low-volume scenarios, it is possible to install both BizTalk Server and SQL Server on the same physical machine. This configuration will work quite well and is fully supported. Issues with this configuration tend to arise when transaction volume increases and additional processing resources are required to service incoming requests.

In high-volume scenarios, it is not realistic to expect to be able to run both BizTalk and SQL Server on the same physical machine. From a performance perspective, SQL Server traditionally is a "RAM hungry" application. This is due mainly to the memory management system used internally within the product. The upside to this is that query executing time within SQL Server is generally extremely fast, and the server engine is able to cache query results to increase performance. It is possible to configure SQL Server to use less memory, but the performance of the database engine could degrade accordingly.

From a fault-tolerance perspective, it would be disastrous to expect maximum uptime and reliability from a shared BizTalk/SQL Server hardware platform. SQL Server enterprise provides clustering support to allow for failover occurring across separate physical machines in the event of a hardware failure. Database clustering is a key component to ensure that the environment achieves maximum uptime despite failures in hardware or software.

A typical SQL Server Enterprise Edition clustered environment is shown in Figure 1-4 and will have a configuration similar to the following:

- Common high-volume database server configuration:
  - 3.0 GHz or higher Pentium IV
  - 4096MB of RAM
  - RAID 5 hard disk array for application installations
  - RAID 0+1 hard disk array for operating system
  - CD-ROM or DVD-ROM drive
  - Shared fiber channel array or storage area network (SAN) for SQL Server database files

---

■ **Note** In a clustered environment, two database server machines are required. In most configurations, the first server accepts database requests, while the other is considered a "hot standby." This configuration is referred to as **active/passive clustering**.

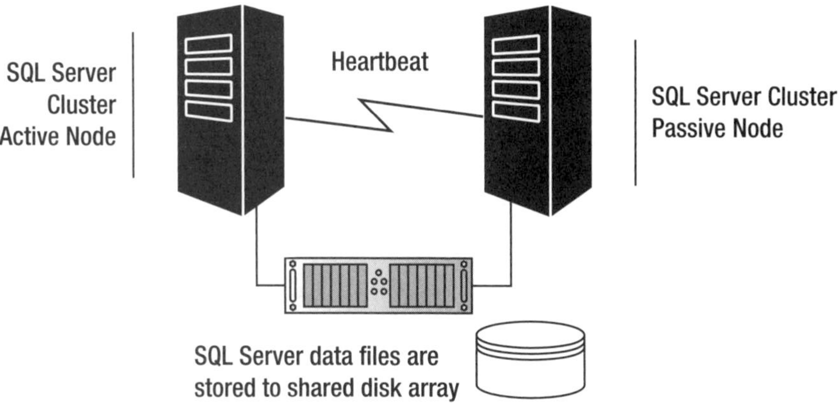

Figure 1-4. *SQL Server clustering configuration*

Software Costs

When estimating costs for a new BizTalk project, it is imperative to consider the total cost of what the software will be. Don't forget, too, that you must consider the cost of both BizTalk *and* SQL Server.

BizTalk Costs

When project managers begin estimating the cost for the solutions hardware environment, many often forget one thing—BizTalk is not freeware. Each edition has it's own per-processor cost. The software licensing costs are shown in Table 1-1.

Table 1-1. *BizTalk Server Pricing*

Edition	BizTalk Server 2006
Enterprise Edition	$29,999 US per processor
Standard Edition	$8,499 US per processor
Developer Edition	$499 US per developer, or as part of an MSDN Universal subscription

SQL Server Costs

SQL Server can be licensed in two modes: per client access license (CAL) or per processor. Per-CAL licensing requires that you purchase a separate license for each concurrent connection to the SQL Server database, whereas per-processor licensing licenses the software based on the number of processors installed in the machine. Given the complex nature of BizTalk and SQL Server processing, it is generally not advisable to license SQL Server based on the CAL model. Developer and testing servers are permitted to use SQL Server Developer Edition. Like BizTalk Developer Edition, this is a full-featured version of the product licensed for use on development and testing machines only and is available through MSDN subscriptions. Per-processor licensing costs are outlined in Table 1-2.

Table 1-2. *SQL Server Pricing*

Edition	SQL Server 2000
Enterprise Edition	$24,999 US per processor
Standard Edition	$5,999 US per processor
Developer Edition	Part of MSDN Universal subscription

How Many Servers Are Required to Implement a BizTalk Solution?

Low-volume systems can be implemented with one BizTalk server machine and one SQL Server machine. High-volume solutions can use eight or more machines depending on the type and volume of processing required.

Typical Low-Volume Solution Configuration

Figure 1-5 shows a configuration that will work for a typical low-volume transaction system.

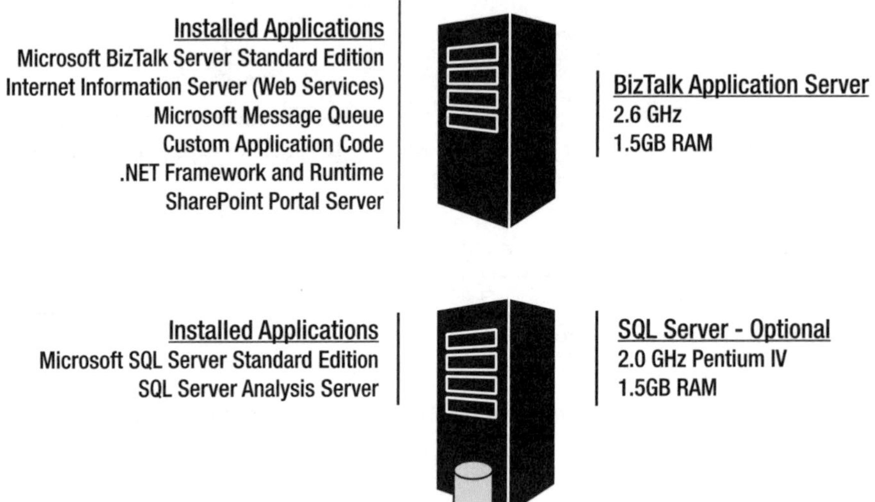

Figure 1-5. *Low-volume BizTalk Server configuration*

Typical High-Volume System Configuration

High-volume transaction systems require a more robust configuration than is shown in Figure 1-5. Figure 1-6 gives one example of how you might configure BizTalk to handle a high volume of transactions.

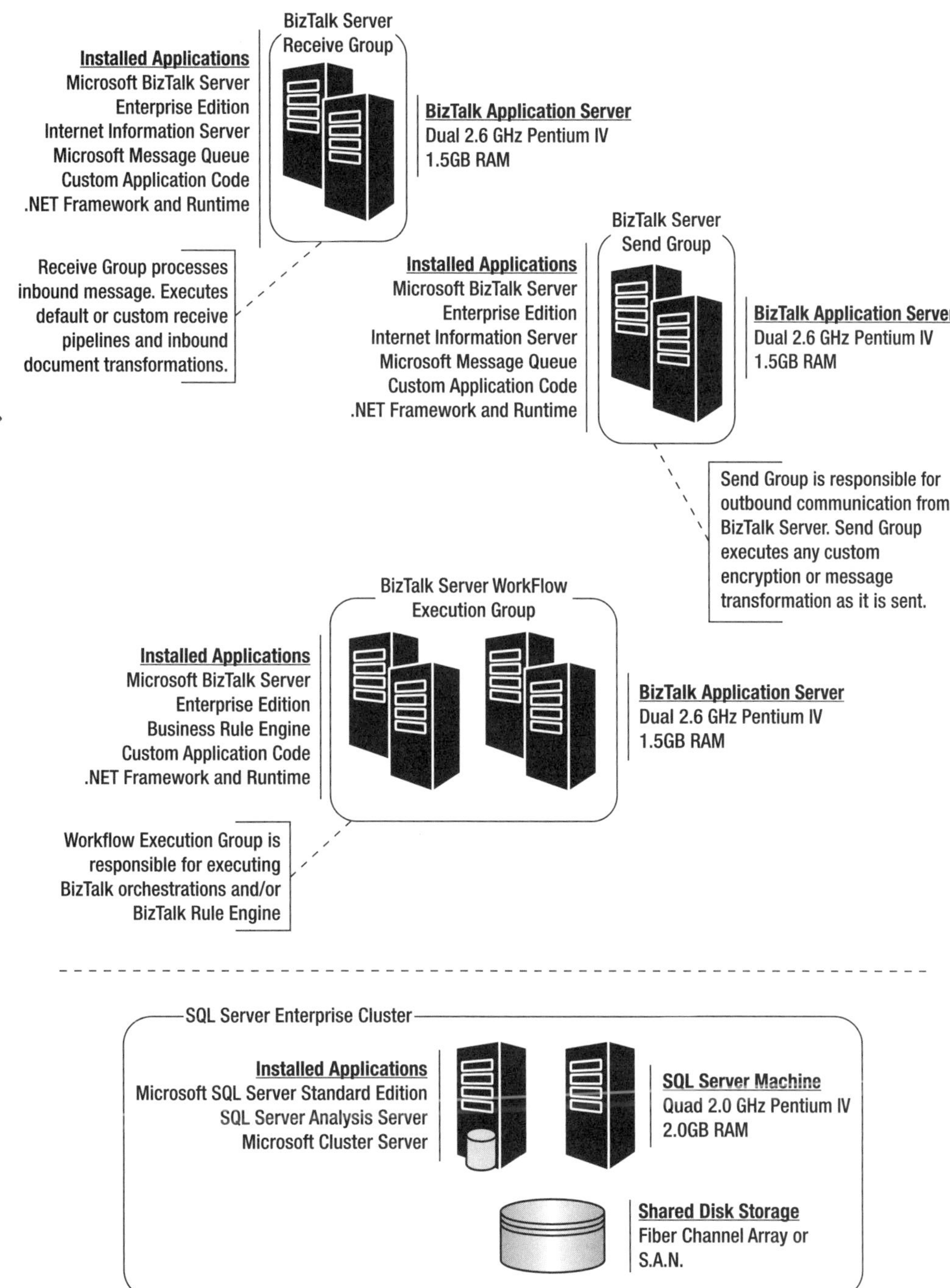

Figure 1-6. *High-volume BizTalk Server implementation*

How Much Custom Code Are You and Your Team Willing to Create? Would You Rather Use Completely Out-of-the-Box Functionality?

Most BizTalk solutions do not require significant amounts (>20,000 lines) of code to implement. Simple projects may not require any. The amount of custom code required will depend greatly on the type of system and the complexity of the business logic that is required.

There are several key types of processing that require a BizTalk solution to implement custom code:

- **Custom message processing logic**: This generally refers to custom pipelines and custom pipeline components. If you need to perform things like custom encryption or decryption, custom digital signature or message verification, compression routines, or custom envelope processing, you will need to write .NET code.

- **Custom transformation logic**: Transformation logic is handled within BizTalk maps. Most transformations can be implemented using the default BizTalk **functoids**. Functoids are pieces of application code that are used to manipulate how values from an incoming message are mapped to the outgoing message within a BizTalk transformation. BizTalk ships with over a hundred default functoids that are able to accommodate most standard tasks. In the case where custom logic needs to be created, most projects will want to code custom functoids to facilitate code reuse. You will want to code custom functoids when you notice that the same scripts or routines are implemented several times across multiple maps.

- **Custom business logic**: .NET components are usually called within orchestrations and contain common business procedures and classes. This is not a BizTalk item per se as the project will need to implement this logic regardless of the platform.

- **Workflow automation**: These are BizTalk orchestrations. In most situations, there is one BizTalk orchestration for each workflow to be automated. In many cases, complicated workflow is broken out into multiple orchestrations so that common pieces can be used in several orchestrations and be coded by multiple developers.

- **Custom adapters**: One of the key selling features of BizTalk is the vibrant adapter partner community that supports it. Adapters allow BizTalk applications to communicate with different transport mechanisms and applications without requiring that the coder understand the details of how this communication will work. Adapters exist for over 300 platforms, operating systems, and ERP applications. In certain circumstances, either an adapter is not available for a desired platform or it is more cost effective to develop a custom adapter from scratch due to licensing costs. In these cases, you will need to create a custom adapter using the BizTalk Adapter Framework classes. Depending on the transaction volume requirements, transport specifics, and protocols involved, this may be a difficult task for the novice developer.

Is BizTalk Suited for the Application in Question?

Refer to the four main types of BizTalk projects—workflow automation, legacy application integration, trading partner exchange, and organizational message broker scenarios. If your application has any of these types of pieces, BizTalk may be a fit. If not, you need to examine where and why BizTalk is being evaluated.

The key thing to remember in this type of situation is to define early in the solution's design phase what data will be exchanged with BizTalk, what the schema definitions are, and how data will be returned to the calling application. Another key decision is to decide whether the main application requires a **synchronous** or an **asynchronous** response from BizTalk and what the threshold values are for an acceptable transaction. If the calling application needs a subsecond synchronous response from BizTalk to process the message, it is imperative that the system be sized properly to ensure that response times are acceptable. If the communication can be asynchronous, it is easier to restrict the flow of messages to an acceptable level either by using a queuing mechanism or some sort of batch processing.

Will Every Transaction in the System Need Monitoring? Will the Tracked Data Need Saving for Archiving Purposes?

This issue is often overlooked when a new project begins. BizTalk provides a very simplistic user interface to view the message specifics and transaction history within the product. This interface, called the Health and Activity Tracker (HAT), is shown in Figures 1-7 and 1-8.

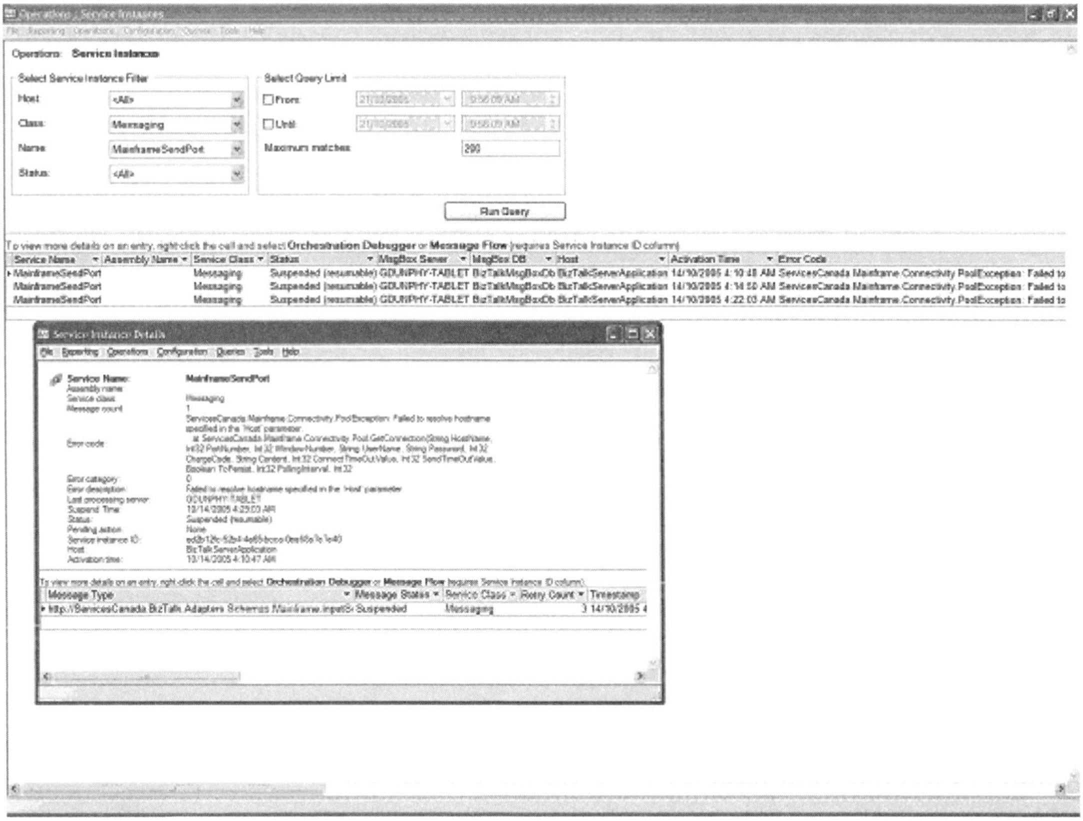

Figure 1-7. *Health and Activity Tracker*

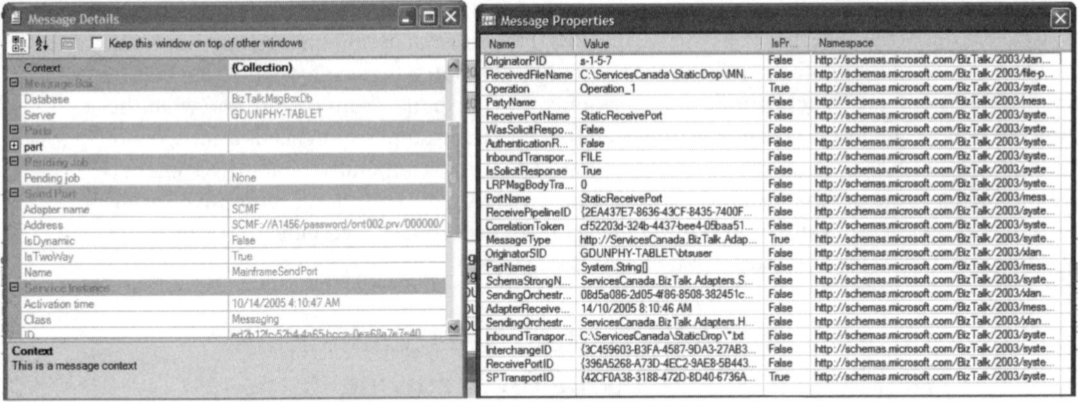

Figure 1-8. *Health and Activity Tracker message details*

The HAT can provide the data that is stored within the message and give the message context properties; however, this data is essentially system-level data. There is no "business-relevant" information in the context other than the message type and any exception information. If there is a requirement to see the transaction from an end-user perspective (i.e., the message is received, processed by system XXX, and failed at updating system YYY), the HAT interface will not be sufficient. Often the type of application that needs to see a transaction from an end-user perspective is integrated into an existing SharePoint portal site using BAS. Developing this application is generally not a trivial task and can add time onto the final product's delivery date. If the type of information is volumetric data (e.g., how many transactions failed, how many were successful, what was the volume at peak processing time), the data can be created using BAM and accessed with Microsoft Excel or another similar tool. Implementing a BAM-based solution is generally less time consuming than creating a customized BAS SharePoint application. Starting in BizTalk 2006, the BAM service ships with a default SharePoint portal application that allows you to view all BAM-related information within the system. This base application is usually then modified or integrated with another main SharePoint site to provide the relevant business-level metrics required.

CHAPTER 2

Starting a New BizTalk Project

Every BizTalk development team, regardless of the size, will encounter the same types of problems. The two most difficult issues that new BizTalk architects face in organizing the development team are how to structure the project in terms of the development/build/test/deploy process and how to appropriately structure the project source tree so that it is optimal for each developer given the task he is working on.

In most cases, a developer on a BizTalk solution will fall into one of three categories:

- Developers who create BizTalk artifacts exclusively
- Developers who create .NET classes exclusively
- Developers who perform a combination of both

In small teams of five developers or less, it is not uncommon to see most developers performing both BizTalk tasks as well as pure .NET coding tasks. For these types of teams, delineation of work becomes simple and is usually based on functional aspects of the system. Small teams can "carve out" pieces of the solution based on some functional aspect, and these solution divides are generally referred to as **subsystems**. In a perfect world, each subsystem can then be coded and tested independent of the rest, which helps to decrease intersolution dependencies and project schedule critical paths. Small teams will also need a **lead**. The lead is responsible for ensuring that coding standards are met, unit test plans are created and executed, and system integration and code promotion into formal application testing happens smoothly and consistently.

In large teams of 15+ developers, the process of managing developer deliverables, subsystem integration and testing, application versioning, and solution builds start to become a nontrivial task. For these teams, it becomes necessary to implement a formal project structure that scales to accommodate large numbers of subsystems while at the same time provide consistency and uniformity across the entire team as a whole. Figure 2-1 shows a simplified diagram for how a development team is structured. Each of the roles within the team is described in Table 2-1.

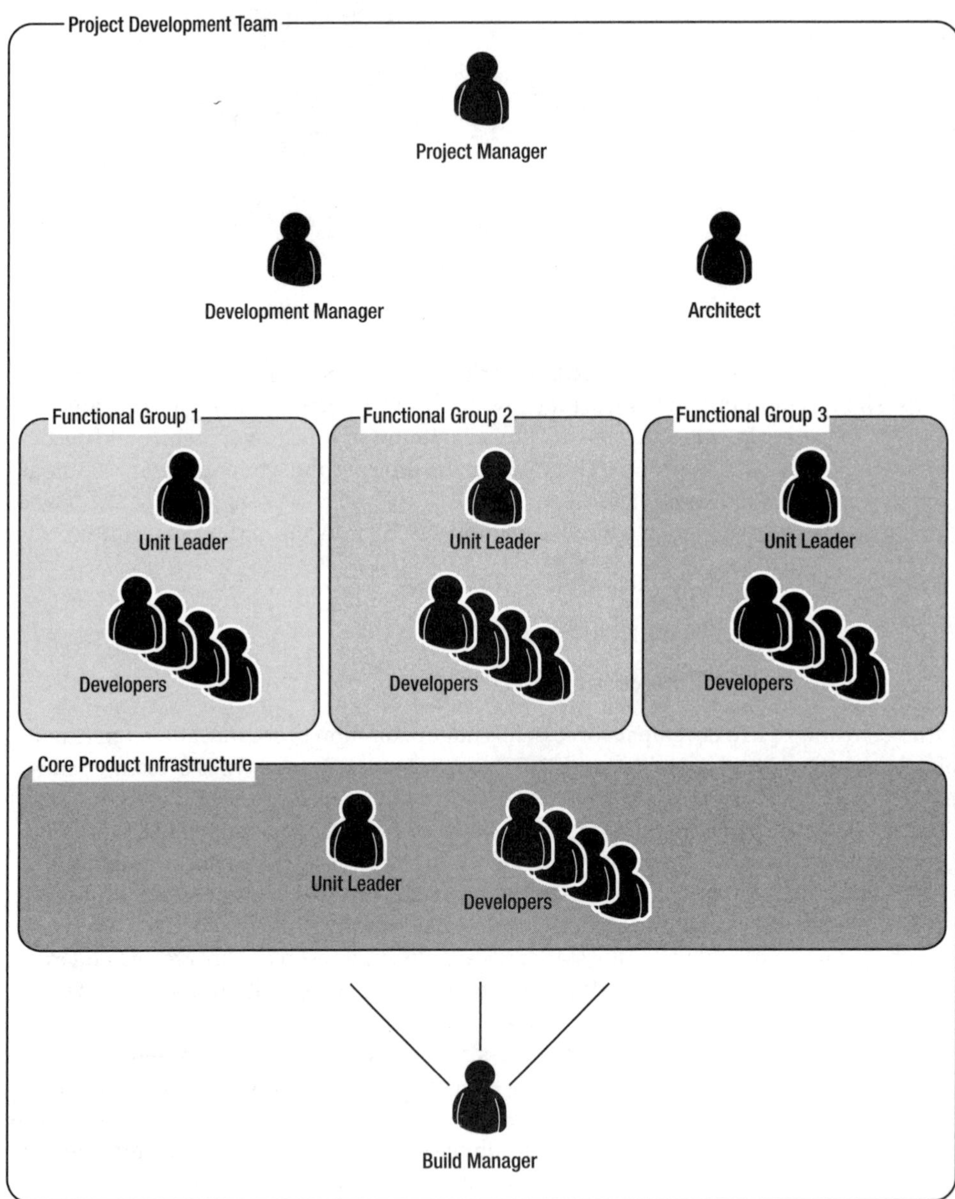

Figure 2-1. *Simplified team structure*

Table 2-1. *Project Roles and Responsibilities*

Role	Key Areas of Responsibility
Project Manager	Ensuring deliverables are to client specifications Ensuring project delivery Creating and managing budget and schedules Managing Change Requests
Development Manager	Integrating features across functional teams Managing Change Requests Working with functional teams to create deliverable lists and ensure timely delivery
Architect	Defining overall system architecture and design Defining development standards and naming conventions Defining source control layout and project solution structure Defining application namespaces Working with Unit Leaders and Development Manager to create developer specifications Defining performance testing metrics Defining subsystem integration points and working with Development Manager to ensure the entire system integrates properly Defining external and internal system interfaces Working with common infrastructure team to define reusable system-level infrastructure components
Build Manager	Ensuring integration between functional teams Performing daily builds into integration and testing environment Creating build scripts/installation packages
Unit Leader	Working with Development Manager to ensure all deliverables within Functional Unit are created Performing code walkthrough and sign-off with Developer Ensuring unit test plans are created and adhered to Depending on nature of team, coding of common subsystem routines
Developer	Producing code according to specification Creating BizTalk artifacts according to development standards Coding .NET classes Creating unit test plans

■ **Caution** Figure 2-1 is a simplified development team model. It is by no means a complete structure as the functions of quality assurance testing and product releases have not been taken into account. For a complete development methodology, Microsoft Solutions Framework is a great place to start: http://lab.msdn.microsoft.com/teamsystem/msf/default.aspx.

Starting Preliminary Design

The team structure outlined previously gives the basics for forming and managing a large group of developers. It also allows the team to scale outwards or inwards depending on new requirements being introduced or having features move out of scope. The key takeaways from this model are the following:

- Break the solution down into functional groups or subsystems. Assign and manage deliverables based on these groupings.
- For projects that require common infrastructure, create a separate team that is responsible for creating and managing this. Ensure that the design for any common components is well defined and used by other functional teams.
- Assign developers to either a functional team or to the common infrastructure team. Assigning developers to more than one team is often problematic as it forces them to split time for multiple deliverables.
- Rotate developers across teams when deliverables are complete. This encourages cross-group collaboration and decreases "knowledge silos."
- Encourage a regular build cycle. This will help to keep the project on track and gives the team members regular code check-in dates that must be met.

On a BizTalk development project, these concepts become even more important. Most BizTalk architects do not take the time necessary to determine how to properly structure the application so that it can be coded using a model like the one defined earlier. Likewise, very few map out what common infrastructure will be needed and what types of artifacts are "feature specific" and which are common infrastructure. Following is an exercise that illustrates this.

Exercise 2-1: Design the Solution

List what features are needed for the solution to be implemented in this exercise scenario. Then list what common components will be required for each subsystem.

Scenario:

ABC Company, Inc., is creating a new solution using BizTalk Server. The system is an order fulfillment application that will receive order information from the public web site, a retail POS (Point of Sale) system, and a custom bulk order solution that is used by large customers. Only customers in good standing are eligible for automatic fulfillment, and presently the project is only piloting customers in four geographic regions. If a customer does not meet the requirements for automatic fulfillment, the order is rejected and manually fulfilled. For orders that can be auto-fulfilled, the solution must first check the stock availability for each product by an SAP ERP system using a custom API. If stock is not available, it must decide whether the order can be split into multiple shipments and fulfill each separately. If the order cannot be split shipped, it must be rejected and processed manually. If an order can be fulfilled, it must update the billing and shipping systems appropriately. The shipping system is a legacy mainframe-based application that requires custom code to be executed to properly authenticate and send transactions to it.

■ **Note** This solution will be the basis for all coding and BizTalk artifact examples given in the book. This is to bring a level of consistency to each example as well as to show how it can be used in a real-world example.

Possible Solution:

In this scenario, the most logical approach would be to separate the solution based on the requirements. There are three key features of this solution:

- Order taking from external sources (POS, web site, and bulk orders)
- Stock checking and rules associated with split shipments
- Updating downstream systems

Each subsystem will have its own pieces and artifacts; however, all of them will need to use the following types of core components:

- Access to customer information
  - Common schema to define customer information
  - Standard way to get access to that customer information
  - Executing customer rules associated with automatic fulfillment
- Coordination to ensure that the fulfillment process is handled in the proper order
- Order rejection subsystem
- Standard way to process exceptions and errors

In this scenario, the solution can be implemented using the architecture in Figure 2-2.

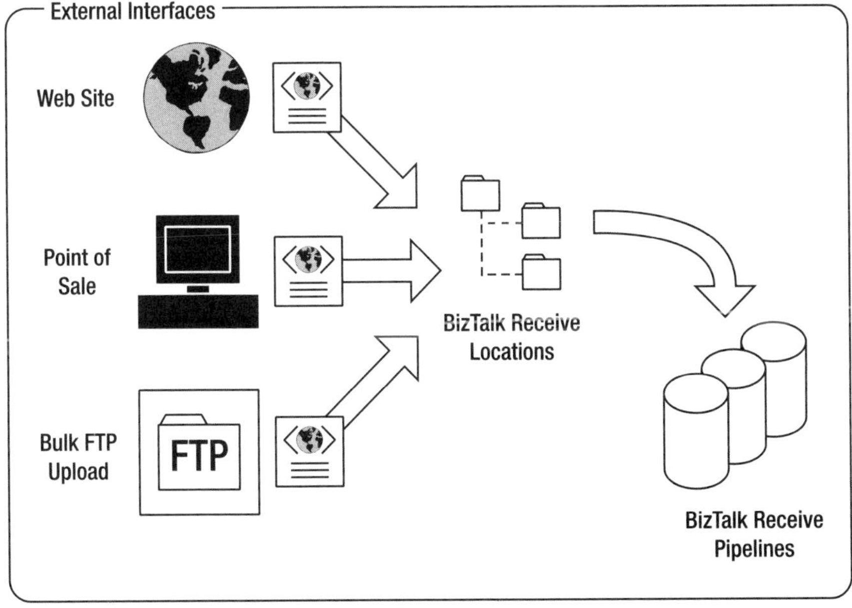

Figure 2-2. *External interfaces design*

Feature 1: External Interfaces

This subsystem is responsible for receiving inbound messages from the three external interfaces. Here, the external interfaces can be XML messages, flat-file messages, or custom inbound API calls.[1] In any case, this subsystem will need to parse the inbound document and transform it to a common schema that represents an "order" within this solution. This order schema will be used by all other subsystems. In the case of the bulk upload, the subsystem will be required to create individual orders based on the entire payload of messages stored within the order file.

This scenario can be implemented using receive ports within BizTalk along with several receive locations. Each receive location will define a custom receive pipeline if the document needs to be examined and/or disassembled before being processed. The port would then have different BizTalk transformations assigned to it to allow it to map the inbound system order schema to the common system order schema that is used by all subsystems.

Feature 2: Check Stock and Associated Rules

The stock-checking subsystem will be responsible for calling the customer lookup system, as shown in Figure 2-3. This will also check whether or not the order can be fulfilled and return the response. Note that in this scenario, the coordination of calling the order rejection system as well as the coordination of this process into the larger fulfillment process is left to the responsibility of the common infrastructure. This subsystem is responsible for determining whether an order can be fulfilled and is not responsible for how or why this information is needed. This is often referred to as **black-boxing** a solution. This will allow the subsystem to be built in isolation of any other subsystem. Only integration points are needed to be defined before development is started, in this case, the schemas for an order and a customer as well as the format of the response.

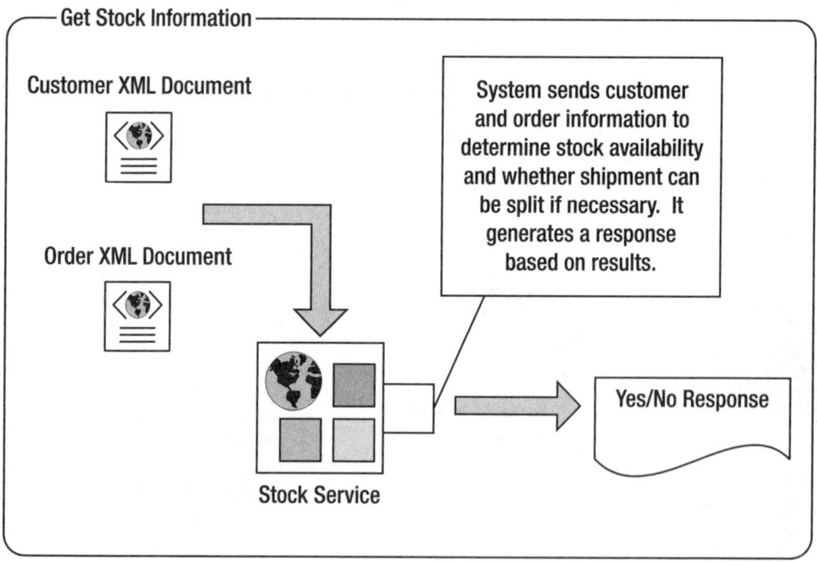

Figure 2-3. *Stock information service design*

---

1. In later chapters, we will explore the scenario of creating a custom **Receive Adapter**. In many cases, the system that will be sending BizTalk messages is either a proprietary COTS (commercial, off-the-shelf) system or requires special transports such as a custom TCP listener. In these scenarios, it may be preferable to buy an external adapter or create a custom one using the Adapter Wizard.

Feature 3: Update Downstream Systems

To update the downstream ERP and shipping systems, the validated order will need to be sent via a BizTalk send port via the appropriate adapter. This is demonstrated in Figure 2-4. The adapter to be used depends on what downstream system is going to be updated. In the case of the ERP system, if this were an SAP application, the port would use the SAP adapter. The same would hold true if it were an MQSeries queue—the port would use an MQSeries adapter. For the custom shipping solution, a custom adapter will need to be created if no off-the-shelf adapter is available. Note that in this system, the send pipelines are responsible for packaging the message into its appropriate format, adding any security information such as digital certificates, and encoding it properly so that the downstream system can read the order information. The send ports also return a response message back that indicates whether or not the update was successful. What to do with that response message is the responsibility of the caller, not the pipeline, adapter, or send port.

These common subsystems also need to be built:

- Coordinate fulfillment process.
- Get customer information.
- Handle errors.
- Handle order rejections.

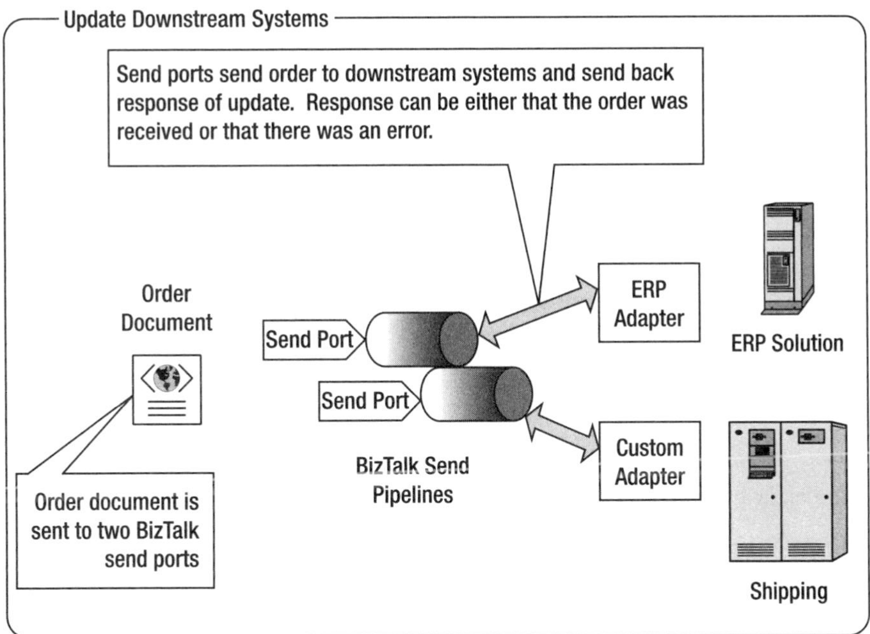

Figure 2-4. *Update Downstream Systems design*

Creating Your Development Environment

Once you have a team established, the next step is to create an environment where you can create, test, and deploy code. Some variables will affect how this is going to be accomplished:

- How are the development servers going to be configured?
- How will source control be configured?
- How are the Visual Studio projects going to be laid out?

The answer to each of these questions can often separate a well-organized and efficient environment from one that can kill a team's productivity. Potential solutions to each of these questions are given in the next sections.

Isolated Development Configuration

BizTalk development is an isolated development model. This model requires each developer to have a stand-alone development environment and not a shared environment such as in web development.

In the isolated model, a developer performs each task independently from other developers on the team. They can code, debug, edit, and restart services without worrying about affecting others on the team. Each developer has a self-contained development workstation with a local BizTalk Server Group. Access to the master source files is controlled via a Visual SourceSafe (VSS) database located on a network file share. Figure 2-5 illustrates an isolated development model.

The isolated model of BizTalk Server development provides the following benefits:

- No chance that BizTalk Server shared configuration information will interfere with another developer's work (for example, XML target namespace clashes occurring from multiple installed versions of shared schema)
- No opportunity for any one individual's BizTalk Server deployment and test processes interrupting other users (for example, the starting and stopping of BizTalk Server host instances, receive locations, or dependent services like IIS, SQL, and SSO)
- Ability to clear resources like event logs and tracking databases without disrupting other users
- Ability for developers to use different versions of shared resources, for example, helper classes and error-handling processes
- Ability for developers to attach and debug the BTNTSvc.exe process without halting other developers' processes

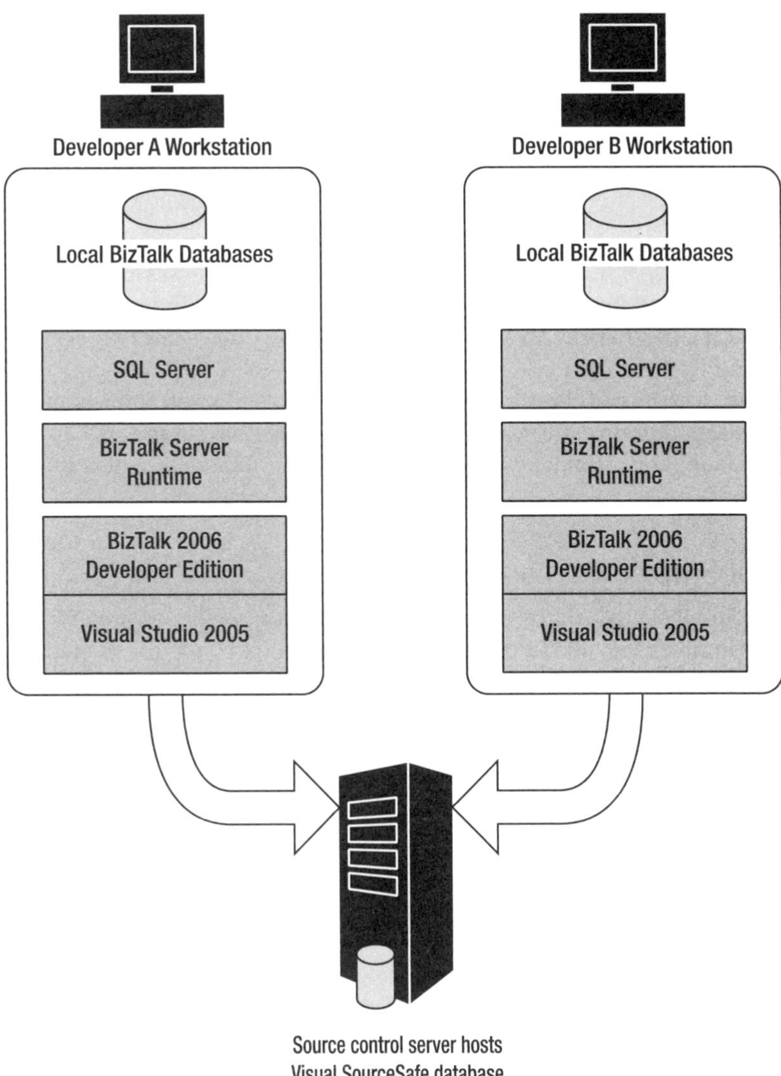

Figure 2-5. *Isolated BizTalk Server development*

Using Virtual Machines

Many organizations use **virtual desktops** for development. In these cases, organizations should look at products such as Virtual PC or VMware to allow developers to have multiple virtual machines running within the same physical hardware. Virtual desktops provide two things well. The most important thing is that they allow your developer to get a fresh install in a matter of minutes rather than hours. How many times have developers needed to rebuild their PCs due to bad code they had written, too much unsupported stuff getting installed, or a bad configuration they might have done? Typically this will happen at least two to three times over the run of a year. Having a fresh virtual image that they can load onto a clean host operating system greatly reduces the time for this to occur. All developers need to do is copy over any files they want to save from the virtual machine onto the host operating system before it is removed.

The second thing that virtual desktops allow for is the ability to host multiple configurations inside one physical box. Often developers need to have separate versions of either the operating system or a development environment. This is often the case when a developer is coding both BizTalk and classic .NET objects. When the BizTalk development tools are installed and the environment is configured, there are significant changes made to the underlying operating system. Developers will often have a "BizTalk" image and a ".NET" image just to keep things separated.

The configuration just described is also often required when creating a web application that targets different browser platforms and versions. Anyone who needs to support IE 5.0, 5.5, and 6.0+ will need to have something similar to this configuration, since these browsers cannot live on the same host OS.

Organizing Visual SourceSafe Source Control

Not implementing a structured source control process is a sure-fire way to derail a project before it gets started. It is important to model the source control directory structure to one that closely simulates the namespaces and assemblies that are actually stored in the project. For example, assuming that your company name is ABC Inc., the easiest place to start would be to create a root directory called ABC in SourceSafe. Each project that is being implemented at ABC would then get its own folder, for example, FulFillment. The structure would look something like that in Figure 2-6.

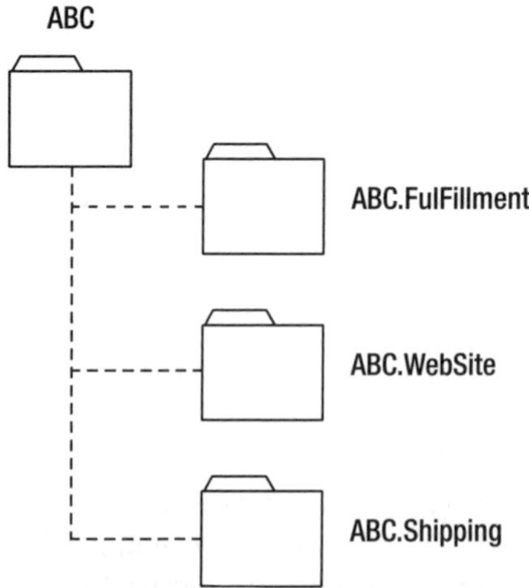

Figure 2-6. *Simple VSS project layout*

Notice that the subfolder names are matching up to the proper namespaces for the projects within that SourceSafe project. Once the high-level folder structure is implemented, it easily allows new projects to be added, and organizational namespaces should be self-enforcing. Consider the example of the FulFillment application; in this scenario you can use subprojects that map to the subsystems you need to create. Each subsystem would then have its own namespace, and the SourceSafe project will be named accordingly. Figure 2-7 illustrates the FulFillment application, its subsystems, and even some sub-subsystems.

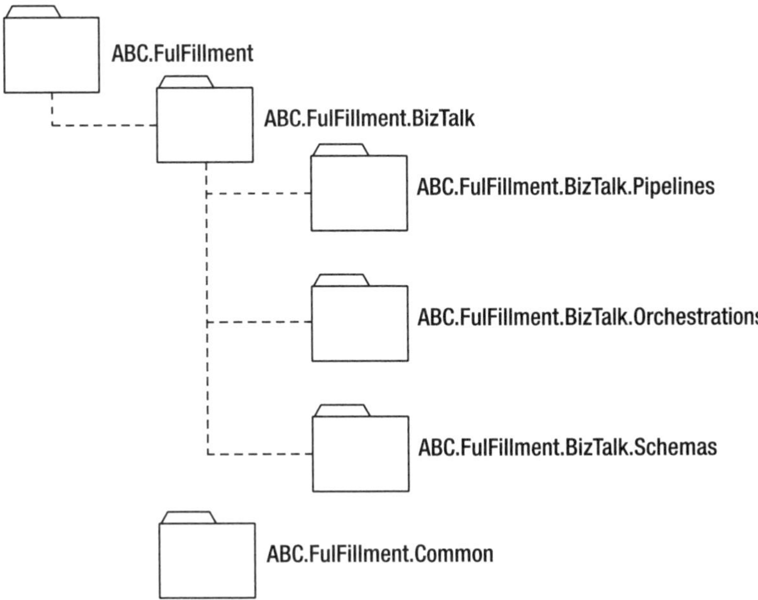

Figure 2-7. *VSS solution layout*

Before beginning with VSS, ensure that the binary file types for *.btm, *.btp, *.xsd, and *.odx have been added to VSS. This is required so that SourceSafe does not attempt to version these file types as text.

Structuring and Integrating with Visual Studio

There is no standard way to structure a Visual Studio solution that has BizTalk projects included. Essentially, a properly defined naming convention will be applicable whether the solution is a complete .NET solution or a mix of .NET classes and BizTalk artifacts. The key decision to make is whether the entire application will be created as a single VS .NET solution or whether it will be broken down into multiple solutions. Another approach is to decide whether or not to have the Visual Studio solution file controlled under source control at all. In this scenario, each developer has a local solution file that is not under source control. The individual developer then adds the Visual Studio projects to his local solution that are required to complete the application being created.

How the Visual Studio solutions are structured will have many ramifications on how developers will use the solution, how it will be built, and how it can be packaged and deployed. Additional things to consider are whether each developer will have the BizTalk development tools installed on their workstation. If a group of developers never code BizTalk artifacts and only create standard .NET classes, then these developers will get errors each time they load a BizTalk development project. A configuration like this will not work for a single-solution scenario where every project is included in the solution and is loaded upon startup. In single-solution scenarios, it is necessary to break the solution up into multiple solutions that can be worked on either by BizTalk developers or by .NET-only developers.

In cases where multiple developers are working on isolated pieces of a solution, a separate integration environment should be created. The purpose of this environment is to allow a common area for each build of the application to be placed. Additionally, the deployment process is developed and tested using this environment in order to minimize deployment errors when the solution is moved from the development environment into testing and finally production.

Since the BizTalk development model is isolated as described in the preceding section, it is crucial that the integration environment provide a place where unit testing can occur in a controlled environment. The integration environment configuration should closely match what will be used in the QA environment. The actual hardware that is used is not as important as the software. In many situations, given that most projects have limited resources, the integration environment is often a small, single-CPU server or spare developer workstation. Following are some things that should be considered when designing this environment:

- **BizTalk Server port configuration**: Often on a developer's local workstation, required BizTalk ports will be simple transports such as the file adapter to facilitate easy testing. Also, port filter criteria may be simplified as the entire list of document filters and transformations may not be required. The integration environment should try to give the developer as controlled and realistic a configuration as possible.

- **Strong name key storage**: When building BizTalk components that will be deployed to the management database, it is necessary to implement a strategy for how to manage the strong name keys. Since BizTalk assemblies that are deployed need to be stored in the Global Assembly Cache (GAC), and all assemblies in the GAC need a strong name, this means that all BizTalk assemblies will need to use a strong name key. How this is managed often depends on the type of solution. If the solution will be a "for sale" commercial product, it is critically important to ensure that access to the strong name key is limited to key team members to ensure that the integrity of the application is maintained. In this case, developers are often given a **test key file** that is used to facilitate their building, deploying, and testing activities. Once the code is promoted, the build master then replaces the test key with a production key file.

- **Restricting code deployed**: Only build and deploy code to the integration environment if it is included in the formal build that will be sent to QA. This also helps to keep the integration environment a "managed" environment and not an isolated sandbox like the developer's local workstation.

- **BizTalk 2006 MSI exports**: Starting in BizTalk 2006, applications can be exported using Windows Installer technology to a Microsoft Installer (MSI) package. This MSI can be customized to include all required BizTalk Server artifacts and referenced assemblies and configuration. The integration environment is the ideal environment for exporting the MSI package to be used for installation in the QA and production environments.

The following sections discuss each of these approaches in turn.

Single Visual Studio Solution

For small- to medium-sized applications (less than 12 VS .NET projects), it is quite feasible to contain all the required Visual Studio projects inside one solution. This one solution is then stored within Visual SourceSafe and is used by all developers, as depicted in Figure 2-8.

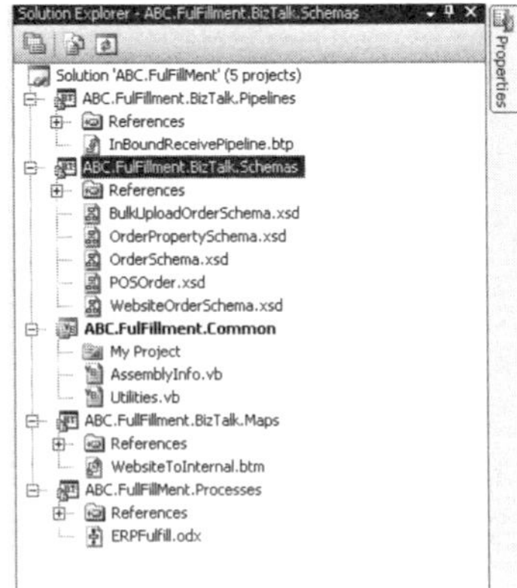

Figure 2-8. *Visual Studio solution layout*

The one solution shared by all developers is often referred to as the **Master solution**, and the solution is bound to the application root in SourceSafe. If the example application were structured as a single-solution configuration, it would most likely be named "ABC.FulFillment.sln" and would be bound to the ABC.FulFillment folder in Visual SourceSafe. This configuration has a number of advantages and disadvantages. First some of the advantages:

- It is simple and easy to manage.
- The entire solution namespace hierarchy is easy to see. Each project will contain only one set of namespaces that will compile to an assembly with the namespace of each class in the assembly equal to the assembly's physical name.
- It allows the entire solution to be built and deployed as a whole without complex build scripts.

- It allows for references between projects to be **project references** and not hard references to a built assembly. This will allow code changes in one project to be automatically reflected in any referenced project and helps to ease version conflict issues.
- Developers will automatically see any checked-in changes from other developer team members. The only action required is to get the latest code check-ins from SourceSafe.

And now some disadvantages:

- It requires the solution file be checked out from SourceSafe if any new projects are added. Each time a project is added to the solution, every developer will be prompted to connect to SourceSafe and get the latest copy of the newly added project.
- Frequent updates to the file cause it to be locked in SourceSafe. Care will need to be taken to ensure that the .sln file in SourceSafe is not checked out for extended periods of time.
- It isn't feasible for teams who don't have BizTalk installed on every development workstation.
- It usually requires that all referenced projects be built along with the main project that is being built. This becomes time consuming as the number of projects increases.
- Solution loading time increases as the number of projects increase. This becomes an issue as the number of BizTalk projects and artifacts within those projects starts to increase.

Multiple Visual Studio Solutions

For larger, more complex projects, it may become necessary to split an application into multiple Visual Studio solutions. In this scenario, there are multiple VS .NET .sln files checked into SourceSafe. Each solution would be logically related to a feature of the application that you are implementing. Each .sln file is bound to a directory in SourceSafe and contains the projects that are required to build the solution. This means that all projects within the solution are part of the solution, and referenced assemblies are referenced in the VS .NET project files as references to assemblies, not references to VS .NET project files.

One of the issues with this approach of carving an application into multiple Visual Studio solutions is how to include common project assemblies within each of the multiple solutions. Consider if there were three VS .NET solutions for each of the three subsystems defined in the earlier example. How would each of these solutions reference the Common Utilities project or the shared BizTalk Schemas project? It is possible to include these common projects within each of the solutions. To have each solution add the project that is needed, you choose the Add Project from Source Control option within the VS .NET solution, as demonstrated in Figure 2-9.

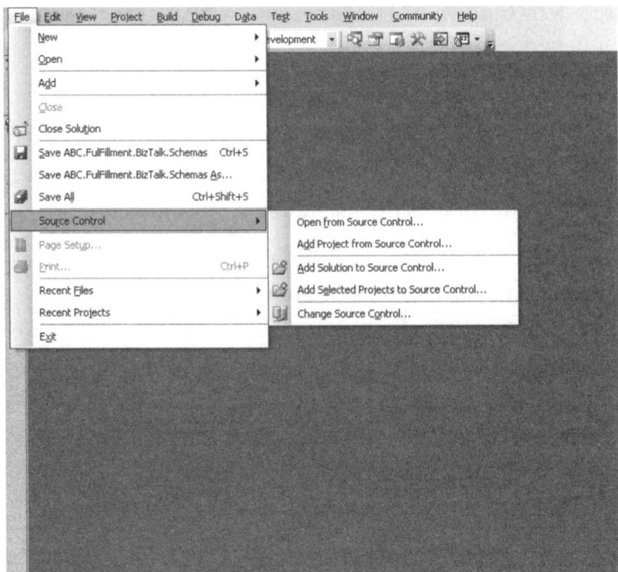

Figure 2-9. *Adding a Visual Studio project from source control*

The issue with adding the common VS .NET projects to each of the solutions becomes a matter of controlling who is allowed to edit and modify the shared source control. If a team of developers is specifically assigned to make additions and modifications to shared library assemblies, it is more advisable to have these assemblies included as references to the built DLL, rather than the VS .NET project file. The team responsible for these assemblies will deploy the correct version to the integration server and publish the correct build number. Each project that references the DLL must be updated to include the new assembly version number, or the reference must not include the version information and a new assembly is simply overwritten.

In a multiple solution configuration, a separate build-and-deploy process is necessary. Since the application is divided into separate VS .NET solutions, there are two approaches to building the solution:

- Build and deploy each solution separately.
- Create a **Master VS .NET solution** that includes all VS .NET projects from each solution. Build and deploy this Master solution as a single unit.

Advantages of the multiple-solutions approach include the following:

- Only projects that are required to build the solution are loaded when the solution is opened in VS .NET. This can help decrease the amount of time required to load the solution.
- Each solution file is based on a logical application subsystem or feature. The .sln file is then maintained and modified by the group that owns that feature.

- Configuration allows application to be built and deployed as pieces. This allows teams to build and test their feature independent of others.
- It allows the application to incorporate new features without having to dramatically change its layout in Visual SourceSafe.
- Contention for Visual Studio .sln files within Visual SourceSafe will be decreased. Each feature team can add/remove VS .NET projects to their solution without affecting developers from other teams.

The list of advantages is long, but there are also a few disadvantages to the multiple-solutions approach:

- It increases build-and-deploy complexity.
- It increases the chances of versioning issues arising from referencing common components.
- Increased management is needed. A formal build-and-deploy process becomes essential.

Developer-Independent Solutions

In some cases, it is possible to not have the VS .NET solution files checked into SourceSafe. In these situations, each developer has a local .sln file that he uses to add/remove projects as he needs; the .sln file is not used to organize the application into its appropriate features. This configuration works well for teams where the .NET assemblies they support are common to several different applications, and the VS .NET project file can be compiled on its own or with minimal references. The build process will need to take this into account by either creating custom build scripts or creating a master .sln file that is used deploy the solution to the integration environment.

Advantages of developer-independent solutions are as follows:

- It is ideal for small teams or projects with very few independencies.
- It is simple.
- It is flexible and gives developers control over development environment.

As always, there are tradeoffs, this time in the form of the following:

- It causes increased build-and-deploy complexity.
- There is a potential loss of control for development leads.
- It still requires a separate build process or Master solution file.

Organizing Artifacts in BizTalk 2006

You're likely to use BizTalk for more than one application. You'll then quickly run into the problem of organizing your application artifacts such as ports, schemas, and so forth. There are two facets to organizing. First you must understand the concept of a **BizTalk application**.

Then you can use the Administration Console to do the actual work of sorting your artifacts so that you can easily see which artifacts go with which application.

BizTalk Applications

In BizTalk 2004, artifacts such as ports and orchestrations were not organized according to what application used them. Each artifact was simply deployed to the management database and was not organized by logical criteria like in Figure 2-10. The result was that the task of managing these artifacts was increasingly difficult and was complicated whenever two or more solutions were installed to the same BizTalk Management Database. The situation has been dramatically improved in BizTalk 2006 with the introduction of BizTalk applications. Applications allow an administrator to logically group artifacts according to the application that uses them. This concept is extended to the improved deployment model within BizTalk 2006 that allows the exporting of a BizTalk application to a Windows Installer package.

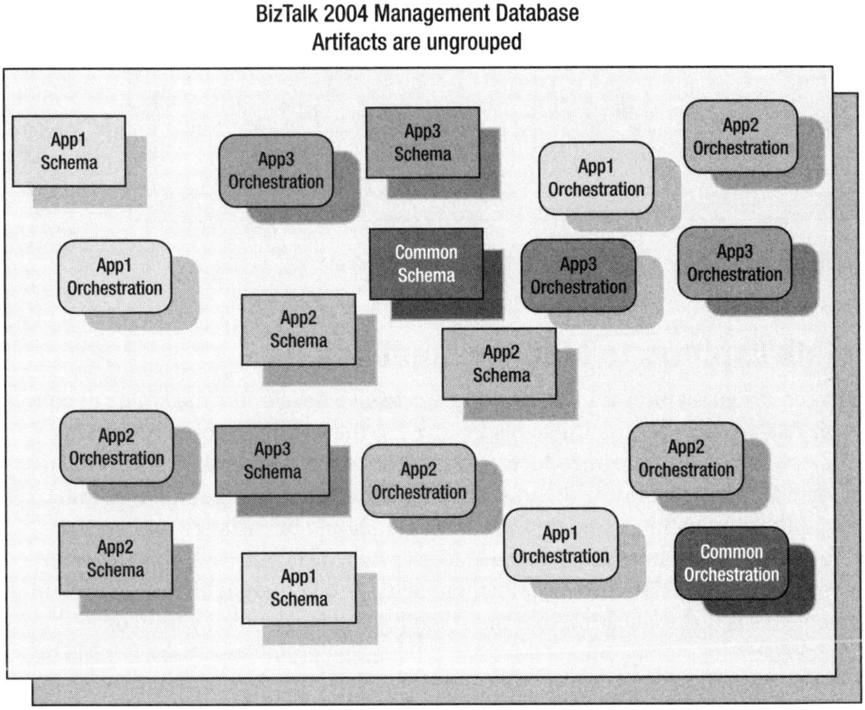

BizTalk 2004 Management Database
Artifacts are ungrouped

Figure 2-10. *BizTalk 2004 artifact organization*

Applications can contain any number of BizTalk artifacts such as schemas, business rules, orchestrations, and ports. To facilitate such organization, the BizTalk Management tools have been redesigned in BizTalk 2006. The top-level logical grouping for BizTalk artifacts becomes the application instead of the artifact type as it was in BizTalk 2004, as shown in Figure 2-11.

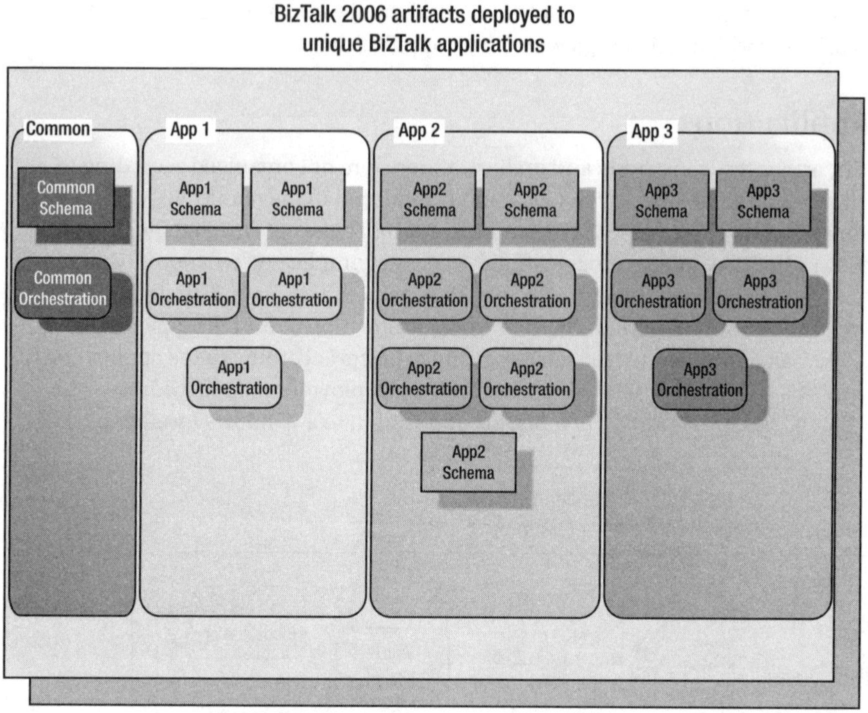

BizTalk 2006 artifacts deployed to unique BizTalk applications

Figure 2-11. *BizTalk 2006 artifact layout*

Using BizTalk Explorer to Manage Applications

One of the most requested features for BizTalk 2006 was to give developers the ability to control how their BizTalk artifacts were going to be deployed to the server. To some extent this existed in BizTalk 2004, but with the introduction of the concept of a BizTalk application, this has been extended. Developers now have the ability to tag their BizTalk assemblies within Visual Studio with the application name that the assembly should be installed within. This is shown in Figure 2-12. In essence, all that is needed is to right-click the assembly in Visual Studio and choose Properties. Under the Deployment Settings tab, there is an option to set the application name. This is the application that the assembly will be installed within once the assembly is deployed to the Management Database. If the application doesn't exist, it will be created upon deployment.

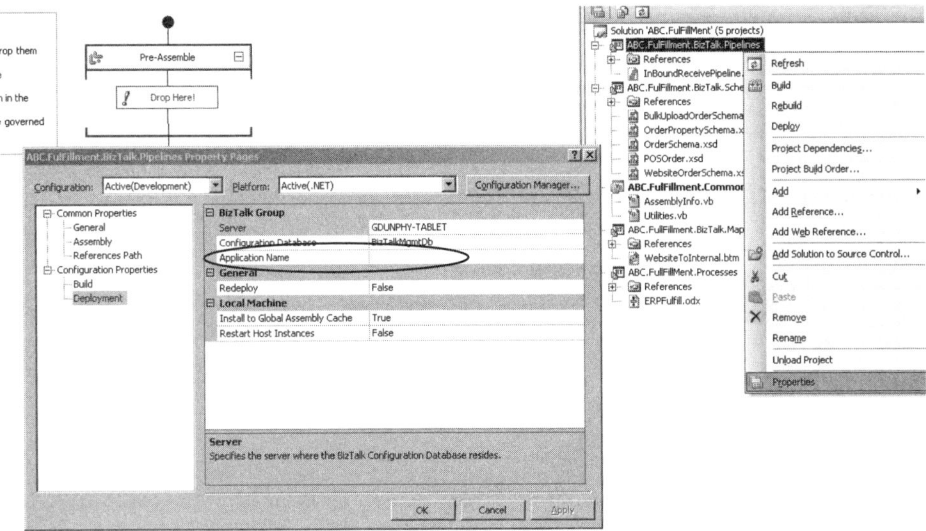

Figure 2-12. *BizTalk Explorer*

BizTalk's Administration Console

BizTalk's **Administration Console** is a Microsoft Management Console (MMC) that allows for the ability to create, configure, and manage one or more applications across multiple servers. Additionally, the MMC includes the ability to import and export applications for installation across multiple servers or to facilitate the moving of applications between staging and production environments. Finally, the console includes the message- and service-monitoring capabilities previously provided by HAT, the Health and Activity Tracking tool introduced in BizTalk Server 2004. While the Administration Console provides runtime monitoring, HAT must still be used for document tracking and orchestration debugging.

In Figure 2-13, you can see the organization of BizTalk applications in the Administration Console. Each application is contained within the **applications root** of the server. Fresh installs of BizTalk Server 2006 create a system application called **BizTalk.System** that contains all global schemas, assemblies, and artifacts and a default application called **BizTalk Application 1**. If you don't explicitly create a new application, each time you deploy, your artifacts will go into the default application.

If you are upgrading from BizTalk Server 2004, your artifacts will also be installed in the BizTalk Application 1 root. After the upgrade is complete, it is advisable to create a new logical application container and move the artifacts to it to avoid confusion.

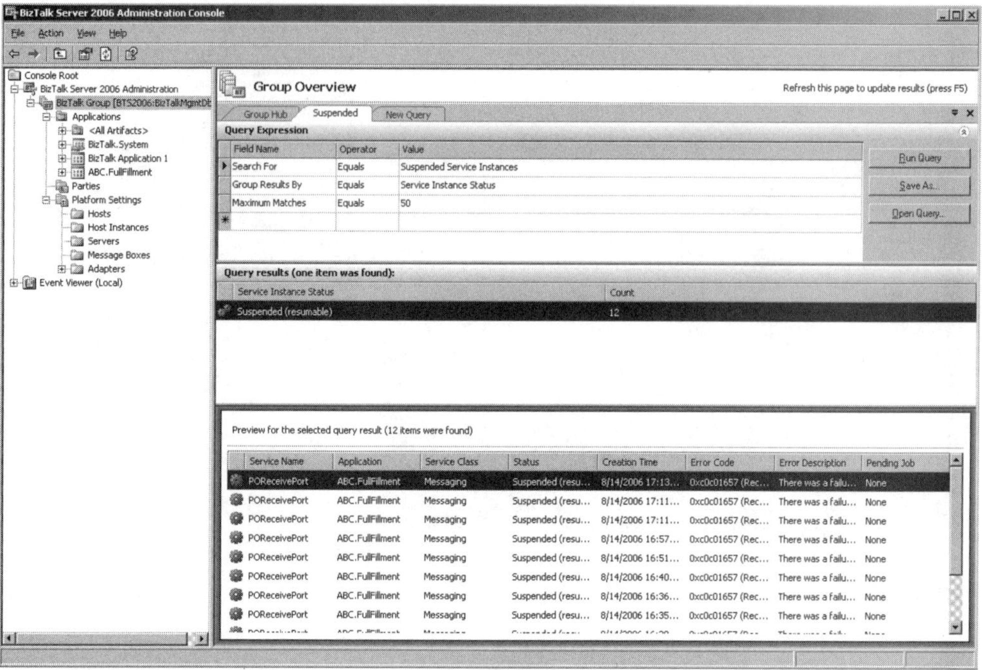

Figure 2-13. *BizTalk 2006 Administration Console*

Creating a Build-and-Integration Environment

As stated in the section "Configuring Your Development Environment," BizTalk development is an isolated model. Because of that, whenever you have a team of people working on a project, you will need to create a build-and-integration environment in which you can deploy and test the unit-tested assemblies and artifacts from each team. You can then use the build-and-integration environment to produce the new version of the installation package through which to update any other environments. It is crucial that this installation package be versioned to allow for bugs/issues to be logged against specific versions of the application to ensure that regression bugs can be tracked down quickly.

The hardware configuration for a build-and-integration environment is usually fairly simple. This usually consists of one machine that is not used for development purposes, generally one small server or developer workstation that is used to get the latest version of the source code from Visual SourceSafe, label the source code, build the code, deploy to the integration environment, and build the MSI deployment package. The environment must be configured as a stand-alone environment with the BizTalk databases installed and configured separately from other environments.

It is critical that the build-and-integration environment not be used for development purposes as this needs to be a "clean" environment that only contains source code to be used in other environments. It is the responsibility of the Build Manager to ensure that this is the case.

Five-Step Build Process

Every development team needs a process to build and test their software. This is as important as the creation of the code itself. Many different build processes exist, but they are all essentially the same with slight twists or enhancements. If your team does not have a formal build process, you need to get one. For this reason, a simplified build process is included here. This process is simple enough that it can be used by even novice teams, yet flexible enough to allow it to scale to larger development groups.

Step 1: Developer Check-In

Pick a regular time each day when unit-tested code needs to be checked into source control. Ideally, this check-in occurs at the same time each day to help enforce a "rhythm" to the project. The most important rule to enforce in this step is *code checked in for a build must compile.*

If code in source control does not compile, there needs to be a process in place to ensure that only compilable code is in source control. If not, the build is considered "broken." Usually there is a special gift for any developer who breaks a build. One of us was once on a team where we would have a dunce cap for the coder who checked in broken code. It was required that he wear the "I Broke the Build" cap for two days while at work. It only took this particular author once to learn to never check bad code in again. Since this form of negative encouragement is often frowned upon by the politically correct, another trick is to have a "swear" jar. Each line of code checked into the build that doesn't work costs $20. At the project's completion, the money goes towards the party.

Step 2: Build Manager Sets Version and Labels Code

Labeling the code is the process of time-stamping all source files with an identifiable tag so that a specific version can be retrieved. In SourceSafe, a label can be anything, but usually the label contains the build number for that day. For example, if the build number for today were 1.0.3.45, then the label would also be 1.0.3.45. This allows the Build Manager to easily retrieve source code for previous builds if there ever is an issue with regression. It is critical that the version label from SourceSafe match the assembly version information that is included in the build. Each .NET assembly must have its AssemblyInfo file updated with the proper build and version number for each build. By default, Visual Studio sets the version number to 1.0.*. This will cause the version to auto-increment each time the solution is built. It is necessary to change this number manually or by using a version structure as outlined in the next section. BizTalk projects must have the assembly information updated in the VS .NET project properties as shown in Figure 2-14.

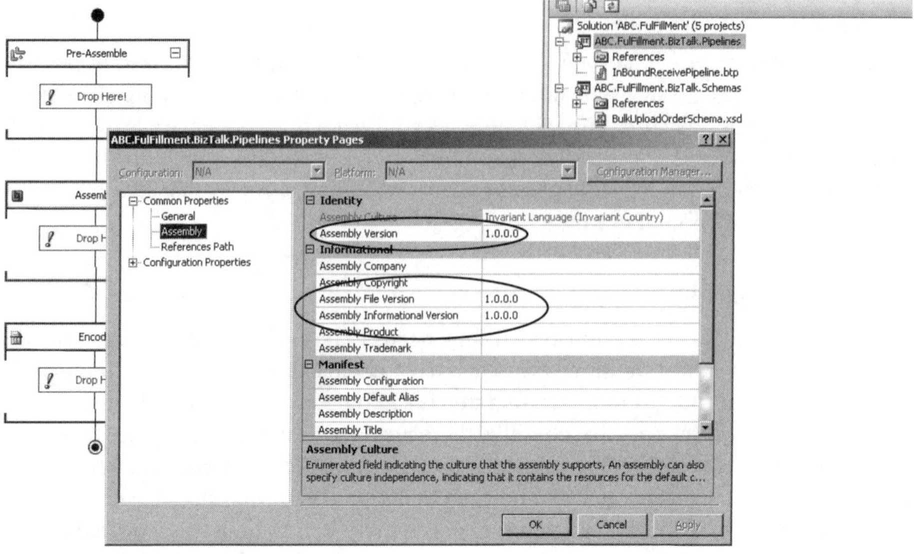

Figure 2-14. *BizTalk project assembling version information*

The dialog boxes are only relevant for BizTalk assemblies. For assemblies that are standard .NET assemblies such as pipeline component projects or utility classes, you need to change the assembly version information using the AssemblyInfo.vb or AssemblyInfo.cs file depending on your language. An example of one is provided here:

```
Common Utilities AssemblyInfo.VB file
Imports System
Imports System.Reflection
Imports System.Runtime.InteropServices

' General information about an assembly is controlled through the following
' set of attributes. Change these attribute values to modify the information
' associated with an assembly.

' Review the values of the assembly attributes

<Assembly: AssemblyTitle("")>
<Assembly: AssemblyDescription("")>
<Assembly: AssemblyCompany("")>
<Assembly: AssemblyProduct("")>
<Assembly: AssemblyCopyright("")>
<Assembly: AssemblyTrademark("")>
<Assembly: CLSCompliant(True)>
```

```
'The following GUID is for the ID of the typelib if this project is exposed to COM
<Assembly: Guid("20E39685-AC83-461A-917F-019D99DFAD20")>

' Version information for an assembly consists of the following four values:
'
'       Major Version
'       Minor Version
'       Build Number
'       Revision
'
' You can specify all the values or you can default the build and revision numbers
' by using the '*' as shown below:

<Assembly: AssemblyVersion("1.0.3.45")>
```

Using an Assembly Info Manager

An assembly info manager is a simple .NET-based structure that can be used to store static properties for assemblies within a solution. This class is then used by all AssemblyInfo.vb files within the solution. This will allow the Build Manager to have to change only one file and have its information reflect in all assemblies within the build. An example implementation is given here:

```
Namespace ABC.FulFillment.Common

    Public Class AssemblyInfoManager
        Public Const Company As String = "ABC Company"
        Public Const ProductName As String = "FulFillment Application"
        Public Const Copyright As String = "Copyright (c) 2006 ABC Inc."
        Public Const Trademark As String = ""
        Public Const MajorVersion As String = "1"
        Public Const MinorVersion As String = "01"
        Public Const BuildNumber As String = "1"
        Public Const RevisionNumber As String = "35"
    End Class

End Namespace
```

In order to use the class a reference to the assembly which contains the class will need to be made. In addition, the AssemblyInfo.vb file will need to be modified to look like the following:

```
Imports System.Reflection
Imports System.Runtime.InteropServices
Imports ABC.FulFillment.Common
```

```
' General Information about an assembly is controlled through the following
' set of attributes. Change these attribute values to modify the information
' associated with an assembly.

' Review the values of the assembly attributes

<Assembly: AssemblyTitle("ABC.BizTalk.PipelineComponents")>
<Assembly: AssemblyDescription("ABC Pipeline Components")>
<Assembly: AssemblyCompany(AssemblyInfoManager.Company)>
<Assembly: AssemblyProduct(AssemblyInfoManager.ProductName)>
<Assembly: AssemblyCopyright(AssemblyInfoManager.Copyright)>
<Assembly: AssemblyTrademark(AssemblyInfoManager.Trademark)>
<Assembly: CLSCompliant(True)>

'The following GUID is for the ID of the typelib if this project is exposed to COM
<Assembly: Guid("6717G042-E07G-6E4f-9G8E-G64370453666")>

' Version information for an assembly consists of the following four values:
'
'       Major Version
'       Minor Version
'       Build Number
'       Revision
'
<Assembly: AssemblyVersion(AssemblyInfoManager.MajorVersion & "." _
AssemblyInfoManager.MinorVersion & "." _ AssemblyInfoManager.BuildNumber & "." _
AssemblyInfoManager.RevisionNumber)>
```

Step 3: Build the Master Solution

Depending on the configuration (single, multiple, or none) of the Visual Studio solution files, this step can either be a single task or a multistep task. Assuming there is a Master Build Visual Studio .NET solution that contains all VS .NET projects to be included in the build, the Build Manager opens this solution within Visual Studio and builds it. Each Visual Studio project should be configured to output its assembly to the proper folder so that it can be loaded from the proper location.

Step 4: Deploy to the Integration Environment

This is a simple step that can be completed by selecting the Deploy build option within Visual Studio as demonstrated in Figure 2-15. The name of the server to deploy the solution is hard-coded in the .sln file. A way around this is to use the "." (dot) as the server name. This will cause Visual Studio to deploy the solution to the local machine. VS .NET will automatically deploy any BizTalk assemblies to the management database without having to create any additional build scripts.

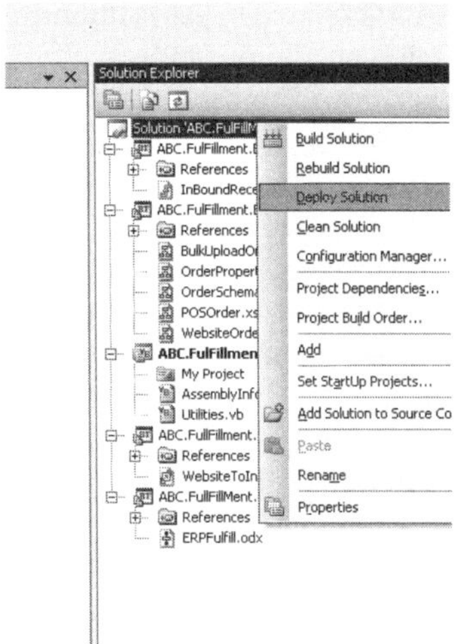

Figure 2-15. *Deploying a BizTalk solution from Visual Studio .NET*

Step 5: Run a Build Verification Test

Once the build is installed in the integration environment, the last task is to perform a test of the build. Generally this is an automated test such as processing a set of test messages and verifying that the output is as expected. This is often called a **build verification test** or **BVT**. An easy way to implement this is to configure a file-based receive location that a set of test messages can be dropped into. These messages would simulate a process that produces a known result such as a set of output messages. A series of messages should be created that model several different test scenarios. Once each of the scenarios has been run and the results verified, the build is said to be "good."

Using Test-Driven Development

Test-driven development is a methodology that states developers should first think about how to test their software before they build it. The software tests are written during the design phase and traditionally take the form of a unit test and unit test plans. **Unit tests** are the "sanity check" tests that developers will create for their software to ensure that all the primary features and test points specified in the unit test plan for the feature are covered. For example, a piece of code that adds two numbers A and B and produces the result will most likely have a unit test plan that states that when you pass in 1 and 2 as parameters, you should get 3 as a result. If not, something is wrong with the code. This is probably the simplest form of a unit test. Extending this example further, unit test plans also should cover error conditions. For example, if your code were to display the result of the division of two numbers, an error check should be made to ensure that the divisor is not zero. In this case, there would be a unit test that attempts to divide by a zero value and check to make sure that this is handled.

To facilitate the creation of unit test plans for BizTalk projects, a good tool to use is **BizUnit**, which is a free tool redistributed from www.gotdotnet.com. BizUnit is an add-on application for **NUnit**, a community-developed tool that allows developers to create unit test harnesses for their source code. For more information on BizUnit and NUnit, see the release package on www.gotdotnet.com.

Once you have created the unit test plans and the associated unit tests using BizUnit and NUnit, you need to think about how to get your test process up and running. In traditional software projects, the unit tests will simply reference the DLL and its methods to be tested. Test data will be passed as arguments to each of the functions in question and the result recorded, which will indicate whether the unit test was successful or not.

This is not the case in a BizTalk project. What you will need to do is create a series of test messages that will simulate the various conditions outlined in your unit test plans. For example, in the previous exercise, you defined the interfaces for the fictitious integration project. If you were to create unit test plans, you would need to create XML documents to be used to simulate real-world messages that would be flowing through the system. These documents would be structured so that they will cause conditions in your unit test plans to be executed. A condition might be to check whether items that are not in stock should be rejected. This is an example of a business requirement being tested. An example of an error condition would be to check that an incoming document conforms to a proper schema. If the document does not, it should be routed to an exception mechanism. Using test-driven development helps you to think about all the potential scenarios that might otherwise go unnoticed. Test-driven development also helps to avoid the "we didn't code for the scenario and it wasn't in your requirements document" argument that often occurs with the end customer of the software. Test-driven development often helps to find these types of issues before coding even begins and allows the customer to decide whether or not the issue is something they want to address.

Creating a BizTalk Installation Package

Significant enhancements have been added to BizTalk 2006 to augment the deployment functionality introduced in BizTalk 2002 and 2004. Previous versions required the creation of a SEED package or a custom Windows Installer package using BTSInstaller. In BizTalk 2006, this functionality has been replaced by simply exporting a BizTalk application into a Windows Installer package that can be imported by any other BizTalk installation. As a result of this enhancement, SEED packages and BTSInstaller scripts are no longer supported.

The MSI package is now created by using the BizTalk Administration Console. Since BizTalk solutions are now organized according to applications, the console provides the functionality to export an MSI package based on the configuration and artifacts that are included within the BizTalk application. Additional files can be included as referenced assemblies, which is ideal for packaging satellite DLL files or configuration files that are not included as artifacts but are still required for the solution to run properly. The MSI file is generated by first right-clicking the BizTalk application in the BizTalk Administration Console and choosing Export MSI to bring up the Export Wizard. The wizard will guide you through the process of creating your export package by having you select the resource(s), dependencies, and destination location for the MSI. During the process, a progress status window is provided and a final summary page appears with any failures encountered during the export process. The MSI package that is created contains the binaries, resources, configuration, and binding file information to import the application on another BizTalk installation as shown in Figures 2-16 and 2-17.

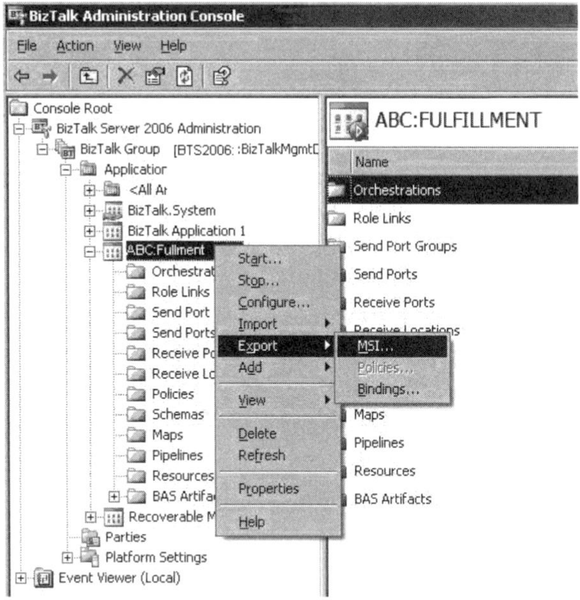

Figure 2-16. *Exporting an MSI using the BizTalk Administration Console*

In order to install the application, you need to first run the MSI package on each machine that will be hosting it. To do this, simply click the MSI package to import all the necessary assemblies and resources and install them into the GAC. This must be done on each BizTalk Server node that will host the application. You then need to import the BizTalk Server artifacts into the system by opening the BizTalk Administration Console, right-clicking the application, and choosing Import as shown in Figure 2-18. For a complete walkthrough of the deployment process within BizTalk 2006, see Chapter 10.

The import process not only imports the BizTalk Server artifacts, but also sets the port bindings and port configurations. This only needs to be performed once per install since these settings are deployed to the BizTalk Management DB.

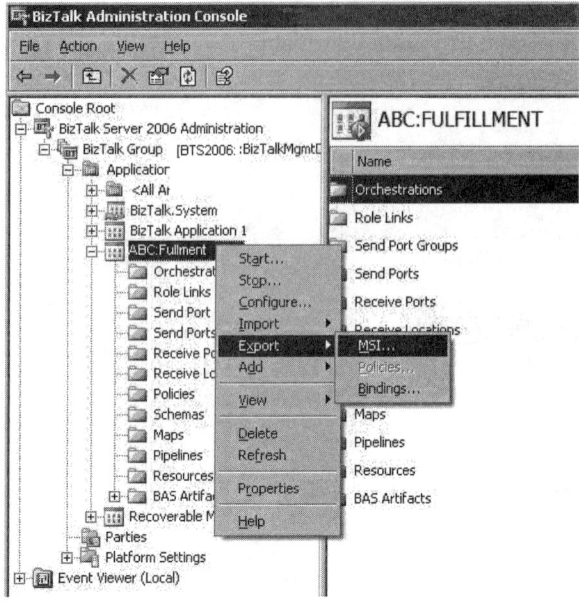

Figure 2-17. *Choosing the MSI destination location*

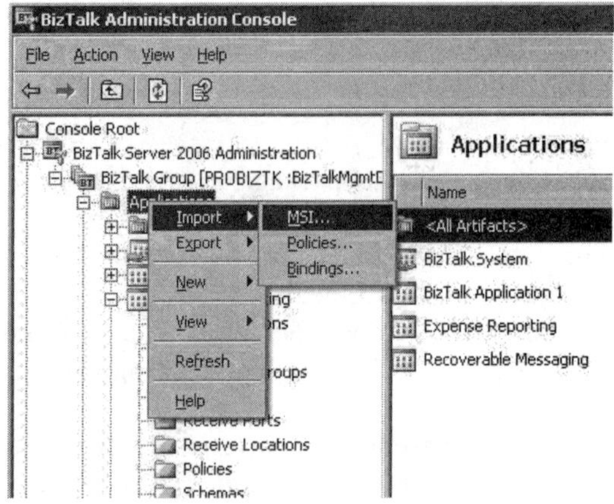

Figure 2-18. *Importing a BizTalk Server MSI*

BizTalk Assembly Naming and Versioning

A BizTalk assembly is created by compiling a BizTalk project using VS .NET.[2] Any artifacts in the project will be included in the compiled assembly that is to be deployed. BizTalk assemblies

2. The material in this section originally appeared in “DotNet, BizTalk, and SQL Team Development,” (REED003675).zip. Copyright by Microsoft Corporation. Reprinted with permission from Microsoft Corporation.

should match the name of their associated namespace. For example, if your namespace is `Company.Project.Subsystem`, then your assembly should be named Company.Project.Subsystem.dll.

In theory, the formal assembly name and the DLL name can be different, but you can only make them different by creating a custom build script outside of Visual Studio. Generally, it isn't necessary to use a DLL name that doesn't correspond to the namespace, and you're better off avoiding the extra work by keeping the names the same.

Note that a division into assemblies such as the following will often be quite suitable for a small- to medium-sized BizTalk project, as in many cases the BizTalk artifacts are shared across all features and subsystems:

- MyCompany.MyProject.Orchestrations.dll
- MyCompany.MyProject.Schemas.dll
- MyCompany.MyProject.Pipelines.dll
- MyCompany.MyProject.Transforms.dll
- MyCompany.MyProject.PipelineComponents.dll

If these artifacts were not shared and were specific to a feature, the namespace would be `MyCompany.MyProject.MySubsystem`.

■ **Note** The Visual Studio solution name will likely be MyCompany.Project.BizTalk in this case.

Often long names such as MyCompany.MyProject.MySubsystem can be difficult to deal with (especially in Visual SourceSafe 6.0, where the file open dialogs do not expand for longer names). The benefits, however, with having the full scoping available when the assemblies and associated artifacts are accessed outside of Visual Studio, especially in a production support and deployment scenario, far outweigh this minor inconvenience.

Side-by-Side Deployments

Within most BizTalk projects, there may be "in-progress" development that can take days, weeks, or even months to complete. In such scenarios, deploying new releases or hot fixes is difficult to achieve. In order to upgrade to a new version of the currently running application, it becomes necessary to allow any in-progress processes to reside **side by side** with the newer releases. When all in-progress processes are complete, then the earlier versions can be safely undeployed without affecting any processes of the newer releases.

In some cases, there may also be a need for multiple versions to reside side by side for an indefinite amount of time. In these scenarios, it becomes vital to ensure the activating logic is unique to guarantee the correct messages are passed on to correct versions. The default versioning process is shown in Figure 2-19.

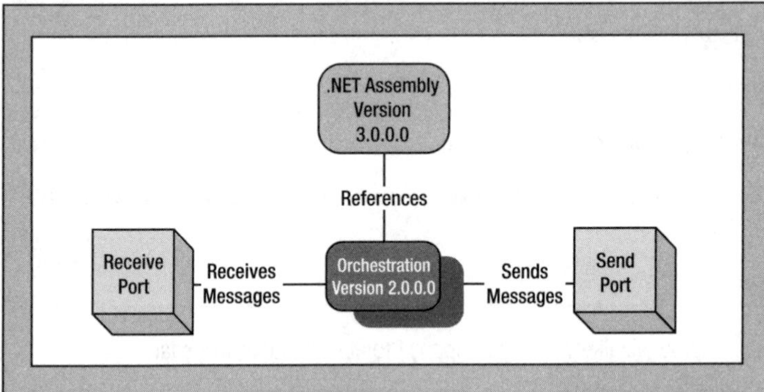

Figure 2-19. *Default versioning*

Following are some unique requirements for side-by-side deployments:

- Provide an ability to deploy new releases.
- Provide an ability to deploy incremental releases (without affecting previous deployments).
- Provide an ability to deploy hot fixes (redeployment of recent deployment installs without affecting previous deployments).
- To ease maintenance, stamp all assemblies with the same version.

Side-by-Side Deployment Strategies

To achieve side-by-side deployment, it is necessary to ensure versioning is maintained appropriately between all referenced assemblies. Without a versioning strategy, any side-by-side deployment strategy is prone to errors. Within .NET, any assembly references (either BizTalk or non-BizTalk) need to match the assembly versions defined within referenced objects at compile time.

The default versioning schema causes a conflict within the BizTalk environment. In a typical BizTalk environment, along with the assemblies, you also have external objects like receive/send ports and schemas that are shared between different versions. Messages meant for one version can be picked up and processed by another version, which may lead to errors or undesired results.

To solve this problem, it becomes necessary to extend .NET's versioning scheme for BizTalk. The following sections describe three common strategies for doing this.

Versioned Deployment Using Versioned Receive/Send Ports

In this strategy, all receive port and send port names are unique across multiple deployments. Hence any messages that arrive at these ports are guaranteed to be processed by the specific versioned modules that are listening to these specific ports. A diagram of this approach is shown in Figure 2-20.

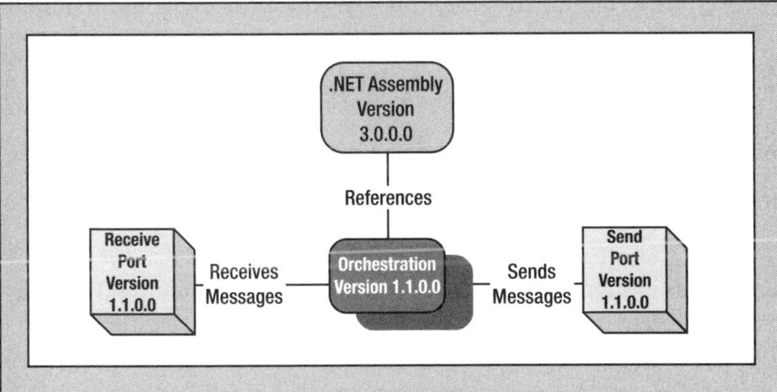

Figure 2-20. *Versioned deployment using ports*

Following are the steps involved:

1. Update the assembly version defined within the specific BizTalk project.
2. Update the assembly version defined within the associated non-BizTalk assemblies.
3. Before compilation, update each binding file associated with the BizTalk modules with appropriate port names (port names will be suffixed with the assembly version). If the binding step is included during deployment, these ports will get created during deployment.

The advantages of this process are as follows:

- The deployment strategy is clean.
- Any number of deployments are guaranteed to process only those messages that arrive at specific binded ports.
- Namespaces of associated schemas do not need to be changed.

The sole disadvantage is this:

- For every release, all associated receive/send ports will need to be updated to reflect the new version. If external partners are submitting messages, new locations will need to be communicated with external partners.

Versioned Deployment Using Versioned Schema Namespaces

This strategy involves changing the namespaces associated with specific schemas. Changing a namespace is easily accomplished by suffixing each schema's namespace with a specific version number before compilation. This strategy solves the correlation error encountered with the preceding approach and is diagrammed in Figure 2-21.

Perform the following procedure to deploy the assemblies in your project using versioned schema namespaces:

1. Update the assembly version defined within the specific BizTalk project.
2. Update the assembly version defined within the associated non-BizTalk assemblies.
3. Update all references for imports and includes within schemas if you have included any.
4. Before compilation, programmatically update namespaces associated with individual schemas to include references to specific versions (e.g., `http://Microsoft.BizTalk/Service/v1.0.0.0`).

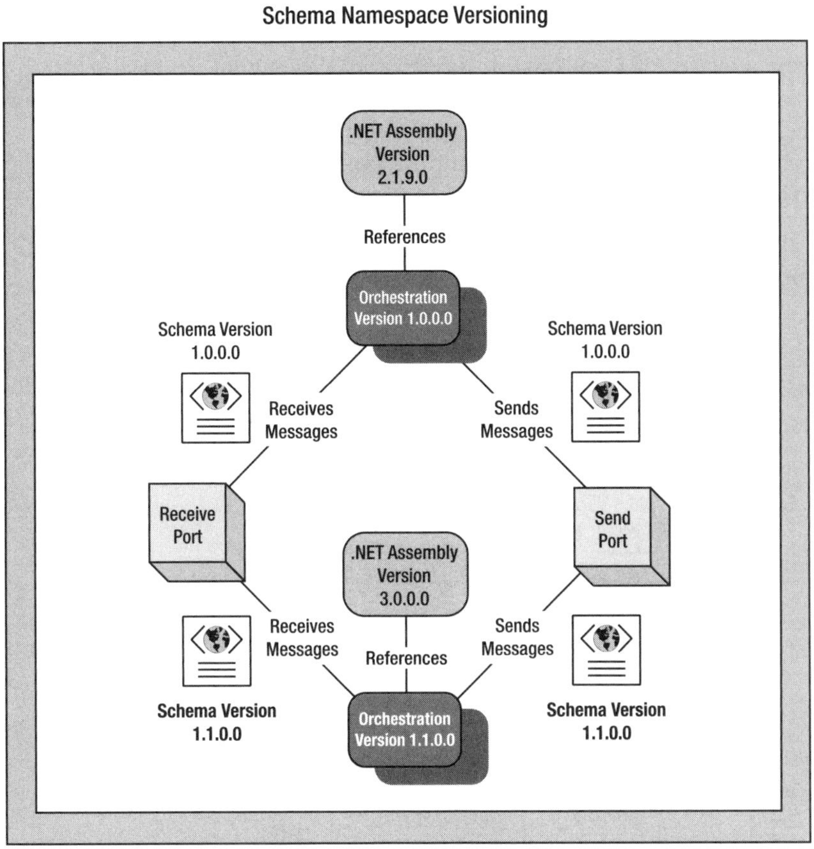

Figure 2-21. *Versioned deployment using namespaces*

Following are the advantages of the versioned deployment approach:

- As BizTalk distinguishes schemas based on namespaces and root node, specific messages are processed by specific versioned assemblies.
- This process works in scenarios where correlation sets are initialized.
- Receive/Send port names do not need to be changed. This is beneficial in scenarios where external partners are submitting messages to specific ports. Using this approach, new port locations do not need to be communicated to external partners.

Disadvantages of the versioned deployment approach include the following:

- Namespaces of associated schemas should be changed even if there are no structural changes to these specific schemas. This is to ease the management of the schemas once they have been deployed. For instance, it is much easier to examine a DLL and know that all the schemas within it contain the same version. If not, the management of the schemas can become cumbersome.
- For every release, all associated schema namespaces will need to be updated to reflect the new version. This could constitute a significant architectural change.

Combining the Two Approaches

You can combine the previous two approaches using versioned schema namespaces in conjunction with versioned receive/send ports. This approach is shown in Figure 2-22.

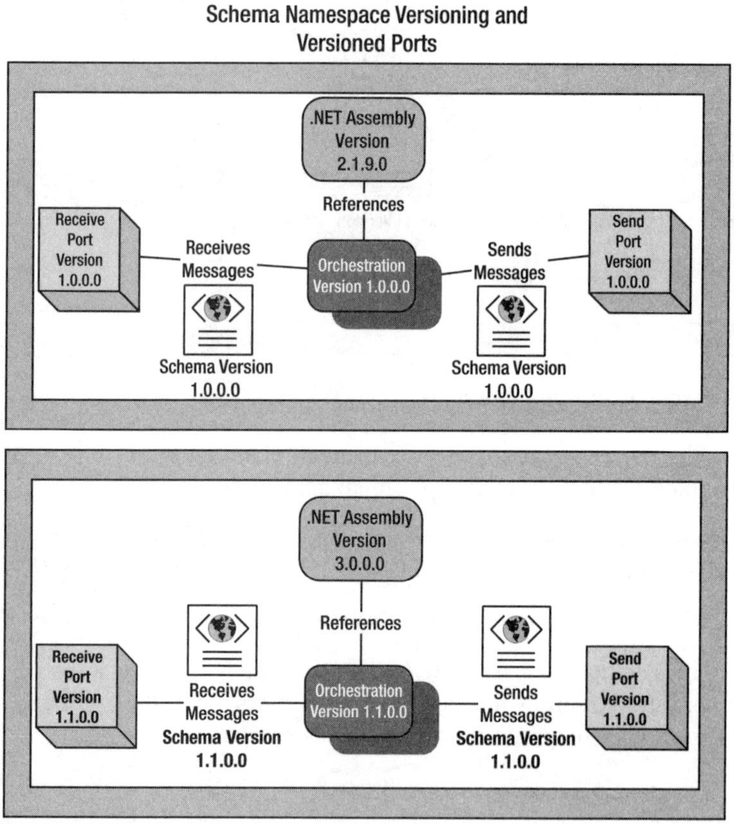

Figure 2-22. *Versioned deployment using ports and namespaces*

The steps involved in the combined approach are as follows:

1. Update the assembly version defined within the specific BizTalk project.
2. Update the assembly version defined within the associated non-BizTalk assemblies.
3. Update all references for imports and includes within schemas if you have included any.
4. Before compilation, programmatically update namespaces associated with each schema to include references to specific versions (e.g., `http://Microsoft.BizTalk/Service/v1.0.0.0`).
5. Before compilation, update each binding file associated with BizTalk modules with appropriate port names (port names will be suffixed with assembly version). These ports will be created if the binding step is included during deployment.

Advantages of the combined approach are as follows:

- It presents a cleaner deployment strategy and easier debugging scenarios.
- As BizTalk distinguishes schemas based on namespaces and root node, specific messages are processed by specific versioned assemblies.
- It works in scenarios where correlation is used.

And the disadvantages:

- Namespaces of associated schemas need to be changed even if there are no structural changes to these specific schemas.
- All receive/send port names also need to be changed.
- For every release, all associated schema namespaces as well as receive/send ports will need to be updated to reflect the new version.

Versioned Deployment Using Filtering

This strategy involves promoting an element within a message (e.g., version) that is used within the filter associated with a Receive shape that gets activated when a message is received by the orchestration. This has the benefit of allowing you to use content-based routing information, which can be changed in a production scenario with no code modification and very little downtime. This approach is shown in Figure 2-23.

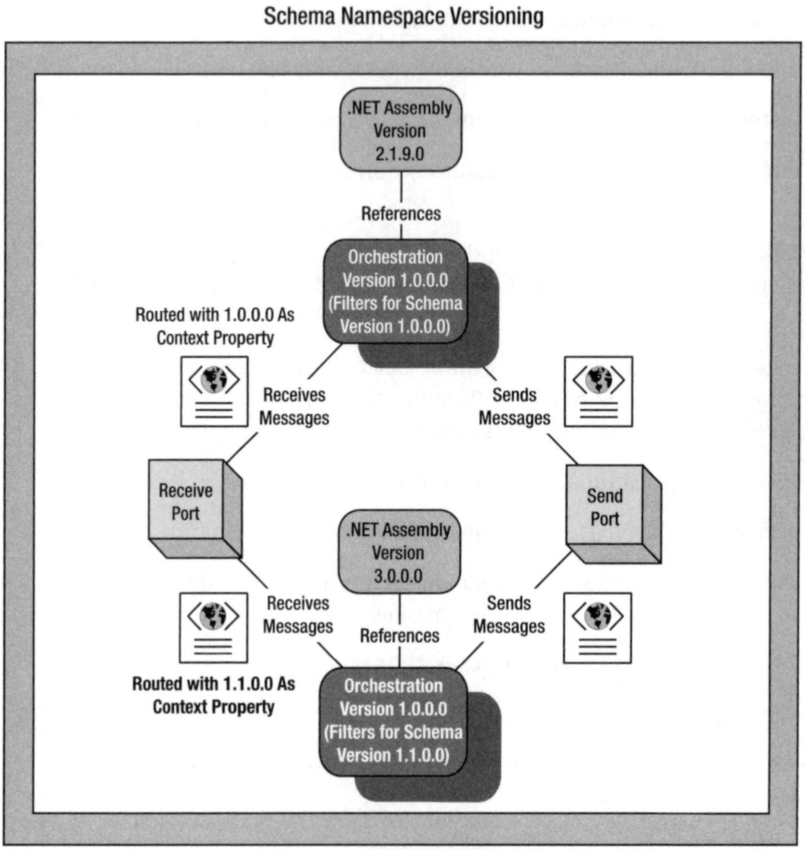

Figure 2-23. *Versioned deployment using filtering*

Use the following steps to implement this strategy:

1. Update the assembly version defined within the specific BizTalk project.
2. Update the assembly version defined within the associated non-BizTalk assemblies.
3. Before compilation, programmatically update the filter expression to check for specific data that contains version information (e.g., Message1.version = "1.0.0.0"). A version-specific message will get picked up by correct versions and processed.

The advantages of this method are as follows:

- Only filter expressions need to be updated.
- Receive/Send port names do not need to be changed.
- Schema namespaces do not need to be changed.

And the disadvantages:

- It will not work for scenarios where orchestrations are required to initialize a correlation set. If correlation sets are being initialized and schemas of the same version are being referenced between different deployments (different assembly versions), BizTalk does not know which combination of assembly and associated schema to use and generates a runtime error.
- An element within the schema that contains the version number will need to be promoted.
- For every release, this filter will need to be changed to reflect the current version.

BizTalk Naming Conventions

One of the key benefits of coding business processes using BizTalk orchestrations is the visual representation of the workflow. When building complex orchestrations, naming conventions are critical for orchestration workflow shapes, and are equally important to naming BizTalk artifacts such as maps, ports, and pipelines properly. Using well-defined naming conventions allows both technical and nontechnical persons to view the orchestration and understand the process it is attempting to model. Well-named and comments orchestration shapes enhance the readability and organization of the workflow and allow the reader to follow the flow of messages through the orchestration and understand the source, destination, and content of the message data.

The following sections provide a guide for naming BizTalk artifacts along with orchestration shapes and types.[3]

A BizTalk artifact is any one of the following:

- **Schema**: This is an XSD schema that defines the data structure. Schemas can define XML or a flat file.
- **Map**: A BizTalk map defines mappings between two different schemas. For instance, a purchase order schema has fields that can be mapped to an invoice schema. The map will transfer the data from the source (purchase order) schema to the destination (invoice) schema.
- **Pipeline**: This can be a send or receive pipeline component. Pipelines are used on the send or receive points of BizTalk to do special processing on a message before it is sent out or as it is received.
- **Orchestration**: An orchestration is where the business process is designed and executed.
- **Property schema**: This is a special type of XSD schema used to define properties to be employed in BizTalk.

---

3. The remainder of this section originally appeared in "DotNet, BizTalk, and SQL Team Development," (REED003675).zip. Copyright by Microsoft Corporation. Reprinted with permission from Microsoft Corporation.

BizTalk Artifact Namespaces

Artifacts in BizTalk server are usually in the end .NET classes. As such, it is generally advisable to follow proper .NET naming conventions as would be followed in any regular .NET development project. Specifically, classes should be named based on the following pattern:

Company.Project.Feature

In the case of BizTalk projects, most developers want a clear delineation between objects that are only used within BizTalk Server and regular .NET classes. In these cases, the ".BizTalk" part of the namespace is added to give the following pattern:

Company.Project.`BizTalk`*.Feature*

As an example of this pattern, if a Pipeline existed within the FulFillment feature, that pipeline would be under the namespace of `ABC.FulFillment.BizTalk.InBoundReceivePipeline`.

A schema uses a namespace to uniquely qualify elements and attributes within that schema to ensure that conflicts do not occur. Ultimately, uniquely identifying your BizTalk artifacts with namespaces is important.

Note that the naming conventions are Pascal cased, and nested namespaces will have dependencies on types in the containing namespace.

BizTalk Messaging Artifacts

All names should follow Pascal-case convention unless mentioned otherwise for the specific artifact, although underscores are used to separate logical entities. For schemas, maps, orchestrations, and pipelines, ensure that the .NET type name matches the file name (without file extension). Table 2-2 gives patterns for properly naming BizTalk artifacts.

Table 2-2. *BizTalk Artifact Naming Conventions*

Artifact	Standard	Notes	Examples
Schema file	<RootNode>_<Standard> *vn-ma*.xsd or <DescriptiveName> *vn-ma*_<Standard>.xsd	Standards include XML, X12, flat file (FF), and other custom formats. If root node does not distinguish the schema or if the schema is for a well-known standard, use a descriptive name. *vn* refers to major version number, *m* refers to minor number. For unreleased schemas, use a letter suffix to the minor version (like "a"). Include version in the version attribute of the schema element. .NET type name should match, without file extension. .NET namespace will likely match assembly name.	ClaimInvoice.xsd PurchaseOrderAcknowledge_FF.xsd FNMA100330_FF.xsd

Artifact	Standard	Notes	Examples
Schema target namespaces	Nonshared schemas should have a target namespace corresponding to the .NET namespace of the associated .NET type, prefixed with "http".	.NET type name should match, without file extension. .NET namespace will likely match assembly name.	For a PatientClaim.xsd file, `http://<Company>.<Function>.PatientClaim` or `http://<Contoso>.HealthClaims.PatientClaim`
Property schema files	<PropSchema>_PropSchema.xsd	Should be named to reflect its common usage across multiple schemas, if needed.	poPropSchema.xsd
Maps	<SourceSchema>_To_<DestinationSchema>.btm	Name should define/describe what is being mapped.	PurchaseOrder_FF_To_PurchaseOrderAcknowledge_XML.btm
Orchestrations	A meaningful name that represents the underlying process, likely with a verb-noun pattern.		EvaluateCredit.odx ProcessHealthClaim.odx
Send/Receive Pipelines	rcv<SchemaName>.btp or rcv<ProjectName>.btp or rcv<Function>.btp snd<SchemaName>.btp or snd<ProjectName>.btp or snd<Function>.btp	A pipeline might be used to ensure reception of particular schema(s) or to perform some other function. A project name might be used when multiple schemas are specified for ASM/DASM.	rcvPOAckPipelineFF.btp rcvCatalogPipeline.btp rcvHealthClaimPipelineEDI.btp rcvInvoiceFromSupplierPipeline.btp sndPaymentPipeline.btp sndClaimProcessPipeline.btp sndOrderToWarehousePipeline.btp
Receive ports	<BizApp><InputSchema>To<OutputSchema>Port or <BizApp><Functional Description> or rcv<InputSchema>To<OutputSchema>Port or rcv<Functional Description>Port	"BizApp" prefix (corresponding to the name of the app deploying to BizTalk) helps when many applications are deployed to the same BizTalk installation. Use functional description if the input schema (and potentially output schema, if request/response) does not adequately describe the port. One-way ports use functional description form.	ERP_PurchaseOrder_XML_To_POAck_XML rcvPurchaseOrderToPOAckPort (for request/response port) ERP_PurchaseOrder_XML (for one-way port) ERP_CheckOrderStatus rcvPurchaseOrderXMLPort rcvERPStatusPort
Receive locations	<ReceivePortName>_<Transport>		ERPCheckOrderStatus_MSMQT rcvERPStatus_File
Send Port Groups	<BizApp>_<Functional Description>	"BizApp" prefix—see the receive ports entry.	CRM_CustomerUpdateNotification

Continued

Table 2-2. *Continued*

Artifact	Standard	Notes	Examples
Send ports	<BizApp><Schema> <Transport> or <BizApp><Func Description><DestApp>_ <Transport> or snd<InputSchema>To <OutputSchema>Port or snd<Functional Description>Port	In some cases, the schema being sent is descriptive enough. In others, a functional description of the action to be taken by a destination app is better suited.	CRM_CustomerUpdate_ERP_ MSMQT sndUpdateToERPSystemPort sndOrderStatusPort
Parties	A meaningful name for a trading partner.	If dealing with multiple entities in a trading partner organization, the organization name could be used as a prefix.	INV_MyTradingPartnerName
Roles	A meaningful name for the role that a trading partner plays.		Shipper

Orchestration Naming Conventions—Workflow Shapes

The BizTalk Orchestration Designer allows you to create complex workflow automations quickly and easily. If you are not careful, however, a large orchestration can often become confusing and difficult to debug. One way to help ensure that your orchestration is maintainable is to properly name the orchestration shapes so that they are easily readable and self-explanatory. Microsoft has published some patterns on how to name orchestration shapes,[4] and Table 2-3 expands upon these.

■ **Note** To add documentation to a group of related workflow shapes, use a Group shape. These will display as much text as you care to associate with them and can add quite a bit of documentation value to the diagram. (Shape names should always follow upper-camel casing after the prefix that is specified in Table 2-3.)

---

4. http://msdn.microsoft.com/library/default.asp?url=/library/en-us/BTS_2004WP/html/ffda72df-5aec-4a1b-b97a-ac98635e81dc.asp

Table 2-3. *Orchestration Workflow Shape Naming Conventions*

Shape	Standard	Notes	Examples
Scope	Scope_<DescriptionOf ContainedWork> or Scope_<DescOfContained Work>_<TxType>	Info about transaction type may need to be included in some situations where it adds significant documentation value to the diagram.	Scope_CreditServiceCall
Receive	Rcv_<MessageName> or Receive_<MessageName>	Typically, MessageName will be the same as the name of the message variable that is being received.	Rcv_rawCreditReport Receive_CreditReport
Send	Snd_<MessageName> or Send_<MessageName>	Typically, MessageName will be the same as the name of the message variable that is being sent.	Snd_poAcknowledge Send_poAck
Expression	<DescriptionOfEffect>	Expression shapes should be named with upper-camel-case convention (no prefix) to simply describe the net effect of the expression, similar to naming a method. The exception to this is the case where the expression is interacting with an external .NET component to perform a function that overlaps with existing BizTalk functionality—use closest BizTalk shape for this case.	GetFindingsReport
Decide	Decide_<DescriptionOf Decision>	Decide shapes should be prefixed with "Decide_" followed by a full description of what will be decided in the "If" branch.	Decide_ApprovalRequired
If Branch	If_<DescriptionOf Decision>	If Branch shapes should be prefixed with "If_" followed by a (perhaps abbreviated) description of what is being decided.	If_ApprovalRequired
Else Branch	Else	Else Branch shapes should always be named "Else".	Else
Construct Message (Message Assignment)	Assign_<Message> (for Construct shape) <ExpressionDescription> (for expression)	If a Construct shape contains a message assignment, it should be prefixed with "Assign_" followed by an abbreviated name of the message being assigned. The actual message assignment shape contained should be named to describe the expression that is contained.	Assign_paymentVoucher which contains the expression CopyPaymentDetails

Continued

Table 2-3. *Continued*

Shape	Standard	Notes	Examples
Construct Message (Transform)	Xform_<SourceSchema>To<DestSchema> (for Construct) or X_<SourceSchema>To<DestSchema> (for expression) or Construct_<DestSchema>	If a Construct shape contains a message transform, it should be prefixed with "Xform_" followed by an abbreviated description of the transform (i.e., source schema to destination schema). The actual message transform shape contained should generally be named the same as the containing shape, except with an "X_" prefix to save space.	Xform_LoanRequestToCreditRequest which contains transform shape X_LoanRequestToCreditRequest or Construct_Invoice
Construct Message (containing multiple shapes)		If a Construct Message shape uses multiple assignments or transforms, the overall shape should be named to communicate the net effect, using no prefix.	
Call Orchestration Start Orchestration	Call_<OrchestrationName> Start_<OrchestrationName>		
Throw	Throw_<ExceptionType>	The corresponding variable name for the exception type should (often) be the same name as the exception type, only camel cased.	Throw_RuleException, which refers to the `ruleException` variable.
Parallel	Parallel_<DescriptionOfParallelWork>	Parallel shapes should be named "Parallel_" followed by a description of what work will be done in parallel.	Parallel_CreditVendorCalls
Delay	Delay_<DescriptionOfWhatWaitingFor>	Delay shapes should be named "Delay_" followed by an abbreviated description of what is being waited for.	Delay_POAcknowledgeTimeout
Listen	Listen_<DescriptionOfOutcomes>	Listen shapes should be named "Listen_" followed by an abbreviated description that captures (to the degree possible) all the branches of the Listen shape.	Listen_POAckOrTimeout Listen_FirstShippingBid
Loop	Loop_<ExitCondition>	Loop shapes should be named "Loop_" followed by an abbreviated description of what the exit condition is.	Loop_AllMsgsSent
Role Link		See "Roles" in Table 2-2 earlier.	

Shape	Standard	Notes	Examples
Suspend	Suspend_<Reason Description>	Suspend shapes describe what action an administrator must take to resume the orchestration. More detail can be passed to an error property—and should include what should be done by the administrator before resuming the orchestration.	Suspend_ ReEstablishCreditLink
Terminate	Terminate_ <ReasonDescription>	Terminate shapes describe why the orchestration terminated. More detail can be passed to an error property.	Terminate_TimeoutsExpired
Call Rule	CallRules_<PolicyName>	The policy name may need to be abbreviated.	CallRules_CreditApproval
Compensate	Compensate or Compensate_<TxName>	If the shape compensates nested transactions, names should be suffixed with the name of the nested transaction—otherwise it should simply be "Compensate".	Compensate_TransferFunds or Comp_TransferFunds
Multi-Part Message Type	<LogicalDocumentType>	Multipart types encapsulate multiple parts. The WSDL spec indicates "Parts are a flexible mechanism for describing the logical abstract content of a message." The name of the multipart type should correspond to the "logical" document type, i.e., what the sum of the parts describes.	InvoiceReceipt (Might encapsulate an invoice acknowledgement and a payment voucher)
Multi-Part Messsage Part	<SchemaNameOfPart>	This shape should be named (most often) simply for the schema (or simple type) associated with the part.	InvoiceHeader
Message	camelCased	This shape should be named using camel casing, based on the corresponding schema type or multipart message type. If there is more than one variable of a type, name it after its use in the orchestration.	purchaseOrderAck
Variable	camelCased		

Continued

Table 2-3. *Continued*

Shape	Standard	Notes	Examples
Port Type	<function>PortType	Port types should be named to suggest the nature of an endpoint, with upper-camel casing and suffixed with "PortType". If there will be more than one port for a port type, the port type should be named according to the abstract service supplied. The WSDL spec indicates port types are "a named set of abstract operations and the abstract messages involved" that also encapsulates the message pattern (e.g., one-way, request-response, solicit-response) that all operations on the port type adhere to.	ProcessPurchaseOrder PortType which might have operations such as SubmitPO or RequestPOStatus
Port	<function>Port	Ports should be named to suggest a grouping of functionality, with upper-camel casing and suffixed with "Port".	ProcessPurchaseOrderPort
Port Operation	<MethodName>	Port operations should be named according to the "method"—i.e., what subset of the port functionality will be exercised. For a port that has one operation, it can be commonly named "Submit". Note that these operation names appear in WSDL for web-service-published orchestrations.	
Correlation Type	UpperCamelCased	Correlation types should be named with upper-camel-case convention, based on the logical name of what is being used to correlate.	PurchaseOrderNumber
Correlation Set	camelCased	Correlation sets should be named with camel-case convention based on the corresponding correlation type. If there is more than one, it should be named to reflect its specific purpose in the orchestration.	purchaseOrderNumber
Orchestration Parameter	camelCased	Orchestration parameters should be named with camel-case convention, and match the caller's names for the corresponding variables where needed.	

PART 2

BizTalk Revealed

Now that you have explored BizTalk at a conceptual level and examined some of the challenges that many teams face in implementing it, let's look at the specifics of the BizTalk toolkit. In Chapters 3 through 8, we discuss the most common tools that you will find within any typical BizTalk solution. Additionally, you get a chance to explore some real-world patterns, examples, and implementations you can use to address specific problems that may be present in your own solutions. Over the course of this part, we will dive into the following topics:

- How BizTalk messaging works
- Specifics of subscriptions and messages
- Pipelines, pipeline components, and example implementations
- Advanced orchestrations and concepts
- Business Rule Engine concepts and examples
- Patterns and practices for solving real-world examples

CHAPTER 3

■ ■ ■

Thinking Inside the Box

The BizTalk Messagebox is the core of the messaging subsystem. It has the responsibility of storing all message items within the product. The Message Bus subsystem queries the Messagebox and looks for messages that match a subscription. The BizTalk Message Bus is a **publisher/subscriber** model, or **pub/sub**. Simply stated, every message going into the Messagebox is "published" so that endpoints with matching message subscriptions can receive the message and send it to the appropriate orchestration or send port and finally to the corresponding adapter. Each BizTalk process that runs on a machine has something called the **Message Agent**, which is responsible for searching for messages that match subscriptions and routing them to the End Point Manager (EPM), which actually handles the message and sends it where it needs to go. The EPM is the broker between the Messagebox and the pipeline/port/adapter combination or orchestration that has a subscription for the message. Both the EPM and Message Agent are executed within the BTSNTSvc.exe process that runs on the host. Figure 3-1 shows the Message Bus architecture.

One thing is crucial to understand: in BizTalk Server, messages are immutable. This means that once a message has entered the Messagebox, it cannot be changed. In order to change the message, you must copy the message payload to a new message, modify the data required, and publish the new message. This is critical, as multiple endpoints may have subscriptions for the published message, and each of them may handle the message differently. If the message payload could be changed, the entire architecture for the product would not work.

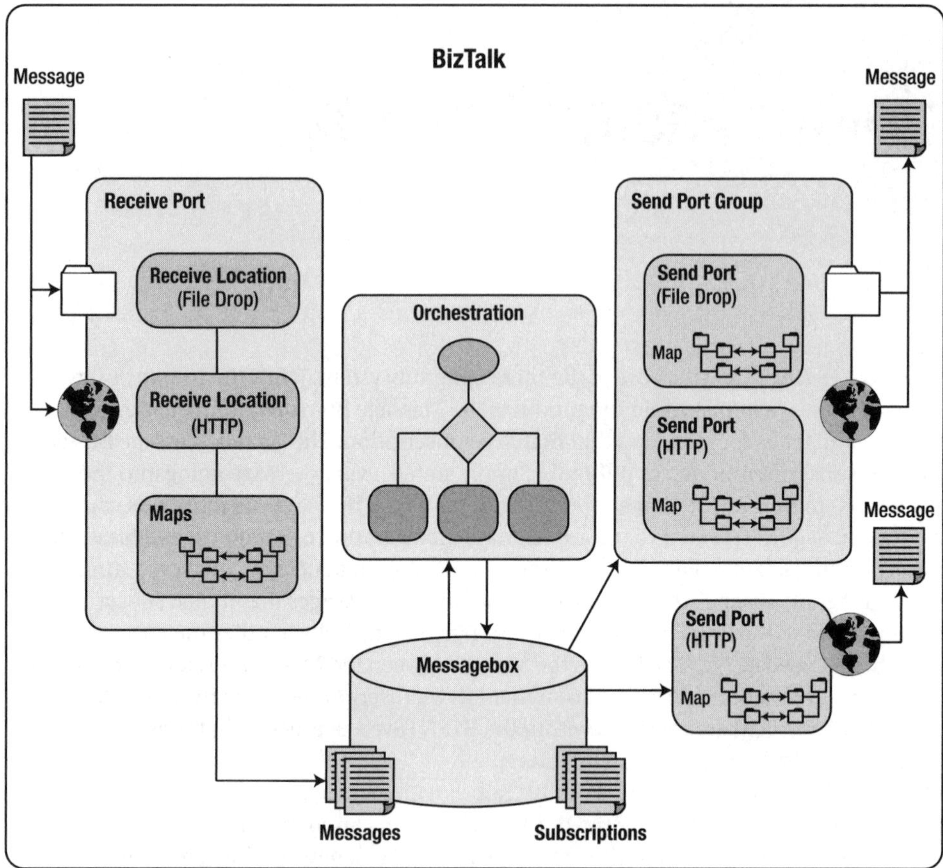

Figure 3-1. *Message Bus architecture in BizTalk Server*

Understanding the Message Bus

The Message Bus is the backbone of the BizTalk Server product. The bus contains unique parts, each of which are explained later in the subsection "Messaging Components." The most obvious of these is the Messagebox, which is explained first. The others include the messages within the Messagebox and messaging components that move messages to their proper endpoints.

The Messagebox

The Messagebox is simply a database. This database has many tables, several of which are responsible for storing the messages that are received by BizTalk. Each message has metadata associated with it called the **message context**, and the individual metadata items are stored in key/value pairs called **context properties**. There are context properties that describe all the data necessary to identify things like

- The inbound port where the message was received from
- The inbound transport type
- Transport-specific information such as `ReceivedFileName` in the case of the file adapter, `InboundQueueName` in the case of MSMQ or MQSeries, etc.
- The `MessageID` of the message so it can be uniquely identified
- The schema type and namespace of the message

Many people generally equate the Messagebox to be the whole of the BizTalk Server messaging infrastructure. This is absolutely false and is similar to saying that a database is basically a set of data files sitting on a hard drive. The messaging infrastructure, or Message Bus, is made of a dozen or so interrelated components, each of which performs a specific job.

Messaging Components

When new architects start designing BizTalk solutions, few stop and think about how the messages are actually going to be sent and received to their proper endpoints. This job belongs to the messaging components within BizTalk, each of which are explained next.

Host Services

A **BizTalk host** is nothing more than a logical container. Hosts provide you with the ability to structure the processing of your application into groups that can be distributed across multiple memory processes and across machines. A host is most often used to separate adapters, orchestrations, and ports to run on separate machines to aid in load balancing. A **host instance** is just that, an instance of the host. The instance is actually just a service that runs on the machine called BTSNTSvc.exe. This process provides the BizTalk engine a place to execute and allows for instances of different hosts to be running on one machine at a given time. Each host will end up being a separate instance of the BTSNTSvc.exe service from within the Windows Task Manager. If you examine the services control panel applet, you will find that each of the hosts that are configured on the machine will show up as a separate service named whatever the host was originally called. The host instance exists simply to allow the BizTalk subservices a place to run. Most people think of the BizTalk service as a single unit, but really it is a container for multiple services, each of which is described in the following text.

The difference between an **Isolated host** and an **In-Process host** is that an Isolated host must run under another process, in most cases IIS, and an In-Process host is a complete BizTalk service alone. Additionally, since In-Process hosts exist outiside of the BizTalk environment, the BizTalk Administration Tools are not able to determine the status of these hosts (stopped, started, or starting). Security is also fundamentially different in an Isolated host versus an In-Process host. In-Process hosts must run under an account that is within the In-Process host's Windows group, and do not maintain security context within the Messagebox. Isolated hosts are useful when a service already exists that will be receiving messages either by some proprietary means or by some other transport protocol such as HTTP. In this case, the Isolated host only runs one instance of the End Point Manager, and is responsible for receiving messages from its transport protocol and sending them to the Messagebox through the EPM. Outside of hosting an IIS process, Isolated hosts could be used to attach to a custom Windows service that is polling a message store looking for new items that it will publish to the Messagebox. Isolated processes provide an architectural advantage for these scenarios. They do not require any interprocess communication (IPC) between the EPM and the Windows service that hosts it. The only real IPC that exists is between the Isolated host and the Messagebox database, which cannot be avoided since . . . it is a database service, hosted most likely on another machine.

In-Process hosts can host all BizTalk subservices depending on how they are configured. They not only can receive messages from the outside world, but they can send them through Send Adapters, poll for messages that match a subscription, and host XLANG engine instances. In the case of a Send Adapter, an In-Process host must be used due to how the security context of the Adapter Framework is built. You can get around this by creating a Send Adapter with custom IPC. This technique is how the HTTP and SOAP adapters interact with the aspnet_wp.exe/w3wp.exe processes within these respective adapters.

Each Isolated host has the set of subservices running within it shown in Table 3-1. These services can also be viewed from the adm_HostInstance_SubServices table in the Management Database.

Table 3-1. *Host Instance Subservices*

Service	Description
Caching	Service used to cache information that is loaded into the host. Examples of cached information would be assemblies that are loaded, adapter configuration information, custom configuration information, etc.
End Point Manager	Go-between for the Message Agent and the Adapter Framework. The EPM hosts send/receive ports and is responsible for excuting pipelines and BizTalk transformations.
Tracking	Service that moves information from the Messagebox to the Tracking Database. See the section "Tracking and Database Management" later in the chapter.
XLANG/s	Host engine for BizTalk Server orchestrations.
MSMQT	MSMQT adapter service; serves as a replacement for the MSMQ protocol when interacting with BizTalk Server. The MSMQT protocol has been deprecated in BizTalk Server 2006 and should only be used to resolve backward-compatibility issues.

Subscriptions

In order to fully understand the Message Bus architecture, it is critical to understand how **subscriptions** work. It is also critical to understand that the process of enlisting a port simply means that a subscription exists for that port within the Messaging Engine. Subscriptions are the mechanism by which ports and orchestrations are able to receive and send messages within a BizTalk Server solution.

Subscribing

According to Microsoft, "A subscription is a collection of comparison statements, known as predicates, involving message context properties and the values specific to the subscription."[1] Following our previous example from Chapter 2 with the ABC Company, the `MessageType`

1. Microsoft MSDN: http://msdn.microsoft.com/library/default.asp?url=/library/en-us/BTS_2004WP/html/1e2e50f7-6609-4eb2-a9a1-3a951700f840.asp

context property would be used to evaluate the subscription criteria. The Message Agent inserts information about a subscription when it creates it. Predicates are inserted into one of the Messagebox's predicate tables, based on what type of operation is specified in the subscription being created. Note the list of predicate tables that follows; these are the same predicates that are used in the filter editor for defining filter criteria on ports. The reason the list of tables is the same as the list of filter predicates is because a filter expression is actually being used to build each subscription. When you are defining a filter expression, what you are actually doing is modifying the underlying subscription within BizTalk to contain the new filter information that is included in your filter expression.

BitwiseANDPredicates

EqualsPredicates

EqualsPredicates2ndPass

ExistsPredicates

FirstPassPredicates

GreaterThanOrEqualsPredicates

GreaterThanPredicates

LessThanOrEqualsPredicates

LessThanPredicates

NotEqualsPredicates

The BizTalk Messaging Engine creates a subscription in the Messagebox by calling two stored procedures. These are `bts_CreateSubscription_{HostName}` and `bts_InsertPredicate_{HostName}`. The subscription is created based on which host will be handling the subscription, which is why these stored procedures are created automatically when the host is created in the Microsoft Management Console.

Enlisting

Most people ask what the difference is between **enlisting** a port and **starting** a port. The difference is simple. Enlisted ports have subscriptions written for them in the Messagebox, while unenlisted ports do not. The same is true for orchestrations. Artifacts that are not enlisted are simply in "deployment limbo" in that they are ready to process messages but no way exists for the Messaging Engine to send them one.The main effect this will have is that ports and orchestrations that are enlisted, but not started, will have any messages with matching subscription information queued within the Messagebox and ready to be processed once the artifact is started. If the port or orchestration is not enlisted, the message routing will fail, since no subscription is available and the message will produce a "No matching subscriptions were found for the incoming message" exception within the Event Log.

When a port is enlisted, the Message Agent will create subscriptions for any message whose context property for `TransportID` matches the port's transport ID. It also creates the subscription based on the `MessageType` of the message that is being sent to the port within the orchestration. Binding an orchestration port to a physical send port will force the EPM to write information about that binding to the Management Database. Should the orchestration send messages through its logical port to the physical port, it will include the transport ID in the context so that the message is routed to that specific send port.

The next point is related to the pub/sub nature of the Message Bus. Since any endpoint with a matching subscription can process the message once it is sent from an orchestration to the send port, it is possible for multiple endpoints to act upon that message. This is critical to understand. Sending a message through an orchestration port to a bound physical port simply guarantees that a subscription will be created so that the message is routed to that particular endpoint. There is nothing that says no other subscriber may also act on that message. This point is often overlooked by most developers. Most people assume that since the port is bound, it simply ends up at the correct send port by magic. In reality, all that is happening is that the Message Agent is writing a subscription that hard-codes the context properties of that message so that it will always end up *at least* at that particular send port. Sending the message through the send port simply publishes the message in the Messagebox, and the engine and subscriptions take care of the rest.

Messages

A message within BizTalk is more than just the XML document. BizTalk has a model where messages contain both data and context. Understanding how messages are stored internally within the Messagebox is crucial to understanding how to architect systems that take advantage of how the product represents messages internally.

What Is a Message?

A **message** is a finite entity within the BizTalk Messagebox. Messages have context properties and zero-to-many message parts. Subscriptions match particular context properties for a message and determine which endpoints are interested in processing it. As mentioned before, there is one critical rule that will never change:

MESSAGES ARE IMMUTABLE ONCE THEY ARE PUBLISHED

Most people who have worked with BizTalk for years do not fully understand this rule. A message must not be changed once it has reached the Messagebox. At this point most developers would say rather proudly, "But what about a pipeline component? I can write a pipeline component that modifies the message and its payload along with the context properties, right?" The answer to this question is already in the response. Modifying the message can only be done in a pipeline, either sending or receiving. A receive pipeline modifies the message before it gets to the Messagebox. At the end of the pipeline, the message is published. A send pipeline operates on the message after it leaves the Messagebox and before it is sent out. The original message is still unmodified in the Messagebox database regardless of what the send pipeline decides to do with the message.

Messages vs. Message Parts

Messages are comprised of zero or more **message parts**. All messages with parts generally have a part that is marked as the **body** part. The body part of the message is considered to contain the data or "meat" of the message. Many adapters will only examine the body part of the message and ignore any other parts. If you look at the Messagebox database, there are two specific tables, one that holds all messages that flow through BizTalk, and one that holds all the message parts. This zero-to-many relationship implies something—message parts can be reused in multiple messages. And that is absolutely true. Each message part has a unique part ID that is stored in the MessageParts table and is associated with the message ID of the main message. The organization of messages and message parts is explored in more detail in Chapter 4 in the discussion on writing custom pipeline components. It is also important to understand that message parts contain message bodies, which are generally XML based. If a message is received on a port that uses a pass-through pipeline, then the message can be anything including binary data. When using a pass-through pipeline, no message context properties are promoted from the data of the message. If you think about it, this is obvious. In the case where you are accepting binary data, BizTalk has no mechanism to examine the message body part and determine the message type, so how can it promote it? In this case, the message will contain one message part whose message body is a stream of binary data.

Message Context Properties

Message context properties are defined in what is called a **property schema**. The properties themselves are then stored into **context property bags**. The context property bags are simply containers for the properties, which are stored as key/value pairs.

Context Property Schemas

The property schema is associated within BizTalk to the schema of the inbound message via the message's schema. There is a global properties schema every message can use by default that contains system-level properties. It is possible to create custom properties schemas that can define application-specific properties that may be required such as an internal organizational key, the customer who submitted the document, etc.

System-level properties defined within global property schemas are essentially the same as custom context properties defined within a custom property schema. Both types have a root namespace that is used to identify the type of property, and both are stored within the context property bag for a given message. In reality there is no real difference to the runtime in terms of whether a context property is a "system-level" property or a "custom" property.

Context properties, whether they are system or custom properties, define part of the subscription that is used to evaluate which endpoint(s) have a valid subscription to the message. The most common message subscription is based on the message type. BizTalk identifies the message type in the message context as a combination of the XML namespace of the message along with the root node name plus the "#". For example, say that you had a document with the declaration in Listing 3-1.

Listing 3-1. *XML Order Request Sample Document*

```
<ns0:Request xmlns:ns0="http://schemas.abccompany.com">
<Header>
            <ReqID>4</ReqID>
            <Date>6/6/2005</Date>
            </Header>
```

```
            <Item>
                  <Description>Description_0</Description>
                  <Quantity>10</Quantity>
                  <UnitPrice>2</UnitPrice>
                  <TotalPrice>2</TotalPrice>
          </Item>
   </ns0:Request>
```

The BizTalk message type in this example would be `http://schemas.abccompany.com#Request`. The subscription would then be evaluated by the Message Agent to determine whether any endpoints have subscriptions for the message in question. The list of all subscriptions can be viewed within the BizTalk MMC snap-in tool by viewing all the subscriptions within the solution. Figure 3-2 shows that each of the message properties can be viewed within the BizTalk Administration Console and selected in the message properties drop-down list, which can be used to search for messages within the tool.

Note The message context properties will only be available if the XML or flat-file pipelines were used. If the pass-through pipeline processed the message, no properties would be available for searching in the BizTalk Administration Console.

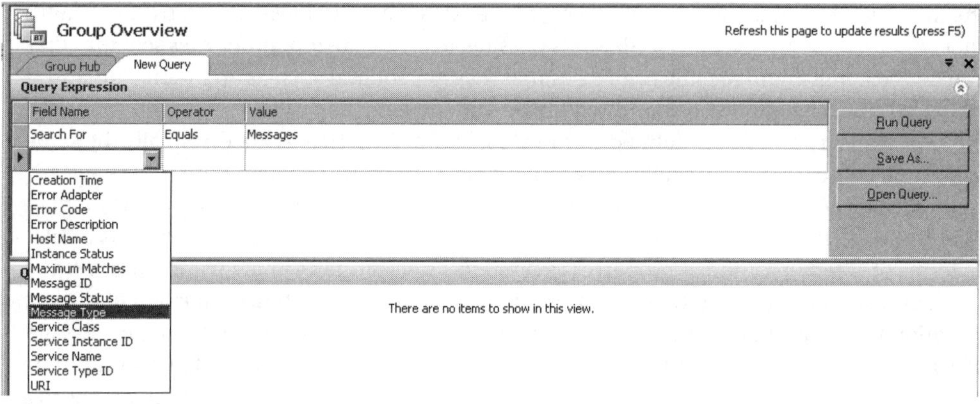

Figure 3-2. *BizTalk Administration Console*

Using subscriptions to route documents to the proper endpoints is called **content-based routing** (**CBR**). Having a thorough understanding of the pub/sub nature of the BizTalk Message Bus is crucial when designing any large messaging-based application, especially in situations where there is going to be significant amounts of routing between organizations and trading partners.

If the message that is received is not schema based, there will be no `MessageType` property promoted. In the case of binary data, the MessageType field will be blank.

The Context Property Bag

As stated previously, context properties are simply key/value pairs stored in an object that implements the IBasePropertyBag interface. As you can see in the following code, the definition of the interface is quite simple:

```
<Guid("fff93009-75a2-450a-8a39-53120ca8d8fa")>
<InterfaceType(ComInterfaceType.InterfaceIsIUnknown)>
Public Interface IBasePropertyBag
```

Public Properties	
CountProperties	Gets the number of properties in the property bag

Public Methods	
Read	Reads the value and type of the given property in the property bag
ReadAt	Reads the property at the specified index value in the property bag
Write	Adds or overwrites a property in the property bag

Given that the context property bag is such a simple structure, it is possible to use the BizTalk API to write any property you want into the property bag. Note that this does not require the property be promoted. Writing a property into the property bag does not mean it is promoted. It is necessary to promote the value in the property bag so that it can be used for routing or within an orchestration. Promoting a property simply means that it is available to the runtime engine for routing, whereas properties that are only written to the message context are not. By using the property schema to promote a property, either by using a custom schema or by promoting a value into a value defined in the global property schemas, what you are doing is first writing the value into the property bag, then marking it as promoted. When doing this within code in a pipeline, writing properties is a different API call than promoting them. This is explored in more detail in the Chapter 4.

■ **Caution** It is critical to understand that everything that is written to the property bag is visible within either the MMC or within HAT. Likewise, it is quite easy to view the subscription information for any ports that route on context properties. If you are promoting properties into the message context, make sure that they *do not contain any sensitive data*. For example, if you have a field in a schema that contains credit card numbers, do not promote this value without taking precautions. If you do store the credit card information in a schema, make sure to make it *sensitive* within the schema definition. This will cause the BizTalk runtime to throw an error should that element's value be promoted. If it is absolutely necessary to promote this value, make sure you encrypt it using a third-party tool.

Using XML Namespaces

BizTalk is heavily dependent on XML namespaces. The worst possible thing that can be done when building BizTalk schemas is to not properly map out what the namespaces are going be for each of the documents. Think of the XML namespaces as the equivilent to .NET namespaces for custom classes. Most architects know to build a proper namespace hierarchy when creating a reusable class library, but most will tend to leave the namespace property of their solution's schemas to the default values. As just stated, the XML namespace is used as part of the values to create the BizTalk `MessageType` context property. This property is the most commonly used property for routing documents, and it makes debugging and maintaining applications much easier if this is a well-thought-out value. As you will see, this becomes even more important when creating and using property schemas.

XML namespaces generally take the following form:

```
http://companyname.com/Project/Subsystem/
```

Defining custom namespaces is crucial for the following reasons:

- They provide unique names for elements and attributes
- They prevent naming conflicts with other schemas
- You can use them for code generation. The namespace will be used to generate the type that represents the schema within the assembly once it is compiled.
- The schema's namespace#root combination must be unique unless you are creating a probing pipeline.[2]
- Other schemas with the same namespace#root can be placed in the GAC *without being deployed* and used by some other components.

When creating a BizTalk schema, the following namespaces are automatically included by default:

```
xmlns:b="http://schemas.microsoft.com/BizTalk/2003"

xmlns:xs="http://www.w3.org/2001/XMLSchema"
```

These namespaces are included to allow the schema to reference common elements that are required by the BizTalk runtime.

Understanding Property Promotions

When new BizTalk developers are asked to "promote a property," they all perform the same task: they open up the schema editor, right-click the element, and choose Quick Promotion. Most have no idea about what is actually happening under the covers or how this element will move into the message's context. Property promotion and the message context are key to the Message Bus architecture within BizTalk and need to be properly understood.

2. For a complete discussion of this issue, see the last section in the chapter entitled "The BizTalk Management Database."

Promoted Properties

Promoted properties are advantageous, as they allow the Messaging Engine to route messages without having to look at the message content since it is already in the message context. If the property that you need to route on does not exist within one of the default property schemas, you will need to create a custom property schema that is used within your project.

Promoted properties are the most common way to enable content-based routing, as promoted properties are available to pipelines, adapters, the Message Bus, and orchestrations. To promote a property within BizTalk Server, you have two options—**quick promotion** and **manual promotion**.

Quick Promotion

Quick promotion is the simplest way to promote an element's value into the message context. To quick promote, all you do is right-click the element's node and choose Quick Promotion. The BizTalk schema editor will create a new property schema and add an XML reference to the new property schema. By default the new schema is called PropertySchema.xml, although this can be changed by editing the properties of the schema file. Each property you promote using a quick promotion will create a corresponding element in the new property schema with the same name and type. When the inbound message is parsed by the pipeline associated with the port, it will move the value from the message's data payload into the message context and assign the namespace of that property to the name defined in the property schema for that element.

Manual Promotion

Manually promoting a property using a custom property schema involves creating a new property schema and creating elements that will hold the promoted values. Once all the elements are created, the property schema is associated to the main content schema by choosing the Show Promotions function in the schema editor. For an example of how to do this, see Exercise 3-1 later in this chapter. Every element that is defined in the promotions section of the schema will be promoted automatically when the message is processed by the pipeline. Manual promotions are also useful when you want to store values in the system property namespaces. The pros and cons of doing this are discussed later in the "Considerations When Promoting Properties" section of the chapter.

Promoting vs. Writing

Promoted properties defined in a property schema can have one of two base types: `MessageDataPropertyBase` and `MessageContextPropertyBase`. If a property is inherited from `MessageDataPropertyBase`, then the value of the property comes from the payload of the message. Properties defined in property schemas are derived of this type. Properties derived from `MessageContextPropertyBase` do not have values from the message payload, but they will generally contain data that relates to the transport of the message and can have configuration information necessary for the subscription to be evaluated. Properties with `MessageContextPropertyBase` as their base type are often promoted by adapters and pipelines and generally include values necessary for the adapter to process the message.

When defining property schemas and coding custom pipeline components and adapters, it is crucial to understand the difference between the two base types and how the BizTalk Messaging Engine treats them. Should the property inherit from `MessageDataPropertyBase`, the orchestration design engine (ODX) examines the property and checks to see whether the namespace and property name match a promoted property. If no promoted property exists in the schema and no matching property is found, the ODX design surface does not allow you to see the property. Inheriting a property from `MessageContextPropertyBase` allows you to see the property regardless of its namespace.

As mentioned previously, the API for writing vs. promoting is essentially the same, but there are two separate methods. On the `IBaseMessageContext` object of every message in BizTalk, there is a `Write()` and a `Promote()` method. Both of these methods take the property name, the namespace, and the value. In order for the property to be available for routing, when promoting a property, the namespace and property name must be the same as those defined in a referenced property schema. This process is different if you want to dynamically write a distinguished field. **Distinguished fields** are special context properties that can be directly accessed from the expression editor through IntelliSense within an orchestration. If you need to write a distinguished field, you must use the distinguished field namespace of `http://schemas.microsoft.com/BizTalk/2003/btsDistinguishedFields`. The name of the property must be a valid XPath expression to the element being written to the context. The following code sample illustrates how to dynamically read and write properties to the message context from code:

```
//BizTalk system properties namespace
Private Const BTSSystemPropertiesNamespace As String = _
"http://schemas.microsoft.com/BizTalk/2003/system-properties"

Private Const BTSDistinguishedFieldsPropertiesNamespace As String = " _
http://schemas.microsoft.com/BizTalk/2003/btsDistinguishedFields"

//Promote the MessageType property
messageType = "http://" + "schemas.abc.com/BizTalk/" + "#" + "Request"
message.Context.Promote("MessageType", BTSSystemPropertiesNamespace, messageType);

//Write a transient value to the message context
message.Context.Write("MyVariable", "SomeNameSpace", SomeData);

//Write a distinguished property
message.Context.Write("OdxProperty", BTSDistinguishedFieldsPropertiesNamespace,
myVar);
```

Considerations When Promoting Properties

Blindly promoting properties is not only inefficient, it can also be costly in terms of both performance and scalability. Following is a short list of items to be considered before promoting a property into the message context.

- **Property size**: To increate routing performance, promoted properties are limited to 255 characters. There is no limit to the size of properties that are simply written to the context. However, writing large properties to the message context will still decrease performance, as the Messaging Engine still needs to process and manage the context regardless of how big it is.

- **Performance**: Large message properties cannot be "streamed" and must be entirely loaded into memory by the runtime. This will become an issue if you write large values for message properties into the message context.
- **Overwriting of promoted properties**: If you have promoted a property to the message context, and you issue a context write operation, the property is no longer promoted.
- **Dealing with Nulls**: Null properties are not persisted to the context. If you set a property's value to Null, it will no longer exist, and you cannot see a context property in the HAT with a value of Null.

Distinguished Fields

There are two types of property promotion: distinguished fields and property fields. The latter type uses property schemas. In the BizTalk schema editor, you manage both of these types of property promotion by using the Promote Properties dialog box, which you access by using the Promote Properties property of the Schema node. Distinguished fields are only useful when they are accessed within orchestration. Promoted properties can be accessed either in orchestrations or from custom code, routing, and pipelines.

Distinguished fields, on the other hand, cannot be used for routing and are only used by the orchestration engine. When dealing with large messages, this can save significant server processing, as the engine would need to use XPath expressions to search through the document to find the piece of data that it needs each time the expression is evaluated. This way, the data is loaded once when the document is parsed by the runtime engine. Distinguished fields are used within orchestrations to move required elements into the context and only read the context property within the orchestration without having to load the entire document into memory. Distinguished fields also offer nice IntelliSense capabilities within the orchestration expression editor and message assignment shapes.

Depending on the type of access that is needed, you can choose to create either promoted properties or distinguished fields depending on how the property will be used. Distinguished fields do not require the creation of a corresponding property schema.

Using Port Filters and Content-Based Routing

As stated in the previous section, subscriptions and context properties are integral to the messaging subsystem. Property schemas are the mechanism by which the context properties are stored in the message context. When creating schemas, you can define a property schema that will hold any custom properties that will be used for routing the inbound message. To create a custom property schema, you need to create a schema and a property schema to hold the properties. In order to move a value from the data of the message into the context, it is necessary to "promote" the property into the context property bag. The BizTalk Message Bus automatically promotes system-level properties from the system property namespaces, depending on the type of inbound and outbound transports that are being used. Each adapter will require and hence promote values that it needs to send and receive the message according to its particular protocol.

In the schema definition of the message, property promotion is done by first associating the property schema to the message and choosing the property to promote. Most architects don't understand how messages are routed within the product or how to use the property schemas to affect the subscription. Exercise 3-1 will show you how you can use the property promotion to implement routing logic.

Exercise 3-1: Using Custom Promoted Properties to Route Messages

Let's continue our example from Chapter 2 of an organization that takes inbound documents from multiple sources, normalizes them to a canonical input schema, and sends them to different outbound locations. Assume that there are three systems: a web site, a POS application, and an automated FTP upload location. Each of these locations takes a different schema and must map it to internal schema. This mapped message then needs to be sent to the ERP system. However, as an added piece of functionality, documents from the web site need to be sent to a separate location as well, and documents from the POS system need to be sent to a file system directory so they can be batch uploaded at a later time. Figures 3-3 and 3-4 define the schema for the internal messages and a possible solution architecture.

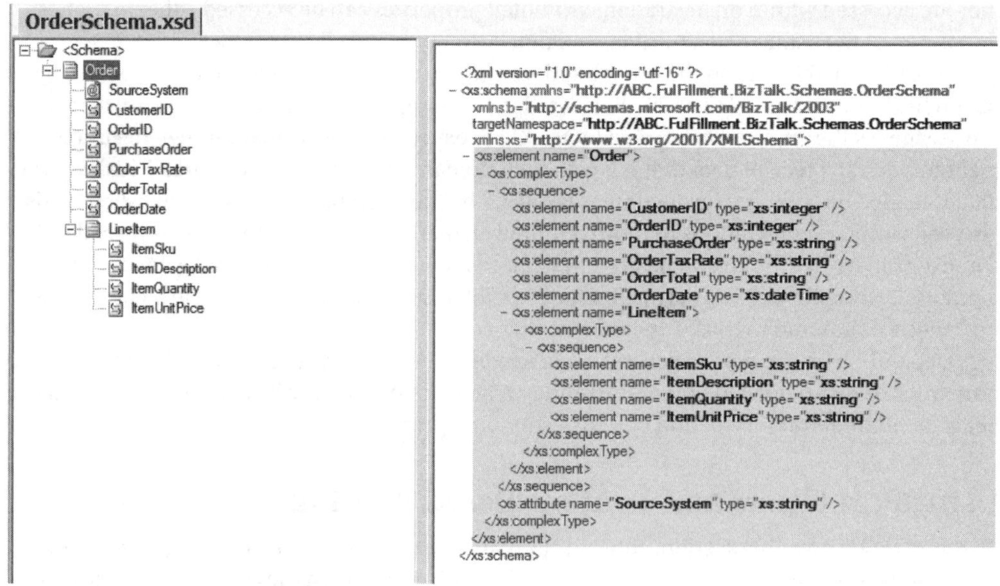

Figure 3-3. *Internal order request schema*

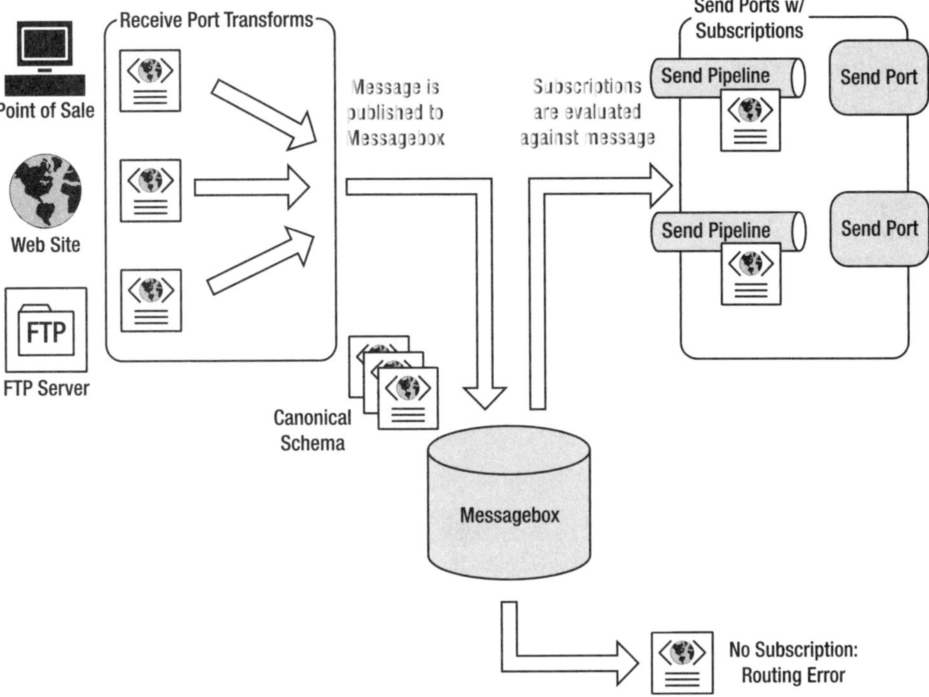

Figure 3-4. *Solution architecture*

The requirements for this solution are quite common in most BizTalk projects, and most new BizTalk architects design it incorrectly. Generally those unfamiliar with the subscription nature of the Message Bus will tend to build an orchestration that has logical ports directly bound to the physical ports. The orchestration would then use Decide shapes to send the message to the appropriate send port, which will then send the message on its way. An even worse solution is to create three orchestrations, each of which receives the inbound message directly from the receive location, executes the map from within the orchestration, and then has a static bound port that is bound to the send port from within the orchestration. This problem requires only messaging to be solved. No orchestrations should be created here since no business logic is needed. Routing the message to the correct location is not business logic, and as such, an orchestration is not the correct tool to use from the BizTalk Server toolbox.

To implement the routing logic, subscriptions need to be created that allow the inbound message, once it has been mapped, to be sent to the correct port. Here, you create filters based on the `MessageType` context property that allow the Messaging Engine to automatically forward any messages of type `http://ABC.FulFillment.BizTalk.Schemas.OrderSchema#Order` to the ERP system. The filter of the port will modify the subscription in the Messagebox accordingly. In the filter properties of the ERPSendPort, the expression shown in Figure 3-5 will be present.

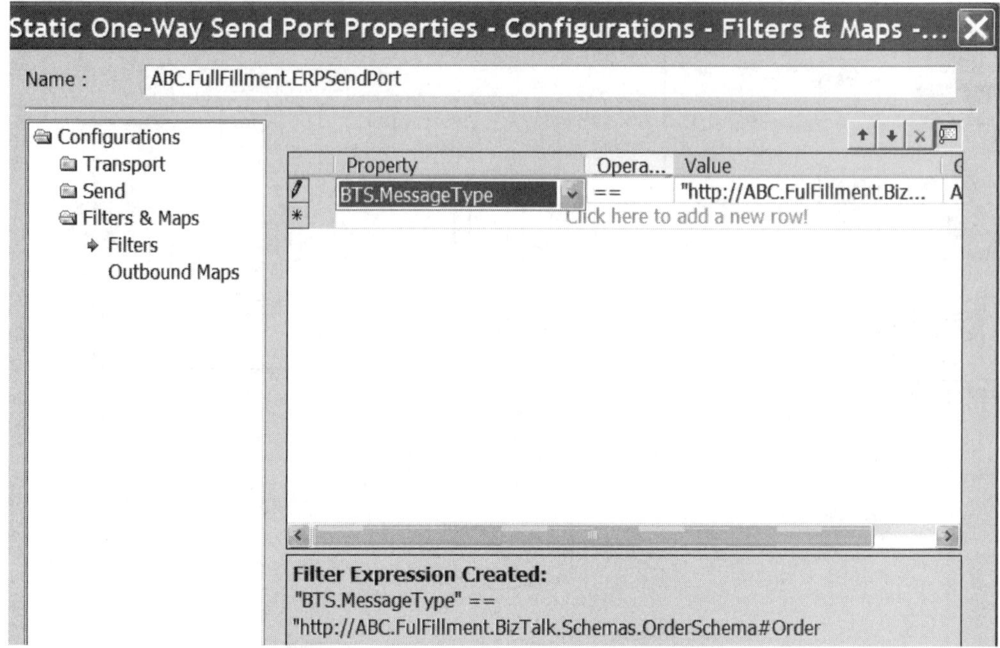

Figure 3-5. *ERPSendPort properties*

You still have not seen how to solve the problem of differentiating messages that are received from each of the three separate order producing systems. Notice that the internal schema definition includes an element that will allow you to store that data should it be available, but there are two problems: a) how do you get the value in this element, and b) how can you route messages based on it. For adding this value into the data document, you use the inbound map defined on the receive port. All you need to do is create a map from the external schema to the internal schema and assign a constant value for the `SourceSystem` element.

To allow you to route on the `SourceSystem` property, you need to create a property schema to define what properties you want to store in the context and to allow the Messaging Engine to promote the value from the data in your inbound document. To do this, add a new item to the schema project: in the list of BizTalk project items, choose Property Schema. Add an attribute to the schema called `SourceSystem`. This can be seen in Figure 3-6.

Figure 3-7 shows the schema for the internal order property schema as viewed in the BizTalk schema editor.

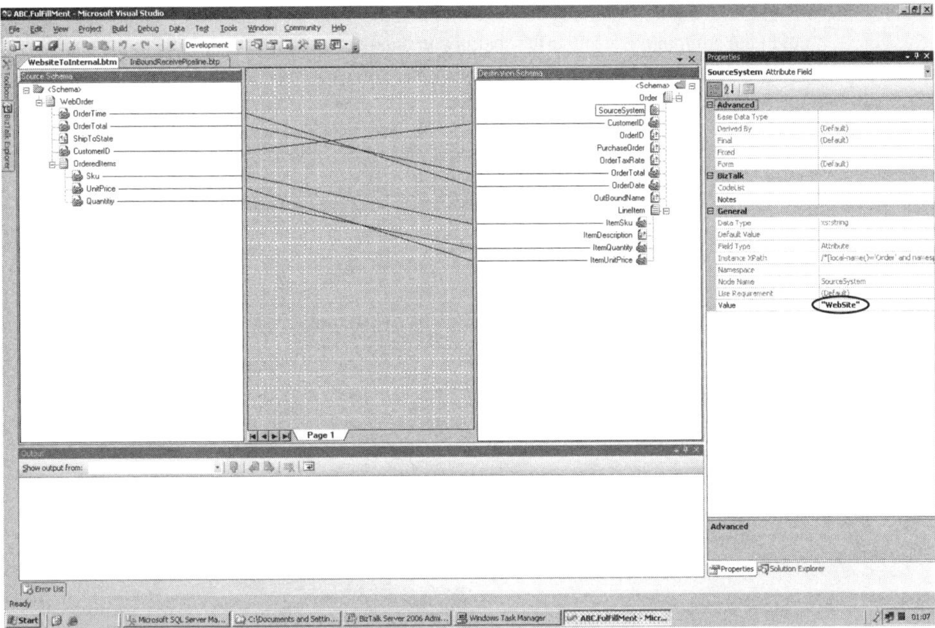

Figure 3-6. *Web site to internal schema map*

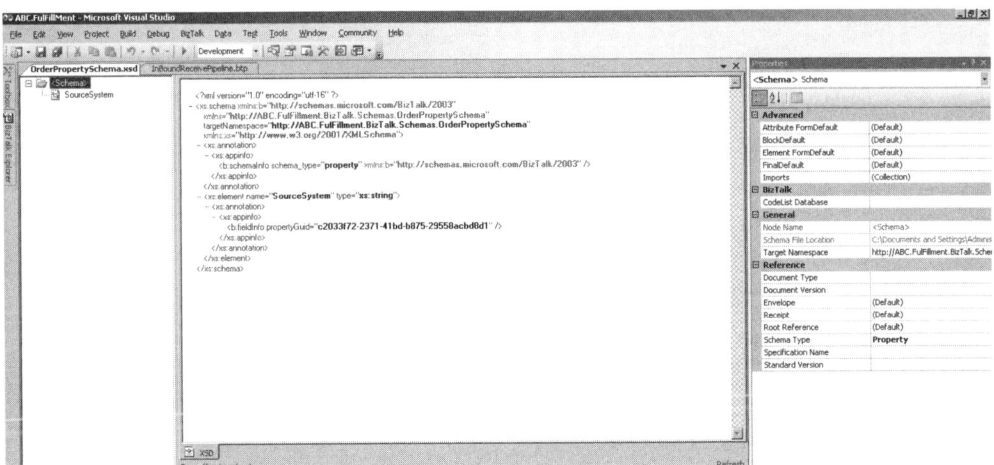

Figure 3-7. *Order property schema*

The next step is to associate the custom property schema to the internal order schema. To do this, right-click the `SourceSystem` element in the internal order property schema and choose Promotions ➤ Show Promotions. This is demonstrated in Figure 3-8. Next, click the Promoted Properties tab and click the open folder icon.

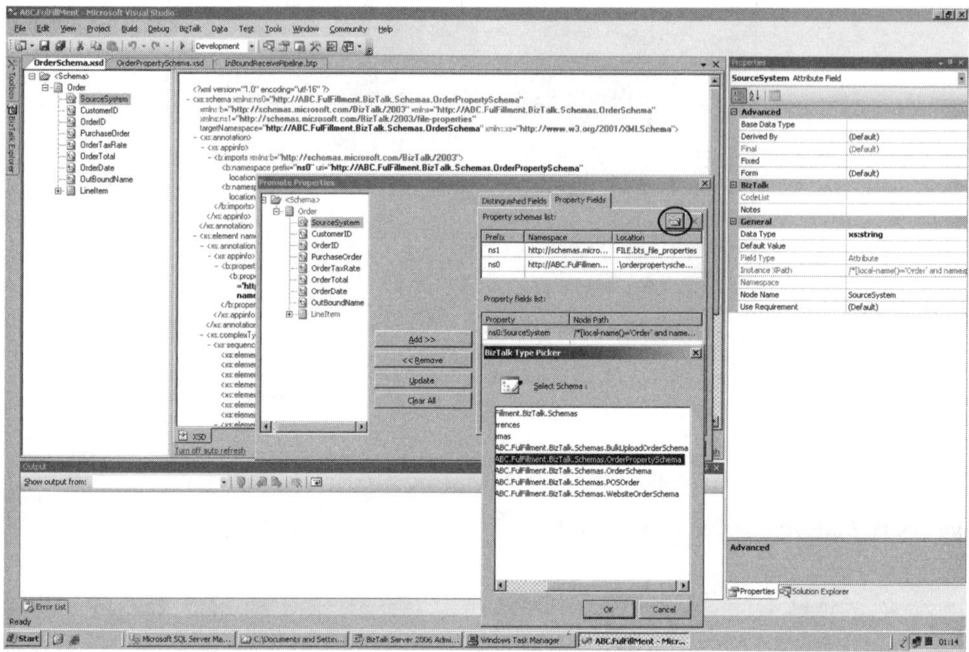

Figure 3-8. *Property Schema Type Picker*

Once you have chosen OrderPropertySchema, highlight the `SourceSystem` element on the left and click the Add associate button. This will add the element to the list of promoted properties. Notice that since there is only one property defined in the property schema, the editor automatically associates this field with the `SourceSystem` property in the property schema. This can be seen in Figure 3-9.

Compile the project and deploy it to the Management Database. Once the schema's assembly is deployed to the Management Database, it will automatically be available in the list of properties in a ports filter. If you create a new send port and want to only send documents from the web site, you can add it as a filter, and this will automatically update the subscription as shown in Figure 3-10.

Another important fact to note is that in this situation, you only need to create one receive port with three receive locations. You also need to create three maps and add them each to the transforms on the port. The pipeline will examine the inbound schema for each map and send the inbound document to the correct map. If no port has a subscription for a matching inbound message type, an error will occur, and the message will become suspended.

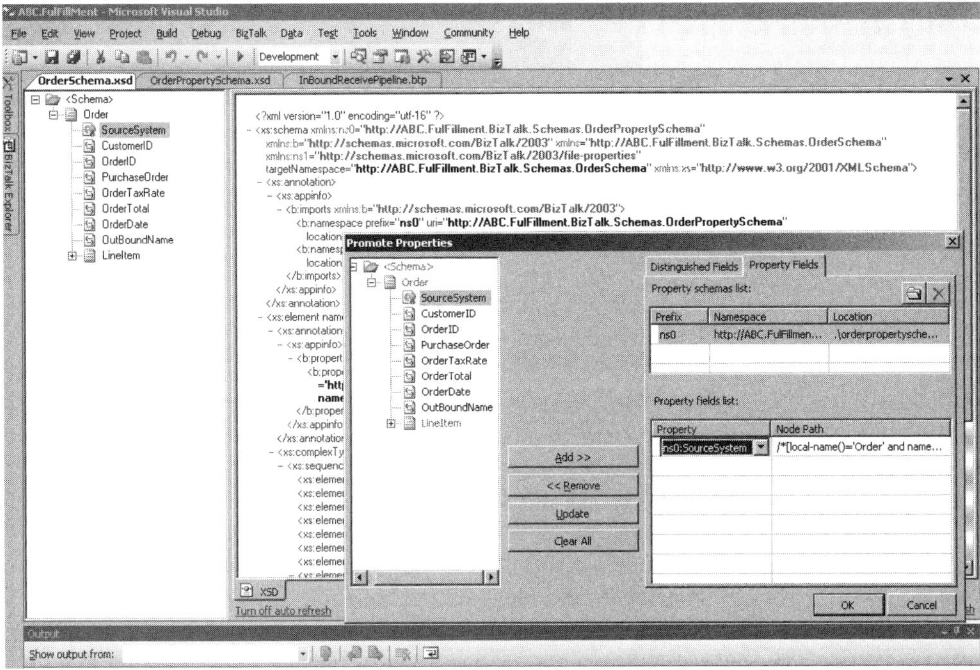

Figure 3-9. *Manually promoting the SourceSystem property*

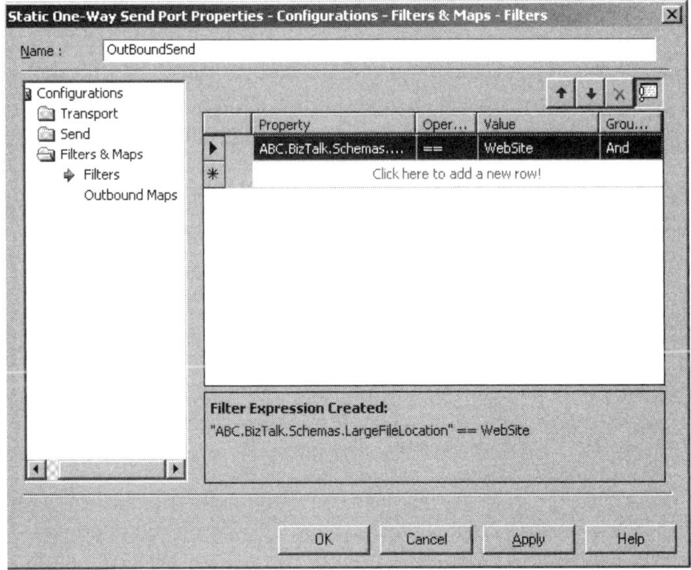

Figure 3-10. *Routing based on a custom promoted property*

Using System Property Schemas

As mentioned previously, a number of system property schemas come with the product. Most of these property schemas exist to support each of the transports and adapters included with the product out of the box. Most of the time, each new transport or application adapter will bring with it a new property schema that is used to define any custom metadata needed to process the message by the adapter. Each of the system property schemas is included in the base assembly Microsoft.BizTalk.GlobalPropertySchemas.dll. Referencing this assembly from a BizTalk project in Visual Studio will allow you to access each of the schemas as you would with any other schema type.

Modifying Values from System Property Schemas: Simple Example

So at this point many people ask the question, "Big deal, I can modify values that BizTalk uses, so why would I need this ability?" In order to fully understand why the creation of property schemas becomes an invaluable tool, let's look at a simple example. Continuing with the scenario from Exercise 3-1, let's assume that an order received from the bulk order system needs to be written to a file location on a server within the organization. Let's also assume that we need to dynamically modify the name of this file depending on some value from the message: the customer ID plus the character "#" and the total amount of the order.

At first, modifying the file name based on a message value seems like an easy thing to do, but it becomes a little more complicated when you look at it. In reality, there are three solutions to the problem. Solution A would be to use an orchestration with a dynamic port and within the orchestration use some XPath expressions to get the data you need from the message; dynamically set the address of the file adapter; and send the file to the dynamic port. However, in reality there is a cost to doing this. First, you are breaking one of the cardinal rules of BizTalk—you are using orchestrations to do routing logic. Second, you have an orchestration that is exclusively bound to a port and has to be deployed, enlisted, and started with the port it is bound to.[3] Third, if this were a large message, using XPath will force the orchestration engine to load the entire document into memory in order to parse out the values from the XPath expression.[4]

Solution B is to use the BizTalk Messaging Engine and have it do the work for you. To implement this solution, you use the macro functionality to write the message in the send port. You need to modify your internal order schema so that there is a new element called `OutBoundName` or something similar, and you need somewhere to promote this property to. For this, use the file adapter property schema. In the internal order schema, there is an element called `ReceivedFileName`. What you do is modify the BulkOrderToInternal.btm map so that the value of the `CustomerID` along with the total is concatenated into your new element in the internal schema. You still have to promote the `CustomerID` property into the context.

---

3. In later chapters, we will discuss orchestrations with direct-bound ports (i.e., not bound to a physical port, but bound to the Messagebox database) vs. orchestrations with static/dynamic bindings. There are pros and cons to each, but there are more pros than cons to a direct port, and generally they are preferable to static or dynamically bound ports.

4. We could use distinguished properties to get around this. The orchestration engine will not load the entire document if the property were distinguished. As stated previously, these would be written into the context when the message is processed by the Messaging Engine. However, the point is that using XPath in orchestrations is costly, especially on large messages.

To do that, in the Property Promotions tab of the schema, add a reference to the file adapter's property schema.

The next step is to create a send port that subscribes to the correct message type, set the outbound destination in the send port to the desired directory, and set the file name to be %sourcefilename%. The BizTalk Messaging Engine will use whatever value is stored in the `ReceivedFileName` message context property when writing this value out. Since you have changed it and promoted it, the engine will use your new value instead of the original one as shown in Figure 3-11.

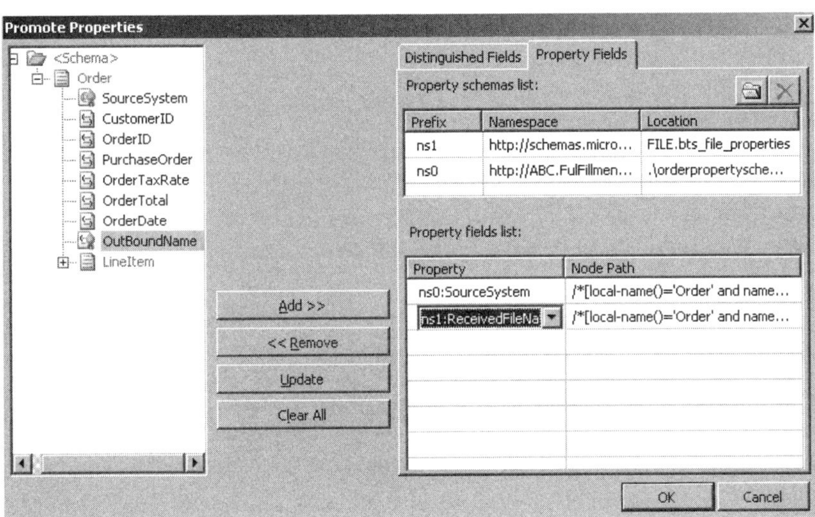

Figure 3-11. *Promoting a value using a system property namespace*

Solution C is to create a custom pipeline component, add it to a stage in a custom receive pipeline, and have it promote the value you want into the context using the message API. The code would look something like the following:

```
Private Sub PromoteProperties(ByVal message As IBaseMessage, ByVal CustomerID As _
String, ByVal OrderTotal As Decimal)

Dim BTSFilePropertiesNamespace As String = _
"http://schemas.microsoft.com/BizTalk/2003/file-properties"
Dim FileName As String

'Get the original directory the file was received from by reading the message _
context and creating a FileInfo object
Dim FileInfoObject As new
System.IO.FileInfo(message.Context.Read("ReceivedFileName", _
BTSFileropertiesNamespace))
```

```
'Replace the original name with the new one
FileName = FileInfoObject.DirectoryName +  "\\ + CustomerID + "#" + _
OrderTotal.ToString() + ".xml"
message.Context.Promote("ReceivedFileName", BTSFileropertiesNamespace, FileName)

End Sub
```

The send port is configured the same as in solution B. Although solution C uses the Messaging Engine to accomplish the task, it requires you to write a custom pipeline and pipeline component that you would then have to maintain. The benefit of solution C is that it does not require you to modify the internal schema or transformation in any way. Solution C would be ideal if you had a production-emergency type of scenario where you needed to implement the proposed change with as little possible downtime or modification to the deployed solution. All you would need to do is deploy the pipeline assembly to each of the BizTalk servers, along with copying the pipeline component to the %Program Files\Microsoft BizTalk Server 2006\Pipeline Components\ directory and changing the pipeline configuration on the receive port. In this scenario, there would be no server downtime and few configuration changes required. The trade-off is that you would have additional custom logic and custom assemblies that must be maintained and deployed with the solution as a whole.

Modifying Values from System Property Schemas: Extended Example

Now that you see a simplistic usage of modifying a system property, we will show you something a little more interesting. Continuing with the previous example, assume that you need to send information to your ERP system with messages received from the web site. Also assume that there have been performance problems calling the ERP solution. Currently the ERP system uses a custom API written in VB 6.0 and exposed through COM+ objects. You need to track how long these calls are taking, but you want the information included within the Messagebox and you want it bundled with all the other tracking information that is stored in the database and accessible through HAT for the server administrators. You also want individual tracking information per message so that you can correlate what types of transactions are taking the most time.

Assume that the code to call the API is fixed and cannot be modified. Due to architectural limitations, you also cannot impose a wrapper (i.e., web service or custom adapter), you must call the API directly as you would be normally, and these calls must be synchronous because the API will not support asynchronous calls due to threading issues. Currently, the API is called from an Expression shape inside an orchestration, and depending on a series of return values, different business logic is executed. As an added bonus, the administrators want a copy of all messages that take more than 5 seconds to process to be sent to a drop location where those messages can be viewed offline. The development team does not want any major logic modifications to the existing receive ports/send ports/orchestrations to implement the logging logic (i.e., you can't store the tracking value somewhere and have the orchestration insert a Decide shape that sends a copy to the send port). Also, message tracking is not enabled, since this is a production system, and the administrators do not want to decrease the performance of the system any further.

Now that your hands are a little more tied, the options are becoming a bit limited. Most people at this point will want to modify the orchestration that logs information either to the event log or to a performance counter, but that still doesn't address the problem of how you can associate a message that you processed with its timing values and have them show up somehow in HAT, nor does it address the problem of how to properly route on those timing values. Also, this breaks one of the cardinal rules: you use orchestrations for something other than business logic. Another option would be to create some custom tracking elements in the document and write these from within the orchestration, but that would require a schema change and some new code. Luckily, there is a better way, and it only requires five lines of code be inserted into the orchestration along with two variables.

BizTalk includes a tracking property schema within the product. Although this schema is very poorly documented (as in not at all), it is possible to write values to it. The property schema is used to define context properties that adapters can write to that will aid in the very type of scenario we're discussing now. The fact that we can write values to the tracking property schema really doesn't help since tracking is not enabled. Also, since the performance bottleneck in this scenario is not based on an adapter, the tracking information is not accurate. However, you can still use the property schema to write information to the context from within the orchestration that will help you as shown in Figure 3-12.

```
InboundDoc(MessageTracking.ActivityIdentity) = "WebSite Order FullFillment";
InboundDoc(MessageTracking.AdapterTransmitBeginTime) = System.DateTime.Now;
ERPAPI.CallERP(InboundDoc);
TotalTime = System.DateTime.Now.Subtract(StartTime);
InboundDoc(MessageTracking.ActivityIdentity) = System.Convert.ToString(TotalTime.Seconds);
```

Figure 3-12. *Orchestration expression*

The system property schema is in the bts-messagetracking-properties.xsd schema file. By default, this schema is populated with values from adapters, but there is nothing that says you can't put your own values in here. Also, since the schema is a property schema, the values will be available for routing. The problem of how you can configure your send port to automatic pickup times that are greater than 5 seconds has now been solved. What you can do is create a little expression in the expression editor that gets the current `Now()` time and substracts it from the time that the operation finished. The `StartTime` variable is a local variable defined as a System.DateTime that is initialized to the current time within the orchestration. Since the result will be of type System.Timespan you cannot simply store it in the property `MessageTracking.AdapterTransmitEndTime` since that property is of type System.DateTime. There is another property called `MessageTracking.ActivityIdentity` that is of type string, which will allow you to store anything you want. You simply store your computed time in that property and use it to route your messages as shown in Figure 3-13.

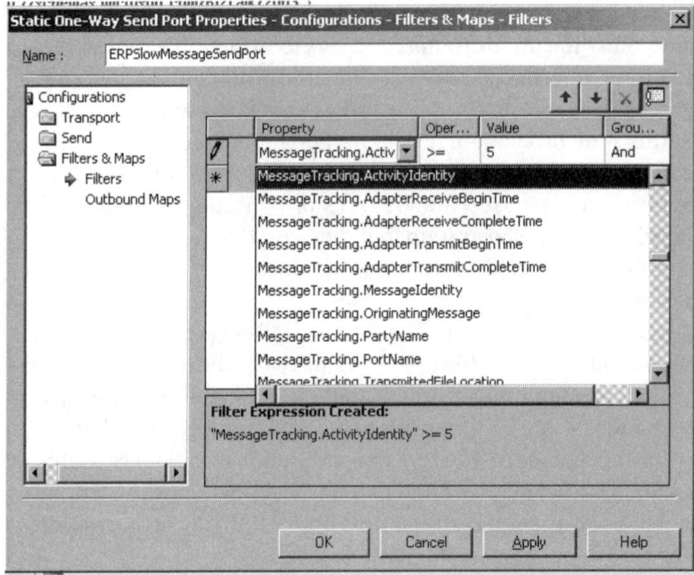

Figure 3-13. *Send port filter expression*

Custom Properties and Orchestration Routing

As demonstrated earlier, custom properties can be very useful in routing scenarios. The previous example showed how to route the message to an orchestration based on a custom property and a subscription created via the filter expression. If you were routing this message to an orchestration based on a filter defined in the receive port of the orchestration, you would get the following error:

```
"message data property 'ABCPropertySchema.CustomProperty' does not exist in
messagetype 'myOrchestrationMessage'"
```

What is happening in this case is that the orchestration engine is examining the message within the orchestration and throwing an error stating that the property you wish to route on does not exist in the message. Typically the engine is correct; however, in this case, you know that this is okay. The solution is to tell the engine that data for your property will not come from the message and that you will provide it.

To fix this, you need to set the Property Schema Base for the property under the Reference section of the schema editor as shown in Figure 3-14.

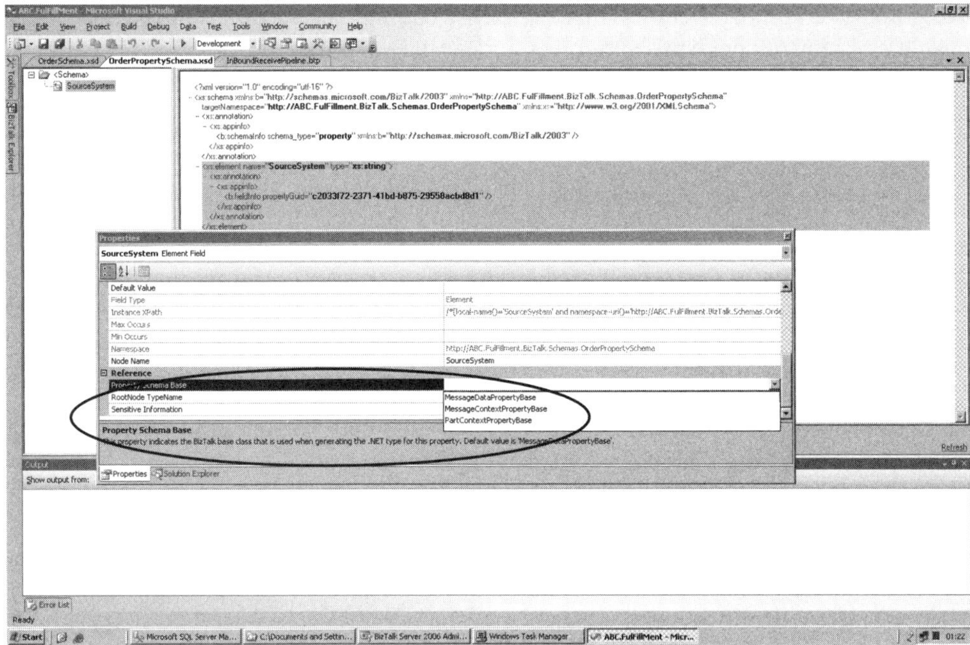

Figure 3-14. *Changing the base type for a property*

To the runtime, this determines what the base type will be used for in the property in question. The base type for the property will be used to determine where the data for the property will come from. The possible values for this are

- **MessageDataPropertyBase (Default)**: The data in this field will come from a message.
- **MessageContextPropertyBase**: The data in this field may not exist in a message (i.e., it could be prompted inside a custom pipeline). The values will not be inside the message.
- **PartContextPropertyBase**: This tells the runtime that the value for the property will be a part of the `MessagePart` context.

The key takeaway is that if you are promoting properties that do not exist in the message, be sure to set the proper base type for the property (i.e., MessageContextPropertyBase).

As you can see, using system properties can solve a number of rather complex scenarios with very little effort. This is explored in further detail later on in the book.

Tracking and Message Management

Now that you have seen how BizTalk stores, routes, and publishes messages, the next step is to understand how those messages can be tracked and what happens to them once they have been processed. Each subscriber of a particular message references the same, single copy of that message. This approach requires that a reference counter be kept for all messages flowing through the system. Although this minimizes storage, it requires that the messages be cleaned up once their reference counters reach 0. To accomplish this, the product includes a set of SQL Agent jobs that perform garbage collection for zero-reference-count messages and message parts. The stored procedures that handle garbage collection are as follows:

- **MessageBox_Message_Cleanup_BizTalkMsgBoxDb**: Deletes all messages that have no references by any subscribers.
- **MessageBox_Parts_Cleanup_BizTalkMsgBoxDb**: Deletes all messages that have no references by any messages. Remember what we stated at the beginning of the chapter—messages are made up of one or more message parts that contain the actual message data.
- **PurgeSubscriptionsJob_BizTalkMsgBoxDb**: Deletes unused subscription predicates leftover from from system-created subscriptions.
- **MessageBox_DeadProcesses_Cleanup_BizTalkMsgBoxDb**: Executed when the runtime detects that a server has crashed. This frees the work that the server was working on so another machine within the group can process it.
- **TrackedMessages_Copy_BizTalkMsgBoxDb**: Copies tracked message bodies from the Messaging Engine spool tables into the tracking spool tables in the Messagebox database.
- **TrackingSpool_Cleanup_BizTalkMsgBoxDb**: Reverses the database table that the TrackedMessages_Copy_BizTalkMsgBoxDb SQL Server Agent job writes to.

The first two items from the preceding list are used to keep garbage messages removed from the Messagebox. When executed, they search the messages and message parts within the Messagebox looking for messages with a reference count of zero. The stored procedures also check for parts that are not referenced by any messages and remove those as well. Once messages are ready to be removed, they are moved to the BizTalk Tracking Database. These two jobs are executed from the machine that hosts SQL Server. In order for these jobs to run, the SQL Server Agent needs to be running. If SQL Server Agent isn't running, tracked message bodies will never be offloaded to the Tracking Database, and hence the Messagebox will grow. As the database grows, performance will suffer, as the number of messages grows unchecked. This is due to the fact that the Message Agent that is running within each BizTalk host will be calling a stored procedure that searches through each of the messages in the Messagebox looking for messages with matching subscription information.

To keep the Messagebox as empty as possible, the tracking subsystem will move completed messages to the Tracking Database on a periodic basis. The Tracking Database is also is where the HAT queries for data and displays its tracking information. This is accomplished by a BizTalk host that has been tagged as a "tracking" host. This is an option in the Host Properties pages.

Handling Failed Messages and Errors

In BizTalk 2004, being able to simply get a copy of a suspended message was a pain. There were a number of very clever design patterns to allow you to get at suspended messages, but each of them required either custom orchestrations or pipeline components to subscribe to the negative acknowledgements (NACKS) in order to look up the suspended message that you were after and route that message dynamically to some endpoint.

In BizTalk Server 2006, getting at suspended messages is a simple problem to resolve. The BizTalk product team added a set of context properties that are available to be subscribed on and routed to. Error handling context properties are defined within the `http://schemas.microsoft.com/BizTalk/2005/error-report` property schema. The new context properties are as follows:

- `Description`
- `ErrorType`
- `FailureCategory`
- `FailureCode`
- `InboundTransportLocation`
- `MessageType`
- `OutboundTransportLocation`
- `ReceivePortName`
- `RoutingFailureReportID`
- `SendPortName`

What needs to be done is to ensure that any receive ports that need to have error handling included have the Generate Error Report check box checked as shown in Figure 3-15. This will signal the runtime engine to generate the routing failure message and publish it to the Messagebox. Since the message is published, there needs to be a subscription available to receive the routing failure message. To that end, you can create an orchestration that is direct-bound[5] to the Messagebox through a receive port. The Receive shape in the orchestration will have a filter criteria specified that sets the subscription information so that it will receive all failed routing messages.

To implement the routing, the filter expression needs to be set to "ErrorReport.ErrorType == Failed Message" as shown in Figure 3-16.

This will cause the subscription to be written that will receive all suspended messages. From here, once you have a copy of the failed message within the orchestration, you can send it wherever you need. An example would be to have the orchestration send the message to an e-mail address or to an offline database for examination. All these options will be quite easy to implement since the message has been parsed and routed to the orchestration.

---

5. Direct binding refers to orchestration ports that are not specifically bound to any physical port but will receive messages solely based on the subscription. As you saw in the "Subscriptions" subsection in the chapter, all this means is that there is no receive port or transport ID information written to the subscription.

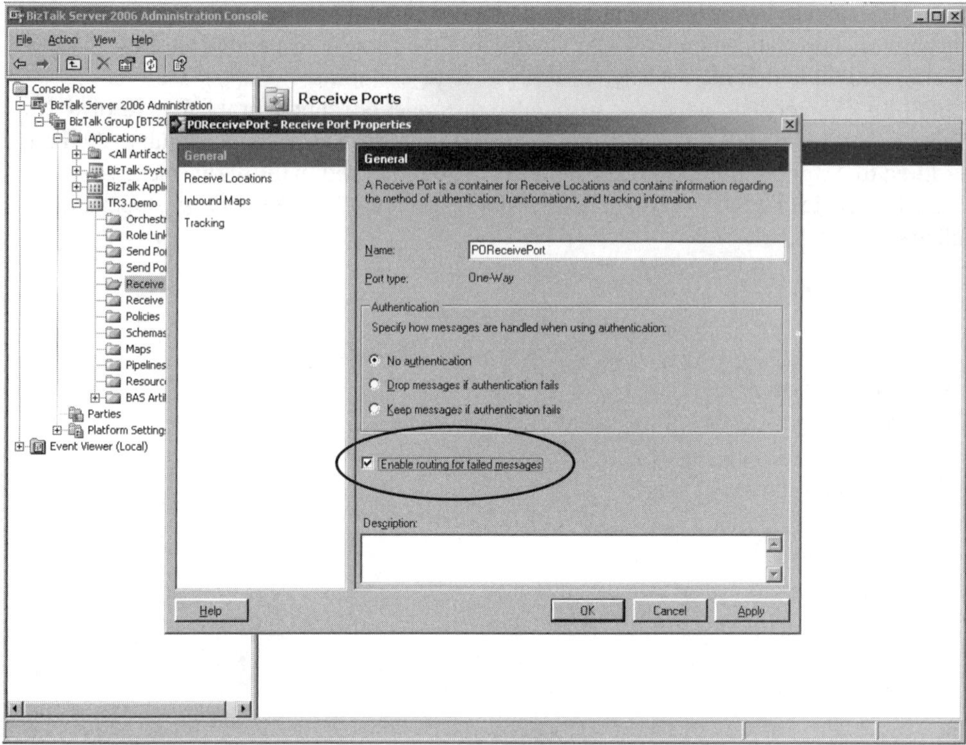

Figure 3-15. *Receive port configuration*

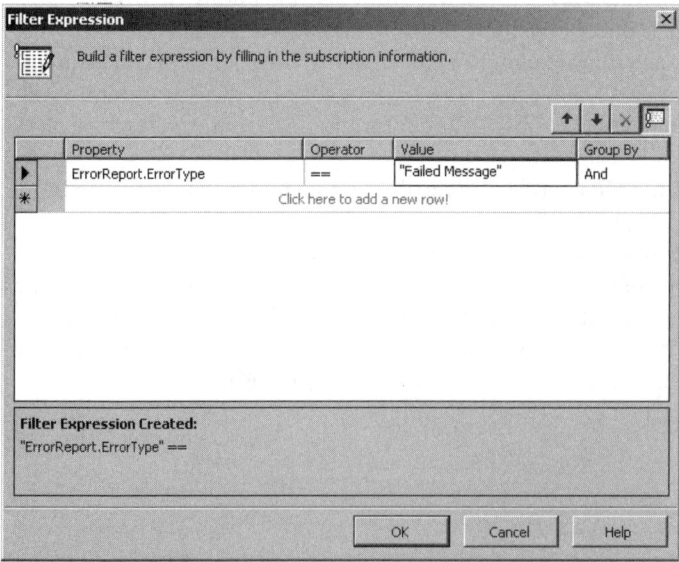

Figure 3-16. *Orchestration Receive shape filter*

The BizTalk Management Database

Up until this point, our discussions regarding BizTalk schemas, deployment, and namespaces have been in the practical sense. We have not discussed where schemas are actually stored, or what is happening within BizTalk when a new schema is deployed. For that, we need to understand the BizTalk Management Database. Unlike the Messagebox, the Management Database is not used to store messages and is not considered to be "working storage." The Management Database is where most configuration and system-level information is stored and accessed from within BizTalk. It is important to understand what's going on behind the scenes when you perform administrative actions using either UI tools or the ExplorerOM/WMI API,[6] as it will give you a good understanding as to how BizTalk artifacts are tied together within the product. Such understanding may save time when dealing with specific issues such as "Why isn't my schema namespace resolving?" or "What version of my schema is this document resolving against?"

The first topic we will cover is how BizTalk Server resolves document/message types, and how/where they are stored in Management Database. If you have worked on a BizTalk project previously, you no doubt have seen the following error messages from the BizTalk Messaging Engine:

> *There was an error executing receive pipeline: Finding the document specification by message type {MessageType} failed. Verify the schema deployed properly.*

or

> *There was a failure executing receive pipeline: Cannot locate document specification because multiple schemas matched this message type [MessageType]*

Knowing how BizTalk handles message types will help you to address this type of problem. We will also provide you with ExplorerOM[7] code for enumerating deployed document specifications, which you can use in your own helper/supplementary utilities tailored for your specific needs.

The second topic we are going to cover is what's going on in the BizTalk Management Database when you deploy a BizTalk assembly. These two discussions should help you troubleshoot any specific issues you may encounter when dealing with schema/version resolution issues.

Let's first create an application containing only one schema file and one orchestration. The document will be received by a receive location, validated against a schema, and routed to the orchestration. Open Visual Studio and create an empty solution. Name the solution ExplorerWMI. Add two BizTalk projects to the solution and name them Schemas and Orchestrations.

---

6. ExplorerOM is the primary API that you will use to work with BizTalk artifacts from within code. WMI is the Windows Management Instrumentation technology we introduced in Chapter 1. For a complete discussion of these techologies as they relate to BizTalk, see Chapter 10.

7. We have included the ExplorerOM code within this chapter for easy reference. For a complete discussion of deploying, managing, and supporting BizTalk using the ExplorerOM API, see Chapter 10.

Choose Add a New Project Item, then choose schema file. Name it TestSchema. Switch to the Properties window, select the root node, and change the Node Name property to ExplorerWMI as shown in Figure 3-17.

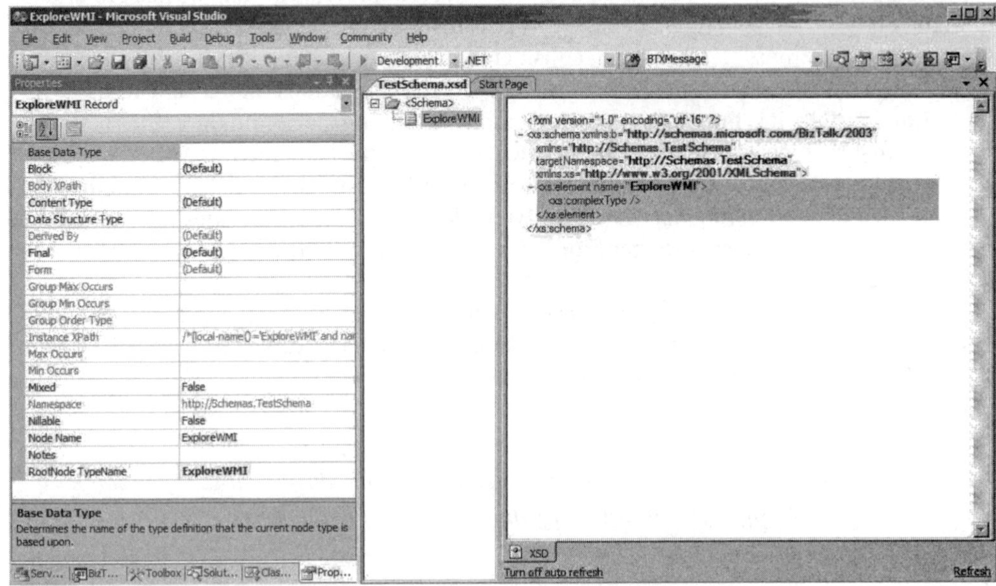

Figure 3-17. *ExplorerWMI project within Visual Studio 2005*

Now switch to Solution Explorer, right-click the Schema project, and select Build. BizTalk compiles the XSD schema and places class definitions in its Schemas.dll assembly. You can see it in the project's output directory. If you are curious, you can load the generated assembly Schemas.dll file into a freeware tool like the .NET Assembly Viewer from Ralf Reiterer[8] to check out the generated .NET class definition matching our TestSchema.xsd schema as shown in Figure 3-18.

Switch to the Orchestrations project, add an orchestration, and configure it to pass through any received messages to a file-based send port as shown in Figure 3-19.

8. http://dotnet.jku.at/applications/course03/Reiterer/

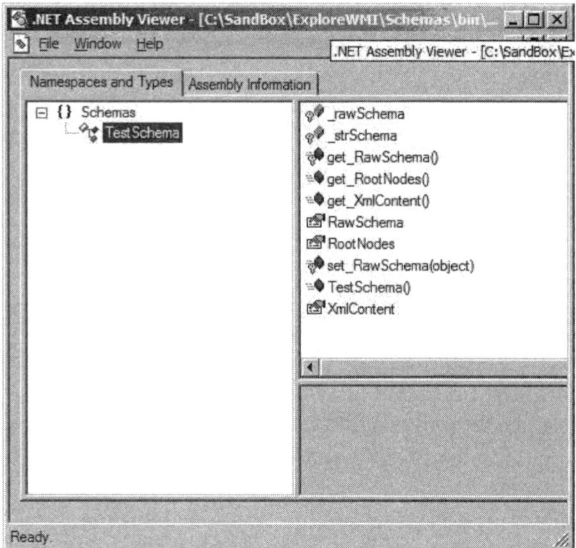

Figure 3-18. *.NET Assembly Viewer*

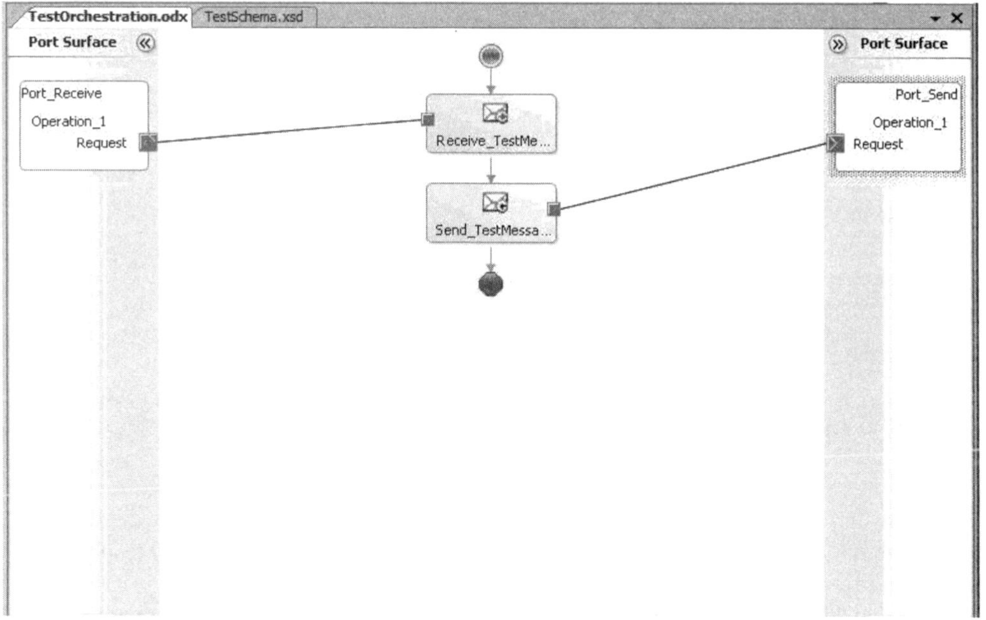

Figure 3-19. *Simple pass-through orchestration*

Right-click the Orchestrations project and select the Build menu item. As you may have guessed, the XLANG compiler compiles the orchestration into a C# class and calls the standard csc.exe C# compiler. This in turn generates the Orchestrations.dll assembly. If you want to look at our generated C# code to see how the orchestration class interacts with the orchestration engine, you can use an undocumented registry setting. Add a registry key named *BizTalkProject* at HKEY_CURRENT_USER\Software\Microsoft\VisualStudio\8.0 for Visual Studio 2005. If you are using BizTalk 2004 and Visual Studio .NET 2003, the key is HKEY_CURRENT_USER\Software\Microsoft\VisualStudio\7.1. Next, create a DWORD value named *GenerateCSFiles* and set it to 1. If you rebuild your project, you will see C# files in your project directory.

Now that all the preliminary steps are complete, you are ready to deploy the solution. Choose the Build menu and select Deploy Solution. Executing the Deploy command within Visual Studio puts assemblies into the GAC (if this option is selected in the project settings) and also updates the Management Database. The first table you want to examine within the BizTalk Management Database is bts_Assembly. This table contains information about system assemblies and assemblies specific to custom applications. They are distinguished by an nSystemAssembly field. A value of 1 in this column indicates that assembly is a system assembly. As you can see in the last row, the deployment procedure put information about the Schemas and Orchestrations assemblies into this table as shown in Figure 3-20.

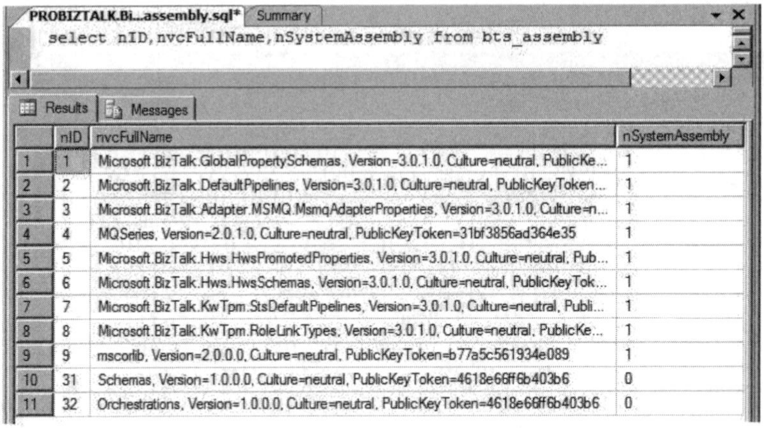

PROBIZTALK.Bi...assembly.sql* | Summary

```
select nID,nvcFullName,nSystemAssembly from bts_assembly
```

Results | Messages

	nID	nvcFullName	nSystemAssembly
1	1	Microsoft.BizTalk.GlobalPropertySchemas, Version=3.0.1.0, Culture=neutral, PublicKe...	1
2	2	Microsoft.BizTalk.DefaultPipelines, Version=3.0.1.0, Culture=neutral, PublicKeyToken...	1
3	3	Microsoft.BizTalk.Adapter.MSMQ.MsmqAdapterProperties, Version=3.0.1.0, Culture=n...	1
4	4	MQSeries, Version=2.0.1.0, Culture=neutral, PublicKeyToken=31bf3856ad364e35	1
5	5	Microsoft.BizTalk.Hws.HwsPromotedProperties, Version=3.0.1.0, Culture=neutral, Pub...	1
6	6	Microsoft.BizTalk.Hws.HwsSchemas, Version=3.0.1.0, Culture=neutral, PublicKeyTok...	1
7	7	Microsoft.BizTalk.KwTpm.StsDefaultPipelines, Version=3.0.1.0, Culture=neutral, Publi...	1
8	8	Microsoft.BizTalk.KwTpm.RoleLinkTypes, Version=3.0.1.0, Culture=neutral, PublicKe...	1
9	9	mscorlib, Version=2.0.0.0, Culture=neutral, PublicKeyToken=b77a5c561934e089	1
10	31	Schemas, Version=1.0.0.0, Culture=neutral, PublicKeyToken=4618e66ff6b403b6	0
11	32	Orchestrations, Version=1.0.0.0, Culture=neutral, PublicKeyToken=4618e66ff6b403b6	0

Figure 3-20. *bts_Assemblies table*

Now switch to the bt_DocumentSpec table and let's look at this table in more detail. The bt_DocumentSpec table is very important and will be the first place to look when resolving BizTalk error messages like the ones mentioned previously.

Next, you'll figure out what your message type is. As stated previously in the chapter, a message type within a BizTalk solution is a concatenation of target namespace property and root node name. When you add a new schema file to your project, Visual Studio automatically sets the target namespace to `http://[ProjectName].[SchemaFileName]`. The schema's root node name is always preset to Root. When you deploy your project containing XSD schemas, the deployment procedure puts the message types into and references the assembly containing the .NET class definitions in bt_DocumentSchemas.

Since you changed the root node name in your project to ExplorerWMI, the message type will be `http://Schemas.TestSchema#ExplorerWMI`.

Open the SQL Server Management Studio and run the query shown in Figure 3-21.

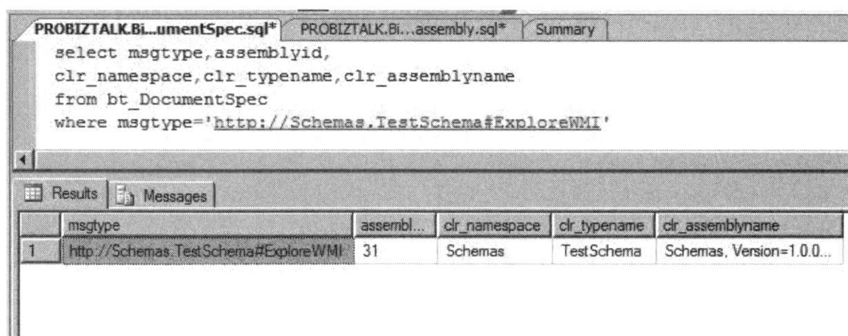

Figure 3-21. *SQL Server Management Studio query*

The output of this query confirms that you defined a new message of type `http://Schemas.TestSchema#ExplorerWMI`, and the class `Schemas.TestSchema` is representing your schema. Its location is in the assembly Schemas, version 1.0.0.0.

Upon startup, the BizTalk runtime caches this table in memory. When a Receive Adapter passes an inbound message to a receive pipeline, it first constructs the message type by concatenating the namespace and root node name of the incoming document. It then checks whether the message type is uniquely presented in the bt_DocumentSpec table. If the check is successful, the receive pipeline proceeds with further execution; if not, you will get an error message similar to the ones we presented at the beginning of this section. The bt_DocumentSpec table will most likely be your first place to look when addressing issues relating to resolving message types.

Since Visual Studio automatically creates a unique namespace for document specification, you shouldn't run into problems. But if for whatever reason you change Target Namespace and Root Node Name properties manually, you have to be careful not to create schemas with conflicting namespaces.

There is another situation you should be aware of that could potentially lead to problems. While working on different projects, we have seen developers make the same mistake and then spend hours trying to figure out what's going on. If the schema namespaces are not set up properly, BizTalk will bounce incoming messages, stating that multiple schemas are matching the same message type. Here is how this might happen and what you can do to address it.

As you may already know, the BizTalk programming model is quite flexible, especially when it comes to message type conversion. When you call methods located in external .NET assemblies from your orchestration and pass the BizTalk message to those methods, you most likely pass the message as either a System.Xml.XmlDocument type or a Microsoft.XLANGs.BaseTypes type. You can then extract the message in the form of a well-typed .NET class, which is very convenient. The inverse applies to when you need to create a new message inside your .NET code and return it to your orchestration. In your orchestration inside a Construct Message shape, you can call a method that returns a .NET class representing an orchestration message. To generate this typed class, which matches your XSD schema, launch the Visual Studio command prompt and then run the following command:

```
Xsd.exe /c TestSchema.xsd
```

This command will generate a file named TestSchema.cs containing the `ExplorerWMI` class. Include this file in your project and you can extract messages and create new ones as a well-formed type as in Listing 3-2.

Listing 3-2. *Type Orchestration Message*

```
using System;
using System.Collections.Generic;
using System.Text;
using Microsoft.XLANGs.BaseTypes ;

namespace CustomClasses
{
    public class MyCustomClass
    {

        public ExplorerWMI  CreateNewMessage(XLANGMessage sourceMessage)
        {
            ExplorerWMI srcClass = sourceMessage[0].RetrieveAs(typeof(ExplorerWMI));
            ExplorerWMI newClass = new ExplorerWMI();
            newClass = srcClass;
return newClass;

        }
    }
}
```

Surely quite a handy technique, but like all conveniences, it can be a source of problems if used indiscriminately. When you declare a message in an orchestration, you are required to specify what type of message it is (not to be confused with the message type routing property). You have four options:

- .NET classes
- Multipart message types
- Schemas
- Web message types

.NET types can be cast to an orchestration message type. So having both .NET classes produced by the XSD.EXE tool and XSD schemas in the same solution technically allows you to choose either when specifying the type of message when creating new orchestration message variables.

Add a new message to the orchestration, switch to the Properties View, and select the Message Type combo box. Expand the .NET class branch and choose Select from Referenced Assembly. This will pop up a Select Artifact Type dialog as shown in Figure 3-22.

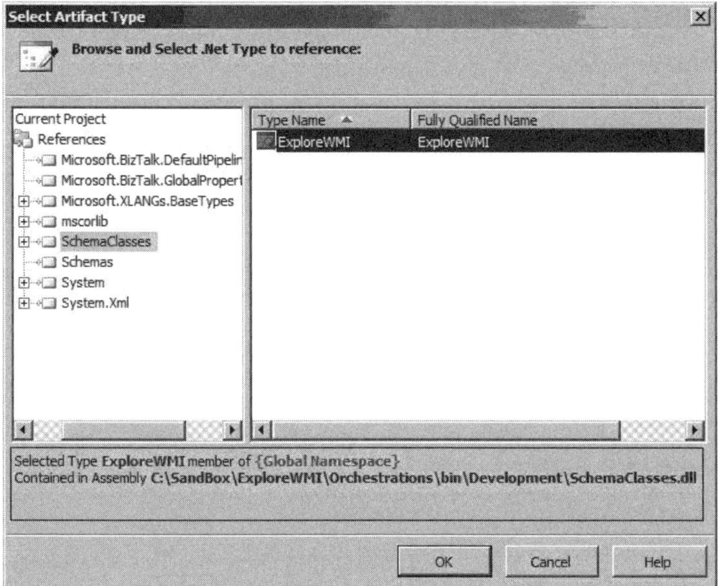

Figure 3-22. *Select Artifact Type dialog box*

Select the ExplorerWMI item in the right pane and compile and deploy the orchestration. Now open the SQL Server Management Studio and run the same query as shown in Figure 3-20 against the bt_DocumentSpec table and check out your results. As you can see in Figure 3-23, the document specification is deployed twice, pointing to different assemblies: one pointing to the assembly created when you deployed XSD schemas, and another to the assembly containing classes produced by the XSD.EXE tool.

PROBIZTALK.Bi...umentSpec.sql | Summary

```
select msgtype,assemblyid,
clr_namespace,clr_typename,clr_assemblyname
from bt_DocumentSpec
where msgtype='http://Schemas.TestSchema#ExploreWMI'
```

Results | Messages

	msgtype	assemblyid	clr_namespace	clr_typename	clr_assemblyname
1	http://Schemas.TestSchema#ExploreWMI	37	Schemas	TestSchema	Schemas, Version=1.0.0.0, Culture=neutral, Public...
2	http://Schemas.TestSchema#ExploreWMI	39		ExploreWMI	SchemaClasses, Version=1.0.0.0, Culture=neutral,...

Figure 3-23. *Multiple assemblies, same namespace*

As you see, the deployment procedure makes no attempts to check for possible duplication and simply deploys everything as is. If you now submit a document instance to the receive location, you will get an error message in the Event Viewer.

Listing 3-3 is the code snippet showing how you can enumerate deployed assemblies and schemas. The product documentation doesn't mention the important properties of the `Schema` class, namely `TargetNamespace` and `RootNode`, which together constitute a message type. So be aware that these properties are available.

Listing 3-3. *Enumerating Deployed Assemblies*

```
using System;
using System.Text;
using Microsoft.BizTalk.ExplorerOM;

namespace Schemas
{
    class Program
    {

        static void Main(string[] args)
        {
            EnumerateSchemas();
            Console.ReadKey();
        }

        public static void EnumerateSchemas()
        {
            BtsCatalogExplorer catalog = new BtsCatalogExplorer();
            catalog.ConnectionString = "Server=.;Initial
Catalog=BizTalkMgmtDb;Integrated Security=SSPI;";_

            foreach (BtsAssembly assembly in catalog.Assemblies )
            {


                foreach (Schema schema in assembly.Schemas)
                {
                   Console.WriteLine("\t{0}#{1}",
                        schema.TargetNameSpace,schema.RootName    );

                }
            }
        }
    }
}
```

Or you can access deployed schemas directly without enumerating assemblies first as shown in Listing 3-4.

Listing 3-4. *Accessing Deployed Schemas Directly*

```
using System;
using System.Text;
using Microsoft.BizTalk.ExplorerOM;

namespace Schemas
{
    class Program
    {

        static void Main(string[] args)
        {
            EnumerateSchemas();
            Console.ReadKey();
        }

        public static void EnumerateSchemas()
        {
            BtsCatalogExplorer catalog = new BtsCatalogExplorer();
           catalog.ConnectionString = "Server=.;Initial
Catalog=BizTalkMgmtDb;Integrated Security=SSPI;";


                foreach (Schema schema in catalog.Schemas)
                {
                   Console.WriteLine("\t{0}#{1}",
                        schema.TargetNameSpace,schema.RootName);

                }
        }
    }
}
```

CHAPTER 4

Pipelining and Components

Pipelines are probably the least properly utilized tools in the BizTalk toolbox. Pipelines are designed to do one thing well:

> *Examine and potentially modify messages or convoys of messages as they are received and sent to/from the Messagebox*

The most important words in the preceding statement are "Examine" and "Modify." As stated previously, messages in BizTalk are immutable once they have entered the Messagebox. The only proper way to affect a message is to change it in a pipeline either on the send side or the receive side. Before starting a new custom pipeline, it is important to understand that a pipeline by itself does nothing. The real work is accomplished by the pipeline components that are attached to the pipeline. If you are building custom pipelines, 99% of your time will be spent in coding the custom pipeline components, not in building the actual pipeline.

Typical out of the box uses of pipelines that are commonly known are

- Breaking up inbound documents into separate individual documents
- Verifying or signing documents with digital signatures
- Processing encoded documents (MIME/SMIME)
- Processing flat text files into XML and back
- Augmenting message data with information from external systems such as a database or mainframe

These scenarios cover about 75% of the typical uses of a BizTalk solution that would need to use a custom pipeline. There are, however, a multitude of other uses that we will dive into later. Pipelines are attached to either a send port or receive location and executed when either a message is received into or sent from the Messagebox. When the port processes a message, the pipeline processing is activated when the message is passed to the start of the pipeline.

■Note If you were to monitor the typical newsgroups relating to BizTalk, you would find that a common question often asked is, "How do I call a pipeline from an orchestration or from custom code?" Although it is possible to do this, try to understand why you need to do this before tackling it. Pipelines are meant to operate on a message or a convoy of messages. A convoy is simply a set of related messages that are logically grouped together by a promoted property called the `InterchangeID`. In BizTalk 2004, calling a pipeline from an orchestration was not a supported scenario. In BizTalk 2006 this has been greatly improved. Unless the application needs to aggregate messages inside the orchestration, there is no real reason to do this. Message aggregation is the primary reason why this feature was improved in BizTalk 2006.

Many new BizTalk architects often ask, "So why not just add all my custom code into the pipeline?" The answer is threefold:

- Pipeline processing does not occur on multiple machines.

  Pipelines only execute on one machine at a time since a message instance is picked up by a host instance. For example, a receive pipeline will execute on the BizTalk machine where the message is processed, not where it is received; if the pipeline has a significant amount of CPU work to accomplish, then this machine can become unavailable while the pipeline is executed. Note that multiple instances of a pipeline can execute simultaneously, but each instance executes on one machine. Likewise, if the messages being processed are quite large, the memory usage on that machine will grow accordingly if the entire document needs to be loaded into memory. This is the primary reason why most BizTalk architectures have receive/send processing servers isolated from orchestration processing servers.

- Pipelines are stateful.

  A pipeline executes in a stateful manner in that once the pipeline starts executing, it doesn't stop until it is completed. Also, if that pipeline instance terminates, that message becomes suspended and does not automatically restart on another machine. This is unlike an orchestration, which can dehydrate itself when the instance is waiting for a task to complete or rehydrate itself on another host if the original machine becomes available. If there are a significant number of messages to process, this can affect how the application will perform.

- Pipeline exception handling is problematic.

  If a pipeline throws an unhandled exception, the pipeline processing stops. This is a major issue for synchronous applications. Synchronous applications that require a notification be sent to the calling application will have issues if the pipeline throws exceptions and no response message is sent back. This issue will be explored later. It is possible in BizTalk 2006 to subscribe to the message failure, but this does not help in a synchronous application scenario.

Getting Started with Pipeline Development

Upon closer inspection, it is clear to see that a pipeline is simply a container for pipeline components. A pipeline has "stages" as shown in the Pipeline Designer. These stages differ for both send and receive pipelines, but they essentially allow you to do two things: first, they provide a way to logically organize the flow of execution logic within the pipeline, and second, they give the pipeline component developer different APIs to code against depending on what type of pipeline component is needed. If custom pipeline development is something that you haven't tackled before, ask yourself the following questions before you get started:

- What is the end result of my pipeline's execution? What types of message are expected?
- Will my pipeline need to look at the message's data? If it does, how big are the messages? Can I stream them using the XMLReader, or do I need to load them into an XML DOM?
- Is the pipeline schema agnostic, or does it need to validate the incoming message type?
- Does my pipeline need to create multiple messages based on the incoming message or just one?
- How do I handle exceptions within the pipeline? Do I need to log them? Can the pipeline throw an exception and stop processing, or does it need to output an error document?
- Do I have all the necessary context properties in the message context?
- Will I be promoting custom properties?

Pipeline Stages

Custom pipelines are divided into receive and send pipelines. Both types of pipelines have stages unique to either sending or receiving messages. Each stage of the pipeline has the ability to contain multiple pipeline components that are designed to be executed within that particular stage. For example, a receive pipeline may have several components within the Decode stage. The components will execute sequentially from the first to last within the stage. In the case of stages with multiple components, the output of one component will be used as the input for the next. The exceptions to this rule are Disassembler components. These types of components execute on a "first match" rule: the rule states that the first component in the Disassemble stage that is able to process the message will be chosen to execute. The remaining components in the stage are then ignored, and processing continues with the next stage in the pipeline.

Receive Pipeline Stages

Receive pipelines have specific stages that help in processing the message in a logical fashion. The surface of the Pipeline Designer is shown in Figure 4-1. Each of the stages of the pipeline is designed to perform a specific task:

- **Decode**: This stage is used to perform operations that are required to "read" the incoming message. Think of the Decode stage as where you would perform things like decryption, decompression, and any processing logic that will be required as input data for the subsequent stages.
- **Disassemble**: Components tagged as Disassemblers are designed to produce multiple messages based on the input message. Disassemblers often are used to de-batch the incoming messages into multiple smaller messages. Each of the messages produced by the Disassembler are then passed to the remaining stages within the pipeline.
- **Validate**: This stage is used to ensure the message that has been decoded and potentially produced by the Disassembler is considered to be "valid" according to the pipeline rules. Often this involves verifying the XML schema of the message to be of a certain type. Custom validators are often created for custom business-level validation logic (i.e., ensuring that the purchase order number of an incoming message is valid and exists within a database).
- **Resolve Party**: This stage is used often in trading partner exchange scenarios. This stage is usually used to examine the digital certificates of a signed message to ensure the validity of the sending party.

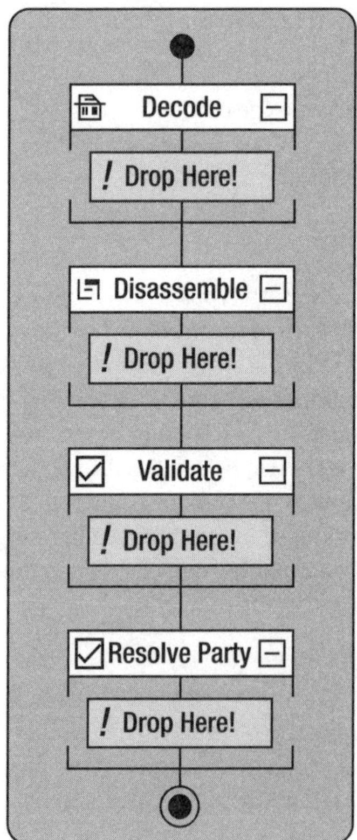

Figure 4-1. *Pipeline Designer stages*

Send Pipeline Stages

Send pipelines have specific stages that are related to preparing the message to be sent out of BizTalk. The surface of the Send Pipeline Designer is shown in Figure 4-2. Each of the stages of the pipeline are designed to perform a specific task:

- **Pre-Assemble**: This stage is often used to gather any specific information that will be needed by an Assembler and add it to the message.
- **Assemble**: Assemblers are responsible for combining multiple smaller messages into one large message. This is often the case when you are aggregating several messages into a batch. Assemblers are also often used in flat-file conversion and EDI scenarios to aggregate the outbound flat file into one large batched file.
- **Encode**: Encoders are responsible for writing the message in a fashion so that it can be read by the downstream system. Often this involves ensuring the proper character set is used, compressing the message, MIME encoding, or attaching a digital certificate.

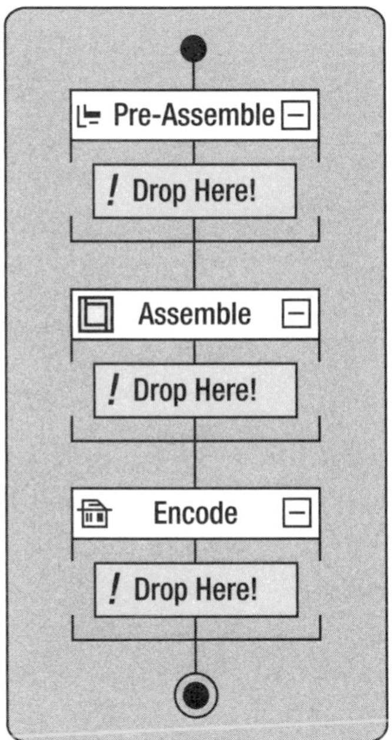

Figure 4-2. *Send Pipeline Designer*

Understanding Pipeline Execution

Pipeline components execute in a sequential order starting from the first stages and working down to the last. The exception to this rule is the Disassembler component, which will execute sequentially within the Disassemble stage of the receive pipeline until a component is found that is able to process the message. The first Disassembler component that accepts the message is executed, and then the resulting messages are passed to the remaining stages of the pipeline. When pipeline components execute sequentially, the output of one pipeline component is used as input to the next one in the sequence. Note the Disassemble stage in Figure 4-3. These components will fire sequentially until one of them determines that they can handle the incoming message. In this scenario, the first component to do this executes.

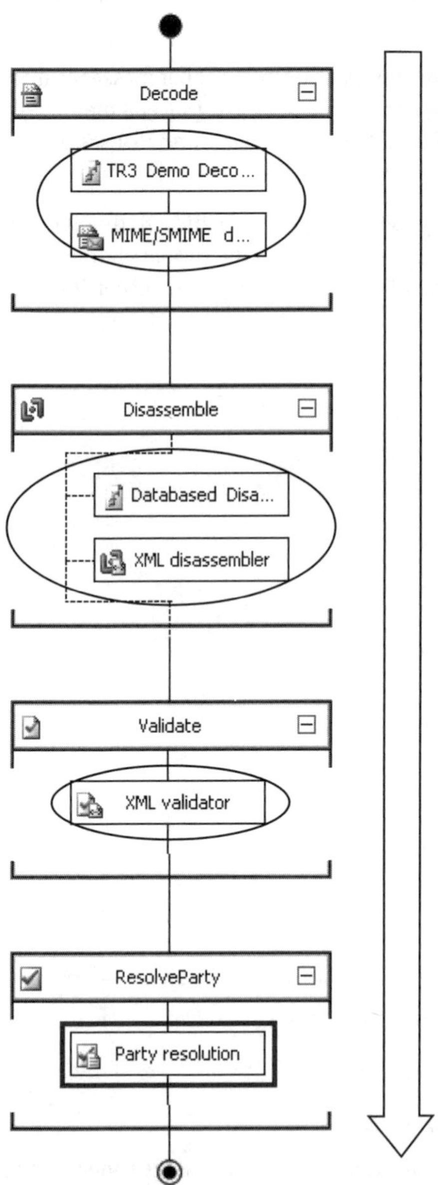

Figure 4-3. *Pipeline execution*

Understanding Interchanges

Most BizTalk developers really do not understand or appreciate fully what an Interchange is. An **Interchange** is a message or series of messages that flow through the Messagebox. Generally one message = one Interchange. The Interchange is uniquely identified by the `InterchangeID` promoted property. In many cases, the Interchange contains more than one message. This is often the case when processing flat-file documents or XML documents that contain envelopes. In this case, there will be one Interchange with as many messages as were contained in the original envelope. Each message would have the same `InterchangeID`; however, they would all have unique `MessageIDs`. In pipeline development, only Disassembler and Assembler components need to be concerned about this, since all other components receive one message and return one message. Disassemblers will receive one message and de-batch it into many messages, and the reverse is the case with Assemblers.

What Is an Interchange?

In terms of BizTalk processing, an Interchange is the message or series of messages that are received by a receive port and run through a receive pipeline. Interchanges with multiple documents generally relate to batch messages that are de-batched by a Disassembler component within a pipeline. If an envelope message was received with 20 documents inside, the Interchange would contain 20 messages. Each message would contain the same `InterchangeIDs` within the message context and distinct `MessageIDs` as shown in Figure 4-4.

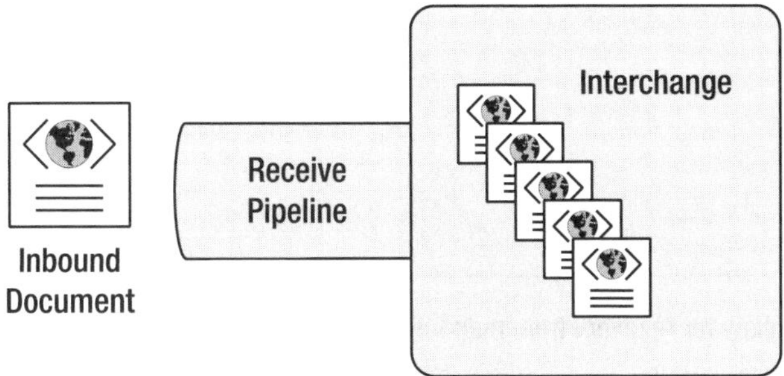

Figure 4-4. *Description of an Interchange*

In BizTalk Server 2004, should a document within the Interchange or "batch" be considered invalid either due to a "subscription not found" error or because the data within the message does not conform to the schema specified, every message within the batch would fail. This had dramatic repercussions for systems that did not want this functionality. In BizTalk 2006, there is an option on the pipeline to allow the pipeline to not fail should one message be bad, continuing processing of the batch and only failing the individual messages that are in error. The remaining messages in the batch would be allowed to proceed. The message that failed can be subscribed to and routed to a generic error-handling mechanism such as an orchestration or a port.

Overview of Recoverable Interchange Handling

Recoverable Interchange Processing (RIP) is a mechanism whereby the Messaging Engine will allow you to subscribe to special properties that are promoted by BizTalk when an error condition occurs. Typically, this is used in de-batching scenarios where a pipeline will be creating multiple messages in an Interchange. Should an error occur, the recoverable Interchange setting will allow the pipeline to throw an error only on the documents that failed and permit the remaining documents to be passed through the pipeline.

Message Suspension

Recoverable Interchange Processing is a function of the Disassembler component configured within the pipeline. If a message is in error and the component is using recoverable Interchanges, the message in error will be suspended and placed in the suspended queue; other messages will be propagated down the pipeline for further processing.

Once the messages within an Interchange are propagated down the pipeline or placed in the suspended queue, the further processing of those messages is treated transactionally as before. If a message fails at any point during its processing path, except in its routing (for example, no matching subscriber), all of the messages within the Interchange are thrown away and the originating Interchange is placed in the suspended queue.

Message Failure Points

Failures in the message stages defined here result in the entire Interchange being suspended:

- Validate
- Resolve Party
- Map

■ **Note** Recoverable Interchanges do not allow for recovery from map failures. If a BizTalk map fails during an Interchange, the entire Interchange stops processing, even if RIP is enabled.

Interchanges that fail processing due to one of these errors will become suspended. These Interchanges can then be resumed from within the BizTalk Administration Console. However, the Interchange will still likely fail unless the underlying cause of the failure is addressed.

Receiving the following errors will not cause the XMLDisassembler component to stop processing messages from an Interchange:

- Schema not found
- Schema ambiguity (more than one schema exists for the same message type)
- XML validation failed
- Flat-file parsing failed

Interchange processing will stop within the XMLDisassembler component if the message data is not well-formed XML. Since the data is read as a stream, a good check is to see whether document properties that would cause `System.Xml.XmlReader` to error are present. If they are, the XMLDisassembler will fail as well.

Messages that are extracted from Interchanges but fail because of a "No matching subscription found" error can be successfully resumed. All that is needed in this case is to ensure the BizTalk port or orchestration that has a subscription for the message is enlisted. The message can then be successfully resumed.

■ **Note** The MSMQT adapter does not support Recoverable Interchange Processing under any circumstance. Unfortunately, there is no user interface restriction on this; however, selecting a receive pipeline that has recoverable Interchanges configured but that gets messages from an MSMQT receive location will generate a runtime error.

The two examples that follow illustrate the differences in Interchange processing as affected by RIP.

Example 1: Standard Interchange Processing Behavior for the XMLDisassembler Component

The following XML is for a document that will be submitted to a receive location, and then to the XMLReceive Pipeline. This XMLDisassembler on the XMLReceive pipeline is configured for Standard Interchange Processing:

```
<MyBatch>
      <SubDoc1>MyDataValue1</SubDoc1>  //No Error
      <SubDoc2>MyDataValue2</SubDoc2> //Routing Error
      <SubDoc3>MyDataValue3</SubDoc3> //No Error
      <SubDoc4>MyDataValue4</SubDoc4> //Pipeline Failure - will be recoverable
      <SubDoc5>MyDataValue5</SubDoc5> //No Error
</MyBatch>
```

This batch of messages contains five messages, all of which will be successfully extracted and put into the Interchange. SubDoc1, SubDoc2, and SubDoc3 process through the pipeline and are ready to be published.

SubDoc 4 creates an error at the Disassemble stage in the pipeline. This causes all the messages that have already been processed to roll back and the original Interchange message to be suspended as resumable. The net effect is that no messages are published to the Messagebox. The batch is suspended because in Standard Interchange Processing, any pipeline failures cause the entire Interchange to be discarded, and any messages that may have been successfully disassembled are to be thrown away and suspended.

Example 2: Recoverable Interchange Processing Behavior for the XMLDisassembler Component

Using the same inbound batch document as shown in Example 1, if we set the XMLDisassembler to use RIP, the execution that will occur in the pipeline processing will be dramatically different. SubDoc1, SubDoc2, and SubDoc3 successfully pass through the pipeline and are ready to be published to the Messagebox. SubDoc4 generates an error in the XMLDisassembler and will be suspended. SubDoc5 passes through the pipeline and is able to be published to the Messagebox.

Once the entire Interchange is processed, SubDoc1, SubDoc2, SubDoc3, and SubDoc5 are successfully published to the Messagebox. SubDoc4 is placed in the suspended queue.[1] SubDoc2 is then sent to the suspended queue due to a "no subscriber found" error.

Configuring Recoverable Interchanges

There are two places where you can configure a recoverable Interchange. The first is in the Receive Pipeline Designer as shown in Figure 4-5. The ability to configure Recoverable Interchange Processing is available at design time when a custom pipeline that contains either a Flat File Disassembler or an XMLDisassembler is being developed. Recoverable Interchanges is a property of that component.

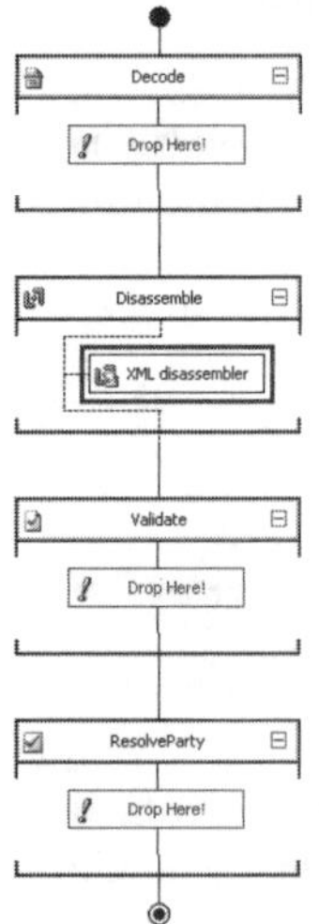

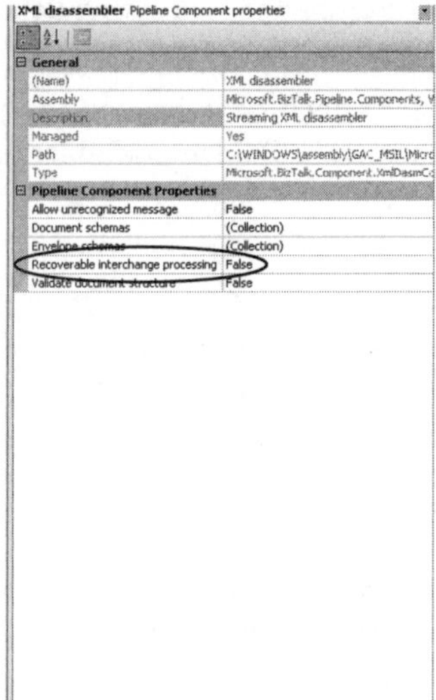

Figure 4-5. *Recoverable Interchanges property*

1. For an example of how to monitor messages that are placed in the suspended queue, see Chapter 6.

The second place to configure Recoverable Interchange Processing is on the receive location that will process the inbound Interchange. The property is part of the per-instance pipeline configuration screen shown in Figure 4-6.[2]

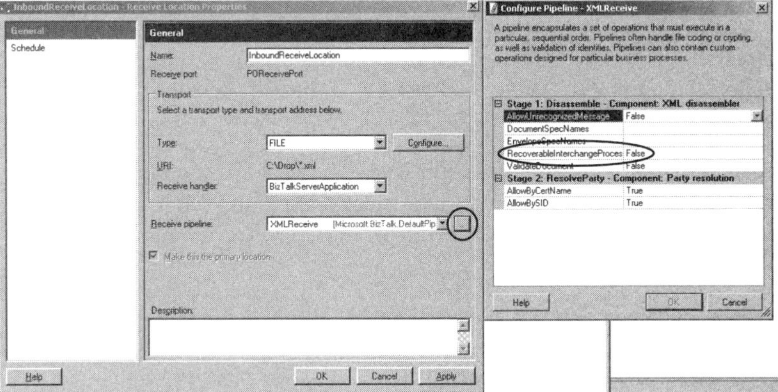

Figure 4-6. *Per-instance pipeline configuration for XMLReceive pipeline*

Using the Default Pipelines

In many circumstances, the default pipelines that ship with BizTalk 2006 are able to handle most common tasks. For example, most do not know the default XMLReceive pipeline not only removes envelopes and disassembles, but also resolves parties and thumbprint certificates. If you examine the documentation as published in the BizTalk Server 2006 product, the default XMLReceive pipeline already includes the default XMLDisassembler and Party Resolution components. Both of these components can be configured in the per-instance pipeline configuration screen as shown in Figure 4-6. In short, if your send or receive pipelines look like those shown in Figure 4-7, you don't need to create them. All you need to do is define an envelope schema inside the schema editor and ensure that each of the documents contained in the envelope are included in the schema as `XSD:Includes` in the case of the receive pipeline. The default XMLReceive pipeline will do the rest of the work for you. In general, it is always preferable to use the default pipelines versus building a custom one. The same is true for the default XMLTransmit pipeline. It contains an Assembler component that will assemble all messages passed to it in the Interchange.

2. This is a good place to note that the property screen in Figure 4-5 is also where you would set the incoming envelope and document schemas for your receive location, which uses the XMLReceive pipeline. Most people would create a custom pipeline with the default XMLDisassembler and set these properties on the component—but starting in BizTalk 2006, the properties for this are exposed in this new UI. This type of setup was also available in BizTalk 2004 but was configured via the BizTalk object model. Alternatively, Jon Flanders has an excellent blog entry about this subject and a tool that allows you to configure these properties without writing additional code. See www.masteringbiztalk.com/blogs/jon/PermaLink,guid,2f6500ae-d832-495f-92a3-f7032ef317ca.aspx for more information.

In many cases, developers will simply default to using the XMLReceive pipeline in all circumstances regardless of what type of document they are processing and the end target for the message. It is important to note that you *do not* need this pipeline to process XML documents. You need the XMLReceive pipeline to promote properties and validate schemas, but if you know the destinations for the messages without having to route them, you can use the pass-through pipeline. The XMLReceive pipeline adds a fair bit of overhead to the receive-side processes due to the fact that it is running the Disassembler and promoting properties into the context. There are several circumstances in which you need the XMLReceive pipeline, some of which are as follows:

- **Need to promote properties from the message's data**: The pass-through pipeline does not promote properties, so any custom properties you define in the schema will not be recognized. Note that default properties that were promoted by the adapter will still be available.
- **Need to route messages to an orchestration**: An orchestration needs to have the message properties promoted in order to determine message types. If the end target for the message is an orchestration, and the orchestration is expecting a specific schema, you need to use the XMLReceive pipeline.
- **Need to validate the schema**: The pass-through pipeline has no concept of schema validation. If you need to verify that the inbound message's data is correct, you cannot use the pass-through pipeline.

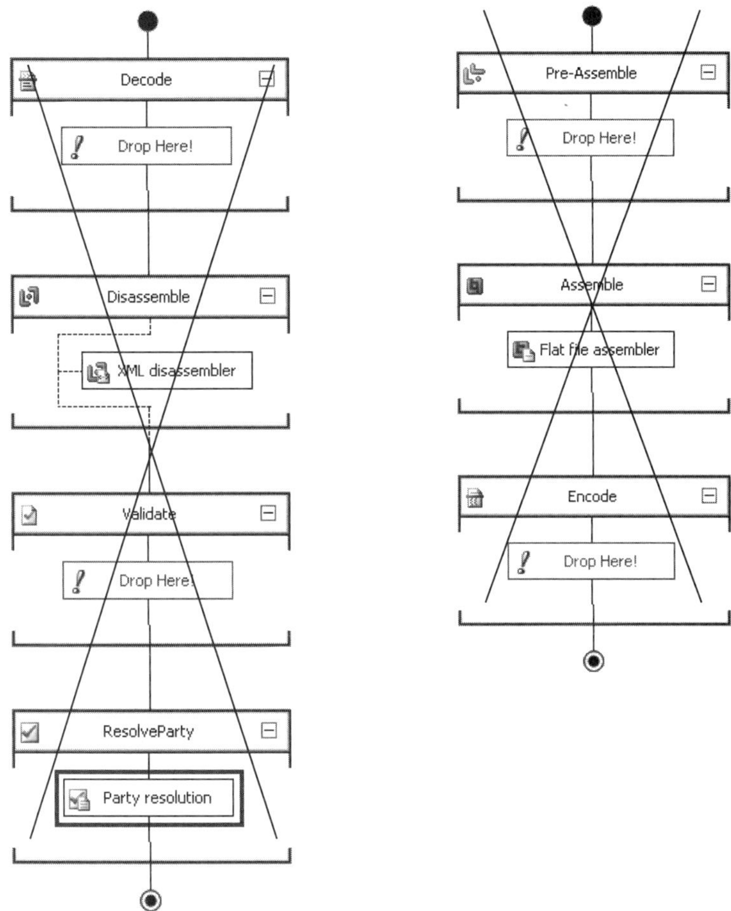

Figure 4-7. *If you have these, you probably don't need them.*

Routing Binary Data

Most people do not think that BizTalk can be used for processing binary data. Since the pass-through pipeline doesn't examine the message data, and the BizTalk Messaging Engine uses streams as its data representation, it is quite easy to move binary data from one source to another. If you need to promote properties for an incoming message, you will need to write a custom Disassembler, but if you know the locations, all you need to do is choose pass-through for both the receive and send ports and ensure that the send port has a valid subscription for the message. Most commonly this is done by creating a filter that matches based on `BTS.ReceivePortName`. If you want to route data based on the `MessageType` context property, you will need to create a custom pipeline component that promotes a value into the context. By default this will not happen with the pass-through pipeline, as technically there is no message to look at since the data is binary. This is explored in detail in the next chapter.

Using BizTalk Framework 2.0 Reliable Messaging

Continuing from the previous examples, let's assume that the order processing system not only needs to update your downstream systems, which are internal to your organization, but also needs to notify a trading partner of the transactions.[3] Let's assume that when an order is placed, you need to order the requested product from a supplier to support your zero inventory objectives. This situation brings about a number of challenges. Assuming for now that the sending and receiving applications are both BizTalk Server applications, you first must ensure that the transaction is completed reliably over inherently unreliable protocols and across network boundaries and firewalls. This is where the BizTalk Framework 2.0 Reliable Messaging scenarios come into play, as shown in Figure 4-8.

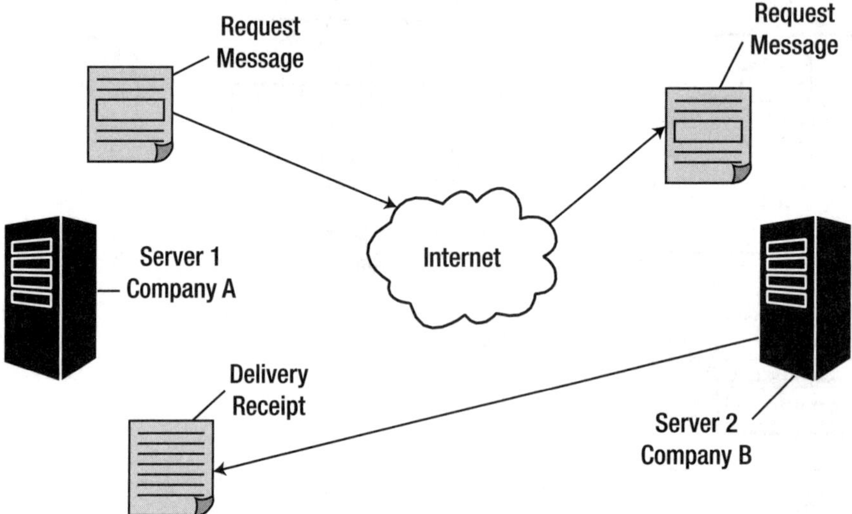

Figure 4-8. *Typical partner exchange scenario*

The BizTalk Framework specification is an XML specification that allows reliable messaging over HTTP and other transports. A BizTalk server according to the definition is a server that implements the BizTalk Framework rules and schemas for processing messages to provide a reliable Interchange mechanism over the wire.

In that sense, the product Microsoft BizTalk Server 2006 is a BizTalk server that implements the BizTalk Framework 2.0 specification. Of course, having BizTalk Server 2006 on both sides will allow you to implement reliable messaging Interchanges and processes with relatively small effort.

Microsoft BizTalk Server 2006 provides custom pipeline components for sending and receiving BizTalk Framework envelopes. The BizTalk Framework properties are configured through these pipeline components and can also be updated at runtime within an orchestration.

---

3. This section and its subsections originally appeared in "Configuring BizTalk Framework Reliable Messaging in BizTalk Server 2004," (REED004872).zip. Copyright by Microsoft Corporation. Reprinted with permission from Microsoft Corporation.

Figure 4-9 shows the required components (channel/ports and pipelines) to implement an Interchange with BizTalk Framework 2.0. The left side shows the sender configuration, which consists of a static one-way send port to send the business document or message and a static one-way receive port to receive BizTalk Framework 2.0 delivery receipts. The right side shows the receiver configuration, which contains a static one-way receive port to receive the message or business document and a dynamic one-way send port that subscribes (using a **filter expression**) to the Messagebox for messages that have the property `BTS.MessageType` with a value of BTF2DeliveryReceipt.

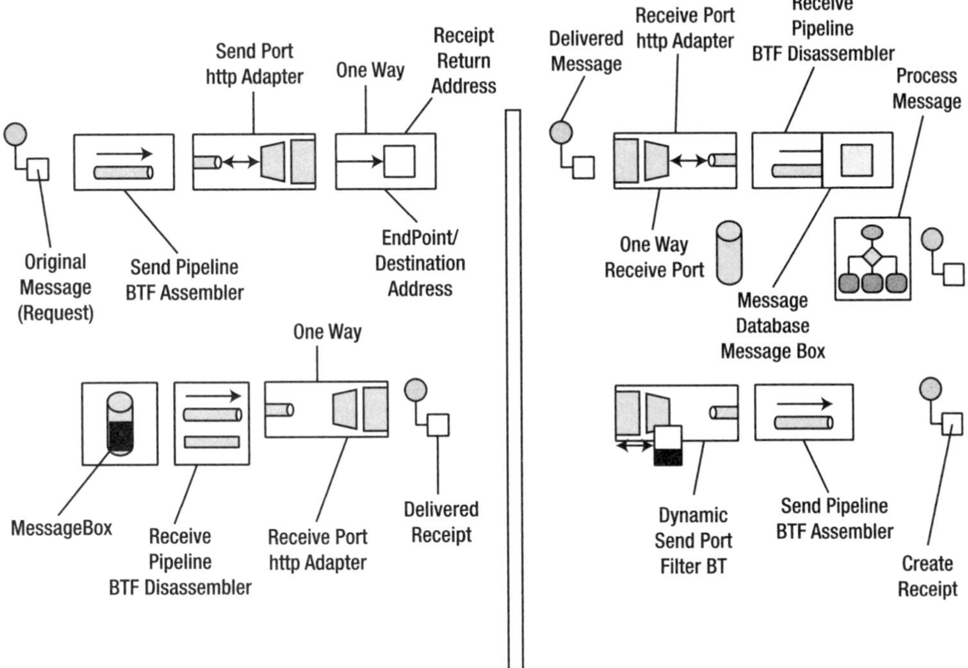

Figure 4-9. *BizTalk reliable messaging configuration*

In all four ports, the BizTalk custom pipeline components are used for receiving (Disassemble) and sending (Assemble) BizTalk Framework envelopes.

BizTalk Framework Assembler and Disassembler Pipeline Components

As mentioned before, BizTalk Server 2006 provides custom pipeline components for BizTalk Framework envelopes. The pipeline component that must be configured for messages going out is the Assembler. In our first scenario, only one of the four ports must be configured.

Note Make sure QFE 1085 (KB 813845) has been installed before trying to configure BizTalk Framework 2.0 Reliable Messaging. The QFE removes the compatibility issues with BizTalk 2002/BizTalk 2000 relating to BizTalk Framework 2.0 Reliable Messaging.

Working with BizTalk Framework Properties Within Orchestrations

In many cases, a business process orchestration will be implemented in either the send or the receive side of a business process, and it is more suitable to configure the BizTalk Framework properties there. On top of that, there are properties that are not accessible as design-time pipeline components. The orchestration is a suitable place to modify the values of these properties at runtime.

The following lines of code show how to assign the values to the property field of the outbound message. These values can be written within a message assignment expression and will override any given value set at design time.

```
//Basic settings for BizTalk Framework Reliable Messaging

msgPSB_ReachEnvelope_Outgoing(XMLNORM.AddXMLDeclaration)=false;
msgPSB_ReachEnvelope_Outgoing(BTF2.IsReliable)=true;
msgPSB_ReachEnvelope_Outgoing(BTF2.svc_deliveryRctRqt_sendBy)=_
vBTFDeliveryReceiptSendBy;
msgPSB_ReachEnvelope_Outgoing(BTF2.svc_deliveryRctRqt_sendTo_address)= _
vBTFDeliveryReceiptAddress;
msgPSB_ReachEnvelope_Outgoing(BTF2.svc_deliveryRctRqt_sendTo_address_type)= _
vBTFDeliveryReceiptAddressType;

//Other settings for BizTalk Framework Reliable Messaging

msgPSB_ReachEnvelope_Outgoing(BTF2.prop_topic)=vBTFDocumentTopic;
msgPSB_ReachEnvelope_Outgoing(BTF2.eps_from_address)=vBTFSourceAddress;
msgPSB_ReachEnvelope_Outgoing(BTF2.eps_from_address_type)=vBTFSourceAddressType;
msgPSB_ReachEnvelope_Outgoing(BTF2.eps_to_address)=vBTFDestinationAddress;
msgPSB_ReachEnvelope_Outgoing(BTF2.eps_to_address_type)=vBTFDestinationAddressType;
msgPSB_ReachEnvelope_Outgoing(BTF2.PassAckThrough)=true;
```

Acknowledgement Verification

One of the easiest ways to verify the acknowledgment of the messages is to look at the following SQL tables in the BizTalk Management Database:

- btf_message_sender
- btf_message_receiver

For outgoing messages, look at the sender table as shown in Figure 4-10. If the message was acknowledged, the acknowledged field will be marked with an *A*.

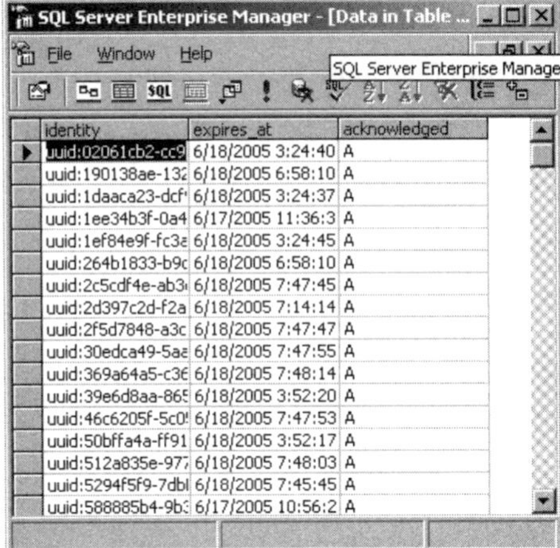

identity	expires_at	acknowledged
uuid:02061cb2-cc9	6/18/2005 3:24:40	A
uuid:190138ae-13	6/18/2005 6:58:10	A
uuid:1daaca23-dcf	6/18/2005 3:24:37	A
uuid:1ee34b3f-0a4	6/17/2005 11:36:3	A
uuid:1ef84e9f-fc3	6/18/2005 3:24:45	A
uuid:264b1833-b9	6/18/2005 6:58:10	A
uuid:2c5cdf4e-ab3	6/18/2005 7:47:45	A
uuid:2d397c2d-f2a	6/18/2005 7:14:14	A
uuid:2f5d7848-a3c	6/18/2005 7:47:47	A
uuid:30edca49-5a	6/18/2005 7:47:55	A
uuid:369a64a5-c3	6/18/2005 7:48:14	A
uuid:39e6d8aa-86	6/18/2005 3:52:20	A
uuid:46c6205f-5c0	6/18/2005 7:47:53	A
uuid:50bffa4a-ff91	6/18/2005 3:52:17	A
uuid:512a835e-97	6/18/2005 7:48:03	A
uuid:5294f5f9-7db	6/18/2005 7:45:45	A
uuid:588885b4-9b	6/17/2005 10:56:2	A

Figure 4-10. *btf_message_sender table*

On the receiver side, look at the receive table. In the table will be the records corresponding to the acknowledged documents.

Custom Components

It is critical to understand that each of the different types of pipeline components is designed to do a specific task. Most pipeline component developers generally only include one custom pipeline component inside a custom pipeline and try to perform all tasks within that one class. Often this becomes problematic and leads to an overly complex class. When starting development, the goal should be to write many small generic components instead of a small number of specialized ones. Pipeline components should be designed to be reused. Additionally, if it makes sense, the components should also accept multiple schema types and allow the user to choose the inbound/outbound schemas. Too often developers will hard-code the schema into the component and assume that the inbound messages will always be of a certain type. The component should first of all be flexible enough to probe the incoming schema and determine that it can handle the document, and second provide a user interface for selecting the desired schema in the Pipeline Designer.

Before starting a new project, the most important thing is to understand what type of component you need to build. This will depend on

- Whether the component is executed in a receive pipeline, a send pipeline, or both
- What type of work needs to be done

Too often developers simply "default" to writing what they know instead of what they should. Having a thorough understanding of how pipeline components work, along with a proper design for what work should take place at which pipeline stage, will help to build more reusable and reliable pipeline components.

Component Categories

As you will soon see, the pipeline component development API is quite heavily based on COM Interop. Most of the specifics of how components are defined are based on what COM category they are tagged with along with what interfaces they implement. Component categories, listed here, exist for each of the different types of pipeline components:

CATID_Any

CATID_AssemblingSerializer

CATID_Decoder

CATID_DisassemblingParser

CATID_Encoder

CATID_Parser

CATID_PartyResolver

CATID_PipelineComponent[4]

CATID_Receiver

CATID_Serializer

CATID_Streamer

CATID_Transmitter

CATID_Validate

These are defined by tagged attributes on the pipeline component's class as shown in the following code:

```
Imports System
Imports System.ComponentModel
Imports Microsoft.BizTalk.Message.Interop
Imports Microsoft.BizTalk.Component.Interop
Imports Microsoft.BizTalk.Component
Imports Microsoft.BizTalk.Messaging

Namespace ABC.BizTalk.FullFillment.PipelineComponents

    <ComponentCategory(CategoryTypes.CATID_PipelineComponent), _
     System.Runtime.InteropServices.Guid("4f1c7d50-e66f-451b-8e94-2f8d599cd013"), _
     ComponentCategory(CategoryTypes.CATID_Encoder)> _
    Public Class MyFirstEncodingComponent
```

4. The CATID_PipelineComponent category is basically a generic "catch-all" category that all pipeline components should implement. It doesn't require any specific interface declarations but is used to identify something as a pipeline component.

Note that it is possible for a component to have more than one category type if it has the proper interface implementation. Also note that the component explicitly defines a GUID for COM Interop.[5] This is done by generating a new GUID using the VS .NET GUID Generation tool, and adding it here as an attribute of the class.

Component Interfaces

The specific interfaces a pipeline component implements are what differentiate that pipeline component from another. BizTalk Server ships with a number of assemblies that define application interfaces for custom components to implement. Once a component has an interface implementation, it can be called by the BizTalk runtime. The basic interfaces are defined in the following list. All components and component categories live in the `Microsoft.BizTalk.Component.Interop` namespace.

- `IBaseComponent`: Defines properties that provide basic information about the component.

  Public properties:

  - `Description`: Gets the component description
  - `Name`: Gets the component name
  - `Version`: Gets the component version

- `IComponent`: Defines the methods used by all pipeline components except Assemblers and Disassemblers.

  Public method:

  - `Execute`: Executes a pipeline component to process the input message and get the resulting message

- `IComponentUI`: Defines methods that enable pipeline components to be used within the Pipeline Designer environment.

  Public property:

  - `Icon`: Gets the icon that is associated with this component

  Public method:

  - `Validate`: Verifies that all of the configuration properties are set correctly

Key BizTalk API Objects

All pipeline components, regardless of what they do, will use the interfaces described in the following subsections. Likewise, most of the pipeline component interfaces defined previously

5. Types including interfaces, classes, and assemblies get a unique GUID even if you don't assign one explicitly. However, they can change between builds/assembly versions, so in this case it's best to explicitly assign them so you don't break binary compatibility between builds/versions.

accept these interfaces as arguments. That being said, it is important to understand these interfaces first before proceeding. The following is based on material from the BizTalk Server documentation on MSDN.

IPipelineContext

`IPipelineContext` is the main interface that defines the operations and properties for the pipeline instance. The MSDN documentation[6] from Microsoft provides good examples for how these interfaces are to be used. Tables 4-1 and 4-2 show the interface's public properties and methods. The key method here is the `GetMessageFactory` method. This method will return a message factory for the pipeline that can be used to create new messages using the `CreateMessage` method.

The `GetMessageFactory` method is the main way to create new messages from within a pipeline component. Also note that you will need to call `IPipelineContext.GetMessageFactory.CreateMessagePart` to create the message part for the message. As we mentioned in Chapter 3, a message is simply a construct that contains zero to many message parts. Once you create the message part, you can assign it to the `IBaseMessage` object through the `AddPart` method.

Table 4-1. *PipelineContext Public Properties*

Property	Description
`ComponentIndex`	Gets the index of the current component in the stage.
`PipelineID`	Gets the ID of the pipeline with which this pipeline context associates.
`PipelineName`	Gets the name of the pipeline.
`ResourceTracker`	Gets the `IResourceTracker` object associated with the pipeline context. This object can be used to track and dispose non-CLR resources.
`StageID`	Gets the ID of the current stage in the pipeline.
`StageIndex`	Gets the index of the pipeline stage where the current component is located.

Table 4-2. *PipelineContext Public Methods*

Method	Description
`GetDocumentSpecByName`	Gets an `IDocumentSpec` object for the specified document name
`GetDocumentSpecByType`	Gets an `IDocumentSpec` object for the specified document type
`GetGroupSigningCertificate`	Gets the signing certificate for the group
`GetMessageFactory`	Get access to the helper interface to work with BizTalk Server message objects

6. http://msdn.microsoft.com/library/default.asp?url=/library/en-us/sdk/htm/frlrfmicrosoftbiztalkcomponentinteropipipelinecontextmemberstopic.asp

IBaseMessage

`IBaseMessage` is the base interface that defines a BizTalk Server message. Tables 4-3 and 4-4 show the public properties and methods. The MSDN documentation[7] from Microsoft provides good examples for how these interfaces are to be used. Note that messages, created using the `IPipelineContext.GetMessageFactory.CreateMessage` method, will implement this interface. This will still need an `IBaseMessagePart` to be assigned through the `AddPart` method for any data to be included with the message.

Table 4-3. *IBaseMessage Public Properties*

Property	Description
`BodyPart`	Gets the body part, or main part, of the message
`BodyPartName`	Gets the name of the body part, or main part, of the message
`Context`	Gets or sets the message context
`IsMutable`	Gets a value indicating whether the message can be changed by components during processing
`MessageID`	Gets the unique message ID for the message
`PartCount`	Gets the total number of parts in the message

Table 4-4. *IBaseMessage Public Methods*

Method	Description
`AddPart`	Adds a part to the message.
`GetErrorInfo`	Gets the exception that caused the error.
`GetPart`	Accesses the message part. This is indexed by `PartName`.
`GetPartByIndex`	Retrieves a part and its name by supplying the part index.
`GetSize`	Gets the size of the message.
`RemovePart`	Removes a part from the message.
`SetErrorInfo`	Sets the error information.

IBaseMessagePart

`IBaseMessagePart` is the interface that defines a BizTalk message part. Tables 4-5 and 4-6 show its public properties and methods. The message part is assigned to an `IBaseMessage` through the `AddPart` method. Note the `Data` property. The MSDN documentation[8] from Microsoft provides good examples for how these interfaces are to be used. This is the property used to assign a value to the message part. The `Data` property accepts and returns only streams. This is incredibly useful, as it allows any stream to be assigned to the message part. This includes XMLReader streams, MemoryStreams, and raw BinaryStreams.

---

7. http://msdn.microsoft.com/library/default.asp?url=/library/en-us/sdk/htm/frlrfmicrosoftbiztalkmessageinteropibasemessagememberstopic.asp

8. http://msdn.microsoft.com/library/default.asp?url=/library/en-us/sdk/htm/frlrfmicrosoftbiztalkmessageinteropibasemessagepartmemberstopic.asp

Another rarely used item is the `PartProperties` property. This is essentially a property bag that can be used to store information and metadata about the part. In reality the `PartID`, `Charset`, and `ContentType` are actually contained in the `PartProperties` `IBasePropertyBag` object.

Table 4-5. *IBaseMessagePart Public Properties*

Property	Description
`Charset`	Gets or sets the character set property for the part
`ContentType`	Gets or sets the content type property for the part
`Data`	Gets or sets the part data
`PartID`	Gets the part with a unique ID
`PartProperties`	Gets or sets one or more properties that describe the part data or contain custom information about the part

Table 4-6. *IBaseMessagePart Public Methods*

Method	Description
`GetOriginalDataStream`	Retrieves the original uncloned version of the part data stream
`GetSize`	Retrieves the size of the part

IBaseMessageContext

`IBaseMessageContext` is the interface used to interact with and manipulate the object context accessible through the `IBaseMessage.Context` property. Tables 4-7 and 4-8 show the public properties and methods. The MSDN documentation[9] from Microsoft provides good examples for how these interfaces are to be used. The main items of interest here are the `Promote`, `Read`, and `Write` methods. Properties that exist in the context can never have a Null value. A Null value means that the property does not exist. For example:

- Attempting to set (or promote) a property value to Null deletes the property and returns the COM result `S_OK`.
- Attempting to read a nonexistent property returns Null.

Table 4-7. *IBaseMessageContext Public Property*

Property	Description
`CountProperties`	Gets the number of properties in the message context

9. http://msdn.microsoft.com/library/default.asp?url=/library/en-us/sdk/htm/frlrfmicrosoftbiztalkmessageinteropibasemessagecontextclasstopic.asp

Table 4-8. *IBaseMessageContext Public Methods*

Method	Description
`AddPredicate`	Adds a message predicate to the message
`GetPropertyType`	Gets the type of the property
`IsMutable`	Indicates whether the message context can be changed by components during processing
`IsPromoted`	Enables the component to determine whether a property has already been promoted in the message context
`Promote`	Promotes a property into the message context
`Read`	Gets a property value from the message context by the name-namespace pair
`ReadAt`	Gets a property from the message context by index
`Write`	Writes a property into the message context

PipelineUtil

`PipelineUtil` is a helper class that exposes the three methods shown in Table 4-9. These methods are invaluable when you need to create a new message. The MSDN documentation[10] from Microsoft provides good examples for how these interfaces are to be used.

Table 4-9. *PipelineUtil Public Methods*

Method	Description
`CloneMessageContext`	Creates a clone of the message context for a given message. This is useful for copying the message context of one message to another.
`CopyPropertyBag`	Creates a clone of the property bag for a given message. This is useful for copying the property bag of one message to another.
`ValidatePropertyValue`	Checks that the object is a valid property value.

■ **Caution** This class is unsupported and is part of the BizTalk product infrastructure. If you run into trouble using it, Microsoft Product Support may not support you. However, it is common knowledge that it exists and makes pipeline component development much easier.

---

10. All of the code snippets in the following sections were generated using the Pipeline Component Wizard, which can be downloaded here: www.gotdotnet.com/Workspaces/Workspace.aspx?id=1d4f7d6b-7d27-4f05-a8ee-48cfcd5abf4a. This is a wonderful tool that we will introduce in the next chapter, but we wanted to specifically reference it here, as the comments and coding styles for the snippets were auto-generated by the tool. The tool dramatically speeds up pipeline component development and generates well-formed and commented code as well. We wanted to specifically *not* discuss it in detail here because it is more important to understand *how* the engine uses pipeline components and how to properly write them versus just running the wizard and having it auto-generate the code for you.

Writing Your First Pipeline Component

The first component most developers want to write is usually some form of simple encoder or decoder. Basically, they want to be passed a message and take some action. This action usually involves updating a piece of data within the message or creating a new message based on some other factors. To implement this behavior is simple. The component in question needs to implement IComponent and populate the IComponent.Execute method with code that takes action. The sample function looks much like this:

```
'<summary>
'Implements IComponent.Execute method.
'</summary>
'<param name="pc">Pipeline context</param>
'<param name="inmsg">Input message</param>
'<returns>Original input message</returns>
'<remarks>
'IComponent.Execute method is used to initiate
'the processing of the message in this pipeline component.
'</remarks>
Public Function Execute(ByVal pContext As _
Microsoft.BizTalk.Component.Interop.IPipelineContext, ByVal inmsg _
As Microsoft.BizTalk.Message.Interop.IBaseMessage) As )
Microsoft.BizTalk.Message.Interop.IBaseMessage _
Implements Microsoft.BizTalk.Component.Interop.IComponent.Execute


            'Build the message that is to be sent out
            DoMyMessageWork(pContext, inmsg)
                ...
                ...
            Return inmsg
End Function
```

Creating More Complex Pipeline Components

Once you master the basics of creating a component, looking at the message, and figuring out what you can do with the data, you may ask yourself, “Okay, so what else can these things do?” We usually answer this with “Pipeline components are much like the Matrix in that you cannot be told what they can do; you must see it for yourself.” In this respect, it is much easier to think about components in terms of specific problems they can solve. We’ll show you a few examples so you can see how you use a pipeline component to solve the issue at hand. In the next chapter, we will dive into advanced pipeline component development and show examples of how you can use pipeline components to extend the base functionality of BizTalk well beyond what is included in the product.

Dynamically Promoting Properties and Manipulating the Message Context

The simplest and most common use of a pipeline component is to promote custom properties into the message context for a message. Often the data for the property is not available in the schema or is not easily accessible—so a simple promotion in the schema editor is not an option. For a simple example, see the Chapter 3 subsection, "Understanding Property Promotions." The code outlined in that subsection demonstrates how to simply write and promote properties to the context.

Dealing with "Out of Order" Message Sequences

When dealing with Interchanges, most often it would be great to know just how many messages are actually in the Interchange and which one is the last one. Preserving order is a major pain for any type of application that needs to do so and potentially resequence messages to an outbound system. Normally selecting ordered delivery is good enough for this task, but two major problems still exist:

- Ordered delivery only works if you receive the messages in the proper order.
- Selecting a port as ordered has a huge performance hit, because messages will essentially be single-threaded as they are dequeued from the Messagebox.

What is needed is a **resequencer pattern** to reorder the messages into the proper order once they are received by an orchestration. The following is a definition and example of a resequencer as given by the Enterprise Integration Patterns site:[11]

> *A* Message Router *can route messages from one channel to different channels based on message content or other criteria. Because individual messages may follow different routes, some messages are likely to pass through the processing steps sooner than others, resulting in the messages getting out of order. However, some subsequent processing steps do require in-sequence processing of messages, for example to maintain referential integrity.*
>
> *How can we get a stream of related but out-of-sequence messages back into the correct order? The figure below logically demonstrates how this concept works.*

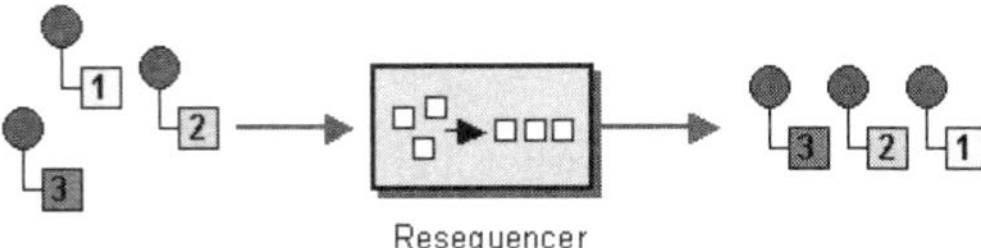

11. Enterprise Integration Patterns site, Resequencer page (www.enterpriseintegrationpatterns.com/Resequencer.html). This site is an excellent resource for all types of patterns that can easily be created using BizTalk Server.

Use a stateful filter, a Resequencer, to collect and re-order messages so that they can be published to the output channel in a specified order.

The Resequencer can receive a stream of messages that may not arrive in order. The Resequencer contains in internal buffer to store out-of-sequence messages until a complete sequence is obtained. The in-sequence messages are then published to the output channel. It is important that the output channel is order-preserving so messages are guaranteed to arrive in order at the next component. Like most other routers, a Resequencer usually does not modify the message contents.

In Chapter 6, we will give a complete example of how to implement custom resequencers using BizTalk orchestrations, convoys, and custom pipeline components. But the most fundamental part of the equation is storing the order. To do that, all you need is a simple pipeline component that can promote what the sequence number is for the current message along with a trigger for determining whether or not it is the last message in the Interchange. Resequencing is most commonly done using a Disassembler component to actually create messages, but can also be implemented using a simple Encoding component if the messages arrive out of order and within different Interchanges.

Custom Distinguished Fields

When you are writing a custom Disassembler, and you want to have distinguished fields that are accessible from within an orchestration, you will need to ensure that they are written to the context of the message before it is stored in the Messagebox. This is because normally when you use an XMLReceive pipeline, it automatically stores these values for you, but when you are writing a custom component, that storing of values doesn't happen auto-magically, so you need to deal with it yourself.[12]

■ **Note** In order to access the distinguished field in the orchestration editor, you still need to tag the field as a distinguished field. This is basically to allow the orchestration engine to read the schema and know at design time what the available distinguished fields are. What needs to happen is that you need to manually populate that field with data at runtime. If you don't, the orchestration will fail with an exception when the XLANG class tries to access the distinguished fields data and finds a Null value.

---

12. People often do not understand what the runtime engine is doing when it processes a distinguished field. Most think that the distinguished field is simply a shortcut to the XPath expression that maps to the field in the document. Actually this is not true. The distinguished field defines what the XPath expression is, but the runtime engine prefetches this data when it processes the message. This is basically done because it is far more performant to do this, and the product team wrote their own XPath navigator component to use streams, making it very efficient to do this as the document is being processed. This is why there is very little performance overhead when you access a distinguished field in an orchestration—it is already loaded and cached. If you used XPath to get the value, the orchestration engine would have to load the entire document and evaluate the XPath expression manually—which is slow and very expensive when dealing with large documents.

The solution to the problem is simple—just write the value to the message context using code as shown in the following snippet. Note the format of the property name and the namespace. In order to be processed by the orchestration engine, they must be named as follows:

Name: The distinguished field location in XPath: `"/*[local-name()='PurchaseOrder' and namespace-uri()='http://ABC.FullFillment']/*[local-name()='UnitPrice' and namespace-uri()='']"`

Namespace URI: `"http://schemas.microsoft.com/BizTalk/2003/btsDistinguishedFields"`

```
//BizTalk System Properties Namespace
Private Const BTSFieldXPathLocation As String =  "/*[local-name()='PurchaseOrder' _
and namespace-uri()='http://ABC.FullFillment']/*[local-name()='UnitPrice' and _
namespace-uri()='']"

Private Const BTSDistinguishedFieldsPropertiesNamespace As String = "_
http://schemas.microsoft.com/BizTalk/2003/btsDistinguishedFields "

//Write a distinguished property
message.Context.Write(BTSFieldXPathLocation, _
BTSDistinguishedFieldsPropertiesNamespace, 10);
```

Checking for Schema Types in Components

As was stated previously, pipeline components that are expecting incoming documents to conform to a particular schema should do two things:

- They should probe the incoming document and determine whether they can process it based on the schema's namespace and root node.
- They should allow the developer to choose the allowed incoming schemas at design time using the Pipeline Designer.

Validating, also called **probing the message**, checks the incoming schema and simply indicates to the runtime that the component will be able to handle the schema—essentially a Boolean value. Ensuring that components validate against the schema is critical, as it often allows the same component code to be reused for multiple applications and also allows for per-instance pipeline configuration. This is done using the `IProbeMessage` interface.

IProbeMessage

The `IProbeMessage` interface has only one method—`Probe`. This method checks whether the incoming message is in a recognizable format. The `Probe` method passes in the pipeline context object as an `IPipelineContext` interface along with the message represented as an `IBaseMessage` Interface and returns a Boolean. If the method returns False, the pipeline component cannot process the message, the current component instance stops executing, and the pipeline component execution sequence continues as defined in Figure 4-3. If it returns True, then the pipeline component executes as normal with its primary operation (Encode, Execute, Disassemble, etc.).

Following is an example of a simple IProbeMessage implementation:

```
Public Class MyProber Implements Microsoft.BizTalk.Component.Interop.IProbeMessage
Private _MyDocSpec As Microsoft.BizTalk.Component.Utilities.SchemaWithNone = New_
Microsoft.BizTalk.Component.Utilities.SchemaWithNone("")

'<summary>
'This property is the document specification for the inbound document. Only
'documents of this type will be accepted. The SchemaWithNone allows the developer to
'select the inbound document type from a pick list.
'</summary>
<Description("The inbound request document specification. Only messages of this _
type will be accepted by the component.")> _
Public Property MyDocSpec() As Microsoft.BizTalk.Component.Utilities.SchemaWithNone
            Get
                Return _MyDocSpec
            End Get
            Set(ByVal Value As Microsoft.BizTalk.Component.Utilities.SchemaWithNone)
                _MyDocSpec = Value
          End Set
End Property

Public Function Probe(ByVal pc As _
Microsoft.BizTalk.Component.Interop.IPipelineContext, ByVal inmsg As _
Microsoft.BizTalk.Message.Interop.IBaseMessage) As Boolean Implements _
Microsoft.BizTalk.Component.Interop.IProbeMessage.Probe

            Dim streamReader As New streamReader(inmsg.BodyPart.Data)
            Dim xmlreader As New Xml.XmlTextReader(inmsg.BodyPart.Data)
            xmlreader.MoveToContent()

            If (_MyDocSpec.DocSpecName = xmlreader.NamespaceURI.Replace("http://", _
"")) Then
                Return True
            Else
                Return False
            End If
End Function
End Class
```

Schema Selection in VS .NET Designer

The property MyDocSpec in the previous section's MyProber class is actually of type SchemaWithNone. SchemaWithNone is a class that lives in the Microsoft.BizTalk. Component.Utilities.dll assembly. Defining a property of type SchemaWithNone will give the user a drop-down list of all deployed schemas within the current BizTalk Management Database. The class has one public constructor, SchemaWithNone, which initializes a new instance of the SchemaWithNone class. Tables 4-10 and 4-11 list the public properties and methods of the class.

Table 4-10. *SchemaWithNone Public Properties*

Property	Description
AssemblyName (inherited from Schema)	Gets or sets the schema assembly name
DocSpecName (inherited from Schema)	Gets or sets the document spec name for the selected schema
RootName (inherited from Schema)	Gets or sets the root node of the selected schema
SchemaName (inherited from Schema)	Gets or sets the selected schema name
TargetNamespace (inherited from Schema)	Gets or sets the target namespace of the selected schema

Table 4-11. *SchemaWithNone Public Methods*

Method	Description
Equals (inherited from Schema)	Overridden. Determines whether the specified Object is equal to the current Object.
GetHashCode (inherited from Schema)	Overridden. Returns the hash code for this instance.
GetType (inherited from System.Object)	For additional information about the System namespace, see the .NET Framework documentation available from Visual Studio .NET or online at http://go.microsoft.com/fwlink/?LinkID=9677.
ToString (inherited from Schema)	Overridden. Converts the value of this instance to its equivalent string representation using the specified format.

As you can see in Figure 4-11, the properties for the SchemaWithNone class are available in the IDE. If you notice the InboundDocSpec property, it is a list of all the schemas that are currently deployed to the BizTalk solution. The SchemaWithNone property allows you to select one and only one schema from the deployed schemas, and this information will be used to populate the properties of the object as defined previously (AssemblyName, DocSpecName, etc.).

In the example from the preceding section, you want your developer to select only one schema, but what if your developer needs multiple? In many cases, your component will be able to handle a variety of schemas; in this case, you need to use the SchemaList property.

In the case where your property needs to select multiple schemas, you need to use the SchemaList object. Such an object will provide developers with an associate window from which they can choose multiple schemas. The selected schemas will be available as a collection of schemas within a main class. The IDE will present a screen as shown in Figure 4-12.

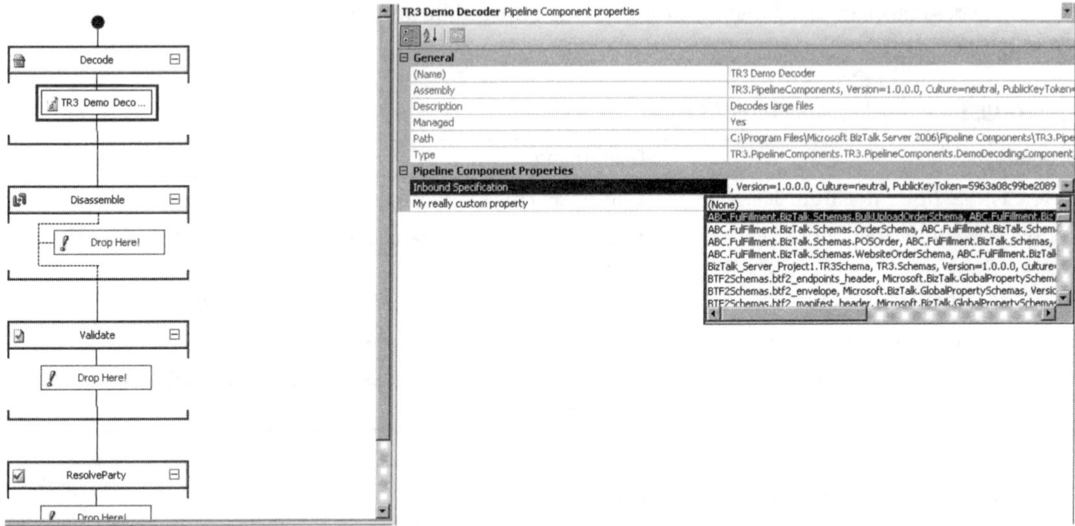

Figure 4-11. *SchemaWithNone example in VS .NET*

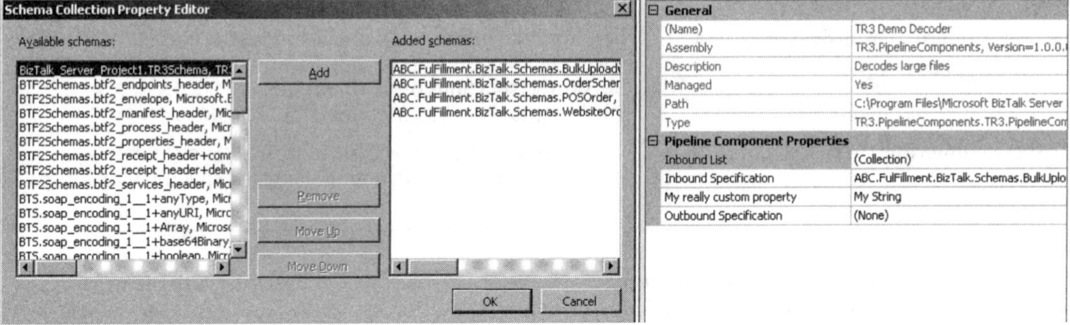

Figure 4-12. *SchemaList example in VS .NET*

Decorating Your Properties

It is important to consider the usability of your components from within the Visual Studio IDE. If you simply expose a public property from within your pipeline component, two things will happen. First, the property name that is displayed in the IDE will be the name of the property (in Figure 4-10 earlier, this would be `InboundDocumentList`, etc.). Second, there is no public description for what the property actually does. In order to make your components usable, you can use custom attributes to decorate your properties with metadata so that the developer experience is improved. The two main attributes you can use to do this are described next.

Using the DisplayName and Description Attributes

The `DisplayName` attribute allows you to set the name for the property that will be displayed in the IDE. The `Description` attribute sets the description box within the VS .NET designer to a friendly description. The effect of these attributes is shown in Figure 4-13. The following code snippet demonstrates how these attributes are to be used:

```
'<summary>
   'this property will contain a single schema
'</summary>
<Description("The inbound request document specification. Only   messages of this _
type will be accepted by the component.")> _
<DisplayName("Inbound Specification")> _
 Public Property InboundFileDocumentSpecification() As _
Microsoft.BizTalk.Component.Utilities.SchemaWithNone
    Get
       Return _InboundFileDocumentSpecification
    End Get
    Set(ByVal Value As Microsoft.BizTalk.Component.Utilities.SchemaWithNone)
    _ InboundFileDocumentSpecification = Value
    End Set
End Property
```

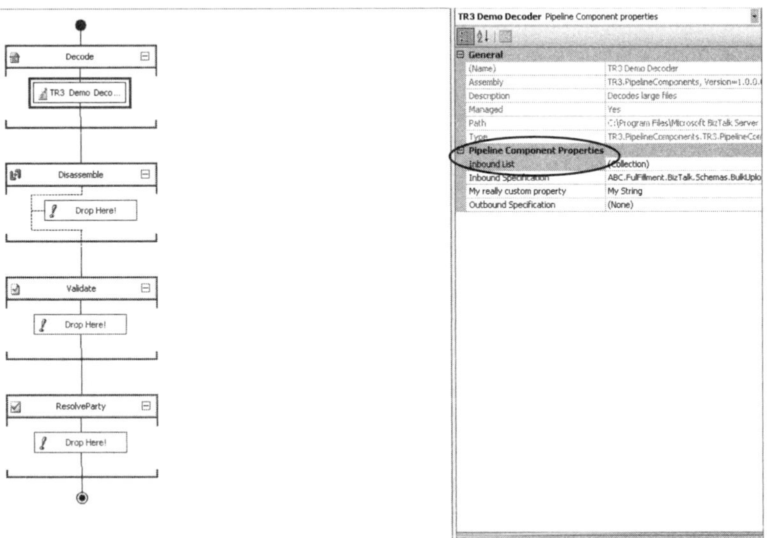

Figure 4-13. *DisplayName and Description attributes set*

Validating and Storing Properties in the Designer

As in any component development model, it is necessary to store properties that a user selects for your component so you can load them at runtime and also validate that the values chosen by the user are appropriate. To perform validation, you need to use the `IComponentUI` interface and implement the `Validate` function. To store and load information for runtime use, you use the `IPersistPropertyBag` interface and implement the `Load` and `Save` functions. Example method implementations are given in the following text.

Validating User Input

IComponentUI.Validate is used to validate any property information and display an error message to the user when the project is compiled. Most implementations use either a collection or an ArrayList to store the errors. You then need to return the IEnumerator object from the ArrayList or collection at the end of the method with all the error messages you want displayed populated.

The following example demonstrates how you can validate a developer's input from within the IDE. Any errors are returned to the user as errors in the IDE's error window.

```
'<summary>
'The Validate method is called by the BizTalk Editor during the build
'of a BizTalk project.
'</summary>
'<param name="obj">An Object containing the configuration 'properties.</param>
'<returns>The IEnumerator enables the caller to enumerate through a collection of
'strings containing error messages. These error messages appear as compiler error
'messages. To report successful property validation, the method should return an
'empty enumerator.</returns>
Public Function Validate(ByVal obj As Object) As System.Collections.IEnumerator_
Implements Microsoft.BizTalk.Component.Interop.IComponentUI.Validate
'example implementation:
Dim errorArray As New ArrayList
errorArray.Add("This is an error that will be shown...")
return errorArray.GetEnumerator
End Function
```

Using the Property Bag to Store Property Information

In order to store property information for pipeline components, you need to implement the IPersistPropertyBag interface and give an implementation to the Save and Load methods. These methods pass in the representative IPropertyBag object that will be used to store the property information. The IPropertyBag is simply a structure that will hold a set of key/value pairs. The key is a string, and the value is of type Object so it can accept any type. You may ask yourself, "Why not store the object itself rather than storing the name of the schema and constructing a New() object in the Load method?" The answer is because the Save function of the component will fail if you do this. When the properties are written to the ContextPropertyBag, they are actually expressed within the BTP file as XML so that they can be used for per-instance pipeline configuration. For more information on this, see the section entitled "Custom Properties and Per-Instance Pipeline Configuration" later on in the chapter. Included within the code sample are two helper functions that encapsulate reading/writing the properties to the property bag.[13] The following code snippet shows how you can use the property bag

13. As you can see in the sample, there are two helper methods included called ReadPropertyBag and WritePropertyBag. These are generated when using the Pipeline Component Wizard, available from www.gotdotnet.com/Workspaces/Workspace.aspx?id=1d4f7d6b-7d27-4f05-a8ee-48cfcd5abf4a. We will introduce this tool in the next chapter, but we wanted to include these helper functions here, as they are quite useful when dealing with IPropertyBag operations.

to read and write custom properties from a pipeline component:

```
'<summary>
'Loads configuration properties for the component
'</summary>
'<param name="pb">Configuration property bag</param>
'<param name="errlog">Error status</param>
Public Overridable Sub Load(ByVal pb As _
Microsoft.BizTalk.Component.Interop.IPropertyBag, ByVal errlog As Integer) _
Implements Microsoft.BizTalk.Component.Interop.IPersistPropertyBag.Load


Dim val As Object = Nothing
val = Me.ReadPropertyBag(pb, "MyDocSpec")
If (Not (val) Is Nothing) Then
        Me._MyDocSpec = New _
Microsoft.BizTalk.Component.Utilities.SchemaWithNone(CType(val, String))
End If
val = Me.ReadPropertyBag(pb, "OutboundDocumentSpecification")
If (Not (val) Is Nothing) Then
        Me._OutboundDocumentSpecification = New _
Microsoft.BizTalk.Component.Utilities.SchemaWithNone(CType(val, String))
End If
val = Me.ReadPropertyBag(pb, "FileRootNode")
If (Not (val) Is Nothing) Then
        Me._FileRootNode = val
End If
val = Me.ReadPropertyBag(pb, "DataElementNode")
If (Not (val) Is Nothing) Then
        Me._DataElementNode = val
End If
End Sub

'<summary>
'Saves the current component configuration into the property bag
'<summary>
'<param name="pb">Configuration property bag</param>
'<param name="fClearDirty">not used</param>
'<param name="fSaveAllProperties">not used</param>
Public Overridable Sub Save(ByVal pb As _
Microsoft.BizTalk.Component.Interop.IPropertyBag, ByVal fClearDirty As Boolean, _
ByVal fSaveAllProperties As Boolean) Implements _
Microsoft.BizTalk.Component.Interop.IPersistPropertyBag.Save

Me.WritePropertyBag(pb, "MyDocSpec", Me.MyDocSpec.SchemaName)
Me.WritePropertyBag(pb, "OutDocSpec", Me.OutboundDocumentSpecification.SchemaName
Me.WritePropertyBag(pb, "FileRootNode", Me.FileRootNode)
```

```
Me.WritePropertyBag(pb, "DataElementNode", Me.DataElementNode)
End Sub

'<summary>
'Reads property value from property bag
'</summary>
'<param name="pb">Property bag</param>
'<param name="propName">Name of property</param>
'<returns>Value of the property</returns>
Private Function ReadPropertyBag(ByVal pb As _
Microsoft.BizTalk.Component.Interop.IPropertyBag, ByVal propName As String) As _
Object
Dim val As Object = Nothing
Try
       pb.Read(propName, val, 0)
       Catch e As System.ArgumentException
Return val
      Catch e As System.Exception
      Throw New System.ApplicationException(e.Message)
End Try
Return val
End Function

'<summary>
'Writes property values into a property bag.
'</summary>
'<param name="pb">Property bag.</param>
'<param name="propName">Name of property.</param>
'<param name="val">Value of property.</param>
 Private Sub WritePropertyBag(ByVal pb As _
Microsoft.BizTalk.Component.Interop.IPropertyBag, ByVal propName As String, ByVal _
val As Object)
Try
      pb.Write(propName, val)
      Catch e As System.Exception
      Throw New System.ApplicationException(e.Message)
End Try
End Sub
```

Custom Properties and Per-Instance Pipeline Configuration

As we discussed earlier in the chapter, per-instance pipeline configuration allows you to change the values of custom properties using the BizTalk Administration Tools. The user interface provides you with a mechanism to set the values for pipeline properties dynamically for a receive location without having to create a new custom pipeline for every new receive location. A few points of interest when attempting to use this feature with a custom pipeline and pipeline components are described here.

Custom pipeline component properties for per-instance pipeline configuration are actually stored within the .btp file for the pipeline definition. A sample of the file follows. If you find that your custom properties are not appearing in the per-instance pipeline configuration document, you can manually add them to the XML of the .btp file and they will appear.

```
<?xml version="1.0" encoding="utf-16"?>
<Document xmlns:xsd="http://www.w3.org/2001/XMLSchema"
xmlns:xsi="http://www.w3.org/2001/XMLSchema-instance"
PolicyFilePath="BTSReceivePolicy.xml" MajorVersion="1" MinorVersion="0">

  <Description />
  <Stages>
    <Stage CategoryId="9d0e4103-4cce-4536-83fa-4a5040674ad6">
      <Components />
    </Stage>
    <Stage CategoryId="9d0e4105-4cce-4536-83fa-4a5040674ad6">
      <Components />
    </Stage>
    <Stage CategoryId="9d0e410d-4cce-4536-83fa-4a5040674ad6">
      <Components>
        <Component>
          <Name>ABC.BizTalk.PipelineComponents.Decoder</Name>
          <Properties>
            <Property Name="MyUnTypedProperty" />
            <Property Name="MyStringProperty">
              <Value xsi:type="xsd:string">My String Value</Value>
            </Property>
          </Properties>
          <CachedDisplayName>Decoding Component</CachedDisplayName>
          <CachedIsManaged>true</CachedIsManaged>
        </Component>
      </Components>
    </Stage>
    <Stage CategoryId="9d0e410e-4cce-4536-83fa-4a5040674ad6">
      <Components />
    </Stage>
  </Stages>
</Document>
```

- In the .btp file for the pipeline definition, you can set the default data of the pipeline component property by inserting a value in the property's <Value> element.
- The <Value> that you insert must be an XSD type. For example, the type must be xsd:string for a string value, or xsd:int for an integer value.

Custom Disassemblers

It's important to call special attention to Disassembler components, as they are often what most developers end up writing. Disassemblers were intended to allow the pipeline to examine the incoming document and break it up into smaller, more manageable documents. The classic example of this is an envelope file. The large document is received that contains an envelope with multiple smaller documents inside it. The envelope is removed, and each of the

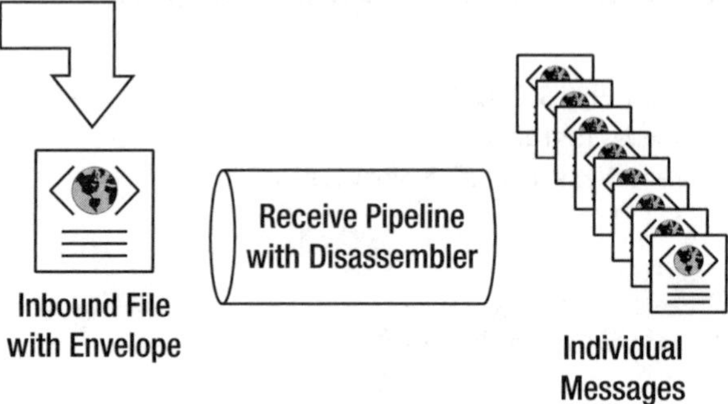

Figure 4-14. *Logical view of a Disassembler*

contained documents is validated against its schema and ends up being a distinct and unique message within BizTalk. This is shown in Figure 4-14. The Disassembler component has one key interface, `IDisassemblerComponent`.

`IDisassemblerComponent` has two methods, `Disassemble` and `GetNext`, which are listed in Table 4-12. What happens is the BizTalk runtime calls the `Disassemble` method first and passes the original message and the pipeline context. It then calls the `GetNext` method after the `Disassemble` method. The `GetNext` method returns new messages of type IBaseMessage until the component decides that all messages are created and then it returns Null. Returning Null from `GetNext` signals the end of the component's execution and signals the runtime that all messages have been properly created.

Table 4-12. *Public Methods of IDisassemblerComponent*

Method	Description
`Disassemble`	Performs the disassembling of incoming document
`GetNext`	Gets the next message from the message set resulting from the Disassembler execution

A couple of design patterns exist that you can use when creating Disassemblers. One pattern is to use the `Disassemble` method to prime any instance variables, setup, and data, and then return and essentially create no messages. The messages will be created in the `GetNext` method, and new messages will be created each time the method is called. Another pattern is to create all messages in the Disassemble stage, enqueue them to a queue structure, and then dequeue the messages from the queue each time `GetNext` is called. Either strategy will work; the second strategy can be more efficient especially if expensive resources need to be instantiated each time a message is created. Using the second method, you only need to create these once at the beginning of the Disassemble method, create all the messages, and then dispose of the resource. Using the first method, the resource will either need to be created for each GetNext() call or stored as an instance member of the class. An example of the second implementation follows. More detailed implementations will be given in the next chapter, but this example shows the basic structure. Also for this example, assume that this code is cumulative with the previous examples. In this case, a variable named _InboundDocumentSpecification is used. This is the SchemaWithNone variable we explained in the previous section that allows us to see the developer-requested "new document schema type."

```
'<summary>
'called by the messaging engine until returned null, after Disassemble has been
'called
'</summary>
'<param name="pc">the pipeline context</param>
'<returns>an IBaseMessage instance representing the message created</returns>
Public Function GetNext(ByVal pc As _
Microsoft.BizTalk.Component.Interop.IPipelineContext) As _
Microsoft.BizTalk.Message.Interop.IBaseMessage Implements _
Microsoft.BizTalk.Component.Interop.IDisassemblerComponent.GetNext
            'get the next message from the Queue and return it
            Dim msg As Microsoft.BizTalk.Message.Interop.IBaseMessage = Nothing
            If (_msgs.Count > 0) Then
                msg = CType(_msgs.Dequeue, _
Microsoft.BizTalk.Message.Interop.IBaseMessage)
            End If
            Return msg
End Function

'<summary>
'called by the messaging engine when a new message arrives
'</summary>
'<param name="pc">the pipeline context</param>
'<param name="inmsg">the actual message</param>
Public Sub Disassemble(ByVal pc As _
Microsoft.BizTalk.Component.Interop.IPipelineContext, ByVal inmsg As _
Microsoft.BizTalk.Message.Interop.IBaseMessage) Implements _
Microsoft.BizTalk.Component.Interop.IDisassemblerComponent.Disassemble

          'This is an example class which gets a simple list of strings. Each of
          'these numbers will be
          'a unique key in the new messages that we create.
          Dim myArrayList As New ArrayList = myHelper.GetArrayofValues
                Dim UniqueCode As String
```

```
'GetDocument is a function we will create in the next chapter. Essentially it is a
'function that returns an empty XML Document as a string given a fully qualified and
'deployed BizTalk
'schema.
                For Each UniqueCode In myArrayList

_msgs.Enqueue(BuildMessage(pc, inmsg.Context, GetDocument _
(InboundSchema.DocumentSpec,UniqueCode)))
                Next
            End If

End Sub
```

Note the following function. This is a general function that can be used in any pipeline component where a new message needs to be created. This function takes the pipeline context, the message context (which is available from the original message), and the content for the document as a string. A new message is returned with a cloned copy of the original message context, and a message type as specified by the SchemaWithNone property.

```
'<summary>
'Returns a new message by cloning the pipeline context and original message context.
'The data to be assigned to the message must be a string value.
'</summary>
'<param name="pContextt">Pipeline context</param>
'<param name="messageContext">Original Message context to be used in the new
'message</param>
'<param name="messageContent">Data to be put in the message</param>
'<returns>New message</returns>
'<remarks>
'Message Content is assigned to the MessageBody by creating a new MemoryStream
'object
'</remarks>
Private Function BuildMessage(ByVal pContext As IPipelineContext, ByVal _
messageContext As IBaseMessageContext, ByVal messageContent As String) As _
IBaseMessage

            ' Build the message with its context
            Dim message As IBaseMessage
            Dim bodyPart As IBaseMessagePart
            Dim messageStream As MemoryStream
            Dim messageBytes As Byte()
            Dim messageType As String

            ' Prepare and fill the data stream
            messageBytes = Encoding.UTF8.GetBytes(messageContent)
            messageStream = New MemoryStream(messageBytes.Length)
```

```
            messageStream.Write(messageBytes, 0, messageBytes.Length)
            messageStream.Position = 0

            bodyPart = pContext.GetMessageFactory().CreateMessagePart()
            bodyPart.Data = messageStream

            message = pContext.GetMessageFactory().CreateMessage()
            message.Context = PipelineUtil.CloneMessageContext(messageContext)
            messageType = "http://" + _InboundDocumentSpecification.DocSpecName + _
"#" + _FileRootNode

            message.Context.Promote("MessageType", BTSSystemPropertiesNamespace,_
messageType)
            message.AddPart("body", bodyPart, True)

            Return message

End Function
```

CHAPTER 5

Pipeline Component Best Practices and Examples

Chapter 4 outlined the "advanced basics" of creating custom pipelines and pipeline components. You should now have the tools that you will need to create well-structured and professional-looking pipeline components. Now that you have learned the internals of how pipelines and pipeline components work, you'll put your new knowledge into practice. This chapter will explore some of the nuances of pipeline component development as well as give you some best practices for creating and implementing them. We will show you some examples of common problems that pipeline components can solve, along with some advanced implementations of cryptography, compression, and decoding.

Creating New Documents

When you look at how a Disassembler component is structured, essentially you are building new documents that get submitted to the Messagebox. In our previous examples, we demonstrated the use of the `SchemaWithNone` and `SchemaWithList` objects as properties to allow users to choose what type of document should be accepted through the `IProbeMessage` interface. If you take this one step further, you could build a generic Disassembler component that allows users to select what type of document they want to accept, and provide them an interface to choose what type of document will be produced. The custom logic will still need to be created to extract the values for the new document, but at least the schema type will be available. But how can you actually create a new message? You will know the schema type of the message, but how do you create a new `XMLDocument` with all the available nodes already inserted but empty?

There are two ways to accomplish this task: the right way and not-so-right way. The not-so-right way is the simplest. What most people do is hard-code the XML for the new empty document in a string and assign it to a new `XMLDocument` object. This approach can be cumbersome for a number of reasons, the most important being that if the structure of the message ever changes, the class will need to be recompiled. Another "wrong," but more correct, way would be to load the XML from a configuration file at runtime or include it as a resource file that is imported when the assembly is loaded. This is still a pain, since you will have to manually keep this in sync with the actual BizTalk schema.

A different way to do this is to use an undocumented API, which allows you to create a new blank XMLDocument based solely on the class file that is generated when you create a new schema. Unfortunately, this class is unsupported and is not made public by the BizTalk product team. It does work well, however, but you need to think about the support implications of using this class in your solution. For most, this isn't an issue, as the other alternative is to create a schema walker class as documented here—http://msdn.microsoft.com/library/default.asp?url=/library/en-us/dnxmlnet/html/xmlgen.asp. Our only issue is that a significant amount of code is required to implement the schema walker. Also, depending on how you create your schema, certain attributes and imports may not be picked up in the new empty document. We have also found a few compatibility issues between the documents that it generates and BizTalk's validation engine. In the end, it is a good solution if you are wary about using an undocumented class, but using the class that exists within the BizTalk Framework guarantees that your documents will match the schema within the engine and will validate properly.

The first thought that comes to many people's minds when they think about this example is "Okay, I have an external resource file that I need to keep in sync with the actual schema, but won't my code that uses the schema need to change anyway if I have a schema change?" The answer to this is maybe. In many cases, the type of code that creates new XML instances only uses certain fields. Often schema changes involve adding new elements to the schema, not removing them or changing element names. In this case, should the BizTalk schema be modified to include new elements, then no code needs modification, and new XML instances will be created with empty elements as you would expect. In the case where fields have been renamed or removed, you will need to determine whether your pipeline component has explicitly added values to those nodes via an XPath expression. If the component has, then you will need a code change.

In order to generate the new empty document, you need to create an instance of the following class: `Microsoft.Biztalk.Component.Interop.DocumentSpec`. This class is found in the `Microsoft.BizTalk.Pipeline` assembly.

An example method follows that can be used to create new documents based on the passed schema name.[1] Note that the name can easily be extracted from the SchemaWithNone property used in the previous chapter.

```
Imports Microsoft.BizTalk.Component.Interop
Public Function CreateNewBTSDoument(ByVal schemaFullName As String) As XmlDocument

    Dim newdocument As XmlDocument = Nothing
    Dim catExplorer As New BtsCatalogExplorer
    Dim Schemas As SchemaCollection
    Dim myDocSpec As DocumentSpec = Nothing
```

1. One of the authors, George Dunphy, originally used this concept in BizTalk 2004 on an engagement after reading about it on a newsgroup posting. Since then Martijn Hoogendoorn has blogged about this technique at http://martijnh.blogspot.com/2005/10/schema-instance-generator-for-use.html. The blog entry also discusses how the class is unsupported and offers the MSDN article as an alternative. Martijn has other excellent entries in his blog and is a wealth of knowledge on BizTalk and pipeline components. In actuality, the method he demonstrates in his entry is much more performant and well written than the one we show here, which should only be used as a learning tool to demonstrate how this can be implemented. For a better implementation, see Martijn's blog.

```
    Dim catExplorer As New BtsCatalogExplorer
    Dim mySchema As Schema
    Dim sbuilder As New StringBuilder()

    catExplorer.ConnectionString = "Integrated Security=SSPI; Persist Security_
Info=false; Server=(local); Database=BizTalkMgmtDb;"
    Schemas = catExplorer.Schemas
    mySchema = Schemas(schemaFullName)

    If Not (mySchema Is Nothing) Then
         myDocSpec = New DocumentSpec(schemaFullName,_
 mySchema.BtsAssembly.DisplayName)
        If Not (myDocSpec Is Nothing) Then
            Dim writer As New StringWriter(sbuilder)
            Try
                newDocument = New XmlDocument()
                'create and load the new instance into the return value
                newDocument.Load(myDocSpec.CreateXmlInstance(writer))
            Finally
                writer.Dispose()
            End Try
        End If
    End If
End Function
```

Using BizTalk Streams

BizTalk Server 2004 and 2006 have been built to use streams as a key part of the products' architecture. A **stream** as a programming construct is a sequence of bytes with no fixed length. When you begin to read a stream, you have no idea how long it is or when it will end. The only control you have is over the size of the data you will read at any one time. So what does this have to do with good programming? It means that when you are dealing with extremely large amounts of data, if you use a stream, you don't need to load all of this data at once. It is almost like reading a book. You can't just read the entire book at once; you must read the pages one at a time. When reading a book, the amount of data you consume at one time is a page; the letters on the page represent bytes. You also don't know how big the book is until you finish the last page and see "The End" (unless you skip to the back of the book).

In this way, streams make dealing with large amounts of data more manageable. If you have worked with BizTalk 2002 or prior, you know that BizTalk would often produce "out of memory" exceptions when processing large XMLDocuments. This was because in BizTalk 2000 and 2002, the XMLDom was used to parse and load XML documents. The DOM is not a streaming-based model. The DOM requires you to load the entire document into memory to use it.

In supporting this paradigm, the BizTalk product team has included three classes that optimize how you can use streams in your pipeline components and allow you to do stream-based XPath queries. Each of these classes is explained in the following sections.

VirtualStream

Included in the BizTalk SDK under the \Program Files\Microsoft BizTalk Server 2006\SDK\Samples\Pipelines\ArbitraryXPathPropertyHandler directory is a class file called VirtualStream.cs. This class is an implementation that holds the data in memory up to a certain threshold (by default 4MB). The remaining data it keeps on disk in temporary files. The ArbitraryXPathPropertyHandler example in the SDK shows you an example of how to use this class.

SeekableReadOnlyStream

`SeekAbleReadOnlyStream` is an implementation of a stream class that provides fast, read-only, seekable access to a stream. It is a wrapper class around a regular stream object and can be used in cases where the base stream object is not seekable, and does not need write access. An example of this class can be found in the \Program Files\Microsoft BizTalk Server 2006\SDK\Samples\Pipelines\Schema Resolver Component directory.

XPathReader

The XPath reader class lives in the Microsoft.BizTalk.XPathReader.dll assembly. This is a class that provides XPath query access to a stream of XML. This is very advantageous as it allows for very fast, read-only access to a stream of data via an XPath expression. Normally, XPath queries require the entire document be loaded into memory such as in an XMLDocument. Using the XPath reader, you can load your document via the `SeekAbleReadOnlyStream` class mentioned previously, and then have this stream wrapped by an `XMLTextReader`. The net effect is that you have a stream-based XPath query that does not require the entire XML document to be loaded into memory. The following example shows how this can be implemented in a pipeline component. Note the use of the `SeekAbleReadOnlyStream` variable in the `Execute` method. This is the means by which you can have your stream of data be seekable and read-only, which improves the performance and usability of the pipeline component.

```
Imports System
Imports Microsoft.BizTalk.Component.Interop
Imports Microsoft.BizTalk.Message.Interop
Imports System.Collections
Imports Microsoft.BizTalk.XPath
Imports System.Xml
Imports System.IO
Imports Microsoft.Samples.BizTalk.Pipelines.CustomComponent

Namespace ABC.BizTalk.Pipelines.Components

 <ComponentCategory(CategoryTypes.CATID_PipelineComponent)> _
 <ComponentCategory(CategoryTypes.CATID_Any)> _
 Public Class PropPromoteComponent
 Implements IComponent
 Implements IComponentUI
 Implements IBaseComponent
```

```
Implements IPersistPropertyBag
  Private _PropertyName As String
  Private _Namespace As String
  Private _XPath As String

  Public Property PropertyName() As String
    Get
      Return _PropertyName
    End Get
    Set
      _PropertyName = value
    End Set
  End Property

  Public Property Namespace() As String
    Get
      Return _Namespace
    End Get
    Set
      _Namespace = value
    End Set
  End Property

  Public Property XPath() As String
    Get
      Return _XPath
    End Get
    Set
      _XPath = value
    End Set
  End Property

  Public Function Execute(ByVal ctx As IPipelineContext, ByVal msg As_
  IBaseMessage)_
    Dim xpathValue As Object = Nothing
    Dim outMessage As IBaseMessage = ctx.GetMessageFactory.CreateMessage
    Dim newBodyPart As IBaseMessagePart = ctx.GetMessageFactory.CreateMessagePart
    newBodyPart.PartProperties = msg.BodyPart.PartProperties
    Dim stream As SeekableReadOnlyStream = New_
SeekableReadOnlyStream(msg.BodyPart.GetOriginalDataStream)
    Dim val As Object = msg.Context.Read(PropertyName, Namespace)
    If val Is Nothing Then
      Throw New ArgumentNullException(PropertyName)
    End If
    msg.Context.Promote(PropertyName, Namespace, val)
    Dim xpc As XPathCollection = New XPathCollection
```

```
    Dim xpr As XPathReader = New XPathReader(New XmlTextReader(stream), xpc)
    xpc.Add(Me.XPath)
    While xpr.ReadUntilMatch = True
      Dim index As Integer = 0
      While index < xpc.Count
        If xpr.Match(index) = True Then
          xpathValue = xpr.ReadString
          ' break
        End If
        System.Math.Min(System.Threading.Interlocked.Increment(index),index-1)
      End While
    End While
    If xpathValue Is Nothing Then
      Throw New ArgumentNullException("xpathValue")
    End If
    msg.Context.Write("SomeValue", "http://ABC.BizTalk.Pipelines", xpathValue)
    stream.Position = 0
    newBodyPart.Data = stream
    outMessage.Context = msg.Context
    CopyMessageParts(msg, outMessage, newBodyPart)
    Return outMessage
  End Function

  Public ReadOnly Property Icon() As IntPtr
    Get
      Return IntPtr.Zero
    End Get
  End Property

  Public Function Validate(ByVal projectSystem As Object) As IEnumerator
    Return Nothing
  End Function

  Public ReadOnly Property Description() As String
    Get
      Return "Description"
    End Get
  End Property

  Public ReadOnly Property Name() As String
    Get
      Return "Property Promote"
    End Get
  End Property
```

```
Public ReadOnly Property Version() As String
  Get
    Return "1"
  End Get
End Property

Public Sub GetClassID(ByRef classID As Guid)
  Dim g As Guid = New Guid("FE537918-327B-4a0c-9ED7-E1B993B7897E")
  classID = g
End Sub

Public Sub InitNew()
  Throw New Exception("The method or operation is not implemented.")
End Sub

Public Sub Load(ByVal propertyBag As IPropertyBag, ByVal errorLog As Integer)
  Dim prop As Object = Nothing
  Dim nm As Object = Nothing
  Dim xp As Object = Nothing
  Try
    propertyBag.Read("Namespace", nm, 0)
    propertyBag.Read("PropertyName", prop, 0)
    propertyBag.Read("XPATH", xp, 0)
  Catch
  Finally
    If Not (prop Is Nothing) Then
      PropertyName = prop.ToString
    End If
    If Not (nm Is Nothing) Then
      Namespace = nm.ToString
    End If
    If Not (xp Is Nothing) Then
      XPath = xp.ToString
    End If
  End Try
End Sub

Public Sub Save(ByVal propertyBag As IPropertyBag, ByVal clearDirty As Boolean_
, ByVal saveAllProperties As Boolean)
  Dim prop As Object = PropertyName
  Dim nm As Object = Namespace
  Dim xp As Object = XPath
  propertyBag.Write("PropertyName", prop)
  propertyBag.Write("Namespace", nm)
  propertyBag.Write("XPATH", xp)
End Sub
```

```
   Private Sub CopyMessageParts(ByVal sourceMessage As IBaseMessage, ByVal _
destinationMessage As IBaseMessage, ByVal newBodyPart As IBaseMessagePart)
      Dim bodyPartName As String = sourceMessage.BodyPartName
      Dim c As Integer = 0
      While c < sourceMessage.PartCount
        Dim partName As String = Nothing
        Dim messagePart As IBaseMessagePart = _
        sourceMessage.GetPartByIndex(c,partName)
        If Not (partName = bodyPartName) Then
          destinationMessage.AddPart(partName, messagePart, False)
        Else
          destinationMessage.AddPart(bodyPartName, newBodyPart, True)
        End If
        System.Threading.Interlocked.Increment(c)
      End While
   End Sub
 End Class
End Namespace
```

Pipeline Component Examples

Now that you are familiar with the steps and key interfaces that define how pipelines and pipeline components work, we'll show you some clever examples of how pipeline components can be used to solve real problems. Most of the examples in this chapter will be the actual class files included in the samples available for download at www.apress.com. The examples we present here will provide you with working solutions to problems that exist today when developing intricate BizTalk applications. These solutions include

- Dealing with large messages
- Receiving and sending ZIP files
- Using PGP to encrypt and decrypt
- Creating new messages based on a stored procedure

Dealing with Extremely Large Messages

A major problem that many have discovered is that accommodating extremely large (200MB+) files can be a major performance bottleneck. The shame is that in many cases the documents that are being retrieved are simply going to be routed to another outbound source. This is typical of the Enterprise Service Bus (ESB) type of architecture scenario.[2] In short, an ESB is software that is used to link internal and partner systems to each other—which basically

2. For an explanation of what an ESB is and how it relates to BizTalk architectures, see http://msdn.microsoft.com/library/default.asp?url=/library/en-us/bts_2004wp/html/47850cbd-63ed-4370-a467-6bd320636902.asp.

is what BizTalk is designed to do out of the box. For these types of architectures, large files are generally routed through the ESB from an external party to an internal party or from internal to internal systems. Most times, the only logic that needs to be performed is routing logic. In many cases, this logic can be expressed in a simple filter criteria based on the default message context data, or by examining data elements within the message, promoting them, and then implementing content-based routing. Also in many cases, the actual message body's content is irrelevant beyond extracting properties to promote. The performance bottleneck comes into play when the entire file is received, parsed by the XMLReceive pipeline, and then stored into the Messagebox. If you have ever had to do this on a 200MB file, even though it works, there is a nasty impact to the CPU utilization on your BizTalk and SQL Server machines, where often the machines' CPU usage goes to 100% and the system throughput essentially goes down the drain.

Now imagine having to process 10 or 20 of these per minute. The next problem is going to be sending the file. The system will essentially take this entire performance hit all over again when the large file needs to be read from SQL Server out of BizTalk and sent to the EPM. You can quickly see how this type of scenario, as common as it is, most often requires either significant hardware to implement or a queuing mechanism whereby only a small number of files can be processed at a time.

You'll find a simple solution in BizTalk Server's capability to natively understand and use streams.[3] The following examples show a decoding component that will receive the incoming message, store the file to disk in a uniquely named file, and store the path to the file in the `IBaseMessagePart.Data` property. The end result will be a message that only contains the path to the text file in its data, but will have a fully well-formed message context so that it can be routed. The component will also promote a property that stores the fact that this is a "large encoded message." This property will allow you to route all messages encoded using this pipeline component to a particular send port/pipeline that has the corresponding encoding component. The encoding component will read the data element for the path to the file, open up a file stream object that is streaming the file stored to disk, set the stream to the 0 byte position, and set the `IBaseMessagePart.Data` property to the `FileStream`. The end result will be that the file is streamed by the BizTalk runtime from the file stored on the disk and is not required to pass through the Messagebox. Also, performance is greatly improved, and the CPU overhead on both the BizTalk Server host instance that is sending the file and the SQL Server hosting the BizTalk Messagebox is essentially nil.

The partner to this is the sending component. In many scenarios, BizTalk is implemented as a routing engine or an Enterprise Service Bus. This is a fancy way of saying that BizTalk is responsible for moving data from one location within an organization to another. In many cases, what does need to be moved is large amounts of data, either in binary format or in text files. This is often the case with payment or EDI-based systems in which BizTalk is responsible for moving the files to the legacy system where it can process them. In this scenario, the same performance problem (or lack of performance) will occur on the send side as on the receive

3. If you have never used or dealt with streams before, read through the article "Streams and .NET" at www.codeguru.com/Csharp/Csharp/cs_data/streaming/article.php/c4223/. Streams essentially allow you to deal with data in a fashion whereby only a piece of the data is read at a time (usually 4K). They allow you to work with large volumes of data in a very reliable and well-performing manner. They also require you to do a little more work to code against them, but in the end, the performance gains are well worth it in this particular application.

side. To account for this, the examples also include a send-side pipeline component that is used to actually send the large file to the outbound destination adapter.

Caveats and Gotchas

The solution outlined previously works very well so long as the issues described in the following sections are taken into account. Do not simply copy and paste the code into your project and leave it at that. The solution provided in this section fundamentally alters some of the design principles of the BizTalk Server product. **The most important one of these is that the data for the message is no longer stored in the Messagebox**. A quick list of the pros and cons is provided here:

- **Pros**:
  - Provides extremely fast access for moving large messages
  - Simple to extend
  - Reusable across multiple receive locations
  - Message containing context can be routed to orchestration, and data can be accessed from the disk
- **Cons**:
  - No ability to apply BizTalk Map
  - No failover via Messagebox
  - Custom solution requiring support by developer
  - Need a scheduled task to clean up old data

Redundancy, Failover, and High Availability

As was stated earlier, the data for the large message will no longer be stored in SQL Server. This is fundamentally different from how Microsoft designed the product. If the data within the message is important and the system is a mission-critical one that must properly deal with failovers and errors, you need to make sure that the storage location for the external file is also as robust as your SQL Server environment. Most architects in this situation will simply create a share on the clustered SQL Server shared disk array. This share is available to all BizTalk machines in the BizTalk Server Group, and since it is stored on the shared array or the storage area network (SAN), it should be as reliable as the data files for SQL Server.

Dealing with Message Content and Metadata

A good rule of thumb for this type of solution is to avoid looking at the message data at all costs once the file has been received. Consider the following: assume that you have received your large file into BizTalk and you need to process it through an orchestration for some additional logic. What happens? You will need to write .NET components to read the file and manually parse it to get the data you need. The worst-case scenario is that you need to load the data into an XMLDom or something similar. This will have performance implications and can negate the entire reason for the special large-file handling you are implementing.

If you know you are going to need data either within an orchestration or for CBR, make sure you write the code to gather this data within either the receiving or sending pipeline components. Only open the large data file at the time when it is being processed within the pipeline if you can. The best approach is to promote properties or create custom distinguished fields using code from within the component itself, which you can access from within BizTalk with little performance overhead.

Cleaning Up Old Data

If you read through the code in the section "Large Message Encoding Component (Send Side)," you will notice that there is no code that actually deletes the message from the server. There is a good reason for this. Normally you would think that once the message has flowed through the send pipeline it would be okay to delete it, but this is not true. What about a send-side adapter error? Imagine if you were sending the file to an FTP server and it was down; BizTalk will attempt to resend the message after the retry period has been reached. Because of this, you can't simply delete the file at random. You must employ a managed approach.

The only real solution to this would be to have a scheduled task that executes every few minutes that is responsible for cleaning up the data directory. You will notice that the name of the file is actually the `InterchangeID` GUID for the message flow. The `InterchangeID` provides you with a common key that you can use to query each of the messages that have been created throughout the execution path. The script that executes needs to read the name of the file and use WMI to query the Messagebox and determine whether there are any suspended or active messages for that Interchange. If there are, it doesn't delete the file; otherwise, it will delete the data file. For examples on using WMI to query BizTalk, see Chapter 10.

Looping Through the Message

As stated previously, if you do know you will need the data within the message at runtime, and this data is of an aggregate nature (sums, averages, counts, etc.), only loop through the file once. This seems like a commonsense thing, but it is often overlooked. If you need to loop through the file, try to get all the data you need in one pass rather than several. This can have dramatic effects on how your component will perform.

Large Message Decoding Component (Receive Side)

This component is to be used on the receive side when the large message is first processed by BizTalk. You will need to create a custom receive pipeline and add this pipeline component to the Decode stage. From there, use the `SchemaWithNone` property to select the desired inbound schema type if needed. If the file is a flat file or a binary file, then this step is not necessary, as the message will not contain any namespace or type information. This component relies on a property schema being deployed that will be used to store the location to the file within the message context. This schema can also be used to define any custom information such as counts, sums, and averages that is needed to route the document or may be required later on at runtime.

```
Imports System
Imports System.IO
Imports System.Text
Imports System.Drawing
Imports System.Resources
Imports System.Reflection
Imports System.Diagnostics
Imports System.Collections
Imports System.ComponentModel
Imports Microsoft.BizTalk.Message.Interop
Imports Microsoft.BizTalk.Component.Interop
Imports Microsoft.BizTalk.Component
Imports Microsoft.BizTalk.Messaging

Namespace ABC.BizTalk.PipelineComponents

<ComponentCategory(CategoryTypes.CATID_PipelineComponent), _
     System.Runtime.InteropServices.Guid("89dedce4-0525-472f-899c-64dc66f60727"), _
     ComponentCategory(CategoryTypes.CATID_Decoder)> _
Public Class LargeFileDecodingomponent
Implements IBaseComponent, IPersistPropertyBag,_
IComponentUI,Microsoft.BizTalk.Component.Interop.IComponent,IProbeMessage

    Private _InboundFileDocumentSpecification As SchemaWithNone = New_
Microsoft.BizTalk.Component.Utilities.SchemaWithNone("")

        Private resourceManager As System.Resources.ResourceManager = New_
System.Resources.ResourceManager("_
ABC.BizTalk.PipelineComponents.LargeFileDecodingComponent", _
[Assembly].GetExecutingAssembly)
        Private Const ABC_PROPERTY_SCHEMA_NAMESPACE=_
"http://ABC.BizTalk.Schemas.ABCPropertySchema"

        '<summary>
        'this variable will contain any message generated by the Disassemble method
        '</summary>
        <Description("The inbound request document specification. Only messages of_
this type will be accepted by the component.")> _
        Public Property InboundFileDocumentSpecification() As_
Microsoft.BizTalk.Component.Utilities.SchemaWithNone
            Get

                Return _InboundFileDocumentSpecification
            End Get
            Set(ByVal Value As Microsoft.BizTalk.Component.Utilities.SchemaWithNone)
                _InboundFileDocumentSpecification = Value
            End Set
```

```
        End Property
        '<summary>
        'Name of the component
        '</summary>
        <Browsable(False)> _
        Public ReadOnly Property Name() As String Implements_
Microsoft.BizTalk.Component.Interop.IBaseComponent.Name
            Get
                Return resourceManager.GetString("COMPONENTNAME",_
System.Globalization.CultureInfo.InvariantCulture)
            End Get
        End Property

        '<summary>
        'Version of the component
        '</summary>
        <Browsable(False)> _
        Public ReadOnly Property Version() As String Implements_
Microsoft.BizTalk.Component.Interop.IBaseComponent.Version
            Get
                Return resourceManager.GetString("COMPONENTVERSION",_
System.Globalization.CultureInfo.InvariantCulture)
            End Get
        End Property

        '<summary>
        'Description of the component
        '</summary>
        <Browsable(False)> _
        Public ReadOnly Property Description() As String Implements_
Microsoft.BizTalk.Component.Interop.IBaseComponent.Description
            Get
                Return resourceManager.GetString("COMPONENTDESCRIPTION",_
System.Globalization.CultureInfo.InvariantCulture)
            End Get
        End Property

        '<summary>
        'Component icon to use in BizTalk Editor
        '</summary>
        <Browsable(False)> _
        Public ReadOnly Property Icon() As IntPtr Implements_
Microsoft.BizTalk.Component.Interop.IComponentUI.Icon
            Get
                Return CType(Me.resourceManager.GetObject("COMPONENTICON",_
System.Globalization.CultureInfo.InvariantCulture), System.Drawing.Bitmap).GetHicon
            End Get
        End Property
```

```
        '<summary>
        'Gets class ID of component for usage from unmanaged code.
        '</summary>
        '<param name="classid">
        'Class ID of the component
        '</param>
        Public Sub GetClassID(ByRef classid As System.Guid) Implements_
Microsoft.BizTalk.Component.Interop.IPersistPropertyBag.GetClassID
            classid = New System.Guid("89dedce4-0525-472f-899c-64dc66f60727")
        End Sub

        '<summary>
        'not implemented
        '</summary>
        Public Sub InitNew() Implements_
Microsoft.BizTalk.Component.Interop.IPersistPropertyBag.InitNew
        End Sub

        '<summary>
        'Loads configuration properties for the component
        '</summary>
        '<param name="pb">Configuration property bag</param>
        '<param name="errlog">Error status</param>
        Microsoft.BizTalk.Component.Interop.IPropertyBag,_
        ByVal errlog As Integer) Implements_
        Microsoft.BizTalk.Component.Interop.IPersistPropertyBag.Load
        End Sub

        '<summary>
        'Saves the current component configuration into the property bag
        '</summary>
        '<param name="pb">Configuration property bag</param>
        '<param name="fClearDirty">not used</param>
        '<param name="fSaveAllProperties">not used</param>
        Public Overridable Sub Save(ByVal pb As_
        Microsoft.BizTalk.Component.Interop.IPropertyBag, ByVal fClearDirty As_
        Boolean, ByVal fSaveAllProperties As Boolean) Implements_
        Microsoft.BizTalk.Component.Interop.IPersistPropertyBag.Save
        End Sub

        '<summary>
        'Reads property value from property bag
        '</summary>
        '<param name="pb">Property bag</param>
        '<param name="propName">Name of property</param>
```

```
        '<returns>Value of the property</returns>
        Private Function ReadPropertyBag(ByVal pb As_
        Microsoft.BizTalk.Component.Interop.IPropertyBag, ByVal propName_
        As String) As Object
            Dim val As Object = Nothing
            Try
                pb.Read(propName, val, 0)
            Catch e As System.ArgumentException
                Return val
            Catch e As System.Exception
                Throw New System.ApplicationException(e.Message)
            End Try
            Return val
        End Function

        '<summary>
        'Writes property values into a property bag.
        '</summary>
        '<param name="pb">Property bag.</param>
        '<param name="propName">Name of property.</param>
        '<param name="val">Value of property.</param>
        Private Sub WritePropertyBag(ByVal pb As_
        Microsoft.BizTalk.Component.Interop.IPropertyBag,_
        ByVal propName As String, ByVal val As Object)
            Try
                pb.Write(propName, val)
            Catch e As System.Exception
                Throw New System.ApplicationException(e.Message)
            End Try
        End Sub

        '<summary>
        'The Validate method is called by the BizTalk Editor during the build
        'of a BizTalk project.
        '</summary>
        '<param name="obj">An Object containing the configuration properties.
        '</param>
        '<returns>The IEnumerator enables the caller to enumerate through a
        'collection of strings containing error messages. These error messages
        'appear as compiler error messages. To report successful property
        'validation, the method should return an empty enumerator.</returns>
        Public Function Validate(ByVal obj As Object) As_
System.Collections.IEnumerator Implements_
Microsoft.BizTalk.Component.Interop.IComponentUI.Validate
            'example implementation:
            'ArrayList errorList = new ArrayList();
```

```
            'errorList.Add("This is a compiler error");
            'return errorList.GetEnumerator();
            Return Nothing
        End Function
        '<summary>
        'called by the messaging engine when a new message arrives
        'checks if the incoming message is in a recognizable format
        'if the message is in a recognizable format, only this component
        'within this stage will be execute (FirstMatch equals true)
        '</summary>
        '<param name="pc">the pipeline context</param>
        '<param name="inmsg">the actual message</param>
        Public Function Probe(ByVal pc As_
Microsoft.BizTalk.Component.Interop.IPipelineContext, ByVal inmsg As_
Microsoft.BizTalk.Message.Interop.IBaseMessage) As Boolean Implements_
Microsoft.BizTalk.Component.Interop.IProbeMessage.Probe

            Dim xmlreader As New Xml.XmlTextReader(inmsg.BodyPart.Data)
            xmlreader.MoveToContent()

            If (InboundDocumentSpecification.DocSpecName = _
xmlreader.NamespaceURI.Replace("http://", "")) Then
                Return True
            Else
                Return False
            End If

        End Function
        '<summary>
        'Implements IComponent.Execute method.
        '</summary>
        '<param name="pc">Pipeline context</param>
        '<param name="inmsg">Input message</param>
        '<returns>Original input message</returns>
        '<remarks>
        'IComponent.Execute method is used to initiate
        'the processing of the message in this pipeline component.
        '</remarks>
        Public Function Execute(ByVal pContext As_
Microsoft.BizTalk.Component.Interop.IPipelineContext, ByVal inmsg As_
Microsoft.BizTalk.Message.Interop.IBaseMessage) As_
Microsoft.BizTalk.Message.Interop.IBaseMessage Implements_
Microsoft.BizTalk.Component.Interop.IComponent.Execute
            'Build the message that is to be sent out
            StoreMessageData(pContext, inmsg)
            Return inmsg
        End Function
```

```
        '<summary>
'Method used to write the message data to a file and promote the
'location to the MessageContext.
        '</summary>
        '<param name="pc">Pipeline context</param>
        '<param name="inmsg">Input message to be assigned</param>
        '<returns>Original input message by reference</returns>
        '<remarks>
        'Receives the input message ByRef then assigns the file stream to the
        'messageBody.Data property
        '</remarks>
        Private Sub StoreMessageData(ByVal pContext As IPipelineContext, _
        ByRef inMsg As_IBaseMessage)
            Dim FullFileName As String = FILE_LOCATION + _
            inMsg.InterchangeID + ".msg"
            Dim dataFile As New FileStream(FullFileName, FileMode.Open, _
            FileAccess.Read_,FileShare.Read, 4 * 1024 * 1024)
            Dim binaryWriter As BinaryWriter = New BinaryWriter(dataFile)
            Dim reader As New StringReader(FullFileName)
            Dim byteRead As Byte
            Dim j As Integer

            If inMsg.BodyPart.Data.CanSeek Then
                inMsg.BodyPart.Data.Position = 0
            Else
                Throw new exception("The stream is not seekable")
            End If

            For j = 0 To inMsg.BodyPart.Data.Length() - 1
                byteRead = inMsg.BodyPart.Data.ReadByte
                bw.Write(byteRead)
            Next
            bw.Close()
            inMsg.BodyPart.Data = reader
            inMsg.Context.Promote("LargeFileLocation", _
            ABC_PROPERTY_SCHEMA_NAMESPACE,FullFileName)
FullFileName)
        End Sub
End Class
End Namespace
```

Large Message Encoding Component (Send Side)

The large message encoding component is to be used on the send side when the large message is sent by BizTalk. You will need to create a custom send pipeline and add this pipeline component to the Encode stage. This component relies on a property schema being deployed that will be used to store the location to the file within the message context.

```
Imports System
Imports System.IO
Imports System.Text
Imports System.Drawing
Imports System.Resources
Imports System.Reflection
Imports System.Diagnostics
Imports System.Collections
Imports System.ComponentModel
Imports Microsoft.BizTalk.Message.Interop
Imports Microsoft.BizTalk.Component.Interop
Imports Microsoft.BizTalk.Component
Imports Microsoft.BizTalk.Messaging

Namespace ABC.BizTalk.PipelineComponents

<ComponentCategory(CategoryTypes.CATID_PipelineComponent), _
     System.Runtime.InteropServices.Guid("4f1c7d50-e66f-451b-8e94-2f8d599cd013"), _
     ComponentCategory(CategoryTypes.CATID_Encoder)> _
Public Class LargeFileEncodingComponent
       Implements IBaseComponent, IPersistPropertyBag, IComponentUI,_
Microsoft.BizTalk.Component.Interop.IComponent

        Private resourceManager As System.Resources.ResourceManager = New_
        System.Resources.ResourceManager("ABC.BizTalk.PipelineComponents._
        LargeFileEncodingComponent", [Assembly].GetExecutingAssembly)
        Private Const ABC_PROPERTY_SCHEMA_NAMESPACE =_
"http://ABC.BizTalk.Schemas.ABCPropertySchema"

        '<summary>
        'Name of the component
        '</summary>
        <Browsable(False)> _
        Public ReadOnly Property Name() As String Implements_
Microsoft.BizTalk.Component.Interop.IBaseComponent.Name
            Get
                Return resourceManager.GetString("COMPONENTNAME",_
System.Globalization.CultureInfo.InvariantCulture)
            End Get
        End Property

        '<summary>
        'Version of the component
        '</summary>
        <Browsable(False)> _
        Public ReadOnly Property Version() As String Implements_
```

```
Microsoft.BizTalk.Component.Interop.IBaseComponent.Version
            Get
                Return resourceManager.GetString("COMPONENTVERSION",_
System.Globalization.CultureInfo.InvariantCulture)
            End Get
        End Property

        '<summary>
        'Description of the component
        '</summary>
        <Browsable(False)> _
        Public ReadOnly Property Description() As String Implements_
Microsoft.BizTalk.Component.Interop.IBaseComponent.Description
            Get
                Return resourceManager.GetString("COMPONENTDESCRIPTION",_
System.Globalization.CultureInfo.InvariantCulture)
            End Get
        End Property

        '<summary>
        'Component icon to use in BizTalk Editor
        '</summary>
        <Browsable(False)> _
        Public ReadOnly Property Icon() As IntPtr Implements_
Microsoft.BizTalk.Component.Interop.IComponentUI.Icon
            Get
                Return CType(Me.resourceManager.GetObject("COMPONENTICON",_
System.Globalization.CultureInfo.InvariantCulture), System.Drawing.Bitmap).GetHicon
            End Get
        End Property

        '<summary>
        'Gets class ID of component for usage from unmanaged code.
        '</summary>
        '<param name="classid">
        'Class ID of the component
        '</param>
        Public Sub GetClassID(ByRef classid As System.Guid) Implements_
Microsoft.BizTalk.Component.Interop.IPersistPropertyBag.GetClassID
            classid = New System.Guid("4f1c7d50-e66f-451b-8e94-2f8d599cd013")
        End Sub

        '<summary>
        'not implemented
        '</summary>
        Public Sub InitNew() Implements_
```

```
Microsoft.BizTalk.Component.Interop.IPersistPropertyBag.InitNew
        End Sub

        '<summary>
        'Loads configuration properties for the component
        '</summary>
        '<param name="pb">Configuration property bag</param>
        '<param name="errlog">Error status</param>
        Public Overridable Sub Load(ByVal pb As_
        Microsoft.BizTalk.Component.Interop.IPropertyBag,_
        ByVal errlog As Integer) Implements_
        Microsoft.BizTalk.Component.Interop.IPersistPropertyBag.Load
        End Sub

        '<summary>
        'Saves the current component configuration into the property bag
        '</summary>
        '<param name="pb">Configuration property bag</param>
        '<param name="fClearDirty">not used</param>
        '<param name="fSaveAllProperties">not used</param>
        Public Overridable Sub Save(ByVal pb As_
        Microsoft.BizTalk.Component.Interop.IPropertyBag, ByVal fClearDirty As_
        Boolean, ByVal fSaveAllProperties As Boolean) Implements_
        Microsoft.BizTalk.Component.Interop.IPersistPropertyBag.Save
        End Sub

        '<summary>
        'Reads property value from property bag
        '</summary>
        '<param name="pb">Property bag</param>
        '<param name="propName">Name of property</param>
        '<returns>Value of the property</returns>
        Private Function ReadPropertyBag(ByVal pb As_
        Microsoft.BizTalk.Component.Interop.IPropertyBag, ByVal propName As_
        String) As Object
            Dim val As Object = Nothing
            Try
                pb.Read(propName, val, 0)
            Catch e As System.ArgumentException
                Return val
            Catch e As System.Exception
                Throw New System.ApplicationException(e.Message)
            End Try
            Return val
        End Function
```

```
        '<summary>
        'Writes property values into a property bag.
        '</summary>
        '<param name="pb">Property bag.</param>
        '<param name="propName">Name of property.</param>
        '<param name="val">Value of property.</param>
        Private Sub WritePropertyBag(ByVal pb As_
Microsoft.BizTalk.Component.Interop.IPropertyBag, ByVal propName As String, ByVal _
val As Object)
            Try
                pb.Write(propName, val)
            Catch e As System.Exception
                Throw New System.ApplicationException(e.Message)
            End Try
        End Sub

        '<summary>
        'The Validate method is called by the BizTalk Editor during the build
        'of a BizTalk project.
        '</summary>
        '<param name="obj">An Object containing the configuration
        ' properties.</param>
        '<returns>The IEnumerator enables the caller to enumerate through a
        'collection of strings containing error messages. These error messages
        'appear as compiler error messages. To report successful property
        'validation, the method should return an empty enumerator.</returns>
        Public Function Validate(ByVal obj As Object) As _
System.Collections.IEnumerator Implements _
Microsoft.BizTalk.Component.Interop.IComponentUI.Validate
            'example implementation:
            'ArrayList errorList = new ArrayList();
            'errorList.Add("This is a compiler error");
            'return errorList.GetEnumerator();
            Return Nothing
        End Function

        '<summary>
        'Implements IComponent.Execute method.
        '</summary>
        '<param name="pc">Pipeline context</param>
        '<param name="inmsg">Input message</param>
        '<returns>Original input message</returns>
        '<remarks>
        'IComponent.Execute method is used to initiate
        'the processing of the message in this pipeline component.
        '</remarks>
```

```
        Public Function Execute(ByVal pContext As_
Microsoft.BizTalk.Component.Interop.IPipelineContext, ByVal inmsg As_
Microsoft.BizTalk.Message.Interop.IBaseMessage) As_
Microsoft.BizTalk.Message.Interop.IBaseMessage Implements_
Microsoft.BizTalk.Component.Interop.IComponent.Execute
            'Build the message that is to be sent out
            BuildMessageData(pContext, inmsg)
            Return inmsg
        End Function

        '<summary>
        'Method used to assign the data to a stream. Method reads path from
         promoted property
        '</summary>
        '<param name="pc">Pipeline context</param>
        '<param name="inmsg">Input message to be assigned</param>
        '<returns>Original input message by reference</returns>
        '<remarks>
        'Receives the input message ByRef then assigns the file stream to the_
 messageBody.Data property
        '</remarks>
        Private Sub BuildMessageData(ByVal pContext As IPipelineContext,_
        ByRef inMsg As IBaseMessage)
            Dim messageBody As IBaseMessagePart = _
pContext.GetMessageFactory().CreateMessagePart()
            Dim data As New FileStream(inMsg.Context.Read("LargeFileLocation", _
ABC_PROPERTY_SCHEMA_NAMESPACE), FileMode.Open, FileAccess.Read, FileShare.Read, 4 *_
1024 * 1024)
            messageBody.Data = data
            If data.CanSeek Then
                data.Position = 0
            End If
            inMsg.BodyPart.Data = data
        End Sub
End Class
End Namespace
```

Dealing with Compressed Files

A common problem that most BizTalk projects encounter is having to either send or receive compressed data in the form of a ZIP file. Often, the incoming ZIP file has multiple entries, each of which need to be submitted to BizTalk. In most cases, these files are XML files, but in some situations, they can be either flat files or binary files instead. The examples in the following sections outline a potential simplified solution for sending and receiving zipped information. Additionally, you'll get a chance to explore ways to augment the solution using new functionality within BizTalk.

Sending Simple Zipped Files

In order to send a ZIP file from BizTalk, you will need to create a custom send pipeline and a custom encoding pipeline component. The pipeline component will be responsible for examining the incoming message, getting access to the message's data, compressing it, and returning it to BizTalk. The simplest scenario is the "single message in/single message out" scenario. Here, a message is sent to the send pipeline, it is compressed, and a single message is sent out. The pipeline component required for this is documented in the following class:[4]

```
Imports Microsoft.VisualBasic
Imports System
Imports System.ComponentModel
Imports System.Collections
Imports System.Diagnostics
Imports System.Drawing
Imports System.IO
Imports System.Reflection
Imports Microsoft.BizTalk.Component.Interop
Imports Microsoft.Utility.PipelinePropertyAttribute
Imports ICSharpCode.SharpZipLib.Zip

Namespace ABC.BizTalk.PipelineComponents

    <ComponentCategory(CategoryTypes.CATID_PipelineComponent),_
ComponentCategory(CategoryTypes.CATID_Encoder),_
System.Runtime.InteropServices.Guid("56C7B68B-F288-4f78-A67F-20043CA4943E")> _

    Public Class ZipEncodingComponent

        Implements IBaseComponent, Microsoft.BizTalk.Component.Interop.IComponent,_
Microsoft.BizTalk.Component.Interop.IPersistPropertyBag, IComponentUI

        Private resourceManager As System.Resources.ResourceManager = New_
System.Resources.ResourceManager("ABC.BizTalk.PipelineComponents",_
System.Reflection.Assembly.GetExecutingAssembly())
        Private _compressionlevel As String
        Private _filename As String
        Private _password As String
```

4. This class uses compression routines that are available from www.sharpdevelop.com. The source for the compression library is available from this web site and is distributed under the GNU Public License. The examples shown here did not require the modification of the source code from SharpDevelop, and as such is not included in the example, but is packaged with the entire sample available from www.apress.com.

```
        Private Const DEFAULT_COMPRESSIONLEVEL_TEXT As String = "5"
        Private Const DEFAULT_COMPRESSIONLEVEL As Integer = 5
        Private Const DEFAULT_FILENAME As String = "ABCBizTalkSendFile"


#Region "IBaseComponent"
        <Browsable(False)> _
        Public ReadOnly Property Name() As String
            Get
                Return "ZIP encoding component"
            End Get
        End Property
        <Browsable(False)> _
        Public ReadOnly Property Version() As String
            Get
                Return "1.0"
            End Get
        End Property
        <Browsable(False)> _
        Public ReadOnly Property Description() As String
            Get
                Return "Pipeline Component which will encode an outgoing_
                message as a ZIP file."

            End Get
        End Property
        <Browsable(False)> _
        Public ReadOnly Property Icon() As System.IntPtr
            Get
                Return (CType(resourceManager.GetObject("IconBitmap"),_
Bitmap)).GetHicon()
            End Get
        End Property
#End Region

        Public Property Password() As String
            Get
                Return _password
            End Get
            Set(ByVal value As String)
                _password = value
            End Set
        End Property
```

```
        Public Property Filename() As String
            Get
                Return _filename
            End Get
            Set(ByVal value As String)
                _filename = value
            End Set
        End Property


        Public Property CompressionLevel() As String
            Get
                Return _compressionlevel
            End Get
            Set(ByVal value As String)
                _compressionlevel = value
            End Set
        End Property

        Private Function Encode(ByVal inStream As Stream) As Stream
            Dim outStream As Stream = inStream
            Dim inFile As String = Path.GetTempFileName()
            Dim outFile As String = Path.ChangeExtension(inFile, "zip")

            Try
                Dim zipStream As ZipOutputStream = New_
ZipOutputStream(File.Create(outFile))

                ' get password, if supplied
                If _password.IsNullOrEmpty Then
                    zipStream.Password = _password
                End If

                ' get compression level, if supplied
                Dim compressionlevel As Integer = DEFAULT_COMPRESSIONLEVEL
                If (Not _compressionlevel Is Nothing) AndAlso (_compressionlevel <>_
"") Then
                    compressionlevel = Convert.ToInt32(_compressionlevel)
                End If
                If (compressionlevel < 0) OrElse (compressionlevel > 9) Then
                    compressionlevel = DEFAULT_COMPRESSIONLEVEL
                End If
                zipStream.SetLevel(compressionlevel)
```

```
            ' get message filename, if supplied
            Dim filename As String
            If ((Not _filename Is Nothing) AndAlso (_filename <> "")) Then
                filename = (_filename)
            Else
                filename = (DEFAULT_FILENAME)
            End If
            Dim entry As ZipEntry = New ZipEntry(filename)
            zipStream.PutNextEntry(entry)

            ' copy the input into the compressed output stream
            Dim buffer As Byte() = New Byte(4095) {}
            Dim count As Integer = inStream.Read(buffer, 0, buffer.Length 0)
            Do While (count <> 0)
                 zipStream.Write(buffer, 0, count)
                 count = inStream.Read(buffer, 0, buffer.Length 0)

            Loop
            zipStream.Finish()
            zipStream.Close()

            outStream = ReadFileToMemoryStream(outFile)
        Catch ex As Exception
            System.Diagnostics.Debug.WriteLine(ex)
        Finally
            If File.Exists(inFile) Then
                File.Delete(inFile)
            End If

            If File.Exists(outFile) Then
                File.Delete(outFile)
            End If
        End Try

        Return outStream
    End Function

#Region "IPersistPropertyBag Members"

    Public Sub InitNew()
    End Sub

    Public Sub GetClassID(<System.Runtime.InteropServices.Out()> ByRef_
    classID As Guid)
        classID = New Guid("0F94CF83-0B04-49a6-B73C-70473E0CF96F")
    End Sub
```

```
        Public Sub Load(ByVal propertyBag As IPropertyBag, ByVal errorLog_
        As Integer)

            Dim value As String

            value = Convert.ToString((ReadPropertyBag(propertyBag, "Password")))
            If Not value Is Nothing Then
                _password = value
            End If
            value = Convert.ToString((ReadPropertyBag(propertyBag, "Filename")))
            If Not value Is Nothing Then
                _filename = value
            End If
            value = Convert.ToString(ReadPropertyBag(propertyBag,_
            "CompressionLevel"))


            If Not value Is Nothing Then
                _compressionlevel = value
            End If
        End Sub

        Public Sub Save(ByVal propertyBag As IPropertyBag, ByVal clearDirty As_
Boolean, ByVal saveAllProperties As Boolean)
            Dim value As String

            value = Convert.ToString(_password)
            WritePropertyBag(propertyBag, "Password", value)

            value = Convert.ToString(_filename)
            WritePropertyBag(propertyBag, "Filename", value)

            value = Convert.ToString(_compressionlevel)
            WritePropertyBag(propertyBag, "CompressionLevel", value)

        End Sub

#End Region


#Region "IComponent Members"
```

```
        Public Function Execute(ByVal pContext As IPipelineContext, ByVal pInMsg As_
Microsoft.BizTalk.Message.Interop.IBaseMessage) As_
Microsoft.BizTalk.Message.Interop.IBaseMessage
            If Not pInMsg Is Nothing Then
                Dim originalStream As Stream = _
pInMsg.BodyPart.GetOriginalDataStream()
                pInMsg.BodyPart.Data = Encode(originalStream)
                pContext.ResourceTracker.AddResource(pInMsg.BodyPart.Data)
            End If

            Return pInMsg
        End Function

#End Region

#Region "IComponentUI Members"

        ' <summary>
        'The Validate method is called by the BizTalk Editor during the build
        'of a BizTalk project.
        ' </summary>
        '<param name="obj">An Object containing the configuration
        'properties.</param>
        '<returns>The IEnumerator enables the caller to enumerate through a
        'collection of strings containing error messages. These error messages
        'appear 'as compiler error messages. To report successful property
        'validation, the method should return an empty enumerator.</returns>
        Public Function Validate(ByVal projectSystem As Object) As IEnumerator
            ' example implementation:
            ' ArrayList errorList = new ArrayList();
            ' errorList.Add("This is a compiler error");
            ' return errorList.GetEnumerator();
            Return Nothing
        End Function
        Public Shared Function ReadFileToMemoryStream(ByVal fromFilename _
        As String) As MemoryStream
            Dim file As FileStream = Nothing
            Try
                file = New FileStream(fromFilename, System.IO.FileMode.Open)
                Dim memStream As MemoryStream = New MemoryStream()
                Dim tmpBuff As Byte() = New Byte(4095) {}
                Dim bytesRead As Integer = 0
                bytesRead = file.Read(tmpBuff, 0, tmpBuff.Length)
                memStream.Write(tmpBuff, 0, bytesRead)
```

```
            Do While bytesRead <> 0
                bytesRead = file.Read(tmpBuff, 0, tmpBuff.Length)
                memStream.Write(tmpBuff, 0, bytesRead)
            Loop

            file.Close()
            file = Nothing

            memStream.Position = 0
            Return memStream
        Finally
            If Not file Is Nothing Then
                file.Close()
            End If
        End Try
    End Function

#End Region

#Region "Private Helpers"
    Public Shared Function ReadPropertyBag(ByVal pb As_
    Microsoft.BizTalk.Component.Interop.IPropertyBag, ByVal propName As_
    String) As Object
        Dim value As Object
        value = Nothing

        Try
            pb.Read(propName, value, 0)

        Catch argException As ArgumentException
            Return value

        Catch ex As Exception
            Throw New ApplicationException(ex.Message)
        End Try

        Return value

    End Function

    ''' <summary>
    ''' Writes property values into a property bag.
    ''' </summary>
    ''' <param name="pb">Property bag.</param>
    ''' <param name="propName">Name of property.</param>
    ''' <param name="val">Value of property.</param>
    Public Shared Sub WritePropertyBag(ByVal pb As _
```

```
Microsoft.BizTalk.Component.Interop.IPropertyBag, ByVal propName As _
String, ByVal val As Object)
            Try
                pb.Write(propName, val)
            Catch ex As Exception
                Throw New ApplicationException(ex.Message)
            End Try
        End Sub
#End Region
    End Class
End Namespace
```

Sending Multiple Zipped Files

In order to accommodate the scenario where a single ZIP file will contain multiple ZIP entries, you need to make some modifications to the preceding example. Specifically, you need to pass in multiple documents and have them all included within the outbound ZIP file. For this, you can write a BizTalk Assembler component. The Assembler component will take an array of messages, loop through them, and compress each of them into the final message output. To actually send the messages to the assembler, you can use the ExecuteSendPipeline from an orchestration feature that is included with BizTalk 2006. What you need to do is build an orchestration that will have a subscription for all messages required to be included within the ZIP file. The orchestration listens for these messages, and when it receives them, it adds them to an `ArrayList` object. At some point, the orchestration will need to call the send pipeline and pass it in the `ArrayList` it has built. From here, the send pipeline will call the Assembler component, which will add each of the messages it has received within the `ArrayList` to the outbound message. An example of this pattern is included in the SDK with BizTalk under the \Program Files\Microsoft BizTalk Server 2006\SDK\Samples\Pipelines\Aggregator\ directory. Chapter 6 in this book also includes a sample of a resequencing aggregator pattern that you can use should the files you receive not be in the correct order in which you want to place them in the ZIP file.

Receiving Zipped Files

The reverse scenario to sending ZIP files is receiving them. When receiving ZIP files, you will need to create a Decoding component, which can extract the files inside and submit them to the pipeline for further processing. This example only addresses the simple example of a ZIP file containing one XML file inside. The following example could be expanded upon to handle ZIP files with multiple files inside and files of binary types.

```
Imports Microsoft.VisualBasic
Imports System
Imports System.ComponentModel
Imports System.Collections
Imports System.Diagnostics
Imports System.Drawing
Imports System.IO
Imports System.Reflection
```

```
Imports Microsoft.BizTalk.Component.Interop
Imports Microsoft.Utility.PipelinePropertyAttribute
Imports ICSharpCode.SharpZipLib.Zip
Namespace Microsoft.Utility.PipelineZip

       <ComponentCategory(CategoryTypes.CATID_PipelineComponent),_
ComponentCategory(CategoryTypes.CATID_Decoder),_
System.Runtime.InteropServices.Guid("67C8CFB9-D89A-4415-A112-76187FC294D1")> _
       Public Class ZipDecodeComponent
              Inherits BaseCustomTypeDescriptor
              Implements IBaseComponent,_
Microsoft.BizTalk.Component.Interop.IComponent,_
Microsoft.BizTalk.Component.Interop.IPersistPropertyBag, IComponentUI

              ' Component information
              #Region "IBaseComponent"
              <Browsable(False)> _
              Public ReadOnly Property Name() As String
                     Get
                            Return "ZIP decoder"
                     End Get
              End Property
              <Browsable(False)> _
              Public ReadOnly Property Version() As String
                     Get
                            Return "1.0"
                     End Get
              End Property
              <Browsable(False)> _
              Public ReadOnly Property Description() As String
                     Get
                            Return "Zip Decode Pipeline Component"
                     End Get
              End Property
              <Browsable(False)> _
              Public ReadOnly Property Icon() As System.IntPtr
                     Get
                            Return (CType(resourceManager.GetObject("IconBitmap"),_
Bitmap)).GetHicon()
                     End Get
              End Property
              #End Region

              Private resourceManager As System.Resources.ResourceManager = New_
System.Resources.ResourceManager_
("Microsoft.Utility.PipelineGnuPG.ZipDecodeComponent",_
System.Reflection.Assembly.GetExecutingAssembly())
```

```
            ' Property: Password
            Private _password As String

            Public Property Password() As String
                Get
                    Return _password
                End Get
                Set
                    _password = Value
                End Set
            End Property

            Private Function Decode(ByVal inStream As Stream) As Stream
                Dim inFile As String = Path.GetTempFileName()
                Dim outFile As String = Path.ChangeExtension(inFile, "txt")

                Try
                    Dim zipStream As ZipInputStream = New_
ZipInputStream(inStream)

                    ' get password, if supplied
                    If (Not _password Is Nothing) AndAlso (_password <> "")_
Then
                        zipStream.Password = _password
                    End If

                    ' this algorithm demands that the ZIP archive contain
                    ' exactly one file
                    Dim entry As ZipEntry = zipStream.GetNextEntry()
                    If entry Is Nothing Then
           Throw New ApplicationException("Input ZIP archive does not contain any _
           files - expecting exactly one file")
                    End If
                    If entry.IsDirectory Then
                        Throw New ApplicationException("Input ZIP _
contains a directory - expecting exactly one file")
                    End If

                    ' copy the compressed stream into the output stream
                    outStream = New MemoryStream()
                    Dim buffer As Byte() = New Byte(4095){}
                    Dim count As Integer = 0
                    count = zipStream.Read(buffer, 0, buffer.Length
                    Do While count <> 0
                        outStream.Write(buffer, 0, count)
                         count = zipStream.Read(buffer, 0, buffer.Length
                    Loop
```

```
                        ' make sure that was the one and only file
                        entry = zipStream.GetNextEntry()
                        If Not entry Is Nothing Then
            Throw New ApplicationException("Input ZIP archive contains multiple files_
            and/or directories - expecting exactly one file")
                        End If

                        zipStream.Close()

#If DEBUG Then
                        outStream.Seek(0, SeekOrigin.Begin)

PipelinePropertyAttribute.FileStreamReadWrite.DumpStreamToFile(outStream,_
outFile)
#End If

                        outStream.Seek(0, SeekOrigin.Begin)
                    Catch ex As Exception
                        System.Diagnostics.Debug.WriteLine(ex)
                        Throw ex
                    Finally
                        If File.Exists(inFile) Then
                            File.Delete(inFile)
                        End If

                        If File.Exists(outFile) Then
                            File.Delete(outFile)
                        End If
                    End Try

                    Return outStream
                End Function

                #Region "IPersistPropertyBag Members"

                Public Sub InitNew()
                End Sub

                Public Sub GetClassID(<System.Runtime.InteropServices.Out()> ByRef_
classID As Guid)
                    classID = New Guid ("19800584-283D-44da-B1EE-0968387DA088")
                End Sub
```

```
            Public Sub Load(ByVal propertyBag As IPropertyBag, ByVal errorLog As_
Integer)
                Dim text As String
                text = CStr(PropertyBagReadWrite.ReadPropertyBag(propertyBag,_
"Password"))
                If Not text Is Nothing Then
                _password = text
                End If
            End Sub

            Public Sub Save(ByVal propertyBag As IPropertyBag, _
            ByVal clearDirty As Boolean, ByVal saveAllProperties As Boolean)
                Dim val As Object
                val = CObj(_password)
                PropertyBagReadWrite.WritePropertyBag(propertyBag, "Password",_
val)
            End Sub

            #End Region


            #Region "IComponent Members"

            Public Function Execute(ByVal pContext As IPipelineContext, _
ByVal pInMsg As Microsoft.BizTalk.Message.Interop.IBaseMessage) As_
 Microsoft.BizTalk.Message.Interop.IBaseMessage
                Try
                    If Not pInMsg Is Nothing Then
                        Dim originalStream As _
Stream = pInMsg.BodyPart.GetOriginalDataStream()
                        pInMsg.BodyPart.Data = Decode(originalStream)
                        pContext.ResourceTracker.AddResource_
(pInMsg.BodyPart.Data)
                    End If
                Catch ex As Exception
                    System.Diagnostics.Debug.WriteLine("Exception caught in_
 ZipDecodeComponent::Execute: " & ex.Message)
    Throw New ApplicationException("ZipDecodeComponent was_
    unable to decompress input stream. This may occur if there is more than_
    one file in the ZIP archive. See inner exception for more information.", ex)
                End Try
                Return pInMsg
            End Function

            #End Region

            #Region "IComponentUI Members"
```

```
        '<summary>
        'The Validate method is called by the BizTalk Editor_
        'during the build of a BizTalk project.
        '</summary>
        '<param name="obj">An Object containing the configuration
        'properties.</param>
        '<returns>The IEnumerator enables the caller to _enumerate through a
        'collection of strings containing error messages. These error_
        'messages appear as compiler error messages. To report successful
        'property validation, the method should return an empty
        'enumerator.</returns>
        Public Function Validate(ByVal projectSystem As Object) As_
IEnumerator
                            ' example implementation:
                            ' ArrayList errorList = new ArrayList();
                            ' errorList.Add("This is a compiler error");
                            ' return errorList.GetEnumerator();
                            Return Nothing
                End Function


                #End Region
        End Class
End Namespace
```

Using PGP

By default, BizTalk ships with no encryption/decryption component. Many organizations need to encrypt the message data as it is sent from BizTalk and decrypt is as well once it is received. A fairly standard way to do this is to use PGP (Pretty Good Privacy). Various vendors sell PGP packages; however, nothing really exists to integrate PGP with BizTalk. The following examples show you a potential implementation for this both on the send side and the receive side.[5]

There is an IMPORTS statement in the beginning of the PGPEncodeComponent. This is the wrapper class that supports the interaction with the GNU Privacy Guard API. The code for this wrapper class is available for download from www.apress.com should you want a full implementation; it is not included in this example due to space constraints. Also, this wrapper class is the logical point where you would implement your own PGP library wrapper should you not want to use the GNU Privacy Guard implementation of the PGP standard.

---

5. This example uses the GNU Privacy Guard package available from www.gnupg.org/. This is an implementation of the OpenPGP standard as defined by RFC2440. In theory, any PGP software package could be used for this example.

PGP Encode Component

The solution for implementing PGP within BizTalk comprises two components, a send-side encoding component and a receive-side decoding component. The following code shows the send-side encoding component.

```
Imports Microsoft.VisualBasic
Imports System
Imports System.ComponentModel
Imports System.Collections
Imports System.Diagnostics
Imports System.Drawing
Imports System.IO
Imports System.Reflection
Imports Microsoft.BizTalk.Component.Interop
Imports ABC.BizTalk.PipelineComponents.PGPUtilities

Namespace ABC.BizTalk.PipelineComponents

    <ComponentCategory(CategoryTypes.CATID_PipelineComponent),_
ComponentCategory(CategoryTypes.CATID_Encoder),_
System.Runtime.InteropServices.Guid("C1917FE1-841B-4583-A59E-B57F76871899")> _

    Public Class PGPEncodeComponent

        Implements IBaseComponent, Microsoft.BizTalk.Component.Interop.IComponent,_
Microsoft.BizTalk.Component.Interop.IPersistPropertyBag, IComponentUI

        ' Component information
#Region "IBaseComponent"
        <Browsable(False)> _
        Public ReadOnly Property Name() As String
            Get
                Return "PGP encoder"
            End Get
        End Property
        <Browsable(False)> _
        Public ReadOnly Property Version() As String
            Get
                Return "1.0"
            End Get
        End Property
        <Browsable(False)> _
        Public ReadOnly Property Description() As String
            Get
                Return "PGP Encode Pipeline Component"
            End Get
        End Property
```

```
        <Browsable(False)> _
        Public ReadOnly Property Icon() As System.IntPtr
            Get
                Return (CType(resourceManager.GetObject("IconBitmap"),_
Bitmap)).GetHicon()
            End Get
        End Property
#End Region

        Private resourceManager As System.Resources.ResourceManager = New_
System.Resources.ResourceManager("ABC.BizTalk.PipelineComponents",_
System.Reflection.Assembly.GetExecutingAssembly())

        ' Property: Recipient
        Private _recipient As String
        Public Property Recipient() As String
            Get
                Return _recipient
            End Get
            Set(ByVal value As String)
                _recipient = value
            End Set
        End Property


        Private _PGPBinDirectory As String
        Public Property PGPBinDirectory() As String
            Get
                Return _PGPBinDirectory
            End Get
            Set(ByVal value As String)
                _PGPBinDirectory = value
            End Set
        End Property

        Private Function Encode(ByVal inStream As Stream) As Stream
            Dim inFile As String = Path.GetTempFileName()
            Dim outFile As String = Path.ChangeExtension(inFile, "gpg")

            Try
                DumpStreamToFile(inStream, inFile)

                Dim GPG As GnuPGWrapper = New GnuPGWrapper(_PGPBinDirectory)
                Dim GPGCommand As GnuPGCommand = GPG.Command
                GPGCommand.Command = Commands.Encrypt
                GPGCommand.Recipient = _recipient
```

```
                GPGCommand.Armor = True
                GPGCommand.InputFile = inFile
                GPGCommand.OutputFile = outFile

                GPG.Execute(Nothing)

                outStream = ReadFileToMemoryStream(outFile)
            Catch ex As Exception
                System.Diagnostics.Debug.WriteLine(ex)
                Throw ex
            Finally
                If File.Exists(inFile) Then
                    File.Delete(inFile)
                End If

                If File.Exists(outFile) Then
                    File.Delete(outFile)
                End If
            End Try

            Return outStream
        End Function

#Region "IPersistPropertyBag Members"

        Public Sub InitNew()
        End Sub

        Public Sub GetClassID(<System.Runtime.InteropServices.Out()> ByRef _
        classID As Guid)
            classID = New Guid("A398E8D1-4213-4438-9010-66F366D4BDF4")
        End Sub

        Public Sub Load(ByVal propertyBag As IPropertyBag, ByVal errorLog _
        As Integer)
            Dim text As String
            text = Convert.ToString(ReadPropertyBag(propertyBag, "Recipient"))

            If Not text Is Nothing Then
                _recipient = text
            End If

            text = Convert.ToString(ReadPropertyBag(propertyBag, "GnuPGBinDir"))
            If Not text Is Nothing Then
                _PGPBinDirectory = text
            End If
        End Sub
```

```
        Public Sub Save(ByVal propertyBag As IPropertyBag, ByVal clearDirty As_
 Boolean, ByVal saveAllProperties As Boolean)
            Dim val As Object
            val = CObj(_recipient)
            WritePropertyBag(propertyBag, "Recipient", val)
            val = CObj(_PGPBinDirectory)
            WritePropertyBag(propertyBag, "PGPBinDirectory", val)
        End Sub

#End Region


#Region "IComponent Members"

        Public Function Execute(ByVal pContext As IPipelineContext, ByVal pInMsg As_
 Microsoft.BizTalk.Message.Interop.IBaseMessage) As_
Microsoft.BizTalk.Message.Interop.IBaseMessage
            Try
                If Not pInMsg Is Nothing Then
                    Dim originalStream As Stream = _
pInMsg.BodyPart.GetOriginalDataStream()
                    pInMsg.BodyPart.Data = Encode(originalStream)
                    pContext.ResourceTracker.AddResource(pInMsg.BodyPart.Data)
                End If
            Catch ex As Exception
                System.Diagnostics.Debug.WriteLine("Exception caught in_
ABC.BizTalk.PipelineComponents.PGPEncodeComponent::Execute: " & ex.Message)
            End Try
            Return pInMsg
        End Function

#End Region

#Region "IComponentUI Members"

        ' <summary>
        'The Validate method is called by the BizTalk Editor during the build
        'of a BizTalk project.
        '</summary>
        '<param name="obj">An Object containing the configuration
        'properties.</param>
        '<returns>The IEnumerator enables the caller to enumerate through a
        'collection of strings containing error messages. These error messages
        'appear as compiler error messages. To report successful property
        'validation, the method should return an empty enumerator.</returns>
        Public Function Validate(ByVal projectSystem As Object) As IEnumerator
```

```
            ' example implementation:
            ' ArrayList errorList = new ArrayList();
            ' errorList.Add("This is a compiler error");
            ' return errorList.GetEnumerator();
            Return Nothing
        End Function

#End Region

#Region "Utility Functions"
        Public Shared Sub DumpStreamToFile(ByVal fromStream As Stream, ByVal _
toFilename As String)
            Dim file As FileStream = Nothing
            Try
                file = New FileStream(toFilename, System.IO.FileMode.Create)
                Dim tmpBuff As Byte() = New Byte(4095) {}
                Dim bytesRead As Integer = 0
                bytesRead = file.Read(tmpBuff, 0, tmpBuff.Length)
                memStream.Write(tmpBuff, 0, bytesRead)

                Do While bytesRead <> 0
                    bytesRead = fromStream.Read(tmpBuff, 0, tmpBuff.Length)
                    file.Write(tmpBuff, 0, bytesRead)
                Loop

                file.Close()
                file = Nothing
            Finally
                If Not file Is Nothing Then
                    file.Close()
                End If
            End Try
        End Sub

        Public Shared Function ReadFileToMemoryStream(ByVal fromFilename As String)_
 As MemoryStream
            Dim file As FileStream = Nothing
            Try
                file = New FileStream(fromFilename, System.IO.FileMode.Open)
                Dim memStream As MemoryStream = New MemoryStream()
                Dim tmpBuff As Byte() = New Byte(4095) {}
                bytesRead = file.Read(tmpBuff, 0, tmpBuff.Length)
                 memStream.Write(tmpBuff, 0, bytesRead)

                Dim bytesRead As Integer = bytesRead = file.Read(tmpBuff, 0, _
tmpBuff.Length)
```

```
                Do While bytesRead <> 0
                    memStream.Write(tmpBuff, 0, bytesRead)
                    bytesRead = file.Read(tmpBuff, 0, tmpBuff.Length)
                Loop

                file.Close()
                file = Nothing

                memStream.Position = 0
                Return memStream
            Finally
                If Not file Is Nothing Then
                    file.Close()
                End If
            End Try
        End Function

        Public Shared Function ReadPropertyBag(ByVal pb As_
 Microsoft.BizTalk.Component.Interop.IPropertyBag, ByVal propName As _
 String) As Object
            Dim val As Object = Nothing

            Try
                pb.Read(propName, val, 0)
            Catch e1 As ArgumentException
                Return val
            Catch ex As Exception
                Throw New ApplicationException(ex.Message)
            End Try

            Return val
        End Function

        ''' <summary>
        ''' Writes property values into a property bag.
        ''' </summary>
        ''' <param name="pb">Property bag.</param>
        ''' <param name="propName">Name of property.</param>
        ''' <param name="val">Value of property.</param>
        Public Shared Sub WritePropertyBag(ByVal pb As_
 Microsoft.BizTalk.Component.Interop.IPropertyBag, ByVal propName As String, ByVal _
val As Object)
            Try
                pb.Write(propName, val)
            Catch ex As Exception
                Throw New ApplicationException(ex.Message)
            End Try
        End Sub
```

```
#End Region

    End Class
End Namespace
```

PGP Decode Component

The following code example is the counterpart to the encoding component shown in the preceding subsection. The Decoding component is used on the receive side of BizTalk and is used when encrypted messages are received into BizTalk.

```
Imports Microsoft.VisualBasic
Imports System
Imports System.ComponentModel
Imports System.Collections
Imports System.Diagnostics
Imports System.Drawing
Imports System.IO
Imports System.Reflection
Imports Microsoft.BizTalk.Component.Interop
Imports ABC.BizTalk.PipelineComponents.PGPUtilities

Namespace Microsoft.Utility.PipelineGnuPG

    <ComponentCategory(CategoryTypes.CATID_PipelineComponent),_
 ComponentCategory(CategoryTypes.CATID_Decoder),_
 System.Runtime.InteropServices.Guid("AEE2E180-8E4F-426d-9E39-C314E09F977E")> _
    Public Class PGPDecodeComponent

        Implements IBaseComponent, Microsoft.BizTalk.Component.Interop.IComponent,_
 Microsoft.BizTalk.Component.Interop.IPersistPropertyBag, IComponentUI

        ' Component information
#Region "IBaseComponent"
        <Browsable(False)> _
        Public ReadOnly Property Name() As String
            Get
                Return "PGP decoder"
            End Get
        End Property
        <Browsable(False)> _
        Public ReadOnly Property Version() As String
            Get
                Return "1.0"
            End Get
        End Property
```

```
        <Browsable(False)> _
        Public ReadOnly Property Description() As String
            Get
                Return "PGG Decode Pipeline Component"
            End Get
        End Property
        <Browsable(False)> _
        Public ReadOnly Property Icon() As System.IntPtr
            Get
                Return (CType(resourceManager.GetObject("IconBitmap"),_
 Bitmap)).GetHicon()
            End Get
        End Property
#End Region

        Private resourceManager As System.Resources.ResourceManager = New_
 System.Resources.ResourceManager("ABC.BizTalk.PipelineComponents",_
 System.Reflection.Assembly.GetExecutingAssembly())

        ' Property: Passphrase
        Private _passphrase As String
        Public Property Passphrase() As String
            Get
                Return _passphrase
            End Get
            Set(ByVal value As String)
                _passphrase = value
            End Set
        End Property

        ' Property: GnuPGBinDir
        Private _PGPBinDirectory As String
        Public Property PGPBinDirectory() As String
            Get
                Return _PGPBinDirectory
            End Get
            Set(ByVal value As String)
                _PGPBinDirectory = value
            End Set
        End Property

        Private Function Decode(ByVal inStream As System.IO.Stream) As Stream
            Dim inFile As String = Path.GetTempFileName()
            Dim outFile As String = Path.ChangeExtension(inFile, "txt")
```

```
            Try
                DumpStreamToFile(inStream, inFile)

                Dim GPG As GnuPGWrapper = New GnuPGWrapper(_PGPBinDirectory)
                Dim GPGCommand As GnuPGCommand = GPG.Command
                GPGCommand.Command = Commands.Decrypt
                GPGCommand.InputFile = inFile
                GPGCommand.OutputFile = outFile
                GPGCommand.Passphrase = _passphrase
                'TODO: support encrypted passphrase, no passphrase is a security
                'risk

                GPG.Execute(Nothing)

                outStream = ReadFileToMemoryStream(outFile)
            Catch ex As Exception
                System.Diagnostics.Debug.WriteLine(ex)
        Throw ex
            Finally
                If File.Exists(inFile) Then
                    File.Delete(inFile)
                End If

                If File.Exists(outFile) Then
                    File.Delete(outFile)
                End If
            End Try

            Return outStream
        End Function

#Region "IPersistPropertyBag Members"

        Public Sub InitNew()
        End Sub

        Public Sub GetClassID(<System.Runtime.InteropServices.Out()> ByRef _
        classID As  Guid)
            classID = New Guid("4FC12033-D0BD-4298-BB31-FBDBA72F5961")
        End Sub

        Public Sub Load(ByVal propertyBag As IPropertyBag, ByVal _
        errorLog As Integer)
            Dim text As String
```

```
            text = CStr(ReadPropertyBag(propertyBag, "Passphrase"))
            If Not text Is Nothing Then
                _passphrase = text
            End If
            text = CStr(ReadPropertyBag(propertyBag, "PGPBinDirectory"))
            If Not text Is Nothing Then
                _PGPBinDirectory = text
            End If
        End Sub

        Public Sub Save(ByVal propertyBag As IPropertyBag, ByVal clearDirty As_
 Boolean, ByVal saveAllProperties As Boolean)
            Dim val As Object
            val = CObj(_passphrase)
            WritePropertyBag(propertyBag, "Passphrase", val)

            val = CObj(_PGPBinDirectory)

            WritePropertyBag(propertyBag, "PGPBinDirectory", val)
        End Sub

#End Region


#Region "IComponent Members"

        Public Function Execute(ByVal pContext As IPipelineContext, ByVal pInMsg As_
 Microsoft.BizTalk.Message.Interop.IBaseMessage) As_
 Microsoft.BizTalk.Message.Interop.IBaseMessage
            Try
                If Not pInMsg Is Nothing Then
                    Dim originalStream As Stream =_
 pInMsg.BodyPart.GetOriginalDataStream()
                    pInMsg.BodyPart.Data = Decode(originalStream)
                    pContext.ResourceTracker.AddResource(pInMsg.BodyPart.Data)
                End If
            Catch ex As Exception
                System.Diagnostics.Debug.WriteLine("Exception caught in_
 ABC.BizTalk.PipelineComponents.PGPDecodeComponent::Execute: " & ex.Message)
                Throw ex
            End Try
            Return pInMsg
        End Function

#End Region
```

```
#Region "IComponentUI Members"

        '<summary>
        'The Validate method is called by the BizTalk Editor during the build
        'of a BizTalk project.
        '</summary>
        '<param name="obj">An Object containing the configuration
        properties.</param>
        '<returns>The IEnumerator enables the caller to enumerate through a_
        'collection of strings containing error messages. These error messages
appear
        'as compiler error messages. To report successful property validation, the
        'method should return an empty enumerator.</returns>
        Public Function Validate(ByVal projectSystem As Object) As IEnumerator
            ' example implementation:
            ' ArrayList errorList = new ArrayList();
            ' errorList.Add("This is a compiler error");
            ' return errorList.GetEnumerator();
            Return Nothing
        End Function


#End Region

#Region "Utility Functions"
        Public Shared Sub DumpStreamToFile(ByVal fromStream As Stream, ByVal_
 toFilename As String)
            Dim file As FileStream = Nothing
            Try
                file = New FileStream(toFilename, System.IO.FileMode.Create)
                Dim tmpBuff As Byte() = New Byte(4095) {}
                Dim bytesRead As Integer = 0
                bytesRead = file.Read(tmpBuff, 0, tmpBuff.Length)
                memStream.Write(tmpBuff, 0, bytesRead)

                Do While bytesRead <> 0
                    bytesRead = fromStream.Read(tmpBuff, 0, tmpBuff.Length)
                    file.Write(tmpBuff, 0, bytesRead)
                Loop

                file.Close()
                file = Nothing
            Finally
                If Not file Is Nothing Then
                    file.Close()
                End If
            End Try
        End Sub
```

```
        Public Shared Function ReadFileToMemoryStream(ByVal fromFilename _
        As String) As MemoryStream
            Dim file As FileStream = Nothing
            Try
                file = New FileStream(fromFilename, System.IO.FileMode.Open)
                Dim memStream As MemoryStream = New MemoryStream()
                Dim tmpBuff As Byte() = New Byte(4095) {}
                Dim bytesRead As Integer = 0
                bytesRead = file.Read(tmpBuff, 0, tmpBuff.Length)
                memStream.Write(tmpBuff, 0, bytesRead)

                Do While bytesRead <> 0
                    bytesRead = file.Read(tmpBuff, 0, tmpBuff.Length)
                    memStream.Write(tmpBuff, 0, bytesRead)
                Loop

                file.Close()
                file = Nothing

                memStream.Position = 0
                Return memStream
            Finally
                If Not file Is Nothing Then
                    file.Close()
                End If
            End Try
        End Function

        Public Shared Function ReadPropertyBag(ByVal pb As_
 Microsoft.BizTalk.Component.Interop.IPropertyBag, ByVal propName As String) _
As Object
            Dim val As Object = Nothing

            Try
                pb.Read(propName, val, 0)
            Catch e1 As ArgumentException
                Return val
            Catch ex As Exception
                Throw New ApplicationException(ex.Message)
            End Try

            Return val
        End Function

        ''' <summary>
        ''' Writes property values into a property bag.
        ''' </summary>
```

```
        ''' <param name="pb">Property bag.</param>
        ''' <param name="propName">Name of property.</param>
        ''' <param name="val">Value of property.</param>
        Public Shared Sub WritePropertyBag(ByVal pb As_
 Microsoft.BizTalk.Component.Interop.IPropertyBag, ByVal propName As String, ByVal _
val As Object)
            Try
                pb.Write(propName, val)
            Catch ex As Exception
                Throw New ApplicationException(ex.Message)
            End Try
        End Sub

#End Region
    End Class
End Namespace
```

The Databased Disassembler

Often, people need to get information from a database and submit it to BizTalk or have BizTalk send it out to a third-party destination. The usual response for this is to use the appropriate database adapter, generate the schemas for the SQL statement or the stored procedure, and use some combination of an orchestration/port and adapter to generate the data, publish it to the Messagebox, and send it to the appropriate destination. While this solution works, it often is met with a response like "But I just want to call a stored procedure and have each row be sent to BizTalk as an XML document."

Our solution to this scenario is called the Databased Disassembler (yes, it is a pun on words as the data is based on a database). The walkthrough for how this solution works is as follows:

1. A receive pipeline is created that hosts the custom Disassembler component.
2. The Disassembler only accepts a primer message. A **primer message** is a message that contains all the parameters needed for the pipeline component to begin executing. It is a primer because it is a message that gets the process going, or "primes" it. The message itself contains data that is not meaningful to anyone but the Databased Disassembler pipeline component.
3. The pipeline component examines the primer message and retrieves all the parameters needed for execution. These parameters can include
    a. The connection string for the database
    b. The stored procedure name
    c. The parameters needed to call the stored procedure
    d. The resulting schema type for the returned data

e. The number of rows to include in an output message (The default is usually 1, but it can contain multiple documents wrapped in an envelope if so desired.)

f. If an envelope is requested, the XPath to the body element in the envelope as well as the schema name for the envelope

4. If no values exist for a given parameter, the pipeline component can have them defaulted to a value when it is placed in the pipeline surface designer.

5. Once all the parameters are gathered, the component calls the stored procedure with the parameters supplied in the primer message.

6. It creates a `DataReader` object from the result of the stored procedure call. If no records were returned, an exception is thrown.

7. If more than one record is requested per created message, then the component generates a new empty instance of the envelope schema that was specified in the primer message. If only one record is requested, then no envelope is used. If more than one document is requested per message but no envelope schema is supplied, then an exception is thrown.

8. For each row that is returned, a new but empty XML document is created based on the requested schema in the primer message. This document is created using the `DocumentSpec` class shown earlier in the chapter.

9. Each element name in the blank XML instance must exist as a named column in the `DataReader` with the same name.[6] This way, the schema instance can change, and all that is required is an update to the stored procedure. In this fashion, you have a logical connection between your XML schema and your database schema.

10. The component continues to create new XML documents in the `GetNext()` method of the Disassembler interface until no more rows exist. When all rows have been processed, the component returns `Nothing`.

The following code shows the schema for the primer message that will be used to signify the start of the processes:

```
<?xml version="1.0" encoding="utf-16"?>
<xs:schema xmlns:b="http://schemas.microsoft.com/BizTalk/2003"
xmlns="http://TR3.Schemas.Primer" targetNamespace="http://TR3.Schemas.Primer"
xmlns:xs="http://www.w3.org/2001/XMLSchema">
```

6. Many other approaches to this problem are available. A second potential solution would be to have a BizTalk transformation that maps the schema created from the component to the requested output schema. A third would be to access the schema and the data columns by index only. This assumes that there is always the same number of elements as the number of columns in the result set and that they are stored in the correct order. Any of these implementations will work; we chose the “named columns” approach as it served the purpose of illustrating this technique the best.

```
  <xs:element name="PrimerData">
    <xs:complexType>
      <xs:sequence>
        <xs:element minOccurs="0" maxOccurs="1" name="ConnectionString"
nillable="true" type="xs:string" />
        <xs:element minOccurs="0" maxOccurs="1" name="StoredProcedureName"
nillable="true" type="xs:string" />
        <xs:element name="StoredProcParams" nillable="true">
          <xs:complexType>
            <xs:sequence minOccurs="0" maxOccurs="1">
              <xs:element minOccurs="0" maxOccurs="unbounded" name="ParamValue"
nillable="true" type="xs:string" />
            </xs:sequence>
          </xs:complexType>
        </xs:element>
        <xs:element minOccurs="0" maxOccurs="1" default="1" name="RecordsPerMessage"
type="xs:integer" />
        <xs:element minOccurs="0" maxOccurs="1" name="OutputMessageSchema"
nillable="true" type="xs:string" />
        <xs:element minOccurs="0" maxOccurs="1" name="EnvelopeSchema"
        nillable="true" type="xs:string" />
        <xs:element minOccurs="0" maxOccurs="1" name="BodyXPath" nillable="true"
type="xs:string" />
      </xs:sequence>
    </xs:complexType>
  </xs:element>
</xs:schema>
```

Figure 5-1 gives a pictorial representation of the message flow that will take place for this process to work. Note one key element in Figure 5-1. The data from which the Disassembler gets its rows is not the BizTalk Messagebox. This is a key feature of this pattern. Since the database can be essentially “anything,” it becomes trivial to get data from any OLEDB-compliant data source such as Oracle, DB2, and Sybase. This technique only requires writing a stored procedure and getting a connection string to access the data source. There is no need to purchase additional adapters for this solution to be used across different databases. This is a key selling point for many projects that might want to use this approach.

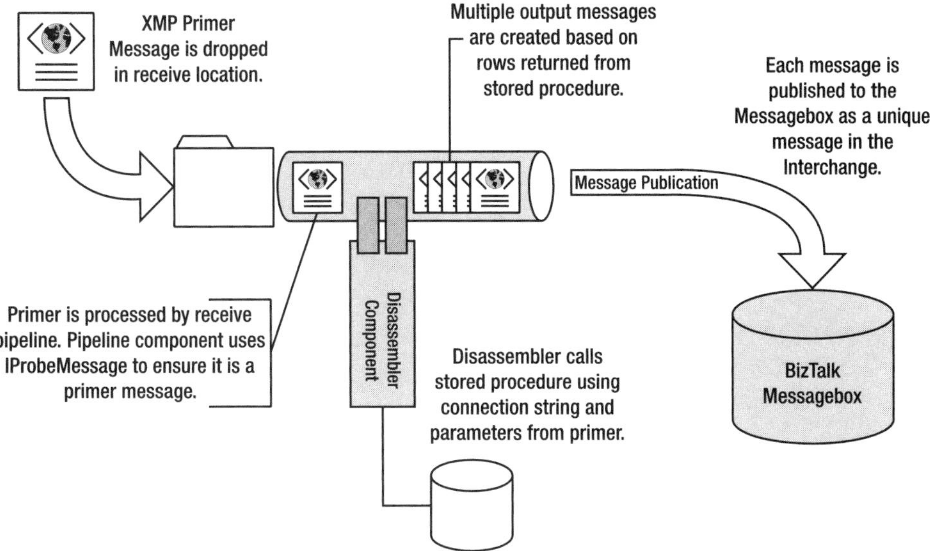

Figure 5-1. *Databased Disassembler execution flow*

Another key architectural component of this solution is that fact that a Disassembler is used to create the messages. Each of the messages that are created from a unique primer message will be tagged as being from the same Interchange. This means that every message that was created from this primer message will have the same `InterchangeID`. This is very useful, as it allows you to easily correlate all the messages in an execution flow within an orchestration using a convoy pattern, because they will all have the same `InterchangeID`. The only issue becomes how to signify that the message received is the last in the sequence. For this, you can use the same pattern that is employed in the resequencing aggregator pattern in Chapter 6. You will need to create a custom property schema that is associated to each of the messages that is created by the Disassembler. Each message will be tagged with a sequence number, and there will be a Boolean flag in the schema that indicates the last message in the sequence. This flag is then used to signal the orchestration that the last message has been received in the convoy.

Note Example code for the Databased Disassembler will be published as a sample, available for download from the Apress web site (www.apress.com).

CHAPTER 6

BizTalk Design Patterns and Practices

The chapters to date have dealt with advanced concepts with regard to pipelines and messaging. Most of the concepts in the previous chapters have involved examining the intricacies of a particular tool within the BizTalk toolkit. Here we'll show you how you can use some of the more advanced concepts within BizTalk to solve some higher-level scenario-based problems.

Implementing Dynamic Parallel Orchestrations

Microsoft BizTalk Server orchestrations allow parallel execution branches, using the native **Parallel Actions** shape.[1] However, the number of branches is static: to add an execution branch, you need to modify and recompile an orchestration.

The behavior for Parallel Actions shapes doesn't fit in scenarios where you know only at runtime the number of execution branches that you can spawn. An example is the travel agent service scenario described at www.w3.org/TR/ws-arch-scenarios/, where a travel agent requests in parallel a list of flights for each airline included in a customer list. This sample can be generalized to scenarios where a client application sends a request to a broker that splits it into individual requests for similar target systems; then the broker collects the responses from the target systems and aggregates them into a single response for the client (see Figure 6-1).

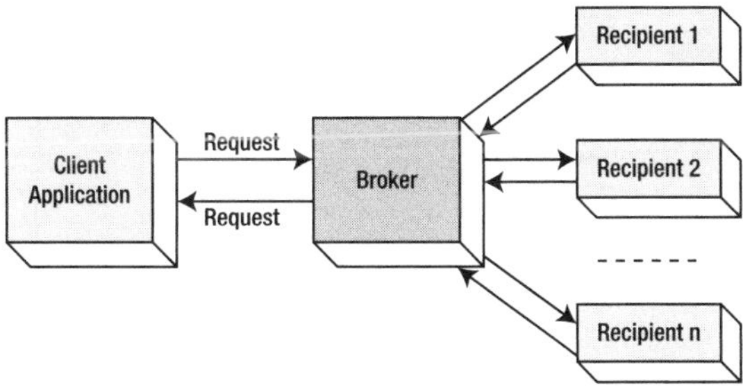

Figure 6-1. *Sample broker implementation*

1. This section originally appeared in "BizTalk Server 2004 Implementing Dynamic Parallel Orchestrations," (REED001965).doc. Copyright by Microsoft Corporation. Reprinted with permission from Microsoft Corporation.

One approach to solve this problem is to use the **Recipient List** pattern as described by Enterprise Integration Patterns. The Recipient List pattern is explained by the Enterprise Integration Patterns site as the following:

> *A Content-Based Router allows us to route a message to the correct system based on message content. This process is transparent to the original sender in the sense that the originator simply sends the message to a channel, where the router picks it up and takes care of everything.*
>
> *In some cases, though, we may want to specify one or more recipients for the message. A common analogy are [sic] the recipient lists implemented in most e-mail systems. For each e-mail message, the sender can specify a list of recipients. The mail system then ensures transport of the message content to each recipient. An example from the domain of enterprise integration would be a situation where a function can be performed by one or more providers. For example, we may have a contract with multiple credit agencies to assess the credit worthiness of our customers. When a small order comes in we may simply route the credit request message to one credit agency. If a customer places a large order, we may want to route the credit request message to multiple agencies and compare the results before making a decision. In this case, the list of recipients depends on the dollar value of the order.*
>
> *In another situation, we may want to route an order message to a select list of suppliers to obtain a quote for the requested item. Rather than sending the request to all vendors, we may want to control which vendors receive the request, possibly based on user preferences*
>
> ***How do we route a message to a list of dynamically specified recipients?***

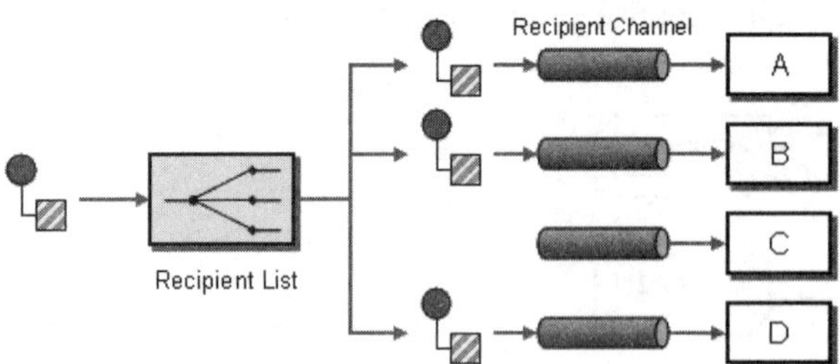

> *Define a channel for each recipient. Then use a Recipient List to inspect an incoming message, determine the list of desired recipients, and forward the message to all channels associated with the recipients in the list.*

> *The logic embedded in a Recipient List can be pictured as two separate parts even though the implementation is often coupled together. The first part computes a list of recipients. The second part simply traverses the list and sends a copy of the received message to each recipient. Just like a Content-Based Router, the Recipient List usually does not modify the message contents.*[2]

This section describes a dynamic parallel implementation of this pattern with a BizTalk orchestration.

An alternative approach would have been using the **Publish-Subscribe** and **Message Filter** patterns. We don't describe here this alternative approach, as this implementation could be more resource consuming in terms of database queries to resolve the filter conditions, and more error prone while setting filter conditions on the channels.

Broker Implementation Overview

Our implementation of the broker requires using two different orchestrations.[3] A parent orchestration builds the list of recipients, based on the received document. The parent orchestration uses the Start Orchestration shape to launch a child orchestration for each recipient. The child orchestration executes the actual flow of messages with the recipient. We assume that all the recipients share a common workflow model and schema documents; otherwise you wouldn't need such a dynamic invocation model, as a manual activity would be needed to introduce each additional recipient! The child orchestration makes use of **dynamic port binding** to send messages to each different recipient.

The parent orchestration collects the results returned by each child and builds an aggregated response document. The parent orchestration makes use of a **self-correlating** binding port to receive the responses from the started child orchestrations.

In Exercise 6-1, we concentrate on the general design and on the orchestration mechanisms involved in the dynamic parallelism implementation; we don't give a complete implementation sample including schemas, maps, ports, and helper Microsoft .NET Framework objects. A working knowledge of the basic orchestration development tasks is required.

---

2. www.enterpriseintegrationpatterns.com/RecipientList.html

3. This subsection and the accompanying exercise originally appeared in "BizTalk Server 2004 Implementing Dynamic Parallel Orchestrations," (REED001965).doc. Copyright by Microsoft Corporation. Reprinted with permission from Microsoft Corporation.

Exercise 6-1: Creating the Implementation

Create the Parent Orchestration:

The following are the steps required to create the parent orchestration as shown in Figure 6-2 for the solution within Visual Studio.

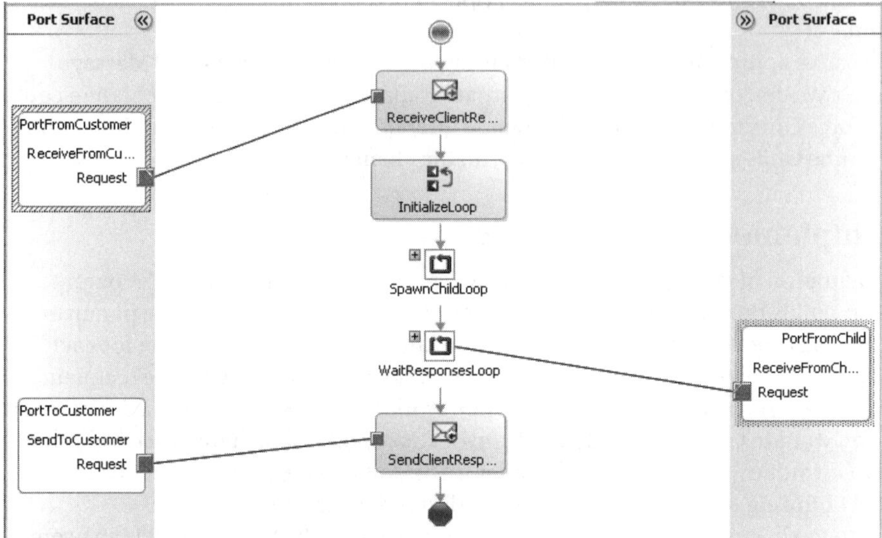

Figure 6-2. *Parent orchestration main blocks*

1. Define the schemas for the Customer Request, Customer Response, Recipient Request, and Recipient Response.
2. Promote a property in the Recipient Request schema that can be used to build the dynamic address of the recipient.
3. Define one message for each of the mentioned schemas, that is, a CustomerRequest, a CustomerResponse, a RecipientRequest, and a RecipientResponse message.
4. Drag a Receive shape to receive a CustomerRequest message from a client application.
5. Define variables to control the two loops of the parent orchestration: the SpawnChild loop and the CollectResponses loop.
6. Drag an Expression shape that you use to calculate the recipient list from the CustomerRequest message and initialize the SpawnChild loop control variable. The customer request message must contain the number of messages to spawn. The SpawnChild variable will contain this number.
7. Drag a Loop shape for the SpawnChild loop and define the Boolean looping control expression.
8. Drag a Loop shape for the CollectResponses loop and define the Boolean looping control expression.
9. Drag a Send shape to return the CustomerResponse message to the client application.

10. Drag two ports to be used as PortFromCustomer and PortToCustomer; their actual properties depend on the particular scenario and are not relevant to the discussion.

11. Drag a port to be used as PortFromChild. In the Port Configuration Wizard, define the following properties:

    a. In the Select a Port Type tab, choose to create a new port type named TypePortFromChild with the communication pattern One-Way.

    b. In the Port Binding tab, choose "I'll always be receiving messages on this port" as port direction of communication.

    c. Choose Direct as port binding and then Self Correlating.[4]

Next, create the SpawnChild loop whose steps are defined here and shown in Figure 6-3.

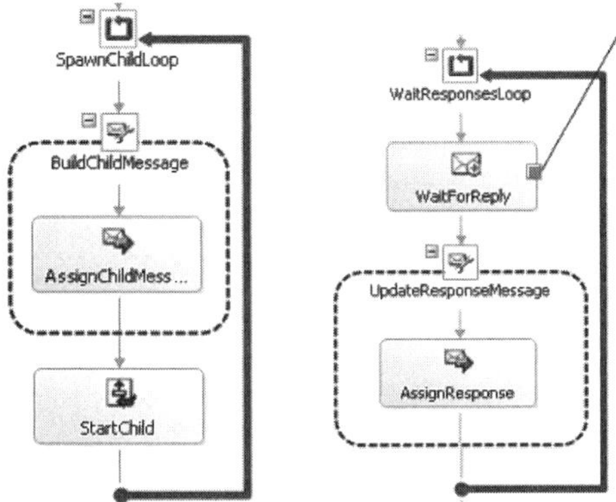

Figure 6-3. *Parent orchestration loops*

1. Drag a Message Assignment shape inside the SpawnChildLoop shape; in the enclosing Construct Message shape, define RecipientRequest as the message to be constructed.

2. In the Message Assignment expression, you will build the RecipientRequest message from the CustomerRequest message according to the current loop cycle; you will probably want to use a helper .NET component to build the message.[5] You will also update an orchestration variable with the number of spawned children.

3. Drag a Start Orchestration shape below the ConstructMessage shape. Leave it unconfigured for the moment.

Once the preceding steps are completed, the final step is to create the wait responses loop as defined here:

1. Drag a Receive shape inside the WaitResponsesLoop shape. Define RecipientResponse as the message that will be received by this shape.

4. Direct port binding and correlation are advanced orchestration topics covered in Chapter 7.

5. Alternatively you could use a BizTalk map to create the new message—either approach will work.

2. Drag a Message Assignment shape below the Receive shape; in the Construct Message shape, define CustomerResponse as the message to be constructed.

3. In the Message Assignment expression, you will build[6] the CustomerResponse message aggregating the RecipientResponse message received in the current loop cycle. You will also update an orchestration variable with the number of received responses that will have to match the number of spawned children to exit the loop.

Create the Child Orchestration:

Once the parent orchestration is created, the next step is to create the child orchestration. The steps for this are defined here and the orchestration is shown in Figure 6-4.

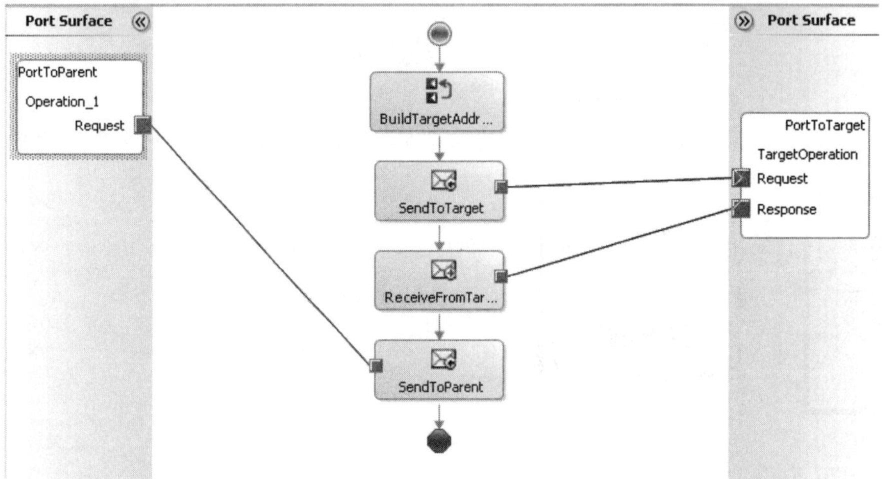

Figure 6-4. *Child orchestration*

You will reuse the Recipient Request and Recipient Response schemas defined before.

1. In the Orchestration View section, right-click Orchestration Parameter and choose New Port Parameter; assign to this port parameter the port type TypePortFromChild, defined previously in the parent orchestration; assign to this port parameter the identifier PortToParent; change the communication direction of this port parameter to Send.

2. Right-click Orchestration Parameter again and choose New Message Parameter; assign to this message parameter the message type RecipientRequest and the identifier MsgFromParent.

3. Define one TargetResponse message that uses the Recipient Response schema.

6. This can be accomplished a number of ways. A potential choice would be to use an aggregating pipeline, collect all the messages to be aggregated, and call the pipeline with the array of messages. An implementation of an aggregating pipeline is given in the BizTalk SDK under the Program Files\Microsoft BizTalk Server 2006\SDK\Pipelines directory. Another choice would be to create a .NET component to accept the messages as they are received and aggregate them together.

4. Drag a port to be used as PortToTarget. In the Port Configuration Wizard, define the following properties:

   a. In the Select a Port Type tab, choose to create a new port type named TypePortToTarget with the communication pattern Request-Response.

   b. In the Port Binding tab, choose "I'll be sending a request and receiving a response" as port direction of communication.

   c. Choose Dynamic as port binding and then choose a receive pipeline and a send pipeline suitable for your Recipient Request and Recipient Response schemas.

5. Drag a Send shape onto the Orchestration Designer surface and name it SendToTarget; configure this shape to send the MsgFromParent message to the PortToTarget port.

6. Drag a Receive shape onto the Orchestration Designer surface that you will name ReceiveFromTarget; configure this shape to receive the TargetResponse message from the PortToTarget port.

7. Drag a Send shape onto the Orchestration Designer surface that you will name SendToParent; configure this shape to send the TargetResponse message to the PortToParent port.

8. Drag an Expression shape at the top of the orchestration that you will name BuildTargetAddress; use this expression to assign the URI to the dynamic port PortToTarget[7] based on the value of a promoted property[8] in the MsgFromParent message.

Bind the Parent Orchestration to the Child Orchestration:

To complete the exercise, you need to add the following additional configuration to the parent orchestration:

1. Double-click the Start Orchestration shape to open its configuration box. In the Select the orchestration you wish to start combo box, select the child orchestration. The Orchestration Parameters grid is automatically updated with the right matches between the variables in scope of the parent orchestration and the parameter name of the child orchestration: the PortFromChild variable is matched with the PortToParent parameter; the RecipientRequest variable is matched with the MsgFromParent parameter.

2. In the Properties pane of the orchestration, change the transaction type to Long Running and set a value for the timeout; otherwise, in case a child orchestration is terminated abnormally, the parent orchestration would wait indefinitely for a response.

The previous exercise shows you how you can use orchestrations to solve a real-world problem. Let's look at another issue that often arises when processing messages—dealing with order.

---

7. The code for the Expression shape will look something like `PortToTarget(Microsoft.XLANGs.BaseTypes.Address) = "Http://wsOrders/Interface.asmx"`.

8. This implementation requires that the address of where the messages are to be sent is known ahead of time. In the original message that was received by the parent orchestration, an element must exist that contains this address. This value must be promoted into the context via either the schema definition or a distinguished field.

Handling Ordered Delivery

As anyone who has worked with HL7[9] would know, ensuring the order of a sequence of messages is a major issue. Most know that BizTalk has a mechanism called Ordered Delivery that is available for a port inside an orchestration or within a messaging port. In short, this setting forces the port to deliver the messages out of the Messagebox in the order in which they were received. This ensures that the First In—First Out pattern is followed when dealing with messages arriving on a port. In BizTalk 2004, this mechanism was only available when using the MSMQT transport adapter. Luckily in BizTalk 2006, ordered delivery has become an adapter-agnostic option and even extends to custom adapters.

Building a Resequencer

Ordered delivery guarantees order in and out of the Messagebox. However, before you can consider the order problem solved, there are a couple of show-stopping things that you need to deal with:

- Using ordered delivery is a major performance bottleneck. As great as this option is, when the rubber hits the road, your overall solution throughput will drop drastically when you use the default End Point Manager (EPM) ordered delivery. This is because the BizTalk engine essentially has to "single-thread" each of the messages as they arrive on the port to their appropriate destination. This means that every message that arrives on the port can only be dequeued, transformed, and delivered one at a time. In many high-throughput scenarios, using the default ordered delivery pattern is simply not an option because of this fact.

- Ordered delivery assumes the messages arrive in the correct order. In many situations, this simply isn't the case. In this scenario, the default ordered delivery pattern simply doesn't work.

As described in Chapter 4, what is needed to implement proper ordering is a **Resequencer** pattern. The job of the resequencer is to examine incoming messages, check the order of the messages (i.e., current message is 7 of 9), and reorder the messages as they arrive into the proper order. To implement such resequencing in BizTalk, you need a couple of components as listed in the following subsections, along with some base assumptions.

Resequencer Assumptions

Like most patterns, the Resequencer pattern is based on a number of assumptions:

- Assuming the messages are arriving out of order, there is a way to examine the incoming message and know

9. Health Level 7 (HL7) is a standard for the exchange of medical information via an electronic format. The standard also has strict requirements about the order in which messages are processed in relation to the order in which they were received. An HL7 accelerator is available for BizTalk and is downloadable from www.microsoft.com/biztalk/evaluation/hl7/default.mspx.

- What number the message is in the sequence to be received
- A flag exists somewhere in the message payload to indicate whether the current fragment is the last in the sequence, or the total number of messages

- Once the messages are received into your resequencer, you can start sending messages out immediately so long as you can preserve the order. For example, assume the messages are arriving into your orchestration in the following order:

  3, 5, 1, 2, 4, 8, 9, 11, 23

  The following diagram illustrates this concept, as it can get a little confusing. Technically once you receive the third message, which is the first message in the logical sequence, you can send it. You then receive the fourth message, which is logical sequence number 2, which you also can immediately send. The resequencer then looks through the list of previously received messages and finds logical sequence numbers 3 and 5, so it immediately sends sequence number 3, since it is next in the logical sequence, and waits for the message that is number 4 in the logical sequence to arrive, since that is the next message that needs to be sent in the logical sequence, but has not yet been received.

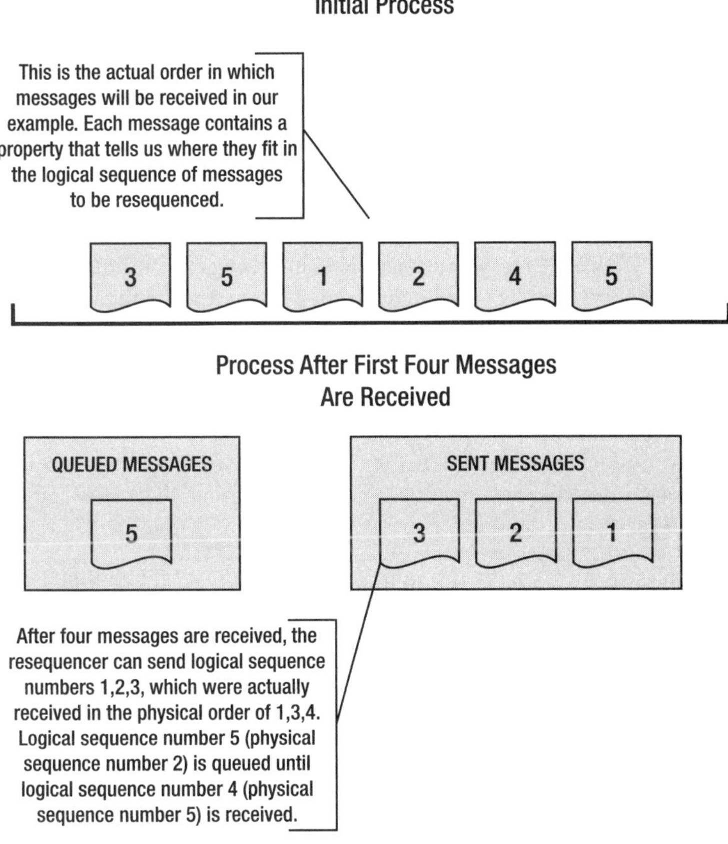
Initial Process
This is the actual order in which messages will be received in our example. Each message contains a property that tells us where they fit in the logical sequence of messages to be resequenced.
3
5
1
2
4
5
Process After First Four Messages Are Received
QUEUED MESSAGES
5
SENT MESSAGES
3
2
1
After four messages are received, the resequencer can send logical sequence numbers 1,2,3, which were actually received in the physical order of 1,3,4. Logical sequence number 5 (physical sequence number 2) is queued until logical sequence number 4 (physical sequence number 5) is received.

- The resequencer is stateful and assists for the life of the sequence. It terminates itself once the last message in the sequence is received.
- The message sequence is atomic. If a message in the sequence cannot be sent, the sequence stops until the issue is fixed.
- In cases where multiple instances of the resequencer are running (i.e., processing multiple distinct sequences), there exists a way to uniquely identify each sequence based on the data in the message. For example, in cases where messages are arriving in distinct interchanges (not from a disassembler or from multiple message parts), there is a way to distinguish which sequence the message belongs to.

BizTalk Components Needed

To implement the resequencer, you will need the following BizTalk components:

- Schema to describe the inbound message
- Custom property schema to hold three properties:
  - The `SequenceID` (GUID that uniquely identifies the sequence)
  - The current `SequenceNumber` (identifies that the message is number XXXX of YYYY in the sequence)
  - `LastMessageInSequence` Boolean, which indicates that the current message is the last in the sequence
- Custom inbound receive pipeline with custom pipeline component:
  - The pipeline component will be responsible for probing the incoming schema and validating whether or not it can handle it, checking for a unique sequence ID in the message as well as the sequence number. Upon finding these, it promotes these values to the message context programmatically. We will call this the **Resequencing Decoder**.
- Orchestration using Convoy pattern with correlation:[10]
  - The orchestration will be initiated by the receipt of the first message received in the sequence. (Note: this message doesn't necessarily need to be the logical first message to be sent.)
  - The orchestration will store the inbound message in a `SortedList` object. The key for the sorted list will be the sequence number.

---

10. Convoys and correlations will be discussed in the next chapter.

- The orchestration will listen for incoming messages after receiving the first one and add them to the array. Upon the receipt of each message, it checks what the next sequence number to be sent is against the list of currently received messages. If the required message hasn't been received yet, it continues to listen for more messages.
- When the required message arrives, it is immediately sent out via the orchestration with a delivery notification.
    - Upon receipt of the delivery notification, the orchestration searches through the `SortedList` of messages to see whether the next sequence number has been received. If it hasn't, it listens for more messages. If it has been received, it is immediately sent, and the loop starts over again.
- The orchestration uses a correlation set that is initialized by the receipt of the first message. The set is correlated based on the `Promoted` property of `SequenceID`, which was promoted in the custom pipeline component.
- When a message arrives that has the `LastMessageInSequence` property set to True, the orchestration stores this message's sequence number in a private variable. When this sequence number is successfully delivered, the orchestration exits the receive messages loop and finishes normally.

The high-level architecture diagram for this pattern is shown in Figure 6-5.

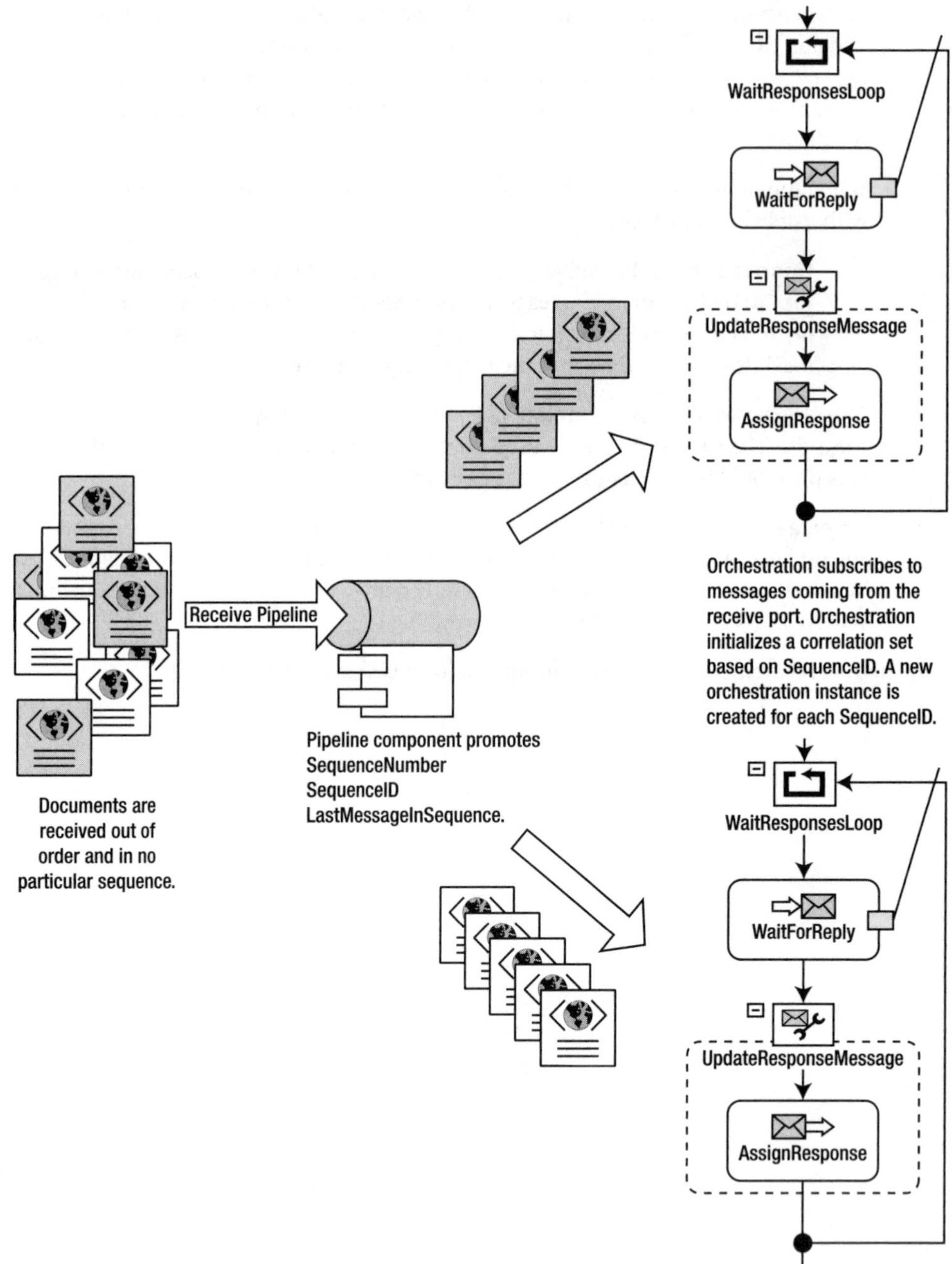

Figure 6-5. *Resequencer implementation*

Building the Solution

As the creation of pipeline components has been well explored in previous chapters and the component implementation is quite simple for this example, let's look at how the orchestration will be implemented. Figures 6-6, 6-7, and 6-8 show how the orchestration will be created.

In the orchestration snippet shown in Figure 6-6, the key areas to observe are at the first Receive shape and the receiving loop. The first Receive shape initializes the correlation set. The correlation set is using the `PropertySchema.SequenceID` that you defined and promoted within your custom pipeline upon receipt of the message. The IsLastFragment Decide shape is checking the Boolean `IsLastMessage` property using an XPath expression.[11] If it is not the last fragment, the Expression shape adds the message to a `SortedList` variable and sets a private integer variable, which stores what the last `SequenceNumber` was for the received message.

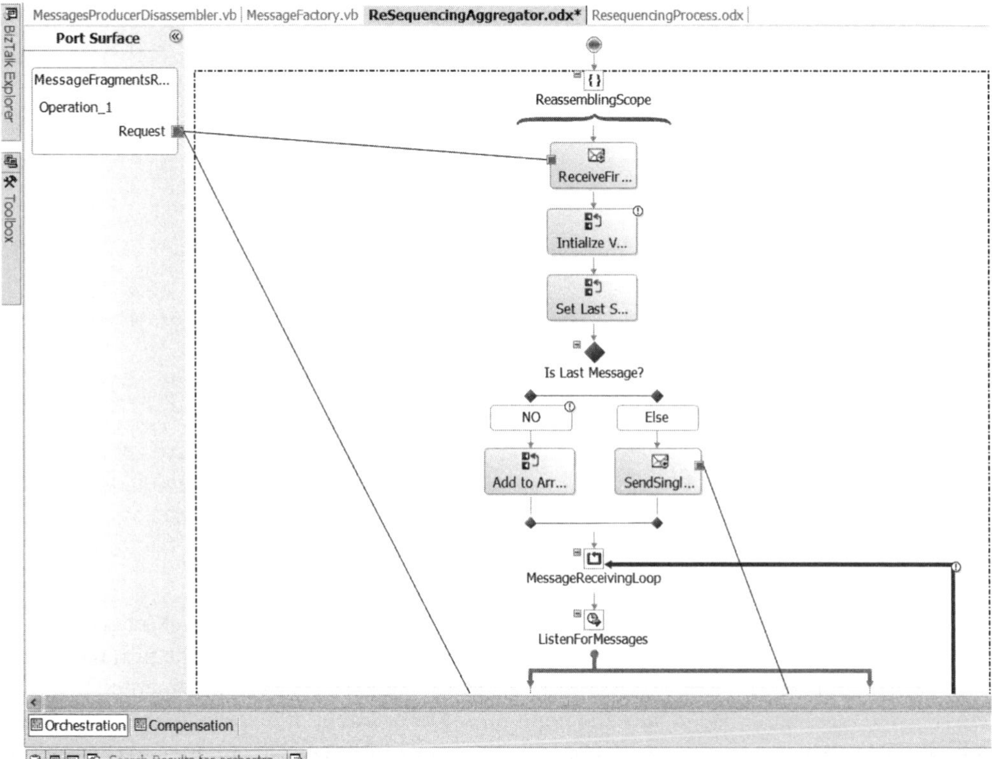

Figure 6-6. *Orchestration beginnning*

11. As stated previously, this is not the optimal way to do this. Checking the property via XPath will cause the whole document to be loaded and parsed by the XLANG engine. A more elegant way to do this would be to change the inbound schema to have an `IsLastMessage` element and add a custom distinguished field as demonstrated in Chapter 4.

The loop illustrated in Figure 6-7 is responsible for receiving incoming messages as they are processed. The second receive message is a follower of the original correlation set that was initialized by the first receive. From this point on, this is a typical Convoy pattern implementation.[12]

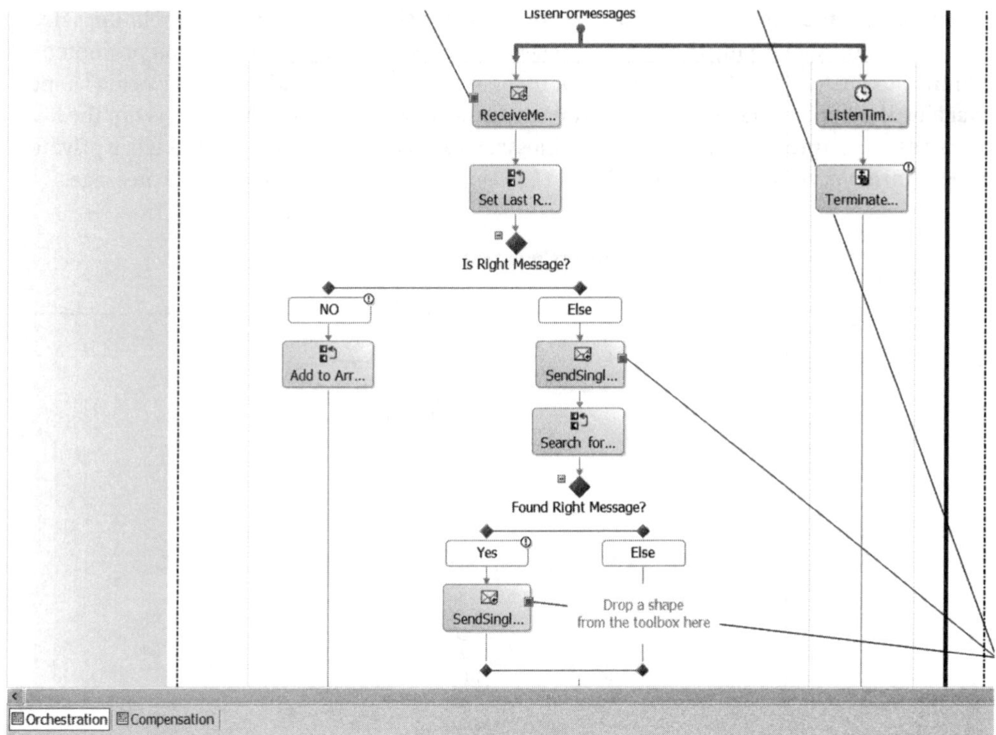

Figure 6-7. *The receiving loop*

What happens next is that when the next message is received, its `SequenceNumber` is checked against the internal variable for the next required `SequenceNumber`. The next required sequence number is simply the last in-order received sequence number incremented by 1. If the received message does not have the required `SequenceNumber`, it is added to the `SortedList` object. If it is, then it is immediately sent and the `SortedList` is checked for the next lowest received sequence number to see whether it should be set as well. This repeats until all messages that could be sent are.

The final step in the process once all the messages have been received and sent in the proper order is to perform cleanup (see Figure 6-8). In this pattern, the received messages were stored to disk in a temporary location as they were received. Cleanup is an optional step

12. See http://msdn.microsoft.com/library/default.asp?url=/library/en-us/BTS_2004WP/html/956fd4cb-aacc-43ee-99b6-f6137a5a2914.asp. The concept of a convoy is not new by any means in BizTalk 2006. Convoys are a simple messaging pattern that exist from the previous version of the product and are documented well in the referenced article.

and isn't required. It is useful, however, when you want to see how many messages were received and verify that all messages have been sent out in cases where you are debugging. The last step in this orchestration is to delete those messages from the location once the resequencer has finished.

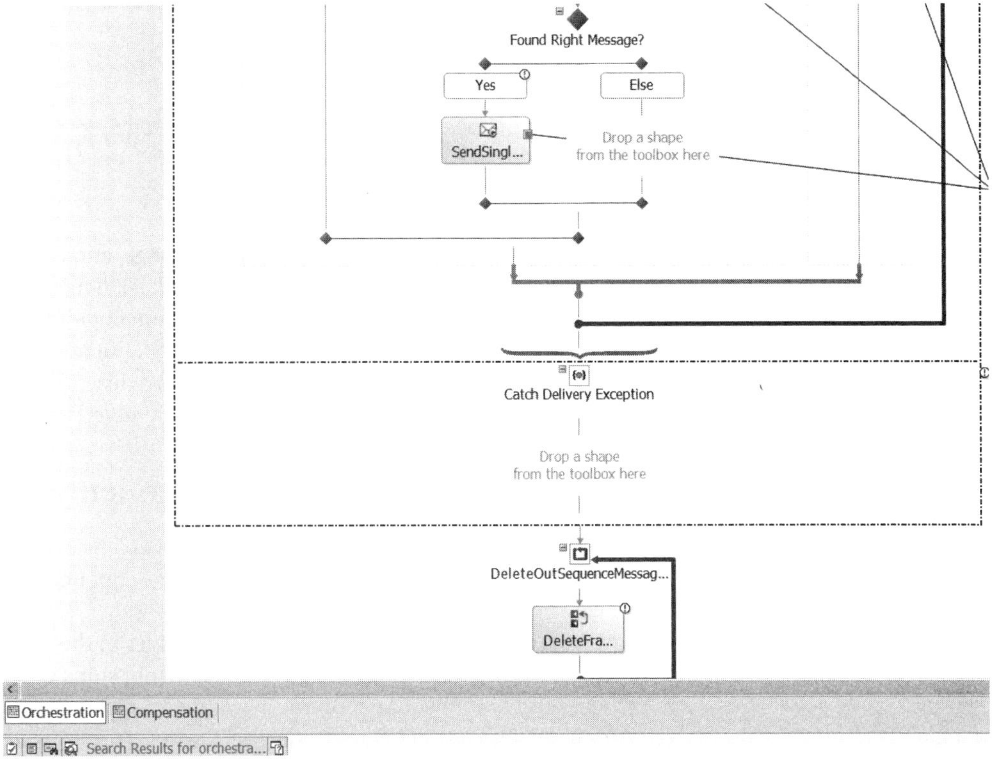

Figure 6-8. *Orchestration finish*

Also note the Catch block illustrated in Figure 6-8. In the described Resequencer pattern, there is no implementation for the scenario where a message in the sequence cannot be delivered. In most cases, the implementation would be a simple Terminate shape or a Throw Exception shape depending on the requirements. In some cases, it may be possible to recover from the scenario in which a message cannot be delivered. If this is the case, you could implement the offline message storage to disk and input a Suspend shape. Logic would be needed to restart the orchestration, remember what messages have already been received and sent, and resend the message that was in error.

Building a Resequencing Aggregator

So now that you know how to solve the problem of receiving messages out of order, you can properly receive messages, resequence them, and send them in the correct order to their destination. But what about batch scenarios—what happens in the case where you need to combine the received messages, order them, and then aggregate them into a batch? This need is quite common in the EDI world where batching has existed for years. Also, in many legacy system integration projects, large aggregated data files are needed to load downstream systems with data. For example, let's look at the company ABC example. Assume that orders received from the FTP bulk upload are compressed and need to be sent as a batch to the fulfillment system, which only understands flat text files. Luckily you have all the pieces you need to solve this except one. To recap, you can

1. Use the Unzip component from Chapter 5 to decompress the files.
2. Use the resequencing pipeline and pipeline component from the resequencing example to add the sequence information.
3. Use the resequencing orchestration to order them properly.

However, you still have no way to A) combine the messages into one message, and B) turn the sorted list of the messages received into a flat file. Luckily, with BizTalk 2006 this becomes a trivial task. There are, however, two possible solutions to this problem depending on how the messages are received. If the messages are not received as described, but are received as independent Interchanges, you need to use the Resequencer pattern described previously. If they are indeed received as a batch, a more elegant solution is available.

Solution 1: Status Quo—Messages Received As Independent Interchanges

If the messages are received independently, a simple change is required to the resequencing orchestration to allow the pattern to work. All you need to do is **not** send the messages as they arrive and wait to receive all messages before sending them. Once all the messages in the batch are received, you can use the new Call Pipeline from Orchestration code that ships with BizTalk 2006 to send the `SortedList` to a send pipeline that contains a flat-file Assembler component. So long as the messages are defined with a schema that uses the flat-file extensions of BizTalk, the pipeline will return a text message with all the messages inside aggregated in their proper order. The orchestration will look something like Figure 6-9.

The code for the Call Send Pipeline Expression shape will look like this:

```
//Initialize pipeline output
AggregatedOutMessage = null;
//Add the messages to the list via a component
PipelineHelper.AddSortedMessages(SortedList, SendPipeMsg)
Microsoft.XLANGs.Pipeline.XLANGPipelineManager.ExecuteSendPipeline
(typeof(ABC.BizTalk.Pipelines.FlatFileSendPipeline),SendPipeMsg,
AggregatedOutMessage);
```

You will need to use a Construct shape, since the shape is creating new messages via the component. The `SendPipeMsg` is of type Microsoft.XLANGs.Pipeline.SendPipelineInputMessages. The reason why you need to add these messages to the `SendPipeMsg` via a component is because within the component you will need to loop through each of the messages stored in the sorted list, and add them one at a time to the `SendPipeMsg` to ensure that the order is properly maintained. Alternatively, you could use a Loop shape in the orchestration, but this is much easier done in code. Once this is done, the send pipeline is called, the messages are aggregated, and the complete message is sent to the send port.

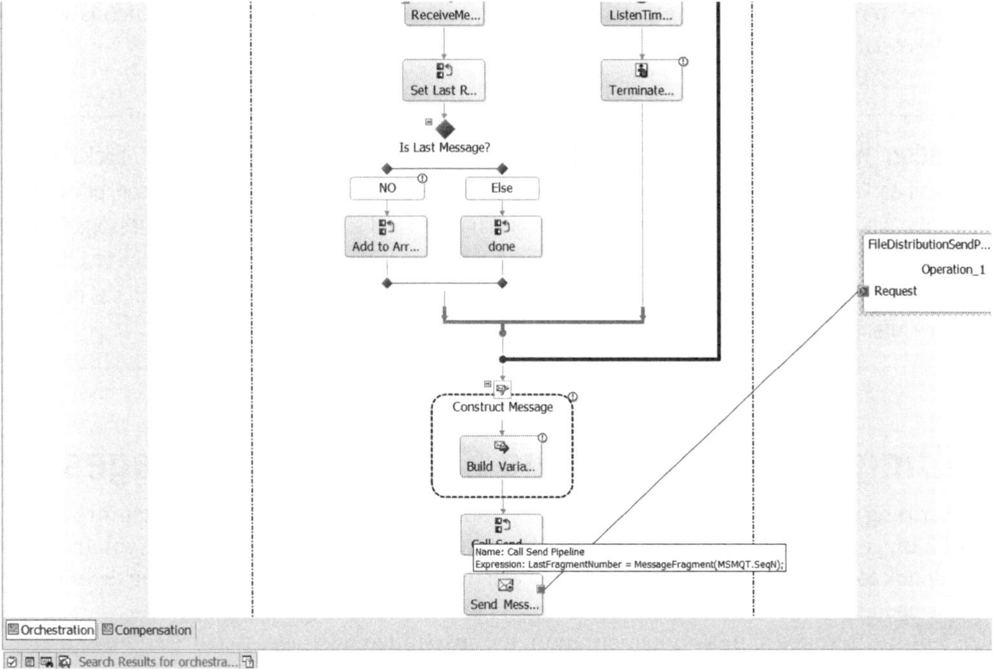

Figure 6-9. *Aggregating resequencing orchestration*

Solution 2: Not So Status Quo—Messages Received As a Batch

In the resequencing aggregator outlined earlier, the messages are received as a complete Interchange. They may be out of order when stored inside the ZIP file, but they are completely batched as a whole. In this case, you actually don't need a resequencing orchestration and can implement this solution entirely within a pipeline and use content-based routing.

Let's reexamine our list of pipeline components from previous examples:

- **Unzip component**: The Unzip component extracts the ZIP file contents and creates a multipart message based on the files included.
- **Resequencing Decoder**: The component examines a message and determines where it fits within a unique sequence.

What if you modified the Resequencing Decoder to handle multipart messages? In this scenario, the component would have additional smarts to know that multipart messages can also be resequenced. In this case, the component would simply loop through each of the message parts, examine its data, determine what number it is in the sequence, and promote that property along with the unique sequence ID and the last message in the sequence property. Also in this case, you need to use another message part feature—they have a property bag. So instead of promoting the values to the message context of the message, you simply write these values as key/value pairs to the parts property bag. Once all the message parts are resequenced properly, the message can flow through BizTalk like any other message. The send port hosting the FlatFileAssembling component would be subscribed for messages of this type, parse the incoming messages, and output one aggregated message, which is sent to the downstream system.

■Caution While the preceding example is technically easier to implement, it has some drawbacks. First, as stated earlier, since pipeline execution is stateful, should the pipeline fail for whatever reason, processing stops. You will manually need to have some error-handling logic and subscribe to the failed message for processing. This is explored in the next section. Also, care should be taken to properly performance test the solution. If the ZIP file is large and contains a high number of individual transactions, the CPU on this machine could be affected. Make sure that you test this scenario properly before implementing it.

Editing and Resubmitting Suspended Messages

Subscribing to an event and pulling messages from BizTalk Server is a fairly straightforward task. A bigger problem is that now that you have the suspended message, how do you fix it and get it back to BizTalk? Ultimately the answer will depend on the roles involved, the technology that is used, and the business process necessary around handling the messages.

For the purpose of this implementation, the suspended messages that are addressed are inbound messages that fail validation. This can often happen when a message is sent into the integration solution that is malformed. Other errors may occur, but this is the most common scenario for resubmitting messages.

Strategy for Edit and Resubmit

Subscribing to the MSBTS_ServiceInstanceSuspendedEvent and calling the `SaveToFile` method allows access to the suspended message and its context.[13] If it has multiple message parts, each is saved to a separate file. The context file contains the message and message part information. This gives developers all the information they need to handle the message. Chapter 10 provides examples for allowing a user to save the files and get the file names. This implementation will use those concepts. After this point, there are a number of different decisions that you will need to make. The rest of this section briefly addresses a number of those decisions.

Pulling Data from the Suspended Queue

In pulling the data from the suspended queue, you could just pull the data itself and try to process the message, but then you are lacking any context for the origination of the message. Most likely this context will be necessary in order to route the message to the appropriate support personnel, resubmit the message, or take other steps with the message. To handle this problem, the same Windows service that you will create to capture the suspended event will create a new canonical format based off the message context and the message data.

---

13. These subsections and upcoming exercise originally appeared in "Edit and Resubmit from Suspend Queue" (REED000632).doc. Copyright by Microsoft Corporation. Reprinted with permission from Microsoft Corporation.

Canonical Format

One strategy this implementation is using is a canonical format for the suspended message, SuspendedMessage.xsd. This schema is provided later in this chapter. This contains a context section for the message that can contain any particular contextual information that needs to be passed along. For example, the receive port name may be included. The other part of the message contains the message parts themselves. In the walkthrough described later in Exercise 6-2, the data is stored in an element that is marked as a CDATA tag. CDATA sections are ignored by XML parsers and allow you to include any data you want in them, regardless of format.

Clients for Editing the Message

For editing a document, there are two obvious options. One is to use an ASP.NET page that will take the raw data file and display it in a text box. The other is to use InfoPath, which could consume the canonical XML document and display that in a form. InfoPath is a natural fit for this, except that the data you want to edit is one element in your XML document, but represents your entire message. If the message is a flat file, it could contain invalid XML characters. To get around this problem, you could place the data in a CDATA section. The challenge though is what control to use in InfoPath. There are restrictions on using a rich text-box control, which would otherwise be a great choice. A text box is possible with XML documents. Also in InfoPath SP1, you can specify the text box to show carriage returns.

Additional Workflow

In this implementation, orchestration is not used to control the flow of the SuspendedMessage XML file. If this example were expanded, it would be advantageous to use an orchestration. With an orchestration, the SuspendedMessage XML document could be sent into the orchestration, do some additional processing, call rules, and then route the document to the appropriate user or group of users who need to fix the message. Once the user fixes the message, it could be routed back to the orchestration, and the orchestration could do further processing. Also, by using an orchestration, you could later leverage BAM to be able to get additional insight into your suspended messages.

Moving Correct Data Back into BizTalk

Once data is corrected, it needs to get back into the Messagebox. One option is to add a web service receive location to the same receive port where the messages were originally sent. This will allow orchestration-bound ports and subscribers to a receive port to still receive the message. The disadvantage is an extra receive location is necessary for each receive port that needs to handle suspended messages.

Another option for moving data back into BizTalk is to have a generic orchestration do a direct binding and send the data directly to the Messagebox. As long as no routing is based on the receive port, you will still be OK. However, if the message is a non-XML file that must first be disassembled, you need to send it back through a receive location for pipeline processing.

Sample Flows for Edit and Resubmit

Figures 6-10 through 6-12 represent possible flows for editing and resubmission of messages to BizTalk Server. These are just possibilities that have their own pros and cons. Hopefully, this will give you some additional ideas on how to best handle suspended messages for your particular solution.

Figure 6-10 illustrates the easiest, although most manual, of the three flows.

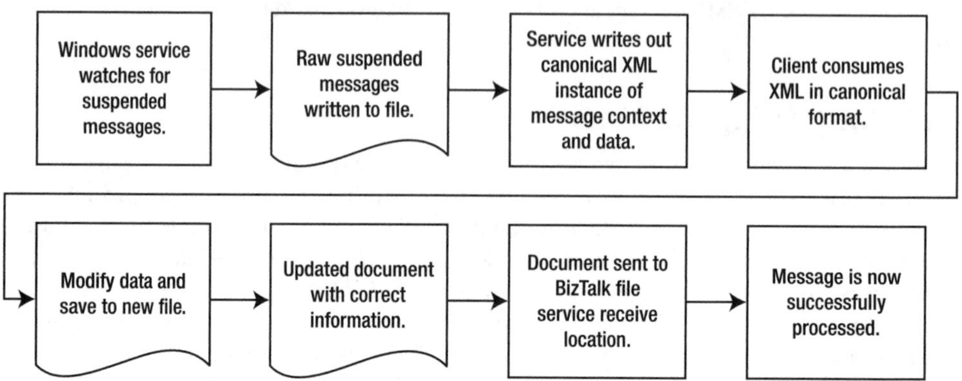

Figure 6-10. *Editing and resubmitting with file receive*

The flow in Figure 6-11 leverages an orchestration to route the message to Windows SharePoint Services. This strategy would allow the solution to be able to route messages to different groups and people based on their roles. The Business Rule Engine could be used to implement the routing logic. The Business Rule Engine could provide the URL and adapter information for message resubmission based upon a given message type. When resubmitting the document back to BizTalk, the client would send the message back to a web service that is specific for that particular message type. A solution could have the flow shown in Figure 6-11.

Finally, the flow in Figure 6-12 builds off of that in Figure 6-11 and uses a long-running orchestration to keep track of the progress of the message. This allows further processing to be done if desired. The solution also submits directly back to the Messagebox, which may or may not be desired depending on whether the message requires processing in a receive pipeline.

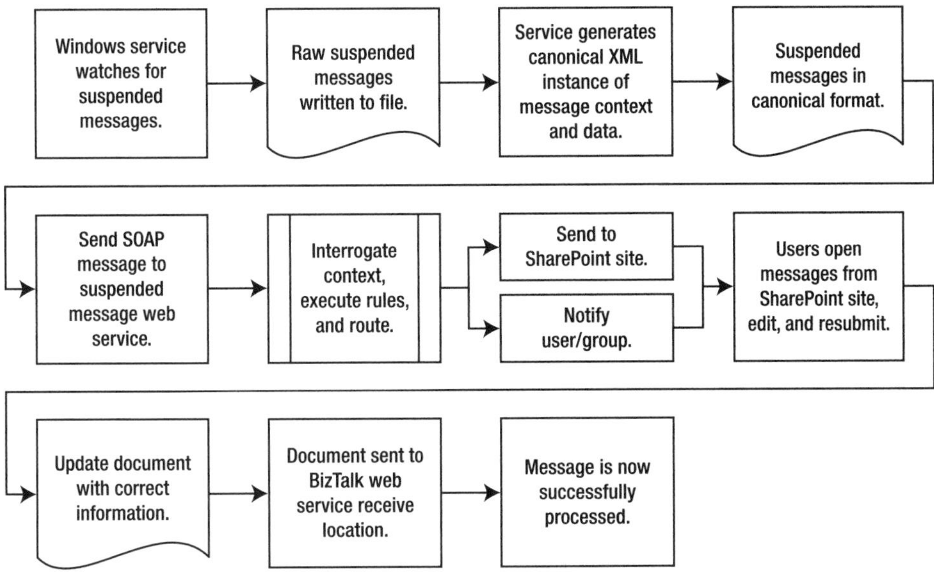

Figure 6-11. *Editing and resubmitting with routing and SharePoint*

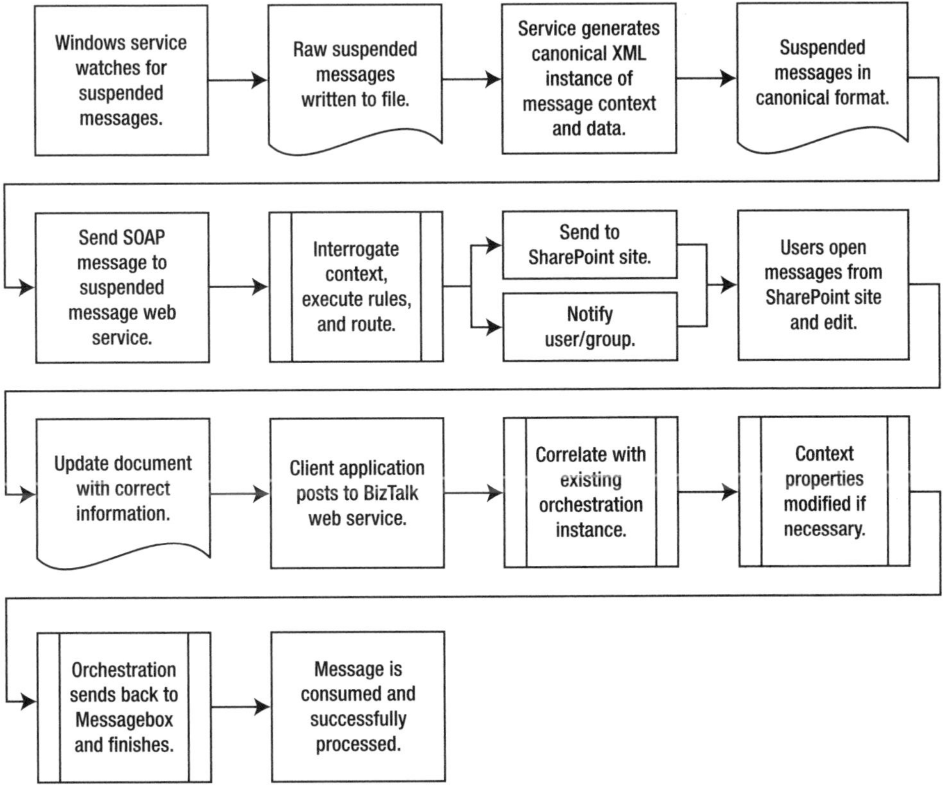

Figure 6-12. *Editing and resubmitting with orchestration correlation*

Pseudo-Walkthrough to Perform Edits and Resubmits

Exercise 6-2 describes in detail the steps to edit and resubmit a suspended message. The walkthrough in Exercise 6-2 follows the steps in Figure 6-11, shown earlier in this section.

Exercise 6-2: Creating a New Windows Service Project and Applying Settings

Create the Suspended Message Handler Service:

The following steps are used to create the Windows service that will poll for suspended messages:

1. Start Microsoft Visual Studio 2005.
2. On the File menu, point to New, and then click Project.
3. Click Visual Basic Projects under Project Types, and then click Windows Service under Templates.
4. Type **BizTalkSuspendedMessageHandlerService** in the Name text box. Change location if necessary. Click OK.
5. In the Code Editor window, right-click Design View, and then click Properties.
6. In the Properties pane, click the Add Installer link.
7. Change the display name to BizTalk Suspended Message Handler Service.
8. In the Properties pane for serviceInstaller1, change the ServiceName property to Service1.

■ **Note** The ServiceName property needs to match the name of the service class.

---

9. Change StartType to Automatic.
10. In the Code Editor window in Design view, click serviceProcessInstaller1.

    Note that the account is set to User. When the service is installed, it will need to be set to an account that has access to the BizTalk resources.

Add a Configuration File:

1. Right-click the project and choose Add New Item.
2. Double-click Application Configuration File in the right-hand pane.
3. Between the configuration tags paste the following XML:

```
<appSettings>
    <add key="SuspendedMessagesTempFileLocation" value="MyDrive:\MyFolder" />
    <add key="SuspendedMessagesFileLocation" value="MyDrive:\MyFolder" />
    <add key="ProcessingInstruction" value="MyInfoPathProcessingInstruction"/>
</appSettings>
```

4. Replace "MyDrive:\MyFolder" with appropriate paths. SuspendedMessagesTempFileLocation is the location where the message parts and context will get saved. SuspendedMessagesFileLocation is the location for the SuspendedMessage instance.

5. Replace processing instructions if desired within the XML file to point to the proper InfoPath form you wish to open. An example of one is

```
solutionVersion='1.0.0.1' productVersion='11.0.5531' PIVersion='1.0.0.0'
href='file:///C:\My%20Documents\EditAndResubmit\InfoPathForms\
SuspendedMessage.xsn' language='en-us'
```

Add References and Class Variables:

1. Add a reference within the project to System.Management.dll and System.Configuration.dll.

2. In Solution Explorer, right-click Service1.vb, and then click View Code.

3. At the top of the page add the following Imports statements:

```
Imports System.Management
Imports System.Xml
Imports System.IOt
Imports System.Configuration
```

4. Within the class declaration, just under

```
private components as System.ComponentModel.Container = nothing
```

add the following:

```
private watcher as ManagementEventWatcher
```

Add Code to OnStart:

1. In Solution Explorer, right-click Service1.cs, and then click View Code.

2. In the OnStart event handler, replace the comments with the following:

```
'Listen for messages
Dim scope as string = "root\\MicrosoftBizTalkServer"
Dim wqlQuery  as string = "Select * from MSBTS_ServiceInstanceSuspendedEvent"
watcher = new ManagementEventWatcher(scope, wqlQuery)
AddHandler watcher.EventArrived, AddressOf MyEventHandler watcher.Start
```

This will start listening for the ServiceInstanceSuspended event.

Add Custom Event Handler:

1. Add the following two procedures to the Service 1 class:

```
Public Shared Sub MyEventHandler(sender As Object, e As EventArrivedEventArgs)
   Try
      ' Read the TempDirectoryName from config file
      Dim TempDirectoryName As String = _
```

```
ConfigurationManager.AppSettings("SuspendedMessagesTempFileLocation")
        ' Read WaitingDirectoryName
        ' This folder is the location for the new XML document that this service
        ' creates based on context and message parts.
        Dim WaitingDirectoryName As String = _
ConfigurationSettings.AppSettings("SuspendedMessagesFileLocation")
        ' If you want to add processing instructions for InfoPath
        ' this will get it.
        Dim pi As String = _
ConfigurationSettings.AppSettings("ProcessingInstruction")

        Dim waitingMessageFileName As String
        ' xwriter for suspended message
        Dim xwriter As XmlTextWriter

        'Look up MSBTS_ServiceInstanceSuspendedEvent
        'in the BTS04/06 documentation for additional properties
        Dim ErrorID As String = e.NewEvent("ErrorID").ToString()
        Dim ErrorCategory As String = e.NewEvent("ErrorCategory").ToString()
        Dim ErrorDescription As String =
e.NewEvent("ErrorDescription").ToString()
        Dim ServiceStatus As String = e.NewEvent("ServiceStatus").ToString()
        Dim ServiceInstanceID As String = e.NewEvent("InstanceID").ToString()
        Dim enumOptions As New EnumerationOptions()

        enumOptions.ReturnImmediately = False

        Dim MessageInstancesInServiceInstance As New _
ManagementObjectSearcher("root\MicrosoftBizTalkServer", _
"Select * from MSBTS_MessageInstance where ServiceInstanceID='" + _
ServiceInstanceID + "'", enumOptions)
        'Enumerate through the result set
        Dim MessageInstance As ManagementObject
        For Each MessageInstance In  MessageInstancesInServiceInstance.Get()
            ' The only way to get at the message body is to utilize the ➥
SaveToFile
            ' method on the BTS_MessageInstance WMI Class.
            ' This saves all of the message information to files.
            ' Each MessagePart making up a message is saved in separate files,
            ' typically you only get a Body, but you must cater to multipart
            ' messages to cover all scenarios.
            ' As well as the MessageParts, a context file is created; you need to
            ' use this to extract the MessagePartIDs and MessagePartNames so you
            ' can then work out the file names to open!
            ' The context file name format is
            ' <MessageInstanceID>_context.xml.
            ' And then the actual message information file name format is
```

```
        ' <MessageInstanceID>_<MessagePartID>[_<MessagePartName>].out
        ' MessagePartName is only required if the MessagePart has a name!
        ' You need to build this file name up so you can load it up -
        ' no hacking here!
        ' Save the files
        MessageInstance.InvokeMethod("SaveToFile", New Object() _
{TempDirectoryName})

        ' Get the MessageInstanceID
        Dim MessageInstanceID As String = _
 MessageInstance("MessageInstanceID").ToString()

        ' You now need to load the context file up to get the MessagePart
        ' information
        Dim ContextFileName As String

        ' Load the context file up
        Dim doc As New XmlDocument()
        doc.Load(ContextFileName)

        ' Pull out context properties that you are interested in
        Dim ReceivedFileName As String = GetContextProperty(doc, _
 "ReceivedFileName")
        Dim InboundTransportLocation As String = GetContextProperty(doc, _
 "InboundTransportLocation")
        Dim InterchangeID As String = GetContextProperty(doc, _
"InterchangeID")
        Dim ReceivePortID As String = GetContextProperty(doc, _
"ReceivePortID")
        Dim ReceivePortName As String = GetContextProperty(doc, _
 "ReceivePortName")

        ' Create an XmlWriter to store the data.
        ' This will get written to a file when complete.
        waitingMessageFileName = [String].Format("")
        xwriter = New XmlTextWriter(waitingMessageFileName, _
 System.Text.Encoding.UTF8)
                xwriter.Formatting = Formatting.Indented
        xwriter.WriteStartDocument()
        'Write the ProcessingInstruction node.
        xwriter.WriteProcessingInstruction("mso-infoPathSolution", pi)
        xwriter.WriteProcessingInstruction("mso-application", _
"progid=""InfoPath.Document""")
        xwriter.WriteComment(String.Format("Created on {0}", _
DateTime.Now.ToString()))
        ' Write the context information
        xwriter.WriteStartElement("ns0", "SuspendedMessage", _
```

```
"http://Microsoft.BizTalk.SuspendQueue.SuspendedMessage")
        xwriter.WriteStartElement("Context")
        xwriter.WriteElementString("ReceivedFileName", ReceivedFileName)
        xwriter.WriteElementString("InboundTransportLocation", _
InboundTransportLocation)
        xwriter.WriteElementString("InterchangeID", InterchangeID)
        xwriter.WriteElementString("ReceivePortID", ReceivePortID)
        xwriter.WriteElementString("ReceivePortName", ReceivePortName)
        xwriter.WriteEndElement() ' Context
        ' Start the Message Element
        xwriter.WriteStartElement("Message")

        ' Use XPath to return all of the MessagePart(s) referenced in the
        ' context
        ' You can then load the file up to get the message information
        Dim MessageParts As XmlNodeList = _
doc.SelectNodes("/MessageInfo/PartInfo/MessagePart")
        Dim MessagePart As XmlNode
        For Each MessagePart In  MessageParts
           ' Pull the MessagePart info out that you need
           Dim MessagePartID As String = MessagePart.Attributes("ID").Value
           Dim MessagePartName As String = ➥
MessagePart.Attributes("Name").Value
           Dim Contents As String
           Dim FileName As String
           ' If you have a MessagePartName, append this to the end of
           ' the file name. It's optional so if you don't have it, don't
           ' worry about it.
           If MessagePartName.Length > 0 Then
              FileName = [String].Format("")
            End If

           ' Load the message, place it in canonical schema, and submit it.
           ' Create an instance of StreamReader to read from a file.
           ' The using statement also closes the StreamReader.
           Dim sr As New StreamReader(FileName)
           Try
              ' Read to end of file
              Contents = sr.ReadToEnd()
           Finally
              sr.Dispose()
           End Try

           ' Write out MessagePart data
           xwriter.WriteStartElement("MessagePart")
           xwriter.WriteElementString("MessagePartId", MessagePartID)
```

```
            xwriter.WriteElementString("Name", MessagePartName)
            xwriter.WriteStartElement("Contents")
            ' Write out contents as CDATA.
            xwriter.WriteCData(Contents)
            xwriter.WriteEndElement() ' Contents
            xwriter.WriteEndElement() ' MessagePart
         Next MessagePart
         xwriter.WriteEndElement() ' Message
         xwriter.WriteEndElement() ' SuspendedMessage
         xwriter.Close()
      Next MessageInstance
   End Try
End Sub 'MyEventHandler

' Helper function to pull out context properties given a property name
Private Shared Function GetContextProperty(doc As XmlDocument, propertyName ➥
As _
String) As String
   Dim MessageContext As XmlNode = _
doc.SelectSingleNode(("/MessageInfo/ContextInfo/Property[@Name='" + _
propertyName"']"))
   If Not (MessageContext Is Nothing) Then
      If Not (MessageContext.Attributes("Value") Is Nothing) Then
         Return MessageContext.Attributes("Value").Value
      Else
         Return "Value no found"
      End If
   Else
      Return "Property not found"
   End If
End Function 'GetContextProperty
```

Compile Project and Install Windows Service:

1. Under the Build menu, select Build Solution.
2. Open a command prompt and change to the project root directory of this project.
3. From the command line type the following:

   "<Drive>:\WINDOWS\Microsoft.NET\Framework\ v2.0.50727\installutil.exe" "bin\Debug\BizTalkSuspendedMessageHandlerService.exe"

   "<Drive>" is the drive letter where Windows is installed. This will install the EXE as a Windows service.
4. A prompt will come up asking you for credentials. Enter credentials that have access to the BizTalk resources. After entering credentials, a message should be returned indicating success and that the install was completed.

5. From Administrative Tools, open Services.
6. Find the new service, Service1. Right-click and select Start. The service will now start, and the system will write out suspended messages from both the SaveToFile procedure and the canonical SuspendedMessage message that the service creates itself.

Create Client to Edit XML in Canonical Format:

The Windows service that you've created generates a new XML document according to the following XSD:

```
<?xml version="1.0" encoding="utf-16"?>
<xs:schema xmlns="http://Microsoft.BizTalk.SuspendQueue.SuspendedMessage"
 xmlns:b=http://schemas.microsoft.com/BizTalk/2003
 targetNamespace=http://Microsoft.BizTalk.SuspendQueue.SuspendedMessage
 xmlns:xs="http://www.w3.org/2001/XMLSchema">
  <xs:element name="SuspendedMessage">
    <xs:complexType>
      <xs:sequence>
        <xs:element name="Context">
          <xs:complexType>
            <xs:sequence>
              <xs:element name="ReceivedFileName" type="xs:string" />
              <xs:element name="InboundTransportLocation" type="xs:string" />
              <xs:element name="InterchangeID" type="xs:string" />
              <xs:element name="ReceivePortID" type="xs:string" />
              <xs:element name="ReceivePortName" type="xs:string" />
            </xs:sequence>
          </xs:complexType>
        </xs:element>
        <xs:element name="Message">
          <xs:complexType>
            <xs:sequence>
              <xs:element minOccurs="1" maxOccurs="unbounded"
 name="MessagePart">
                <xs:complexType>
                  <xs:sequence>
                    <xs:element name="MessagePartId" type="xs:string" />
                    <xs:element name="Name" type="xs:string" />
                    <xs:element name="Contents" type="xs:string" />
                  </xs:sequence>
                </xs:complexType>
              </xs:element>
            </xs:sequence>
          </xs:complexType>
        </xs:element>
      </xs:sequence>
    </xs:complexType>
  </xs:element>
</xs:schema>
```

In order to consume the XML document generated in accordance with this schema, you need to load the document into some type of editor and modify the contents of the original message contained in the `<Contents>` element. One option for this is InfoPath. Specifically InfoPath with SP1 may be more useful because it has a Paragraph Breaks option for text boxes that allows for easier viewing of data. You may also experience problems when trying to perform changes on flat files, since most flat files use CR and LF. Flat files will need to be tested to see whether they work with this scenario.

If you are going to use InfoPath, you can easily create a new form based on the preceding schema, modify the app.config file of the Windows service to point to the processing instruction for the InfoPath form, and then be able to open the SuspendedMessage XML files that get generated. Once modified, you can just save the app.config file.

Send Document to BizTalk File Service Receive Location:

The data within the `<Contents>` element represents the actual data for each suspended message part. Once this data has been repaired, there are two easy options for resubmitting the file:

- Copy and paste the value within the `<Contents>` element into a new file within Notepad. Place this new file within the receive location drop directory to be processed by BizTalk.
- Create a simple submit button on your InfoPath form that reads the `<Contents>` element and submits the file to BizTalk based upon the `ReceivedFileName` and `InboundTransportLocation` context property values.

Managing Exceptions in Orchestrations

Designing consistent reusable patterns for exception management within any development project is a fundamental necessity to ensure maintainability and supportability of the application once it's deployed. BizTalk development introduces somewhat new challenges due to the distributed nature of the BizTalk infrastructure. For example, a typical BizTalk application may leverage the BizTalk messaging features, then optionally start an orchestration for processing, call the Business Rule Engine, interact with several lines of business LOB (Line of Business) or ERP systems, and return a response back to another third-party system. This is the typical scenario shown in the previous fictitious examples in the previous chapters. In addition, the execution runtime of these components, including the BizTalk subsystems, may be distributed across one or more servers within the current environment.

The use case just described is not atypical, and would entail catching and reporting on exceptions possibly generated by several decoupled subsystems within BizTalk as well as numerous third-party LOB systems with their own exception-handling constraints. Building on the previous scenario of the fictitious company ABC, what if the mainframe rejected errors while accepting orders from the web site? How does the web site compensate for this, and how should the user be notified? The developer is faced with several exception-reporting options in a BizTalk environment:

- Health Activity and Tracker (HAT)
- BizTalk Administration Console
- Microsoft Event Log
- Custom development options

Given the complexity, the development of a consistent solution for application exception management should embody several common design goals:

- Standardize how application exceptions are detected and caught in the BizTalk environment, i.e., messaging and orchestration subsystems.
- Provide common patterns that allow automated processes to react and manage application exceptions.
- Provide a loosely coupled exception management pattern that facilitates reuse.
- Develop a common reporting paradigm of application exceptions and their available message state that applies to any BizTalk subsystem.

The BizTalk product team considered some of these points during the development of BizTalk Server 2006. For example, BizTalk Server 2006 introduced the **Failed Message Routing** feature. This essentially allowed users to create orchestration processes or messaging send ports that could be configured to "subscribe" to any exceptions that occurred at the messaging subsystem level.

Consider the following scenario:

A user submits financial records to BizTalk. During the parsing and validation stage, an exception is thrown.

Using BizTalk Server 2004, the message would be moved to a suspended queue where limited options were available. For instance, an operator would first have to independently detect that an exception did in fact occur. Then, the message would have to be manually saved to disk from the HAT user interface. Next, the message would have to be manually corrected and resubmitted to the system.

In BizTalk Server 2006, an operator can simply create either an orchestration or a messaging send port that subscribes to any failed message, thereby solving the issue of automated error detection and routing the original message state for processing. Unfortunately, there was no time to build a similar feature for orchestrations. This leaves you today with two very different ways in which exceptions are processed and managed within a BizTalk system. It's up to the developer to customize the exception handling as necessary.

Failed Message Routing was not the only new feature that shipped with BizTalk Server 2006. A new BizTalk Administration Console provides a set of Group Hub pages that allows the query of suspended instances and exceptions grouped by either application, service name, error code, or URI, as shown in Figure 6-13. Although this provides a common user interface to view exceptions, its views are limited to "live" service instances, and examining state can be a bit cumbersome due to the drill-down required.

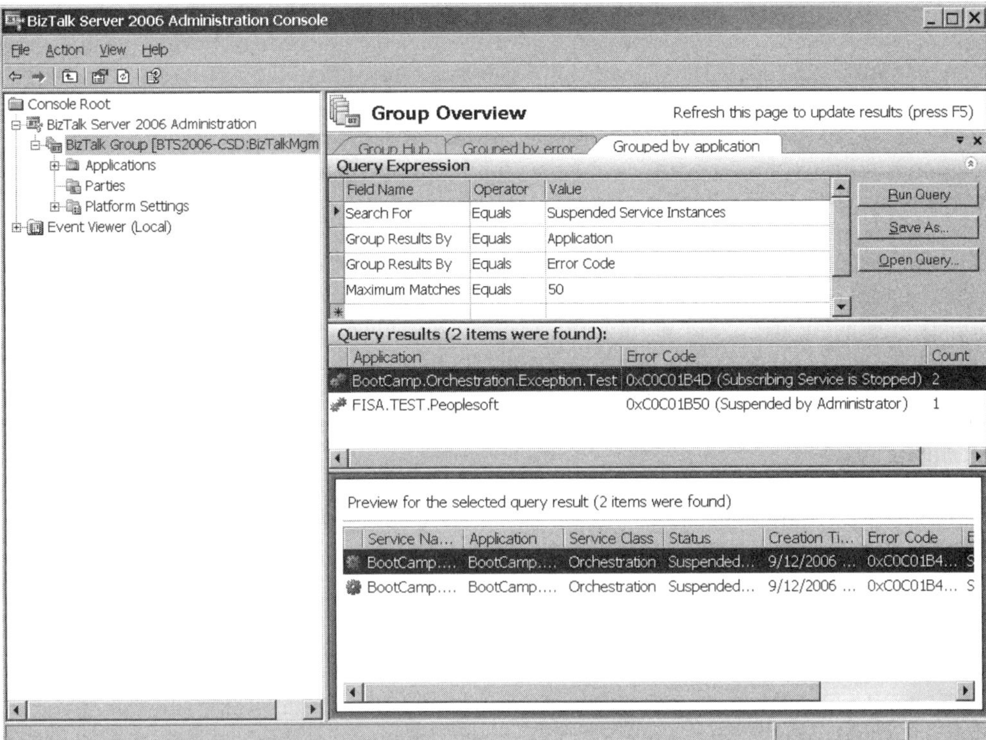

Figure 6-13. *BizTalk Server 2006 Administration Console Group Hub query page showing all suspended services grouped by application*

Several other factors also limit the BizTalk Administration Console in its application exception reporting role:

- There is no way to mine the data for business intelligence. For instance, how does someone query to see what the worst offending applications are on a monthly basis or examine quarterly trends of application exceptions?
- The business may want to be alerted when certain application exceptions occur or when specific thresholds are reached. How does someone subscribe to such exception events? The MMC as a reporting tool is not the ideal interface, since it's not very convenient to access in production environments. You need at minimum to be in the BizTalk Operator's role, and, in production environments, access to the MMC is usually limited to a terminal server client interface, reducing the audience significantly.
- Only unhandled exceptions, i.e., suspended service instances, are displayed in the Administration Console. If the developer handles the exception within the orchestration, exiting the service, the exception information will never be displayed in the Administration Console.

An obvious suggestion would be to build a custom web portal interface to replace the MMC. However, because of the way data is stored, exposed, and accessed by the BizTalk Administration Console, this is a nearly impossible task. Any unified reporting system would really need to feed off the several sources, including the Microsoft Event Log and HAT.

With BizTalk, you're working in a message-oriented paradigm. Everything in a BizTalk solution is message oriented, and developers think in a message-oriented mindset. Wouldn't it seem natural that exception handling also be done in a message-oriented manner?

Fortunately, BizTalk Server 2006 provides you with a sophisticated infrastructure and object model that will allow you to build a simple API that should address your common goals for application exception management in a message-oriented fashion, for both the BizTalk messaging and orchestration subsystems. The API you build can then be used to take advantage of other features within BizTalk, such as the subscription model and event-based Business Activity Monitoring. Coupled with Windows SharePoint Services, you should be able to provide a fairly robust reporting portal for all application exceptions that occur within BizTalk.

The remainder of this chapter we'll dedicate to examining how current challenges are addressed today, but more importantly we'll drill into building the API that can address these issues for you tomorrow.

The Exception Management Challenge

In BizTalk Server 2004, there was no built-in mechanism to make this an easy accomplishment for the developer. For instance, if an error occurred in the BizTalk messaging subsystem, the message would simply be written to BizTalk's suspended queue. If the developer needed to view, repair, or resubmit the message, it entailed some rather elaborate custom development work. In addition, developers would have to write their own solution, subscribing to WMI events, to detect that the suspension of the message actually took place. The end product would look almost exactly like the example shown previously in this chapter in the "Editing and Resubmitting Suspended Messages" section.

This forced some developers to design their applications not with business considerations in mind, but rather with exception management in mind. For instance, because there was no way to trap the exception that a BizTalk map could generate in the messaging subsystem, many developers opted to put maps in the orchestration, rather than in the receive and send ports where they logically should have been placed. They did so simply because BizTalk offered a graphical mechanism for catching and reacting to application exceptions within an orchestration. Some developers even took this a step further: incorporating more code within the orchestration, code that logically should be placed within a custom pipeline component, for no better reason than to have the ability to catch the exception and react to it.

When using an orchestration, developers could graphically define a Scope shape with one or more exception handlers, similar to the `Try...Catch...Finally` functionality you would incorporate writing any pure .NET application. This gave the developer a way to catch the exceptions, but custom code would still have to be written within the Exception Handler shape to process the exception. By default, just as with a .NET application, BizTalk doesn't do anything with the .NET exception it catches. An example of this is shown in Figure 6-14. It's up to the developer to do something, i.e., write to `Debug.Trace`, incorporate custom logging, write to the Microsoft Event Log, and/or write the exception to HAT.

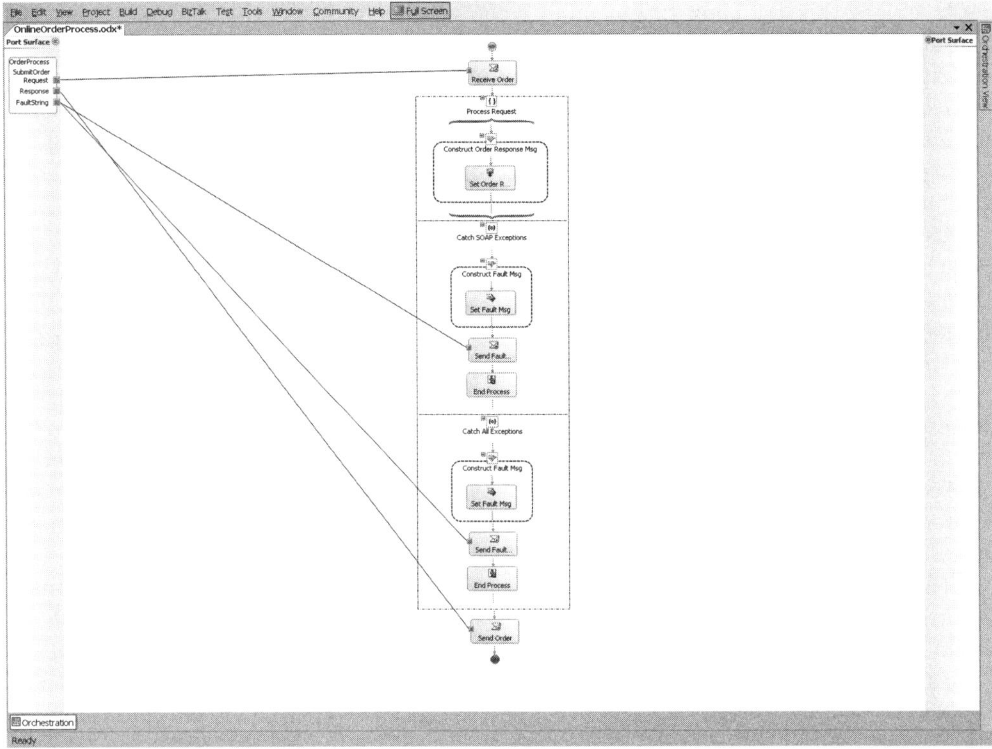

Figure 6-14. *BizTalk Server 2006 Orchestration Designer demonstrating the inclusion of multiple exception handlers*

We've seen some fairly well-thought-out and elaborate exception handling implemented in BizTalk, but usually just at the orchestration level. For example, it wasn't uncommon to see the Exception Management Application Block (posted on the Microsoft Patterns and Practices web site)[14] used as a common way to control exception reporting. Using it was a little challenging, though due to the overhead and configuration files, it was necessary. Other times we've seen custom exception reporting to a database.

However, none of the exception management options we've just described provide a unified pattern for managing and reporting application exceptions in a BizTalk environment that includes both orchestration and messaging subsystems. And neither addresses the issue of managing the state involved in a misbehaving process.

Managing state, or to be clearer, making the state available as part of the exception management process, is fairly important when you consider scenarios that require the current

14. www.microsoft.com/downloads/details.aspx?displaylang=en&FamilyID=8CA8EB6E-6F4A-43DF-ADEB-8F22CA173E02

message state when handling the exception. A common scenario that would require message state availability as well as a robust exception management process would be the following:

A user submits an invoice to the system. During the course of processing the invoice within an orchestration, the Business Rule Engine throws an application exception because a piece of the data is incorrect. The business process should catch the exception and send the offending message to another person or system. That person or system can correct and resubmit the message for processing.

Using existing exception management techniques, the exception management logic could be maintained in the current Exception Handler shape on the existing orchestration. Alternatively, you could tightly couple the current orchestration to a secondary orchestration and pass the message over to it for processing.

The downside to the former approach is that handling more elaborate exception use cases is done within the current Orchestration Exception Handler shapes. This means an orchestration starts to grow in complexity due to exception correction logic being embedded in it. What happens if you have five, ten, or even more Exception Handler shapes that need corrective action or management? This slowly becomes difficult to manage as it limits the development of all exception logic to a single developer (due to the single orchestration handling the exception logic).

The latter approach would move the logic out of the exception handlers and into secondary orchestrations by using either the Start Orchestration or Call Orchestration shapes. This would allow additional developers to work with the exception logic but would maintain a fairly tightly coupled process.

Now consider the following scenario where message state is part of the exception reporting process:

There are several BizTalk applications deployed in the environment. Some are generating application exceptions at the messaging subsystem level, while others are generating application exceptions at the orchestration level. The internal IT Operations department needs to be able view a central portal for all exception messages, their state, and application exception trends by fiscal quarter across applications.

Today, there is no BizTalk feature that provides this functionality, since there is no standard and consistent way of reporting and logging all exceptions generated in a BizTalk environment.

Clearly, you would want to accomplish several things by developing a unified pattern and API for business exception handling. The goals of this approach would be

- Develop loosely coupled asynchronous orchestration processes that have the ability to subscribe to specific business exceptions generated by either the messaging subsystem or an orchestration.
- Enable identification of common exceptions generated from either orchestration- or messaging-based applications.
- Allow the development of common business exception orchestration handlers that function across multiple orchestration applications.
- Provide the ability to create these business exception orchestration handlers independent of the currently deployed orchestration-based applications.
- Provide a web-based portal that displays application and business exception trends using optional BAM observations models as well as exception messages and application state driven from both orchestration- and messaging-based applications.

BizTalk Server 2006 Failed Message Routing As a Blueprint

In BizTalk 2006, the BizTalk product team tried to alleviate some of the issues that occurred when application exceptions were generated in the messaging subsystem. As mentioned earlier, the team introduced a new feature called Failed Message Routing. For example, if the Enable routing on failed messages check box option was enabled on either the BizTalk send or receive port and a pipeline or routing failure occurred, then the BizTalk EPM would do the following instead of suspending the message:

1. Create a cloned message and de-promote all the promoted properties.
2. Put an error description on the message context (e.g., "The Assembler component cannot load the schema named mySchema.xsd.").
3. Promote the failure-specific properties (e.g., `ReceivePortName == "MyReceivePort"`, `MessageType == "msgtype#mynamespace"`, `FailureCode == "0x1824"`, etc.).
4. Try to publish this message.
5. Discard the original message if publishing succeeds.
6. Suspend the original message and generate NACK as usual if publishing fails because there is no subscription.

If you examine this feature closely, you can see that it touches upon several of the common goals that were previously defined. A similar feature, if created for use in an orchestration, would provide a standard way to trap and report all exceptions in a BizTalk environment.

For instance, consider the following scenario:

A user submits an invoice to the system. During the course of processing the invoice within an orchestration, the Business Rule Engine throws an application exception because some piece of the data is incorrect. The business process should catch the exception, send the offending message to another person or system that can correct the message, and resubmit the message for processing.

If a similar Failed Message Routing feature existed for orchestrations, perhaps it would work something like this:

1. The user creates a Fault message in the exception handler.
2. The system puts an error description on the Fault message context (e.g., "The Business Rule Engine threw a divide/zero error processing the LoanProcessing policy.").
3. The system promotes failure- and application-specific properties such as
    - `Application` (supplied by the developer)
    - `Description` (auto-populated—exception message)
    - `ErrorType` (auto-populated—exception type)
    - `FailureCategory` (supplied by the developer)
    - `FailureCode` (supplied by the developer)

- `FailureSeverity` (supplied by the developer)
- `FailureDescription` (supplied by the developer)
- `Scope` (auto-populated—Scope shape of current exception handler)
- `ServiceName` (auto-populated—orchestration name)
- `ServiceInstanceID` (auto-populated—orchestration instance ID [GUID])

4. The system serializes the current `Exception` object into the Fault message.
5. The user optionally adds current orchestration messages to the Fault message, which are serialized and persisted (including their message context properties), for example, `AddMessage(FaultMsg, SomeMessage)`.
6. The user publishes the Fault message.
7. If publishing succeeds, orchestration or send port subscriptions can be deployed to process the Fault, rehydrating the `Exception` object as well as any added messages and message context properties.
8. If publishing succeeds, a global exception handler (send port) publishes the Fault message to a web portal.

Given this description of a proposed Failed Message Routing feature for an orchestration, we'll walk you through how you can provide a simple solution for the scenario we just described. This approach would look something like the following:

1. A developer is assigned responsibility for the recently deployed Financial Reporting BizTalk application.
2. A new exception message arrives in the SharePoint-based exception management portal indicating a data integrity issue with an orchestration in the Financial Reporting BizTalk application.
3. The developer is notified of the new exception either through his subscription to the SharePoint application list or because the exception exceeded a threshold predefined in BAM.
4. The developer navigates to the SharePoint-based exception management portal and examines the Fault message posted as well as the individual orchestration messages and their context properties that were persisted.
5. The developer determines that this will be a common error that will require manual intervention and correction by the Finance team and resubmission to the system.
6. The developer creates and deploys an independent BizTalk orchestration project that subscribes to the specific exception and application information.
7. The project is designed to retrieve the invalid message from the Fault message, send the message to the Finance team for correction, and correlate the corrected message back to the orchestration and resubmit.
8. A week later, the developer navigates to the SharePoint-based exception management portal to view that the application exception trends for invalid messages have decreased dramatically since the deployment of his solution.

A close examination reveals obvious similarities between this proposed orchestration functionality and the existing Failed Message Routing feature of BizTalk Server 2006. In fact, if you were somehow able to incorporate this feature, you would address the four design goals we discussed earlier in the section, which we list again here for your convenience:

- Standardize how application exceptions are detected and caught in the BizTalk environment, i.e., messaging and orchestration subsystems.
- Provide common patterns that allow automated processes to react and manage application exceptions.
- Provide a loosely coupled exception management pattern that facilitates reuse.
- Develop a common reporting paradigm of application exceptions and their available message state that applies to any BizTalk subsystem.

Additionally, you could use the same mechanism that would feed the exception metrics and portal of your proposed solution to process all failed messages from the messaging subsystem (provided Failed Message Routing is enabled). So given the solution, we'll walk you through what it takes to develop it.

Failed Orchestration Routing API for BizTalk 2006

We'll show you what the Failed Orchestration Routing API looks like when used to catch an exception within an orchestration. First, you need to design a simple orchestration that receives a message, does some processing, and then simulates the generation of an exception within a Scope shape. Figure 6-15 depicts a simple orchestration named EAIProcess. Within this orchestration, you have two messages available, one you receive that is named ApprovedRequest, the other, DeniedRequest, that is created via a map. Following the creation of the second message, you generate an exception by dividing by zero by using the UnitPrice value located in the incoming message. This orchestration would be like the one shown in Figure 6-15.

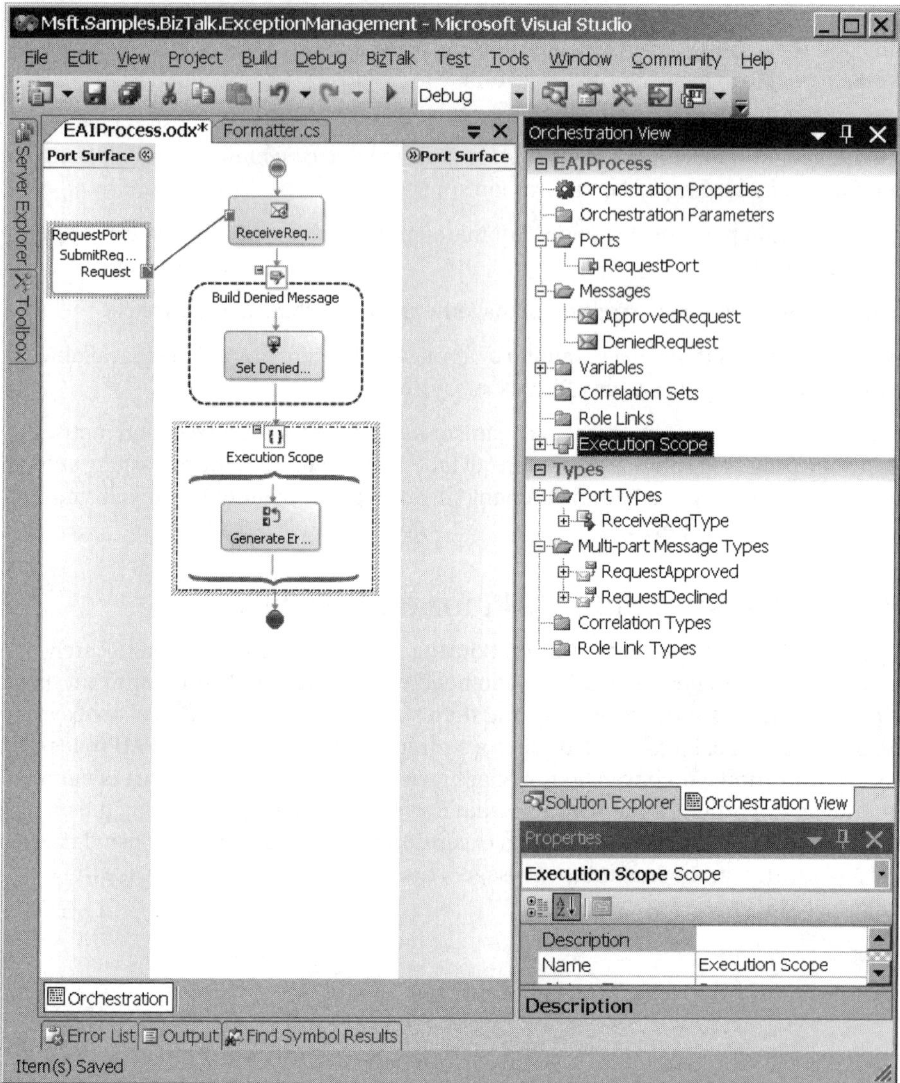

Figure 6-15. *Msft.Samples.BizTalk.ExceptionManagement solution displaying the EAIProcess orchestration*

The orchestration in Figure 6-15 receives the ApprovedRequest message and executes a map to create the DeniedRequest message. It then generates an exception by dividing by zero. The EAIProcess sample resides with three projects within the Msft.Samples.BizTalk.Exception-Management solution. These are listed in Table 6-1.

Table 6-1. *List of Projects Within Exception Management Solution*

Project Name	Description
BootCamp.Orchestration.Exception.Process	Contains the EAIProcess orchestration schedule and references the BootCamp.Orchestration.Exception.Schemas and Msft.Samples.BizTalk.Exception.Schemas projects as well as the Msft.Samples.BizTalk.Exception.dll assembly.
BootCamp.Orchestration.Exception.Schemas	Contains the schemas and maps used by the EAIProcess orchestration.
BootCamp.Orchestration.Exception.FaultHandler	Contains two orchestrations (EAIGenericHandler, EAIProcessHandler) that demonstrate strongly-typed and typeless options of using the Failed Orchestration Routing API. References the BootCamp.Orchestration.Exception.Schemas and Msft.Samples.BizTalk.Exception.Schemas project as well as the Msft.Samples.BizTalk.Exception.dll assembly.

Add an exception handler to the Execution Scope shape and configure it to capture all `System.Exceptions`. Once the exception is generated, control will jump to the exception handler.

Within the exception handler, you need to follow a fairly simple methodology:

1. Create a Fault message.
2. Add the ApprovedRequest message to the Fault message.
3. Add the DeniedRequest message to the Fault message.
4. Add the `Exception` object (caught by the exception handler) to the Fault message.
5. Publish the Fault message to the Messagebox.

So, how would you do this? By using an API to enable this functionality, which is embodied within the two projects listed in Table 6-2.

Table 6-2. *Failed Orchestration Routing API Projects*

Project Name	Description
Msft.Samples.BizTalk.Exception	Contains all public methods for handling Fault-message processing within orchestrations. The public methods are `CreateFaultMessage`, `AddMesssage`, `SetException`, `GetException`, `GetMessage`, and `GetMessages`. This assembly must be registered in the local GAC.
Msft.Samples.BizTalk.Exception.Schemas	Contains Fault message schema and system property schema. Deploys to the BizTalk.Sample.ExceptionMgmt application container.

The Msft.Samples.BizTalk.Exception.Schemas project assembly must be referenced by every BizTalk project that references or uses the Fault message schema. It contains two schemas, one that defines an instance of a Fault message (FaultMessage.xsd) and one that defines the property schema (System-Properties.xsd). These must be deployed in the BizTalk environment. The class outline is shown in Figure 6-16.

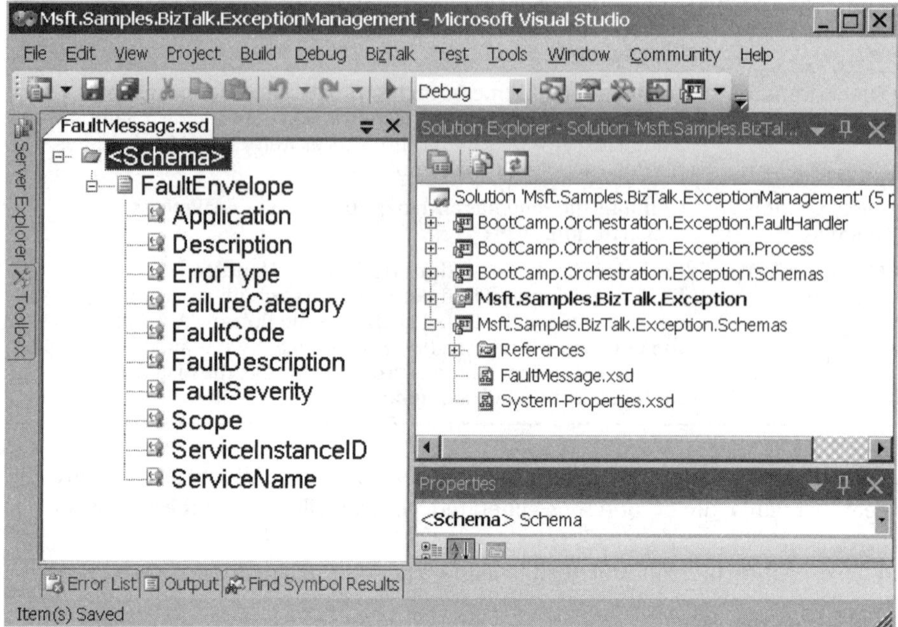

Figure 6-16. *Msft.Samples.BizTalk.Exception.Schemas project displaying the FaultMessage.xsd schema*

The Msft.Samples.BizTalk.Exception.Schemas project must be referenced by all BizTalk projects that need to create an instance of the Fault message for publication. Many of the properties have been promoted or defined as distinguished properties.

For the developer, the next step would be to define a Fault message using the FaultMessage.xsd schema reference. Once the message variable is created (name it `FaultMsg`) within the orchestration view window, an instance of it needs to be created within the Exception Handler shape using the API exposed in the Msft.Samples.BizTalk.Exception project.

Just as in the case of the Msft.Samples.BizTalk.Exception.Schemas project, the Msft.Samples.BizTalk.Exception project assembly must be referenced as well by all BizTalk projects that need to use the API. The API exposes public methods to create Fault messages, and manage and retrieve them for processing, as described in Table 6-3.

Table 6-3. *Public Failed Orchestration Routing API*

Class.Method	Use Case	Description
`ExceptionMgmt.CreateFaultMessage`	Exception handler scope	`public static XmlDocument CreateFaultMessage()` Accepts no arguments. Returns an instance of the Fault message (XmlDocument), populated with the current orchestration name and the orchestration instance ID (GUID).
`ExceptionMgmt.AddMesssage`	Exception handler scope	`public static void AddMessage(XLANGMessage faultMsg, XLANGMessage message)` Accepts the created Fault message as the first argument. Accepts any existing message instance within the orchestration as the second argument. This method will persist the added message instance and its message context properties into the Fault message and make it available for later retrieval via the `GetMessage()` API. Returns void.
`ExceptionMgmt.SetException`	Exception handler scope	`public static void SetException(XLANGMessage faultMsg, Object exception)` Accepts the created Fault message as the first argument. Accepts the existing `Exception` object caught within the exception handler as the second argument. This method will persist the `Exception` object into the Fault message and make it available for later retrieval via the `GetException()` API. Returns void.
`ExceptionMgmt.GetMessage`	Subscriber/processor	`public static XLANGMessage GetMessage (XLANGMessage faultMsg, string msgName)` Accepts the received (via subscription) Fault message as the first argument. Accepts the name of the message previously added to the Fault message from the originating Orchestration Exception Handler shape. Returns the fully typed XLANGMessage that matches the `msgName` argument. The XLANGMessage will contain all original context properties, including custom promoted properties.
`ExceptionMgmt.GetMessages`	Subscriber/processor	`public static MessageCollection GetMessages (XLANGMessage faultMsg)` Accepts the received (via subscription) Fault message as the argument. Returns a `MessageCollection` class populated with **all** XLANGMessages previously added to the Fault message from the originating Orchestration Exception Handler shape. The XLANGMessages will contain all original context properties, including custom promoted properties.

Continued

Table 6-3. *Continued*

Class.Method	Use Case	Description
`ExceptionMgmt.GetException`	Subscriber/processor	`public static System.Exception GetException (XLANGMessage faultMsg)` Accepts the received (via subscription) Fault message as the argument. Returns the `System.Exception` object previously added to the Fault message from the originating Orchestration Exception Handler shape.
`FaultSeverity`	Exception handler scope and subscriber/processor	Exposes public properties simulating the following enumeration: `enum FaultCodes { Information = 0, Warning = 1, Error = 2, Severe = 3, Critical = 4 }` Used to either set or compare against the FaultSeverity value in the Fault message.
`MessageCollection`	Subscriber/processor	Returned by the `ExceptionMgmt.GetMessages` API. This class derives from an `ArrayList` and implements an enumerator allowing `MoveNext()` operations.

Using the APIs listed in Table 6-3, you can add the following shapes to your exception handler and execute the methodology previously discussed. Add the following to the EAIProcess orchestration's exception handler:

- Message Assignment shape enclosed within the Construct shape
- Send shape (for Fault message)
- Outbound Direct Bound Port (one-way) shape
- Terminate shape
- Send shape (for ApprovedRequest message)

Next, set the Construct shape to create a new Fault message. Name the Fault message variable `FaultMsg`.

Within the Message Assignment shape, add the following code:

```
// Create Fault exception message
FaultMsg.Body = Msft.Samples.BizTalk.Exception.ExceptionMgmt.CreateFaultMessage();

// Set Fault message properties
FaultMsg.Body.Application = "EAI Process Application";
FaultMsg.Body.FailureCategory = "MessageBuild";
FaultMsg.Body.FaultCode = "1001";
FaultMsg.Body.FaultDescription = "Some error occurred";
FaultMsg.Body.FaultSeverity = Msft.Samples.BizTalk.Exception.FaultSeverity.Severe;
FaultMsg.Body.Scope = "Execution Scope";
```

```
// Add each message you want to process later to the Fault message
Msft.Samples.BizTalk.Exception.ExceptionMgmt.AddMessage(FaultMsg,
ApprovedRequest);
Msft.Samples.BizTalk.Exception.ExceptionMgmt.AddMessage(FaultMsg,
DeniedRequest);

// Add the exception object you may want to inspect later to the Fault message
Msft.Samples.BizTalk.Exception.ExceptionMgmt.SetException(FaultMsg, _
sysExc);
```

Lastly, set the `Message` property of the Send shape to use the FaultMsg message and connect the Send shape with the Outbound Direct Bound Port. Once complete, the orchestration should look like the one shown in Figure 6-17.

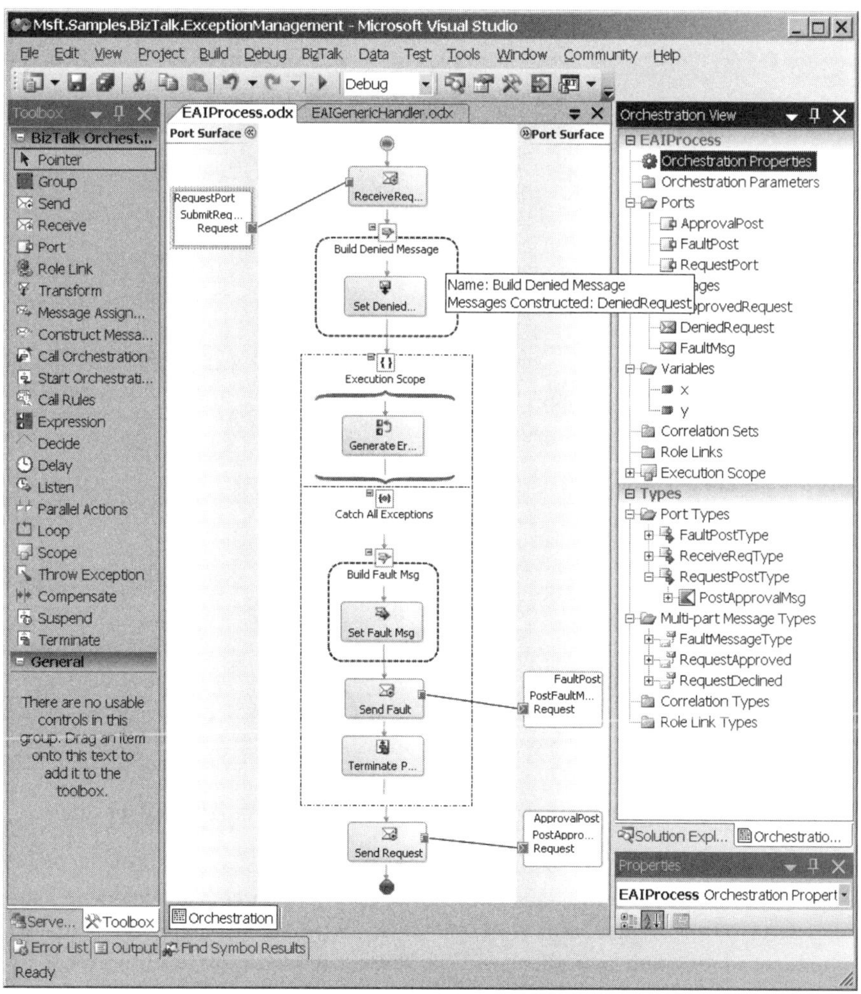

Figure 6-17. *Msft.Samples.BizTalk.ExceptionManagement solution displaying the EAIProcess orchestration*

The orchestration described in Figure 6-17 receives the ApprovedRequest message and executes a map to create the DeniedRequest message. Within the execution scope it generates an exception by dividing by zero. An exception handler has been added to the scope to build the Fault message, set the properties on it, and publish it directly to the BizTalk Messagebox.

Running the EAIProcess

The EAIProcess orchestration can be started by binding the logical RequestPort port to a physical port configured to receive files from a folder. Once the project is built and deployed, ensure that there is a subscriber (send port) built for the Fault message and that it is enlisted and stopped; otherwise a persistence exception will be reported. Post a sample file into the folder being monitored, execute the orchestration, and generate the exception, thereby publishing the Fault message. You can inspect the properties of the generated Fault message using the BizTalk Server 2006 Administration Console as displayed in Figure 6-18.

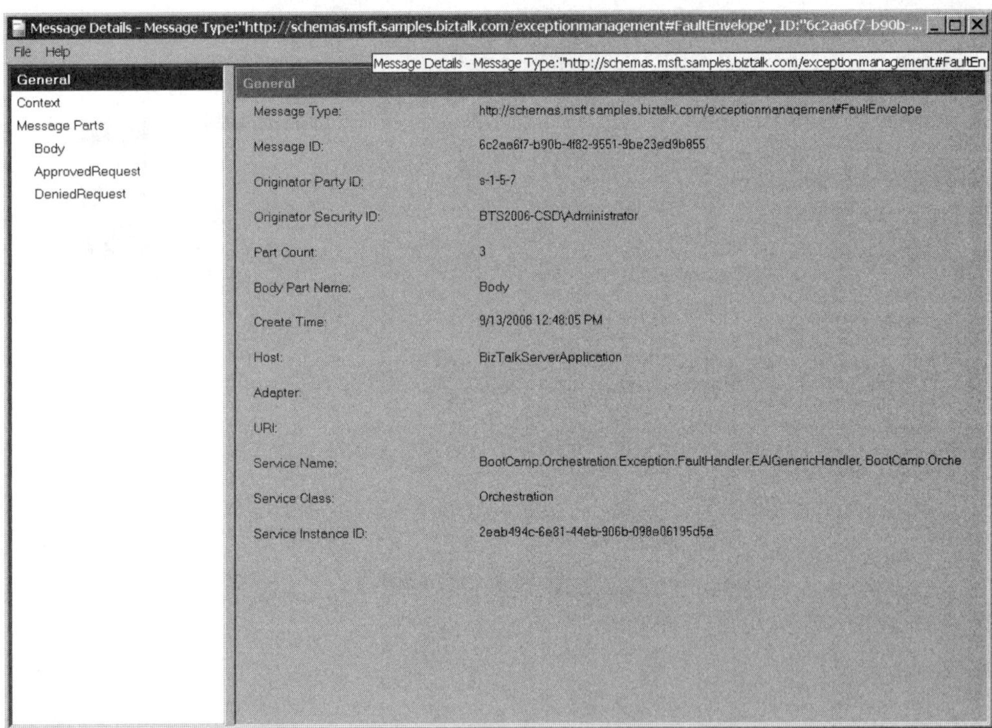

Figure 6-18. *Message Details dialog box displaying properties of the suspended Fault message*

Each message added to the Fault message in the exception handler gets persisted as dynamic message parts to the original Fault message. The Message Details dialog box illustrates some of the niceties resulting from the use of the Failed Orchestration Routing API. First, the message published from the exception handler is still defined as the Fault message derived from your FaultMessage.xsd schema as shown by the message type context property. However, notice two additional message parts listed in the left-hand pane. In the EAIProcess orchestration, the `FaultMsg` message variable was set to a multipart message type of one part, body. The API dynamically adds the individual messages as message parts to the current Fault message.

If you examine the context properties of the Fault message (as shown in Figure 6-19), you can see all of the fault properties you set in the Message Assignment shape, as well as some that the API sets for you (i.e., `ServiceName` and `ServiceInstanceID`).

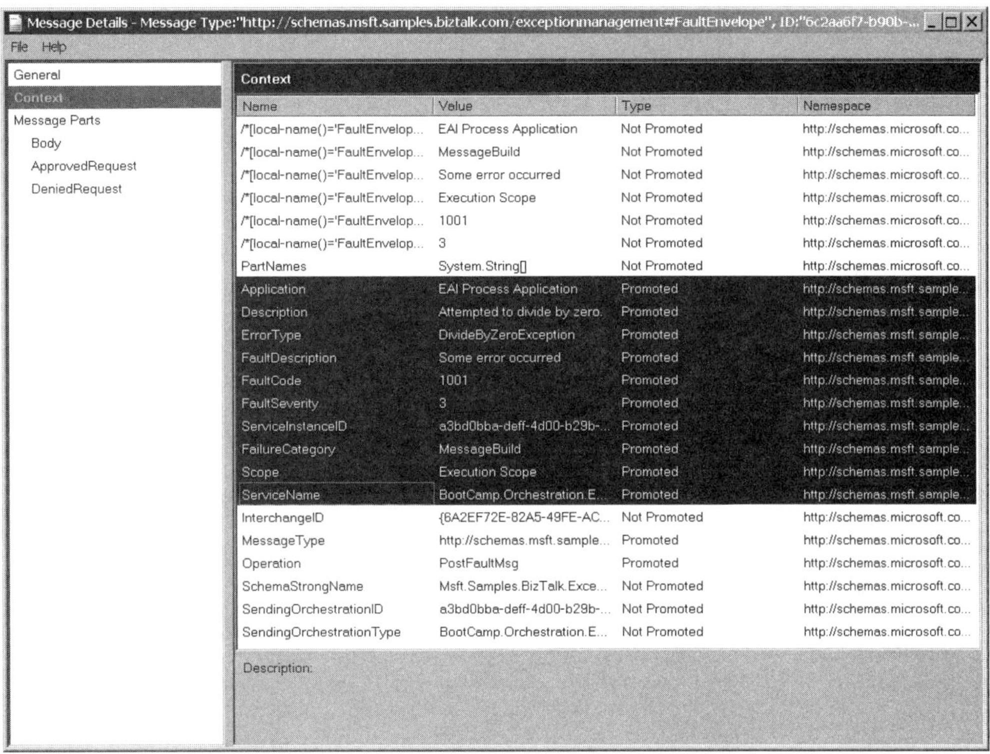

Figure 6-19. *Message Details dialog box displaying the promoted properties of the suspended Fault message. These properties were set in the exception handler as well as within the API.*

Figures 6-20, 6-21, and 6-22 show the Message Details dialog box displaying the content of the original ApprovedRequest and DeniedRequest messages.

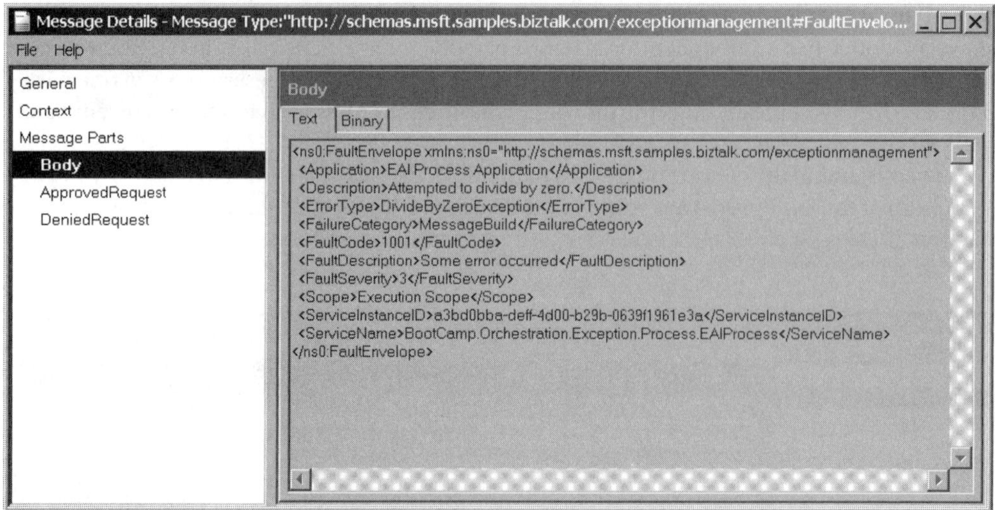

Figure 6-20. *Message Details dialog box displaying the content of the original Fault message published from the EAIProcess exception handler*

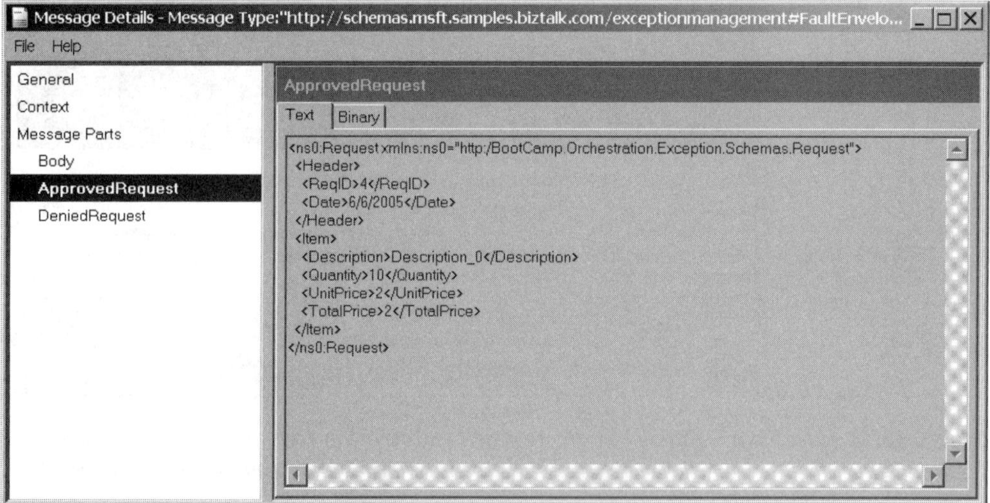

Figure 6-21. *Message Details dialog box displaying the contents of the ApprovedRequest message that was added to the Fault message*

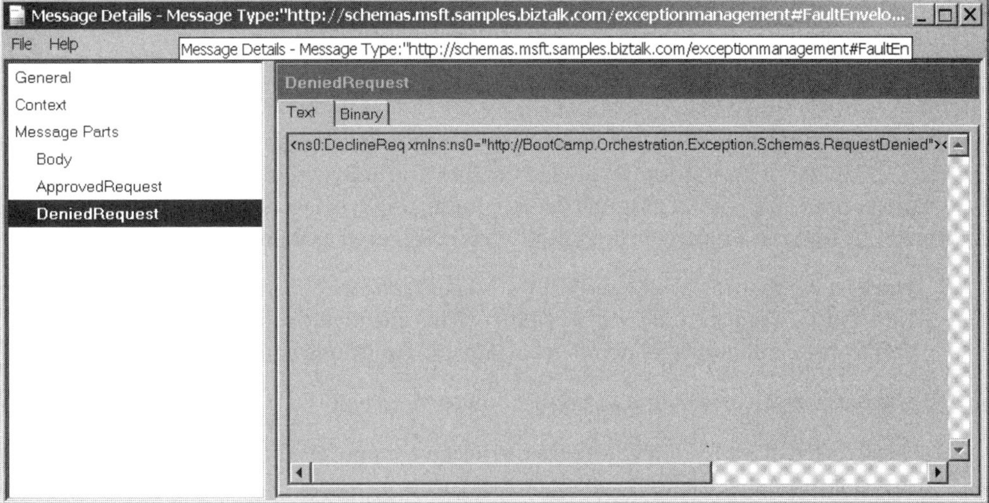

Figure 6-22. *Message Details dialog box displaying the contents of the DeniedRequest message that was added to the Fault message*

Processing and Retrieving Messages and Exceptions from the Fault Message

Having published the Fault message with the two persisted messages (ApprovedRequest and DeniedRequest) and a persisted `Exception` object from the EAIProcess orchestration, we'll move forward and demonstrate how to extract the messages and the `Exception` objects in secondary orchestration schedules.

There is really only one method for extracting an `Exception` object: the `GetException()` API. However, there are two methods for extracting messages. One provides a typeless method to retrieve all messages persisted to the Fault message. The other provides a strongly-typed approach.

Typeless Message Retrieval

The typeless approach is useful if you have a general logging need, or you don't have access to the schema assembly used in the originating orchestration that persisted the messages. In this case, a collection of messages can be returned using `MoveNext()` to enumerate through them.

This allows developers to inspect the message context properties and do whatever they want with them, e.g., process them, send them out to a SharePoint site, etc. For example, a generic orchestration exception process may do the following:

- Retrieve array of messages from Fault message.
- Inspect context properties to determine message type or retrieve other context values.

- Based on message type or other criteria, look up processing instructions via Business Rule Engine.
- Process individual messages per business rule evaluation.

This makes for an extremely decoupled exception processing solution. The EAIGenericHandler orchestration, located in the BootCamp.Orchestration.Exception. FaultHandler project, is a good example demonstrating the typeless approach and is shown in Figure 6-23. In this example, the orchestration is configured as follows:

1. The Receive shape is configured with a filter expression: ("Msft.Samples.BizTalk. Exception.Schemas.FaultCode" == "1001"). This effectively subscribes the orchestration to any Fault messages published where the FaultCode equals 1001.
2. The Receive shape is bound to a direct bound receive port.
3. The Expression shape directly below the Receive shape has the following code snippet that calls the `GetMessages()` API:

   ```
   msgs =  Msft.Samples.BizTalk.Exception.ExceptionMgmt.GetMessages(FaultMsg);
   ```

   The `msgs` variable is declared of type MessageCollection. This returns an array of messages, including their original context properties, from the Fault message.
4. A Loop shape is configured to call

   ```
   msgs.MoveNext()
   ```
5. Within the Loop shape, an Expression shape is configured to retrieve the current message in the collection by calling

   ```
   TmpMsg = msgs.Current;
   ```

   `TmpMsg` is a message variable declared as a `System.Xml.XmlDocument`.
6. Each message in the collection is then published to a direct bound port.
7. A physical send port is configured to serialize each message to a folder.

Note Message Construct shapes are not necessary within the example. The API for the exception handler takes care of constructing new messages within the BizTalk runtime.

When this orchestration executes, it will retrieve all the messages from the Fault message (i.e., ApprovedRequest and DeniedRequest) and serialize them to disk via the send port subscription.

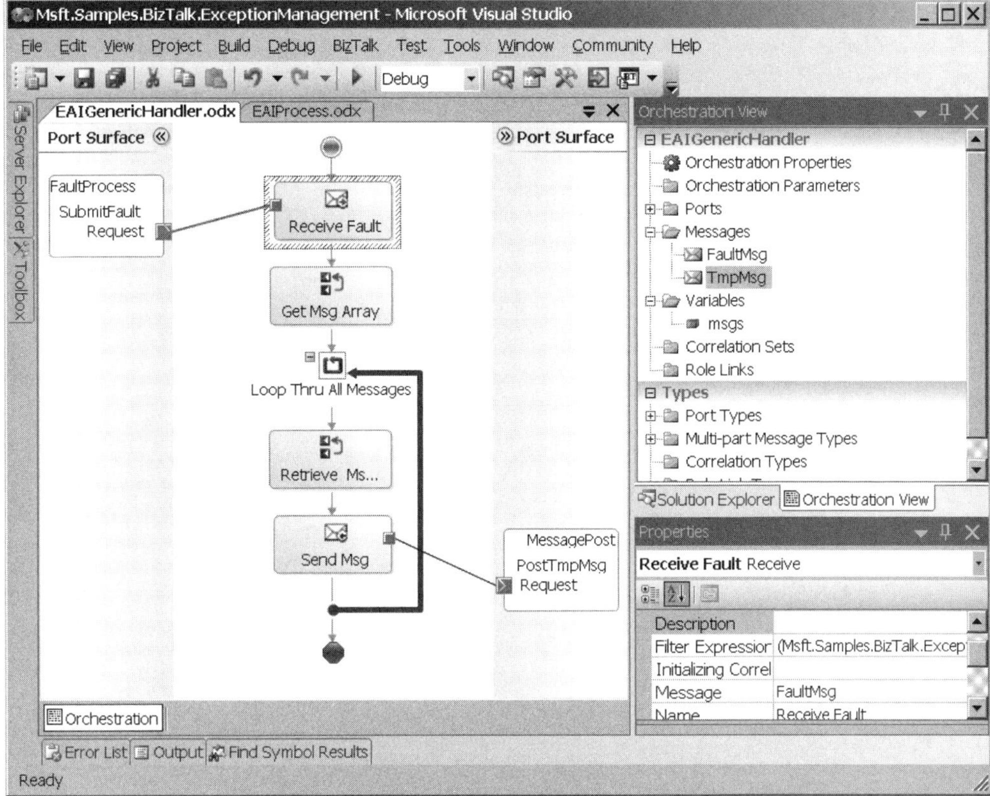

Figure 6-23. *EAIGenericHandler orchestration demonstrating typeless message retreival and handling using the Failed Orchestration Routing API*

Strongly-Typed Message Retrieval

Another effective approach is retrieving the messages from the Fault message as strongly-typed messages. This is done by referencing the schema assemblies used by the originating orchestration.

The EAIProcessHandler orchestration, located in the BootCamp.Orchestration.Exception.FaultHandler project, is a good example demonstrating the strongly-typed approach. The orchestration flow is shown in Figure 6-24.

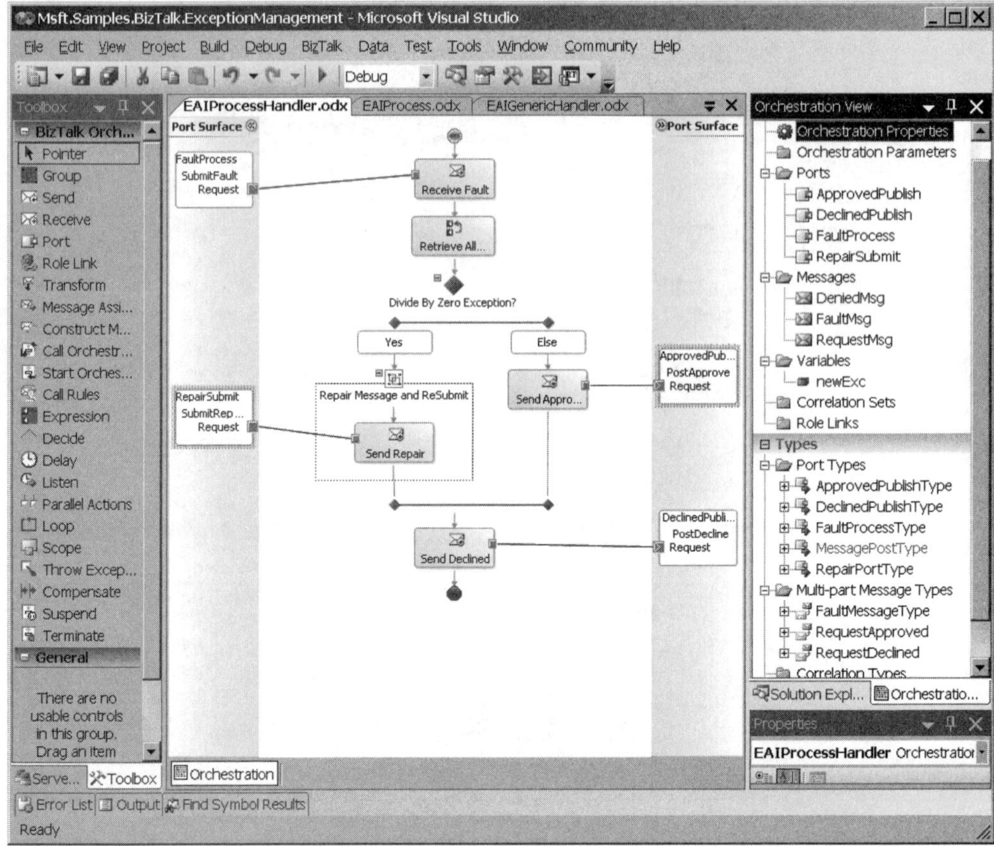

Figure 6-24. *EAIProcessHandler orchestration demonstrating strongly-typed message retreival and handling using the Failed Orchestration Routing API*

In this example, the orchestration is configured as follows:

1. The Receive shape is configured with a filter expression: ("Msft.Samples.BizTalk. Exception.Schemas.FaultCode" == "1001"). This effectively subscribes the orchestration to any Fault messages published where the FaultCode equals 1001.

2. The Receive shape is bound to a direct bound receive port.

3. The Expression shape directly below the Receive shape has the following code snippet, which calls the `GetMessage()` and `GetException()` APIs:

```
//Retrieve the two original messages from the Fault message
RequestMsg = Msft.Samples.BizTalk.Exception.ExceptionMgmt.GetMessage(FaultMsg,
"ApprovedRequest");
DeniedMsg = Msft.Samples.BizTalk.Exception.ExceptionMgmt.GetMessage(FaultMsg,
"DeniedRequest");
```

```
//Retrieve the System.Exception from the original service
newExc = Msft.Samples.BizTalk.Exception.ExceptionMgmt.GetException(FaultMsg);

// Write the error value to event log (need admin rights)
System.Diagnostics.EventLog.WriteEntry _
("EAIProcessHandler",newExc.Message.ToString());
```

Both `RequestMsg` and `DeniedMsg` are strongly typed using the schemas in the originating orchestration.

`newExc` is declared as a variable of type System.Exception.

4. If repair is needed:

   a. `RequestMsg` is sent to the folder drop via a port.

   b. An InfoPath processing instruction is added to it to facilitate editing as shown in Figure 6-25.

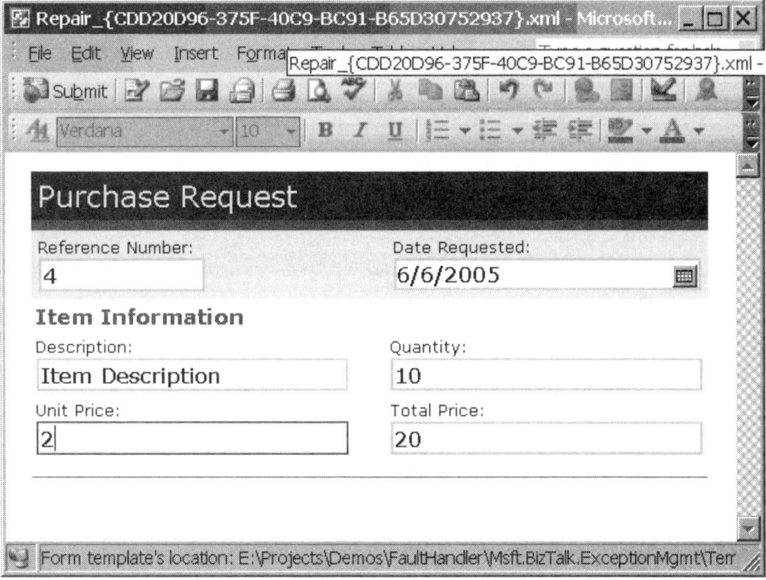

Figure 6-25. *RepairReSubmitForm.xsn Infopath form*

   c. The InfoPath form is designed to submit repaired data to a BizTalk HTTP receive location configured under the receive port for the EAIProcess orchestration.

   d. `DeniedMsg` is published to a direct bound port.

   e. A physical send port is configured to serialize the message to a folder.

5. If repair is **not** needed:

   a. Each message is then published to a direct bound port.

   b. A physical send port is configured to serialize each message to a folder.

■ **Note** Message Construct shapes are not necessary within the example. The API for the exception handler takes care of constructing new messages within the BizTalk runtime.

The form in Figure 6-25 is configured to use a BizTalk HTTP receive location URL as its submit data source. Once submitted, it will activate a new instance of the EAIProcess orchestration.

When this orchestration executes, it will retrieve all the messages from the Fault message (i.e., ApprovedRequest and DeniedRequest) and set them into strongly-typed message variables. In fact, if you stop the send port subscriptions and run the orchestration, you can see the original context property values on the messages; the context properties were set from the originating orchestration (see Figure 6-26).

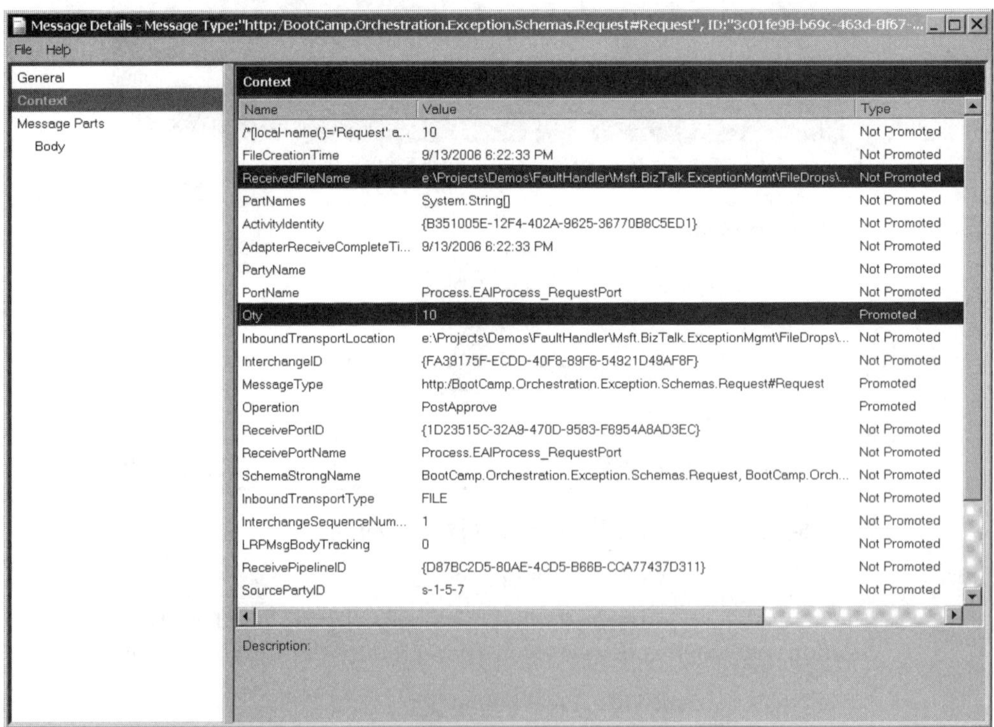

Figure 6-26. *Message Details dialog box displaying the properties of the ApprovedRequest message retreived from the Fault message using the GetMessage() API*

Note In Figure 6-26, the `ReceivedFileName` property that was set before the originating orchestration processed the message and threw the exception. Also, the API persists all custom `Promoted` properties as noted by the `Qty` property. This is an incredibly handy feature to have.

Beyond the Next Horizon

As can be seen from the previous sections, the Failed Orchestration Routing API is powerful enough to allow developers to handle orchestration-generated exceptions. With a little work and a good design, you can handle orchestration exceptions the same way you would handle messaging subsystem exceptions using the Failed Message Routing feature of BizTalk Server 2006.

The samples provided online,[15] specifically the EAIGenericHandler and EAIProcessHandler orchestrations, demonstrate simple patterns for accessing both the exception messages as well as the state from the original processing orchestration. This state, in the form of the original messages, can be accessed as strongly-typed or typeless XLANG messages. This satisfies at least three of the four original common design goals we listed earlier in the chapter, specifically

- Standardize how application exceptions are detected and caught in the BizTalk environment, i.e., messaging and orchestration subsystems.
- Provide common patterns that allow automated processes to react and manage application exceptions.
- Provide a loosely coupled exception management pattern that facilitates reuse.

If you take this pattern a step further and extend the API, you could provide another method that creates canonical Fault messages generated either by the Failed Message Routing feature of BizTalk Server 2006 or the Failed Orchestration Routing API. A generic, BizTalk Group–wide send port could be configured to subscribe to all Fault messages, regardless of source, call the method, and then post all canonical Fault messages to a central web-based portal. That would satisfy the last design goal:

- Develop a common reporting paradigm of application exceptions and their available message state that applies to any BizTalk subsystem.

The final step would be to dynamically generate business intelligence data from the Fault messages going through the BizTalk environment. That's right; you call that BAM in BizTalk Server 2006.

15. Samples and compiled API to be provided for download at www.apress.com.

Remember the following scenario we described earlier and the solution walkthrough we proposed:

> *A user submits an invoice to the system. During the course of processing the invoice within an orchestration, the Business Rule Engine throws an application exception because some piece of the data is incorrect. The business process should catch the exception, send the offending message to another person or system that can correct the message, and resubmit the message for processing.*

To implement the use case, we envisioned a sequence of events would need to happen, as presented earlier in the subsection "BizTalk Server 2006 Failed Message Routing As a Blueprint" and repeated here for your convenience:

1. A developer is assigned responsibility for the recently deployed Financial Reporting BizTalk application.
2. A new exception message arrives in the SharePoint-based exception management portal indicating a data integrity issue with an orchestration in the Financial Reporting BizTalk application.
3. The developer is notified of the new exception either through his subscription to the SharePoint application list or because the exception exceeded a threshold predefined in BAM.
4. The developer navigates to the SharePoint-based exception management portal and examines the Fault message posted as well as the individual orchestration messages and their context properties that were persisted.
5. The developer determines that this will be a common error that will require manual intervention and correction by the Finance team and resubmission to the system.
6. The developer creates and deploys an independent BizTalk orchestration project that subscribes to the specific exception and application information.
7. The project is designed to retrieve the invalid message from the Fault message, send the message to the Finance team for correction, and correlate the corrected message back to orchestration and resubmit.
8. A week later the developer navigates to the SharePoint-based exception management portal to view that the application exception trends for invalid messages have decreased dramatically since the deployment of his solution.

If you extend the Failed Orchestration Routing API, you could make the solution walkthrough a reality with very little effort. This need is not unique to a specific BizTalk application; it tends to be ubiquitous in BizTalk environments to provide operational visibility into the health of the applications deployed. This becomes a vital function in Enterprise Service Bus (ESB)[16] type deployments.

In the upcoming release of the Microsoft ESB Toolkit, this API will be extended to accommodate the scenarios we described previously. This should prove invaluable for anyone deploying applications in the future.

---

16. http://en.wikipedia.org/wiki/Enterprise_Service_Bus

CHAPTER 7

■ ■ ■

What the Maestro Needs to Know: Advanced Orchestration Concepts

Orchestrations are series of ordered operations or transactions that implement a business process. To interact with entities outside the boundaries of this business process, orchestrations can use **send** or **receive ports**. You can perform transactions in parallel, execute business rules from within orchestrations, call complex logic in managed .NET assemblies, or call and start other orchestrations. They are by far the most powerful tool in a BizTalk architect's tool belt. To perform complex routing in BizTalk or do any process automation work, you need to use orchestrations.

What an Orchestration Is

BizTalk orchestrations are used to visually model workflows and provide the primary mechanism to implement business process automation within a solution. They are the equivalent of the good-old flowcharts programmers used to detail algorithms in functional specifications before sequence diagrams and object-centric design. Orchestrations are the most powerful tool within the BizTalk Server toolbox, as they allow for the rapid development and deployment of complex processes that in many circumstances can be implemented with little to no coding. They are created within Visual Studio and are compiled into .NET assemblies that are deployed to the Global Assembly Cache and registered in the BizTalk Management Database.

Just like in any subroutine, you can declare and use variables within an orchestration. Orchestrations started or called programmatically or through a caller orchestration may also be passed parameters. In those aspects, an orchestration is no different from a procedure or function. Orchestrations may also receive and send messages, due to the integration of the orchestration engine, known as the **XLANG engine**, and the BizTalk messaging subservice. The orchestration engine's constructs in the Orchestration toolbox allow developers to construct, modify, and transform messages that an orchestration sends and receives. Developers can add C#-like expressions[1]—**XLANG expressions**—to an orchestration flow to perform complex logic or call external assemblies. Orchestration developers may declare transaction scopes within an orchestration and define compensation blocks that will be implicitly called to roll back the transaction if an exception occurs.

What the Orchestration Engine Provides

The BizTalk orchestration engine, the XLANG engine, consists of a set of SQL Server stored procedures, jobs that run on the BizTalk Messagebox database—msgbox DB—and Management Database as well as a set of managed assemblies that run within BizTalk host instances. The XLANG engine is the maestro that schedules, manages, and monitors orchestration execution across host instances. It manages orchestration instantiation, execution, termination, and migration across host instances using a predefined amount of system resources, like memory and threads. For the engine to be able to perform its functions, it needs to be able to interrupt the executions of orchestration instances regularly. Instead of resorting to a language that gets interpreted at runtime to run on top of the engine, visual orchestration constructs (shapes) that form the flow of an orchestration are compiled into a set of calls to the XLANG APIs in a managed assembly. This allows the engine to control the scheduling and execution of orchestration instances without the performance hit associated with interpreted languages. In essence, the XLANG engine and orchestration instances are running side by side in the BizTalk host instance.

The integration of the XLANG engine and the rest of the BizTalk Server components, as illustrated in Figure 7-1, helps provide the basic services required for building and running reliable enterprise-grade orchestrations:

- The ability to scope transaction and designate compensation blocks and exception handlers.
- Support for atomic or long-running transactional scopes. **Atomic scopes** mean that the engine will cease to dehydrate[2] the running orchestration instance until it exits the atomic scope. Long-running scopes mean that the execution time of each step in the scope is undetermined or very long. The engine persists the instance's state on each operation that crosses the instance boundary, like sending messages, and eventually dehydrates the orchestration instance if it is idle and meeting the dehydration thresholds.[3]

---

1. XLANG expressions constitute the subset of C# expressions that can be used within the orchestration. The XLANG engine performs a fair amount of housecleaning and state management after each expression statement. A simple C#-like statement in an Expression shape results in several other operations performed by the XLANG engine.
2. The **dehydration** of a running orchestration instance is the act of persisting the current orchestration instance state to the BizTalk Messagebox database and releasing all transient system resources, memory, and threads back to the resource pools. **Rehydration** of a dehydrated orchestration instance is the act of loading the persisted orchestration instance state into memory and consuming resources from the pools to continue execution of that instance at its last persisted state.
3. A more detailed explanation of dehydration thresholds will follow in this chapter in the section "The Dehydration Algorithm and Thresholds."

- Fault tolerance. Leveraging state persistence of orchestration instances, the BizTalk orchestration engine can recover from a failure by recycling or restarting a failed host and resuming execution of previously running instances from the last persisted state. If the orchestration is deployed on a BizTalk Server Group running multiple host instances on different servers, the engine may also resume such instances on a different host instance running on a different server. This ensures absolute resilience in the case of a catastrophic failure of a server.
- Scalability and load balancing. The power of orchestration instance state persistence allows the engine to dehydrate an orchestration instance on one host instance and resume its execution on another host instance on a different server if the original host instance it was running on is overloaded. It can also balance the load across the running host instances on multiple servers.
- Activity tracking and monitoring. If designed by the Orchestration Designer, an orchestration can log and track activity execution that later can be monitored and reviewed through the Business Activity Monitor.
- Integration with the Business Rule Engine and firing business policies from within orchestrations.
- Integration with the BizTalk Messaging Engine and sending and receiving messages from within orchestrations.
- Leveraging XSLT maps and performing message transformation from within orchestrations.
- Leveraging the BizTalk Messaging Engine to allow for correlation of sent and received messages to ensure their delivery to the proper orchestration instance for the implementation of complex execution flows that span multiple requests.

In short, the BizTalk orchestration engine allows for the implementation and deployment of resilient transactional business processes that are scalable, fault tolerant, and able to send and receive messages or execute business rules.

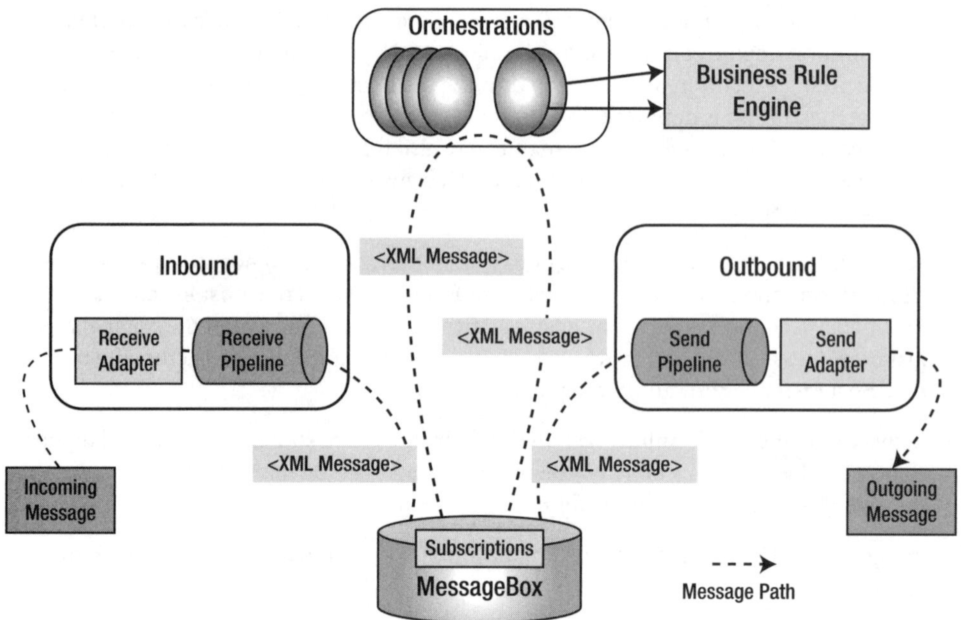

Figure 7-1. *Where the orchestration engine fits in BizTalk Server*

Do You Really Need an Orchestration?

Like all eager developers, you probably want to know the answer to this question right away. After all, an orchestration often seems like the best tool for you to use, as it is simply a procedural algorithm in a visual form. Before identifying when you should and should not use an orchestration, however, we need to explain the rationale behind some of the wrong decisions that some new BizTalk developers make, as well as the reason they are wrong.

The Orchestration Designer is the tool that new BizTalk developers are most comfortable with, as it is simply a visual procedural language. It provides a natural transition from VB .NET or C# to BizTalk development. Almost every new BizTalk developer or architect tends to think of a BizTalk solution as a set of orchestrations with defined external entry and exit points—ports—glued together to perform a business function. Although this visual development approach is the natural transition from procedural or object-oriented development, to leverage BizTalk to its full potential, solutions have to be architected differently. Unfortunately, designing a BizTalk solution is not as simple as abiding by object-oriented design guidelines, applying service-oriented architecture, or defining data structures and schemas. It is a combination of all of the foregoing, but couched in terms of message processing patterns. For the unfamiliar, the combination of these design approaches is a new paradigm shift in solution design.

Fortunately, this combination lends itself easily to business analysis. The mapping from a defined business process or collection of processes including cross-platform transactions to a BizTalk solution is usually a one-to-one mapping. It is a matter of finding the proper set of BizTalk tools—**messaging patterns**—to perform the defined function.[4]

Orchestrations are a powerful tool. However, they come at a high cost. For the orchestration engine to properly manage and maintain an orchestration instance, the engine has to perform multiple round-trips to the Messagebox to persist its state. Message subscription resolution is mostly implemented through stored procedures running on the Messagebox directly. We therefore highly advise you to resort to content-based routing (CBR), as illustrated in Figure 7-2, whenever possible rather than using orchestrations to implement message-routing logic. With the support for CBR of SOAP ports in BizTalk 2006, the use of orchestrations is not required anymore to consume web services and route messages to and back from web services. Simple message routing can be done using content filtering on ports. Unless it is unavoidable, message transformations should be implemented using maps on the ports as well. Use orchestrations if you must correlate multiple messages to fulfill business needs.

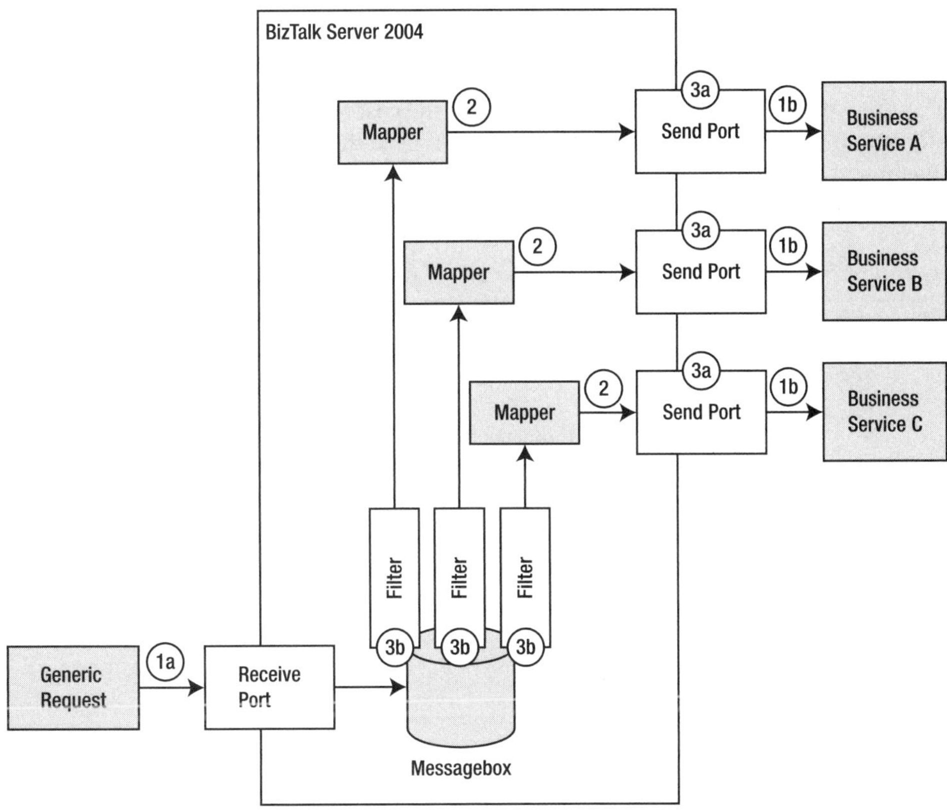

Figure 7-2. *The power of CBR*

4. Enterprise Application Integration patterns and Process Automation patterns were discussed in detail in Chapter 6.

In short, orchestrations should **not** be used to

- Simply route messages between ports.
- Perform simple or conditional transformations on messages.
- Simply call remote systems through expressions and managed code.
- Define complex business rules and policies.

Orchestrations **should** be used to

- Correlate multiple messages to fulfill the required business needs.
- Fire business rules in the Business Rule Engine.
- Manage and scope business transactions.

Know Your Instruments (Shapes)

Just as any C++ or C# developer needs to understand the cost of an API call or a statement to properly optimize their algorithms, BizTalk developers need to understand the use and cost of orchestration shapes to properly optimize their orchestrations. Table 7-1 lists the different orchestration shapes and describes what they are used for and what their cost is.

Table 7-1. *Orchestration Shapes (Microsoft, "BizTalk Server 2006 Documentation," 2006)*[5]

Icon	Shape	Description
	Implicit Start	Indicates the beginning of an orchestration instance.
	Implicit End	Indicates the termination of an orchestration instance. The engine persists the orchestration instance's state for the last time as it reaches the end of the orchestration.
Group_Pro Drop a shape from the toolbox here	Group	Enables you to group operations into a single collapsible and expandable unit for visual convenience.

5. Copyright © 2006 by Microsoft Corporation. Reprinted with permission from Microsoft Corporation.

Icon	Shape	Description
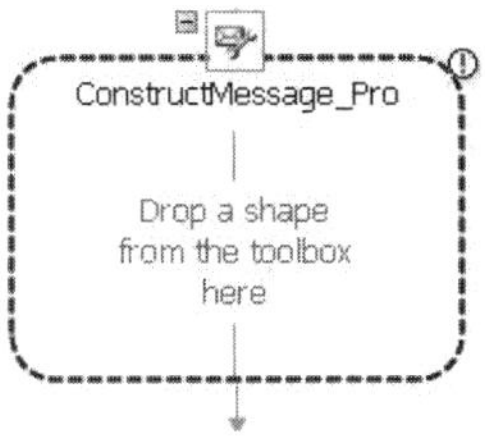 ConstructMessage_Pro Drop a shape from the toolbox here	Construct Message	Constructs a new message instance. It must contain either a Message Assignment shape or a Transform shape, and can contain any number of either, but no other shapes. You specify the message variable that you want to construct and make assignments to the message or its parts. Messages are immutable. Once created and persisted to the Messagebox database, they cannot be changed. All assignments to any given message must take place within the same Construct Message shape. If you want to modify a property on a message that has already been constructed—such as a message that has been received—you must construct a new message instance by assigning the first to the second and then modifying the property on the new message instance; both the construction and modification occur within the same Construct Message shape.
 Transform_Pro	Transform	Moves data from one message into another. The Transform shape is the only way to map one-to-many or many-to-one messages in BizTalk. You need to define one or more input messages, one or more output messages, and an XSLT map for the transform. All messages identified for the transform need to comply with a defined schema. The map assigns message parts from the input messages to message parts in the output messages. Transforms are usable only in the construction of messages, so the Transform shape always appears inside a Construct Message shape.
 MessageAssi...	Message Assignment	Constructs messages by assigning one message to another, assigning individual message parts, or calling a .NET class to construct the message. The Message Assignment shape must be enclosed within a Construct Message shape.
 CallOrchestra...	Call Orchestration	Synchronously instantiates and runs another orchestration. The caller is blocked until the called orchestration terminates. The called orchestration as well as the caller can only consume a maximum of one thread from the engine's thread pool.
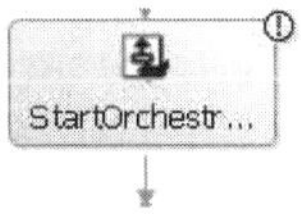 StartOrchestr...	Start Orchestration	Asynchronously instantiates and invokes another orchestration. The invoked orchestration is running on its separate thread and the calling orchestration continues execution. The calling orchestration instance's state is persisted at this point.
	Orchestration Parameters	Port, Message, Variable, Correlation Set, Role Link

Continued

Table 7-1. *Continued*

Icon	Shape	Description
RoleLink_Pro / Provider / PortType_BizTa... / Op_BTSPro / Request / Consumer / Insert Send Ports	Role Link	Contains placeholders for an implements role and a uses role. It can include one of either or one of each. You can add port types directly to a Role Link shape using either existing roles or new roles, and existing or new port types.
Correlation_Pro	Correlation Set	Indicates a set of properties with specific values. This is different from a correlation type, which is simply a list of properties. Correlation sets are used to match an incoming message with the appropriate instance of an orchestration. You can create any number of instances of a given orchestration, and while each of them will perform the same actions, they will do so on different data. If an incoming message does not have all of the properties listed in the correlation set, with matching values for each, correlation will fail and the message will not be received by the orchestration instance.
Variable_Pro	Variable*	Indicates a scoped orchestration variable. Scoped orchestration variables are used the same way as in conventional programming languages. (Variables can be of any .NET class type. The assembly that the class is part of has to be deployed to the GAC and referenced by the BizTalk project. The class has to be serializable unless the variable is being declared within an atomic scope.)
Port_BizTalkPro / Op_BTSPro / Request	Port	Indicates an instance of a definition of a set of message interaction patterns called operations that are permitted at that endpoint (port). An operation can be one-way, in which case one message is sent or received; or it could be two-way, in which case a message is sent (or received) and a response is received (or sent).
Receive_1	Receive Message	Receives a message from a port. It may be used to start an orchestration by setting the **`Activate`** property to true so that a message-matching criteria specified in a filter expression will be received and the orchestration instance will execute. Correlation sets may be applied to a Receive shape to ensure that messages corresponding to a given orchestration instance are correctly received by that instance.
Send_1	Send Message	Sends a given message to a specified port. If an indirect response (not using a request-response port) to the sent message is expected to be received, the message has to be correlated with the currently running instance of the orchestration, so that the respondent can get the response to the correct instance. A following correlation set for a previously initialized correlation or an initializing correlation set may be applied to the Send shape. A persistence point is performed after the execution of a send, except within an atomic scope.

Icon	Shape	Description
Listen_1	Listen	Makes an orchestration instance wait for any one of several possible events before proceeding. The first branch with a condition that evaluates to true (a delay is reached or a message is received) is followed, and none of the other branches will run. The first shape within a Listen branch must be either a Delay shape or a Receive shape. No other shape may be placed below the initial Receive or Delay shape. An activation receive may be used in a Listen shape, but if one branch contains an activation receive, all branches must contain activation receives, and no timeout can be used. The activation receive must be the first action in each branch.
Delay_Pro	Delay	Enables you to control the timing of the orchestration progress. A timeout may be set on the Delay shape so that an orchestration instance pauses before resuming execution. The timeout is specified using **`System.DateTime`** (refer to the definition of DateTime Structure in Microsoft Visual Studio's online help), which causes the orchestration instance to pause until the specified date or time is reached. The timeout may also be specified using **`System.TimeSpan`**, which causes the orchestration instance to pause for the specified length of time (refer to the definition of TimeSpan Structure in Microsoft Visual Studio's online help). Delay shapes are regularly used within Listen shapes to implement a timeout.
ParallelActions_Pro	Parallel Actions	Contains branches. Any shape may be placed in a parallel branch. Each branch of a parallel runs concurrently but independently. It is possible that more than one branch of a Parallel Actions shape will attempt to access the same data. To avoid errors, shapes that access the data should be placed inside synchronized scopes. You can specify in the properties of a Scope shape whether it be synchronized or not. (If a Terminate shape is placed inside a Parallel Actions shape, and the branch with the Terminate on it is run, the instance completes immediately, regardless of whether other branches have finished running. Depending on the orchestration design, results might be unpredictable in this case.)
Decide_Pro	Decide	Represents a decision based on if/else logic. The shape always has a branch for the "if" statement and a branch for the "else" statement; you can add additional branches for "else if" statements as needed. You may use the Expression editor to add a rule to each branch except the "else" branch. If the rule evaluates to true, the branch will be taken. Below the rule or "else" clause, a branch of a Decide shape can contain additional shapes, just like any other part of the orchestration.
Loop_Pro	Loop	Enables your orchestration to loop until a condition is met.
Scope_Pro	Scope	Provides a contextual framework for its contents. The first block of a Scope shape is the context block, or body, in that the basic actions of the scope take place; it is analogous to the **`try`** block in a **`try/catch`** statement. Following the body, the Scope shape may also include one or more exception-handler blocks and a compensation block (refer to the "Scopes" sidebar later in this chapter for more details).

Continued

Table 7-1. *Continued*

Icon	Shape	Description
Compensation_1	Compensation	Enables you to call code to undo or compensate for operations already performed by the orchestration when an error occurs.
CatchException_Pro	Catch Exception	Represents an exception handler and is attached to the end of a Scope shape. You can attach as many Catch Exception blocks as you need. If an exception is thrown that matches the type specified, the exception handler will be called. If some other exception is thrown, it will be handled by the default exception handler. To add a Catch Exception block to a Scope shape, the **`Transaction Type`** property of the Scope shape must be set to None or Long Running.
ThrowExcepti...	Throw Exception	You can explicitly throw exceptions in an orchestration with the Throw Exception shape. The runtime engine searches for the nearest exception handler that can handle the exception type. It first searches the current orchestration for an enclosing scope, and then considers in order the associated exception handlers of the scope. If the engine does not find an appropriate handler, it searches any orchestration that called the current orchestration for a scope that encloses the point of the call to the current orchestration. (Do not select `GeneralException` in the Throw Exception shape. This type should only be used for rethrowing exceptions in a Catch Exception block.)
Expression_T...	Expression	Enables you to enter any expression you choose in your orchestration. For example, you can make a .NET-based call to run an external library or manipulate the values of your orchestration variables. It is generally not good practice to use it to perform high-level orchestration logic that preferably would be visible in the orchestration flow itself. Your orchestration is easier to understand and maintain if your Expression shapes contain simple and modular expressions.
Suspend_My...	Suspend	Makes an orchestration instance stop running until an administrator explicitly intervenes—you do so by setting it to a suspended resumable state,** perhaps to reflect an error condition that requires attention beyond the scope of the orchestration. All of the state information for the orchestration instance is saved, and it will be reinstated when the administrator resumes the orchestration instance. When an orchestration instance is suspended, an error is raised. You can specify a message string to accompany the error to help the administrator diagnose the situation. All of the state information for the orchestration instance is saved, and it is reinstated when the administrator resumes the orchestration instance. If a Suspend shape exists in an orchestration that has been called synchronously (as with the Call Orchestration shape) by another orchestration, the nested instance and all enclosing orchestration instances will be suspended.

Icon	Shape	Description
Terminate_M...	Terminate	The Terminate shape is used to end an orchestration instance instantly. You can specify a message string to accompany the shape when viewed in HAT. If a Terminate shape is encountered in an orchestration that has been called synchronously (as with the Call Orchestration shape) by another orchestration, the nested instance and all enclosing orchestration instances will be terminated.

* *If the developer wants to process a binary object in an orchestration, the message type should be set to* `System.XMLDocument`. *The orchestration engine treats it as an agnostic type, and it does not care what it is, so it does not have to be valid XML. Cool, huh?*

** *If the engine encounters an error or unhandled exception while executing an orchestration, it will set the orchestration to a suspended nonresumable state. This will maintain the orchestration information in the BizTalk Messsagebox database for an administrator to review using HAT and clean up once the information has been examined by the administrator.*

Tip You can pass a gigantic message to an orchestration, and as long as XPath statements are not called, the orchestration will never load the document. Use distinguished and promoted properties to access a message within an orchestration, and the message in use will never be put in memory.

What Transactions Mean and Cost

Transactions guarantee that any partial updates are rolled back automatically[6] in the event of a failure during a transactional update and that the effects of the transaction are erased. Transactions in BizTalk may be **atomic** or **long running**.

Atomic Transactions

In BizTalk, orchestrations are similar to distributed transaction coordinator (DTC) transactions in that they are generally short-lived and have the four **ACID** attributes—(atomicity, consistency, isolation, and durability). The BizTalk Server 2006 documentation (Microsoft, 2006) describes these as follows:[7]

- **Atomicity**: A transaction represents an atomic unit of work. Either all modifications within a transaction are performed or none.
- **Consistency**: When committed, a transaction must preserve the integrity of the data within the system. If a transaction performs a data modification on a database that was internally consistent before the transaction started, the database must still be internally consistent when the transaction is committed. Ensuring this property is largely the responsibility of the application developer.

6. Non–long-running transactions will only persist their state to store when the transaction completes, thus achieving auto-rollback. Long-running transactions require the explicit declaration of a compensation block by the Orchestration Designer.
7. Copyright © 2006 by Microsoft Corporation. Reprinted with permission from Microsoft Corporation.

- **Isolation:** Modifications made by concurrent transactions must be isolated from the modifications made by other concurrent transactions. Isolated transactions that run concurrently perform modifications that preserve internal database consistency exactly as they would if the transactions were run serially.
- **Durability:** After a transaction is committed, all modifications are permanently in place in the system by default. The modifications persist even if a system failure occurs.

According to the BizTalk Server 2006 documentation (Microsoft, 2006), "Atomic transactions guarantee that any partial updates are rolled back automatically in the event of a failure during the transactional update, and that the effects of the transaction are erased (except for the effects of any .NET calls that are made in the transaction)." Atomic transactions dictate to the engine that their scope should be fully executed before the resources allocated to the orchestration instance are released and reused by another instance. Therefore, the XLANG engine does not persist the orchestration instance state until the transaction is fully committed.[8] This allows for the isolation and consistency of the transaction. This also implies that, in the case of a server failure or a manual host instance recycle while the transaction is executing, the orchestration instance will resume execution at the beginning of the atomic transaction scope. An atomic transaction cannot contain any other transaction within it nor can it contain an exception handler.

Crossing the process boundary within an atomic transaction scope is highly undesirable. For example, a call to a receive port within the atomic scope will not allow the engine to dehydrate if there are no messages to receive.[9] Such a design decision might lead to the quick depletion of processing threads in the host instance's thread pool and the inability of the host instance to instantiate new orchestrations. On the other hand, if an atomic transaction contains a Receive shape, a Send shape, or a Start Orchestration shape, the corresponding action will not be performed until the transaction is committed. Therefore, scoping multiple consecutive sends within an atomic scope is very useful. The XLANG engine will not persist the orchestration instance's state on every send, instead batching the round-trips to the Messagebox database to be performed once at the end of the atomic transaction. Atomic transaction scopes are also handy for wrapping nonserializable managed variables; although such wrapping is poor design, sometimes it is inevitable, especially when leveraging third-party managed assemblies or legacy components.

■ **Note** **DTC transactions**, mentioned early in this section, are atomic transactions using COM+ objects derived from `System.Enterprise Services.ServicedComponents` and agreeing isolation levels between transaction components.

---

8. "BizTalk Server ensures that state changes within an atomic transaction—such as modifications to variables, messages, and objects—are visible outside the scope of the atomic transaction only upon commitment of the transaction. The intermediate state changes are isolated from other parts of an orchestration" (Microsoft, "BizTalk Server 2006 Documentation"). Copyright © 2006 by Microsoft Corporation. Reprinted with permission from Microsoft Corporation.
9. An atomic transaction cannot contain matching send and receive actions—that is, a request-response pair or a send and receive that use the same correlation set.

Long-Running Transactions

Long-running transactions provide you with great flexibility in designing robust transaction architecture through custom scope-based compensation, custom scope-based exception handling, and the ability to nest transactions. Long-running transactions are the right candidate if transactions might run for an extended time and full ACID properties are not required (that is, you do not need to guarantee isolation of data from other transactions). A long-running transaction might have long periods of inactivity, often due to waiting for external messages to arrive. The XLANG engine might dehydrate the running orchestration instance at this point and release its resources back to the pool. Long-running transactions impose consistency and durability, but not atomicity and isolation. The data within a long-running transaction is not locked; other processes or applications can modify it. The isolation property for state updates is not maintained because holding locks for a long duration is impractical.

By declaring variables, messages, and .NET components, a scope can define its own state. A long-running transaction has access to the state information of its own scope, any scope that encloses it, and any state information globally defined within the orchestration. It does not have access to the state information of any scopes that do not enclose it.

The following sidebar, based on material from the BizTalk Server 2006 documentation (Microsoft, 2006), discusses scopes in detail.[10]

SCOPES

A scope is a framework for grouping actions. It is primarily used for transactional execution and exception handling. A scope contains one or more blocks. It has a body and can optionally have appended to it any number of exception-handling blocks. It may have an optional compensation block as well, depending on the nature of the scope. Some scopes will be purely for exception handling, and will not require compensation. Other scopes will be explicitly transactional, and will always have a default compensation handler, along with an optional compensation handler that you create for it. A transactional scope will also have a default exception handler and any number of additional exception handlers that you create for it.

BizTalk developers can specify that scopes are synchronized or not synchronized. By synchronizing a scope, developers will ensure that any shared data that is accessed within it will not be written to by one or more parallel actions in their orchestration, nor will it be written to while another action is reading it. Atomic transaction scopes are always synchronized. All actions within a synchronized scope are considered synchronized, as are all actions in any of its exception handlers. Actions in the compensation handler for a transactional scope are not synchronized.

You can nest Scope shapes inside other Scope shapes. The rules for nesting scopes are as follows:

- Transactional and/or synchronized scopes cannot be nested inside synchronized scopes, including the exception handlers of synchronized scopes.
- Atomic transaction scopes cannot have any other transactional scopes nested inside them.
- Transactional scopes cannot be nested inside nontransactional scopes or orchestrations.
- You can nest scopes up to 44 levels deep.

10. Copyright © 2006 by Microsoft Corporation. Reprinted with permission from Microsoft Corporation.

- Call Orchestration shapes can be included inside scopes, but the called orchestrations are treated the same as any other nested transaction, and the same rules apply.
- Start Orchestration shapes can be included inside scopes. Nesting limitations do not apply to started orchestrations.

You can declare variables such as messages and correlation sets at the scope level. You cannot use the same name for a scope variable as for an orchestration variable; however; name hiding is not allowed.

■ **Caution** You can still run into a deadlock condition if you do not design your processes carefully. Example: two branches of a parallel action in orchestration A access the same message, one to send it and one to receive it, so both must have a synchronized scope. A second orchestration receives the message and sends it back. It is possible that the sending branch in orchestration A will receive its locks before the receiving branch, and you will end up with a deadlock.

Threading and Persistence

Threads are a limited resource in BizTalk hosts and persisting a running instance state to the Messagebox is an expensive operation. The orchestration engine balances the use of threads and orchestration persistence and dehydration delicately to ensure the continued execution of the maximum number of instances possible with the minimum overhead required.

Dehydration

The XLANG engine saves to persistent storage the entire state of a running orchestration instance at various points so that the instance can later be completely restored in memory. The state includes

- The internal state of the engine, including its current progress
- The state of any .NET components—variables—that maintain state information and are being used by the orchestration
- Message and variable values

The XLANG engine saves the state of a running orchestration instance at various points. If it needs to rehydrate the orchestration instance, start up from a controlled shutdown, or recover from an unexpected shutdown, it will run the orchestration instance from the last persistence point as though nothing else occurred. For example, if a message is received but an unexpected shutdown occurs before state can be saved, the engine will not record that it has received the message and will receive it again upon restarting.

According to the BizTalk Server 2006 documentation (Microsoft, 2006), the orchestration state is persisted under the following circumstances:[11]

- The end of a transactional scope. The engine saves state at the end of a transactional scope to ensure transactional integrity and to ensure that the point at which the orchestration should resume is defined unambiguously, and that compensation can be carried out correctly if necessary. The orchestration will continue to run from the end of the scope if persistence was successful; otherwise, the appropriate exception handler will be invoked. If the scope is transactional and atomic, the engine will save state within that scope. If the scope is transactional and long running, the engine will generate a new transaction and save the complete state of the runtime.
- A debugging breakpoint is reached.
- A message is sent. The only exception to this is when a message is sent from within an atomic transaction scope.
- The orchestration starts another orchestration asynchronously, as with the Start Orchestration shape.
- The orchestration instance is suspended.
- The system shuts down under controlled conditions.[12] Note that this does not include abnormal termination; in that case, when the engine next runs, it will resume the orchestration instance from the last persistence point that occurred before the shutdown.
- The orchestration instance is finished.
- The engine determines that the instance should be dehydrated.

Transactions have an impact on the number of persistence points within an orchestration and the overall performance of the BizTalk Messagebox, SQL Server, and BizTalk server. An increasing number of persistence points may impede the performance of the BizTalk solution, due to the contention on access to the Messagebox database while storing orchestration instances' state. When using atomic and long-running transactions, the BizTalk developer needs to understand the performance impact of each. Although atomic transactions hold limited system resources, like threads and memory, during the lifetime of the transaction scope, they could be used to minimize the number of persistence points in an orchestration and to minimize the contention and round-trips to the database. Long-running transactions, on the other hand, may be used to optimize the use of limited system resources—threads and memory, as the XLANG engine can dehydrate an orchestration instance within the scope of a long-running transaction and reclaim its memory and threads if it meets the dehydration criteria. For this to be achieved, the XLANG engine needs to persist the orchestration instance's state at various points throughout the long-running

---

11. Copyright © 2006 by Microsoft Corporation. Reprinted with permission from Microsoft Corporation.
12. During a controlled shutdown, the engine saves control information as well as the current state of all running orchestration instances so that it can resume running them when it is started again. The engine will continue to run the instance until it reaches the next persistence point, when it will save the orchestration state and shut down the instance before shutting itself down.

transaction scope. Proper solution load testing and load modeling can give you indications of the number of persistence points over time, and contention over the database may be predicted and proper sizing of the servers implemented to mitigate the risk of these contentions.[13]

The Dehydration Algorithm and Thresholds

So, how does the engine determine that an orchestration should be dehydrated? If an orchestration instance is idle, waiting at Receive, Listen, or Delay shapes, and the engine predicted that it will be idle for a longer period than the dehydration threshold, it will get dehydrated. The decision that an orchestration instance needs to be dehydrated and the prediction that it might become idle for a long period at the current shape is made based on the configurable maximum, minimum, and static thresholds. Those settings may be configured in the BTSNTSvc.exe.config file.[14] The estimated service idle time,[15] used to predict whether an orchestration instance should be dehydrated or not, is averaged out over time. As more instances of the same orchestration get instantiated, the more realistic that average becomes. If a constant dehydration threshold or a memory threshold is used, the check whether an orchestration instance should be dehydrated or not is simple, it is simply

Dehydrate = (Estimated instance idle time > `StaticThreshold`)

or

Dehydrated = (Used host memory > `MemoryThreshold`)

If constant dehydration thresholds are not used, the engine checks whether the estimated instance idle time is greater than `MinThreshold` + `Stress_scaling_factor`[16] * (`MaxThreshold` – `MinThreshold`).

In BizTalk 2006, other than the check when an orchestration instance hits Receive, Listen, or Delay shapes, the engine checks periodically for instances that are passed the dehydration threshold by replacing the estimated instance idle time with the actual instance idle time in the preceding checks. Orchestration instances with actual instance idle time past the dehydration threshold are dehydrated immediately.

Caution The checks for constant dehydration thresholds do not use the `Stress_scaling_factor`. This means that the thresholds do not decrease as the server is under increasing stress!

---

13. For proper scalability and sizing techniques, refer to the BizTalk Performance and Stress Team's white paper on scalability and performance tuning.

14. The section "Orchestration Engine Configuration" covers the different thresholds and their syntax.

15. The estimated service idle time is calculated for instances of the same orchestration type. If a host instance is recycled or the server is rebooted, that value is reset and is averaged out again from scratch.

16. `Stress_scaling_factor` is a number between 0 and 1 that converges to zero with stress. This will ensure that orchestration instances get dehydrated at a much lower estimated idle time if the system is under stress.

The Cost of Parallel Shapes

If you were to ask seasoned developers whether to use a multithreaded approach to respond to a set of requests, each resulting in a series of calculations followed by the formatting of a response, or simply resorting to using a limited number of threads to respond to these requests, they would likely say that a single threaded approach would be their method of choice. An alternative would be using a limited pool of prespawned threads to perform these transactions, and they would warn against the use of a single worker thread per request. This is because the act of spawning threads and allocating their proper resources and soft context switching is somewhat expensive, but mostly because of the complexity associated with multithreaded design and the uncertainty of the order of execution.

You should also be wary of using Parallel Actions shapes for the same reasons. There are hidden costs associated with using Parallel Actions shapes. The engine decides whether new threads need to be allocated to perform the parallel branches and implements a persistence point before the parallel action, then one at the ending synchronization point. Figures 7-3, 7-4, and 7-5 illustrate three different ways to perform the same action and highlight that using parallel actions would result in the worst performance. There is also the risk of corrupting data, as interleaved data access from multiple parallel branches might lead to unexpected behavior and undesirable values. To avoid data corruption, the logic accessing data should be encapsulated within synchronized scopes. Synchronized scopes will ensure that the data is being accessed by one thread or branch at a time. Using synchronized scopes will result in parallel branches being blocked on each other to ensure data integrity. This will slow down execution to ensure the predictability of the outcome. Depending on how complex and interdependent the logic is, it might be simpler to serially perform the data access instead of using parallel actions.

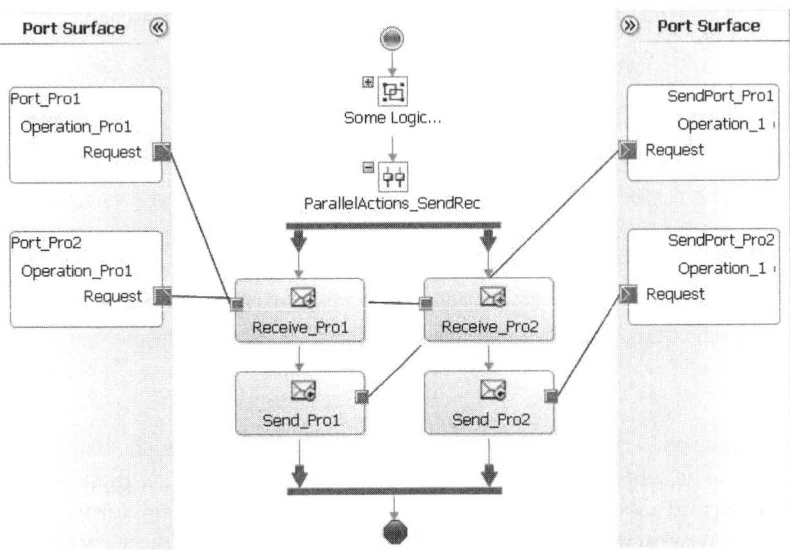

Figure 7-3. *Parallel actions—slowest solution*

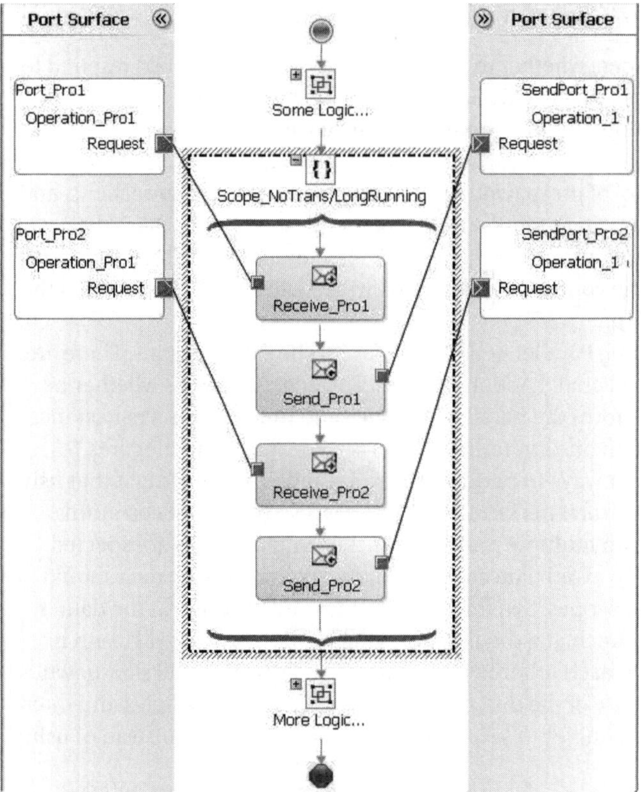

Figure 7-4. *Single long-running transaction or scope with no transaction—second slowest solution*

■ **Caution** The use of parallel branches in orchestrations does not mean that these branches will run on parallel threads. It is simply an indication to the XLANG engine that operations in these branches may be interleaved if necessary! The engine then makes the decision to run them on separate threads or interleave them. For example, if you place a Terminate shape inside a Parallel Actions shape, and the branch with the Terminate shape on it is run, the instance completes immediately, regardless of whether other branches have finished running. Depending on your design, results might be unpredictable in this case.

One of us, Ahmed, once got a call from a developer who was seeing his BizTalk host instance recycle every time he sent more than five concurrent messages to his solution. The problem was reproducible and easy to diagnose, as the error message in the event log was "not enough threads" to create new orchestration instances. Although BizTalk dehydrates orchestration instances to manage its resources and the number of active threads versus the number of available threads in the thread pool, if all current running instances are active, BizTalk may not be able to dehydrate them to free up some resources.

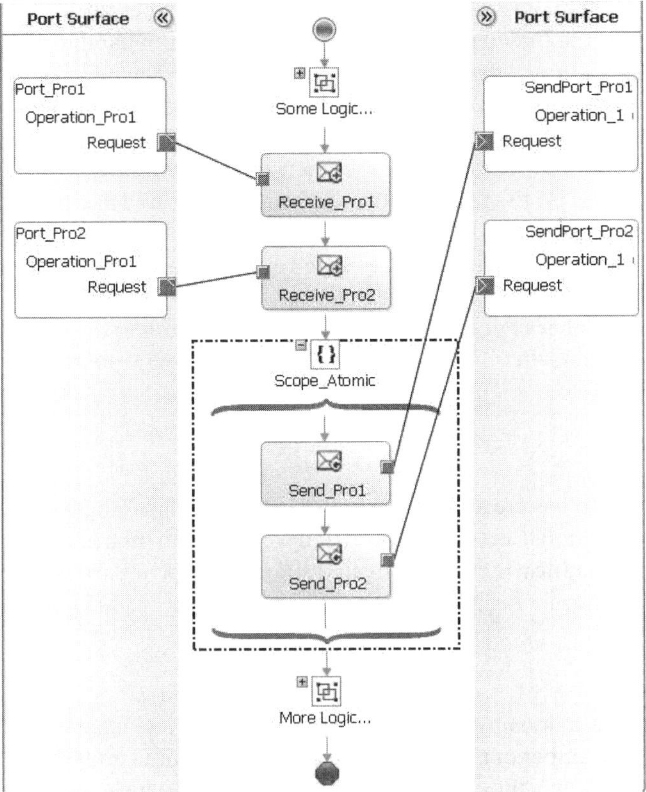

Figure 7-5. *Sends in atomic scope—fastest solution*

In the scenario we're talking about, the developer had an orchestration subscribed to a receive port and upon activating a receive would issue five calls to an external managed .NET assembly on five parallel branches in a Parallel Actions shape. The external assembly performed a set of calculations and eventually called a web service to perform a transaction.[17] The test was being implemented on the developer's machine that luckily was set to have a pool of 25 threads max per CPU.[18] Had the settings been higher, it would have taken longer for the developer to find the problem.

We are sure that by now you are aware of the point we are trying to make. Although calling a web service from within an expression instead of using the messaging subsystem would not

17. Calling external logic that might take a considerable amount of time to perform its task before returning should be implemented through the messaging subsystem. A call to an external assembly from within an expression means that the call is executing on the XLANG engine's thread currently assigned to that particular orchestration instance. Making such calls from within expressions means that the engine threads will not be able to manage its threads and dehydrate them as required.

18. Using the BizTalk 2006 Server Administration Console, you can set the thresholds for the number of threads per CPU through the throttling thresholds settings on the Advanced tab of the host property pages.

be considered wise, making the calls in parallel from within Parallel Actions shapes results in the exhaustion of available threads in the thread pool and prevents the host from handling new instances. BizTalk uses the default thread pool provided by the .NET common language runtime (CLR); tuning the thread pool is simply a matter of setting the proper values in the BizTalk Server 2006 Administration Tools for the particular BizTalk host. With automatic throttling in BizTalk 2006, you will not have to worry as much about their servers recycling, but tuning the server with the proper values for the thread pool based on the projected and modeled loads will lead to an optimal application performance.

In short, BizTalk application performance can be easily optimized by monitoring and tuning the minimum and maximum number of threads in the thread pool and the number of in-flight messages; monitoring the number of persistence points and their effect on the overall performance; and tweaking orchestrations to minimize the number of persistence points.

Correlation

Automating a business process tends to require associating multiple messages together to achieve the necessary business transaction. **Correlations** are used whenever an orchestration does not have an explicit way of associating a message with an instance, such as an activating receive, a request-response, or a self-correlating port.

What Is Correlation?

Correlation is the process of matching an incoming message with the appropriate instance of an orchestration. You can create any number of instances of a given orchestration, and while each of them will perform the same actions, they will do so on different data. To have the same **orchestration instance** perform a set of actions on different incoming messages to complete a complex transaction, you will need to leverage **correlation sets** and correlate those incoming messages. If, for example, an orchestration developed to automate a purchase from a partner is designed to issue a purchase order, receive an invoice, and send payment, you need to be sure that the invoice is received by the same orchestration instance that the corresponding purchase order was sent from. Imagine ordering a single item and getting back an invoice for 1,000 items, or vice versa, and you will understand the value of correlation.

This sort of correlation of messages with orchestration instances may be achieved by defining correlation sets. A **correlation set** is a set of properties with specific values. If an incoming message does not have all of these properties, with matching values for each, correlation will fail, and the message will not be received by the orchestration instance. Correlation sets are initialized in a receive action or a send action.

Each correlation set is based on a **correlation type**, which is simply a list of properties. These properties might be data properties, which are found in the message itself, or context properties, which describe details of the system or messages that are unrelated to the data being conveyed in the message.

A correlation type may be used in more than one correlation set. If you need to correlate on different values for the properties in a correlation type, you must create a new correlation set—each correlation set can be initialized only once.[19]

19. Correlation sets may be passed as in parameters to other orchestrations.

■ **Caution** Do not set the system-defined property `BTS.CorrelationToken` associated with each message. This is used by the engine in correlating messages, and setting it could result in your orchestration losing messages.

The properties of a message sent from an orchestration may be validated by the engine to ensure that it reflects the properties in its correlation set. By default, this validation is disabled.[20]

Convoys: Serial vs. Parallel

Convoys are groups of related messages that are intended by a partner business process to be handled in a specific order within an orchestration. For example, an orchestration might need to receive five different messages before any processing can begin.

When a group of correlated messages could potentially be received at the same time, a race condition could occur in that a correlation set in a particular orchestration instance must be initialized by one of the messages before the other messages can be correlated to that orchestration instance. To ensure that all of the correlated messages will be received by the same orchestration instance, BizTalk detects the potential for such a race condition and treats these messages as a convoy.

There are two main types of convoys: **concurrent correlated receives** and **sequential correlated receives**. A convoy set is a group of correlation sets that are used in a convoy.

Note the following general restrictions on convoys:

- A convoy set can contain no more than three properties.
- Concurrent and sequential convoys can coexist in an orchestration, but they cannot use any shared correlation sets.
- Correlation sets passed into started orchestrations do not receive convoy processing in the started orchestration.
- You cannot initialize two or more correlation sets with one receive to be used in separate convoys. For example, if receive r1 initializes correlation sets c1 and c2, receive r2 follows c1, and receive r3 follows c2, then the orchestration engine will not treat these as convoys. It is a valid convoy scenario if both r2 and r3 follow both c1 and c2, both follow c1 only, or both follow c2 only.

Concurrent correlated receives are correlated receive statements in two or more branches of a Parallel Actions shape. If a correlation is initialized in more than one parallel task, each correlated receive must initialize exactly the same set of correlations. The first such task that receives a correlated message will do the actual initialization, and validation will be done on the others.

---

20. Refer to the "Orchestration Engine Configuration" section near the end of this chapter for more information on how to enable and disable correlation validation.

Sequential correlated receives are receives that are correlated to previous receives. Convoy processing takes place for cases in which the correlation sets for a receive are initialized by another receive.

■ **Note** Any correlation set that is being followed by a send statement (chronologically) prior to the particular receive statement is not considered a part of the convoy set.

For receives that require convoy processing, the following restrictions apply:

- The correlation sets that constitute a sequential convoy set for a particular receive must be initialized by one preceding receive.
- The port for a receive that requires sequential convoy processing must be the same as the port for the receive initializing the convoy set. Cross-port convoys are not supported.
- Message types for a particular receive that require convoy processing must match the message type for the receive initializing the convoy set, unless the receive statement is operating on an ordered delivery port.
- All receives participating in a sequential convoy must follow all the correlation sets that are initialized (or followed) by the initializing receive, unless operating on an ordered delivery port.
- If a sequential convoy is initialized by an Activating Receive statement, then the Activating Receive cannot have a filter expression unless operating on an ordered delivery port.
- If a sequential convoy is initialized by an Activating Receive, the following receives cannot be inside a nested orchestration. Otherwise the preceding rules apply for nested orchestrations.

Pitfalls of Orchestration Development

Some BizTalk artifacts lend themselves nicely to particular patterns of solutions, while their use could be devastating to the performance of a different solution. The following sections describe some of these solution patterns and the pitfalls that you as a BizTalk developer need to watch out for.

Batch Processing and Legacy Systems

Legacy mainframe systems excel in what they were designed to do best, batch processing. With the emergence of online applications and progressive automation of internal processes, the load onto these legacy systems is exponentially increasing. Instead of handling a handful of requests concurrently, they are now expected to handle hundreds and thousands of concurrent requests as business goes online and customers perform actions resulting in transactions executing on these back-end legacy systems. EAI platforms such as BizTalk facilitate the integration of newly developed interactive systems with legacy back ends such as those batch-processing mainframes. Third-party or custom adapters could be used to communicate with the mainframes, and transformation maps could be used to translate data back and forth. BizTalk-based solutions developed to integrate with the mainframe will leverage the Messagebox as a queue to throttle and batch transaction requests to the mainframes to ensure their ability to handle the incoming load of requests.

Such a solution works perfectly fine, but should be stress and load tested to ensure that the queuing and throttling does not affect the overall performance of the solution. With BizTalk 2006 auto-throttling, queuing is not a big problem, but with previous versions of BizTalk, queuing leads to the growth of the spool table in the Messagebox, which affects the overall performance of the Messagebox and consequently the BizTalk server.

Interactive Orchestrations (The Request/Response Approach)

The response time in interactive orchestrations such as workflows exposed as web services could be critical to the correctness of the complete solutions. For example, a call from an ASP.NET web app to an orchestration exposed as a web service might be expected to return within 2 seconds or less so that the web application can complete its response to the client within the required timeout period. To ensure that BizTalk is not holding incoming web service requests from being submitted to the proper orchestration instance as soon as they arrive, the batch size should be set to 1 in the adm_serviceclass table in the Management Database for the web service receive host. To minimize the time spent by the engine performing its plumbing functions, you should use atomic transaction scopes whenever possible to minimize the number of persistence points in the orchestration.

If tuning is not enough to improve the response time, you should consider redesigning the interaction with the orchestration to support polling. For example, the web application will call a one-way web method as soon as the data needed to pass to the orchestration is available to that web application, passing in a parameter that the orchestration will use for correlation. The web application would then call a two-way request-response web method, right before the web application really needs the response from the orchestration instance, passing in the same parameter used for correlation and receiving the expected response from the orchestration. This request/poll method allows the orchestration instance extra time to execute and formulate the response while the web application is still executing and promptly responding to client requests.

Calling an Assembly or Sending a Message to a Web Service

Complex logic in a process is usually wrapped in an external assembly called by the orchestration at different points in its execution. The called logic in those external assemblies will execute on the same thread assigned to the orchestration instance by the engine. The engine cannot dehydrate the thread while it is executing within the external assembly. Also, if a failure occurs and the server is restarted, the orchestration instance will continue execution from the last persistence point, meaning that it will issue the same call to the external assembly again, resulting in the execution of the same logic twice. Logic in those external assemblies should not be affecting state in permanent data stores.

In the rare circumstances that logic in those external assemblies does affect state in permanent data stores, those assemblies should be wrapped in protective transactions that prevent those permanent data stores from being altered until the transaction fully executes successfully. Those assemblies should then be exposed as web services and called through the messaging infrastructure to ensure that they are called once and only once.

For complex logic in external assemblies called by orchestrations that are expected to take a considerable amount of time to execute or pause in idle state for an event to occur and complete, execution should also be isolated and exposed as a web service. This ensures that the orchestration instance calling that logic can dehydrate while waiting for a response to come back from the web service and relinquish its resources instead of holding them while waiting for the response.

Error Handling and Suspended Instances

It's Murphy's Law that in a production environment errors are bound to occur. BizTalk solutions not designed to handle and recover from errors are going to suffer a performance degradation that might lead to an eventual catastrophic failure. You might be thinking, "Impossible, I have fault tolerance built into every part of the solution," but consider the following scenario. A BizTalk orchestration running within your application is issuing solicit/response calls to an external web service through the SOAP adapter. One of the web services that you are calling happens to fail intermittently and throws an exception. What will happen to your orchestration? If you are not properly handling exceptions in your orchestration, it is going to fail with an unhandled exception, and you will end with a suspended-unresumable instance on your hands. What is worse is that you just had a business transaction fail, and the only way to retry it is to have the logic to recover from it and retry it all from the beginning. So, lesson number 1: handle exceptions, including those raised by external assemblies, expressions, or the messaging subsystem caused by external systems.

OK, so now you have learned your lesson and are handling exceptions throughout the orchestration. What about those suspended-resumable message instances being accumulated in the queue every time the called web service throws an exception? If not handled, those are going to keep on piling up in the queues and spool and eventually negatively affect the overall system performance. So, lesson number 2: configure and handle error reports.[21] As the BizTalk Server 2006 documentation (Microsoft, 2006) states, "At each point along the pathway that a message follows through the BizTalk Server messaging subsystem, failures can occur in the BizTalk Server infrastructure and in custom pipeline components, orchestrations, and so forth. If you have specified error reporting for the port through which a message is entering or will leave, BizTalk Server publishes an error report message derived from the failing message. The error report message is routed to the subscribing routing destination, such as a send port or orchestration; all previously promoted properties are

21. In BizTalk 2004, the messaging subsystem publishes negative acknowledgments (NACKs) whenever a message fails and its instance is suspended. Orchestrations should be able to subscribe to those NACKs and perform the required recovery and consequent cleanup of those suspended instances. The handling of those NACKs and cleanup of suspended messages is essential to ensure the system's overall healthy operation as well as the sanity of the business transaction.

demoted and selected properties related to the specific messaging failure are promoted to the message context."[22]

BizTalk Server does not suspend the message when failed message routing is enabled, it routes the message instead. Failed message routing can be enabled on both receive and send ports. Any failure that occurs in adapter processing, pipeline processing, mapping, or message routing results in an error message if routing for failed messages is enabled. Also, when a messaging error occurs while an orchestration is receiving from a receive port or sending to a send port, the resulting error message is associated with the messaging ports to which the orchestration is bound. The error message is a clone of the original message. When a failed message is generated, BizTalk Server promotes error-report–related message context properties and demotes regular message context properties before publishing the failed message. If failed message routing is not enabled, messages that fail are simply suspended.

"Error messages are delivered to orchestrations or send ports that have subscribed to receive them. A subscription typically selects an error message based on the name of the port in which the messaging error occurred (either a send or a receive port). A subscription might also filter on other properties promoted to the error's message context (for example, InboundTransportLocation or FailureCode)" (Microsoft, "BizTalk Server 2006 Documentation," 2006).

In short, to ensure the sanity of your business transactions and healthy operation of the system, handle exceptions and configure your application to handle error reports to recover from errors and prevent suspended message instances.

Orchestration Engine Configuration

The orchestration engine uses an XML file called BTSNTSvc.exe.config to determine certain behaviors. A service reads this configuration information once, when it is started. Any changes to it will not be picked up unless the service is stopped and restarted.

See the examples that follow for different nodes and potential values.

Example: All Validations On

The following configuration example illustrates how to enable assembly, schema, correlation, and logging validation.

```
<?xml version="1.0" ?>
<configuration>
      <configSections>
            <section
                  name="xlangs" type="Microsoft.XLANGs ➥
.BizTalk.CrossProcess.XmlSerializationConfigurationSectionHandler, ➥
Microsoft.XLANGs.BizTalk.CrossProcess" />
      </configSections>
```

22. "An error message is a clone of the original failed message, with all previously promoted properties demoted and with a set of error-specific properties promoted to the message context. . . . Previously promoted properties are demoted to avoid unintended delivery to subscribers not designated to receive the error message. The error message is published for distribution to subscribers (orchestrations, send ports, and send port groups)" (Microsoft, "BizTalk Server 2006 Documentation"). Copyright 2006 by Microsoft Corporation. Reprinted with permission from Microsoft Corporation.

```
        <runtime>
                <assemblyBinding xmlns="urn:schemas-microsoft-com:asm.v1">
                        <probing privatePath="BizTalk Assemblies;Developer Tools; ➥
Tracking" />
                </assemblyBinding>
        </runtime>

        <xlangs>
                <Configuration>
                        <Debugging
                                ValidateAssemblies="true"
                                ValidateSchemas="true"
                                ValidateCorrelations="true"
                                ExtendedLogging="true"
                        />
                </Configuration>
        </xlangs>
</configuration>
```

Example: Assembly Validation Only

The following configuration example illustrates how to enable assembly validation only.

```
<?xml version="1.0" ?>
<configuration>
        <configSections>
                <section
                        name="xlangs"
                        type="Microsoft.XLANGs.BizTalk ➥
.CrossProcess.XmlSerializationConfiguration ➥
SectionHandler, Microsoft.XLANGs.BizTalk.CrossProcess"
                />
        </configSections>
        <runtime>
                <assemblyBinding xmlns="urn:schemas-microsoft-com:asm.v1">
                        <probing privatePath="BizTalk Assemblies;Developer Tools; ➥
Tracking" />
                </assemblyBinding>
        </runtime>

        <xlangs>
                <Configuration>
                        <Debugging
                                ValidateAssemblies="true"
                                ExtendedLogging="false"
                        />
                </Configuration>
        </xlangs>
</configuration>
```

Example: Dehydration

The following configuration example illustrates how to configure dehydration settings.

```
<?xml version="1.0" ?>
<configuration>
       <configSections>
              <section name="xlangs" type= "Microsoft.XLANGs ➥
.BizTalk.CrossProcess.XmlSerializationConfigurationSectionHandler, ➥
Microsoft.XLANGs.BizTalk.CrossProcess" />
       </configSections>
       <runtime>
              <assemblyBinding xmlns="urn:schemas-microsoft-com:asm.v1">
                     <probing privatePath="BizTalk Assemblies;Developer Tools; ➥
Tracking" />
              </assemblyBinding>
       </runtime>
       <xlangs>
              <Configuration>
                     <!--
                     MaxThreshold: the maximal time, in seconds,
                     that a dehydratable orchestration
                     is retained in memory before being dehydrated.
                     MinThreshold: the minimum time, in seconds, that a
                     dehydratable orchestration is retained in memory before
                     it is considered for dehydration.
                     ConstantThreshold: the dynamic threshold usually
                     fluctuates between the min and max values specified.
                     However, you can make the threshold
                     a fixed value by setting this. A value of -1
                     tells the engine not to use a constant threshold.
                     -->
                     <Dehydration MaxThreshold="1800" MinThreshold="1"
                       ConstantThreshold="-1">
                            <!--
                            Currently, virtual memory can become a bottleneck
                            on 32-bit machines due to unmanaged heap fragmentation,
                            so you should throttle by this resource as well.
                            You should reconfigure if /3GB is set.
                            Optimal and maximal usage are in MB.
                            -->
                            <VirtualMemoryThrottlingCriteria OptimalUsage="900"
                              MaximalUsage="1300" IsActive="true" />
```

```
                        <!--
                         This is a useful criterion for throttling, but
                         appropriate values depend on whether the box is being
                         shared among servers. If the machine has a lot of RAM
                         and is not being shared with other functions,
                         then these values can be significantly increased.
                         Optimal and maximal usage are in MB.
                         -->
                         <PrivateMemoryThrottlingCriteria OptimalUsage="50"
                           MaximalUsage="350" IsActive="true" />
                    </Dehydration>
                </Configuration>
            </xlangs>
</configuration>
```

Example: AppDomain Configuration

Assemblies are assigned to named domains using assignment rules (more about which appears in the comments within the code). If no rule is specified for some assembly, the assembly will be assigned to an ad hoc domain. The number of such assigned assemblies per ad hoc domain is determined by the value of AssembliesPerDomain.

```
<?xml version="1.0" ?>
<configuration>
    <configSections>
        <section name="xlangs"
          type="Microsoft.XLANGs.BizTalk.CrossProcess.XmlSerialization ➥
ConfigurationSectionHandler, Microsoft.XLANGs.BizTalk.CrossProcess" />
    </configSections>
    <runtime>
        <assemblyBinding xmlns="urn:schemas-microsoft-com:asm.v1">
            <probing privatePath="BizTalk Assemblies;Developer Tools;Tracking" />
        </assemblyBinding>
    </runtime>
    <xlangs>
        <Configuration>
            <!--
                <!--
AppDomain configuration.
                Assemblies are assigned to named domains using assignment. If no ➥
rule is specified for some assembly, the assembly will be
assigned to an ad hoc domain. The number of such assigned assemblies per ad hoc
domain is determined by the value of AssembliesPerDomain.
            -->-->
            <AppDomains AssembliesPerDomain="10">
                <!--
                    <!--
```

```
                In this section, the user may specify default configuration
                for any app domain created that does not have a named
                configuration associated with it (see AppDomainSpecs later in
                this example). SecondsEmptyBeforeShutdown is the number of
                seconds that an app domain is empty (that is, it does not
                contain any orchestrations) before being unloaded. Specify -1
                to signal that an app domain should never unload, even when
                empty. Similarly, SecondsIdleBeforeShutdown is the number of
                seconds that an app domain is idle (that is, it contains only
                dehydratable orchestrations) before being unloaded. Specify -1
                to signal that an app domain should never unload when idle but
                not empty. When an idle but nonempty domain is shut down, all
                of the contained instances are dehydrated first.
            -->
            -->
<DefaultSpec SecondsIdleBeforeShutdown="1200" SecondsEmptyBeforeShutdown="1800">
              <!--
                <!--
                BaseSetup is a serialized System.AppDomainSetup object.
                This is passed as is to AppDomain.CreateAppDomain()
                and can be used to influence assembly
                search path, etc.
              -->
              -->
<BaseSetup>
 <ApplicationBase>c:\myAppBase</ApplicationBase>
 <ConfigurationFile>c:\myAppBase\myConfig.config</ConfigurationFile>
 <DynamicBase>DynamicBase_0</DynamicBase>
 <DisallowPublisherPolicy>true</DisallowPublisherPolicy>
 <ApplicationName>ApplicationName_0</ApplicationName>
 <PrivateBinPath>PrivateBinPath_0</PrivateBinPath>
 <PrivateBinPathProbe>PrivateBinPathProbe_0</PrivateBinPathProbe>
 <ShadowCopyDirectories>ShadowCopyDirectories_0</ShadowCopyDirectories>
 <ShadowCopyFiles>ShadowCopyFiles_0</ShadowCopyFiles>
 <CachePath>CachePath_0</CachePath>
 <LicenseFile>LicenseFile_0</LicenseFile>
 <LoaderOptimization>NotSpecified</LoaderOptimization>
</BaseSetup>
</DefaultSpec>
            <!--
              - <!--
In this section the user may specify named configurations for specific app domains,
identified by their "friendly name". The format of any app-domain spec is identical
to that of the default app-domain spec.
```

```
                -->-->
                <AppDomainSpecs>
                    <AppDomainSpec Name="MyDomain1" SecondsIdleBeforeShutdown= ➥
"-1" SecondsEmptyBeforeShutdown="12000">
                        <BaseSetup>
                            <PrivateBinPath>c:\PathForAppDomain1</PrivateBinPath>
                        <PrivateBinPath>PrivateBinPath_0</PrivateBinPath>
<PrivateBinPathProbe>PrivateBinPathProbe_0</PrivateBinPathProbe>
</BaseSetup>
                    </AppDomainSpec>
                    <AppDomainSpec Name="MyFrequentlyUnloadingDomainMyTrashyDomain"
                      SecondsIdleBeforeShutdown="60" SecondsEmptyBeforeShutdown=
"60" />
                </AppDomainSpecs>
                <!-- The PatternAssignmentRules and ExactAssignmentRules control
                     assignment of assemblies to app domains. When a message
                     arrives, the name of its corresponding orchestration's assembly
                     is determined. Then, the assembly is assigned an app domain
                     name. The rules guide this assignment. Exact rules are
                     consulted first, in their order of definition, and then the
                     pattern rules. The first match is used. If no match is found,
                     the assembly will be assigned to an ad hoc domain. The
                     configuration and number of assemblies per ad hoc domain is
                     controlled by the AssembliesPerDomain attribute and the
                     DefaultSpec section. -->
<ExactAssignmentRules>

<!-- An exact assembly rule specifies a strong assembly name and an app domain name.
 If the strong assembly name equals the rule's assembly name, it is assigned to
 the corresponding app domain.-->
                    <ExactAssignmentRule AssemblyName="BTSAssembly1, ➥
 Version=1.0.0.0, Culture=neutral, PublicKeyToken=9c7731c5584592ad ➥
                      AssemblyName_0" AppDomainName="MyDomain1" />
AppDomainName_1" />
                    <ExactAssignmentRule AssemblyName=
                      "BTSAssembly2, Version=1.0.0.0, Culture=neutral, ➥
PublicKeyToken=9c7731c5584592ad AssemblyName_0"
 AppDomainName="AppDomainName_1" />
                <ExactAssignmentRule AssemblyName=
"AssemblyName_0" AppDomainName="AppDomainName_1" />
</ExactAssignmentRules>
                <PatternAssignmentRules>
                    <!-- A pattern assignment rule specifies a regular expression
                    and an app domain name. If the strong assembly name matches the
                    expression, it is assigned to the corresponding app domain.
                    This allows version-independent assignment, assignment by
                    public key token, or assignment by the custom assembly key.
```

```
                    -->
                    <!--
                        Assign all assemblies with name BTSAssembly3,
                        regardless of version and public key,
                        to the MyDomain1 app domain.
                    -->
                    <PatternAssignmentRule AssemblyNamePattern= ➥
" BTSAssembly3, Version=\d.\d.\d.\d, Culture=neutral, ➥
 PublicKeyToken=.{16}"AssemblyNamePattern_0"
                        AppDomainName="AppDomainName_1" />
                         AppDomainName="MyDomain1" />
                <PatternAssignmentRule
                  AssemblyNamePattern="AssemblyNamePattern_0"
                  AppDomainName="AppDomainName_1" />
</PatternAssignmentRules>
            </AppDomains>
        </Configuration>
    </xlangs>
</configuration>
```

In addition to BizTalk-specific configuration information, the BTSNTSvc.exe.config file is also the place where .NET application components that run in the context of an orchestration, an adapter, or a pipeline obtain their configuration information at runtime using the standard .NET `<appSettings>` tag under the `<configuration>` tag. Because BizTalk already provides a mechanism for custom adapters and pipeline components to obtain configuration information, the `<appSettings>` tag in the BTSNTSvc.exe.config file would most likely be used by custom .NET components called from within an orchestration.[23] For example:

```
<appSettings>
<add key="configParamName" value="configParamValue" />
</appSettings>
```

---

23. A separate custom config file may be specified per app domain using the `<ConfigurationFile/>` key to hold the required configuration and app settings for custom application components.

CHAPTER 8

Playing By the Rules? Use the Business Rule Engine.

The Business Rule Engine (BRE) enables you to encapsulate the creation and management of complex rules to be used from within your applications. These rules can be modified and updated in real time without having to update any assemblies in the solution, thereby providing a great deal of flexibility.

What Is a Business Rule Engine?

An organization's most important assets are the products/services it provides to its customers as well as the business model and internal processes it uses to differentiate itself from its competition. An organization's IT department's most valuable assets are the data on products/services and customers of the organization as well as the workflows and business rules that drive the internal processes and business model. It is the IT department's main responsibility to ensure the security and agility of those assets.

While data management and portability is being addressed by database management systems like SQL Server, and workflow management and portability is usually addressed by business process management services like the BizTalk orchestration engine, business rules are usually neglected. Most business rules today are implemented in procedural languages and code that is maintained by application developers and programmers. This ties up one of the most critical organizational assets and limits its agility. The cost and time required to update the business rules and underlying IT services within an organization that implements its business rules in procedural languages is too high for such an organization to react quickly to its business units' needs.

The BRE addresses these pains. It allows IT departments to properly isolate and manage their business rules and policies in a simple manner so that they can react to their organization's business process changes swiftly at low cost points. The Business Rule Engine allows business analysts to describe business policies and rules in a simple graphical or textual form without the need to use a typical procedural programming language. Those rules are then stored away from the rest of the enterprise applications in a separate business rule store managed by the Business Rule Engine. Isolating business rules from the invoking applications in such a manner allows business analysts and business rule authors to update the business rules dynamically to meet the changes required by their business units. Updating those business rules does not require any changes to enterprise applications or business orchestrations that invoke them. Running applications will seamlessly fire the latest version of the updated business rules the next time they invoke them. Applications leveraging the BRE invoke business rules through the **Business Rules Framework**.

As stated in the BizTalk Server 2006 documentation (Microsoft, 2006),[1]

> *The Business Rules Framework is a Microsoft .NET-compliant class library. It provides an efficient inference engine that can link highly readable, declarative, semantically rich rules to any business objects (.NET components), XML documents, or database tables. Application developers can build business rules by constructing rules from small building blocks of business logic (small rule sets) that operate on information (facts) contained in .NET objects, database tables, and XML documents. This design pattern promotes code reuse, design simplicity, and modularity of business logic. In addition, the rule engine does not impose on the architecture or design of business applications. In fact, you can add rule technology to a business application by directly invoking the rule engine, or you can have external logic that invokes your business objects without modifying them. In short, the technology enables developers to create and maintain applications with minimal effort.*

Rule engines optimize rule resolution performance. They can evaluate rules within the same policy in parallel and cache their results until the facts involved in their evaluation change. **Business policies**, or **rule sets**, are composed of multiple business rules. Figure 8-1 illustrates this composition. The order of the evaluation of the different rules within a policy may be controlled by setting priorities to these different rules. **Rules** are composed of a **condition** followed by a set of **actions** that are executed if the condition in question is evaluated to be true. Conditions are composed of **operations**—predicates—that can be performed on **facts** to result in a Boolean value. Facts may be part of an XML document, an entry in a relational database, a basic .NET type, or a .NET component. To retrieve the values of complex facts, **fact retrievers**, which are .NET components that implement a particular interface, may be used.

The Business Rule Engine is composed of multiple components:

- The Business Rule Composer allows business rule authors to identify the sources for the different facts used within their business rules as well as define and version their business policies and business rules.
- The Business Rule Store holds the definition of those business policies and facts.
- The in-memory cache holds the results of the evaluation of the different business rule conditions.
- The Business Rules Framework is used by application developers or orchestration developers to call business policies and execute different business rules from within their applications or orchestrations.
- The Business Rules Update Service monitors the Business Rule Store for published updates of policies and rules to deprecate older versions from the cache and reevaluate conditions as needed.

---

1. Copyright © 2006 by Microsoft Corporation. Reprinted with permission from Microsoft Corporation.

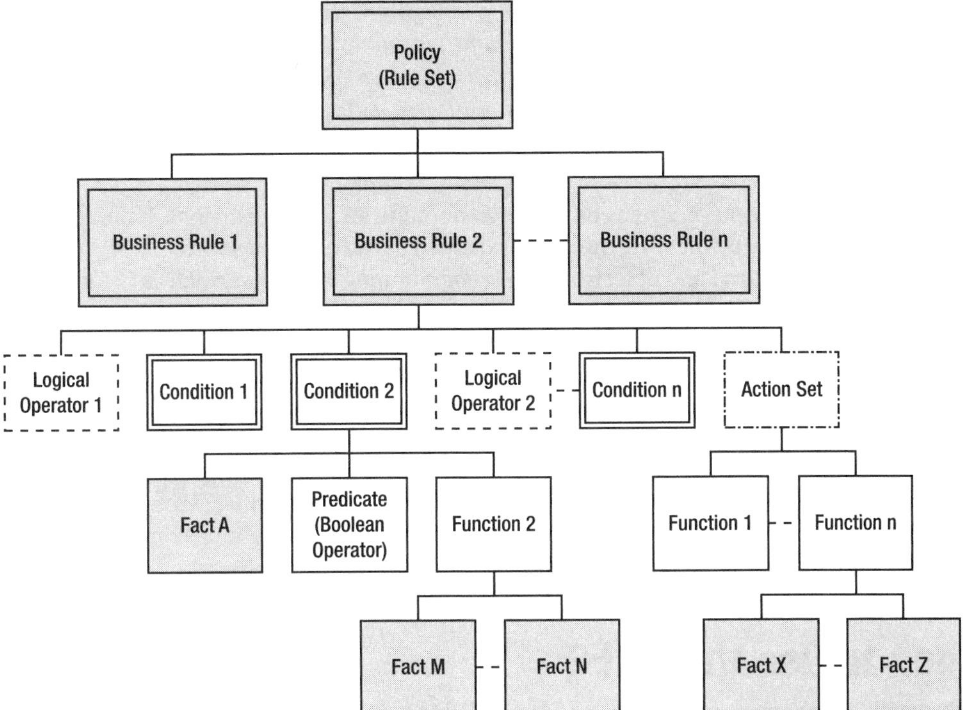

Figure 8-1. *The composition of a business policy*

Studies show that 15% to 50% of annual IT budgets are spent on compiling, testing, and implementing rule changes in applications. Rule engines allow the separation of business rules from the applications that use them and enable the maintenance of business logic without having to resort to code changes and software modification. This reduces application development time and significantly reduces maintenance and enhancement cost by 15% to 50%. IT organizations leveraging rule engines can increase the flexibility of their applications and services and reduce their time to production. Rule engines promote visibility and understanding of business policies and procedures as well as consistent decision making, since a business rule update in a rule engine directly updates the behavior of all enterprise applications and services that call the common business rules managed by the rule engine. This enforces order to the rules and policies that govern business (eFORCE).

What Are Business Rules?

As explained in "Implementation Guide of BizTalk's Business Rules" (Xi, 2005),

> *Business rules (or business policies) define and control the structure, operation, and strategy of an organization. Business rules may be formally defined in procedure manuals, contracts, or agreements, or may exist as knowledge or expertise embodied in employees. Business rules are dynamic and subject to change over time, and can be*

> *found in all types of applications. Finance and insurance, e-business, transportation, telecommunications, Web-based services, and personalization are just a few of the many business domains that are governed by business rules. Each of these business domains shares the need to convey business strategies, policies, and regulations to information technology (IT) personnel for inclusion into software applications.*

As mentioned previously, a rule consists of a condition and a set of actions. If the condition is evaluated to true by the BRE, the actions defined in the rule are executed.

Traditional procedural and object-oriented programming languages, such as C, C++, and Microsoft Visual Basic, are oriented toward programmers. Even advanced object-oriented languages, such as Java and C#, are still primarily programmers' languages. The traditional software development cycle of design, develop, compile, and test requires substantial time and coordination, and limits the ability of nonprogrammers to participate in the maintenance of automated business policies. The Business Rule Engine and the Business Rules Framework address this problem by providing a development environment that enables rapid application creation without the lengthy cycle of traditional application programming. For example, business policies constructed by using this framework can be updated without recompiling and redeploying the associated orchestrations (Xi, 2005).[2,3]

When to Use the BRE?

Traditionally, rule engines have been used for such things as credit scoring and underwriting in financial organizations because of the number and complexity of business rules that these applications require. Using a procedural programming language to code such rules directly into an application makes application maintenance difficult and expensive, as these rules change often. The difficulty in maintaining these rules is encountered even in the initial release of the application, since such rules often change between the time the code is written and the time it's deployed. Hence, rule engines were devised to separate business rules from application logic (Moran).[4]

Virtually every application includes some logic that needs to change often or needs to change in ways not anticipated in the original design. The real question then is not whether you need a rule engine, but how much time and money the rule engine will save you. Even if only a small subset of your rules is subject to change, your project can benefit greatly by separating these rules from the rest of the program logic. This is particularly true during user acceptance testing when missed requirements and incorrect assumptions become evident. A rule engine enables you to make dramatic changes in system behavior without dramatic changes in your code, and it enables you to make changes at runtime.

---

2. Copyright © 2005 by Microsoft Corporation. Reprinted with permission from Microsoft Corporation.
3. Despite the simplicity of creating and updating business rules, you should not be tempted to do so in your product environment directly. You should never short-circuit your testing cycle. Proper product testing is required with every change including business rule updates before they are implemented in production.
4. Copyright by Microsoft Corporation. Reprinted with permission from Microsoft Corporation.

Although simple runtime rule customization can be implemented by using database tables or configuration files to store values for facts used in business rules, a rule engine offers much greater flexibility than simple database tables or configuration files. A rule engine allows you to isolate the condition as well as the action from the application flow. You can simply update a rule's condition, change values associated with facts, or change actions in a rule altogether without the need to recompile and redeploy the application.

So when do you use the BRE and when do you keep your rules outside the BRE? A rule engine is suitable when your application involves significant decision making; the rules are complex or change frequently; the rules need to be shared across multiple applications and organizations; or you are in a volatile industry sector where change is the norm or regulation is extensive and complex. Maintaining your rules in custom code that may be configured through database value lookups or configuration files is suitable when the rules are mostly static and computational, or are simple, even if numerous; speed and throughput are more important than flexibility and maintenance cost; or your business rules are never expected to change in the future (eFORCE).

A rule engine provides the flexibility to change not only what is being evaluated, but also how, when, where, or any other basis you can imagine. In the main application flow or logic, there is no query, no table, and no rule-specific code. There is only a call to the rule engine passing raw data and getting back processed data. The whole logic of what to change and the basis for that change is controlled by the rule engine. Before business rule engines, you were limited to the tweaking of values; now you can change the way the system lets you do business (Moran).

What Are the Artifacts That Constitute a Business Rule?

In the "What Is a Business Rule Engine?" section, we touched briefly on the structure of a business rule and the fact that it is composed of facts (no pun intended), conditions, and actions (see Figure 8-2). In this section, we give you a detailed look at these artifacts.

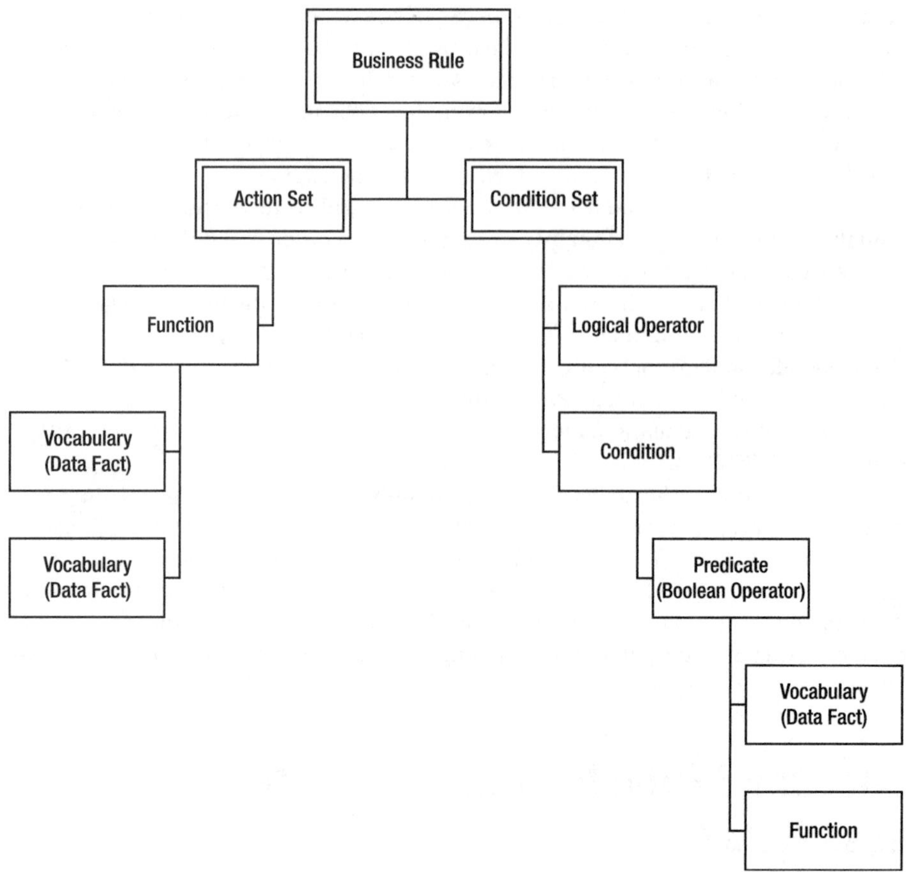

Figure 8-2. *Business rule structure*

Facts and Vocabularies

Before embarking on the creation of business rules, the business analyst should identify the different data facts involved in the evaluation or execution of a particular rule. Those facts are usually aliased using a domain-specific nomenclature understood by peers in that domain. Such domain-specific definitions are referred to in the Business Rule Composer as a *vocabulary*,[5] as in the vocabulary specific to the problem domain for which you are creating the business rules.[6]

---

5. A vocabulary is a collection of definitions consisting of friendly names for the facts used in rule conditions and actions. These definitions make the rules easier to read, understand, and share by people in a particular business domain (Microsoft, "BizTalk Server 2006 Documentation"). Copyright © 2006 by Microsoft Corporation. Reprinted with permission from Microsoft Corporation.

6. Business rule creators may decide to skip vocabulary definition and embed the facts in their business rules directly. They can reference constants, data in a SQL database, or an XML message directly from within the business rules without resorting to a vocabulary definition. Although this is doable, it is not advisable, as it might render the rules unreadable by future resources maintaining the business rules.

Vocabularies are a wonderful way to abstract facts from their implementation. Although a vocabulary set can be composed of different types of facts, the business analyst and business rule creator can deal with them all in the same fashion while creating or updating their business rules.

These types of facts can be included when composing a vocabulary:

- Constant values, ranges of values, or value sets used to validate and constrain rule parameters.
- .NET classes or class members, which may be used to wrap other vocabularies and/or define bindings and binding parameters. "For example, a vocabulary definition might refer to a .NET method that takes two parameters. As part of the definition, one parameter may be bound to the value in an XML document and the other may be defined by the user at design-time but limited to the valid values defined in another definition that defines a 'set'" (Microsoft, "BizTalk Server Business Rules Framework," 2003).[7]
- XML document elements or attributes.
- Data tables or columns in a database.
- Custom managed facts to be retrieved through a .NET object that implements the fact retriever interface.

Using the Business Rule Composer, you may define vocabularies and store them in the shared rule store. Vocabularies can also be consumed by tool developers responsible for integrating rule authoring into new or existing applications.

■ **Note** The requirement to define vocabularies and facts before the definition of the business rules within a policy can be cumbersome and annoying for most business analysts, and usually results in them creating and publishing multiple versions of their vocabularies as they are developing the business rules. Hopefully in the future, the Business Rule Composer will allow the composition of business rules based on unpublished vocabularies that business analysts can create and edit while creating their rules, and restrict users from publishing policies until the vocabulary they use is published.

Before being used in business rules, vocabularies must be stamped with a version number and published in the rule store. Once published, a vocabulary version is immutable. This guarantees that the definitions in the vocabulary will not change. It preserves the referential integrity between policies and the vocabulary. This prevents any policies that use a particular version of the vocabulary from failing unexpectedly due to changes in the underlying vocabulary (Microsoft, "BizTalk Server 2006 Documentation," 2006).

Users can define two types of vocabulary items or facts, **short-term** and **long-term** facts. A short-term fact is specific to a single execution cycle of the Business Rule Engine and does not need to exist beyond that execution cycle. A long-term fact is loaded into memory for use over an arbitrary number of execution cycles. In the BizTalk BRE, the only

---

7. Copyright © 2003 by Microsoft Corporation. Reprinted with permission from Microsoft Corporation.

real distinction between the two is in implementation (Microsoft, "BizTalk Server 2006 Documentation," 2006).[8]

To use long-term facts, you must configure your policy to know where to find them and implement a fact retriever object that can fetch those facts from an external store and present them to the policy. According to the BizTalk Server 2006 documentation (Microsoft, 2006), there are three ways to supply fact instances to the rule engine:[9]

- The simplest way to submit fact instances to the rule engine is with short-term, application-specific facts that you pass in to the policy object as an array of objects or as XML messages from an orchestration at the beginning of every execution cycle.
- You can use your rule actions to assert additional facts into the engine during execution when those rules evaluate to true.
- You can write a fact retriever—an object that implements a standard interface and typically uses them to supply long-term and slowly changing facts to the rule engine before the policy is executed. The fact retriever may cache these facts and use them over multiple rule execution cycles.

■ Note If your data changes frequently between execution cycles and must be reinstantiated and asserted again, you likely want to represent this data as short-term facts.

XML Facts

As we mentioned previously, facts asserted into the rule engine's working memory can be .NET objects, XML documents, or data tables. These facts contain fields called **slots** in the world of rule engines. If a business rule requires access to a slot in a fact to evaluate a condition and that slot is not defined—for example, an optional XML element that is not defined in the XML message—the BRE will throw an exception. The engine will attempt to perform this evaluation because the relevant fact has been asserted. However, when it looks for the slot, it will not find it.

In this situation, why does the engine throw an exception?

When you create a vocabulary definition for a node in your schema, two properties are set: **XPath Selector** and **XPath Field**. These properties are the way the engine can refer to data fields or slots in a given fact. The vocabulary definition maps these to business-friendly terms defined by the **Name** and **Display Name** properties.

The XPath Selector defines and selects a fact. If a vocabulary definition is referring to a fact rather than a slot, the XPath Field property will be empty. However, there will be an additional XPath expression in the XPath Field property if the vocabulary definition is referring to a slot. This XPath expression is used to select a descendant node of the fact. The engine will throw an exception if a fact exists and it tries to evaluate a business rule condition depending on this fact, but the vocabulary in the condition refers to a slot that does not exist in the message instance asserted into the engine's working memory.

---

8. Copyright © 2006 by Microsoft Corporation. Reprinted with permission from Microsoft Corporation.

9. Copyright © 2006 by Microsoft Corporation. Reprinted with permission from Microsoft Corporation.

If the fact does not exist, no error would occur in the first place. Very simply, the engine would not be able to assert the fact and would therefore realize that it cannot evaluate any rule conditions that depend on this fact. If the fact exists, the engine assumes that the child element exists and throws an error when it tries to access the nonexistent element.

To ensure that you do not run into such situations, you can edit the XPath Selector so that it only selects fact instances with the required slots defined. XPath supports filters that you can use to amend the XPath Selector to ensure those required slots exist.

For example, if you had a message like this one:

```
<MyMessage>
   <Fields>
      <Field1/>
      <Field2> MyFiled2 value </Field2>
</Fields>
</MyMessage>
```

a vocabulary named MyDataField defined to reference `Field2` will have an XPath Selector value of

```
/*[local-name()='My_Message' and namespace
uri()='http://schemas.test.com/20060307/MyMessageSchema']/*
[local-name()='MyMessage' and namespace
uri()='']/*[local-name()='Fields' and namespace-uri ()='']
```

and an XPath Field value of

```
*[local-name()='Field2' and namespace-uri()='']
```

To avoid exceptions if an asserted `My_Message` instance does not have a `Field2` element defined, you can modify the Xpath Selector to

```
/*[local-name()='My_Message' and namespace-
uri()='http://schemas.test.com/20060307/MyMessageSchema']/*
[local-name()='MyMessage' and namespace-
uri()='']/*[local-name()='Fields' and namespace-uri()=''][Field2]
```

You can improve this filtering process further by modifying the XPath Selector to select `My_Message` nodes with a `Field2` child element, which has a nonempty text node only:

```
/*[local-name()='My_Message' and namespace-
uri()='http://schemas.test.com/20060307/MyMessageSchema']/*
[local-name()='MyMessage' and namespace-
uri()='']/*[local-name()='Fields' and namespace-uri()=''][Field2=""]
```

The key to effectively using the BRE and using XML facts is to understand XPath and the difference between facts and slots, and to edit your XPath Selectors and XPath Fields accordingly to meet your needs. A good example is a business rule that should perform an action only if a certain number of fields have the same value. For instance, an institute that wants to automate the selection of courses it offers to its students would use a business rule that looks at a feedback summary report for a class and adds the class to the offered courses roster only if ten students or more responded that the course was "Very Good". This could be implemented through a set of complex business rules or custom code. A better alternative is to leverage XPath to define a vocabulary item that represents the count of "Very Good" responses.

Assuming the feedback summary is as follows:

```
<CourseFeedback>
   <Course title="Introduction to BizTalk 2006" />
   <Instructor>John Smith</Instructor>
   <WasThisCourseUseful>
      <answer value="Good"/>
      <answer value="Bad"/>
      <answer value="Very Good"/>
      <answer value="Good"/>
      <answer value="Very Good"/>
      <answer value="Very Good"/>
      <answer value="Very Good"/>
      <answer value="Very Good"/>
      <answer value="Very Good"/>
      <answer value="Very Good"/>
      <answer value="Very Good"/>
      <answer value="Very Good"/>
      <answer value="Very Good"/>
   </WasThisCourseUseful>
...
   <WouldYouRecommendThisCourseToAFriend>
      <answer value="Good"/>
      <answer value="Bad"/>
      <answer value="Very Good"/>
      <answer value="Good"/>
      <answer value="Very Good"/>
      <answer value="Very Good"/>
      <answer value="Very Good"/>
      <answer value="Very Good"/>
      <answer value="Very Good"/>
      <answer value="Very Good"/>
      <answer value="Very Good"/>
      <answer value="Very Good"/>
      <answer value="Very Good"/>
   </ WouldYouRecommendThisCourseToAFriend >
...
</CourseFeedback>
```

you could define a vocabulary item that counts the number of "Very Good" answers as follows:

```
XPath Selector: /*[local-name()='CourseFeedback' and namespace-
uri()='http://schemas.test.com/20060307/
CourseFeedbackSchema']/*[local-name()=' CourseFeedback'
and namespace-uri()='']/*[local-
name()='WouldYouRecommendThisCourseToAFriend' and namespace-uri()='']

XPath Field: Count(//answer[@value="Very Good"])
```

You can then define a business rule as part of the policy that checks whether the count is greater than 10, and if so sets the course to be "OnRoster".

```
SetCourseOnRoster (priority = 0)
IF WouldYouRecommendThisCourseToAFriend:Count(//answser[@value="Very Good"])
     is greater than or equal to 10
THEN CourseOnRoster = "Yes"
ELSE CourseOnRoster = "No"
```

Leveraging XPath queries in the definition of XPath Field properties is a great way to minimize custom code and optimize the execution of the BRE to evaluate complex rules.

Custom Fact Retrievers

To expose long-term facts to the BRE and leverage them in the definition of business rules and policies, you may use custom fact retrievers, which are custom .NET classes that implement the `Microsoft.RuleEngine.IFactRetriever` interface. This interface has a single public method, `UpdateFacts`. A particular fact retriever may be associated with a particular policy version through the policy property settings. This indicates to the BRE that an instance of that fact retriever object should be instantiated and the method `UpdateFacts` called to update all custom facts associated with that particular policy. It is the responsibility of the fact retriever to determine when the fact base has changed.

Note A long-term fact only needs to be asserted once for the same rule engine instance. For example, when you use the Call Rules shape in an orchestration, the policy instance is moved into an internal cache. At this time, all short-term facts are retracted and long-term facts are kept. If the same policy is called again, either by the same orchestration instance or by a different orchestration instance in the same host, this policy instance is fetched from the cache and reused. In some batch processing scenarios, several policy instances of the same policy could be created. If a new policy instance is created, you must ensure that the correct long-term facts are asserted.

Fact retrievers are used to manage long-term facts used by business policies. "If a fact changes infrequently, rule processing efficiency can be obtained by saving it as a long-term fact and loading it into memory to reuse. By referencing this fact retriever in a policy, the user ensures that the engine (more accurately the policy class) will call the fact retriever to get long-term facts" (Microsoft, "BizTalk Server Business Rules Framework," 2003).[10]

Caution BizTalk Server 2006 contains two interfaces with the name `IFactRetriever`. The BizTalk Server 2006 documentation also indexes the term "fact retriever" under two different topics. Essentially when dealing with the BRE, ensure that you are dealing with the `IFactRetriever` interface in the `Microsoft.RuleEngine` namespace and referencing the documentation related to the BRE, not the Human Workflow Services (HWS).

---

10. Copyright © 2003 by Microsoft Corporation. Reprinted with permission from Microsoft Corporation.

The following custom fact retriever, DbFactRetriever, selects a set of rows from a database table, adds them to a typed data table, and asserts it as a fact.

```
...
public class DbFactRetriever:IFactRetriever
{
      public object UpdateFacts(RuleSetInfo rulesetInfo,
 Microsoft.RuleEngine.RuleEngine engine, object factsHandleIn)
      {
         object factsHandleOut;

         // The following logic asserts the required DB rows only once and always
         // uses the the same values (cached) during the first retrieval in
         // subsequent execution cycles
         if (factsHandleIn == null)
         {
            string strCmdSqlCon = "Persist Security Info=False;"+
             "Integrated Security=SSPI;database=mydatabasename;server=myservername";
            SqlConnection conSql = new SqlConnection(strCmdSqlCon);

            // Using data connection binding
            // DataConnection dcSqlCon = new DataConnection("Northwind", "CustInfo",
            // conSql);

            // Using data table binding
            SqlDataAdapter dAdaptSql = new SqlDataAdapter();
            dAdaptSql.TableMappings.Add("Table", "CustInfo");
            conSql.Open();
            SqlCommand myCommand = new SqlCommand("SELECT * FROM CustInfo", conSql);
            myCommand.CommandType = CommandType.Text;
            dAdaptSql.SelectCommand = myCommand;
            DataSet ds = new DataSet("Northwind");
            dAdaptSql.Fill(ds);
            TypedDataTable tdtCustInfo = new TypedDataTable(ds.Tables["CustInfo"]);

            engine.Assert(tdtCustInfo);
            factsHandleOut = tdtCustInfo;
         }
         else
         {
            factsHandleOut = factsHandleIn;
         }
         return factsHandleOut;
      }
}
...
```

Conditions

After creating the vocabulary and publishing it to the rule store, the business rule creator can now create the business rules constituting the business policies. The creation of the business rules constitutes creating a set of conditions and actions for each rule.

A condition is simply a Boolean expression that consists of one or more **predicates** applied to **facts**. "Predicates can be combined with the logical connectives AND, OR, and NOT to form a logical expression that can be potentially quite large, but will always evaluate to either true or false" (Microsoft, "BizTalk Server Business Rules Framework," 2003).[11]

A set of predefined predicates are available in the Business Rules Framework:

- `After`: Tests whether a date/time fact happens after another date/time fact
- `Before`: Tests whether a date/time fact happens before another date/time fact
- `Between`: Tests whether a date/time fact is in the range between two other date/time facts
- `Exists`: Tests for the existence of an XML node within an XML document[12]
- `Match`: Tests whether the specified text fact contains a substring that matches a specified regular expression or another fact
- `Range`: Tests whether a value is within a range defined by the lower-bound value (inclusive) and upper-bound value (inclusive)
- `Equal`: The equality relational operator
- `GreaterThan`: The greater than relational operator
- `GreaterThanEqual`: The greater than or equal relational operator
- `LessThan`: The less than relational operator
- `LessThanEqual`: The less than or equal relational operator
- `NotEqual`: The not equal to relational operator

Actions

Actions are the functional consequences of condition evaluation. If a rule condition is met, a corresponding action or multiple actions will be initiated. Actions can result in more rules being evaluated and trigger a chain effect. They are represented in the Business Rules Framework by invoking methods or setting properties on objects, or by performing set operations on XML documents or database tables. The Business Rules Framework provides a set of predefined functions that can be used in actions:

- `Assert`: Adds a new fact to the current rule engine instance.

---

11. Copyright © 2003 by Microsoft Corporation. Reprinted with permission from Microsoft Corporation.

12. Although the predicate is called `Exists`, it will only check whether a given node is empty. If the node does not exist in the XML document, an exception will be thrown and the processing will stop.

Note To assert a .NET object from within a rule, you can add the built-in `Assert` function as a rule action. The rule engine has a `CreateObject` function, but it is not displayed explicitly with the rest of the functions in the Facts Explorer window in the Business Rule Composer. By simply dragging the constructor method of the object you wish to create from the .NET Class view of the Facts Explorer to the action pane, the Business Rule Composer will translate the constructor method into a `CreateObject` call in the rule definition (Moons, 2005).[13]

- `Update`: Refreshes the specified fact in the current rule engine instance. If this fact is used in business rule conditions in the current policy, this will result in those rules being reevaluated. Rules that use the fact being updated in their actions will not be reevaluated and their actions will remain on the agenda.[14]

Caution A rule with an action that updates the value of a fact being used in its condition evaluation might result in a cyclical valuation loop, if the value used to update the fact always results in the condition being evaluated to true. By default, the Business Rule Engine will cycle through 2^32 loops before it exits the match–conflict resolution–action cycle (more about which you'll find in the "How Does the BRE Work?" section). This value is a configurable property per policy version.

- `Retract`: Removes the specified fact from the current rule engine instance.
- `RetractByType`: Removes all existing facts of the specified fact type from the current rule engine instance.
- `Clear`: Clears all facts and rule firings from the current rule engine instance.
- `Halt`: Halts the current rule engine execution and optionally clears all rule firings. The facts remain unaffected so that values are returned.
- `Executor`: Returns a reference to the current rule engine instance of type IRuleSetExecutor.
- `FindAll`: Returns a string containing all substrings that match a specified regular expression in the specified text.
- `FindFirst`: Returns a string containing the first substring that matches a specified regular expression in the specified text.
- `Add`: Adds two numeric values.

---

13. Copyright © 2005 by Microsoft Corporation. Reprinted with permission from Microsoft Corporation.

14. To force the engine to reevaluate rules with an XML element in their condition, you have to update its immediate parent; if you update the element itself or its grandparent, the engine will not pick up on the fact that the element got updated and the rule needs to be reevaluated. We are not sure if this is a bug or a feature by design, as the `Update` function is inherently efficient in modifying facts and invalidating the agenda. A description of the agenda and how the engine uses it will be provided in the "Rules and Priorities" section.

- `Subtract`: Subtracts two numeric values.
- `Multiply`: Multiplies two numeric values.
- `Divide`: Divides two numeric values.
- `Power`: Returns the result of a number raised to a power.
- `Remainder`: Returns the remainder after a number is divided by a divisor.
- `Year`: Returns the year component of the specified date/time fact, a value in the range 1 to 9999.
- `Month`: Returns the month component from the specified date/time fact, a number from 1 to 12.
- `Day`: Returns the day of the month component from the specified date/time fact, a number from 1 to 31.
- `Hour`: Returns the hour component from the specified date/time fact, a number from 0 (12:00 a.m.) to 23 (11:00 p.m.).
- `Minute`: Returns the minute component from the specified date/time fact, a number from 0 to 59.
- `Second`: Returns the second component from the specified date/time fact, a number from 0 to 59.
- `TimeOfDay`: Returns the time component from the specified date/time fact.
- `DayOfWeek`: Returns the day of the week from the specified date/time fact, a number from 0 (Sunday) to 6 (Saturday).

Rules and Priorities

The BRE implements the RETE algorithm.[15] By default the execution of rule actions is nondeterministic. The engine evaluates all rules in the policy and creates an agenda of actions for rules with valid conditions to be executed. The execution of actions on the agenda might result in condition reevaluation or more conditions being evaluated, if those actions update or assert new facts. With all rules having the same priority, there is no guaranteed order of execution for the actions on the agenda. To guarantee an order of execution, you need to resort to using **rule priorities**.

The default priority for all rules is zero. Priority for execution is set on each individual rule. The priority is a positive or negative integer value, with larger numbers having higher priority. Actions added to the agenda for rules with valid conditions are executed in order from highest priority to lowest priority.

15. The RETE algorithm, designed by Dr. Charles L. Forgy of Carnegie Mellon University in 1979, is an efficient pattern-matching algorithm for implementing Business Rule Engines. For more information on the RETE algorithm, please refer to the Wikipedia article at http://en.wikipedia.org/wiki/Rete_algorithm.

To see how priority affects the execution order of rules, take a look at the following example from the BizTalk Server 2006 documentation (Microsoft, 2006):[16]

```
Rule1 (priority = 0)
IF Fact1 == 1
THEN Discount = 10%


Rule2 (priority = 10)
IF Fact1 > 0
THEN Discount = 15%
```

Although the conditions for both rules have been met, Rule2, having the higher priority, is executed first. The action for Rule1 is executed last, and so the final discount is 10%, as demonstrated here:

Working Memory	Agenda
Fact1 (value=1)	**Rule2** Discount = 15%
	Rule1 Discount = 10%

The Business Rule Composer

The Business Rule Composer, illustrated in Figure 8-3, is the environment used by business rule authors to create, update, version, publish, and deploy vocabularies and policies. Policy authors may also test their policies using the testing tool in the Business Rule Composer and review the execution output as well as error messages in the Output window. As mentioned earlier, creating the required vocabularies is necessary before the rule creation, as the vocabulary needs to be published before it can be used in a rule. However, if you like to create your rules top down, you can get around this by simply creating all the business rules with fake arguments using the taxonomy of your domain, then start creating the vocabulary following that nomenclature. The drawback here of course is that you will not be able to save your policy unless you add and publish the vocabulary and update the rules with the right facts.

We will not discuss the mechanics of creating vocabularies, policies, and rules in this chapter, since the Business Rule Engine and the Business Rule Composer did not change in BizTalk 2006.[7] However, we will go over some of the hazards of rule development that business rule authors go through.

16. Copyright © 2006 by Microsoft Corporation. Reprinted with permission from Microsoft Corporation.

17. If you are interested in learning more on your own, this is well covered in the BizTalk Server 2006 product documentation and in *Microsoft BizTalk 2004 Unleashed* by Scott Woodgate, Stephen Mohr, and Brian Loesgen (SAMS, 2004).

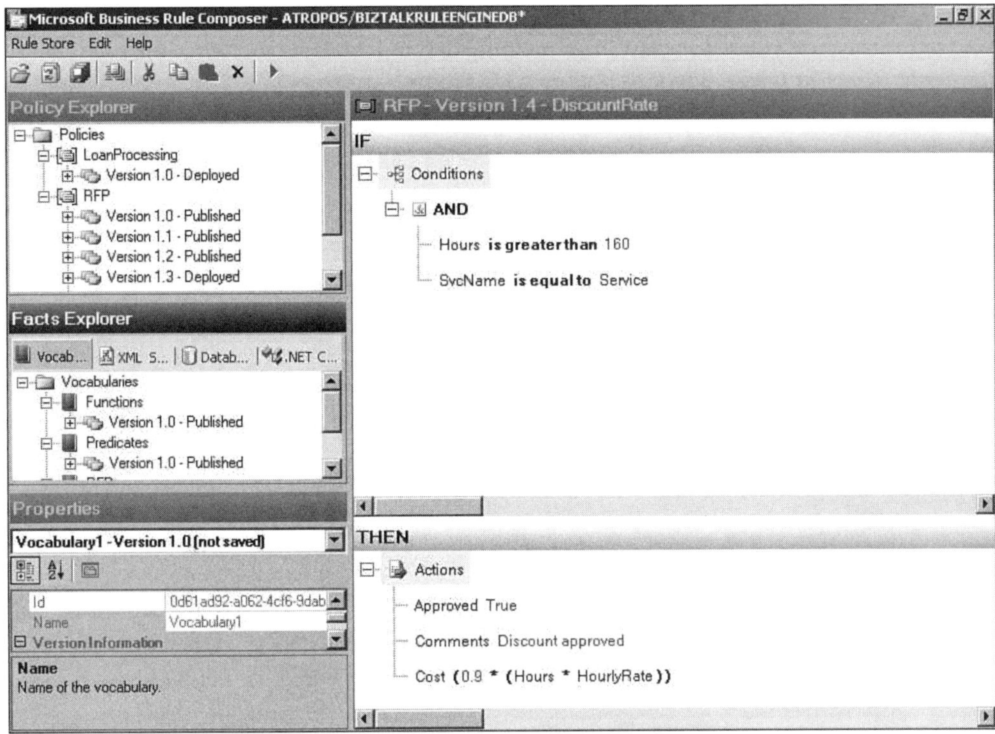

Figure 8-3. *The Business Rule Composer*

Caution Multiple users of the Business Rule Composer can connect to the shared rule store at the same time. However, the Business Rule Composer does not prevent users from overwriting each other's work. Potentially, a user could see a policy or a vocabulary that is out of sync because another user may have modified the policy or vocabulary.

Creating Vocabularies

Even if building a vocabulary is not your immediate concern, you should know how to work with the Facts Explorer, as most of the tasks there apply to rule development. You can use the XML Schemas, Databases, and .NET Classes tabs to construct names and drag them into conditions and actions in the Rule Editor (Woodgate, 2005). Although you can add facts directly from the XML Schemas, Databases, or .NET Classes tabs to your rules, it is not advisable to do so. This greatly impedes the readability of the business rules and thus their future portability. As explained in the section "When to Use a BRE?" earlier, one of the main advantages of using a Business Rule Engine is to abstract and package the business rules that are valuable assets to the IT organization in a highly managable and portable format. Introducing facts from different data sources directly into the business rules creates a dependency between the business rules and those data sources and hinders the portability of those rules.

It is therefore advisable to create a vocabulary to represent the facts in a nomanclature relevant to the business rules' domain. While defining different vocabulary items, the user has the choice to select the item type as illustrated in Figure 8-4.

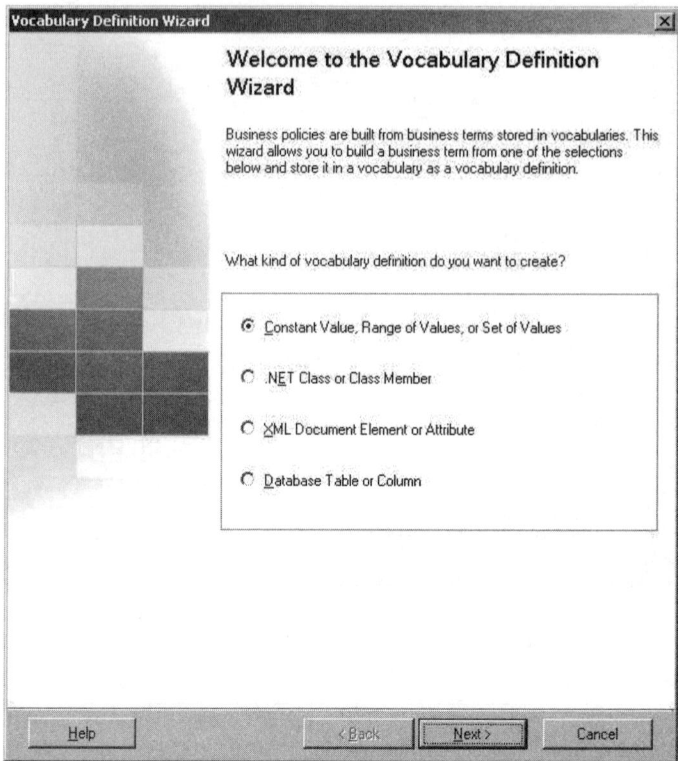

Figure 8-4. *Vocabulary Definition Wizard*

To create a vocabulary item based on a .NET class member, the .NET assembly containing that class should be deployed to the Global Assembly Cache (GAC). The assembly needs to be deployed to the GAC to ensure that the rule engine can always get to the class definition at runtime.

When creating a vocabulary item based on an XML node in an XML document, ensure that the schema file defining the XML document in question is in a location that will be accessible when the rule set or vocabulary is deployed. If they will be exported to another server, or if the development machine is not the BizTalk Server that will make use of your definitions, the schema must be copied to a disk that is accessible under the file path given.

■ **Tip** If you are not able to pass the required messages to a business policy execution from within an orchestration, ensure that the XML document type specified while creating the vocabulary item is valid. The Business Rule Composer is in the habit of simply adding the document type instead of the fully qualified type name prefixed with all the namespaces if any.

Creating Rules

Creating a policy to encapsulate related rules is the first task in rule creation. If you are updating the rules in the policy or adding onto the existing rules of an already published version of the policy instead of simply creating a new version and starting from scratch, copy the latest version of the policy you need to update and paste it as a new policy version. To create policy rules, you can drag and drop predicates and vocabulary items from the Facts Explorer into the IF pane to create conditions and drag and drop functions and vocabulary items into the THEN pane to create actions. If required, different priorities can be assigned to different rules to affect the order of their actions' execution upon their successful evaluation. Applications executing deployed policies will execute the latest version of the policy by default. However, they may explicitly execute a particular version of the policy instead.

■ **Caution** If you redefine a particular vocabulary item in a new version of a policy, the rules will not pick up the latest version. Rules are explicitly bound to the vocabulary item that was dragged and dropped on the action or condition. This means that if you update your vocabulary, you need to manually update the rules to use the new version of the vocabulary.[18]

How Does the BRE Work?

The main activities of the Business Rule Engine fall into one of two main user experience categories, the design-time experience and the runtime experience. At design time, business rule creators can use the business policy authoring tool, namely the Business Rule Composer in BizTalk, to create and update the business rules and policies. As mentioned previously, business rule authors use the Business Rule Composer to first create the vocabulary required to define the different business rules and then proceed to define their business rules grouped in the form of policies. The different artifacts created by the business rule creator are then compiled and persisted in the Business Rule Store. A service, the Rule Engine Update Service, periodically checks the Business Rule Store for changes to update the rule engine runtime.[19] Applications and orchestrations calling the rule engine to execute policies use the interfaces exposed by the Business Rules Framework to do so. Figure 8-5 shows the separation between the two experiences and how the different components interact together to allow for the auto-update of business rules at runtime.

---

18. The Vocabulary Upgrader for the Rule Engine tool, available on GotDotNet at www.gotdotnet.com/Workspaces/Workspace.aspx?id=236732a5-9f8d-48f7-a7af-25d9b6cc9b46, updates fact references in policies to the latest version of the vocabulary.

19. To configure how often the Rule Engine Update Service polls the Rule Store for changes to update the engine, define the registry value *PollingInterval* under the registry key HKEY_LOCAL_MACHINE\SOFTWARE\Microsoft\BusinessRules\3.0. The *PollingInterval* value defines the number of seconds that the Rule Engine Update Service waits between Rule Store polls for changes. The default value for this setting is 1 minute.

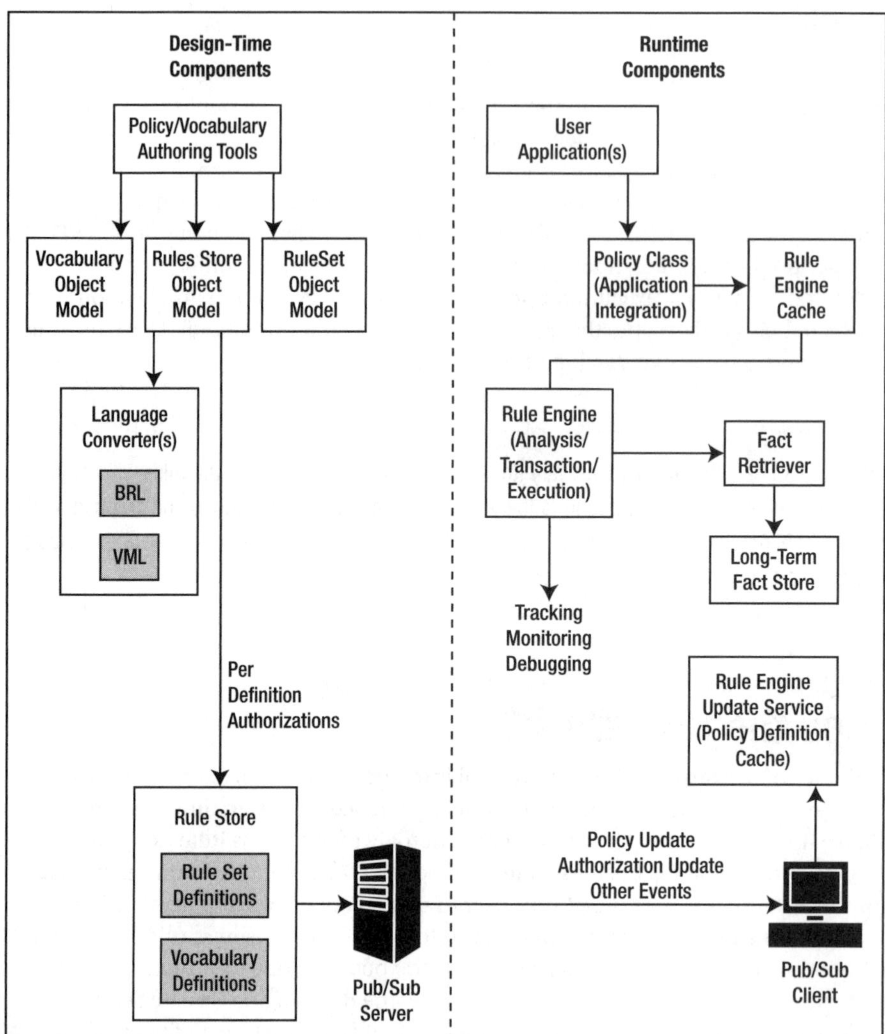

Figure 8-5. *The interaction between the different Business Rules Framework components (Microsoft, "BizTalk Server 2006 Documentation," 2006)*[20]

As we mentioned earlier, a highly efficient rule inference engine serves as the core component of the Business Rules Framework, and it provides the execution context for a policy. The rule engine is primarily composed of three main components:

20. Copyright © 2006 by Microsoft Corporation. Reprinted with permission from Microsoft Corporation.

- An **inference engine**, also called the **rule set executor**, is responsible for the evaluation of rule conditions and action execution. The default rule set executor, implemented as part of the Business Rules Framework, is a "discrimination network-based forward-chaining inference engine designed to optimize in-memory operation" (Microsoft, "BizTalk Server 2006 Documentation," 2006). The inference engine uses forward chaining[21] of rules and conditions to evaluate and action the rules in a rule set. Weighted priorities assigned to the different rules will affect the engine's processing and reorder the execution of their actions.

- A **rule set translator** takes as input a rule set definition—a RuleSet object—and "produces an executable representation of the rule set. The default in-memory translator creates a compiled discrimination network from the rule set definition" (Microsoft, "BizTalk Server 2006 Documentation," 2006). A custom translator can be assigned to a particular policy version through the policy translator property. To assign a custom translator, the policy author needs to identify the .NET assembly containing the rule translator as well as the class implementing the `IRuleSetTranslator` interface in that assembly.

- A **rule set tracking interceptor** receives output from the inference engine—rule set executor—and forwards it to the rule set tracking and monitoring tools that facilitate the tracking and debugging of business rules' execution (Microsoft, "BizTalk Server 2006 Documentation", 2006).[22]

The discrimination network-based forward-chaining logic of the inference engine consists of a three-stage algorithm for policy execution. The stages are as follows (Microsoft, "BizTalk Server 2006 Documentation," 2006):[23]

1. *Match.* In the match stage, facts are matched against the predicates that use the fact type[24] using the predicates defined in the rule conditions. To improve efficiency, pattern matching occurs over all the rules in the policy, and conditions that are shared across rules are matched only once. Partial condition matches may be stored in working memory to accelerate subsequent pattern-matching operations. The output of the pattern-matching phase consists of updates to the rule engine agenda. An agenda is completed when all facts that are simultaneously present in working memory are matched to all active policy rules. The agenda is used by the engine to queue rules and schedule them for execution.

2. *Conflict resolution.* In the conflict resolution stage, the rules that are candidates for execution are examined to determine the next set of rule actions to execute based on a predetermined resolution scheme. All candidate rules found during the matching stage are added to the rule engine's agenda. The default conflict resolution scheme is based on rule priorities within a policy. . . . Therefore if multiple rules are triggered, the higher-priority actions are executed first.

---

21. Forward chaining, often called data driven, is one of the two main methods of reasoning when using inference rules in artificial intelligence. The other is backward chaining. For more information on forward chaining, please refer to the Wikipedia article at http://en.wikipedia.org/wiki/Forward_chaining.

22. Copyright © 2006 by Microsoft Corporation. Reprinted with permission from Microsoft Corporation.

23. Copyright © 2006 by Microsoft Corporation. Reprinted with permission from Microsoft Corporation.

24. The fact type is an object reference maintained in the rule engine's working memory.

3. *Action*. In the action stage, the actions in the resolved rule are executed. Note that rule actions can assert new facts into the rule engine, which causes the engine to cycle again and start at the matching stage. This is also known as forward chaining. It is important to note that the algorithm never preempts the currently executing rule. All actions for the rule that is currently firing will be executed before the match phase is repeated. However, other rules on the agenda will not be fired before the match phase begins again. The match phase may cause those rules on the agenda to be removed from the agenda before they ever fire.

   An agenda exists per engine instance, and acts on a single policy only. A rule's actions are placed on the agenda and executed according to their priority, when facts are asserted and the rule's conditions are satisfied. A rule's actions are executed as a block and in order from top to bottom, before the execution of the actions of the next rule on the agenda.

■ **Note** It is important to note that if a rule's action asserts new facts into the rule engine, causing it to cycle again starting at the match stage, the engine will never preempt the currently executing rule. The block of actions for the current firing rule will continue executing before the match phase is repeated. After the current action block has executed, the engine will proceed to the match phase again before other rules on the agenda fire, as the match phase may result in the removal of those rules from the agenda before they ever fire.

The example shown next illustrates the Business Rule Engine's three-stage logic of match–conflict resolution–action:[25]

A policy is defined with two rules. The rules and their facts are detailed in Tables 8-1 and 8-2, respectively.

Table 8-1. *Rules Definition*

Declarative Representation	IF—THEN Representation Using Business Objects
Rule 1: Evaluate Income	
An applicant's credit rating should be obtained only if the applicant's income-to-loan ratio is less than 0.2.	`IF Application.Income / Property.Price < 0.2` `THEN Assert new CreditRating( Application)`
Rule 2: Evaluate Credit Rating	
An applicant should be approved only if the applicant's credit rating is more than 725.	`IF Application.SSN = CreditRating.SSN AND CreditRating.Value > 725` `THEN SendApprovalLetter(Application)`

---

25. This example is extracted from the BizTalk Server 2006 online documentation available at http://msdn.microsoft.com/library/default.asp?url=/library/en-us/sdk/htm/ebiz_prog_rules_srtz.asp.

Table 8-2. *Facts Definition*

Fact	Field
Application: An XML document representing a home loan application	Income = $65,000 SSN = XXX-XX-XXXX
Property: An XML document representing the property being purchased	Price = $225,000
CreditRating: An XML document containing the loan applicant's credit rating	Value = 0 – 800 SSN = XXX-XX-XXXX

Initially, the rule engine working memory and agenda are empty. After the application asserts the Application and Property facts with the values detailed in Table 8-2 to the rule engine, the engine's working memory and agenda are updated, as shown in Table 8-3. Rule 1 is added to the agenda because its condition (Application.Income / Property.Price < 0.2) evaluated to true during the match phase. There is no CreditRating fact in working memory, so the condition for Rule 2 was not evaluated.

Table 8-3. *Engine's Working Memory and Agenda Before Execution*

Working Memory	Agenda
Application Property	Rule 1 `Assert new CreditRating(Application)`

Because the only rule in the agenda is Rule 1, the rule is executed and then disappears from the agenda. The single action defined for Rule 1 results in a new fact (CreditRating document for the applicant) being added to working memory. After the execution of Rule 1 completes, control returns to the match phase. Because the only new object to match is the CreditRating fact, the results of the match phase are as shown in Table 8-4.

Table 8-4. *Engine's Working Memory and Agenda After the Execution of Rule 1*

Working Memory	Agenda
Application Property CreditRating	Rule 2 `SendApprovalLetter(Application)`

At this point Rule 2 is executed, resulting in the invocation of a function that sends an approval letter to the applicant. After Rule 2 has completed, execution of the forward-chaining algorithm returns to the match phase. Because there are no longer new facts to match and the agenda is empty, forward chaining terminates, and policy execution is complete (Microsoft, "BizTalk Server 2006 Documentation," 2006).[26]

Testing Business Rules

Once all business policies and their required vocabularies are defined, you need to test and debug them before deploying them in production. Although the Business Rule Composer does

26. Copyright © 2006 by Microsoft Corporation. Reprinted with permission from Microsoft Corporation.

not provide the same testing, tracing, and debugging functionality as procedural development environments such as Visual Studio, due to the nonsequential nature of business rule execution, it does provide a testing tool—depicted in Figure 8-6. You can simply select fact instances for the testing tool to assert into the engine for your policy or select a *FactCreator*[27] that the testing tool will instantiate and call to create the facts required for the policy execution. The testing tool then uses the *DebugTrackingInterceptor*[28] to track the execution of the Business Rule Engine and display it in the output window.

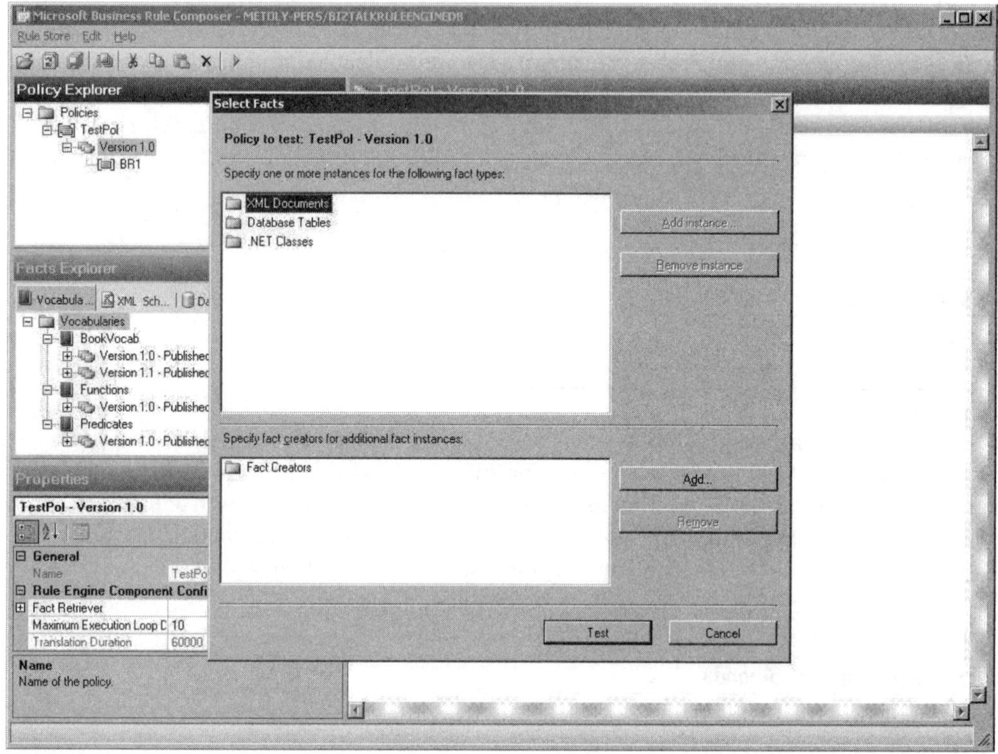

Figure 8-6. *The Business Rule Composer testing tool interface*

The following extract of output was produced by the Business Rule Composer testing tool when testing the Loans Processing policy from the Loans Sample in the SDK. It shows the details of the tracked information by the *DebugTrackingInterceptor*.

27. A fact creator, used to generate facts for policy testing, implements the `Microsoft.RuleEngine.IFactCreator` interface. The fact creator needs to implement the `GetFactTypes` and `CreateFacts` methods, which return an array of object types and objects respectively for a given rule set.

28. The Business Rule Engine allows for the registration of tracking interceptors that implement the `Microsoft.RuleEngine.IRuleSetTrackingInterceptor` interface to be notified along with the execution of the engine and track its progress.

```
RULE ENGINE TRACE for RULESET: LoanProcessing 5/19/2005 12:46:13 PM

FACT ACTIVITY 5/19/2005 12:46:13 PM
Rule Engine Instance Identifier: fb330399-15f0-4dc7-9137-4463a32f580e
Ruleset Name: LoanProcessing
Operation: Assert
Object Type: DataConnection:Northwind:CustInfo
Object Instance Identifier: 782

FACT ACTIVITY 5/19/2005 12:46:13 PM
Rule Engine Instance Identifier: fb330399-15f0-4dc7-9137-4463a32f580e
Ruleset Name: LoanProcessing
Operation: Assert
Object Type: TypedXmlDocument:Microsoft.Samples.BizTalk.LoansProcessor.Case
Object Instance Identifier: 778

FACT ACTIVITY 5/19/2005 12:46:13 PM
Rule Engine Instance Identifier: fb330399-15f0-4dc7-9137-4463a32f580e
Ruleset Name: LoanProcessing
Operation: Assert
Object Type: TypedXmlDocument:Microsoft.Samples.BizTalk.LoansProcessor.Case:Root
Object Instance Identifier: 777

CONDITION EVALUATION TEST (MATCH) 5/19/2005 12:46:13 PM
Rule Engine Instance Identifier: fb330399-15f0-4dc7-9137-4463a32f580e
Ruleset Name: LoanProcessing
Test Expression: NOT(TypedXmlDocument:Microsoft.Samples.BizTalk.LoansProcessor.Case:
                                            Root.Income/BasicSalary > 0)
Left Operand Value: 12
Right Operand Value: 0
Test Result: False

CONDITION EVALUATION TEST (MATCH) 5/19/2005 12:46:13 PM
Rule Engine Instance Identifier: fb330399-15f0-4dc7-9137-4463a32f580e
Ruleset Name: LoanProcessing
Test Expression: NOT(TypedXmlDocument:Microsoft.Samples.BizTalk.LoansProcessor.Case:
                                            Root.Income/OtherIncome > 0)
Left Operand Value: 10
Right Operand Value: 0
Test Result: False

CONDITION EVALUATION TEST (MATCH) 5/19/2005 12:46:13 PM
Rule Engine Instance Identifier: fb330399-15f0-4dc7-9137-4463a32f580e
Ruleset Name: LoanProcessing
Test Expression: TypedXmlDocument:Microsoft.Samples.BizTalk.LoansProcessor.Case:
                                      Root.PlaceOfResidence/TimeInMonths >= 3
```

```
Left Operand Value: 15
Right Operand Value: 3
Test Result: True
[.. cut for brevity ..]
```

If you are testing or executing policies outside of BizTalk or in a component consumed within BizTalk, you can specify an alternative custom interceptor that implements the `IRuleSetTrackingInterceptor` interface.[29] Creating your custom interceptor allows you to track and log as much information as your application requires. It allows you to step through the rule processing and view fact details through the facts you pass to the policy. The following code snippet demonstrates how to invoke your custom interceptor—`MyInterceptorClass`.

```
...
xmlDocument = IncomingXMLMessage.XMLCase;
typedXmlDocument = new
Microsoft.RuleEngine.TypedXmlDocument("Microsoft.Samples.BizTalk.LoansProcessor.
                                                                   Case",xmlDocument);
policy = new Microsoft.RuleEngine.Policy("LoanProcessing");
policy.Execute(typedXmlDocument,new MyInterceptorClass());
OutgoingXMLMessage.XMLCase = xmlDocument;
policy.Dispose();
...
```

The RuleTesterApp project accompanying this book implements a simple rule testing tool. The tool's user interface allows the user to load XML policy definitions, specify the destination trace output file, and then execute those policies. To experiment with your own custom tracking interceptor, instantiate your interceptor in the method `FireRule RulesTesterFrm` class on line 267 instead of the current instantiation of the DebugTrackingInterceptor.

```
...
// Change the following line to instantiate your own custom Tracking Interceptor
DebugTrackingInterceptor dti = new DebugTrackingInterceptor(traceFileName);
try
{
   for( int i = 0 ; i < policies.Length; i++ )
   {
      string PolicyName = policies[i].Trim();
      lblProcessing.Text = PolicyName;
      ProcessingTxtBx.Text = ProcessingTxtBx.Text +  "Processing ... " + policies[i]
                           + " " +  DateTime.Now + "\r\n";
      Application.DoEvents();
```

29. A custom tracking interceptor that implements the `Microsoft.RuleEngine.IRuleSetTrackingInterceptor` interface needs to implement the `SetTrackingConfig`, `TrackAgendaUpdate`, `TrackConditionEvaluation`, `TrackFactActivity`, `TrackRuleFiring`, and `TrackRuleSetEngineAssociation` methods, which allow it to intercept the execution sequence, agenda, and facts updates for a specified rule set.

```
        Microsoft.RuleEngine.Policy tstPolicy = new
                                        Microsoft.RuleEngine.Policy(PolicyName);
        ArrayList shortTermFacts = null;
        shortTermFacts =GetFacts(PolicyName);
        shortTermFacts.Add(doc1);
        // Change the following line to pass in your own custom Tracking Interceptor
        // to the rule set Execute method
        tstPolicy.Execute(shortTermFacts.ToArray(), dti );
        tstPolicy = null;
    }
}
...
```

Going to Production

Once all business policies and their required vocabularies are defined and well tested, you can deploy them to your production environment. You can use the Business Rule Deployment Wizard to package the policies and/or vocabulary for deployment. The Business Rule Deployment Wizard will allow you to export a particular version of a vocabulary definition or policy definition to an XML file. After exporting all the required policies and vocabulary definitions, remember to package all fact retrievers and custom .NET classes used as facts in the solution. You will need to deploy those to the Global Assembly Cache on your production server running the BRE. You will also need to copy the XML schema definitions used by facts in your policies and vocabulary to the same directory path in your production environment as your development and testing environments.

■ **Note** Remember to modify your database facts to point to your production database before deploying the business policies and vocabulary in production. If not, your rules with either fail or read and write to your test database environment.

To streamline the deployment process to production, application developers might like to package the rules as well as all other collateral material in an interactive setup for the system administrator to use while deploying the application to production. Such a setup package should also contain schema files, .NET assemblies referenced by the business policies, as well as fact retrievers or policy translators used by the policies meant to be deployed. Using an interactive setup, the application developer can prompt the system administrator for the directory location in which he would like to deploy schemas and other collateral files used by the business policies as well as the production database server and database to be used for different database facts.

POLICY DEFINITION IN XML

The following is a dump of a business policy exported to XML. Note the references to the fact retriever assembly and fully qualified class name, the database server information and table names, as well as the schema file location in the fact definitions.

```
<brl xmlns="http://schemas.microsoft.com/businessruleslanguage/2002">
  <ruleset name="RFP">
    <version major="1" minor="4" description=""
         modifiedby="myserver\user"
         date="2004-02-15T00:29:02.6381024-05:00" />
    <configuration>
      <factretriever>
        <assembly>DbFactRetriever, Version=1.0.1505.34508,
         Culture=neutral, PublicKeyToken=d4e488d64aff1da4</assembly>
        <class>
          Que.BizTalk.RFP.myFactRetriever.RFPDbFactRetriever
        </class>
      </factretriever>
    </configuration>
    <bindings>
      <xmldocument ref="xml_0" doctype="RFPEstimateXML.RulesRFP"
          instances="16" selectivity="1" instance="0">
        <selector>/*[local-name()='RFP' and namespace-uri()=
          'http://RFPEstimateXML.RulesRFP"] </selector>
        <schema>C:\RulesRFP.xsd</schema>
      </xmldocument>
      <datarow ref="db_1" server="myserver\Consulting"
              dataset="Consulting" table="Rates" instances="16"
              selectivity="1" isdataconnection="true"
              instance="0" />
    </bindings>
```

EXPORTING/IMPORTING A POLICY TO/FROM AN XML FILE

The following code snippet uses the Business Rules Framework to export a policy version to an XML file.

```
using System;
using Microsoft.RuleEngine;
using Microsoft.BizTalk.RuleEngineExtensions;
namespace SimpleExport
```

```
{
    class ExportPolicy
    {
        [STAThread]
        static void Main(string[] args)
        {
            if (args.Length != 3)
                Console.WriteLine("Format: PolicyName MajorVersion MinorVersion");
            else
            {
                string policyName = args[0];
                int majorRev = Convert.ToInt16(args[1]);
                int minorRev = Convert.ToInt16(args[2]);
                RuleSetInfo rsi = new RuleSetInfo(policyName,majorRev,minorRev);
                Microsoft.BizTalk.RuleEngineExtensions.RuleSetDeploymentDriver dd;
                dd = new
                Microsoft.BizTalk.RuleEngineExtensions.RuleSetDeploymentDriver();
                string fileName = (rsi.Name + "-" + rsi.MajorRevision +
                                                "." + rsi.MinorRevision + ".xml");
                dd.ExportRuleSetToFileRuleStore(rsi,fileName);
            }
        }
    }
}
```

The following code snippet uses the Business Rules Framework to import a policy version from an XML file into the Rule Store and deploy it.

```
using System;
using Microsoft.RuleEngine;
using Microsoft.BizTalk.RuleEngineExtensions;
namespace SimpleImport
{
    class ImportPolicy
    {
        [STAThread]
        static void Main(string[] args)
        {
            if (args.Length != 1)
            {
                Console.WriteLine("Format: ""XML File Name""");
                return;
            }
            String filename = args[0];
            Microsoft.BizTalk.RuleEngineExtensions.RuleSetDeploymentDriver
            dd = new
```

```
            Microsoft.BizTalk.RuleEngineExtensions.RuleSetDeploymentDriver();
            SqlRuleStore sqlRuleStore = (SqlRuleStore) dd.GetRuleStore();
            FileRuleStore fileRuleStore = new FileRuleStore(filename);
            RuleSetInfoCollection rsic =
                    fileRuleStore.GetRuleSets(RuleStore.Filter.All);
            foreach (RuleSetInfo rsi in rsic)
            {
               RuleSet ruleSet = fileRuleStore.GetRuleSet(rsi);
               bool publishRuleSets = true;
               sqlRuleStore.Add(ruleSet,publishRuleSets);
               dd.Deploy(rsi);
            }
        }
    }
}
```

Executing Business Rules

Application developers can call upon the BRE to execute business policies from within their .NET code or through the Call Rules shape in their BizTalk orchestrations. At runtime, the Business Rules Framework provides a caching mechanism for *RuleEngine* instances. Each RuleEngine instance contains an in-memory representation of a specific policy version.

According to the BizTalk Server 2006 documentation (Microsoft, 2006), when a new policy instance is instantiated, either through a direct call from a .NET application through the API or the execution of the Call Rules shape in an orchestration,[30]

1. *The Policy object requests a RuleEngine instance from the rule engine cache.*
2. *If a RuleEngine instance for the policy version exists in the cache, the RuleEngine instance is returned to the Policy object. If a RuleEngine instance is not available, the cache creates a new instance. When a RuleEngine instance is instantiated, it does, in turn, create a new fact retriever instance if one is configured for the policy version.*

Likewise, when the `Execute` method is called on the `Policy` object, the following steps occur:

1. *The Policy object calls the UpdateFacts method on the fact retriever instance if a fact retriever exists. The fact retriever's implementation of the method may assert long term facts into the working memory of the RuleEngine.*
2. *The Policy object asserts the short term facts contained in the Array that was passed in the Execute call.*
3. *The Policy object calls Execute on the RuleEngine.*

30. Copyright © 2006 by Microsoft Corporation. Reprinted with permission from Microsoft Corporation.

4. *The RuleEngine completes execution and returns control to the Policy object.*
5. *The Policy object retracts the short term facts from the RuleEngine. The long term facts asserted by the fact retriever will remain in the working memory of the rule engine.*

After the Dispose method is called on the Policy object, the RuleEngine instance is released back to the rule engine cache.

The rule engine cache will have multiple rule engine instances for a given policy version if the load requires it, and each rule engine instance has its own fact retriever instance.

Calling the Engine from Within an Orchestration

Orchestration developers can use the Call Rules shape to call upon the Business Rule Engine to execute a business rule policy. They can assert facts to the policy that they wish to execute by passing them as parameters to the Call Rules shape. This is done by double-clicking the Call Rules shape, which brings up the parameters dialog depicted in Figure 8-7.

■ **Caution** Some logic might require an Orchestration Designer to use the Call Rules shape in a loop. If the loop executes quickly—i.e., it only takes seconds or minutes—then this is fine. If the loop spans days and the logic is hanging on to a specific policy instance, then "policy version updates will not be picked up by the rule engine instance executing the policy . . ." and "the overall application performance may suffer as the rule engine instance held onto by the policy will be tied up and not returned to the pool to be reused by other orchestrations".

Parameters to an orchestration's Call Rules shape are implicitly defined in the policy. These facts can be XML schema instances, .NET classes, or database elements. If a schema is referenced in a policy's rule, the Orchestration Designer is required to pass in an instance of that schema as a parameter as a fact that will be evaluated.

In their orchestrations, the developers will have to select a message that matches the same type from the drop-down list in the Call Rules shape. Oftentimes developers run into the issue where they are not allowed to add any parameters in the Call Rules shape. This means there are no messages defined in the orchestration with the same type as the schema used in the policy. The problem is that the document type in the Business Rule Engine and the message type in the schema do not match, so the designer cannot find any messages with the appropriate type to populate the drop-down lists in the parameter selection dialog.

■ **Note** We mentioned this before, but so many developers run into the issue that it is worth mentioning again. If you expect to be able to assign messages as parameters to a Call Rules shape in an orchestration and the Orchestration Designer is not allowing you to do so, then most probably the document type defined in the Facts Explorer is not fully qualified; you need to fix that before you add the fields to your rules.

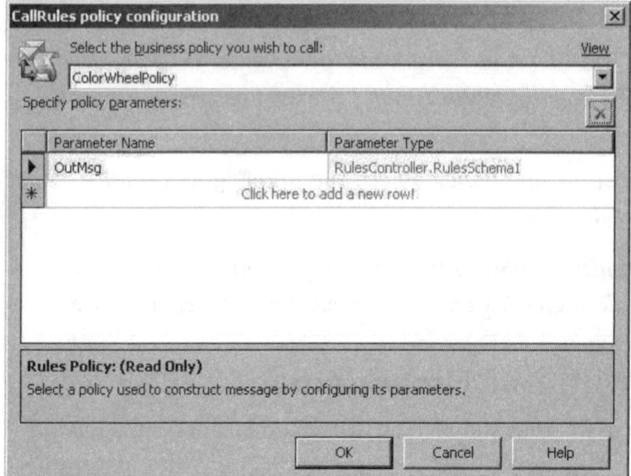

Figure 8-7. *CallRules policy configuration dialog in the Orchestration Designer*

Referencing a .NET Class from a Policy That Is Being Called from an Orchestration

A developer might want to reference and use a .NET class in the business policies. The class could provide helper functions to add nodes to an XML document, the ability to store rule results in an array or a hash table, or make calls to another set of libraries (Moons, 2005).

If the policies are using a .NET class member as a fact in the business rules, and you need to call these policies from within an orchestration using a Call Rules shape, you need to do two things:

- At design time, reference the assembly in the Business Rule Composer to use the methods and/or properties in the policy rules, so that you can create vocabulary items based on that class, or simply use properties and member functions of that class in your rule's conditions and actions.
- Pass an object instance of that class into the policy at runtime. This needs to be done even if you are just referencing static members of the class.
    a. Add a reference to your .NET class in the BizTalk project that contains the orchestration making the call to the business rule policy.
    b. Add a variable to the orchestration of that .NET class type.
    c. Create an instance object of the class in an Expression shape.
    d. Select the policy in the Call Rules shape and select the variable you defined previously in the orchestration as a parameter to that policy. "The messages or variables that are available to you in the rules shape parameter list are determined by the XML Schemas or classes referenced in the policy. When you select the .NET class variable you will be asserting the class instance into the rules engine at runtime" (Moons, 2005).[31]

---

31. Copyright © 2005 by Microsoft Corporation. Reprinted with permission from Microsoft Corporation.

Returning a Value from the BRE to the Calling Orchestration

Sometimes a developer needs a return value from the business rules policy for his code to execute a different piece of logic depending on the policy's results.[32] The returned object could be an XML document; in this case an orchestration simply passes through a message of that document type to be modified and returned[33] by the Business Rule Engine. Or, it could be either a complex structure or a simple single value, for example, a Boolean value. In either case, it is not efficient to use an XML document—a BizTalk message—to pass those values back and forth; using an object instance of a .NET class would be the right approach. The following example of using a .NET class in a policy will illustrate how an object instance of a .NET class can be used to act as a return value from a policy. A policy will be executed and an action fired that sets a Boolean public property on a class.

You start off by writing a simple class that has a public Boolean property:

```
public class MyReturn
{
  private bool approved;
  public bool Approved
  {
    get{ return approved; }
    set{ approved = value; }
  }
}
```

After compiling this class into a .NET library and deploying its assembly to the GAC, reference that assembly from the Business Rule Composer and set the property of this class in an action to true or false, either by dragging the property from the .NET Class Facts Explorer or by creating and using a vocabulary definition. Your rule should look something like Figure 8-8.

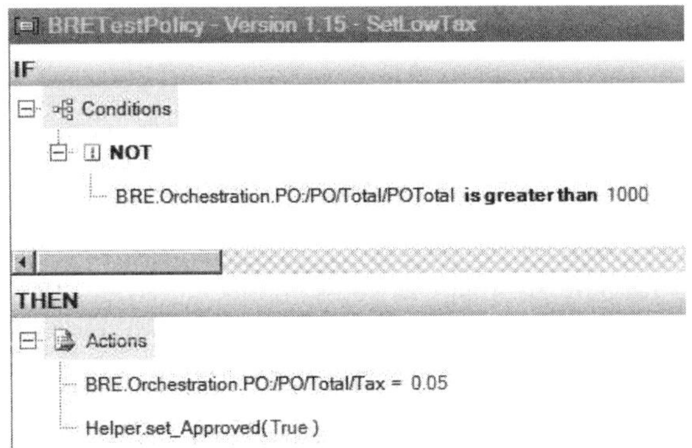

Figure 8-8. *Setting a Boolean value*

---

32. This discussion is based on material presented in "BizTalk Business Rules Engine Quick Tips" by Jonathan Moons (Microsoft Corporation). Copyright © 2005 by Microsoft Corporation. Reprinted with permission from Microsoft Corporation.

33. BizTalk messages are immutable. The document being returned is a new instance and needs to be assigned to a new document.

Reference that assembly in the BizTalk project hosting the orchestration that will call the policy and create a variable of type MyReturn. Assign a reference of a new object instance of this class to the variable in an Expression shape and pass it as a parameter to the policy in the Call Rules shape as in Figure 8-9.

```
hlpr = new RulesHelper.Helper();
```

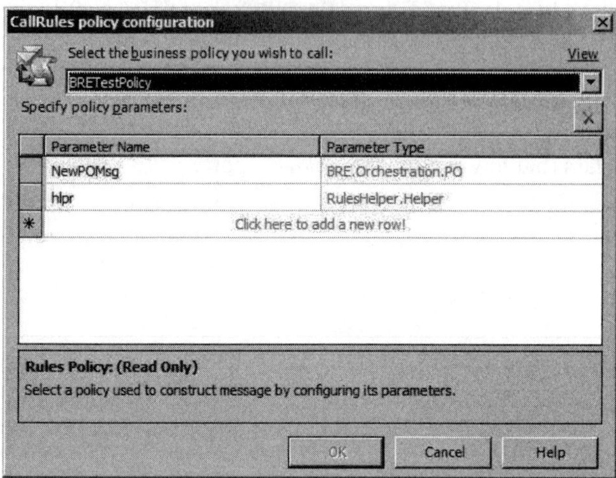

Figure 8-9. *Call Rules shape*

The orchestration can access the class's Boolean property in a Decision shape to find out what value it was set to in the Business Rule Engine.

```
hlpr.Approved == true
```

To test the policy from the Business Rule Composer, you can write a fact creator[34] to create an object instance of the `MyReturn` class.

Calling the Engine from a .NET Application

Application developers can use the APIs exposed by the Business Rules Framework to call upon the BRE to execute a business rule policy. They can assert facts to the policy that they wish to execute. This is simply done by passing the engine an array of objects and/or XML document as parameters.

The following code snippet illustrates how the application developer can call the Business Rule Engine to execute the latest version of a particular policy simply by creating a `Microsoft.RuleEngine.Policy` object with the particular rule name passed as a parameter to the policy's constructor.

34. For a detailed description of how to create a fact creator implementing the `IFactCreator` interface, refer to the BizTalk Server 2006 online help.

■ **Note** Calling an older version of a policy is only possible through the Business Rules Framework APIs. The Call Rules shape in the Orchestration Designer only calls the latest version of the policy. To call an older version from within an orchestration, the orchestration developer needs to use the Business Rules Framework APIs from within an expression or an external assembly.

```
using Microsoft.RuleEngine;
using BTSSampleLibrary;
...
// create an instance of the policy (gets the latest version by default)
Microsoft.RuleEngine.Policy policy = null;
policy = new Microsoft.RuleEngine.Policy("Contoso Policy");
```

The developer can then pass the short-term facts as well as objects that will contain return values required for the policy's execution by packaging them in an array and passing it as a parameter to the `Policy.Execute` method.

```
// Create an Employee fact as an example of setting up a fact
StaffMember staff = new Employee();
staff.PersonnelNumber = "123456";
staff.PrimaryRole = "Engineer";
SupportTicket  orderTicket = new SupportTicket();

// create the array of short-term facts
object[] shortTermFacts = new object[3];
shortTermFacts[0] = staff;
shortTermFacts[1] = new SupportTransaction();
shortTermFacts[2] = orderTicket;

//Execute Policy
policy.Execute( shortTermFacts );
```

Once the rule engine instance executing the policy returns, the developer can check for return values from the policy by inspecting the objects whose references were passed in the array.

```
// Process outcome by checking the modified fact, i.e., the authorization ticket
if (orderTicket.IsAuthorized)
{
      MessageBox.Show("Order approved");
}
else if ( orderTicket.RequiresSupervisor)
{
      MessageBox.Show("Support Supivisor Approval is Required");
}
else
{
      MessageBox.Show("Order Rejected: " + orderTicket.FailureReason);
}
```

Policy Chaining

Policy chaining is the ability to call one policy from another. Policy chaining is not natively supported through the Business Rule Engine, but can still be accomplished through additional coding. Essentially, a policy can call .NET code that executes another policy.

The following steps walk through calling one policy from another policy using a console application. It modifies the Loan Processing Sample in the BizTalk SDK. This same sample could be used to call the rule from an orchestration.[35]

1. Create an `Executer` class with the following code snippet. When its `Execute` method is called, the class will use the policy name that is passed to it to assert the facts that were previously passed in via its constructor. In this case it is passing an array to allow multiple objects to be asserted into the engine.

```
using System;
using Microsoft.RuleEngine;
namespace PolicyExecutor
{
        public class Executor
        {
                public Executor(Array passedFacts)
                {
                        facts = passedFacts;
                }
                public void Execute(string policyName)
                {
                        Policy policy = new Policy(policyName);
                        policy.Execute(facts);
                        policy.Dispose();
                }
                private Array facts;
                public Array Facts
                {
                        get{return facts;} set{facts = value;}
                }
        }
}
```

2. Create a console application with the following code snippet:

```
using System;
using System.Xml;
using Microsoft.RuleEngine;
using System.Collections;
using PolicyExecutor;
namespace PolicyChaining
```

35. This example is based on material presented in "BizTalk Business Rules Engine Quick Tips" by Jonathan Moons (Microsoft Corporation). Copyright© 2005 by Microsoft Corporation. Reprinted with permission from Microsoft Corporation.

```
{
 class Class1
 {
  [STAThread]
  static void Main(string[] args)
  {
      string filename = "sampleLoan.xml";
      string policyName = "LoanProcessing";
      // Build TXD
      XmlDocument xd1 = new XmlDocument();
      xd1.Load(filename);
      TypedXmlDocument doc1 = new
        TypedXmlDocument("Microsoft.Samples.BizTalk.LoansProcessor.Case",xd1);
      // Build short term fact array and provide to Executor object
      object[] facts = new object[2];
      PolicyExecutor.Executor executor = new PolicyExecutor.Executor(facts);
      facts[0] = doc1;
      facts[1] =executor;
      // Call parent policy
      Policy policy = new Policy(policyName);
      policy.Execute(facts);
      policy.Dispose();
      // Write out updated XML
      XmlTextWriter writer1 = new XmlTextWriter("sampleLoan_Out.xml",null);
      writer1.Formatting = Formatting.Indented;
      doc1.Document.WriteTo( writer1 );
      writer1.Flush();
  }
 }
}
```

3. Set up and modify the Loan Policy SDK sample.
4. Run the Setup.bat file to set up the Loan Processing SDK sample.
5. Open the Business Rule Composer and create a new policy called LoanPolicyChained.
6. Copy and paste the "Income Status Rule" and the "Negation of Income Status Rule" from LoanPolicy to LoanPolicyChained.
7. Add a new rule to the LoanPolicy called Chain to Income Rules. Set the condition to always be true and in the action call the `Execute` method of the `Executor` class. Set the parameter to the same name as the chained policy, LoanPolicyChained. The new policies will look something like Figure 8-10.
8. Compile and run the console application to have it call the two policies.

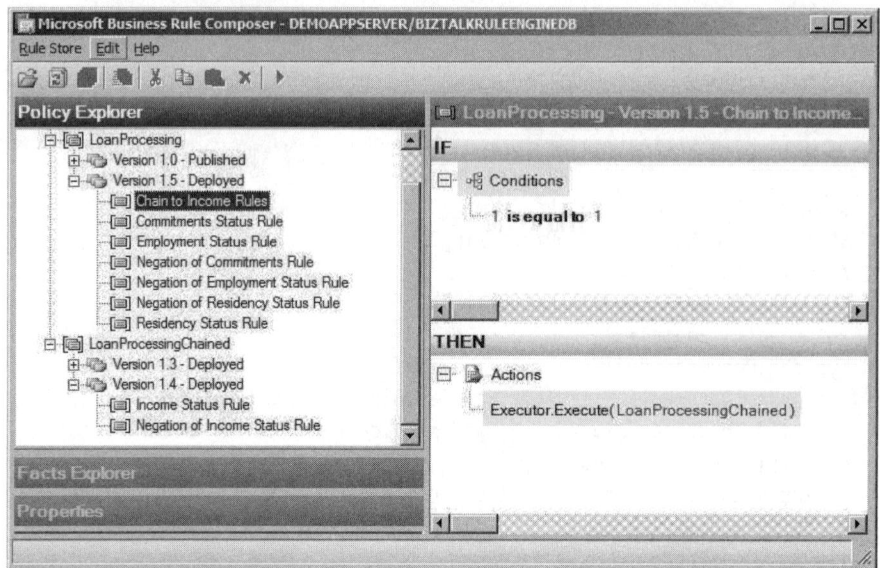

Figure 8-10. *Policy chaining*

■ **Note** If the policy caller is an orchestration and not an application, the same `Executor` class and policies can still be used. Just replace the console app with an orchestration. One way to do this is to set up the `Executor` class in an Expression shape and then call the Loan policy normally through a Call Rules shape, while passing in the XML message and the `Executor` class instance. The Expression shape would include the following code:

```
facts = new System.Collections.ArrayList();

// Build TXD
xmlDoc = LoanMsg;
typedXmlDoc = new
Microsoft.RuleEngine.TypedXmlDocument("Microsoft.Samples.BizTalk.LoansProcessor
                                                                .Case",xmlDoc);

// Build short term fact array and provide to Executor object
facts.Add(typedXmlDoc);
executor = new PolicyExecutor.Executor(facts.ToArray());
```

The code also depends on four variables that can be defined within the Scope shape that is required for the Call Rules shape: `executor` of type PolicyExecutor.Executor, `facts` of type ArrayList, `xmlDoc` of type XmlDocument, and `typeXmlDoc` of type TypedXmlDocument.

PART 3

You Mean You Aren't a Developer?

Chapters 1 through 8 were primarily targeted toward the developer. As you no doubt have come to realize, BizTalk is a developer-centric product. The tools within BizTalk are built for and are designed to be used by developers. This is a major source of pain for system administrators who are ultimately responsible for ensuring that a BizTalk solution is supported and managed properly once it is commissioned into production. "Productionalizing" a BizTalk Server–based solution is a task that is often overlooked, but one we are going to address. In Part 3, we will dive into these antideveloper topics:

- Performance tuning
- BizTalk Server scripting through WMI and ExplorerOM
- Deploying BizTalk Server applications
- Backup and disaster recovery options
- High-availability configurations

CHAPTER 9

BizTalk Server 2006 Operations

In this chapter, we cover BizTalk Server 2006 operations, which include configuration, management, scalability, high availability, backup, restore, and disaster recovery. A well-designed and developed BizTalk system can only realize its full potential when married with a well-architected and managed BizTalk operations environment. BizTalk Server 2006 provides a number of new features and tools to improve the operations experience for IT staff. This chapter covers the critical management tasks necessary to ensure a BizTalk system is operating at a high level of performance and availability. In this chapter, you will find discussions of the following topics:

- **Configuration and management**: We discuss the many improvements in the administrative features in BizTalk Server 2006 involving configuration and management. Enhancements to the BizTalk Server Administration Console functionality such as the management of groups, applications, parties, and platform settings will be detailed. In BizTalk, the addition of new and reorganization of existing administration tools and artifacts provides both developers and IT staff with more intuitive means to manage, deploy, monitor, and secure production BizTalk systems.
- **Scalability and high availability**: We present the various features of BizTalk Server 2006 and options to consider when designing and implementing a BizTalk system to be both performant and robust in support of a productive and profitable business. Options around scaling out to additional servers for performance and redundancy or scaling up the power of existing hardware to improve throughput will be presented. BizTalk Server 2006 now provides features such as support for native 64-bit execution on x64 and Windows clustering that can improve performance and uptime.
- **Backup/restore**: We show you how to back up and restore BizTalk Server databases as well as other databases that are part of the overall solution. We also cover how to maintain, archive, and purge data from the BizTalk Tracking database. Plan to test backup and restore procedures before entering production and on a recurring basis.

- **Disaster recovery**: We provide the specific steps and procedures for developing a disaster recovery plan for a BizTalk Server 2006 application, covering both the BizTalk runtime servers and the BizTalk Group hosted in SQL Server. You should plan to test application-specific disaster recovery procedures to ensure the procedures have been successfully tailored to meet application requirements before entering production. Our discussion does not cover procedures for disaster recovery for the following related topics:

  - Non-BizTalk applications
  - Application source code
  - Certificates
  - Personnel

  There may be additional areas that require documentation in a specific application's disaster recovery plan not listed here that must be addressed on an application-by-application basis.

Configuration and Management

BizTalk Server 2006 includes many new features that make administration quicker and easier than in previous releases of BizTalk Server. Core administrative tools such as the BizTalk Administration Console and BizTalk Deployment Wizard have been reorganized with many new options and features added. Specifically, the concept of a BizTalk application has been added to provide a container in which to organize related messaging artifacts to ease their management and deployment as Microsoft Installer (MSI) files. These changes enhance the BizTalk operations experience for both the developer and IT professional, especially in large and complex BizTalk environments.

Administration Tools

The following list defines the tools used to configure and manage BizTalk Server groups, deploy BizTalk Server applications, troubleshoot errors, control security settings, define trading partners, monitor business activities, and administer workflows:

- **BizTalk Server Administration Console**: Is the Microsoft Management Console (MMC) snap-in that has been significantly enhanced to serve as the primary management tool for BizTalk Server. The BizTalk Administration MMC provides a graphical user interface for performing all of the deployment operations for a BizTalk application. It also provides BizTalk group management, message and orchestration troubleshooting such as resume/retry messages and terminate suspended messages/instances, as well as party definition and platform settings.
- **BTSTask command-line tool**: Is the new command-line administration and deployment tool in BizTalk Server 2006 that supersedes BTSDeploy.

- **BTSDeploy command-line tool**: Was the command-line tool in BizTalk Server 2004 for deploying/undeploying assemblies and importing/exporting port and orchestration binding settings to/from the BizTalk Management Database. BTSDeploy is included in BizTalk Server 2006 to support scripts that administrators had developed for BizTalk Server 2004.

■ **Caution** While BTSDeploy scripts will continue to work, BizTalk administrators should use BTSTask commands when creating new scripts and consider converting existing scripts. BTSDeploy may be removed in subsequent versions of BizTalk Server.

- **Scripting and Programmability APIs**: Are exposed as Microsoft Windows Management Instrumentation (WMI) or BizTalk Explorer Object Model objects. Along with the BTSTask command-line tool, these APIs facilitate creation and execution of scripts to automate very detailed administrative tasks.

■ **Note** The WMI object model exposes and simplifies administrative APIs. All administration APIs expose some form of the following operations on every object they manage: create, enumerate, modify, and delete. WMI exposes this functionality in a consistent manner for all WMI objects.

- **BizTalk Explorer toolbar**: Is used in Microsoft Visual Studio 2005 to allow developers to perform common administrative tasks from a single integrated development environment (IDE).
- **BizTalk Server Configuration tool**: Allows each installed BizTalk Server feature to be fully configured, exported, imported, and unconfigured. Configuration of a feature typically involves defining a SQL database to hold setting information, NT service accounts and groups for runtime access permissions, and other feature-specific settings.
- **Business Activity Services (BAS) web site:** Is a Microsoft Windows SharePoint Services (WSS) web site that provides business users with a friendly interface for interacting with trading partners and business processes in a familiar environment.
- **Business Activity Monitoring (BAM):** Is set up and configured through the Visio-based Orchestration Designer for Business Analysts (ODBA), the Microsoft Office Excel workbook (BAM.xls), the Tracking Profile Editor (TPE), the BM.exe command-line deployment tool, and the BAM portal web site. BAM provides business users with a way to see a real-time or aggregated holistic view of their business processes.

- **Health and Activity Tracking (HAT)**: Tracks the health and run history of your BizTalk messages and orchestration processes and aids in identifying errors and bottlenecks in the BizTalk Server environment. Use HAT to view the technical details of a particular orchestration, pipeline, or message instance, as well as see the message flow of a particular message from end to end within the BizTalk system. Business users can also view, monitor, and query completed messages and processes via tracked data, saving these queries as custom views for reuse. Business analysts and end users can track the state of their business processes by viewing both live and archived data.

Tip Some features previously in BizTalk Server 2004 HAT such as retry/resume messages have been moved to the Group Hub and Query pages in the improved BizTalk Server 2006 Administration Console.

- **Enterprise Single Sign-On (SSO) Administration**: Is a Microsoft Management Console snap-in that enables SSO Administrators, SSO Affiliate Administrators, and Application Administrators to update the SSO database; to add, delete, and manage applications; to administer user mappings; and to set credentials for the affiliate application users. Some operations can be performed only by the SSO Administrators and others by the SSO Affiliate Administrators. All operations that can be performed by the BizTalk Application Administrators can also be performed by the SSO Administrators and SSO Affiliate Administrators.
- **Enterprise SSO Client Utility**: Enables end users to manage their own mappings and set their credentials using this UI tool.
- **Enterprise SSO command-line tools**: Consists of three different command-line utilities to perform Enterprise Single Sign-On tasks:
    - **SSOConfig**: Enables an SSO Administrator to configure the SSO database and to manage the master secret.

Note The Configuration Wizard creates the SSO database and the master secret server.

    - **SSOManage**: Enables SSO Administrators, SSO Affiliate Administrators, and Application Administrators to update the SSO database to add, delete, and manage applications; administer user mappings; and set credentials for the affiliate application users. The SSOManage command-line tool contains similar functionality to the SSO Administration MMC snap-in.
    - **SSOClient**: Enables SSO users to manage their own user mappings and set their credentials.
- **BizTalk Web Services Publishing Wizard**: Is a wizard for generating an IIS virtual directory and web service for publishing BizTalk orchestrations and schemas via SOAP.

- **Business Rule Engine Deployment Wizard**: Is a wizard for importing/exporting policies and vocabularies. This tool can also deploy or undeploy a policy in a Rule Engine database.
- **Human Workflow Services (HWS) Server Administration Console**: Is used to manage human workflow objects. WMI can be used to create and run scripts that perform HWS administrative tasks.

■ **Note** Human Workflow Services is fully supported with no feature enhancements in BizTalk Server 2006 but is planned for removal in future versions.

Application Concept

BizTalk Server 2006 formalizes the concept of a BizTalk **application** by providing a logical container for housing all the artifacts for a given solution. This BizTalk application container can hold design-time artifacts (schemas, maps, pipelines, and orchestrations), messaging components (receive ports, receive locations, and send ports), and other related items (rules policies, pre-processing or post-processing scripts, assemblies, and BAS artifacts) that comprise an integrated business process. By leveraging this new concept, the effort to deploy and manage applications is significantly reduced compared to previous versions of BizTalk.

Even as the number of artifacts and components within several complex applications increases, each application can still be managed separately in a simple and intuitive manner. The effect is a streamlining of many everyday tasks, because developers and IT professionals are now able to deploy, manage, start/stop, and troubleshoot at the application level. This results in less confusion and fewer errors. In order to take advantage of the application concept, use the new deployment features in BizTalk Server 2006 or update WMI deployment scripts as necessary. Otherwise, artifacts will deploy to the default application for the BizTalk Group.

BizTalk Server Administration Console

The newly designed BizTalk Server Administration Console was built with applications in mind. The Administration Console provides a complete view of one or more BizTalk Server environments. The BizTalk Administration Console is an MMC snap-in that allows the ability to create, configure, and manage one or more applications across multiple servers. Additionally, the MMC includes the ability to import and export applications for installation across multiple servers or for facilitating moving between staging and production environments.

The console also includes the message- and service-monitoring capabilities previously provided by HAT, the Health and Activity Tracking tool introduced in BizTalk Server 2004. While the Administration Console provides the runtime monitoring, HAT must still be used for document tracking and orchestration debugging.

The enhanced BizTalk Server Administration Console is used to manage the following artifacts:

- **BizTalk Group**: The BizTalk Group node in the console tree contains additional nodes that represent the artifacts (applications, parties, and platform settings) for that BizTalk Group (see Figure 9-1). BizTalk groups are units of organization that usually represent enterprises, departments, hubs, or other business units that require a contained BizTalk Server implementation. A BizTalk Group has a one-to-one relationship with a BizTalk Management Database.

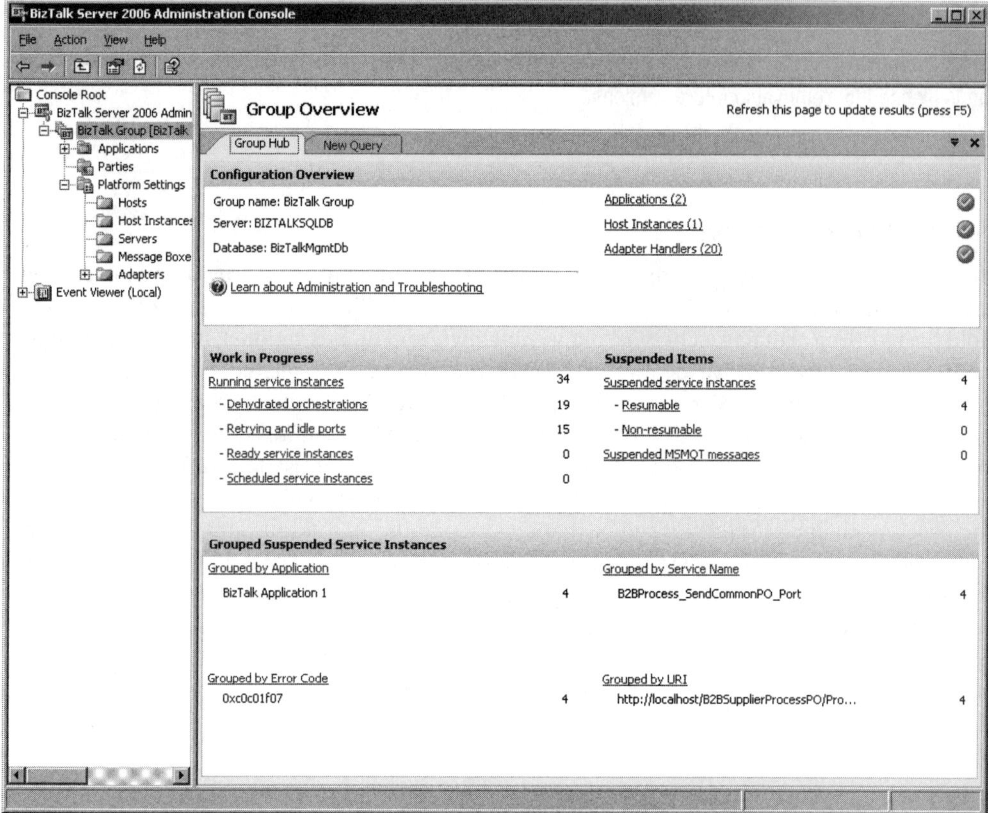

Figure 9-1. *BizTalk Group Hub page in the BizTalk Server Administration Console*

When you select the BizTalk Group node in the BizTalk Server Administration Console, the BizTalk Server Group Hub page is displayed in the details pane. The BizTalk Server Group Hub page, shown in Figure 9-1, provides an overall view of the health of your BizTalk Server system.

Use the Group Hub page in the BizTalk Server Administration Console to investigate orchestration, port, and message failures. The Group Hub page provides access to the current real-time state of the system, accessing data in the Messagebox database to view all service instances such as orchestrations, ports, and messaging, along with their associated messages.

■ **Tip** The BizTalk Server Administration Console in BizTalk Server 2006 now allows management of multiple BizTalk Groups from a single console. To connect to an additional existing group in an environment, right-click the BizTalk Server 2006 Administration node below Console Root. Choose Connect to Existing Group from the pop-up menu. In the dialog box that appears, enter the SQL Server name and database name for the additional BizTalk Management Database to connect to. The connection will use Windows Authentication. If the account under which the Administration Console is run is part of the added BizTalk Server Administrators group, then the connection will succeed and an additional BizTalk Group will be available to manage.

Use the Group Hub page to

- See currently running service instances such as orchestrations and messaging, and their associated messages.
- Look into the Messagebox database for a view of the current data and the real-time state of the system.
- Suspend, terminate, and resume service instances.
- Troubleshoot application configuration errors and view subscriptions.

Use the Query tab on the Group Hub page in the BizTalk Server Administration Console shown in Figure 9-1 to find specific running and suspended service instances, messages, or subscriptions. Queries performed using the Administration Console search through active items, which are stored in the Messagebox database. A new query tab will appear each time you run a new query. To locate tracked, archived, or completed messages or service instances, use the HAT tool.

- **Applications**: BizTalk applications are new with BizTalk Server 2006. Applications are managed through the BizTalk Server 2006 Administration Console under the Applications node. BizTalk applications provide a way to view and manage the items, or artifacts, that make up a BizTalk business solution. For a new BizTalk Server 2006 installation, a default application named BizTalk Application 1 is created. When upgrading to BizTalk Server 2006 from BizTalk Server 2004, all existing artifacts are placed into BizTalk Application 1. Examples of artifacts are BizTalk assemblies, .NET assemblies, schemas, maps, bindings, and certificates. Artifacts are organized for each application in folders described in the following list:
  - **Orchestration**: Orchestrations are designed using the Orchestration Designer in Visual Studio and are deployed to the BizTalk Group under which they appear in the Administration Console.
  - **Role links**: A role link defines the relationship between roles defined by the message and port types used in the interactions in both directions.
  - **Send port groups**: A send port group is a named collection of send ports used to send the same message to multiple destinations in a single binding configuration.

- **Send ports**: A send port is a BizTalk object that sends outbound messages to a specific address combined with a BizTalk Server send pipeline.
- **Receive ports**: A receive port is a logical grouping of similar receive locations.
- **Receive locations**: A receive location is defined as a specific address at which inbound messages arrive combined with a BizTalk Server receive pipeline that processes the messages received at that address.
- **Policies**: A policy is a versioned collection of business rules.
- **Schemas**: A schema is the structure for a message. A schema can contain multiple subschemas.
- **Maps**: A map is an XML file that defines the corresponding transformations between the records and fields in one or more source schema and the records and fields in one or more destination schema. A map contains an Extensible Stylesheet Language (XSL) stylesheet that is used by BizTalk Server to perform the transformation.
- **Pipelines**: A pipeline is a software infrastructure that defines and links one or more processing stages, running them in prescribed order to complete a specific task such as decode, disassemble validate, etc. Pipelines divide processing into stages, abstractions that describe a category of work. They also determine the sequence in which each category of work is performed.
- **Resources**: A resource is a pre-processing or post-processing script, deployed assembly, or other file associated with a BizTalk application.
- **BAS artifacts**: Business Activity Services artifacts provide a way for applications to communicate with outside partners. BAS artifacts are made up of partner profiles (also known as parties), partner groups, agreements, and Microsoft Office InfoPath templates. BAS artifacts must first be created using the BAS site before they can be imported and appear in the BizTalk Server Administration Console.

- **Parties**: A party is an entity outside of BizTalk Server that interacts with an orchestration. All of the partners an organization deals with are considered parties. An organization may have tens to thousands of partners.
- **Platform settings**: The Platform Settings node contains subnodes that represent globally configurable settings that apply across the farm of BizTalk servers in the Group. Those subnodes are
    - **Hosts**: The Hosts node contains all of the in-process and isolated hosts in the BizTalk Server environment. A BizTalk host is a logical container for items such as adapter handlers, receive locations (including pipelines), and orchestrations. Additional hosts can be created by right-clicking the Hosts node and choosing New ➤ Host.

- **Host Instances**: The Host Instances node contains all of the host instances in the current BizTalk Server Group. Host instances are physically manifested as one or more copies of the BizTalk Server runtime process (i.e., NT service instance) that executes application components. New host instances can be created by right-clicking the Host Instances node and choosing New ➤ Host Instance.
- **Servers**: The Servers node lists all servers that are joined to the selected BizTalk Server group. These are the computers where BizTalk Server is installed and configured, and where host instances are running. Host instances are created by associating a server with a particular host.
- **Message Boxes**: The Message Boxes node contains all Messagebox databases used by the current BizTalk Server Group. Right-clicking the Message Boxes node and choosing New ➤ Message Box allows for creation of additional Messagebox databases. The Messagebox database is the basis for work item load balancing across servers that do cooperative processing. A work item can pass through a Messagebox database more than once during its processing life. The name of the Messagebox database cannot exceed 100 characters.
- **Adapters**: The Adapters node contains subnodes for all the Send and Receive Adapters configured for the BizTalk Server Group and the associated adapter handlers. Adapters are the messaging middleware used to send and receive messages between endpoints.

Scalability and High Availability

BizTalk Server 2006 has fundamentally the same underlying architecture as BizTalk Server 2004, so the approach to scalability and high availability is very similar. BizTalk Server 2006 does include new features in these areas, specifically

- Support for clustering BizTalk hosts
- Clustering of BizTalk messaging services
- Support for native execution on 64-bit Windows platforms (x64 not IA64)

64-bit native execution allows BizTalk Server 2006 to take advantage of the benefits of the x64 Windows platform such as a larger memory address space, support for larger RAM, and faster I/O. The white paper "Benefits of Microsoft Windows x64 Editions" located at the following link covers the benefits of the Windows x64 platform in detail: www.microsoft.com/windowsserver2003/techinfo/overview/x64benefits.mspx.

We highly recommend implementing BizTalk on Windows x64 editions to take advantage of these benefits where appropriate. With x64, even 32-bit Windows applications can benefit from running on x64 Windows; however, note that BizTalk Server 2006 host instances can run x64 natively.

■ **Tip** There are no additional licensing costs from either a BizTalk or Windows perspective to take advantage of the x64 platform.

Scalability

Even after tuning an application, bottlenecks in performance can develop, especially if load increases, which may require upgrading or adding hardware to the existing BizTalk solution architecture. Thankfully, BizTalk Server 2006 provides options to easily scale up or scale out the solution architecture.

Depending on where a bottleneck exists, it might be necessary to scale out or scale up either the BizTalk tier or the SQL Server tier. This is why it is extremely important to monitor a BizTalk solution to help identify trends in hardware resource utilization such as memory, CPU, or disk before the problem occurs. Microsoft Operations Manager (MOM) 2005 with the MOM 2005 management pack for BizTalk Server 2006 can greatly assist with this task.

The white paper "BizTalk Server 2004 Performance Characteristics" is a great document to review in order to get a feel for how application design can affect resource utilization/ performance. This white paper can be found here: http://msdn.microsoft.com/library/ default.asp?url=/library/en-us/bts_2004wp/html/04d20926-20d2-4098-b701-52238a267eba. asp?frame=true.

While the preceding white paper is for BizTalk Server 2004, the scalability concepts still apply in BizTalk Server 2006. A more recent white paper on BizTalk Server 2006 adapter performance, "BizTalk Server 2006 Comparative Adapter Study," is available at this link: www. microsoft.com/downloads/details.aspx?FamilyID=fdae55db-184b-4d93-ad79-a113b5268ee2&DisplayLang=en.

In addition to the details on adapter performance, this white paper provides detail on how to determine Maximum Sustainable Throughput (MST), which is a critical step for understanding the performance characteristics of any BizTalk application.

The next subsections cover when to choose an option and the steps involved.

Scaling Out the BizTalk Tier

Scaling out the BizTalk tier is a good option when BizTalk Server is the bottleneck in terms of high CPU, memory, or heavy disk I/O and adding additional servers makes economic sense and can solve the issue. High CPU can result from intensive pipeline processing, message maps converting between complex schemas, or large/complex orchestrations. High memory or disk I/O can occur under high load and can generally be addressed through scale-out, but not always. See the "Scaling Up of the BizTalk Tier" subsection later for more information. In many cases, scaling out by adding another BizTalk Server is more cost effective than replacing an existing machine with a more powerful one as long as it can solve the issue.

Scaling out the BizTalk tier does not help when the Messagebox database is the bottleneck, which again highlights how important it is to monitor resource utilization on both the BizTalk tier and the SQL tier. Another scenario of when scaling out the BizTalk tier may not help is when an adapter is a bottleneck. For example, if the FTP adapter is the bottleneck, adding more BizTalk servers does not help if the limit exists on the other end of the FTP communication.

Scaling out the BizTalk tier is achieved through managing BizTalk hosts and host instances. BizTalk hosts are logical groupings where artifacts such as receive locations, send ports, and orchestrations execute. Hosts are physically implemented as host instances, which are .NET Windows Services. A typical way to organize a BizTalk application is to create a receive host, a send host, a tracking host, and an orchestration host. This type of organization can isolate processing so that if a receive problem is occurring, troubleshooting and debugging can be focused on the receive host instance(s), and it is a good idea even when there is just a single BizTalk server.

Note Hosts can be configured to run host instances under separate service accounts/Windows groups as a security boundary to provide security isolation between host processing, if needed to meet business requirements.

The way scale-out works is that when a receive adapter (or a send port or orchestration) is configured to run in a host such as a receive host, the adapter physically runs on every BizTalk server where an instance of the receive host is deployed. So to scale-out the host where the receive adapter executes, a new BizTalk server is configured to join the BizTalk Group and a host instance of the receive host is deployed to the new server. Deploying a new instance of a host takes a few clicks in the BizTalk Server 2006 Administration Console. For information on managing hosts and host instances, please refer to the BizTalk Server 2006 documentation.

Scaling Out the SQL Tier

Scale-out of the SQL tier is primarily focused on the Messagebox database. The Messagebox database is where BizTalk application processing occurs from a database perspective. The first Messagebox database is created during initial BizTalk configuration and is the master Messagebox database. The master Messagebox contains the master subscription information and routes messages to the appropriate Messagebox database if there is more than one Messagebox.

When it is determined that scaling out the Messagebox database is required, Microsoft recommends dedicating the master Messagebox to do routing only by selecting Disable new message publication for the master Messagebox database in the BizTalk Server 2006 Administration Console, and then having the other Messagebox databases perform application processing. Microsoft also recommends going from one Messagebox to three Messagebox databases to benefit from scaling out the SQL tier and to overcome the additional processing overhead that occurs when there is more than one Messagebox database. For more information on scaling out the Messagebox, please refer to the BizTalk Server 2006 documentation.

Scaling Up the BizTalk Tier

Scaling up the BizTalk tier is a good option when BizTalk Server is the bottleneck, if it can solve the issue and is a good alternative economically. Scaling up the BizTalk tier makes sense in the following scenarios:

- Large message transforms
- Large number of messages per Interchange
- High memory utilization by some BTS components such as pipelines or adapters
- A transport-related issue, such as EDI

Scaling up includes adding additional CPUs, adding memory or faster disk I/O to an existing BizTalk server, or replacing an existing BizTalk server with a more powerful machine.

Next, we cover scale-up of the SQL tier.

Scaling Up the SQL Tier

Scaling up the database tier avoids the overhead of adding additional Messagebox databases that results from message routing and can be a good option if it makes economic sense and addresses the issue. In general, scale-up should be considered before scale-out for the SQL tier.

Scaling up the database tier can include adding CPUs, memory, or a faster disk as well as replacing the existing server with a more powerful server. One scenario that scale-up cannot address is when there is SQL lock contention on the SQL tier. In this case, scaling out of the SQL tier should be considered.

High Availability

Most BizTalk Server solutions are mission critical to a company and require high availability to meet business requirements. Therefore, BizTalk Server 2006 provides features for high availability as well as takes advantage of high-availability capabilities in the underlying operating system such as clustering to provide a robust architecture.

Both BizTalk and SQL Server must be highly available in order for the solution to function, and we cover this in the next two subsections. In addition, the master secret server must also be highly available for a BizTalk solution to function. Clustering the master secret server is covered in the following text as well.

BizTalk Tier High Availability

As with scalability, BizTalk hosts are the key feature to provide high availability for the BizTalk tier. As mentioned previously, BizTalk artifacts such as receive locations, send ports, and orchestrations are configured to run in a logical host but actually execute in host instance Windows Services that can be deployed to multiple BizTalk servers in the BizTalk Group.

If there are two BizTalk servers with an instance of a particular host, but one server becomes unavailable, processing will continue on the other BizTalk server with the instance of the host, providing processing redundancy or availability.

BizTalk Server 2006 introduces Windows clustering for host instances. Host clustering is necessary for integrated BizTalk adapters that should not be run in multiple host instances simultaneously such as the FTP receive handler or potentially the POP3 receive handler. The FTP does not have file locking, so if there were two FTP host instances running, both could potentially receive the same file, resulting in duplicate processing. Therefore, only one FTP receive host instance should be configured, which is why it should be clustered because it is a single instance. For POP3, the scenario is similar to FTP's. If the POP3 server allows multiple simultaneous connections to the same mailbox such that duplicate messages may be received, the POP3 adapter should be run as a single host instance and should therefore be clustered for high availability.

Caution Running the EDI adapter handlers in a clustered BizTalk host is not supported.

Another scenario where host clustering is necessary for high availability is when a single host instance is required to maintain ordered delivery for the MSMQ or the WebSphere MQ–integrated adapters. For these adapters, the single host instance can be clustered to provide high availability. For more information on implementing high availability for the BizTalk tier, please refer to the BizTalk Server 2006 documentation.

The next subsection covers SQL tier high availability.

SQL Tier High Availability

The BizTalk Group exists in the SQL tier in SQL Server database instances, which can be clustered for high availability. From a BizTalk standpoint, it is transparent whether the SQL Server instance is clustered or not, so SQL tier high availability is a matter of implementing SQL Server in a highly available manner by configuring the BizTalk Group databases on a SQL Server instance that is clustered. For more information on SQL Server high availability, please refer to the SQL Server documentation installed as part of the product or available online here:

- **SQL Server 2000 Books Online**: www.microsoft.com/downloads/details.aspx?familyid=a6f79cb1-a420-445f-8a4b-bd77a7da194b&displaylang=en.
- **SQL Server 2005 Books Online**: www.microsoft.com/technet/prodtechnol/sql/2005/downloads/books.mspx.

Next, we cover how to implement the master secret server for high availability.

Master Secret Server High Availability

If the master secret server becomes unavailable, all runtime operations already running will continue to run, but SSO servers will not be able to encrypt new credentials. Since there can be only one master secret server in the SSO system, Microsoft recommends clustering the master secret server, and the BizTalk Server 2006 documentation covers the steps in detail.

■ **Tip** Though many organizations implement Enterprise SSO with a master secret server on a per–BizTalk Group basis, a single master secret server can be shared between multiple BizTalk Groups as well as with Microsoft Host Integration Server.

Clustering the master secret consists of installing Enterprise Single Sign-On on a Windows cluster. Quite often, customers choose to cluster the master secret server on the same Windows cluster that hosts the BizTalk Group databases to avoid the cost of having a separate Windows cluster just for Enterprise SSO. Where you install Enterprise SSO depends on the business requirements of the solution as well as economic considerations. Just ensure that the master secret is installed in a Windows cluster to ensure high availability whether on a stand-alone Windows cluster or in the same Windows cluster where the BizTalk Group SQL Server database instances are clustered.

Maintaining the BizTalk Group

A BizTalk Group consists of the set of databases hosted in SQL Server. SQL Server provides high availability for BizTalk Server 2006 applications through Windows cluster installations hosting the BizTalk configuration and operation databases. For BizTalk applications, the servers with BizTalk installed provide the runtime environment with SQL Server as the persistent store. Therefore, BizTalk Server 2006 backup, restore, and disaster recovery procedures are heavily focused on procedures related to SQL Server.

A BizTalk Server solution's availability and performance are highly dependent on maintaining the SQL Server–based back end where the BizTalk Group is located. Every message that is received by a BizTalk host instance enters the SQL Server Messagebox database, tracked to some degree, retrieved from SQL Server by the host instance where the subscribing orchestration is executed with the results put back into SQL Server for transmission on a host instance send port. As you can see, overall BizTalk performance is highly dependent on the underlying SQL Server performance.

■ **Caution** Changes to the BizTalk Group SQL Server schema are not supported. Do not modify the SQL Server schema for any tables or stored procedures that are part of the BizTalk Group.

Luckily the BizTalk product team provides several SQL Agent jobs to assist with keeping the BizTalk Group running in top form. SQL Server Agent makes message bodies available to HAT and WMI, and enables you to run jobs to clean up the Messagebox databases.

The SQL Agent jobs are created when the BizTalk Group is configured using Configuration.exe. The user who runs Configuration.exe is also designated as the SQL Agent job owner. The account designated as the job owner is the security context that the SQL Agent job executes under. If any SQL Agent jobs are failing, consider changing the job owner to a different account that has the required privileges to folders or UNC shares, etc., so that the job can complete successfully.

The SQL Agent jobs and a description of each are listed in Table 9-1. Do not alter the schedule for any jobs except possibly for the Backup BizTalk Server SQL Agent job. Details configuring the Backup BizTalk Server SQL Agent job are covered in the subsection titled "Configuring the Backup BizTalk Server SQL Agent Job."

Table 9-1. *BizTalk Group SQL Agent Jobs*

SQL Agent Job	Remarks
Backup BizTalk Server (BizTalkMgmtDb)	Performs backup operations on BizTalk databases that participate in Distributed Transaction Coordinator (DTC) transactions. Not all BizTalk databases are part of this job. Also, additional databases can be added to this job. This job is disabled by default and must be configured in order to run. Scheduled to perform full backup daily and log backup every 15 minutes by default.
CleanupBTFExpiredEntries Job_<BizTalkMgmtDb>	New in BizTalk Server 2006, this SQL Agent job cleans up expired BizTalk Framework (BTF) entries in the BizTalk Management Database. Scheduled to run every 12 hours and enabled by default.
DTA Purge and Archive (BizTalkMsgBoxDb)	New in BizTalk Server 2006, this SQL Agent job automatically archives data in the BizTalk Tracking (BizTalkDTADb) database and purges obsolete data. This job is disabled by default and must be configured in order to run. Scheduled to run every minute by default.
MessageBox_DeadProcesses_ Cleanup_<BizTalkMsgBoxDb>	Detects when a running BizTalk host instance has stopped. This SQL Agent job releases all in-progress work for that host instance so that it can be picked up by another host instance. Scheduled to run every minute and enabled by default.
MessageBox_Message_ Cleanup_<BizTalkMsgBoxDb>	Removes messages that are no longer referenced by any subscribers in the Messagebox database tables. This job is disabled by default, but it should **not** be manually run. This job is started when needed by the MessageBox_Message_ManageRefCountLog_ <BiztalkMsgBoxDb> job.
MessageBox_Message_ ManageRefCountLog_ <BizTalkMsgBoxDb>	Manages the reference count logs for messages. It determines when a message is no longer referenced by a subscriber. Scheduled to run every minute and enabled by default.
MessageBox_Parts_Cleanup_ <BizTalkMsgBoxDb>	Removes message parts that are no longer referenced by any messages in the Messagebox database tables. Scheduled to run every minute and enabled by default.
MessageBox_UpdateStats_ <BizTalkMsgBoxDb>	New in BizTalk Server 2006, this SQL Agent job manually updates database statistics for the BizTalk Messagebox database. Scheduled to run every 5 minutes and enabled by default.
Operations_OperateOn Instances_OnMaster_ <BizTalkMsgBoxDb>	New in BizTalk Server 2006, this SQL Agent job is required for multiple Messagebox database deployments. It performs operational tasks on Messagebox databases. Scheduled to run every minute and enabled by default.
PurgeSubscriptionsJob_ <BizTalkMsgBoxDb>	Purges unused subscription predicates from the Messagebox database. Scheduled to run every minute and enabled by default.
Rules_Database_Cleanup <BizTalkRuleEngineDb>	New in BizTalk Server 2006, this SQL Agent job purges old audit data from the Rule Engine database every 90 days. It also purges old history data from the Rule Engine database every 3 days. Scheduled to run every hour and enabled by default.
TrackedMessages_Copy_ <BizTalkMsgBoxDb>	Copies message bodies of tracked messages from the Messagebox database to the Tracking database. Scheduled to run every minute and enabled by default.

Microsoft strongly recommends monitoring the SQL Agent service and the individual jobs using a monitoring tool such as MOM or similar enterprise monitoring product. If any of these jobs starts failing, it is a strong indication that there are performance issues with the application. It is also a good idea to monitor how long it takes for the SQL Agent jobs to run, perhaps on a weekly basis. If the jobs are taking longer and longer to run over time, it is another indication that there may be performance issues.

For completeness, the BizTalk Server 2004 SQL Agent job TrackingSpool_Cleanup_<BizTalkMsgBoxDb is no longer present in BizTalk Server 2006.

The next step is to configure the necessary SQL Agent jobs to perform backups and to maintain the BizTalk Group.

SQL Agent Job Configuration

The following jobs from Table 9-1 require configuration before they can be enabled and can run successfully:

- Backup BizTalk Server (BizTalkMgmtDb)
- DTA Purge and Archive (BizTalkMsgBoxDb)

■Note The SQL Agent job MessageBox_Message_Cleanup_<BizTalkMsgBoxDb> is disabled by default. It is not supported to enable this job or run it manually. This SQL Agent job is managed by the MessageBox_Message_ManageRefCountLog_<BiztalkMsgBoxDb> SQL Agent job.

The following two subsections cover how to configure these SQL Agent jobs.

Configuring the Backup BizTalk Server SQL Agent Job

The Backup BizTalk Server SQL Agent job is a critical job that must be configured in order to be able to successfully back up the BizTalk Server 2006 databases that participate in Distributed Transaction Coordinator transactions. Databases that participate in DTC transactions such as with BizTalk must be backed up and restored as a set to ensure consistency.

■Note Not all BizTalk databases are backed up as part of the Backup BizTalk Server job. Backing up these databases is covered in the next subsection.

The following databases are backed up as part of the Backup BizTalk Server SQL Agent job:

- BizTalk Configuration (BizTalkMgmtDb)
- BizTalk Messagebox (BizTalkMsgBoxDb)
- BizTalk Tracking (BizTalkDTADb)

- Rule Engine (BizTalkRuleEngineDb)
- BAM Primary Import (BAMPrimaryImport)
- Trading Partner Management (TPM)
- HWS Administration (BizTalkHWSDb)
- BizTalk EDI (BizTalkEDIdb)

These databases **must** be backed up by the Backup BizTalk Server SQL Agent job and cannot be backed up using the normal SQL Server backup procedures. The reason is because BizTalk uses SQL Server log marks to keep the set of databases consistent as part of DTC transactions. The Backup BizTalk Server job creates a log mark and then backs up the database log for each database that is part of the Backup BizTalk Server SQL Agent job. This log mark is used when restoring the last log file for each database so that transactional consistency is maintained. Here are the steps to configure the Backup BizTalk Server SQL Agent job:

1. In SQL Server 2000 Enterprise Manager or SQL Server 2005 Management Studio, navigate to the SQL Agent jobs list.
2. Right-click Backup BizTalk Server (BizTalkMqmtDb) and select Properties.
3. In the Job Properties dialog under Select a page, click Steps to view the job steps.
4. In the Job step list, click BackupFull, and then click Edit.
5. On the General page, in the Command box, replace '<destination path>' with the full path (the path must include the single quotes) to the computer and folder where you want to back up the BizTalk Server databases. Also add a new parameter by typing a comma and then a number one (",1") at the end of the parameter list for the stored procedure `sp_BackupAllFull`. Adding this parameter enables an automatic full backup after a backup failure. Click OK when finished.

Note The default frequency for the BackupFull job is d for daily. Other values are hourly (h/H), weekly (w/W), monthly (m/M), or yearly (y/Y). The first time the job is run during a new period, a full backup is performed. Also, the default name is BTS, which will be part of the backup file name. Change this to reflect a better name for the application such as OrdSys for an application named Order System.

---

6. In the Job step list, click MarkAndBackupLog, and then click Edit.
7. On the General page, in the Command box, replace '<destination path>' with the full path (including single quotes) to the computer and folder where you want to store the BizTalk Server database logs and then click OK. The <destination path> may be local or a UNC path to another server.

Note We recommend a UNC share to store the backup files on a different file system than where the databases reside for production environments. For a dev or test environment, if you are not concerned with maintaining offsite backup sets or multiple backup sets, you can consider using a local path instead of a UNC path.

Also, for the job step MarkAndBackupLog, Log Mark Name is part of the naming convention for backup files:

```
<Server Name>_<Database Name>_Log_< Log Mark Name >_<Timestamp>
Replace "BTS' with a more appropriate name for the solution.
```

8. In the Job step list, click Clear Backup History, and then click Edit.
9. On the General page, in the Command box, change DaysToKeep=<number> to the number of days (default is 14) you want to keep the backup history, and then click OK twice to close the Job Properties dialog box.

Note The DaysToKeep setting is not related to how many sets of backup files are maintained. Backup file sets must be handled manually by copying to another system for long-term archival.

Change the backup schedule for MarkAndBackupLogSched if desired and then right-click the Backup BizTalk Server SQL Agent job and select Enable. The default schedule is to perform a log backup every 15 minutes.

Once the Backup BizTalk Server job is configured and enabled, right-click and select Start Job to test. Click F5 to refresh the status on the Jobs node. If the result is not successful, check the following:

- Verify that the destination folder exists and is reachable if a UNC share.
- Check that the job owner has permissions on the destination folder.
- Ensure that linked servers are configured properly if BizTalk databases are present in multiple SQL Server database instances.

Tip For SQL Server 2005, there are additional security settings for linked servers. When configuring linked servers in SQL Server 2005 as part of the Backup BizTalk Server SQL Agent job, click the Security tab and select the "Be made using the login's current security context" option. Next click Server Options, set RPC Out to True, and then click OK.

Be aware that the file name includes the date/time from when the backup file was created. This date/time is GMT time, not local time. If you look at the Date Modified field in Windows Explorer, you will see the local time.

Also, the Backup BizTalk Server SQL Agent job does not manage disk space, meaning it will continue to copy files into the same directory until the drive runs out of space. This allows the administrator to decide how many backup sets to keep on disk as well as how many to archive to an offsite location, deleting the files from disk after archival.

The next subsection covers how to configure the DTA Purge and Archive SQL Agent job.

Configuring the DTA Purge and Archive SQL Agent Job

With companies having to comply with IRS, general accounting, and legislative requirements for business reporting, BizTalk Server provides extensive tracking capabilities to help with complying with these mandates. This data must be kept for various periods of time to meet reporting requirements. BizTalk Server 2006 adds the DTA Purge and Archive job to help automate the backup of tracking data including the ability to perform on-the-fly validation of tracking data backups using another instance of SQL Server to ensure that a complete record of activity is maintained and available.

In addition to providing data archival, the DTA Purge and Archive SQL Agent job performs data pruning to help keep the system running smoothly. As with any database system, unchecked growth in table size will eventually push the limits of the hardware. In general, there are two solutions to this problem, buy more disks or a faster disk or have a purge and archival policy to "prune" the databases where it makes sense. While all database-based systems benefit from more and faster disks, BizTalk has a process to keep the BizTalk Tracking and Messagebox databases performing optimally by automating purging and archival tasks through the DTA Purge and Archive SQL Agent job.

The DTA Purge and Archive job purges various tracking information such as service instance and message information, orchestration event information, and rule engine tracking data. The purge process is based on the age of the tracking data, which is maintained by having a time stamp added when tracking information is inserted into the database. The DTA Purge and Archive job has a **soft purge** and **hard purge** process. The soft purge processes completed instances, while the hard purge processes incomplete instances. Note that both soft purge and hard purge process just the tracking data, not the actual running instances, so they have no effect on actual data processing data. The purge process helps to optimize tracking processes and HAT operations when looking at historical data. Here are the steps to configure the DTA Purge and Archive SQL Agent job:

1. Depending on whether you are on SQL Server 2000 or SQL Server 2005, navigate to the Management node and view the SQL Agent jobs.

2. In the details pane, right-click DTA Purge and Archive (BizTalkDTADb), and then click Properties.

3. In the Job Properties dialog box, click the Steps tab, click Archive and Purge, and then click Edit.

4. On the General tab, in the Command box, edit the following parameters as appropriate, and then click OK.

■ **Note** For the soft purge, the sum of LiveHours and LiveDays is the live window of data that will be maintained for the BizTalk Tracking database. All tracking data associated with completed instances older than the live window will be deleted and archived.

- `@nLiveHours tinyint`: Default is 0 hours.
- `@nLiveDays tinyint`: Default is 1 day.
- `@nHardDeleteDays tinyint`: Default is 30 days.
- `@nvcFolder nvarchar(1024)`: Specify the folder or UNC share to put the tracking data backup files.
- `@nvcValidatingServer`: SQL Server instance where validation is performed. Default is null.
- `@fForceBackup int`: Default is 0. This is not currently implemented.

Here is an example command that specifies that soft purge occurs every 12 hours and hard purge occurs every 7 days:

```
exec dtasp_BackupAndPurgeTrackingDatabase 12, 0, 7, '\\BizTalkBackupServer\data',
null, 0
```

In the preceding example, we left the validation server value as null; however, we recommend that you set up a validation server for the tracking data to ensure that the backup files of the tracking data for reporting and compliance purposes are valid. Also, the data can be queried on the validation server, offloading potentially long-running queries from the production BizTalk databases. To configure a validation server for the DTA Purge and Archive SQL Agent job, you must have a separate instance of SQL Server available. Having a validation server requires that the `@nvcFolder` variable in the DTA Purge and Archive job points to a UNC share reachable by the validation server. The SQL Server instance where the BizTalk databases are configured cannot also act as the validating server. On the server designated as the validation server, perform these steps:

1. In either ISQL on SQL Server 2000 or in SQL Management Studio on SQL Server 2005, open a file to execute a SQL file. Connect to the SQL instance that is the validation server.
2. Select File ➤ Open and then browse to this SQL script on the server/drive where BizTalk Server 2006 is installed: \Program Files\Microsoft BizTalk Server 2006\Schema\BTS_Tracking_ValidateArchive.sql.
3. Execute the query to create a SQL Agent job called ValidateArchive on the validating server.

4. Open either Enterprise Manager for SQL Server 2000 or SQL Management Studio for SQL Server 2005 to set up the required linked servers. Linked servers must be created between the following:

    - Each of the BizTalk Messagebox (BizTalkMsgBoxDB) SQL Server instances and the BizTalk Tracking (BizTalkDTADb) SQL Server instances. The SQL instance hosting the DTA database requires a linked server to each SQL instance hosting a BizTalk Messagebox and vice versa.

    - The BizTalk Tracking (BizTalkDTADb) SQL Server instance and the validating server SQL Server instance. Create a linked server on each SQL instance to the other SQL instance so that the SQL instance hosting the DTA database has a linked server to the validating server and vice versa.

Next, we turn our attention to monitoring best practices for the SQL Agent jobs.

Monitoring the BizTalk Group SQL Agent Jobs

Because the SQL Agent jobs are critical to maintaining BizTalk performance, the jobs must be monitored so that operations personnel can be alerted if a job fails. The Microsoft SQL Server Management Pack contains MOM rules for monitoring SQL databases, SQL Server Agent jobs, etc., for comprehensive monitoring of SQL Server items. The BizTalk Server 2006 Management Pack for Microsoft Operations Manager 2005 includes two rules, disabled by default, for monitoring the health of two of the most important BizTalk SQL Server Agent jobs. The rule names as defined in the Management Pack are

- Critical Error: A BizTalk SQL Server Agent job failed—Backup BizTalk Server
- Critical Error: A BizTalk SQL Server Agent job failed—Tracked Message Copy

To monitor all BizTalk Server SQL Server Agent jobs from within the BizTalk Server 2006 Management Pack, enable these rules and create additional rules for other jobs that you want to monitor. To enable these rules, perform the following steps in the MOM Administrator Console:

1. Create a copy of the two rules just listed in the BizTalk Server Core Rule group and rename each rule appropriately.
2. In the criteria section for the MOM rule, change the wildcard comparison for Parameter 1 because the job names are specific to the BizTalk Group configuration.

You need to add the SQL Server computers into the BizTalk Server 2006 Computer Group in MOM. This is because the MOM rule needs to be evaluated on the SQL Server computer, and the SQL Server computer will not be recognized as a BizTalk Server computer unless BizTalk and SQL Server happen to be installed on the same machine.

Backup Procedures

This subsection covers the backup procedures for BizTalk applications; however, a BizTalk application is usually just one part of an overall solution that includes other applications, servers, and databases. In general, backup of an application solution that includes BizTalk requires the following general procedures:

- Back up application code, artifacts, documentation.
- Back up server configuration documentation.
- Back up BizTalk servers and BizTalk Group databases.
- Back up related non-BizTalk databases.

Steps and procedures for backing up the first two items listed are outside the scope of this chapter; however in general, application code, artifacts, code documentation, and server configuration documentation should be kept in a source code control system that is backed up automatically with rotating backup sets maintained at an offsite location.

The following subsections focus on the last two items listed including backup procedures for BizTalk runtime servers and for the BizTalk Group.

BizTalk Servers

The servers where BizTalk is installed and configured should be backed up using your corporate standards for server backup. In addition, the config.xml file used to configure each server should be backed up along with documentation on what host instances, receive ports, and send ports are installed on the server. This information can be stored in your source code control system as solution artifacts. Essentially the procedures used to perform the following steps must be in a format that administrators can use to perform a restore or disaster recovery event:

- **BizTalk installation**: Document what features/service pack/hotfixes are installed on the BizTalk runtime server. Document what other products such as SharePoint, IIS, or third-party adapters are installed.
- **BizTalk configuration**: Back up the config.xml that was used to configure the server. This file can be reused to configure the server with minor edits depending on whether the BizTalk Windows server name changed or the SQL instance location of the databases has changed.
- **Master secret**: This is an extremely important backup item that is covered later in this chapter. Without the master secret, a BizTalk Group cannot be restored. The master secret is encrypted and stored in the registry of the master secret server. It is required in order to access the credential (SSOdb) database.
- **BizTalk application configuration**: Document host instances, receive ports, send ports, and of course versions of BizTalk application binaries.

Maintaining the preceding documentation is the minimum requirement necessary to restore the BizTalk runtime servers. It is recommended to automate installation, configuration, and application deployment as much as possible to support normal operations as well as to provide an automated method to restore the BizTalk runtime servers.

The next subsection covers procedures for backing up the master secret.

The Master Secret

BizTalk Server 2006 includes a new Microsoft Management Console (MMC) snap-in for managing Enterprise SSO and the master secret, as shown in Figure 9-2. To launch the SSO Administration tool, go to Start ➤ All Programs ➤ Microsoft Enterprise Single Sign-On ➤ SSO Administration. To back up the master secret, right-click the System node and select Backup Secret within the GUI.

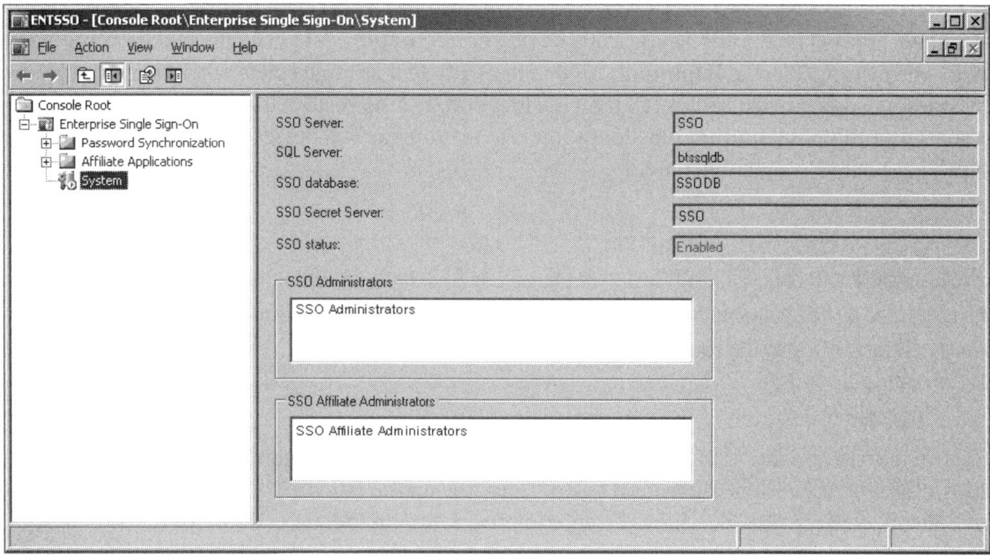

Figure 9-2. *SSO Administration MMC console*

Clicking Backup Secret displays the dialog box shown in Figure 9-3, where you enter a location for the backup file, a password, and optionally a password reminder. This file should be removed from the server and stored in a safe place such as a source control system locally as well as at an offsite location.

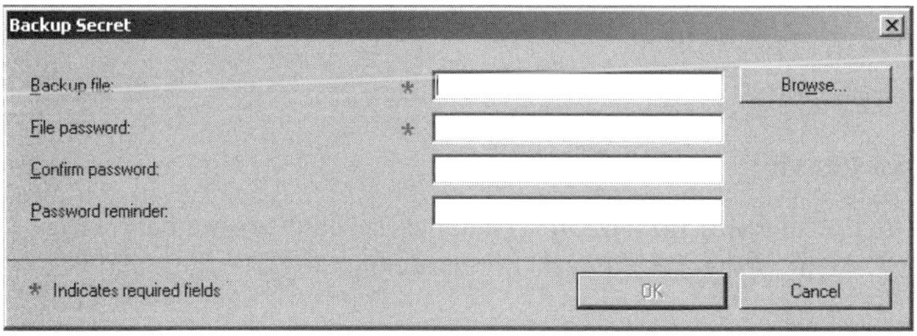

Figure 9-3. *Backup Secret dialog*

The Enterprise SSO tools SSOManage.exe and SSOConfig.exe are still available in the C:\Program Files\Common Files\Enterprise Single Sign-On directory to support scripting, so the master secret can be backed up using the command-line tool SSOConfig.exe with the `-backupSecret` switch as well.

Next, we cover procedures for backing up the BizTalk Group.

BizTalk Group

This subsection covers backup procedures for the BizTalk Group, which consists of a set of databases created by BizTalk Server 2006 during configuration. All of the normal requirements when performing SQL backups apply: allocating sufficient storage space where backup files are stored, copying backup files to an offsite location, testing restore files on a regular basis such as monthly, etc. Another consideration is to ensure backup devices and media are secure to protect business-sensitive data.

■ **Note** BizTalk Server includes a SQL Server role named BTS_BACKUP_USERS so that BizTalk databases can be backed up without requiring System Administrator permissions within SQL Server, except for the primary server controlling the backup process.

If not done already, configure the Backup BizTalk Server SQL Agent job following the instructions in the earlier subsection titled "Configuring the Backup BizTalk Server SQL Agent Job." The Backup BizTalk Server SQL Agent job backs up the following databases:

- BizTalk Configuration (BizTalkMgmtDb)
- BizTalk Messagebox (BizTalkMsgBoxDb)
- BizTalk Tracking (BizTalkDTADb)
- Rule Engine (BizTalkRuleEngineDb)
- BAM Primary Import (BAMPrimaryImport)
- Trading Partner Management (TPM)
- HWS Administration (BizTalkHWSDb)
- BizTalk EDI (BizTalkEDIdb)
- Credential Database (SSOdb)

You must also back up the following BizTalk Group databases, which are not part of the Backup BizTalk Server SQL Agent job because they do not participate in DTC transactions:

- BAM Archive (BAMArchive)
- BAM Star Schema (BAMStarSchema)

These databases can be backed up using normal SQL Server backup procedures because they do not participate in distributed transactions; however, these databases require special consideration, described in the next subsection, if BAM is configured with BM.exe and used as part of a BizTalk solution.

BizTalk Server 2006 includes a table named adm_OtherBackupDatabases in the BizTalk Management database (BizTalkMgmtDb). Other application databases that participate in DTC transactions (i.e., accessed within an atomic scope in an orchestration) should be added to adm_OtherBackupDatabases to remain transactionally consistent with the BizTalk databases. Table 9-2 lists the column names.

Table 9-2. *Columns in the adm_OtherBackupDatabases Table*

Field Name	Value
DefaultDatabaseName	The alias for the database. Can be the same as the database name or the application name.
DatabaseName	The actual name of the database.
ServerName	The name of the SQL Server instance hosting the database.
BTSServerName	Name of a BizTalk server. Not used, but required.

Databases added to the adm_OtherBackupDatabases table will automatically be backed up by the Backup BizTalk Server SQL Agent job.

■ Caution You *must* add any non-BizTalk custom database that performs distributed transactions with BizTalk to this table so that the table can be restored to the same log mark and remain transactionally consistent. For example, if you have an orchestration that updates a database named App1 within an atomic scope in BizTalk, the database App1 must be added to the adm_OtherBackupDatabases table.

The next step is to add the necessary schema changes to the databases added to the adm_OtherBackupDatabases table. Otherwise, the Backup BizTalk Server SQL Agent job will fail. Browse to the <installation directory>\Program Files\Microsoft BizTalk Server 2006\Schema directory, and then run Backup_Setup_All_Procs.sql and Backup_Setup_All_Tables.sql in the destination database. This creates the necessary procedures, tables, and roles to participate in the Backup BizTalk Server SQL Agent job and assigns permissions to the stored procedures.

Now let's take a look at backup procedures for the SQL Server Analysis Services databases.

BAM Analysis Services and Supporting Databases

BizTalk leverages SQL Server Analysis Services for reporting and analysis functionality as part of the Health and Activity Tracking and Business Activity Monitoring features. In BizTalk Server 2006, the Tracking Analysis Server OLAP database is available in BizTalk installations as part of HAT to support the service metrics and message metrics functionality for SQL Server

2000 Analysis Services only. The Tracking Analysis Server database is not supported on SQL Server 2005 Analysis Services and is not available as an option when configuring the BizTalk Group with a SQL Server 2005 database back end.

A BizTalk Group configured with BAM enabled in the BizTalk Configuration Wizard results in two additional SQL Analysis Services OLAP databases if the Tracking Analysis Server database is present:

- BAM Analysis (BAMAnalysis)
- Tracking Analysis Server (BizTalkAnalysisdb)

These Analysis Services databases must be backed up following the procedures for backing up SQL Analysis Services databases.

There are two scenarios for backing up BAM SQL Server databases when BAM is enabled through the BizTalk Configuration Wizard:

- BAM enabled for the BizTalk Group but not configured
- BAM enabled and configured with BM.exe (i.e., the BizTalk solution includes BAM features)

The next two subsections cover these scenarios.

BAM Enabled but Not Configured in a BizTalk Group

Since BAM is not configured with BM.exe, there are not any BAM-related Data Transformation Services (DTS) packages present in the solution. Therefore, the BAM SQL databases can be backed up using regular SQL Server backup procedures or can be added to the Backup BizTalk Server SQL Agent job by adding the table to the adm_OtherBackupDatabases table for convenience. Here is a list of the BAM SQL databases that must be backed up:

- BAM Archive (BAMArchive)
- BAM Star Schema (BAMStarSchema)

This will ensure that a full set of databases for the BizTalk Group are maintained. The next subsection covers backup procedures when BAM is enabled and configured with BM.exe.

BAM Enabled and Configured in a BizTalk Group

When BAM is enabled and configured for a BizTalk Group using BM.exe, it results in the creation of one or more DTS packages that must be backed up in case they are accidentally deleted as well as duplicated on the disaster recovery site. (Disaster recovery is covered in its own section later in this chapter.) Backup procedures for DTS packages are documented in SQL Server Books Online.

Before backing up the BAM databases, ensure that neither the BAM cube process nor data maintenance DTS packages are running when the backup package is scheduled to run. Ensure consistent schema across all BAM databases by backing up the BAM databases and DTS packages each time a BAM activity is deployed and not deployed.

The BAM Analysis and BAM Star Schema databases should be backed up each time a BAM view is deployed and undeployed. Follow these procedures when backing up BAM databases:

1. Run the Backup BizTalk Server job to back up the BAM Primary Import database as well as the other BizTalk Server databases.

2. Run the BAM data maintenance DTS package for all activities.

■ **Tip** Incorporate these steps into a DTS package, scheduling it to run on a regular basis. To guarantee data integrity, ensure no other BAM cubing or DTS packages run when this DTS package is scheduled.

Back up the BAM Archive database after the partition is copied into the BAM Archive database but before the partition is deleted from the BAM Primary Import database so that a complete set of archived data is maintained. This can be achieved by modifying the data maintenance DTS package for each activity to add a step to back up the BAM Archive database before the last step in the DTS package called End Archiving.

3. Back up the BAM Archive database, and then the BAM Star Schema database.

Next, we cover backup procedures for Business Activity Services.

BAS Site and Databases

Business Activity Services is an optional installation option and may not be part of a solution. If BAS is part of a solution, it requires special backup procedures because the BAS environment consists of the following:

- A web site hosted in Microsoft Windows SharePoint Services and InfoPath templates. Windows SharePoint Services and InfoPath provide a common user interface for all of the services included in BAS.

- A Trading Partner Management database. This database stores trading partner data for BAS. It is not a runtime database.

- Two Windows SharePoint Services databases: the Configuration and Content databases. These databases store the global settings for the WSS server as well as site content. Perform the following steps to back up the BAS site and database:

    1. After BAS is configured, back up all of the changes made to the web application configuration files and Windows SharePoint Services site templates so these can be recovered later. There may be modifications in other places, for example, in client-side JavaScript files if the site has been customized by the development team. These changes must be documented and backed up to a source code control system as well.

2. Ensure the Backup BizTalk Server SQL Agent job is configured since it backs up the Trading Partner Management database.
3. Follow the instructions in the "Windows SharePoint Services Administrator's Guide" to back up the Windows SharePoint Services Configuration and Content databases. This guide is available for download here: www.microsoft.com/downloads/details.aspx?amp;displaylang=en&familyid=a637eff6-8224-4b19-a6a4-3e33fa13d230&displaylang=en.

The next subsection covers steps to back up the Base EDI adapter.

Base EDI Adapter

Additional backup steps are required in order to completely restore the EDI adapter. The first step is to back up the DocumentsHome directory. This directory is located here by default: <root>\Documents and Settings\All Users\Application Data\Microsoft\BizTalk Server 2006\EDI\Subsystem.

■ **Note** Path references to BizTalk Server 2006 may actually be in the BizTalk Server 2004 directory if an in-place upgrade was performed when BizTalk Server 2006 was installed.

In this directory are subdirectories and folders containing EDI adapter settings, sent and received documents in EDI and XML format, log files, in-flight files, and the compiled engine input file (EIF).

The entire DocumentsHome directory should be backed up frequently using a file-based high-capacity backup system. Ideally, the DocumentsHome directory is mirrored using a robust high-capacity storage technology. This also allows fast restore time because the system automatically switches to the mirrored disk when necessary. If disk mirroring is not an option, the DocumentsHome directory should be backed up very frequently to minimize data loss.

Depending on legal requirements with partners, incoming EDI documents can be configured to be received at an alternate receive location that makes a copy of the incoming document before sending the document to the EDI receive location. This provides an additional layer of archive for inbound documents. Another option is to enable message body tracking on inbound EDI documents. Legal implications may surround message body tracking depending on the legal agreements with trading partners. Be sure to review all legal agreements before enabling message body tracking. Also, message body tracking greatly increases database growth, which must be taken into account because of potential performance impact.

Now let's look at backup procedures for DTS packages related to the BizTalk solution.

DTS Packages

All DTS packages that are part of the solution must be duplicated at the disaster recovery site. The BizTalk Configuration Wizard does not create any DTS packages. However, if Business Activity Monitoring is part of the solution and is configured with the BAM monitoring tool

(BM.exe), there will be DTS packages created that generate/update the OLAP cubes. The DTS packages have names like the following:

- BAM_AN_<ViewName>
- BAM_DM_<activity name>

Note There are no DTS packages that require backing up if BAM is not configured using the BM.exe tool.

To back up the DTS packages with SQL Server 2000, follow these steps:

1. Navigate to the Data Transformation Services folder in SQL Server 2000.
2. Click Local Packages to see a list of DTS packages for the server.
3. In the right pane, right-click each package and select Design Package.
4. In the menu, click Package and then Save As.
5. Click the drop-down for Location and select Structure Storage File.
6. Click the button with the caption ... and enter a path/file name.
7. Click OK to generate the DTS file for the package.
8. Connect to the destination disaster recovery server using Enterprise Manager.
9. Expand the target server/instance.
10. Right-click the Data Transformation Services folder and select Open Package.
11. Browse to the package exported in the preceding steps and import the package to the target server.
12. Perform the preceding steps for all DTS packages that are part of the solution.

To back up SSIS packages with SQL Server 2005, follow these steps:

1. Open SQL Server Management Studio and connect to Integration Services.
2. Expand the Stored Packages folder in Object Explorer.
3. Expand the subfolders to locate the package that needs to be exported.
4. Right-click the package, click Export, select File System, and then browse to a location to save the package.

To back up SQL Server Integration Services packages with SQL Server 2005, follow these steps:

1. Open SQL Server Management Studio and connect to Integration Services.
2. Expand the Stored Packages folder in Object Explorer.

3. Expand the subfolders to locate the package that needs to be exported.

4. Right-click the package, click Export, select File System, and then browse to a location to save the package.

There may be additional non-BizTalk DTS packages related to the solution. These DTS packages must also be duplicated at the disaster recovery site as well.

Backing Up SQL Agent Jobs

BizTalk Server 2006 Log Shipping will re-create the SQL Agent jobs running in production on the disaster recovery site; however, it is still a best practice to maintain backups of the SQL Agent jobs in case they need to be restored outside of a disaster recovery event. Here are the steps to back up a SQL Agent job in SQL Server 2000:

1. Open SQL Server 2000 Enterprise Manager.

2. Expand the database server/instance.

3. Expand the Management folder.

4. Expand SQL Server Agent, and then click Jobs.

5. In the right pane, right-click each job listed, select All Tasks, and then Generate SQL Script.

6. Choose a location by clicking the button with the caption ... and enter a file name.

7. Click OK to generate the script.

8. Run the script using SQL Server Query Analyzer on the target disaster recovery site SQL Server instance where the BizTalk Configuration database is located.

9. Go through the preceding steps for each job.

For SQL Server 2005, the steps are similar:

1. Connect to the database instance using SQL Server Management Studio.

2. Expand SQL Server Agent and click Jobs.

3. Right-click each job and select Script Job as ➤ Create To ➤ File.

4. Enter a file name and click Save.

5. Go through the preceding steps for each job.

The next subsection covers backup procedures for related non-BizTalk applications and databases.

Related Non-BizTalk Applications and Databases

How related non-BizTalk application databases are backed up depends on the BizTalk solution. As mentioned earlier, if an orchestration updates another database from within an atomic scope that results in a distributed transaction, the other database must be added to the adm_OtherBackupDatabases so that it is backed up by the Backup BizTalk Server SQL Agent job and can be restored to the same log mark as all other databases that participate in distributed transactions as part of the solution.

For applications and databases that do not participate in distributed transactions with BizTalk but are still part of the overall application solution, these applications and databases should be backed up following your corporate standards/guidance. Essentially, the same requirements apply in that the source code, code documentation, runtime environment, etc., must be backed up such that the application and database can be restored successfully. Always practice a restore in a lab environment to confirm that enough information is available to be successful as well as automate as much of the process as possible.

Next, we cover restore procedures for a BizTalk solution.

Restore Procedures

Restoring a BizTalk-based solution, or any large application environment, is a challenging process if not well documented, tested, and periodically rehearsed from an operations training standpoint. BizTalk Server 2006 has its own set of unique steps required for successful restore. This subsection covers steps for recovering from various failure scenarios that do not require transitioning to the disaster recovery site. In some scenarios, this discussion leverages the destination system databases and the SQL Agent automation available in order to safely perform restore procedures minimizing manual steps. This discussion covers restore steps for the following scenarios:

- Restore procedures when refreshing the BizTalk databases in a development or test environment
- Restore procedures when migrating the production BizTalk databases to a more powerful production database server without switching to the disaster recovery site
- Restore procedures when recovering the production database environment from a hardware failure such as a SAN failure without switching to the disaster recovery site (destination system)
- Restore procedures for a BAS site when recovering from a hardware failure
- Restore procedures for SQL Agent jobs and DTS packages
- Restore procedures for the master secret
- Restore procedures for the BizTalk runtime environment

The next subsection covers how to stop and start BizTalk processing while performing any of the restore scenarios listed previously.

Stopping and Starting BizTalk Application Processing

This subsection lists the steps to stop, start, pause, or resume BizTalk processing using either the Services administration tool or the command line. Depending on the features configured on a BizTalk runtime server, there are up to six services that must be managed:

- BizTalk Base EDI Service (edi subsystem)
- BizTalk Service BizTalk Group: <BizTalkServerApplication> (btssvc$BizTalkServerApplication)
- Enterprise Single Sign-On Service (Entsso)
- Rule Engine Update Service (ruleengineupdateservice)
- BAM Event Notification Service (NS$BamAlerts)
- World Wide Web Publishing Service (W3SVC)

Using the Services administration tool in the Control Panel, simply click Start, Stop, Pause, or Resume as needed for the scenario. From a command prompt, enter the following commands (where *ServiceName* corresponds to the values in parentheses in the preceding list):

- Start a service: **net start *ServiceName***
- Stop a service: **net stop *ServiceName***
- Pause a service: **net pause *ServiceName***
- Resume a service: **net continue *ServiceName***

These commands can of course be scripted by placing the commands in a batch file or using WMI so that all services can be controlled by a single step. For example, a Stop.cmd file could contain the following:

```
Net stop "edi subsystem"
Net stop Entsso
Net stop ruleengineupdatservice
Net stop btssvc$BizTalkServerApplication
Net stop NS$BamAlerts
Net stop w3svc
```

When writing scripts such as this, you may need multiple `Net stop btssvc$BizTalkServerApplication` lines depending on how many host instances are running on the BizTalk runtime server. Also, the services that are actually present on a BizTalk runtime server depend on the BizTalk configuration. For more information on the BizTalk services, go to the BizTalk Server 2006 core documentation and search for the topic titled "How to Start, Stop, Pause, Resume, or Restart BizTalk Server Services."

The next subsection covers restore procedures for refreshing a development or test environment.

Refreshing a Development or Test Environment

Here we cover the steps to restore a development environment or test environment back to a "known" or "initial state." These procedures can be used to help ensure that a testing environment remains consistent between test runs or as new functionality is added to the application. This scenario requires a consistent full backup set of the following items:

- BizTalk databases
- Related non-BizTalk application databases
- Analysis Services databases for BAM or for Tracking Analysis Server
- DocumentsHome directory for EDI
- Windows SharePoint Services site customizations such as configuration files, site templates, client-side scripts, etc.
- Windows SharePoint Services Configuration and Content databases for BAS

■ **Note** To create the "initial state" full backup files, configure the development or test BizTalk Group as needed, ensure no processing is occurring by following the procedures to stop processing listed in the preceding subsection, and then perform a full backup on all databases, analysis services databases, and the DocumentsHome directory if using EDI by following the guidance detailed in the earlier subsection titled "Backup Procedures."

This procedure is based on "Moving BizTalk Server Databases" and related documentation in the BizTalk Server 2006 core documentation. Please be sure to review this section of the BizTalk documentation before proceeding. This is actually a simpler scenario than described in the documentation, because the BizTalk runtime servers and SQL Server database instance server names remain the same, so the steps to update database names and database locations via script are not required.

1. Stop all processing using the guidance listed in the earlier subsection titled "Stopping and Starting BizTalk Application Processing."
2. Obtain a copy of the "initial state" backup set and restore each BizTalk database and related non-BizTalk application database (if applicable) using SQL Server database restore procedures.
3. Restore the applicable Analysis Services databases if using BAM or the Tracking Analysis Server database for HAT metrics with SQL Server 2000.
4. Restore the BAS site if using BAS by following the guidance in the subsection titled "Restore Procedures for BAS Site and Database" in the "Disaster Recovery" section later in this chapter.
5. Restore the DocumentsHome directory using the full backup that is part of the "initial state" backup set if using EDI.
6. Enable application processing by following the steps in the earlier subsection titled "Stopping and Starting BizTalk Application Processing." The development or test environment is now restored to the "initial state."

Migrating Production Databases to More Powerful Servers

Migration is probably the most common scenario that a BizTalk application operations team will encounter with respect to having to move a database. In this scenario, application processing is stopped using the procedure listed in the subsection titled "Stopping and Starting BizTalk Application Processing" earlier. The next step is to perform a full backup on the applicable database that is being migrated. Then perform the steps necessary to update references to the new database location for the BizTalk Group. The specific steps are covered in the BizTalk Server 2006 core documentation in the section titled "Moving BizTalk Server Databases" for the following databases:

- BAM Primary Import database
- BAM Archive database
- BAM Star Schema database
- BAM Analysis database
- BAM Notification Services database
- Messsagebox database

Please refer to the BizTalk Server 2006 core documentation for the specific steps to move these databases.

Recovering Production Database Environment from Hardware Failure

This scenario covers restoring the BizTalk Group databases that are backed up by the Backup BizTalk Server SQL Agent job. There are two options for this scenario. The first is to perform a full disaster recovery event by following the procedures listed in the section titled "Disaster Recovery" later in this chapter. This is the option available when reviewing the BizTalk Server 2006 core documentation.

Another option that leverages the disaster recovery infrastructure without actually performing a full disaster recovery is to obtain a copy of the databases from the disaster recovery destination system database instances and perform a restore of the databases at the production site. The second option is available if the BizTalk application operations team is able to correct the hardware failure in a timely manner in accordance with availability and corporate requirements and those server and database instance names do not change. Since this scenario requires that BizTalk Log Shipping is configured, before proceeding with either option, review the section that follows titled "Disaster Recovery."

■ **Caution** The second option is not documented in the BizTalk Server 2006 documentation and therefore is not supported by Microsoft. However, choosing the second option does not remove the first option. When performing the second option, a copy of the databases is maintained at the destination system so that if that procedure fails, a full disaster recovery can be performed by completing the steps in the first option to bring the destination system online.

The second option assumes that the BizTalk runtime servers, database servers, and all related servers and sites are back to fully operational, but the most up-to-date version of the application databases are required in order to restart processing. The disaster recovery site (destination system) will generally have the latest copy of the database available, so this scenario leverages the availability of those databases to quickly restore processing at the production site.

■ **Note** Performing option two will require that BizTalk Log Shipping be removed and then reconfigured at the destination system once the production system is back online. Otherwise an error will be received in the destination system that states "The databases have already been restored to a mark" and the destination system SQL Agent job "BTS Log Shipping—Restore Databases" will fail.

In order to obtain the latest version of the databases from the destination system, the operations team must ensure that all of the log backup sets (except for the latest set available) have been successfully restored to the databases. To determine the last successful backup set restored, review the contents of the Master.dbo.bts_LogShippingHistory table on each database instance in the destination system. This table is populated by the Get Backup History job and updated by the Restore Databases job. When a backup is successfully restored, the Restored column is set to 1 and the RestoredDateTime is set to the current date and time. When all of the databases being restored to the server from a particular backup set have been successfully restored, that backup set ID is written to the Master.dbo.bts_LogShippingLastRestoreSet table. Once all of the log backup sets except for the last available have been confirmed to have been successfully restored, follow these steps:

1. Stop application processing by following the procedures in the subsection titled "Stopping and Starting BizTalk Application Processing" to prevent any database activity from occurring until the production database environment is fully configured.

2. Depending on whether you are on SQL Server 2000 or SQL Server 2005, navigate to the SQL Agent Jobs view on the destination system SQL Server database instances.

3. Right-click and select Disable Job to disable the following SQL Agent jobs on the destination system disaster recovery SQL Server database instances:

   - BTS Log Shipping—Get Backup History
   - BTS Log Shipping—Restore Databases

4. Right-click BTS Log Shipping—Restore To Mark and select **Start Job** on the destination system SQL Server database instances.

5. Once you have verified that the job BTS Log Shipping—Restore To Mark has completed, detach each database from the destination system SQL Server database instance, and copy each database file over to the appropriate storage area on the source system (production) so the databases can be attached to the correct production SQL Server database instance in order to bring the production database instances online.

Caution Ensure that a copy of the database files remains at the destination system in case it is needed in the event of an unsuccessful attempt to restore production processing, and the destination system must be brought online by completing the steps in option one.

---

6. Disable the following SQL Server Agent jobs on the source system SQL Server database instances (this step assumes that the Backup BizTalk Server and DTA Purge and Archive jobs have been configured and enabled):
   - Backup BizTalk Server (BizTalkMgmtDb)
   - CleanupBTFExpiredEntriesJob_<BizTalkMgmtDb>
   - DTA Purge and Archive (BizTalkMsgBoxDb)
   - MessageBox_DeadProcesses_Cleanup_<BizTalkMsgBoxDb>
   - MessageBox_Message_ManageRefCountLog_<BizTalkMsgBoxDb>
   - MessageBox_Parts_Cleanup_<BizTalkMsgBoxDb>
   - MessageBox_UpdateStats_<BizTalkMsgBoxDb>
   - Operations_OperateOnInstances_OnMaster_<BizTalkMsgBoxDb>
   - PurgeSubscriptionsJob_<BizTalkMsgBoxDb>
   - Rules_Database_Cleanup<BizTalkRuleEngineDb>
   - TrackedMessages_Copy_<BizTalkMsgBoxDb>
7. Attach the databases copied from the destination system disaster recovery SQL Server database instances to the correct source system production SQL Server database instances.

Note If the BAM Archive, BAM Star Schema, or BAM Analysis databases were affected by the hardware failure as well, then these databases should be restored by using a backup older than the BAM Primary Import database backup.

---

8. Enable the following SQL Agent jobs on the source system production SQL Server database instances:

Note Do not enable the SQL Agent job MessageBox_Message_Cleanup_<BizTalkMsgBoxDb> by mistake. It is always disabled by default.

- Backup BizTalk Server (BizTalkMgmtDb)
- CleanupBTFExpiredEntriesJob_<BizTalkMgmtDb>
- DTA Purge and Archive (BizTalkMsgBoxDb)
- MessageBox_DeadProcesses_Cleanup_<BizTalkMsgBoxDb>
- MessageBox_Message_ManageRefCountLog_<BizTalkMsgBoxDb>
- MessageBox_Parts_Cleanup_<BizTalkMsgBoxDb>
- MessageBox_UpdateStats_<BizTalkMsgBoxDb>
- Operations_OperateOnInstances_OnMaster_<BizTalkMsgBoxDb>
- PurgeSubscriptionsJob_<BizTalkMsgBoxDb>
- Rules_Database_Cleanup<BizTalkRuleEngineDb>
- TrackedMessages_Copy_<BizTalkMsgBoxDb>

9. After confirming that the SQL Agent jobs are running successfully in the source system, enable application processing by following the steps in the subsection titled "Stopping and Starting BizTalk Application Processing."

10. Remove and then reconfigure BizTalk Log Shipping at the destination system.

Next we cover another restore scenario when the BAS site is not available.

When Recovering from Hardware Failure of a BAS Site

In the event that a BAS site encounters a hardware failure, but otherwise the BizTalk solution is fully functional, then only the steps to restore BAS are required. These steps are detailed in the subsection titled "Restore Procedures for BAS Site and Database" in the "Disaster Recovery" section later in this chapter.

SQL Agent Jobs

The SQL Agent jobs are a critical tool for maintaining the BizTalk Group. If one of these jobs is accidentally deleted or needs to be restored as part of restoring the BizTalk Group, obtain the backed-up script file for the SQL Agent job and execute the script for the SQL Agent job in a query window. Check the status of the SQL Agent jobs in SQL Server. Ensure the correct account is configured to run each job.

DTS Packages

If the BizTalk solution has BAM configured with BM.exe, BM.exe will create a set of DTS packages to produce the OLAP cubes. For each DTS package, import the package using SQL Server 2000 Enterprise Manager or SQL Server 2005 Integration Services. Check the status of the DTS package in Enterprise Manager.

The Master Secret

The master secret is a critical item that must be backed up and stored in a safe place. It is not possible for BizTalk Server to function or to be restored without the master secret. There are two scenarios where the master secret server must be restored:

- Failure of the master secret server for an existing BizTalk Group
- Restoration of the master secret server as part of restoring a BizTalk Group to another set of servers

This subsection covers the procedures to restore the master secret server for the BizTalk Group. If the original master secret server fails and cannot be recovered, but the BizTalk Group is still available and functioning except for the master secret server, another server can be promoted as the master secret server. To promote a Single Sign-On Server in the BizTalk Group to master secret server, follow these steps:

1. Create an XML file that includes the name of the SSO server that will be promoted to master secret server. For example:

```
<sso>
  <globalInfo>
     <secretServer>SSO Server name</secretServer>
  </globalInfo>
</sso>
```

2. On the Start menu, click Run, and then type **cmd**.
3. At the command-line prompt, go to the Enterprise Single Sign-On installation directory. The default installation directory is <*drive*>:\Program Files\Common Files\Enterprise Single Sign-On.
4. Type **ssomanage -updatedb <*update file*>**, where <*update file*> is the name of the XML file created in step 1.
5. Type **ssoconfig -restoresecret <*restore file*>**, where <*restore file*> is the path and name of the file where the master secret backup is stored.

Now let's move on to the procedures for restoring the BizTalk runtime environment.

BizTalk Runtime Environment

If the BizTalk runtime environment is intact, then restoring the BizTalk runtime environment is a matter of verifying connectivity by opening the BizTalk Administration Console and then restarting processing by starting the items stopped in the subsection titled "Stopping and Starting BizTalk Application Processing" earlier.

Caution If the BizTalk applications are dependent on related non-BizTalk applications and databases, then these related applications and databases must be available before restarting processing.

If the BizTalk runtime environment must also be rebuilt, and the server names will be the same, first install BizTalk following the same procedures originally used to install BizTalk. Once BizTalk is installed, run Configuration.exe and join the BizTalk Group that has been previously restored.

Note Do not create a new BizTalk Group. This will result in a new set of databases, whereas the goal is to use the existing BizTalk Group that was restored.

Restore the master secret on the server with the same server name as the original master secret server. Or, restore the master secret to a new server and then perform the steps to designate the new server as the master secret server. Redeploy the BizTalk applications and bindings into the environment as needed.

Next, you'll learn the restore procedures for non-BizTalk, but related, applications and databases.

Related Non-BizTalk Applications and Databases

A BizTalk solution may update or receive data from non-BizTalk applications as part of the overall solution. If the related non-BizTalk applications include a database that participates in distributed transactions with BizTalk, this database should be added to the Backup BizTalk Server SQL Agent job and restored to the same log mark as the BizTalk databases. Otherwise, restore the non-BizTalk application and databases following the documentation for that application.

This wraps up our discussion on maintaining the BizTalk Group. Next we discuss disaster recovery procedures for BizTalk applications.

Disaster Recovery

Business-critical software solutions must have a disaster recovery plan in order to protect against major system disruptions. A disaster recovery plan must include steps to bring the backup site online as well as steps to deal with potential data loss as a result of the major system disruption. BizTalk Server 2006–based solutions require a comprehensive disaster recovery plan that covers both the BizTalk servers and the BizTalk Group running in SQL Server. BizTalk Server 2006 disaster recovery requirements include the following:

- BizTalk Server 2006 Log Shipping configuration for disaster recovery
- BizTalk Server 2006 Log Shipping procedures for restoring the BizTalk Group as part of disaster recovery
- BizTalk runtime environment disaster recovery procedures

These items make up the core disaster recovery requirements for BizTalk Server 2006. Additional disaster recovery procedures are required for any additional application databases, application code, other middleware products, etc.

Note Application teams must plan to test disaster recovery procedures before entering production and on a recurring basis to ensure current operations personnel understand the process and can implement it successfully.

There is better automation of the required tasks to configure and implement disaster recovery for a BizTalk Server 2006 solution that helps to simplify the process. Also, the BizTalk Server 2006 core documentation greatly increases the amount of documentation regarding BizTalk Server Log Shipping and disaster recovery. The procedures in this section are based on the product documentation and should be reviewed along with this chapter. In addition, this section details additional configure steps encountered while testing out the procedures not found in the BizTalk Server 2006 core documentation.

Caution The steps to manually update the required database fields in order to move a BizTalk Group to a new set of database server instances without using BizTalk Log Shipping are not documented for BizTalk Server 2006. Therefore we strongly recommend configuring BizTalk Log Shipping as part of any BizTalk Server 2006 production environment.

Next, let's take a look at how BizTalk Log Shipping works.

How Does BizTalk Log Shipping Work?

Because BizTalk Server 2006 implements distributed transactions between BizTalk databases in the BizTalk Group through log marks, typical SQL Server disaster recovery technology such as SQL Server Log Shipping cannot be used for BizTalk databases that participate in DTC transactions. Therefore, BizTalk Server 2006 provides BizTalk Log Shipping.

Tip When referring to BizTalk Log Shipping, the **source system** is the production SQL Server database instances and the **destination system** is the disaster recovery SQL Server database instances.

BizTalk Log Shipping uses capabilities within SQL Server that takes into account log marks and DTC transactions while providing very similar functionality to SQL Server Log Shipping. As with SQL Server Log Shipping, BizTalk Log Shipping performs log backups at the specified interval in the Backup BizTalk Server SQL Agent job. The log backups are then continuously applied to a SQL Server instance that is the disaster recovery server.

The primary difference between SQL Log Shipping and BizTalk Log Shipping is that when performing a disaster recovery event with BizTalk Group databases, the last log is applied with the `STOPATMARK` SQL Server `RESTORE` command option to restore all databases to the same point by the SQL Agent job named BTS Log Shipping—Restore To Mark for each database instance in the destination system. Figure 9-4 describes how BizTalk Log Shipping works.

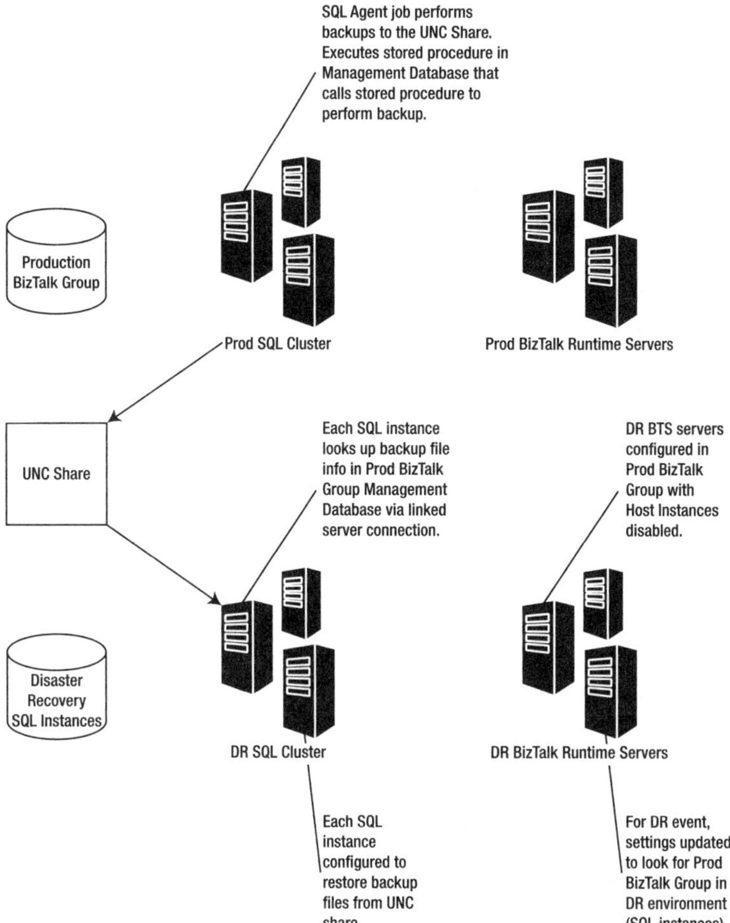

Figure 9-4. *BizTalk Log Shipping process*

When the disaster recovery SQL Server instances in the destination system are configured for BizTalk Log Shipping, the backup files created by the Backup BizTalk SQL Agent job are restored at the disaster recovery site every 15 minutes. The backup files are copied over the network by a SQL `RESTORE` command. Full backup files are only copied in the following situations:

- When BizTalk Log Shipping is first configured
- When a new database is added to the BizTalk Log Shipping SQL Agent job
- When a `RESTORE` failure occurs

Each SQL instance at the disaster recovery site is configured individually as part of BizTalk Log Shipping. When a SQL instance is configured for BizTalk Log Shipping and the SQL Agent job is enabled, the SQL Agent job will connect to the management database on the production BizTalk Group, find the most recent full backup set at the UNC share, and attempt to restore the database.

■ **Note** If you move the full or log backups for a source database from the location in which the Backup BizTalk Server job put them, the associated row for that database in the bts_LogShippingDatabases table on the destination system must be updated by setting LogFileLocation or DBFileLocation to the new location where the destination system should retrieve them. By default these values are Null, which tells the destination system to read the backup files from the location stored in the adm_BackupHistory table.

On the disaster recovery SQL instances configured for BizTalk Log Shipping, the databases will be displayed in a "loading" state in SQL Server 2000 and "restoring" state in SQL Server 2005. This is because the last log in a backup set is never restored automatically. Once a new log is available, BizTalk Log Shipping restores the next-to-last log. When a disaster recovery event occurs and the disaster recovery site must be brought online, the last log is restored automatically using the `STOPATMARK` command by the SQL Agent job named BTS Log Shipping—Restore To Mark on each destination system SQL instance to recover the databases, and the databases will no longer be in a "loading" or "restoring" state.

BizTalk Server 2006 Log Shipping supports two scenarios: In one scenario, all databases on all BizTalk databases on all production SQL server instances are log-shipped to a single disaster recovery SQL server database instance. The other scenario maps all source databases on each source SQL Server instance to an associated destination SQL Server instance. Note that it is fully supported to have the same number of SQL Server database instances in the disaster recovery site as there is in production, but on fewer physical servers—i.e., it is not required to have the same number of physical servers, just the same number of database instances for the second option.

The next subsection covers configuration of the destination system SQL Server instance for BizTalk Log Shipping.

Configuring the Destination System for Log Shipping

Here we cover the steps to configure BizTalk Log Shipping. As mentioned previously, ensure that the same path where database files are located in production exists on the destination system. So, in the earlier example where there are three SQL Server database instances in production, all three database instances must store the database files (MDF and LDF files) in the same path on each server, and this path must also exist on the destination system SQL Server database instances. The database file path can be set or changed within SQL Server.

Another configuration step on the destination system SQL instances is to create a linked server that points to the source system SQL instances. There should be a linked server created that points to the production SQL instance hosting the management database. This will allow the SQL Agent job running on the destination system SQL Server instances to access the BizTalk Management Database to retrieve the backup history and database and log backup file location.

Caution A key requirement for BizTalk Log Shipping to function is that the same file path where the BizTalk database files (MDF and LDF files) are installed must exist on the destination system. Therefore, if a database in the production BizTalk Group is stored at F:\Data, the drive/path F:\Data must exist on the server where the destination system SQL Server instance is configured. Otherwise, an error message similar to this one will occur: "File 'DBFileName' cannot be restored to 'drive\path'. Use WITH MOVE to identify a valid location for the file." BizTalk Log Shipping does **not** support `WITH MOVE`, so the path must be present on the destination system for BizTalk Log Shipping to work.

Note Path references to Microsoft BizTalk Server 2006 may actually be located in the Microsoft BizTalk Server 2004 directory if an in-place upgrade was performed when BizTalk Server 2006 was installed.

Follow these steps to configure BizTalk Log Shipping:

1. In either ISQL on SQL Server 2000 or in SQL Management Studio on SQL Server 2005, open a query window to execute a SQL file. Connect to the SQL instance on the destination system that must be configured for Log Shipping.
2. Select File ➤ Open, and then browse to the location of the script LogShipping_Destination_Schema.sql. This script is located on the drive where BizTalk Server 2006 is installed in the following default directory location: \Program Files\Microsoft BizTalk Server 2006\Schema\LogShipping_Destination_Schema.sql.
3. Execute the query.
4. Select File ➤ Open, and then browse to the following SQL script LogShipping_Destination_Logic.sql. This script is located on the drive where BizTalk Server 2006 is installed in the following directory: \Program Files\Microsoft BizTalk Server 2006\Schema\LogShipping_Destination_Logic.sql.

Note This script is located on the server where BizTalk Server 2006 is installed in the directory \Program Files\Microsoft BizTalk Server 2006\Schema\ by default, so you may need to copy it to the SQL Server machine.

5. Execute the query.
6. In SQL Server 2005 or in SQL Server 2000 SP4 or later, the Ad Hoc Distributed Queries option is disabled by default. This must be enabled on the destination system or disaster recovery SQL Server database instances in order to allow the disaster recovery SQL Server database instances to perform the necessary steps. To enable this option, execute the following SQL command in the master database on each production SQL Server database instance:

```
sp_configure 'show advanced options', 1;
GO
RECONFIGURE;
GO
sp_configure 'Ad Hoc Distributed Queries',1;
GO
RECONFIGURE
GO
```

To confirm the change, run this query to view the configured value:

```
SELECT * FROM sys.configurations ORDER BY name
```

Ad Hoc Distributed Queries should now be set to a value of 1.

7. Open a new query window and enter the following command:

```
exec bts_ConfigureBizTalkLogShipping @nvcDescription =
'<MyLogShippingSolution>',
@nvcMgmtDatabaseName = '<BizTalkServerManagementDatabaseName>',
@nvcMgmtServerName = '<BizTalkServerManagementDatabaseServer>',
@SourceServerName = null,
-- null indicates that this destination server restores all databases
@fLinkServers = 1
-- 1 automatically links the server to the management database
```

8. Replace `<MyLogShippingSolution>` in the preceding command with a description of the solution, surrounded by single quotes. Also, replace `<BizTalkServerManagement➥DatabaseName>` and `<BizTalkServerManagementDatabaseServer>` with the name and location of your source BizTalk Management Database, surrounded by single quotes.

9. If there are multiple SQL Server instances in the source system, each source SQL instance can be restored to its own destination SQL instance. On each SQL instance in the destination system, run the preceding scripts and command, but in the `@SourceServerName = null` parameter, replace `null` with the name of the appropriate source server, surrounded by single quotes: `@SourceServerName = 'SQLSvrInstance1'`.

10. Execute the preceding command in the query window. The BizTalk Server 2006 documentation has this information: If the command fails, after you fix the problem with the query, you must start over from step 1 of this procedure to reconfigure the destination system.

■ **Note** When you execute the preceding command, this warning will occur, which can be ignored: "Warning: The table '#Servers' has been created but its maximum row size (25059) exceeds the maximum number of bytes per row (8060). INSERT or UPDATE of a row in this table will fail if the resulting row length exceeds 8060 bytes."

---

11. View the Jobs node in either Enterprise Manager or SQL Management Studio depending on which version of SQL you are running. There will be three new jobs:

    - **BTS Log Shipping Get Backup History**: This SQL Agent job copies backup history records from the source system to the destination every minute, and it is enabled by default.

    - **BTS Log Shipping Restore Databases**: This SQL Agent job restores backup files for the specified databases from the source system SQL Server instance on to the destination system SQL Server instance. It is enabled by default and runs continuously.

    - **BTS Log Shipping Restore To Mark**: This SQL Agent job restores all of the databases to a log mark in the last log backup. It ensures that all databases are transitionally consistent. It also re-creates the SQL Server SQL Agent jobs on the destination system saving the administrator from having to manually re-create the SQL Agent jobs running on the source system.

12. Create SQL Server security logins for the disaster recovery site that correspond to the production site so that in the event that a failover to the disaster recovery site is required, all required security logins are present on the destination system.

13. Once everything is configured, check the status of the newly created SQL Agent jobs to make sure that they are running successfully. Here are a couple of items to check in the event a SQL Agent job is failing:

    - Ensure that the system time and time zone are consistent between all servers.

    - Ensure that the job has the correct account as the owner.

    - Ensure that NETWORK COM+ and NETWORK DTC are enabled in Add/Remove Windows Components.

    - Ensure that the MSDTC security configuration in Control Panel ➤ Administrative Tools ➤ Component Services is configured correctly for your environment. Try checking Network DTC Access, Allow Remote Clients, and Transaction Manager Communication Allow Inbound and Allow Outbound to see if doing so resolves connectivity issues.

14. The last step is to edit the update scripts and XML files to prepare for a disaster recovery event by following these steps:

    a. On a computer running BizTalk Server 2006, browse to the following folder: \Program Files\Microsoft BizTalk Server 2006\Schema\Restore.

    b. Right-click SampleUpdateInfo.xml, and then click Edit.

    c. For each database listed, replace "SourceServer" with the name of the source system SQL Server database instance, and then replace "DestinationServer" with the name of the destination system SQL Server instance.

Caution Do not perform a blanket search and replace, since databases may be present on different SQL Server instances in the source system and may be restored to different SQL Server instances in the destination system. Be sure to include the quotation marks around the name of the source and destination SQL Server instances. Also, if you renamed any of the BizTalk Server databases, you must also update the database names as appropriate.

d. If you have more than one Messagebox database in the source system, add another MessageBoxDB line to the list, and then set `IsMaster="0"` for the non-master databases.

e. If the source system is using BAM, HWS, SSO, the Rules Engine, or EDI, uncomment these lines as appropriate.

f. If custom databases have been added to the Backup BizTalk Server SQL Agent job, add the custom databases as appropriate under the <OtherDatabases> section.

g. When finished editing the file, save it and exit.

This completes the configuration of BizTalk Log Shipping. The next two subsections cover disaster recovery procedures for the BizTalk Group and for BizTalk servers, respectively.

BizTalk Group Disaster Recovery Procedures

This discussion assumes that BizTalk Log Shipping is configured and working correctly by following the guidance in the earlier subsection titled "Configuring the Backup BizTalk Server SQL Agent Job" as well as the guidance in the earlier subsection titled "Configuring the destination system for Log Shipping." Once that is verified, the next step is to prepare for performing a disaster recovery event. A disaster recovery event for the BizTalk Group consists of restoring the BizTalk Group databases as well as related non-BizTalk databases on the Destination System SQL Server instances. This also includes any DTS packages as well as SQL Agent jobs that exist in the source system (production).

The first step is to ensure that the last backup set has been restored to all SQL Server instances that are part of the destination system. This can be confirmed by reviewing the Master.dbo.bts_LogShippingHistory table that is populated by the Get Backup History SQL Agent job. When a backup is successfully restored, the Restored column is set to 1 and the RestoreDateTime is set to the date/time the restore was completed. When all of the databases that are part of a backup set have been successfully restored, the backup set ID is written to the Master.dbo.bts_LogShippingLastRestoreSet table. Once you have confirmed that available backup files have been applied, follow these steps on each SQL Server instance in the destination system:

1. Depending on whether you are on SQL Server 2000 or SQL Server 2005, navigate to the SQL Agent Jobs view.

2. Right-click and select Disable Job to disable the following SQL Agent jobs:

- BTS Log Shipping—Get Backup History
- BTS Log Shipping—Restore Databases

3. Right-click BTS Log Shipping—Restore To Mark and select Start Job.
4. Once you have verified that the job BTS Log Shipping—Restore To Mark has completed, copy the script and XML files UpdateDatabase.vbs and SampleUpdateInfo.xml to the server where the SQL Server instance is running and execute the following command:

```
cscript UpdateDatabase.vbs SampleUpdateInfo.xml
```

Note On 64-bit servers, run the UpdateDatabase.vbs script from a 64-bit command prompt.

As promised, we next cover the disaster recovery procedures for the BizTalk runtime servers. Later subsections cover disaster recovery procedures for BAM, BAS, and EDI functionality.

BizTalk Runtime Server Disaster Recovery Procedures

The BizTalk runtime servers in the destination system should have BizTalk Server 2006 as well as any required third-party adapters or software installed using the same guidelines for the production BizTalk runtime servers. There are generally two methods for setting up the BizTalk runtime servers:

- **Method one**: Restore BizTalk Group, and then configure BizTalk servers in BizTalk Group and deploy applications.
- **Method two**: Configure disaster recovery BizTalk servers in production BizTalk Group, disable services, keep server up to date, and run update script to update locations of databases in destination system.

Both methods have advantages and disadvantages, which you'll find out more about in our detailed discussion of these methods next.

Method One

To proceed with method one, first verify that procedures to restore the BizTalk Group databases and related application databases have been completed. Once completed, proceed with restoring the BizTalk runtime servers using method one. Method one has all software preinstalled, but not configured, and without any applications deployed on the BizTalk servers in the destination system. When the BizTalk Group is restored in the destination system, and the BizTalk severs are configured using Configuration.exe, select Join for the BizTalk Group, not Create. The first server configured should have the master secret restored on it and then designated as the master secret server for the BizTalk Group using the Enterprise SSO management tools. Once all of the BizTalk servers are configured in the BizTalk Group at the destination system, deploy the BizTalk applications (assemblies and bindings).

While many of the steps can be scripted, this method essentially brings online a new environment when recovering from a disaster. At the same time, it reduces the amount of ongoing maintenance work for the destination system to a degree, since just the latest version of the application is deployed.

Method Two

Method two also has all software preinstalled, but takes it a step further and actually configures the BizTalk servers in the destination system to be member servers in the production BizTalk Group. Applications (assemblies and bindings) are deployed to the destination system BizTalk servers just like in production, except that the BizTalk host instances and all other BizTalk-related Windows Services are disabled and do not perform any processing in the destination system. During a disaster recovery event, a script is run on the destination system BizTalk servers to update the new location of the BizTalk Group in the destination system SQL instances. Once updated, processing can be enabled. Method two is recommended because it results in a faster recovery and less change overall. To proceed with method two, first verify that procedures to restore the BizTalk Group databases and related application databases have been completed.

■ **Note** Path references to Microsoft BizTalk Server 2006 may actually be located in the Microsoft BizTalk Server 2004 directory if an in-place upgrade was performed.

Once verification is completed, perform these steps:

1. Copy the edited SampleUpdateInfo.xml file to the \Program Files\Microsoft BizTalk Server 2006\Schema\Restore directory on every BizTalk server in the destination system.

2. On each BizTalk Server, open a command prompt (must be 64-bit if on a 64-bit OS) by selecting Start ➤ Run, typing **cmd**, and then clicking OK.

3. At the command prompt, navigate to the location of the edited SampleUpdateInfo.xml file and the script (\Program Files\Microsoft BizTalk Server 2006\Schema\Restore is the default) and enter this command:

   ```
   cscript UpdateRegistry.vbs SampleUpdateInfo.xml
   ```

4. Enable and restart all BizTalk host instances and all other BizTalk services on the BizTalk servers in the destination system.

5. Restart WMI on each BizTalk server in the destination system by selecting Start ➤ Run, typing **services.msc**, and clicking OK. Then right-click Windows Management Instrumentation and select Restart.

6. On each BizTalk server, open the BizTalk Server Administration Console, right-click BizTalk Group, and select Remove.

7. Right-click BizTalk Server 2006 Administration, select Connect to Existing Group, select the SQL Server database instance and database name that corresponds to the BizTalk Management database for the BizTalk Group, and click OK.

8. Restore the master secret on the master secret server in the destination system if not already completed by following the steps detailed in the subsection titled "The Master Secret" earlier.

Next, we show you how to restore BAS, if BAS was configured in the BizTalk Group.

Restore Procedures for BAS Site and Database

This subsection covers the procedures to restore BAS and is only required if BAS was configured in the source system. BAS exists in a Windows SharePoint Services web site. Refer to the Windows SharePoint Services Administrators guide for further information, available for download here: www.microsoft.com/downloads/details.aspx?amp;displaylang=en&familyid=a637eff6-8224-4b19-a6a4-3e33fa13d230&displaylang=en.

If BAS is part of the BizTalk solution, follow these steps:

1. Restore the Windows SharePoint Services Configuration and Content databases using SQL Server tools.

2. Open SharePoint Central Administration and on the WSS Central Administration page, click Configure Virtual Server settings.

3. On the Virtual Server List page, select the WSS virtual server.

4. Unextend the WSS virtual server by clicking Remove, delete Content databases by clicking Remove Windows SharePoint Services from virtual server on the Virtual Server Settings page under Virtual Server Management, and then click OK.

5. Click Set Configuration Database Server under Server Configuration.

6. On the Set Configuration Database Server page, enter the name of the SQL Server instance hosting the Configuration database, enter the database name in the SQL Server Database Name field, and then select Connect to Existing Database followed by clicking OK.

7. Under Virtual Server Configuration, select Extend or upgrade virtual server, then in the Virtual Server List, click Default Web Site.

8. Under Provisioning Options, click Extend and map to another virtual server.

9. In Extend and Map to Another Virtual Server, select Use an existing application pool, and then click OK.

10. On the Virtual Server Settings page, under Virtual Server Management, click Manage Content databases, and then on the Manage Content Databases page, click Add a Content database.

11. On the Add Content Database page, under Database Information, click Specify database server settings. In Database server, type the name of the restored database server name. In Database name, type the name of the restored database.

12. On the Manage Content Databases page, click the previous Content database. This is the database that was backed up.

13. On the Manage Content Database Settings page, under Remove Content Database, click Remove Content database to remove this old database link from the Manage Content Databases page.

14. Open the Internet Information Services Manager snap-in by selecting Start ➤ Run and then type **%SystemRoot%\system32\inetsrv\iis.msc**.

15. Select the local computer, and then click Web Sites ➤ Default Web Site ➤ _layouts ➤ <locale identifier> (1033 for En-US), right-click BAS, and then click Properties.

16. In the BAS Properties dialog box, on the Directory tab, next to the Application name box click Create, and then click OK. Verify that the BAS application pool is unchanged after you restore the BAS site and database.

17. Apply any other Windows SharePoint Services customizations such as web.config files, JavaScript files, site templates, etc., as required.

The next subsection covers restore procedures for Business Activity Monitoring.

Restore Procedures for BAM

The BizTalk Server 2006 documentation covers these procedures extensively so we won't repeat them here. BAM consists of SQL Server databases, SQL Analysis databases, and DTS packages. Refer to the section titled "Backing Up and Restoring BAM" in the BizTalk Server 2006 documentation for the details. It is also available online here: http://msdn.microsoft.com/library/default.asp?url=/library/en-us/BTS06CoreDocs/html/5d477492-fdb7-4866-92a8-2720fea15839.asp?frame=true.

Next, we cover the restore procedures for the Base EDI adapter.

Restore Procedures for the Base EDI Adapter

The Base EDI adapter, unlike the other adapters in BizTalk Server, has its own database and stores files in a directory (DocumentsHome) during runtime. The DocumentsHome directory is located here by default: <root>\Documents and Settings\All Users\Application Data\Microsoft\BizTalk Server 2006\EDI\SubsystemThe Base EDI adapter.

Restoring the Base EDI adapter requires following a precise order of steps to ensure that the system comes back online in an orderly fashion with successful message processing and tracking from the point of failure with minimal risk of data loss. There are three primary steps when restoring the Base EDI adapter:

- Restore the DocumentsHome directory.
- Recover data and resynchronize the audit trail.
- Generate the engine input file.

The detailed tasks for the preceding steps are available in the BizTalk Server 2006 core documentation in the section titled "Backing Up and Restoring the Base EDI Adapter" available at this link: http://msdn.microsoft.com/library/default.asp?url=/library/en-us/BTS06CoreDocs/html/92ee1636-c2bd-4965-b949-4a24d99b7956.asp?frame=true.

Now let's take a look at the additional tasks related to disaster recovery for a BizTalk Server solution.

Other Disaster Recovery Tasks

This subsection covers other tasks and recommendations related to disaster recovery. As mentioned in the subsection titled "Configuring the DTA Purge and Archive SQL Agent Job" earlier in the chapter, tracking data is an important part of a BizTalk solution, since that data can be used for reporting and as part of recordkeeping regulations compliance. It can also be used to help recover from a disaster, because it is a record of data processing activity. For this reason, we recommend separating your tracking databases from the runtime databases that generate tracking data by configuring your databases in separate SQL Server instances on different disks in production. Data in the tracking databases can be used to help determine the state of the system up to the point of failure for the runtime databases. Tracked messages and events can indicate what processes may have already happened and what messages have been received or sent.

■ **Note** Tracking data is not written directly to the tracking databases. Instead, it is cached on the Messageboxes and moved to the Tracking database. Therefore, in the event of a Messagebox data loss, some tracking data may be lost as well.

The next subsection covers steps to evaluate data loss for the BizTalk Group with tips on how to recover data.

Evaluating Data Loss for the BizTalk Group

After data loss has occurred, recovering it is often difficult or impossible. For these reasons, using a fault-tolerant system to prevent data loss is extremely important. In any case, a disaster may occur, and even the most fault-tolerant system has some chance of failure. This subsection covers methods to help determine the state of the system when the failure occurred and how to evaluate corrective action.

Managing In-Flight Orchestrations

The Messagebox databases contain the state of orchestrations that are currently in progress. When data is lost from the Messagebox databases, it is not possible to tell exactly what data has been lost. Therefore, it will be necessary to examine external systems to see what activities have occurred in relation to the in-progress orchestrations.

Once it is determined what has occurred, steps can be taken to restore processes. For example, if upon looking at external systems or logs it is determined that an orchestration was activated but didn't perform any work, the message can be resubmitted to complete the operation.

It is important to consider what information will be available to compare with in-flight orchestrations in order to decide whether to terminate or resume particular in-flight orchestrations. Available information is largely determined by the architecture and design of the system such as what logging is performed "out-of-band" so as to not impact performance but at the same time provide an audit of events for comparison purposes.

Health and Activity Tracking Operations Tool

The HAT Operations tools can be used to determine what services were active at the time the Messagebox was recovered. Because there is a gap between the time of the recovered database and the time of the failure, the state of these and other transactions that may have started is in doubt and will need to be evaluated with available information.

Health and Activity Tracking Reporting Tools

HAT provides reporting tools for viewing system events. These tools can show which service instances completed and started after the point of recovery. HAT can positively report on any service that completed, and it can indicate that a service started. However, HAT cannot reveal everything because tracking data is first staged to the Messagebox and then moved to the Tracking database. The data that was staged may have been lost to the backlog of the TDDS service.

Viewing After the Log Mark in Tracking Databases

While all databases need to be restored to the same mark for operational reasons in order to restore a consistent BizTalk Group, administrators can use a Tracking database that was not lost in Archive mode to see what happened after the mark. The process of evaluating the data begins by comparing services that are in flight in the HAT Operations views against their state in HAT Reporting. If HAT Reporting shows it as having completed, the instances can be terminated.

HAT Reporting may show instances that started after the point of recovery. If so, any actions these instances took must be compensated, and then the initial activation messages can be submitted.

Reporting may also show that instances have progressed beyond the point at which the Operations view indicates. In this case, use the Orchestration Debugger in Reporting to see the last shapes that were executed, and then use Message Flow to see what message should have been sent or received. If they do not match the state in the Operations view, corrective action is required. Options are to terminate, compensate and restart, or resubmit any lost messages.

■ **Note** If the BizTalk Tracking database is lost, all discovery of what happened past the point of recovery will need to be done using the external system's reporting mechanisms.

Marking In-Flight Transactions As Complete in BAM

BAM maintains data for incomplete trace instances in a special active instance table. If some instance records were started before the last backup but completed after the backup, those records will remain in the active instance table because the completion records for the instance will have been lost. Although this does not prevent the system from functioning, it may be desirable to mark these records as completed so that they can be moved out of the active instance table. To accomplish this, manual intervention is necessary.

A list of incomplete ActivityIDs for a given activity can be determined by issuing the following query against the BAM Primary Import database:

```
Select ActivityID from bam_<ActivityName> where IsComplete = 0
```

If data from external systems indicates that the activity instance is in fact completed, use the following query to manually complete the instance:

```
exec bam_<ActivityName>_PrimaryImport @ActivityID=N'<ActivityID>', @IsStartNew=0,
@IsComplete=1
```

Related Non-BizTalk Application Disaster Recovery Procedures

There may be additional non-BizTalk applications that must be restored as part of the overall application solution. If these application databases participate in distributed transactions with the BizTalk Group databases, the databases should be part of the Backup BizTalk Server SQL Agent job and restored to the same mark as the other BizTalk Group databases. In general, each individual application should have a disaster recovery plan tailored to the application that should be part of the overall solution disaster recovery plan.

CHAPTER 10

Deploying and Managing BizTalk Applications

In the previous chapters, you have seen how to create schemas to define the different messages that your BizTalk applications send and receive, how to create orchestrations for the implementation of business workflows, how to create custom pipelines to customize the different stages of message processing, and finally how to create and maintain ports to receive and send messages. In a nutshell, you have seen how to develop each of the major artifacts present in a BizTalk solution.

Now that you are able to develop BizTalk solutions in a development environment, it is time to learn how to deploy your solution onto other environments such as a testing or production environment.

In this chapter, you will first learn how a BizTalk solution is organized. Then we will talk about different deployment methods to install your BizTalk applications on other target environments. Finally, you will learn about the different tools available to manage or deploy a BizTalk application.

BizTalk Applications

Prior to BizTalk 2006, it was impossible to know which BizTalk artifacts belonged to what BizTalk solution. Even if developers, administrators, and architects used a clever naming convention, the Administration Tools did not allow viewing of different artifacts for a specific BizTalk solution. A BizTalk Server Group that has multiple BizTalk solutions installed can easily have hundreds of ports, orchestrations, and other artifacts for different BizTalk solutions.

In order to solve this problem, Microsoft created a new entity named the **BizTalk application**. The purpose of a BizTalk application is to group BizTalk artifacts. Figure 10-1 depicts a BizTalk application along with the artifacts associated with it.

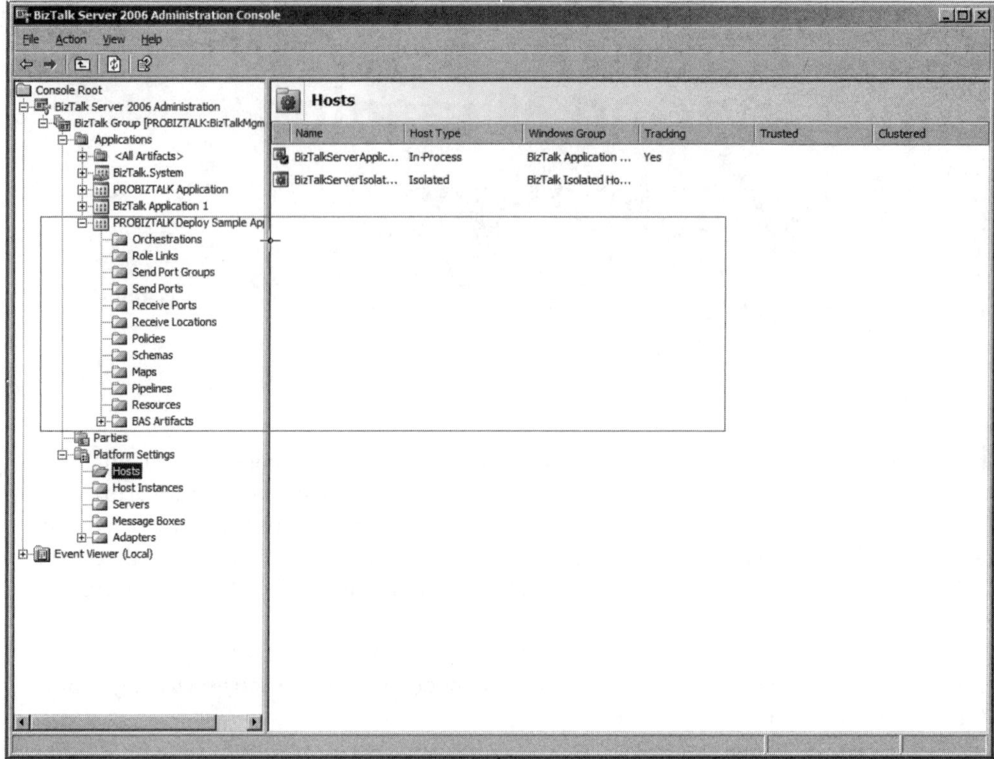

Figure 10-1. *BizTalk application and associated artifacts*

You can perform the following actions on a BizTalk application:

- Enumerate, add, and remove BizTalk artifacts from a BizTalk application. Table 10-1 shows BizTalk resource artifacts that can be associated with a BizTalk application.
- Export or import all the BizTalk artifacts related to a single business solution to an MSI file.
- Start or stop all the BizTalk artifacts that can be enlisted, started, unenlisted, and stopped within a BizTalk application.
- Create or remove dependencies between BizTalk applications by adding or removing references from one application to another.

Table 10-1. *BizTalk Application Resource Artifacts*

Artifact	Fully Qualified Resource Type	Description
.NET assembly	System.BizTalk:Assembly	All .NET assemblies that are used within the BizTalk application.
BAM definition	System.BizTalk:Bam	All BAM definition files used within the BizTalk application.
BAS artifact	System.BizTalk:Bas	BAS artifacts encompass the self profiles, partner profiles, partner groups, agreements, and templates. These artifacts are used to describe relationships between your company and trading partners.
BizTalk assembly	System.BizTalk:BizTalkAssembly	Assembly that contains BizTalk schemas, maps, orchestrations, or pipelines.
BizTalk binding file	System.BizTalk:BizTalkBinding	XML files that contain a snapshot of the binding as seen at that instant. It does not contain details about the completeness of the binding with respect to the orchestration.
Security certificate	System.BizTalk:Certificate	BizTalk artifact used to verify the identities and to establish secure communications. Certificates are associated to ports.
COM component	System.BizTalk:Com	COM components that are used by the BizTalk application.
Ad hoc file	System.BizTalk:File	Any file that is used by the BizTalk application or that provides information about the BizTalk application.
Post-processing script	System.BizTalk:PostProcessingScript	Scripts that are executed after a BizTalk application has been installed on a host instance.
Pre-processing script	System.BizTalk:PreProcessingScript	Scripts that are executed before a BizTalk application has been installed on a host instance.
Policy or rule	System.BizTalk:Rules	XML files that contain all the different policies and rules contained in the BizTalk rule engine.
Virtual directory	System.BizTalk:WebDirectory	Any IIS Virtual Directories that must deploy on the target host instance to allow the BizTalk application to function properly.

BizTalk 2006 requires all BizTalk artifacts to belong to a BizTalk application. When configuring a BizTalk Server Group, a default BizTalk application named BizTalk Application 1 is created. BizTalk artifacts are deployed to the default BizTalk application in the following situations:

- When upgrading a BizTalk Server 2004 to BizTalk Server 2006. All the BizTalk 2004 artifacts will be found under the default application.
- When deploying BizTalk artifacts using the deprecated BTSDeploy command-line tool.
- When deploying BizTalk assemblies using Visual Studio 2005 without specifying an application name in the deployment configuration properties.

- When creating ports using BizTalk Explorer in Visual Studio 2005.
- When adding BizTalk artifacts using the BTSTask command-line application without specifying a BizTalk application name.
- When importing an MSI file using the BTSTask command-line application without specifying a BizTalk application name.

Important Deployment Artifacts

In this section, you will learn about binding files and processing scripts. These two artifacts play a vital role in deploying and managing BizTalk applications. After reading this section, you may still wonder when these artifacts come into play upon deploying applications. We will cover this in more detail when we discuss deployment scenarios. For now the most important thing is for you to understand what binding files and processing scripts are.

Binding Files

Binding files are XML files describing the different BizTalk artifacts stored in the BizTalk Management Database and the relationship between these artifacts. Binding files are useful because they provide a way for an administrator to export the settings from a BizTalk Server Group, modify them if necessary, and import them to another BizTalk Server Group. You can choose to export either all the information related to a BizTalk Server Group, or a BizTalk application, or a specific BizTalk assembly.

The easiest way to understand what binding files are and what they look like is to export one from an existing BizTalk application and to look at its content. One of the ways to export a binding file is to open the BizTalk Server Administration Console, right-click a BizTalk application, and select the Export ➤ Bindings context menu item. When the Export Bindings window appears, simply select where you wish to export the binding file and that you only wish to export the bindings for the currently selected application. Open the exported file in a text editor. You should see an XML document similar to the partial binding file shown in Listing 10-1.

Listing 10-1. *Partial Binding File*

```
<?xml version="1.0" encoding="utf-8"?>
<BindingInfo
   xmlns:xsi="http://www.w3.org/2001/XMLSchema-instance"
   xmlns:xsd="http://www.w3.org/2001/XMLSchema"
   Assembly="Microsoft.BizTalk.Deployment, Version=3.0.1.0, Culture=neutral, ➥
PublicKeyToken=31bf3856ad364e35"
   Version="3.0.1.0"
   BindingStatus="FullyBound"
   BoundEndpoints="2"
   TotalEndpoints="2">
  <Timestamp>2005-07-15T17:44:04.9787774-07:00</Timestamp>
```

```
  <ModuleRefCollection>
    ...
  </ModuleRefCollection>
  <SendPortCollection>
    ...
  </SendPortCollection>
  <DistributionListCollection>
    ...
  </DistributionListCollection>
  <ReceivePortCollection>
    ...
  </ReceivePortCollection>
  <PartyCollection>
    ...
  </PartyCollection>
</BindingInfo>
```

There are five important XML elements under the `BindingInfo` document element:

- `ModuleRefCollection`: Declares all the BizTalk assemblies and orchestrations used within the application. It also specifies which physical ports are used for each orchestration.
- `SendPortCollection`: Contains all the information necessary to create or update all the send port groups.
- `DistributionListCollection`: Contains all the information necessary to create or update all the send port groups.
- `ReceivePortCollection`: Contains all the information necessary to create or update all the receive ports and receive locations.
- `PartyCollection`: Contains all the information necessary to create or update all the parties.

Please refer to the product documentation for the full list of attributes and elements available in a binding file. If you need to validate binding files, you can generate the XML schema for binding files by running the following command in the Visual Studio 2005 command prompt:

```
xsd.exe "C:\Program Files\Microsoft BizTalk Server 2006\ ➥
Microsoft.BizTalk.Deployment.dll" /type:BindingInfo
```

The XML schema will be generated in the directory where the command was run.

Processing Scripts

Processing scripts are scripts or executables that are run when installing, importing, or removing a BizTalk application. Table 10-2 displays the different types of files that can be used as processing scripts. **Pre-processing scripts** run at the beginning of an import or installation process. **Post-processing scripts** run at the end of an import or installation process.

Table 10-2. *Valid Processing Script Files*

Scripts or Executables	Extension
MS-DOS application	.com
Application	.exe
MS-DOS batch file	.bat
Windows NT command script	.cmd
VBScript script file	.vbs, .vbe
JScript script file	.js, .jse
Windows Script Host setting and Script file	.wsh, .wsf

Processing scripts are useful to perform simple or complex operations to reduce the number of manual operations that must occur when installing or removing a BizTalk application. Here are a few examples showing what you can do with processing scripts:

- Create a directory structure.
- Create a database.
- Register COM components.
- GAC .NET components.
- Start or stop BizTalk applications.
- Enlist, start, stop, or unenlist ports and orchestrations.

Listing 10-2 shows the content of a pre-processing script used to create and remove a directory structure when installing and removing a BizTalk application.

Listing 10-2. *Directories Preprocessing Script*

```
REM Creates and Removes Directories to receive or
REM send files

@setlocal
REM ### For verifying BTAD_* environment variables when script is called.
set LogFile=C:\PROBIZTALK\Log.txt

echo Script Log %DATE% %TIME% > "%LogFile%"
echo Install Directory: %BTAD_InstallDir% > "%LogFile%"
echo Install Mode: %BTAD_InstallMode% > "%LogFile%"
echo Change request action: % BTAD_ChangeRequestAction% > "%LogFile%"
```

```
REM ### Create directories prior to BizTalk assembly deployment
if "%BTAD_InstallMode%"=="Install" AND "%BTAD_ChangeRequestAction%"=="Update" (
            REM ### Create the folders which will drop messages
            mkdir %BTAD_InstallDir%\TestDocuments\In\
            mkdir %BTAD_InstallDir%\TestDocuments\Out\
)

REM ### Remove directories after undeploying at the end of uninstallation process
if "%BTAD_InstallMode%"=="Uninstall" AND "%BTAD_ChangeRequestAction%"=="Delete" (
     del %BTAD_InstallDir%\TestDocuments\ /s /q
)

REM ### Return exit code of 0 to indicate a success.
echo Script Executed sucessfully > "%LogFile%"
exit /B 0
@endlocal
```

As you can see, Listing 10-2 uses several environment variables containing a context for a script developer. Some variables can be set by a developer, and others are set by the BizTalk Server Installer. Refer to Table 10-3 for the complete list of the environment variables accessible through processing scripts and their description. Table 10-4 displays the values for the environment variables set by the BizTalk Server Installer at different stages of the installation or uninstallation process.

Table 10-3. *Processing Script Environment Variables*

Environment Variable	Description
BTAD_ChangeRequestAction	Specifies whether the installer is creating, updating, or removing BizTalk artifacts. The possible values are **Create**: Imports or installs artifacts without overwriting previous ones **Update**: Imports or installs artifacts overwriting previous ones **Delete**: Deletes artifacts
BTAD_HostClass	Specifies whether the operation is being applied on the BizTalk Management Database or on the BizTalk host instance. The possible values are ConfigurationDb BizTalkHostInstance
BTAD_InstallMode	Specifies whether a BizTalk application is being imported, installed, or uninstalled. The possible values are Import Install Uninstall
BTAD_InstallDir	Specifies the installation directory of a BizTalk application.
BTAD_ApplicationName	Specifies the name of a BizTalk application. If the name was not provided when launching the BizTalk Server Installer, it will contain the default BizTalk application name.

Continued

Table 10-3. *Continued*

Environment Variable	Description
`BTAD_SilentMode`	Specifies options for running the script in silent mode. The most commonly used values are **0**: Does not change the user interface (UI) level. **1**: Uses the default UI level. **2**: Performs a silent installation (the default). **3**: Provides simple progress and error handling. **4**: Provides authored UI; suppresses wizards.
`BTAD_Server`	Specifies the name of a SQL Server instance hosting the BizTalk Management Database for a group.
`BTAD_Database`	Specifies the name of the BizTalk Management Database for a group.

Table 10-4. *Environment Variable Values at Different Deployment States*

	Environment Variables		
Deployment State	**BTAD_ChangeRequest Action Values**	**BTAD_Install Mode Values**	**BTAD_Host Class Values**
Import without overwrite flag	Create	Import	ConfigurationDb
Import with overwrite flag	Update	Import	ConfigurationDb
Install	Update	Install	BizTalkHostInstance
Uninstall	Delete	Uninstall	BizTalkHostInstance
Import rollback	Delete	Import	ConfigurationDb
Install rollback	Delete	Install	BizTalkHostInstance

Deploying a BizTalk Solution

In this section, you will learn the different methods of deploying BizTalk applications. First, you will discover how to deploy a BizTalk application manually. Then, you will see how to export, import, or install a BizTalk application using an MSI package. Finally, you will investigate a BizTalk application deployment process that allows you to move your BizTalk solution from your development environment all the way to your production environment.

Steps in Deploying a BizTalk Application

There are two major steps in order to deploy an application. First, you must import the BizTalk application to a BizTalk Server Group. Importing a BizTalk application registers all the BizTalk artifacts for a BizTalk application in the Management Database. Once a BizTalk application has been imported into the Management Database, all other BizTalk servers in the BizTalk Server Group are now aware of the new BizTalk application and its artifacts.

However, before they can run the application themselves, they must have a physical copy of all the BizTalk artifacts that are referenced in the Management Database. Consequently, the second step is to install all artifacts on each of the BizTalk servers in a BizTalk Server Group. This step includes copying all artifacts to the target servers, registration of COM libraries, registration of .NET assemblies in the Global Assembly Cache, installing certificates in servers' certificate store, and the configuration of virtual directories if needed.

Exercise 10-1 demonstrates how to perform some of the steps just mentioned.

Exercise 10-1: Deploying a BizTalk Application Manually

The purpose of this exercise is to illustrate how to deploy a BizTalk application manually using the BizTalk Administration Console. You will learn how to

- Create a BizTalk application.
- Deploy a BizTalk assembly manually.
- Create ports manually.
- Start a BizTalk application.

1. Copy all the files located in the Chapter10\DeploymentSampleApplication sample application provided as part of the download files for this book to C:\DeploymentSampleApplication.
2. Open the BizTalk Administration Console:
   a. Select Start ➤ All Programs ➤ Microsoft BizTalk Server 2006 ➤ BizTalk Server and then click the Administration icon.
   b. In the BizTalk Server 2006 Administration Console, expand BizTalk Server 2006 ➤ BizTalk Group ➤ Applications.
3. Create a new application:
   a. Right-click Applications, point to New, and then click Application.
   b. In the Applications Properties window shown in Figure 10-2, type **PROBIZTALK Deploy Sample Application** in the Name field.
   c. In the Applications Properties window, type **PROBIZTALK's Deployment Sample Application** in the Description field.
   d. In the Applications Properties window, click OK.

Note You can add references to other BizTalk applications by clicking the reference section.

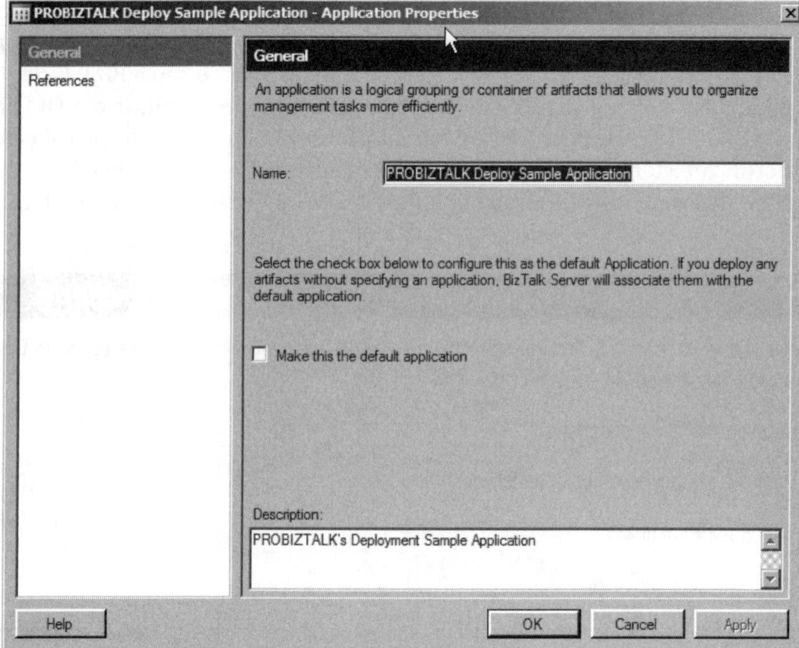

Figure 10-2. *Application Properties dialog*

4. Add the BizTalk assembly:

   a. In the BizTalk Server 2006 Administration Console, expand BizTalk Server 2006 ➤ BizTalk Group ➤ Applications ➤ PROBIZTALK Deploy Sample Application.

   b. Right-click Resources, point to Add, and click BizTalk Assemblies.

   c. In the Add Resources window, click the Add button.

   d. Browse to the C:\DeploymentSampleApplication\DeploymentSampleApplication.dll, and then click Open.

   e. In the Add Resources window, click the OK button.

   f. Notice in the right pane of the BizTalk Server 2006 Administration Console the newly added assembly.

5. Create a receive port:

   a. In the BizTalk Server 2006 Administration Console, expand BizTalk Server 2006 ➤ BizTalk Group ➤ Applications ➤ PROBIZTALK Deploy Sample Application.

   b. Right-click Receive Ports, point to New, and click One-way Receive Port.

   c. In the Receive Port Properties window shown in Figure 10-3, type **ReceiveGreetingsPort** in the Name field.

   d. Click Receive Locations on the left pane, then click the New button on the right pane.

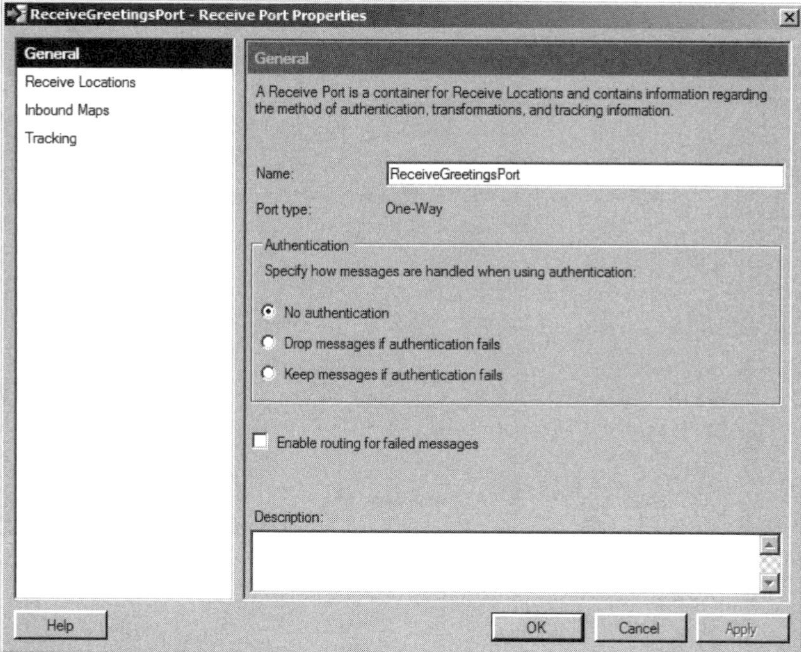

Figure 10-3. *Receive Port Properties dialog*

e. In the Receive Location window shown in Figure 10-4, type **ReceiveGreetingsPortFILE** in the Name field.

f. Select FILE in the Type field.

g. Click the Configure button.

h. Type **C:\DeploymentSampleApplication\Documents\In** in the Receive folder field.

i. Click the OK button.

j. Select BizTalk Server Application from the Receive Handler drop-down menu.

k. Select XMLReceive in the Receive Pipeline field, and click the OK button.

l. Click the OK button one more time to close the Receive Properties Window.

6. Create a send port:

a. In the BizTalk Server 2006 Administration Console, expand BizTalk Server 2006 ➤ BizTalk Group ➤ Applications ➤ PROBIZTALK Deploy Sample Application.

b. Right-click Send Ports, point to New, and click Static One-way Send Port.

c. In the Send Port Properties window shown in Figure 10-5, type **SendGreetingsResponsePort** in the Name field.

d. Select FILE in the Type field.

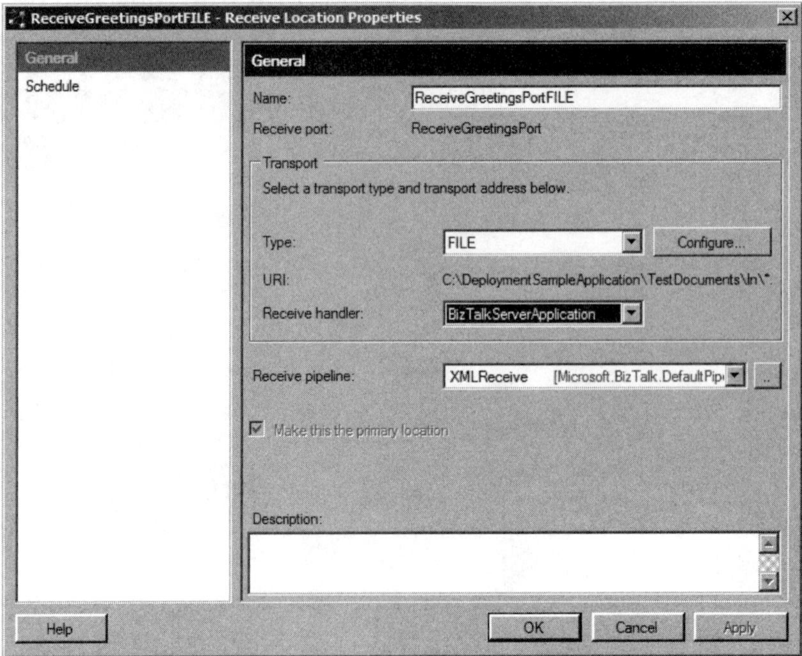

Figure 10-4. *Receive Location Properties dialog*

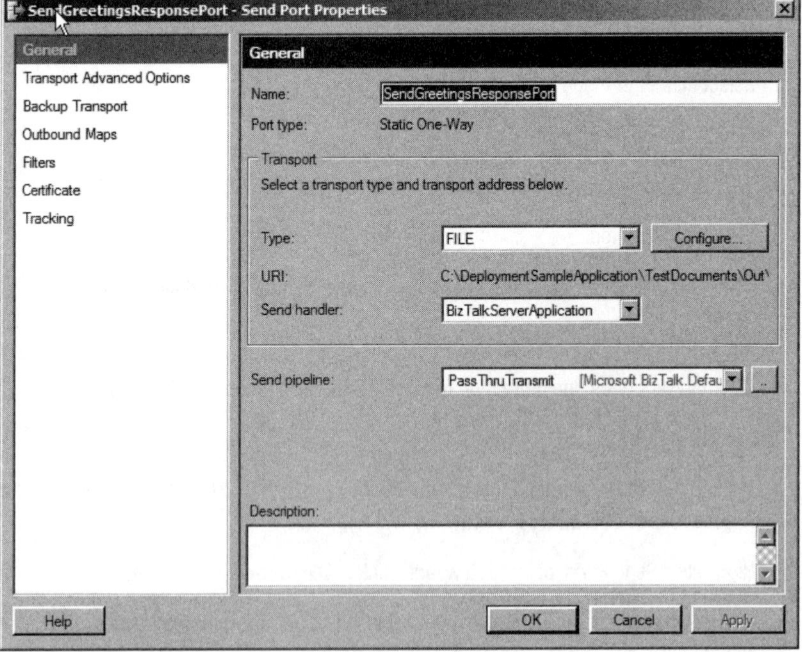

Figure 10-5. *Send Port Properties dialog*

e. Click the Configure button.

f. Type **C:\DeploymentSampleApplication\Documents\Out** in the Destination folder field.

g. Click the OK button.

h. Select PassThruTransimit in the Send Pipeline field.

i. Select BizTalk Server Application in the Sebd Handler drop-down menu

j. Click the OK button.

7. Configure the PROBIZTALK Deploy Sample Application:

   a. In the BizTalk Server 2006 Administration Console, right-click PROBIZTALK Deploy Sample Application, and click Configure.

   b. In the Configure Application window, click the ProcessGreetingsOrchestration orchestration.

   c. Select BizTalkApplication in the Host drop-down menu.

   d. In the Inbound Logical Ports section, select the ReceiveGreetingsPort port in the port drop-down menu.

   e. In the Outbound Logical Ports section, select the SendGreetingsResponsePort port in the port drop-down menu.

   f. In the Configure Application window, click the OK button.

8. Start the PROBIZTALK Deploy Sample Application:

   a. In the BizTalk Server 2006 Administration Console, right-click PROBIZTALK Deploy Sample Application, and click Start.

   b. In the Start 'PROBIZTALK Deploy Sample Application' window, click Start.

   c. Copy C:\DeploymentSampleApplication\Documents\GreetingsSchemaInstance.xml to the C:\DeploymentSampleApplication\Documents\In folder. The file will be picked up by a BizTalk Server for processing, and shortly an output document will be created in the C:\DeploymentSampleApplication\Documents\Out folder.

MSI Export/Import/Install

You have seen in the previous section how to import and install a BizTalk application manually. Soon you will realize, if you have not already, that deploying an application manually is a long and error-prone process. In order to simplify the process of exporting, importing, and installing a BizTalk application, Microsoft provides with BizTalk 2006 a way to do all the preceding using MSI packages.

Exporting a BizTalk application consists of taking all BizTalk artifacts for a particular application and packaging them into an MSI file. Exercise 10-2 walks you through the process. You do not have to export all the different BizTalk artifacts into a single MSI. You can also decide to split your BizTalk artifacts into multiple MSI packages. This is convenient for BizTalk applications that contain too many artifacts.

Exercise 10-2: Exporting a BizTalk Application

This exercise shows how to export an MSI application. To perform this exercise, please ensure that you completed Exercise 10-1 successfully. Then follow these steps:

1. Open the BizTalk Administration Console:

   a. Select Start ➤ All Programs ➤ Microsoft BizTalk Server 2006 ➤ BizTalk Server and then click the Administration icon.

   b. In the BizTalk Server 2006 Administration Console, expand BizTalk Server 2006 ➤ BizTalk Group ➤ Applications ➤ PROBIZTALK Deploy Sample Application.

2. Add the testing binding file to the PROBIZTALK Deploy Sample Application:

   a. Right-click PROBIZTALK Deploy Sample Application, point to Export, and then click Bindings.

   b. In the Export Bindings window shown in Figure 10-6, type **C:\DeploymentSampleApplication\TestingBindings.xml** in the Export to file field and select Export all bindings from the current application.

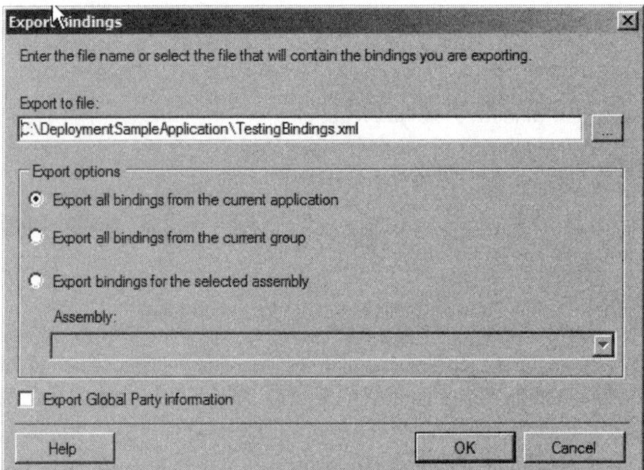

Figure 10-6. *Export Bindings dialog*

   c. Click the OK button.

   d. Open C:\PROBIZTALK\DeploymentSampleApplication\TestingBindings.xml with Notepad.

   e. Replace all occurrences of the text "\Documents\" with "\TestDocuments\".

   f. Save the file and close Notepad.

   g. In the BizTalk Server 2006 Administration Console, expand BizTalk Server 2006 ➤ BizTalk Group ➤ Applications ➤ PROBIZTALK Deploy Sample Application.

   h. Right-click the PROBIZTALK Deploy Sample Application, point to Add, and then click Resources.

i. In the Add Resources window, click the Add button and select the C:\PROBIZTALK\DeploymentSampleApplication\TestingBindings.xml file.

j. In the Add Resources window, type **Testing** in the Target Environment text box. This text box allows you to specify which environment a binding file is applied to upon installation of the BizTalk MSI application.

k. In the Add Resources window, click the OK button.

3. Add a pre-processing script to the PROBIZTALK Deploy Sample Application:

   a. In Notepad, create a new file and insert content of the command file presented in Listing 10-2.

   b. Save the file as C:\PROBIZTALK\DeploymentSampleApplication\TestingDirs.cmd.

   c. In the BizTalk Server 2006 Administration Console, expand BizTalk Server 2006 ➤ BizTalk Group ➤ Applications ➤ PROBIZTALK Deploy Sample Application.

   d. Right-click the PROBIZTALK Deploy Sample Application, point to Add, and then click Pre-processing scripts.

   e. In the Add Resources window shown on Figure 10-7, click the Add button, and select the C:\PROBIZTALK\DeploymentSampleApplication\TestingDirs.cmd file.

   f. In the Add Resources window, click the OK button.

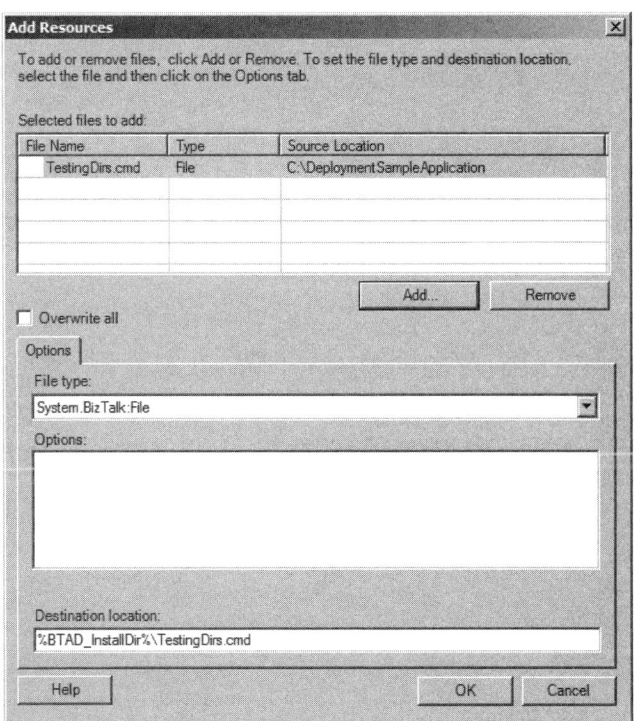

Figure 10-7. *Add Resources dialog*

4. Export the PROBIZTALK Deploy Sample Application to an MSI file:

   a. In the BizTalk Server 2006 Administration Console, expand BizTalk Server 2006 ➤ BizTalk Group ➤ Applications ➤ PROBIZTALK Deploy Sample Application.

   b. Right-click the PROBIZTALK Deploy Sample Application, point to Export, and then click MSI.

   c. When the Welcome window appears as shown on Figure 10-8, click the Next button.

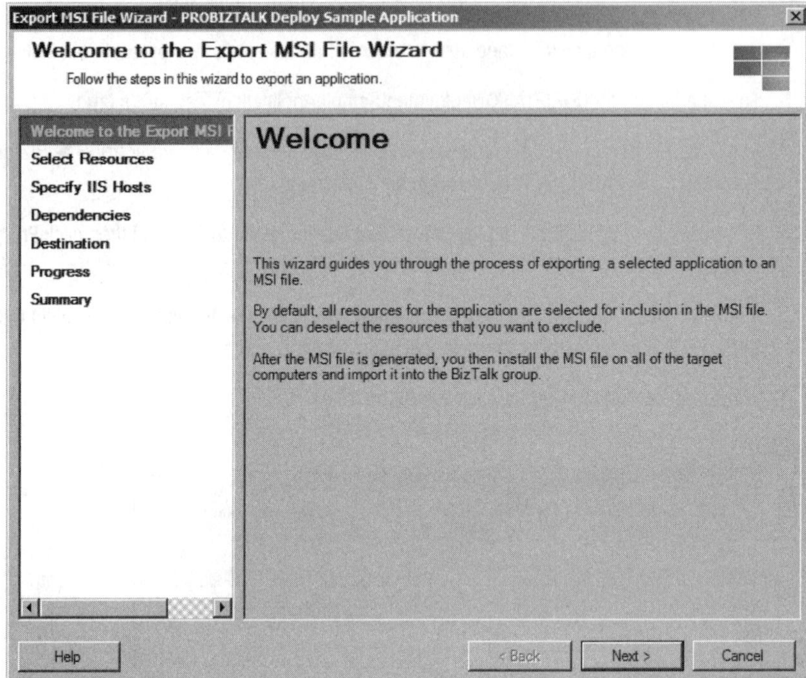

Figure 10-8. *Export MSI File Wizard Welcome screen*

   d. In the Select Resources window shown on Figure 10-9, ensure that all BizTalk artifacts are checked, and then click the Next button.

   e. Since the application does not have any virtual directories, click the Next button in the Specify IIS Hosts window as shown on Figure 10-10.

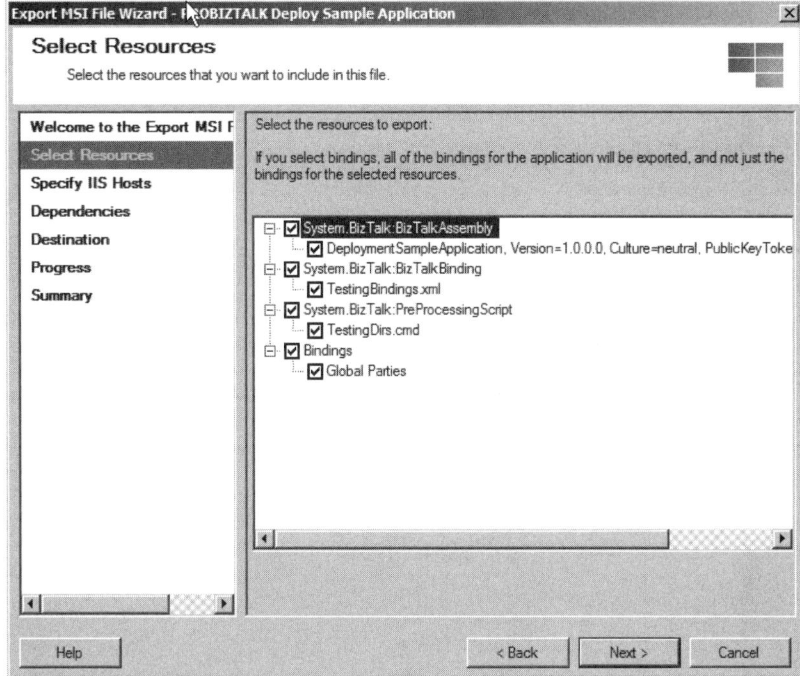

Figure 10-9. *Export MSI File Wizard Resources screen*

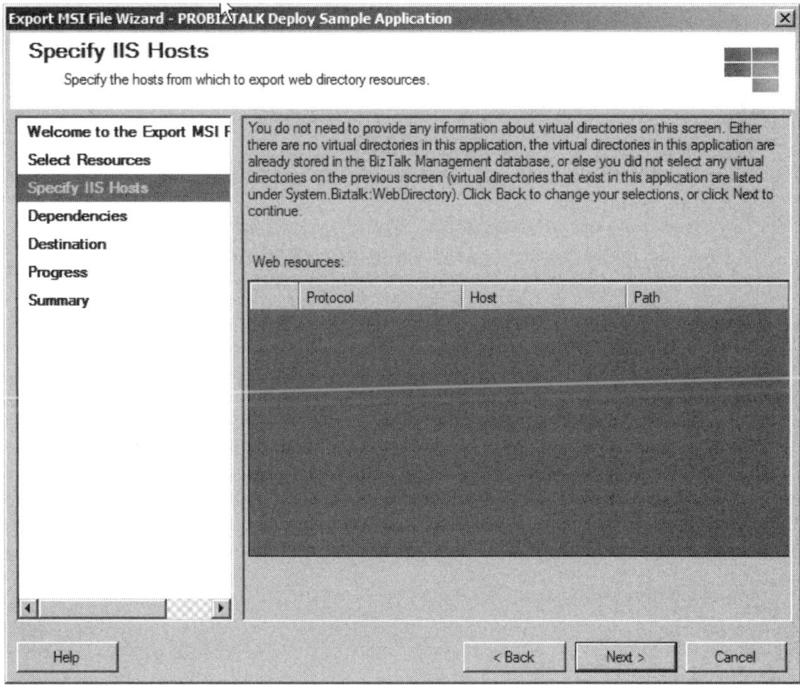

Figure 10-10. *Export MSI File Wizard—Specify IIS Hosts screen*

f. The Dependencies window shown in Figure 10-11 enumerates all the dependencies for the application. As you can see in this particular case, this application depends only on the BizTalk.System application. Click the Next button.

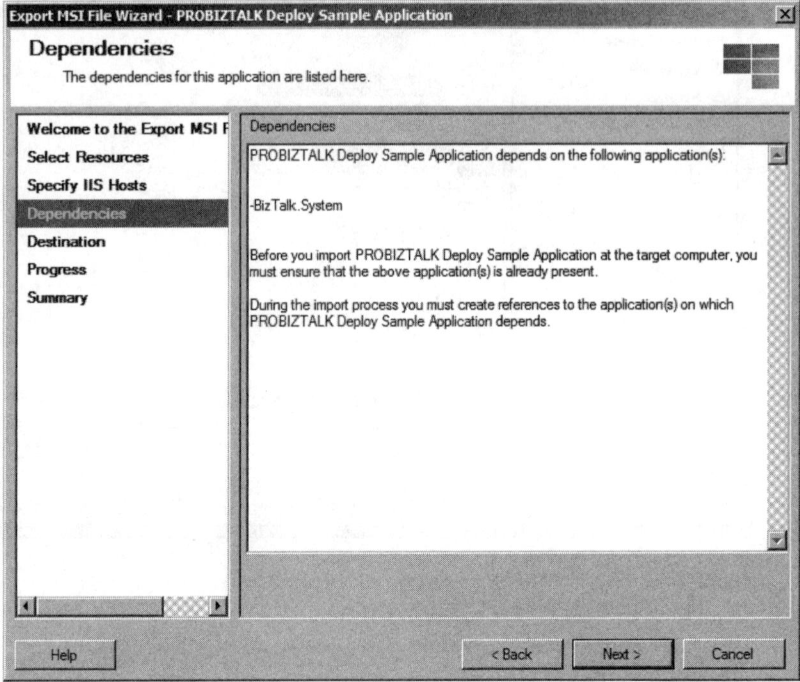

Figure 10-11. *Export MSI File Wizard—Dependencies screen*

g. Type **C:\ProBizTalkSample.msi** and then click the Export button in the Destination window as shown in Figure 10-12.

h. In the Summary window shown in the Fig 10-13, click the Finish button.

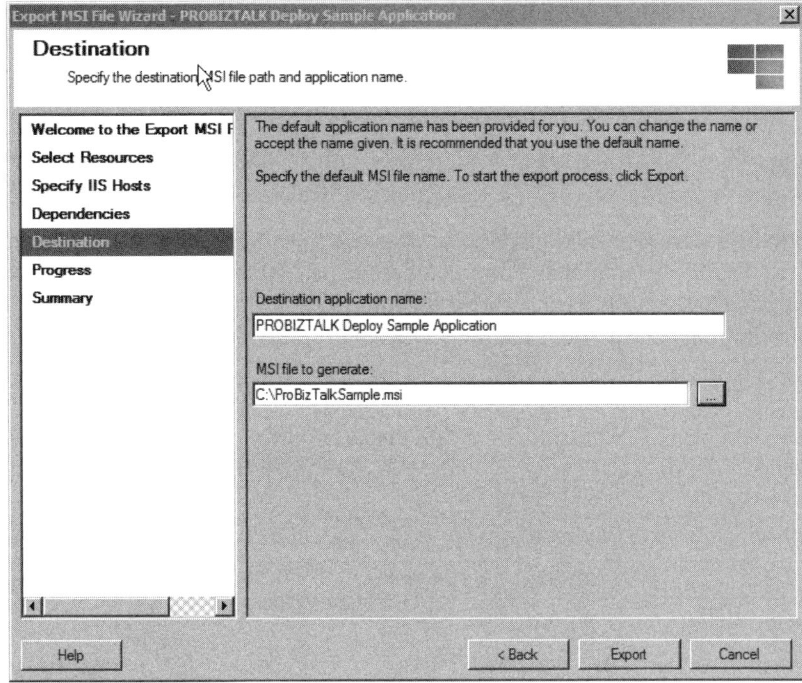

Figure 10-12. *Export MSI File Wizard—Destination screen*

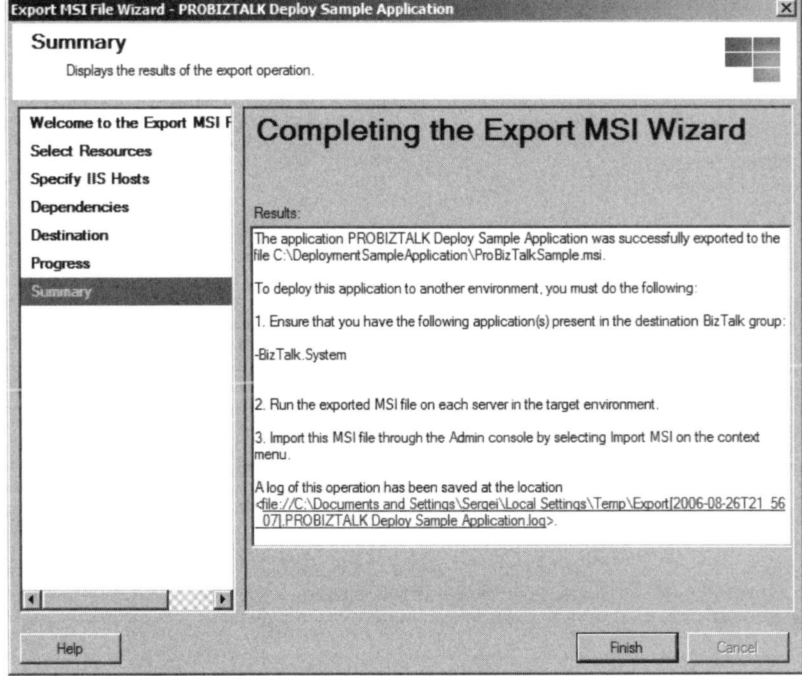

Figure 10-13. *Export MSI File Wizard—Summary screen*

Once you have exported your BizTalk application to an MSI package, you can import or install it onto a new BizTalk Server Group. When importing or installing an MSI BizTalk application, you can specify the following parameters:

- **Application name**: The name of the application used to import or install the MSI package. If the application name is not provided, the default BizTalk application name will be used.
- **Environment**: The target environment where the MSI package is being imported or installed. This parameter allows all binding files for the specified environment to be applied to the BizTalk server. If the environment parameter is not specified, all the binding files that do not specify a target environment will be applied.
- **Overwrite**: This flag specifies whether or not to overwrite the existing artifacts.

Table 10-5 displays what operations are executed when a BizTalk application is imported or installed.

Table 10-5. *Operations Executed When Importing or Installing a BizTalk Application*

Operation	Occurs While Importing	Occurs While Installing
Add references in the BizTalk Management Database.	X	
Copy BizTalk artifacts to the BizTalk server.	X	X
Apply binding files for the specified target environment.	X	X
Execute pre- or post-processing scripts.	X The scripts will only perform actions that will run when the `BTAD_InstallMode` is equal to Import.	X The scripts will only perform actions that will run when the `BTAD_InstallMode` is equal to Install.
Store file-based artifact (assemblies, virtual directories, files, scripts, certificates, BAM artifacts, and BAS artifacts) data in the BizTalk Management Database.	X	
Store policies in the Rule Engine database.	X	
Store BAM artifacts in the BAM Primary Import database. Deploy BAM definitions.	X	
Add BAS artifacts to the BAS site.	X	
Add BizTalk assemblies to the Global Assembly Cache.	Only if BizTalk assemblies were added to the BizTalk application with the "Add to global assembly cache on MSI import" option.	Only if BizTalk assemblies were added to the BizTalk application with the "Add to global assembly cache on MSI install" option.

The BizTalk Administration Console and BTSTask command-line application are the two applications that allow a user to export, import, and install a BizTalk MSI file. Please note that the BTSDeploy tool from BizTalk Server 2004 is also available to perform these tasks, but it has been deprecated and scripts should be migrated to the BTSTask tool. Exercise 10-3 walks you through the process of importing a BizTalk application using the BTSTask tool.

Exercise 10-3: Importing a BizTalk Application

To perform this exercise, please ensure that you completed Exercise 10-2 successfully. Then follow these steps:

1. Remove the PROBIZTALK Deploy Sample Application:

   a. In the BizTalk Server 2006 Administration Console, expand BizTalk Server 2006 ➤ BizTalk Group ➤ Applications ➤ PROBIZTALK Deploy Sample Application.

   b. Right-click the PROBIZTALK Deploy Sample Application and then select Stop.

   c. In the Stop 'PROBIZTALK Deploy Sample Application' window shown in Figure 10-14, select the Full Stop – Terminate instances radio button and then click Stop.

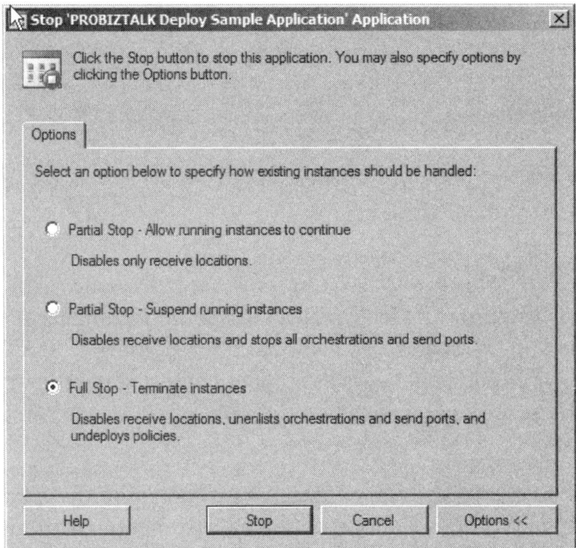

Figure 10-14. *Stop Application dialog*

   d. In the BizTalk Server 2006 Administration Console, right-click the PROBIZTALK Deploy Sample Application and then select Delete.

   e. In the confirmation message box, click the OK button. Then, close the BizTalk Server 2006 Administration Console.

2. Import the PROBIZTALK Deploy Sample Application:

   a. Open the Visual Studio 2005 Command Prompt.

   b. In the Visual Studio 2005 Command Prompt, execute the following command: `BTSTask ImportApp /Package:C:\ProBizTalkSample.msi /Environment:Testing /ApplicationName:"PROBIZTALK Deploy Sample Application" /Overwrite`.

   c. If the script was executed successfully, the content of the command prompt will resemble Figure 10-15.

```
Visual Studio 2005 Command Prompt
Information: Updating binding information.
ConnectionString="Data Source=PROBIZTALK;Initial Catalog=BizTalkMgmtDb;Integrate
d Security=True;Enlist=True;Application Name=Microsoft.BizTalk.ApplicationDeploy
ment.Engine"
Information: Updating send ports, send port groups, and receive ports...
Information: Updated "[Send port "SendGreetingsResponsePort"]"
Information: Updated "[Receive location "ReceiveGreetingsPortFILE"]"
Information: Updated "[Receive port "ReceiveGreetingsPort"]"
Information: Updating parties and enlistments...
Information: Updating orchestration bindings...
Information: Successfully updated binding information.
Information: Commit the change requests...
* Performing EndTypeChangeRequest for resource type "System.BizTalk:PreProcessin
gScript".
* Performing EndTypeChangeRequest for resource type "System.BizTalk:BizTalkAssem
bly".
* Performing EndTypeChangeRequest for resource type "System.BizTalk:BizTalkBindi
ng".
Information: Imported package into application "PROBIZTALK DeploySample Applicat
ion".

Command succeeded with 0 errors, 0 warnings.

C:\Program Files\Microsoft Visual Studio 8\VC>
```

Figure 10-15. *BizTalk Server MSI import using the BTSTask console application*

Typical Deployment Cycle

In the previous sections, you learned how to deploy a BizTalk solution manually and using the MSI export and import method. In this section, you will learn how to move a BizTalk application from the development environment all the way to production using the steps outlined in the preceding two sections. There are five main steps to move an application from one environment to another:

1. **Deploy from Visual Studio 2005 the assemblies in a BizTalk solution**: In this step, the BizTalk developers deploy a BizTalk solution on their development environment. Once the developers have tested their BizTalk application adequately, they proceed to the next step.

2. **Add BizTalk artifacts to the deployed BizTalk application**: In this step, the BizTalk developers or the integrators add artifacts to the BizTalk application in order to deploy their solution to another environment or BizTalk Server Group. Typically, this step involves creating new binding files specific to the next target environment, adding processing scripts to automate as much as possible the installation of the BizTalk MSI application to the next target environment, and adding any other BizTalk artifact (like certificates and readme files) necessary on the target environment.

3. **Export the BizTalk application to an MSI file**: In this step, the developers or the integrators proceed to export the modified BizTalk application to an MSI file using the BizTalk Administration Console or the BTSTask command-line tool. They will have to decide whether or not they want to create one or more MSI packages and what BizTalk artifact they wish to include in them.

4. **Import and install the MSI file**: Once the MSI package or packages are ready, it is time to import and install them on the target environment. The MSI file will register all BizTalk artifacts in the target environment's BizTalk Management Database. It will also copy and register in the GAC or in the Windows' registry all .NET assemblies and COM libraries on the BizTalk servers where the packages are installed. Please keep in mind that you must install the MSI file on each BizTalk server in a BizTalk Server Group.

5. **Start the application and verify that it is functioning correctly**: At this point, the BizTalk developer or integrator starts and tests the newly installed BizTalk application. Once that person is satisfied with the results, he can repeat steps 2 through 5 to deploy the BizTalk application to other staging environments until he eventually releases the BizTalk application to production.

Administrative Tools

BizTalk 2006 provides different tools to manage BizTalk Server applications:

- BizTalk Administration Console MMC
- BTSTask command-line tool
- BTSDeploy command-line tool (deprecated and its usage is not recommended by Microsoft)
- WMI and the ExplorerOM APIs

Each of these tools allows you to deploy and manage your solutions. While BizTalk Administration Console has been changed and improved significantly in BizTalk Server 2006, it is, as most UI tools, not intended to automate administration tasks. The BTSTask and BTSDeploy command-line tools can be used in batch files to perform automation tasks, but batch files are still not as flexible as full-featured programming languages like C# or VB .NET. If you are an experienced developer, you know that real-world projects can easily contain hundreds and even thousands of artifacts. Managing them manually is a daunting and error-prone task and in many cases simply hardly possible. To address these kinds of problems, Microsoft provides two APIs—Windows Management Instrumentation (WMI) and ExplorerOM, which allow you to write your own custom utilities to address all aspects of managing and configuring a BizTalk Server and a BizTalk Server Group.

As shown in Tables 10-6 to 10-15, the tools have an overlapping functionality, and for the most common BizTalk tasks you can use any of them. However, for some tasks you will have a more limited set of tools to choose from. Tables 10-6 through 10-15 list common management tasks and indicate what tools are available to perform each of them.

Table 10-6. *Application Tasks*

Task	Administration Console	BTSTask Tool	WMI	ExplorerOM
Creating a new application	X	X		X
Modifying application properties	X	X		X (but you can't modify the `Default Application` property)
Deleting an application	X	X		X

Table 10-7. *Assembly Tasks*

Task	Administration Console	BTSTask Tool	WMI	ExplorerOM
Deploying an assembly	X	X	X	
Undeploying an assembly	X	X		

Table 10-8. *Host Tasks*

Task	Administration Console	BTSTask Tool	WMI	ExplorerOM
Creating a new host	X		X	
Modifying a host	X		X	
Deleting a host	X		X	
Starting/stopping/modifying host instances	X		X	

Table 10-9. *Orchestration Tasks*

Task	Administration Console	BTSTask Tool	WMI	ExplorerOM
Browsing orchestration artifacts	X	X	X	X
Finding roles used or implemented by orchestration				X
Binding/enlisting/starting orchestrations	X	Only if BTSTask makes use of processing scripts that internally use WMI or ExplorerOM	X	X
Stopping/unenlisting/unbinding orchestrations	X	Only if BTSTask makes use of processing scripts that internally use WMI or ExplorerOM	X	X

Table 10-10. *Send Port Tasks*

Task	Administration Console	BTSTask Tool	WMI	ExplorerOM
Adding/enlisting/starting a send port	X		X	X
Stopping/unenlisting/deleting a send port	X		X	X
Modifying port properties	X	Only if BTSTask applies binding files	X	X
Managing send port certificates	X	Only if BTSTask applies binding files	X	X
Adding/editing filtering expressions	X	Only if BTSTask applies binding files	X	X
Adding/removing maps for inbound/outbound transformation	X	Only if BTSTask applies binding files	X	X

Table 10-11. *Send Port Group Tasks*

Task	Administration Console	BTSTask Tool	WMI	ExplorerOM
Adding/enlisting/starting a send port group	X		X	X
Stopping/unenlisting/deleting a send port	X		X	X
Adding/deleting a port to/from a send port group	X	Only if BTSTask applies binding files	X	X
Adding a filter to a send port group	X	Only if BTSTask applies binding files	X	X

Table 10-12. *Receive Port Tasks*

Task	Administration Console	BTSTask Tool	WMI	ExplorerOM
Adding/modifying/deleting a receive port	X	Only if BTSTask applies binding files	X	X
Adding a map to inbound/outbound transformations	X	Only if BTSTask applies binding files	X	X

Table 10-13. *Receive Location Tasks*

Task	Administration Console	BTSTask Tool	WMI	ExplorerOM
Adding/editing/deleting a receive location	X	Only if BTSTask applies binding files	X	X
Enabling/disabling a receive location	X	Only if BTSTask applies binding files	X	X

Table 10-14. *Party Tasks*

Task	Administration Console	BTSTask Tool	WMI	ExplorerOM
Adding/deleting a party	X	X		X
Enlisting/unenlisting a party	X	X		X
Adding/deleting a send port to/from a party		Only if BTSTask applies binding files		X
Adding an alias to a party		Only if BTSTask applies binding files		X
Adding a certificate for a party		Only if BTSTask applies binding files		X

Table 10-15. *Messagebox Tasks*

Task	Administration Console	BTSTask Tool	WMI	ExplorerOM
Adding/deleting a Messagebox	X		X	
Editing Messagebox properties	X		X	

BizTalk Administration Console

The BizTalk Administration Console, shown in Figure 10-16, is a Microsoft Management Console (MMC). This tool is the only one that comes with a Windows graphical UI. It is also the easiest one to use for novices.

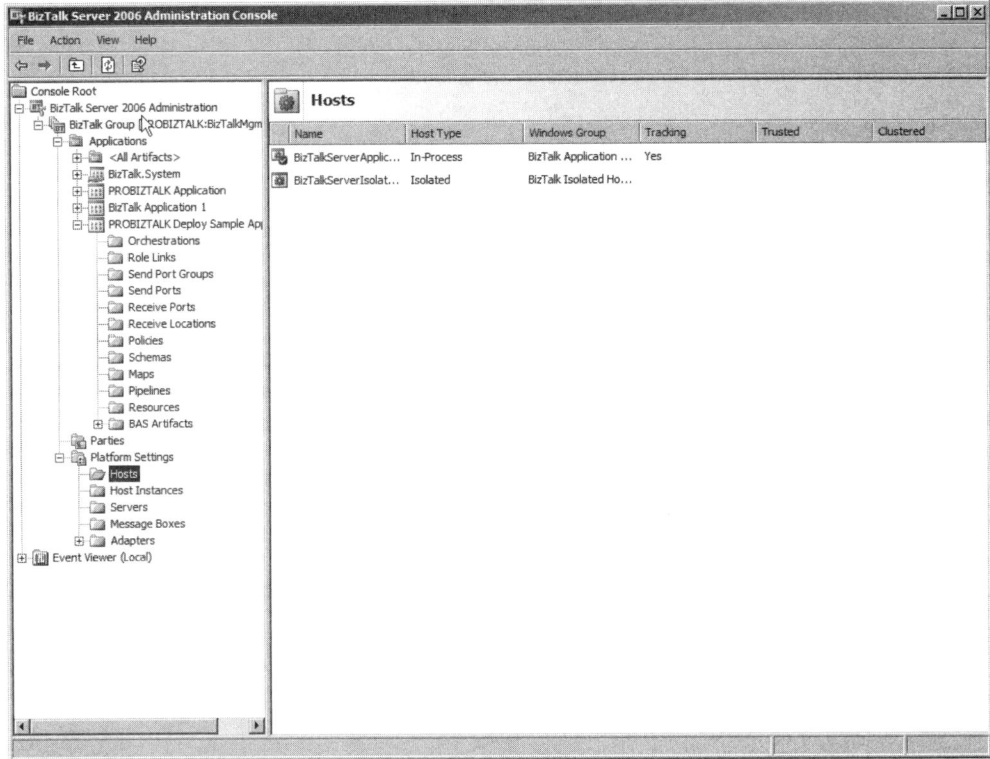

Figure 10-16. *BizTalk Server 2006 Administration Console*

If you have used the Administration Console with BizTalk Server 2004, you will be pleased to know that the new Administration Console has gone through a major overhaul. It now has a new slick look, and most importantly you can finally administer every aspect of your BizTalk Server Groups and BizTalk servers. With the Administration Console you can

- Add, configure, remove, and uninstall a BizTalk application.
- Import and export a BizTalk application as an MSI.
- Import and export binding files.
- Create, configure, and delete ports and receive locations.
- Configure, start, stop, enlist, and unenlist ports and orchestrations.
- Create, configure, delete, and install hosts and host instances.
- Manage and configure parties.

■Note If you are working on a BizTalk Server 2004 project, we suggest that you download the BizTalk 2004 Management Tool by Paul Somers available on the GotDotNet web site (www.gotdotnet.com/workspaces/workspace.aspx?id=992ca223-553c-475a-ac87-da7ae2c9016a). This tool will allow you to administer your BizTalk servers from a Windows application without having to install development tools (like Visual Studio) on your integration, testing, and production environments.

BTSTask

BTSTask is the new command-prompt application that replaces BizTalk 2004's BTSDeploy command-prompt application. Unlike BTSDeploy, BTSTask does not come with a wizard. If developers or administrators want to use a GUI, they must use the BizTalk Administration Console.

This application allows you to

- Add, enumerate, remove, and uninstall BizTalk applications.
- Add, list, and remove artifacts (assemblies, bindings, pre-processing scripts, and post-processing scripts) from a BizTalk application.
- Export and import BizTalk applications from an MSI file.
- Export and import binding information from BizTalk binding files.
- List all BizTalk applications in the BizTalk Management Database for the BizTalk Group.
- List the resources in an MSI file.

The sample shown in Figure 10-17 creates an application named PROBIZTALK Application using the BTSTask command-line application. If you open the BizTalk Administration Console, you will see the newly created application. For the full list of the command options, please refer to the product documentation.

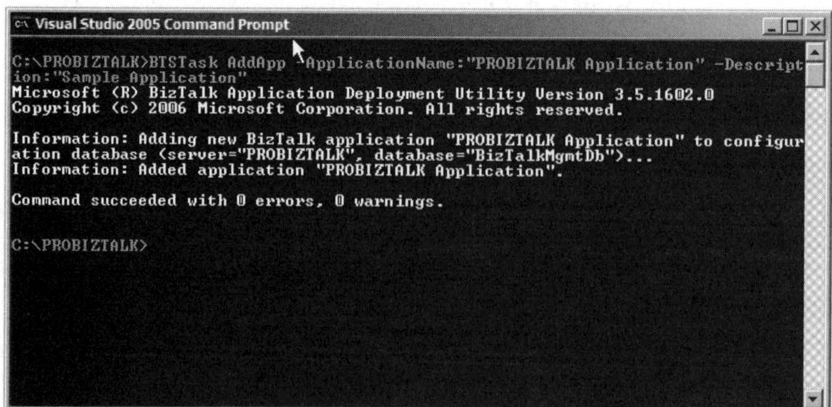

Figure 10-17. *BTSTask add application example*

BTSDeploy

In BizTalk 2004, the BTSDeploy command-line application allowed you to

- Deploy and remove assemblies from the Management Database.
- Import and export bindings.

BizTalk 2006 still includes the BTSDeploy tool (minus the BTSDeploy Wizard) for backward compatibility. However, BTSDeploy is now deprecated, and Microsoft recommends converting all scripts or applications to use BTSTask instead of BTSDeploy.

WMI

Windows Management Instrumentation provides a standard way of managing a computer system. WMI allows you to

- Gather information about systems.
- Configure systems.
- Fire or consume specific WMI events occurring on computers or servers.

Tables 10-16 and 10-17 describe the different BizTalk WMI classes and events. To utilize these classes, you must use the WMI COM API or the System.Management assembly, which is a .NET COM Interop assembly. Listing 10-3 demonstrates how to create a host using WMI API from managed code.

Table 10-16. *BizTalk WMI Classes*

WMI Class Name	Specific Methods	Purpose
`MSBTS_AdapterSetting`	None	Registers new adapters.
`MSBTS_DeploymentService`	`Deploy`, `Export`, `Import`, `Remove`	Deploys/undeploys assemblies and imports/exports binding files.
`MSBTS_GroupSetting`	`RegisterLocalServer`, `UnRegisterLocalServer`	Represents information about BTS Groups.
`MSBTS_Host`	`Start`, `Stop`	Represents a host. Used to start/stop all host instances in a given BizTalk host. It is also used to get/set host properties.
`MSBTS_HostInstance`	`GetState`, `Install`, `Start`, `Stop`, `Uninstall`	Represents a host instance. Used to install/uninstall and start/stop a specific host instance in a given BizTalk host.
`MSBTS_HostInstanceSetting`	None	Represents host settings.
`MSBTS_HostQueue`	`ResumeServiceInstancesByID`, `SuspendServiceInstancesByID`, `TerminateServiceInstancesByID`	Resumes, suspends, or terminates service instances.
`MSBTS_HostSetting`	None	Sets host settings.

Continued

Table 10-16. *Continued*

WMI Class Name	Specific Methods	Purpose
MSBTS_MessageInstance	SaveToFile	Represents a message instance.
MSBTS_MsgBoxSetting	ForceDelete	Represents a single Messagebox setting in the BizTalk Server Group.
MSBTS_Orchestration	Enlist, QueryDependencyInfo, QueryInstanceInfo, Start, Stop, Unenlist	Represents an orchestration. Used to start/stop and enlist/unenlist orchestrations.
MSBTS_ReceiveHandler	None	Represents a receive handler. Used to configure receive handlers.
MSBTS_ReceiveLocation	Disable, Enable	Represents a receive location. Used to enable and disable the receive location.
MSBTS_ReceiveLocation Orchestration	None	Represents all possible combinations of orchestrations and receive locations.
MSBTS_ReceivePort	None	Represents a receive port. Used to configure receive ports.
MSBTS_SendHandler	None	Represents a send handler. Used to configure send handlers.
MSBTS_SendPort	Enlist, Start, Stop, Unenlist	Represents a send port. Used to configure send ports.
MSBTS_SendPortGroup	Enlist, Start, Stop, UnEnlist	Represents a send port group. Used to start/stop and enlist/unenlist send port groups.
MSBTS_SendPortGroup2 SendPort	None	Represents a many-to-many relationship between send port groups and send ports.
MSBTS_Server	CheckIfCanInstallHost Instances, Start, Stop	Represents a computer within a BizTalk Server Group. Used to start services on a given server.
MSBTS_ServerHost	ForceUnmap, Map, Unmap	Represents a mapping between BizTalk hosts and host instances. Used to map and unmap relationships.
MSBTS_ServiceInstance	Resume, Suspend, Terminate	Represents an instance of a service. Used to resume, suspend, and terminate services.
MSBTS_TrackedMessage Instance	SaveToFile	Represents a tracked message instance saved in the Messagebox or Archive databases. Used to save a message to a file.

Table 10-17. *BizTalk WMI Events*

WMI Event Name	Specific Properties	Purpose
MSTBS_MessageInstance SuspendentEvent	ErrorCategory, ErrorDescription, ErrorId, HostName, Message InstanceID, MessageType, ReferenceType, ServiceClass, ServiceClassID, Service InstanceID, ServiceTypeID	Represents a suspended event for a BizTalk Message Queuing (MSMQT) message instance
MSTBS_ServiceInstance SuspendentEvent	ErrorCategory, ErrorDescription, ErrorId, HostName, InstanceID, ServiceClass, ServiceClassID, ServiceStatus, ServiceTypeID	Represents a suspended event for a service instance

Listing 10-3. *Create Host Example Using Managed Code*

```
[C#]
using System.Management;

      // Basic WMI operation - Create
      // sample to show MSBTS_HostSetting instance creation
      public void CreateHost(string ServerName, string HostName, int HostType, ➥
string NTGroupName, bool AuthTrusted)
      {
         try
         {
            PutOptions options = new PutOptions();
            options.Type = PutType.CreateOnly;

            // Create a ManagementClass object and spawn a ManagementObject instance
            ManagementClass objHostSettingClass = new ManagementClass("\\\\" + ➥
ServerName + "\\root\\MicrosoftBizTalkServer", "MSBTS_HostSetting", null);
            ManagementObject objHostSetting  = objHostSettingClass.CreateInstance();

            // Set the properties for the Host
            objHostSetting["Name"] = HostName;
            objHostSetting["HostType"] = HostType;
            objHostSetting["NTGroupName"] = NTGroupName;
            objHostSetting["AuthTrusted"] = AuthTrusted;

            // Creating the host
            objHostSetting.Put(options);
            System.Console.WriteLine(string.Format("The Host '{0}'has been ➥
created successfully", HostName ));
         }
         catch(Exception ex)
```

```
        {
            System.Console.WriteLine("CreateHost - " + HostName + ➥
" - failed: " + ex.Message);
        }
    }
```

The same example using VBScript instead of managed code is shown in Listing 10-4.

Listing 10-4. *Create Host Example Using VBScript*

```
[VBScript]
Option Explicit
' wbemChangeFlagEnum Setting
const UpdateOnly = 1
const CreateOnly = 2
Sub CreateHost (ServerName, HostName, HostType, NTGroupName, AuthTrusted)
   On Error Resume Next
   Dim objLocator, objService, objHostSetting, objHS

   ' Connects to local server WMI Provider BizTalk namespace
   Set objLocator = Createobject ("wbemScripting.SwbemLocator")
   Set objService = objLocator.ConnectServer(ServerName, ➥
"root/MicrosoftBizTalkServer")

   ' Get WMI class MSBTS_HostSetting
   Set objHostSetting = objService.Get ("MSBTS_HostSetting")

   Set objHS = objHostSetting.SpawnInstance_

   objHS.Name = HostName
   objHS.HostType = HostType
   objHS.NTGroupName = NTGroupName
   objHS.AuthTrusted = AuthTrusted

   ' Create Host
   objHS.Put_(CreateOnly)

   CheckWMIError
   wscript.echo "Host - " & HostName & " - has been created successfully"
end Sub
```

Another interesting task you can accomplish with WMI is to subscribe to the `MSTBS_MessageInstanceSuspendentEvent` and `MSTBS_ServiceInstanceSuspendentEvent`. Consuming these events will allow you to handle certain situations gracefully in your BizTalk solution. For instance, when a mapping error occurs on a send or receive port, you could decide to send an e-mail to an administrator and automatically terminate the service instance. Listing 10-5 shows how to subscribe to a WMI event.

Listing 10-5. *Subscribing to a BizTalk WMI Event*

```
using System.Management;

static public void ListenForSvcInstSuspendEvent()
 {
     try
     {
        // Set up an event watcher and a handler for the ➥
MSBTS_ServiceInstanceSuspendedEvent event
       ManagementEventWatcher watcher = ➥
new ManagementEventWatcher( new ManagementScope("root\\MicrosoftBizTalkServer"),➥
new EventQuery("SELECT * FROM MSBTS_ServiceInstanceSuspendedEvent") );

        watcher.EventArrived += new EventArrivedEventHandler(MyEventHandler);

        // Start watching for MSBTS_ServiceInstanceSuspendedEvent events
        watcher.Start();

        Console.WriteLine("Press enter to quit");
        Console.ReadLine();
        watcher.Stop();
     }
     catch (Exception ex)
     {
        Console.WriteLine("Error: " + ex.Message);
     }
  }

  static public void MyEventHandler(object sender, EventArrivedEventArgs e)
  {
     // Print out the service instance ID and error description upon receiving
     // of the suspend event
     Console.WriteLine("A MSBTS_ServiceInstanceSuspendEvent has occurred!");
     Console.WriteLine(string.Format("ServiceInstanceID: {0}", ➥
e.NewEvent["InstanceID"]));
     Console.WriteLine(string.Format("ErrorDescription: {0}", ➥
e.NewEvent["ErrorDescription"]));
     Console.WriteLine("");
  }
```

ExplorerOM

The ExplorerOM object model is a set of classes and interfaces from the `ExplorerOM` namespace used by BizTalk Explorer to configure applications. You can consider ExplorerOM as an API to the Management Database that allows you to perform application management and configuration tasks. To use it in your .NET applications, you have to add a reference to the [BizTalk Installation directory]\Developer Tools\Microsoft.Biztalk.ExplorerOM.dll assembly. All artifacts in ExplorerOM are stored in collections, and there are three classes hosting collections of artifacts, as listed in Table 10-18.

Table 10-18. *ExplorerOM Container Classes*

Class	Description
`BtsCatalogExplorer`	Provides methods and properties to manipulate artifacts at the BizTalk Server Group level
`BtsApplication`	Provides methods and properties to manipulate artifacts at the BizTalk application level
`Assembly`	Provides properties to access artifacts at the assembly level

BtsCatalogExplorer Class

This class provides access to all artifacts in the Management Database, regardless of their association with a specific BizTalk application or assembly. You can also use this class to add or remove artifacts from the different collections and then commit changes to the Management Database. This class is the most fundamental, since all ExplorerOM code you write will have one thing in common: instantiating the `BtsCatalogExplorer` class and setting the `ConnectionString` property to access the Management Database.

Table 10-19 lists the properties of the `BtsCatalogExplorer` class. As you can guess, all these properties except the `ConnectionString` property are collections of different BizTalk artifacts stored in the Management Database.

Table 10-19. *BtsCatalogExplorer Properties*

Property Name	Description
`ConnectionString`	Connection string to the Management Database.
`Applications`	Read-only. Returns a collection of applications in the Management Database. This property is specific to BizTalk Server 2006 and absent in BizTalk 2004.
`Assemblies`	Read-only. Returns a collection of deployed assemblies.
`Certificates`	Read-only. Returns a collection of certificates installed on the computer.
`Hosts`	Read-only. Returns a collection of hosts in the Management Database.
`Parties`	Read-only. Returns a collection of parties in the Management Database.
`Pipelines`	Read-only. Returns a collection of pipelines in the Management Database.
`ProtocolTypes`	Read-only. Returns a collection of protocol types in the Management Database.
`ReceiveHandlers`	Read-only. Returns a collection of receive handlers in the Management Database.
`ReceivePorts`	Read-only. Returns a collection of receive ports in the Management Database.
`Schemas`	Read-only. Returns a collection of schemas in the Management Database.

Property Name	Description
SendPortGroups	Read-only. Returns a collection of send port groups in the Management Database.
SendPorts	Read-only. Returns a collection of send ports in the Management Database.
StandardAliases	Read-only. Returns a collection of standard aliases.
Transforms	Read-only. Returns a collection of transforms.

Let's put everything mentioned previously in practice and write a utility that enumerates all send ports in the Management Database and prints out the port name and status as shown in Listing 10-6.

Listing 10-6. *Enumeration of Send Ports*

```
using System;
using System.Text;
using Microsoft.BizTalk.ExplorerOM;

namespace SendPorts
{
    class Program
    {

        static void Main(string[] args)
        {
            EnumerateSendPorts();
            Console.ReadKey();
        }

        public static void EnumerateSendPorts()
        {
            BtsCatalogExplorer catalog = new BtsCatalogExplorer();
            catalog.ConnectionString = "Server=.;Initial Catalog=BizTalkMgmtDb; ➥
Integrated Security=SSPI;";


            foreach (SendPort sendPort in catalog.SendPorts )
            {
                Console.WriteLine("\tPortName:{0},Status:{1}",
                     sendPort.Name ,sendPort.Status);


            }
        }
    }
}
```

Alternatively, you can get access to the collections of artifacts exposed by the BtsCatalog-Explorer class by calling the GetCollection method and passing as a parameter values from the CollectionType enumeration. The member names of this enumeration are exactly the same as the names of the properties of the BtsCatalogExplorer class. Listing 10-7 shows how to print out port names and status using the GetCollection method.

Listing 10-7. *Enumeration of Send Ports Using the GetCollection Method*

```
using System;
using System.Text;
using Microsoft.BizTalk.ExplorerOM;

namespace SendPorts
{
    class Program
    {

        static void Main(string[] args)
        {
            EnumerateSendPorts();
            Console.ReadKey();
        }

        public static void EnumerateSendPorts()
        {
            BtsCatalogExplorer catalog = new BtsCatalogExplorer();
            catalog.ConnectionString = "Server=.;Initial Catalog=BizTalkMgmtDb; ➥
Integrated Security=SSPI;";
            SendPortCollection spCollection = ➥
(SendPortCollection)catalog.GetCollection(CollectionType.SendPort);

            foreach (SendPort sendPort in spCollection)
            {
                Console.WriteLine("\tPortName:{0},Status:{1}",
                    sendPort.Name, sendPort.Status);

            }
        }
    }
}
```

The BtsCatalogExplorer class not only allows you to walk through existing artifacts, but also provides methods to add, delete, and configure them and commit changes to the Management Database. Table 10-20 lists such methods.

Table 10-20. *BtsCatalogExplorer Methods*

Method Name	Description
AddNewApplication	Creates and adds a new Application object to the Application collection. Specific to BizTalk Server 2006.
RemoveApplication	Removes the specified application from Application collection. Specific to BizTalk 2006.
AddNewParty	Creates and adds a new Party object to the Parties collection.
RemoveParty	Removes the specified party from the Parties collection.
AddNewReceivePort	Creates and adds a new ReceivePort object to the ReceivePorts collection.
RemoveReceivePort	Removes the specified receive port from the ReceivePorts collection.
AddNewSendPort	Creates and adds a new SendPort object to the SendPorts collection.
RemoveSendPort	Removes the specified send port from the SendPorts collection.
AddNewSendPortGroup	Creates and adds a new SendPortGroup object to the SendPortGroups collection.
RemoveSendPortGroup	Removes the specified send port group.
SaveChanges	Commits all BtsCatalogExplorer object changes to the Management Database.
DiscardChanges	Discards all BtsCatalogExplorer object changes.

The code in Listing 10-8 shows how to create a send port using the AddNewSendPort method of the BtsCatalogExplorer class.

Listing 10-8. *Creating a New Send Port Using the AddNewSendPort Method*

```
using System;
using Microsoft.BizTalk.ExplorerOM

namespace AddSendPort
{
    class Program
    {
        static void Main(string[] args)
        {
            CreateSendPort();

        }


        private static void CreateSendPort()
        {
            // Connect to the BizTalk configuration database
           BtsCatalogExplorer catalog = new BtsCatalogExplorer();
            catalog.ConnectionString = "Server=PROBIZTALK;Initial Catalog= ➥
BizTalkMgmtDb;Integrated Security=SSPI;";
```

```
            try
            {
               // Create static one-way send port
                SendPort myStaticOnewaySendPort = ➥
catalog.AddNewSendPort(false, false);
                myStaticOnewaySendPort.Name = "PROBiztalkSendPort";
                myStaticOnewaySendPort.PrimaryTransport.TransportType = ➥
catalog.ProtocolTypes["HTTP"];
                myStaticOnewaySendPort.PrimaryTransport.Address = ➥
"http://DestinationUrl";
                myStaticOnewaySendPort.SendPipeline = ➥
catalog.Pipelines["Microsoft.BizTalk.DefaultPipelines.XMLTransmit"];

                // Commit changes to BizTalk configuration database
                catalog.SaveChanges();
            }
            catch (Exception ex)
            {
                catalog.DiscardChanges();
            }
        }

    }
}
```

In the beginning of this chapter, we mentioned that in BizTalk Server 2006 all artifacts must be associated with a BizTalk application. It is important to note that the code in Listing 10-8 adds a new port and associates it automatically with the current default application. How to associate artifacts with a specific application will be discussed in the next section, which we devote to the `Application` class.

Application Class

The second class hosting collections of BizTalk artifacts is the `Application` class. As you can guess, this class provides similar methods and properties as the `BtsCatalogExplorer` class. The main difference is that the `Application` class deals with the artifacts belonging to a specific application.

If you want to perform actions on the artifacts belonging to a specific BizTalk application, you have to obtain a reference on the desired application and then use the methods and properties of the `Application` class listed in Tables 10-21 and 10-22.

Table 10-21. *Application Class Properties*

Property Name	Description
`Assemblies`	Read-only. Returns a collection of assemblies associated with the application.
`BackReferences`	Read-only. Returns a collection of applications referencing the application.
`BtsCatalogExplorer`	Read-only. Returns the `BtsCatalogExplorer` object containing the `Application` object.
`Description`	Gets or sets the application description.
`IsConfigured`	Read-only. Returns a Boolean value indicating that all orchestrations' ports in the application are bound.
`IsDefaultApplication`	Read-only. Returns a Boolean value indicating whether or not the application is the default application.
`IsSystem`	Read-only. Returns a Boolean value indicating whether or not the application is the system application.
`Name`	Gets or sets the name of the application.
`Orchestrations`	Read-only. Returns a collection of the orchestrations associated with the application.
`Pipelines`	Read-only. Returns a collection of the pipelines associated with the application.
`Policies`	Read-only. Returns a collection of the policies associated with the application.
`ReceivePorts`	Read-only. Returns a collection of the receive ports associated with the application.
`References`	Read-only. Returns a collection of the applications referenced by the application.
`Roles`	Read-only. Returns a collection of the roles associated with the application.
`Schemas`	Read-only. Returns a collection of the schemas associated with the application.
`SendPortGroups`	Read-only. Returns a collection of send port groups associated with the application.
`SendPorts`	Read-only. Returns a collection of the send ports associated with the application.
`Status`	Read-only. Returns the status of the application.
`Transforms`	Read-only. Returns a collection of the maps associated with the application.

Table 10-22. *Application Class Public Methods*

Method Name	Description
AddNewReceivePort	Adds a new receive port to the ReceivePorts collection
AddNewSendPort	Adds a new send port to the SendPorts collection
AddNewSendPortGroup	Adds a new send port group to the SendPortGroups collection
AddReference	Adds a BizTalk application to the References collection
RemoveReference	Removes a BizTalk application from the References collection
Start	Starts all orchestrations, send ports, and send port groups, and enables all receive locations belonging to this and referenced applications
Stop	Stops all orchestrations, send ports, and send port groups, and disables all receive locations belonging to this and referenced applications

Assuming you have an application named PROBIZTALK Application, the code in Listing 10-9 shows how you can obtain a reference to this application and to add a send port to it.

Listing 10-9. *Adding a New Send Port to a Specific BizTalk Application*

```
using System;
using Microsoft.BizTalk.ExplorerOM

namespace AddSendPort
{
    class Program
    {
        static void Main(string[] args)
        {
            CreateSendPort();

        }


        private static void CreateSendPort()
        {
            // Connect to the BizTalk configuration database
           BtsCatalogExplorer catalog = new BtsCatalogExplorer();
            catalog.ConnectionString = "Server=PROBIZTALK;Initial Catalog= ➥
BizTalkMgmtDb;Integrated Security=SSPI;";

            try
            {
               // Get a reference on existing BizTalk Application
               Application app = catalog.Applications["PROBIZTALK Application"]
```

```
                // Create static one-way send port
                SendPort myStaticOnewaySendPort = app.AddNewSendPort(false, false);
                myStaticOnewaySendPort.Name = "PROBiztalkSendPort";
                myStaticOnewaySendPort.PrimaryTransport.TransportType = ➥
catalog.ProtocolTypes["HTTP"];
                myStaticOnewaySendPort.PrimaryTransport.Address = ➥
"http://DestinationUrl";
                myStaticOnewaySendPort.SendPipeline = ➥
catalog.Pipelines["Microsoft.BizTalk.DefaultPipelines.XMLTransmit"];

                // Commit changes to BizTalk configuration database
                catalog.SaveChanges();
            }
            catch (Exception ex)
            {
                catalog.DiscardChanges();
            }
        }
    }
}
```

If you happened to work with previous versions of BizTalk Server, you are no doubt aware that starting BizTalk solutions was not easy. For example, if one orchestration called another, they had to be started and stopped in the following strict order: called orchestrations first, calling orchestrations last in case of starting, and in reverse order in case of stopping. Not a problem if you only had a few orchestrations, but what if there were dozens of them and they were interdependent? And how about starting dozens or even hundreds of ports one by one manually? Fortunately, BizTalk Server 2006 provides an easy solution. Simply use the `Start` and `Stop` methods of the `Application` class, taking values from the `ApplicationStartOption` and `ApplicationStopOption` enumerations as parameters. Available values are listed in Tables 10-23 and 10-24.

Table 10-23. *ApplicationStartOption Enumeration*

Enumeration Value	Description
DeployAllPolicies	Specifies all policies to be deployed
EnableAllReceiveLocations	Specifies all receive locations to be enabled
StartAllOrchestrations	Specifies all orchestrations to be started
StartAllSendPortGroups	Specifies all send port groups to be started
StartAllSendPorts	Specifies all send ports to be started
StartReferencedApplications	Specifies all referenced applications to be started
StartAll	Specifies all of the preceding to be enabled and started

Table 10-24. *ApplicationStopOption Enumeration*

Enumeration Value	Description
UndeployAllPolicies	Specifies all policies to be undeployed
DisableAllReceiveLocations	Specifies all receive locations to be disabled
UnenlistAllOrchestrations	Specifies all orchestrations to be unenlisted and stopped
UnenlistAllSendPortGroups	Specifies all send port groups to be unenlisted and stopped
UnenlistAllSendPorts	Specifies all send ports to be unenlisted and stopped
StopReferencedApplications	Specifies referenced applications to be stopped
StopAll	Specifies all of the preceding options

In order to start your application, you can use the code shown in Listing 10-10.

Listing 10-10. *Starting Biztalk Application*

```
using System;
using Microsoft.BizTalk.ExplorerOM;

namespace BTSApplication
{
    class Program
    {

        static void Main(string[] args)
        {
            BtsCatalogExplorer catalog = new BtsCatalogExplorer();
            catalog.ConnectionString = "Server=.;Initial Catalog=BizTalkMgmtDb; ➥
Integrated Security=SSPI;";
            Application app = catalog.Applications["PROBIZTALK Application"]
            app.Start(StartApplicationOptions.StartAll);

        }

    }
}
```

BtsAssembly

The last class we are going to consider in this section is the `BtsAssembly`. Using the properties of this class listed in Table 10-25, you can get access to the collections of compiled artifacts contained in the assembly.

Table 10-25. *BtsAssembly Class Properties*

Property Name	Description
`Application`	Read-only. Returns the application this assembly is associated with.
`BtsCatalogExplorer`	Read-only. Returns the `IBtsCatalogExplorer` interface, which represents the database hosting the assembly.
`Culture`	Read-only. Returns the culture of the assembly.
`DisplayName`	Read-only. Returns the display name of the assembly.
`IsSystem`	Read-only. Indicates whether or not the assembly is system (deployed during Biztalk installation).
`Name`	Read-only. Returns the name of the assembly.
`Orchestrations`	Read-only. Returns the collection of orchestrations in the assembly.
`Pipelines`	Read-only. Returns the collection of pipelines in the assembly.
`PortTypes`	Read-only. Returns the collection of port types in the assembly.
`PublicToken`	Read-only. Returns the public token of the assembly.
`Roles`	Read-only. Returns the collection of roles in the assembly.
`Schemas`	Read-only. Returns the collection of schemas in the assembly.
`Transforms`	Read-only. Returns the collection of maps in the assembly.
`Version`	Read-only. Returns the version of the assembly.

Assuming you have a deployed assembly named BTSOrchestrations, Listing 10-11 shows how you can print out orchestration names contained in this assembly using properties of the `BtsAssembly` class.

Listing 10-11. *Enumerating Orchestrations*

```
using System;
using System.Text;
using Microsoft.BizTalk.ExplorerOM;

namespace EnumerateOrchestrations
{
    class Program
    {

        static void Main(string[] args)
        {
            EnumerateOrchestrations();
            Console.ReadKey();
        }
```

```
        public static void EnumerateOrchestrations()
        {
            BtsCatalogExplorer catalog = new BtsCatalogExplorer();
            catalog.ConnectionString = "Server=.;Initial Catalog=BizTalkMgmtDb; ➥
Integrated Security=SSPI;";
            BtsAssembly assembly = catalog.Assemblies["BTSOrchestrations"];

            foreach (BtsOrchestration orch in assembly.Orchestrations )
            {
                Console.WriteLine("\tOrchestrationName:{0}",
                     orch.FullName);

            }
        }
    }
}
```

As you see, programming using ExplorerOM is not very complicated. Once you get a fundamental idea how classes representing BizTalk artifacts are related to each other, the rest will be quite straightforward. For the full list of classes and interfaces, please refer to the product documentation.

CHAPTER 11

To Tune or Not to Tune? Nobody Should Ask That Question.

Gathering metrics to serve as the baseline for your stress and performance tests should be part of your requirements gathering. Such metrics will help you identify the maximum load that the application and environment can handle before they break as well as the maximum sustainable load that can be processed, which will become the performance goals for your solution and constitute your performance release criteria.

What You Should Do First

The solution is fully developed and ready; now what? Well, since you are about to go to production, the assumption is that the application went through rigorous functional and integration testing. So what is next? Performance testing and performance tuning! To ensure a successful deployment in production, you need to gather performance statistics and come up with the proper configuration to tune your production environment.

Gather Metrics on Expected Loads

Metrics should have been gathered as part of the requirements, but if this did not happen, now would be the right time for it. If this solution is replacing an existing application or set of applications in your production environment, gathering statistics should be an easy task, and you most probably had them before you started. If this is a brand new business application, you have to base your numbers on the expected number of users and transactions to extrapolate the number of messages and concurrent requests going through your applications.

Those metrics will then serve as the baseline for your stress and performance tests. You have to identify the maximum load that the application and environment can handle before they break as well as the maximum sustainable load that can be processed. The **maximum sustainable load** is the maximum load that your application can handle indefinitely in the production environment. This is not only a function of your solution, but also a function of the environment; and if that is a shared environment, your solution's performance is affected by other applications sharing resources with yours on the same servers. This means that your performance testing environment should be as close as possible to your production environment, including other applications and solutions running on the same servers as your solution.

Prepare the Proper Environment and Gather Performance Metrics

Before immersing yourself in a tuning exercise, make sure first that you have the proper environment setup. If your organization's IT governance policies include guidelines for deploying BizTalk solutions, there is not much to do here. You simply have to follow the guidelines and use the metrics gathered earlier to ensure the availability of the proper capacity in production.

On the other hand, if this is the first time BizTalk is being used in your enterprise environment, and there are no IT standards, some capacity planning and server allocation is required. It would be best if this is done early on in the development process, but this absolutely must be finalized after analyzing the results of preliminary performance tests. One of the major pitfalls that many BizTalk newbies fall into is lumping BizTalk and SQL Server on one big iron server, which is not a good investment to make. It is best to separate BizTalk Server and SQL Server on separate hardware. Depending on your High Availability requirements, you may want to look into a SQL Server cluster in the back end as well. Scaling out BizTalk into a multiserver group might be an option if High Availability is a requirement or if a single BizTalk server is not enough to handle the expected load.[1]

After allocating the proper servers for the platform, you should consider using BizTalk hosts to isolate and better manage your application. Separating the send, receive, and processing functionality in different hosts is a good idea, allowing for better memory and thread management. Leveraging BizTalk hosts to isolate Send or Receive Adapter instances expected to handle a high load or large messages, or orchestrations expected to consume a considerable amount of resources, would be a good idea as well. It is also highly recommended to create a separate host to handle tracking in order not to overload a processing host with that functionality. Figure 11-1 illustrates basic solution partitioning across hosts.

Now that the proper environment[2] is in place and your performance testing vertical is ready, you next start the load tests. In your test vertical, you need to simulate the production environment along with its relative load. This would allow for the collection of realistic performance metrics.[3] Stop the processing and sending hosts so that you gather timing metrics for message receives. Then start the processing hosts to gather timing metrics for message receives and orchestration processing. Last of all, start the sending hosts to gather metrics for the full process. Now you have the ability to estimate which part of the process is taking more time than it should and can start your tuning.

---

1. For more information on High Availability and how to scale BizTalk Server, refer to the BizTalk planning and architecture resources at http://msdn.microsoft.com/biztalk/learning/planarch/.

2. Make sure that you have the proper testing tools in place as well. BizUnit may be the right tool for unit testing, but you might want to look at LoadGen for stress testing. A link to the latest LoadGen version is available on the performance team's BizTalk blog.

3. Use the Performance Monitor or MOM to monitor and log performance counters, as well as the Performance tab on the Task Manager to monitor resource utilization.

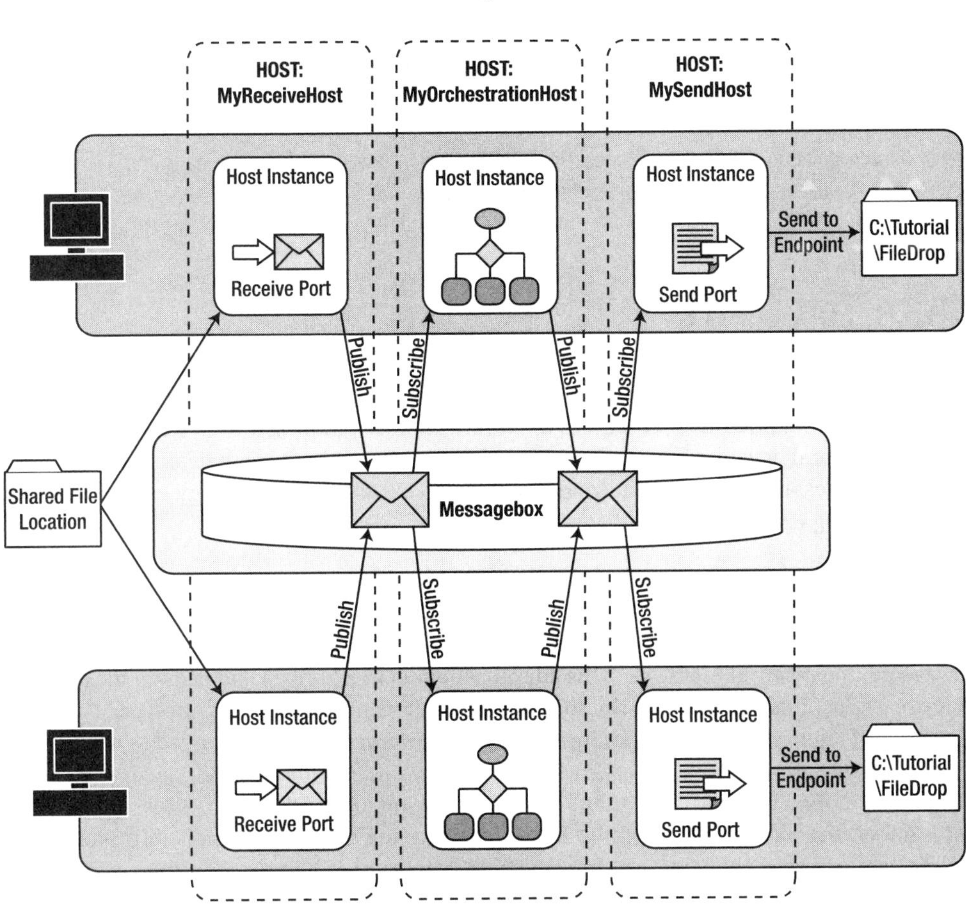

Figure 11-1. *Basic solution partitioning across hosts to optimize resource usage*

WHAT HAPPENED OVER THE LAST TWO YEARS?

For those who have been working with BizTalk 2004 for a while, it is good to know that a few things changed for the better between BizTalk Server 2004 and BizTalk Server 2006. Apart from the advancements in deployment and management, throttling and tuning have improved.

BizTalk Server 2004 Tuning

Tuning BizTalk 2004 applications is not a task for the fainthearted. The property pages for the different BizTalk artifacts in the management console had very limited capabilities if any. Tuning the server was mainly about dabbling with obscure registry keys and changing values in the Management Database tables in SQL Server—yes, for example, the infamous adm_ServiceClass table with the magical entries to control host settings. These facts, coupled with the difficulty in understanding how the server is behaving in the first place, made BizTalk tuning closer to black magic than a science.

BizTalk Server 2006 Tuning

OK, maybe not all the obscure registry keys have disappeared. We hope that will happen one day, though. For some HTTP and SOAP adapter tuning, you still have to use the registry. But, in BizTalk Server 2006, throttling is automatic. You can control it through a set of variables in property pages, or if you like, you can still mess with config files and/or registry settings. The adm_ServiceClass table did not disappear, but it is being deprecated. You can set most of these values today using property pages.

Where You Start

Now that you have your performance metrics, you are ready to do some tuning. You have to identify the different adapters and hosts used by the solution. This allows you to focus your attention on the components that require the tuning. Before jumping into that though, you need to understand how to decipher those gathered metrics and ensure that your solution follows coding best practices and the guidelines, which eliminate unnecessary extra configuration and tuning work.

What to Keep in Mind When Tuning

Out of the box, BizTalk Server 2006 is optimized for high throughput by adaptively managing its rate of polling received messages. This adaptive polling mechanism can cause a maximum latency of 0.5 seconds by default. If the solution at hand includes interactive scenarios where 0.5 seconds of latency is an issue, that internal polling interval could be changed to a value as low as 0.1 seconds by modifying the *MaxReceiveInterval* value in the adm_ServiceClass table, which is part of the BizTalk Management Database (*BizTalkMgmtDb*).

Managing the incoming throughput is one of the tuning options to handle bottlenecks whether they are internal or external. Internal bottlenecks could be caused by long execution times for a transform or a poorly designed orchestration resulting in extra persistence points. External bottlenecks are usually caused by legacy back-end systems or poorly designed services that cannot keep up with the load.

To properly tune the server, you need to know the expected throughput of the application; whether there are external bottlenecks or not; and what the expected peak input and its duration are. Knowing these, you need to analyze the gathered performance counters accordingly and identify which counters are showing problem areas. Table 11-1 highlights important performance counters and common causes for undesirable performance values for these counters as well as some troubleshooting options to rectify them.

Table 11-1. *Main Bottleneck Analysis*

Performance Counter	Analysis	Options
Low % CPU Idle on BizTalk Server	Too many hosts running on the server. Improper use of custom pipelines. Custom components requiring optimization.	Isolate the receive, process, and send functionality into different hosts and run host instances on different servers within the BizTalk Server Group. Move message transformation out of orchestrations to your ports to avoid the creation of new copies. Move message filters to your ports and receive locations. Optimize your schemas. Large schemas reduce performance. Use distinguished fields in orchestrations rather than properties or XPath. Use pass-through pipelines whenever possible.
Low % CPU Idle on SQL Server	Check if DBA changed any of the default database settings set by the BizTalk installation. Auto-Update Statistics and Max Degree of Parallelism are set to off and 1 respectively on purpose.	Minimize the number persistence points* in your orchestrations. Use static methods instead of wrapping nonserializable components in atomic scopes. Avoid using Parallel shapes, except when needed.** In a multi-Messagebox scenario, ensure that you have at least three Messageboxes. The master Messagebox is doing all the routing to secondary Messageboxes, which is CPU intensive. Whenever you are using multiple Messageboxes, Microsoft's Distributed Transaction Coordinator (DTC) is involved, therefore you need to jump from one Messagebox to three instead of only two to offset that overhead.
Low % Disk Idle on SQL Server High Avg. Disk Queue Length on SQL Server	Check whether the tracking database and Messagebox are on the same disks. Check whether the data and log files are on the same disks. Check the log sizes. Check the SQL Agents to ensure that the databases are being backed up. Check whether the tracked messages' bodies are being archived.	Use a SAN. Ensure that the tracking and Messagebox databases are on different servers. If they are on the same server, ensure that they are on different disks. Ensure that the data and log files are not sharing the same disks. Make sure the BizTalk agents are enabled on the server. The agents copy tracking data from the Messagebox to the tracking database. They also back up the databases and clean up the logs.

* *Persistence points also represent a performance metric that can be monitored using the BizTalk performance counter named Persistence Points.*

** *Parallel shapes are usually used to allow for the execution of independent flows upon the arrival of different messages, when the order of delivery is unknown.*

If any of the scenarios outlined in Table 11-1 hold true, this means that the whole BizTalk platform is underperforming, not just your solution, as these counters influence the performance of the core BizTalk subsystems. Problems or inefficiencies in one BizTalk solution could affect all other solutions sharing the same environment with that problematic solution. It is therefore a good idea to look at the overall platform when troubleshooting performance issues in a BizTalk solution.

IMPORTANT MESSAGEBOX METRICS

Other important metrics that you can gather directly from your Messagebox are your spool table and queue length. This gives you a complete understanding of what is happening on the Messagebox level. The following is a set of code snippets that you can use in a SQL script to gather this information; another way to get this data is to create your SQL custom counters to gather it.[4] It is a good idea when doing any server analysis or troubleshooting a problem to use a similar script to gather metrics on your production environment before you start going through endless logs.

```
-- ---------------------------------------------------
-- Get the number of rows in the spool table (backlog)
-- ---------------------------------------------------
SET NOCOUNT ON
SET TRANSACTION ISOLATION LEVEL READ COMMITTED
SET DEADLOCK_PRIORITY LOW
SELECT  COUNT(*) as Messages,
        'Spooled Messages' as State
FROM [BizTalkMsgboxDb]..[spool] WITH (NOLOCK)
-- ---------------------------------------------------


-- ---------------------------------------------------------
-- Get the number of orchestrations and their state per host
-- ---------------------------------------------------------
SET NOCOUNT ON
SET TRANSACTION ISOLATION LEVEL READ COMMITTED
SET DEADLOCK_PRIORITY LOW
SELECT  o.nvcName AS Orchestration, COUNT(*) as Count,
        CASE i.nState
                WHEN 1 THEN 'Ready To Run'
                WHEN 2 THEN 'Active'
                WHEN 4 THEN 'Suspended Resumable'
                WHEN 8 THEN 'Dehydrated'
                WHEN 16 THEN 'Completed With Discarded Messages'
                WHEN 32 THEN 'Suspended Non-Resumable'
        END as State
```

4. The following SQL code snippets assume that the BizTalk databases were installed using the default names.

```
FROM [BizTalkMsgboxDb]..[Instances] AS i WITH (NOLOCK)
JOIN [BizTalkMgmtDb]..[bts_Orchestration] AS o
WITH (NOLOCK) ON i.uidServiceID = o.uidGUID
--WHERE dtCreated > '2004-08-24 00:00:00'
--AND dtCreated < '2004-08-24 13:30:00'
GROUP BY o.nvcName, i.nState
-- -----------------------------------------------------------



-- ------------------------------------------------------------
-- Get the number of Messages per host Q
-- IMPORTANT! Replace each instance of Q with the name of the
-- host that you are inspecting.
-- and the number of messages in the spool that are in that Q
-- ------------------------------------------------------------
SET NOCOUNT ON
SET TRANSACTION ISOLATION LEVEL READ COMMITTED
SET DEADLOCK_PRIORITY LOW

SELECT COUNT(*) as Messages, 'Suspended Non-Resumable' as State,
                'BizTalk Server Isolated Host' as Server
FROM [BizTalkMsgBoxDb]..[BizTalkServerIsolatedHostQ_Suspended]
WITH (NOLOCK)
--WHERE dtCreated > '2004-08-24 00:00:00'
--AND dtCreated < '2004-08-24 13:30:00'
SELECT  COUNT(*) as Messages,
        'Spooled Suspended Non-Resumable' as State,
        'BizTalk Server Isolated Host' as Server
FROM [BizTalkMsgboxDb]..[spool] AS i WITH (NOLOCK)
JOIN [BizTalkMsgboxDb]..[BizTalkServerIsolatedHostQ_Suspended] AS o
WITH (NOLOCK) ON i.uidMessageID = o.uidMessageID
--WHERE dtCreated > '2004-08-24 00:00:00'
--AND dtCreated < '2004-08-24 13:30:00'

SELECT COUNT(*) as Messages, 'Scheduled' as State,
        'BizTalk Server Isolated Host' as Server
FROM [BizTalkMsgBoxDb]..[BizTalkServerIsolatedHostQ_Scheduled]
WITH (NOLOCK)
--WHERE dtCreated > '2004-08-24 00:00:00'
--AND dtCreated < '2004-08-24 13:30:00'
```

```
SELECT  COUNT(*) as Count, 'Spooled Scheduled' as State,
        'BizTalk Server Isolated Host' as Server
FROM [BizTalkMsgboxDb]..[spool] AS i WITH (NOLOCK)
JOIN [BizTalkMsgboxDb]..[BizTalkServerIsolatedHostQ_Scheduled]
AS o WITH (NOLOCK) ON i.uidMessageID = o.uidMessageID
--WHERE dtCreated > '2004-08-24 00:00:00'
--AND dtCreated < '2004-08-24 13:30:00'

SELECT COUNT(*) as Messages, 'Active' as State,
        'BizTalk Server Isolated Host' as Server
FROM [BizTalkMsgBoxDb]..[BizTalkServerIsolatedHostQ]
WITH (NOLOCK)
--WHERE dtCreated > '2004-08-24 00:00:00'
--AND dtCreated < '2004-08-24 13:30:00'

SELECT  COUNT(*) as Count, 'Spooled Active' as State,
        'BizTalk Server Isolated Host' as Server
FROM [BizTalkMsgboxDb]..[spool] AS i WITH (NOLOCK)
JOIN [BizTalkMsgboxDb]..[BizTalkServerIsolatedHostQ] AS o
WITH (NOLOCK) ON i.uidMessageID = o.uidMessageID
--WHERE dtCreated > '2004-08-24 00:00:00'
--AND dtCreated < '2004-08-24 13:30:00'
-- ----------------------------------------------------------
```

What to Keep in Mind About Your Code

A few simple things to keep in mind before jumping into tuning your BizTalk solution as well are your current coding practices. Coding is a constant improvement process. While coding and performing code reviews, since the Assembly/C/C++ days, we have constantly written and seen comments like, "// —TBD: refactor or rewrite in next rev". This is an obvious sign that no matter what stage you are in, there is always some code in your application or library that, given the time, you would revisit, rewrite, or repackage.

Some of the BizTalk coding caveats that tend to apply to most BizTalk developers, and that generally represent quick performance wins, are as follows:

- **Move your message transformations to the ports**: This minimizes the number of message copies created in your orchestration.
- **Avoid using `XmlDoc` objects in your orchestration and use distinguished fields on a message**: `XmlDoc` objects load the full message into a DOM and consume a considerable amount of memory resources. Each transformation from an `XmlDoc` to a message object and back results in copies of these objects being created in memory. Using distinguished fields simply references the existing message and minimizes memory churn.

- **Move data validation to the pipeline or schema**: If you are performing any data validation on your input messages, for example, validating that an order number is numeric and within a prespecified range, you are better off specifying this form of validation when defining the data types in the schema. If you require other forms of contextual validation, you are better off doing that in a pipeline. It is better to do this before persisting the message to the Messagebox, running the routing logic to find the proper schedule subscribed to the message instance, and then spawning an orchestration instance and allocating the required resources for it to run, only to realize that the data was not good enough to start with and issues an exception or sends back an error. You can save a lot of system resources and processing time by handling this in the pipeline and generating an error message there that you can then route back to the sender using content-based routing.
- **Avoid using orchestrations for routing**: If all your orchestration is doing is checking message fields to route the message to the proper handler or another worker orchestration to perform a particular task, strongly consider redesigning that piece of your application as a set of port filters. Leverage receive ports with multiple receive locations and send groups to route messages coming in from multiple sources and send messages to multiple destinations instead of relying on orchestrations to achieve that.
- **Avoid calls to external assemblies that perform extensive processing, especially if they call web services or make calls to a database**: Avoid calling slow external assemblies from within your orchestrations.[5] This holds the processing host resources and valuable host threads from servicing other orchestration instances while waiting for that external logic to terminate and return. If these calls stall or take a considerable amount of time, there is no way for the BizTalk engine to dehydrate that orchestration instance and use the resources assigned to it to service another one, as the engine sees the instance's state as running while in fact the external code that it called is idle. Leverage the messaging infrastructure to issue such calls that span multiple processes boundaries.
- **Do not wrap calls to .NET objects in atomic transactions because they are nonserializable**: Do not create transaction scopes around an expression to simply get around the shortcoming of an external object that you are using. If it makes sense, make this object serializable, or if it is simply a utility, use static methods instead of instantiating an object. Change the class's implementation or implement a façade that provides you with the required interface[6] if needed.
- **Use Parallel shapes carefully**: As illustrated in Figure 11-2, Parallel shapes should be used to parallelize receives if the order of incoming messages is unknown. The cost of persistence points associated with Parallel shapes is high.

---

5. Ensure that all external assemblies being called are not making calls to web services or communicating with external systems or back-end databases that might hold the calling thread until they complete. Also, ensure that all external assemblies adhere to the.NET development guideline and best practices.

6. For more details on implementing a façade, refer to *Design Patterns: Elements of Reusable Object-Oriented Software* by Erich Gamma, Richard Helm, Ralph Johnson, and John Vlissides (Addison-Wesley, 1995). The definition of the Façade pattern can be found at Wikipedia: http://en.wikipedia.org/wiki/Facade_pattern.

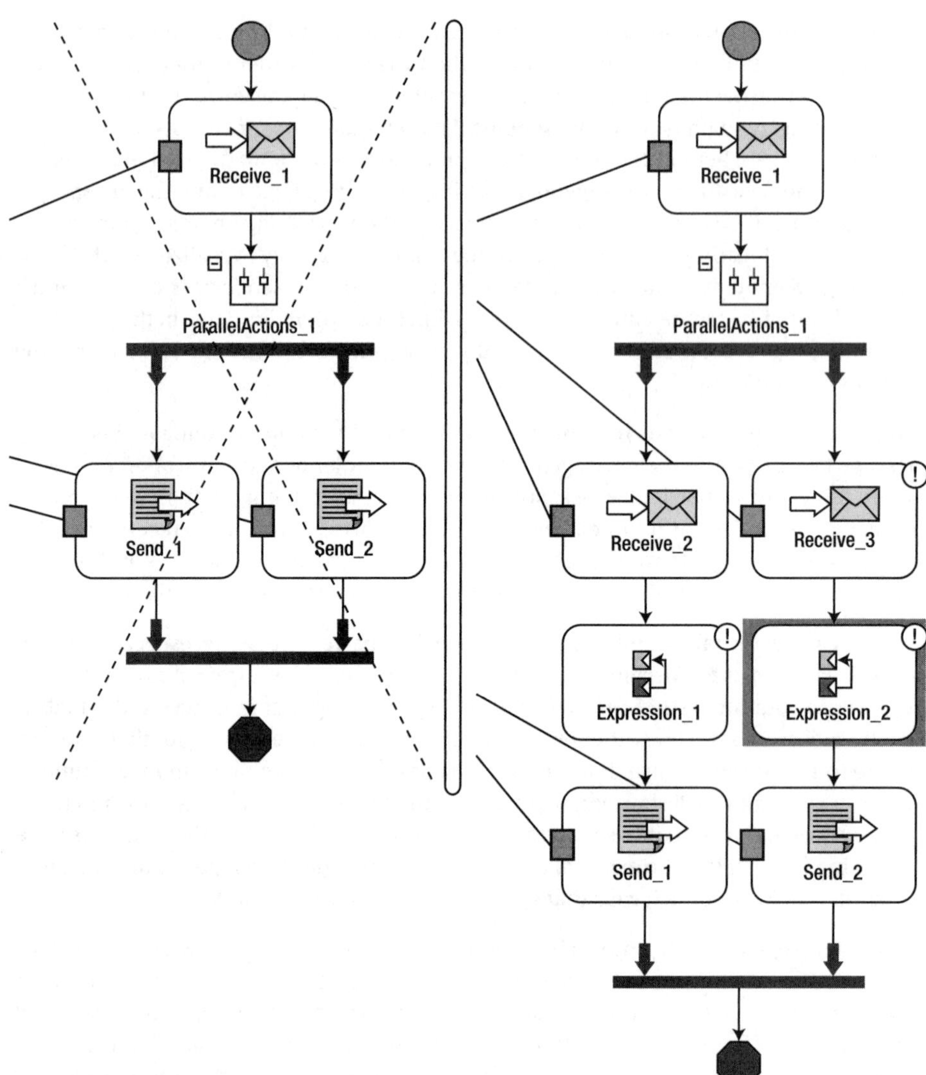

Figure 11-2. *The proper use of Parallel shapes in an orchestration*

- **Differentiate between scopes and transactions**: Transaction scopes affect persistence points. Atomic transactions batch state persistence points and write them to the database in a single call. Long-running transactions, on the other hand, persist state at different points along the process. If you are not really running a transaction, do not assign a transaction type to your scope.
- **Use pass-through pipelines where possible**: The XMLSend or XMLReceive pipelines do a fair amount of work to validate and assemble the data going through them. If you are sure that outgoing and incoming messages are in a valid XML form, use a pass-through pipeline to eliminate this unneeded overhead.

■ **Note** The pass-through pipeline does not promote any message properties. You might still want to use the XMLReceive pipeline if you want to access promoted properties.

- **Clean up suspended messages**: Suspended messages are held in the suspended queue and thus retain an entry in the Messagebox spool table. An unexpected growth in the spool table affects overall performance, as all instances added to, changed, or removed from the system touch the spool table. It is therefore wise to help maintain as small a size as possible for the spool table. Suspended-resumable instances have a worse impact on the system as they are considered by the engine as dehydrated messages on a server recovery from an unexpected failure and are rehydrated back to memory, consuming valuable threads and resources. Leverage exception handlers in orchestrations and subscribe to negative acknowledgements or use a cleanup script to clear your system from suspended instances regularly.[7]

Regular code reviews during the development cycle should ensure that these guidelines are being followed and save the development team valuable time spent in performance testing and bug fixing to meet performance requirements.

SUSPENDED INSTANCES CLEANUP SCRIPT

The following script can be used to periodically clean up suspended messages. Add it to your task scheduler on the server to run periodically—every day or couple of days—and clean up suspended messages. The script needs to be configured with the different hosts to inspect and clean up. The approved way of cleaning up suspended messages programmatically is using the WMI APIs exposed by BizTalk, which is unfortunately a resource-intensive way to perform this task. To avoid locking up the server, the script cleans up instances in batches. The number of instances in a batch—*nMaxInstancesToClean*—as well as the hosts—*aryHostNames*—to clean up suspended instances for and the log file location—*strDirectory* and *strFile*—can be easily modified. The script also generates and appends data to the same log file with each run for administrators to track its progress and keep track of cleaned-up messages. Enter your host names in order of priority, such that the one that needs to be cleaned first will run first.

---

7. Although you should not be seeing suspended instances in your system, as they are signs of an error and you should be handling all errors, sometimes the occurrence of suspended instances is out of your hands. For example, you may be making a request/response call to a web service that was unavailable or issuing a query to a database that was taken offline during a valid change window for maintenance. Such actions, though valid, will result in suspended instances on the host instance running those adapters. The recommended approach to handle these suspended instances is to handle error reports or to create a context-sensitive orchestration that subscribes to NACK, inspects the instances' details and archives them, and then cleans them up.

```
dim objServices, objMsg, svcinsts, inst, msg, ndx, size, nHostCount

Dim aryClassIDs()
Dim aryTypeIDs()
Dim aryInstanceIDs()

Dim aryClassIDsTemp()
Dim aryTypeIDsTemp()
Dim aryInstanceIDsTemp()
'-----------------------------------------------
Dim strKey2Instance
Dim strQuery2Msg
Dim objQueue

'-----------------------------------------------
'-- Creating and opening log file to append info
'-----------------------------------------------
Dim strDirectory, strFile, objFSO, objTextFile
strDirectory = "c:"
strFile = "\TermallScriptResults.txt"
'Create the File System Object
Set objFSO = CreateObject("Scripting.FileSystemObject")

'Check that the folder and file exists
If objFSO.FileExists(strDirectory & strFile) Then
    'OpenTextFile Method needs a Const value
    'ForAppending = 8 ForReading = 1, ForWriting = 2
    Const ForAppending = 8
    Set objTextFile = objFSO.OpenTextFile(strDirectory & strFile,
                                          ForAppending, True)
Else
    Set objTextFile = objFSO.CreateTextFile(strDirectory & strFile)
End If

'--------------------------
'-- Set the object reference
'--------------------------
set objServices = GetObject("winmgmts:\\.\root\MicrosoftBizTalkServer")

'-------------------------------------------------------------------
'-- Create array of hostnames to loop over hosts
'-- increase the array's size,
'-- add as many hostnames as required to the array,
'-- and initialize the corresponding aryHostSuspendedMessages entries
'-------------------------------------------------------------------
```

```
Dim aryHostNames(1)
Dim aryHostSuspsendedMessages(1)
aryHostNames(0) = "BizTalkServerApplication"
aryHostNames(1) = "BizTalkServerIsolatedHost"
aryHostSuspsendedMessages(0) = 0
aryHostSuspsendedMessages(1) = 0
'-----------------------------------------------------------------------
'-- The maximum number of suspended instances to clean up in a single batch
'-----------------------------------------------------------------------
Dim nMaxInstancesToClean
nMaxInstancesToClean = 500


Dim strHost
nHostCount = 0

objTextFile.WriteLine("------- SCRIPT EXECUTION STARTED -------")

'-----------------------------------------------------------------
'-- Terminate instance in each suspended Queue for the selected hosts
'-----------------------------------------------------------------
for each strHost in aryHostNames

    'wscript.echo "Host: " & strHost
    objTextFile.WriteLine("----------------------------------------")
    objTextFile.WriteLine(Now() & " :    Host: " & strHost)

'-------------------------------
'-- Query for Suspended instances
'-------------------------------
    wbemFlagReturnImmediately = 16
    wbemFlagForwardOnly = 32
    IFlags = wbemFlagReturnImmediately + wbemFlagForwardOnly
    set svcinsts = objServices.ExecQuery(
             "select * from MSBTS_serviceinstance
              where (servicestatus=32 or servicestatus=4)
              and HostName="""&strHost&"""",, IFlags)

    'Using a semi-synchronous therefore the count property doesn't
    'work with wbemFlagForwardOnly
    'size = svcinsts.Count
    'wscript.echo "Suspended Message: " & size

    strKey2Instance = "MSBTS_HostQueue.HostName=""" & strHost & """"
```

```
    set objQueue = objServices.Get(strKey2Instance)

    If Err <> 0 Then

        wscript.echo Now() & " :    Failed to get MSBTS_HostQueue instance"
        wscript.echo Now() & " :    " & Err.Description & Err.Number
        objTextFile.WriteLine(Now() & " :
                              Failed to get MSBTS_HostQueue instance")
        objTextFile.WriteLine(Now() & " :    " + Err.Description & Err.Number)

    Else

        ndx = 0

        redim aryClassIDs(nMaxInstancesToClean)
        redim aryTypeIDs(nMaxInstancesToClean)
        redim aryInstanceIDs(nMaxInstancesToClean)

        'Loop through all instances and terminate nMaxInstancesToClean at a
        'time.
        'This number was choosen for optimization, so it can be changed if
        'desired.
        for each inst in svcinsts

             If ndx > nMaxInstancesToClean Then
                  'Currently 500 entries are ready to be terminated

                  'wscript.echo "Attempting to terminate "
                  '& ndx & " suspended instances in host"
                  objTextFile.WriteLine(Now() &
                         " :    Attempting to terminate "
                         & ndx & " suspended instances in host")

                  objQueue.TerminateServiceInstancesByID aryClassIDs,
                                  aryTypeIDs, aryInstanceIDs

                  If Err <> 0 Then
                       wscript.echo Now() & " :    Terminate failed"
                       wscript.echo Now() & " :    " & Err.Description
                                          & Err.Number
                       objTextFile.WriteLine(Now() & " :    Terminate failed")
                       objTextFile.WriteLine(Now() & " :    " + Err.Description
                                                & Err.Number)
```

```
            Else
                'wscript.echo "SUCCESS> " & ndx &
                '" Service instance terminated"
                objTextFile.WriteLine(Now() &
                  " :    SUCCESS> " & ndx &
                  " Service instance terminated")
            End If

            'Reinitialize the arrays and counter
            'to ensure we store non-terminated
            'Entries for the next round of termination
            ndx = 0
            redim aryClassIDs(nMaxInstancesToClean)
            redim aryTypeIDs(nMaxInstancesToClean)
            redim aryInstanceIDs(nMaxInstancesToClean)

            'Suspends script execution for 30 seconds,
            'then continues execution
            'wscript.echo "Suspending script execution for 30 seconds"
            objTextFile.WriteLine(Now() &
              " :    Suspending script execution for 30 seconds")
            Wscript.Sleep 30000

        End If

        aryClassIDs(ndx) = inst.Properties_("ServiceClassId")
        aryTypeIDs(ndx) = inst.Properties_("ServiceTypeId")
        aryInstanceIDs(ndx) = inst.Properties_("InstanceId")

        ndx = ndx + 1

    next

    'If count <> zero then the arrays are still populated
    'and the messages need to be terminated one last time.
    If ( ndx > 0 ) then

        redim aryClassIDsTemp(ndx-1)
        redim aryTypeIDsTemp(ndx-1)
        redim aryInstanceIDsTemp(ndx-1)
```

```
            for i=1 to ndx
                aryClassIDsTemp(i-1) = aryClassIDs(i-1)
                aryTypeIDsTemp(i-1) = aryTypeIDs(i-1)
                aryInstanceIDsTemp(i-1) = aryInstanceIDs(i-1)
                aryHostSuspsendedMessages(nHostCount) =
                   aryHostSuspsendedMessages(nHostCount) + 1
            next

            'wscript.echo "Attempting to terminate " &
            'ndx & " suspended instances in host"
            objTextFile.WriteLine(Now() &
                 " :    Attempting to terminate " & ndx &
                 " suspended instances in host")

            objQueue.TerminateServiceInstancesByID aryClassIDsTemp,
                      aryTypeIDsTemp, aryInstanceIDsTemp

            If Err <> 0 Then
                wscript.echo Now() & " :    Terminate failed"
                wscript.echo Now() & " :    " & Err.Description & Err.Number
                objTextFile.WriteLine(Now() & " :    Terminate failed")
                objTextFile.WriteLine(Now() &
                                " :    " + Err.Description & Err.Number)
            Else
                'wscript.echo "SUCCESS> " & ndx &
                '" Service instance terminated"
                objTextFile.WriteLine(Now() &
                   " :    SUCCESS> " & ndx & " Service instance terminated")
            End If
        Else
            'wscript.echo "No suspended instances in this host"
            objTextFile.WriteLine(Now() &
                    " :    No suspended instances in this host")
        End If
    End If

    nHostCount = nHostCount + 1

Next

objTextFile.WriteLine("")
objTextFile.WriteLine("-------       SUMMARY START       -------")
```

```
nHostCount = 0
for each strHost in aryHostNames
    wscript.echo Now() & " :    Total of " &
                 aryHostSuspsendedMessages(nHostCount) &
                 " suspended messages were terminated in " &
                 strHost & " host"
    objTextFile.WriteLine(Now() & " :    Total of " &
                          aryHostSuspsendedMessages(nHostCount) &
                          " suspended messages were terminated in " &
                          strHost & " host")
    nHostCount = nHostCount + 1
Next
objTextFile.WriteLine("-------        SUMMARY END        -------")
objTextFile.WriteLine("")

wscript.echo Now() & " :    Script Execution Completed"
objTextFile.WriteLine(Now() & " :    Script Execution Completed")
objTextFile.WriteLine("-------  SCRIPT EXECUTION ENDED  -------")
objTextFile.Close
Set objTextFile = nothing
```

A sample log file output with multiple batch runs to clean the hosts:

```
 ------- SCRIPT EXECUTION STARTED -------
----------------------------------------
12/13/2005 3:42:31 PM :    Host: BizTalkServerApplication
12/13/2005 3:42:37 PM :    Attempting to terminate 500 suspended instances in
                           host
12/13/2005 3:42:43 PM :    SUCCESS> 500 Service instance terminated
12/13/2005 3:42:43 PM :    Suspending script execution for 30 seconds
12/13/2005 3:43:13 PM :    Attempting to terminate 162 suspended instances in
                           host
12/13/2005 3:43:14 PM :    SUCCESS> 162 Service instance terminated
----------------------------------------
12/13/2005 3:43:14 PM :    Host: BizTalkServerIsolatedHost
12/13/2005 3:43:15 PM :    No suspended instances in this host

-------      SUMMARY START      -------
12/13/2005 3:43:25 PM :    Total of 662 suspended messages were terminated in
                           BizTalkServerApplication host
12/13/2005 3:43:30 PM :    Total of 0 suspended messages were terminated in
                           BizTalkServerIsolatedHost host
-------       SUMMARY END       -------

12/13/2005 3:43:32 PM :    Script Execution Completed
-------  SCRIPT EXECUTION ENDED  -------
```

How to Tune Each Subsystem

A typical BizTalk solution includes adapters, pipelines, maps, message schemas, orchestrations, and ports. Figure 11-3 shows a logical illustration of a BizTalk solution detailing the different components that might be involved in it and dividing them into their logical containers, inbound Receive Adapters and receive pipelines, processing orchestrations and business rules, as well as outbound send pipelines and Send Adapters. The illustration highlights the constant reliance on the Messagebox and a typical message flow within the solution. The receive locations and send locations are implied as the **Inbound** and **Outbound** containers. The maps and filters are applied to the implied ports. To properly tune the environment and the solution, you need to identify the different components used by your solution.

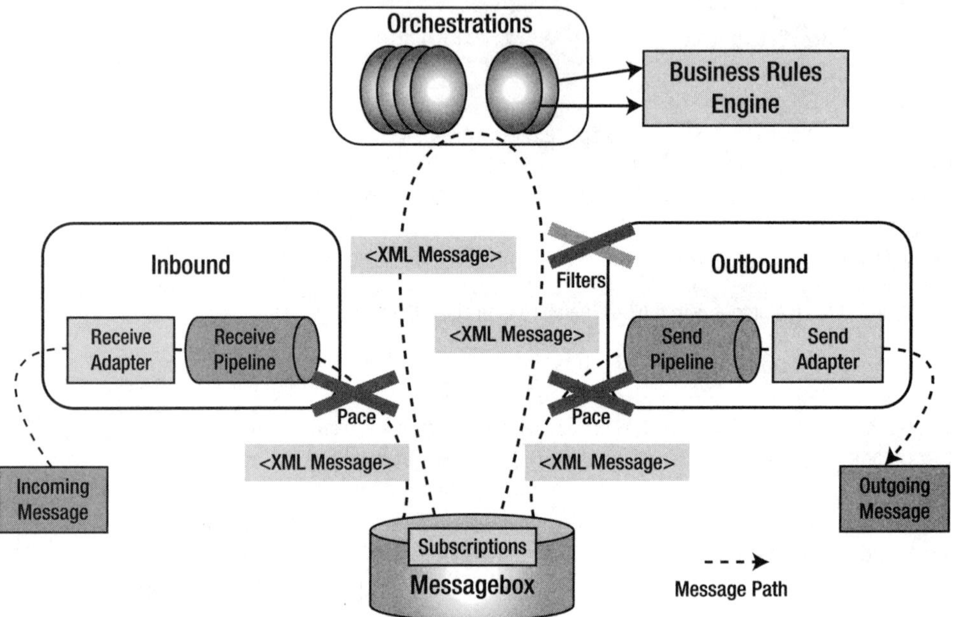

Figure 11-3. *The different components constituting a BizTalk solution*

ASP.NET, SOAP, and HTTP

To tune HTTP as well as SOAP Send and Receive Adapters, you have to fiddle around with ASP.NET web.config and machine.config files as well as BTSNTSvc.exe.config and the registry keys for the BTSNTSvc.exe service instance that is hosting the adapter.

Receive Adapter Tuning

Tuning the SOAP receive host is mostly about tuning web services, IIS, and the ASP.NET worker process. You can use LoadGen or the Microsoft Web Application Stress (WAS) Tool[8] to stress test the isolated host and gather performance metrics. Table 11-2 shows a set of performance metrics to monitor while load testing the web services. Web services use ASP.NET thread pooling to process requests. To ensure that your web services use the thread pool most effectively, consider the following guidelines (Meier, 2004):[9,10]

- Set the maximum thread-pool thresholds to reduce contention:
  - Set *maxIOThreads* and *maxWorkerThreads* in machine.config to 100. The *maxIOThreads* setting controls the maximum number of I/O threads in the common language runtime (CLR) thread pool. This number is then automatically multiplied by the number of available CPUs. The recommendation is to set this to 100. The *maxWorkerThreads* setting controls the maximum number of worker threads in the CLR thread pool. This number is then automatically multiplied by the number of available CPUs. The recommendation is to set this to 100.
  - Set *minFreeThreads* in machine.config to 88 × number of CPUs. The worker process uses this setting to queue up all the incoming requests if the number of available threads in the thread pool falls below the value for this setting. This setting effectively limits the number of concurrently executing requests to *maxWorkerThreads* – *minFreeThreads*. The recommendation is to set this to 88 times the number of CPUs. This limits the number of concurrent requests to 12 (assuming *maxWorkerThreads* is 100).
  - Set *minLocalRequestFreeThreads* to 76 × the number of CPUs.[11] This worker process uses this setting to queue up requests from localhost (where a web application calls a web service on the same server) if the number of available threads in the thread pool falls below this number. This setting is similar to *minFreeThreads*, but it only applies to requests that use localhost. The recommendation is to set this to 76 times the number of CPUs.
- Set the minimum thread-pool thresholds to handle load bursts. Set *minIOThreads* and *minWorkerThreads* to prep the thread pool for incoming large loads instead of creating new threads as requests come in to fill up the pool.

---

8. A free stress testing application that can simulate loads of 100s or 1000s of users accessing your ASP.NET application or web service and generates a summary report with performance information. The tool is downloadable from www.microsoft.com/downloads/details.aspx?familyid=e2c0585a-062a-439e-a67d-75a89aa36495&displaylang=en.
9. The following settings' values should be used as guidelines and a starting point. They should be tuned either up or down based on the results of the load tests.
10. Copyright © 2004 by Microsoft Corporation. Reprinted with permission from Microsoft Corporation.
11. The difference between *minFreeThreads* and *minLocalRequestFreeThreads* is intentional to ensure that local requests have a higher priority than remote requests. This allows remote calls to web service A, which calls local web service B, to acquire the required resources to make the second web service call and complete successfully. Had both settings been the same, a sudden spike in concurrent calls to web service A would result in a timeout and eventually a process recycle, as the process would consume the available threads to service the calls to web service A and would not find enough resources to service the calls from web service A to web service B.

Table 11-2. *Basic Counters to Monitor for ASP.NET (Northrup)*[12]

Object	Counter	Description
Processor	% CPU Utilization	The overall measure of total processor utilization on a web server. The processor is the most common bottleneck on ASP.NET web servers. If this counter peaks near 100% while the web server is under load, you should add the % Processor Time counter for the Process object to isolate which process is bogging down the server.
Process	% Processor Time	This counter provides similar information to the % CPU Utilization counter but identifies which specific process is using the most CPU time. To be certain you gather all the information you need, you should select the All Instances radio button in the Add Counters dialog box when adding this counter. If the aspnet_wp process is consuming most of the processor, it is a good indication that rendering ASP.NET pages is the bottleneck. If the inetinfo process is to blame, IIS itself is the cause of the problem. These conditions can be remedied by upgrading the web server's processor, adding multiple processors, or adding more web servers. If your ASP.NET application is database-driven and you run a Microsoft SQL Server on the same system, you will very likely discover that the process named sqlservr is causing the CPU bottleneck. The best remedy for this situation is to move the SQL Server software to another physical server. Alternatively, upgrading the processor or adding more processors will help.
ASP.NET Applications	Requests/Sec	This counter measures the current rate of incoming ASP.NET requests and is a useful way to measure the peak capacity of your web application while under load. The counter will report on only the number of requests for files with extensions configured in IIS to be passed to ASP.NET—most commonly, .aspx and .asmx files. To view the total number of requests, including requests for images, add the Get Requests/Sec counter from the Web Service object instead.
ASP.NET Applications	Sessions Active	This counter measures the current number of active ASP.NET sessions. A session is created by an ASP.NET application when a new user makes the first request. The session lives until 1) the application explicitly abandons it when the user logs out, or 2) no requests are received from the user for the period of the session timeout. By default, ASP.NET sessions timeout after 20 minutes. This setting can be adjusted by modifying the `timeout` attribute of the `sessionState` element in the web.config or machine.config files.

12. Copyright © 2004 by Microsoft Corporation. Reprinted with permission from Microsoft Corporation.

Object	Counter	Description
ASP.NET	Requests Queued	Requests are queued when the time required to render a page is greater than the time between incoming client requests. In normal web traffic, request rates are very erratic, and queuing might occur for a few seconds during a busy moment. This will cause page load times to increase temporarily, but the queue is quickly eliminated during the next quiet moment. Traffic generated by a load-testing tool such as WAS might not have the same erratic patterns and might cause the ASP.NET Requests Queued counter to climb before it would do so under real traffic conditions. To simulate these random peaks and valleys in web traffic, enable the Use Random Delay check box on the script settings page of WAS. If this counter still increases with this setting enabled, the server is currently above its peak capacity, and a bottleneck should be identified and resolved before continuing testing. By default, ASP.NET is configured to queue a maximum of 100 requests. This limit is defined by the `appRequestQueueLimit` attribute of the `httpRunTime` element of the web.config or machine.config files.
ASP.NET	Requests Rejected	After the ASP.NET request queue is full, new requests are rejected. This process is generally a good way for ASP.NET to behave under extremely heavy load because it is better to return an error to the user immediately and remove the request from the web server's queue than to force users to wait for their browser to timeout. Monitoring this counter gives you a running total of the requests received while the queue length was at the maximum.

Send Adapter Tuning

The default number of maximum concurrent outgoing SOAP connections is two. This can cause outgoing SOAP requests to timeout and create a bottleneck in scenarios where a high volume of outgoing SOAP requests is expected. If not treated, this problem can cause a buildup of messages in the Messagebox and entries in the spool table resulting in overall performance degradation. It may also cause the host instances running the SOAP Send Adapter to recycle because eventually, if the load is high enough and the time taken for the called web method to complete is long enough, all threads in that host instance's thread pool will be exhausted, and the host instance will be unable to service new requests as it runs out of threads. Increasing the batch size in this scenario will only make the situation worse. Decreasing it might eliminate the errors, but it will not improve the performance of the solution.

To rectify this problem, you need to increase the maximum number of connections for the host instances hosting the SOAP Send Adapter. The recommended value is 25 connections

× the number of CPUs on the server.[13] This is done by adding a maxconnection element to the ConnectionManagement node in the BTSNTSvc.exe.config file on each of the BizTalk Servers in the BizTalk Server Group. This file holds the common configuration for the BizTalk host services. If the solution needs to call web services with performance issues that cannot handle more than a specific number of concurrent transactions, the same setting can be used to specify a low number of maximum concurrent connections for that specific web service and ensure that you do not overdrive that service to failure. As per the config file fragment that follows, the maxconnection key could be defined multiple times with different name attributes identifying different endpoints, thus allowing for the customization of different maximum values for the concurrent number of connections for different endpoints. To specify the default value used for all web service endpoints not specifically called out by name, use "*" as the name attribute for the default key value.

```
<configuration>
...
   <system.net>
      <connectionManagement>
         <add name = "www.MyLowThroughputWebService.com" maxconnection = "4" />
         <add name = "*" maxconnection = "50" />
      </connectionManagement>
   </system.net>
</configuration>
```

Web services located on the same computer as your BizTalk solution share the same thread pool with web services exposed by the BizTalk solution if running within the same application pool. Therefore, the client-facing web services and the web service being called through the SOAP Send Adapter share the same threads and other related resources, such as CPU for request processing. Calling a local web service also means that your request travels through the entire processing pipeline and incurs overhead, including serialization, thread switching, request queuing, and deserialization.

In addition, the maxconnection attribute of machine.config has no effect on the connection limit for making calls to local web services. Therefore, local web services always tend to give preference to the requests that come from the local computer over requests that come from other machines. This degrades the throughput of the web service for remote clients (Meier, 2004). If the local web services are not making calls to any external systems and their web method processing time is considerably low, package them into a .NET library and call them from within your orchestrations. If those web services are calling external systems or take a considerable amount of processing time, move them off the BizTalk Server Group servers.

By default, the .NET thread pool used by BizTalk host instances is 100 threads per CPU. To configure the maximum number of threads allocated by the thread pool, set the *MaxWorkerThreadsPerProcessor* DWORD registry key under software\Microsoft\BizTalk Server\3.0\Administration.

13. The actual maximum number of connections entered to the configuration file should be a factor of the total number of CPUs on the server running the BizTalk host instance, as the thread-pool size in each host depends on the number of CPUs on the server.

HTTP-Specific Tuning

Several configuration and tuning parameters are accessible for the HTTP adapter through registry key entries and through the modification of the BTSNTSvc.exe.config file that is located in the root BizTalk installation directory. Table 11-3 describes the registry settings that affect the performance of the HTTP adapter. Note that by default there are no HTTP adapter keys in the registry, so the HTTP adapter uses the default settings. To change the default settings, you need to create the following registry keys under the following locations in the registry:

> *DisableChunkEncoding, RequestQueueSize,* and *HttpReceiveThreadsPerCpu* must be defined in HKEY_LOCAL_MACHINE\SYSTEM\CurrentControlSet\Services\BTSSvc.3.0\HttpReceive.

> *HttpOutTimeoutInterval, HttpOutInflightSize,* and *HttpOutCompleteSize* must be defined in HKEY_LOCAL_MACHINE\SYSTEM\CurrentControlSet\Services\BTSSvc{$HostName}.[14]

Table 11-3. *HTTP Adapter Settings (Microsoft, "BizTalk Server 2006 Documentation," 2006)*[15]

Key Name	Type	Default Value	Description
DisableChunkEncoding	DWORD	0	Regulates whether or not the HTTP Receive Adapter uses chunked encoding when sending responses back to the client. Set to a nonzero value to turn off chunked encoding for HTTP Receive Adapter responses. Minimum value: 0 Maximum value: Any nonzero value
RequestQueueSize	DWORD	256	Defines the number of concurrent requests that the HTTP Receive Adapter processes at one time. Minimum value: 10 Maximum value: 2048
HttpReceiveThreadsPerCpu	DWORD	2	Defines the number of threads per CPU that are allocated to the HTTP Receive Adapter. Minimum value: 1 Maximum value: 10
HttpOutTimeoutInterval	DWORD	2,000	Defines the interval in seconds that the HTTP Send Adapter will wait before timing out. Minimum value: 500 Maximum value: 10,000,000

Continued

14. {$Host Name} is the actual host name. In BizTalk Server 2004 or a BizTalk Server 2006 upgrade from BizTalk 2004, the key may be HKEY_LOCAL_MACHINE\SYSTEM\CurrentControlSet\Services\BTSSvc{GUID}, where GUID is the ID of the host for the HTTP send handler.

15. Copyright © 2004 by Microsoft Corporation. Reprinted with permission from Microsoft Corporation.

Table 11-3. *Continued*

Key Name	Type	Default Value	Description
HttpOutInflightSize	DWORD	100	This is the maximum number of concurrent HTTP requests that a BizTalk Server HTTP Send Adapter instance will handle. The recommended value for latency is between three to five times that of the *max-connection* configuration file entry. Minimum value: 1 Maximum value: 1024
HttpOutCompleteSize	DWORD	5	This is the size of the batch of messages that is returned from the HTTP Send Adapter. If the buffer is not full and there are outstanding responses, the adapter will wait for 1 second until it commits the batch. For low-latency scenarios, this should be set to 1, which will allow the adapter to send response messages immediately to the Messagebox for processing. This will have the greatest effect during times of low-throughput activity with varied response times from back-end systems. Minimum value: 1 Maximum value: 1024

The number of concurrent connections that the HTTP adapter opens for a particular destination server is configured by modifying the *maxconnection* entry in the BTSNTSvc.exe.config file that is located in the root BizTalk installation directory.

■ **Caution** This property will be applied to both the HTTP and SOAP adapters if they send messages to the same destination HTTP server. By default the maximum connections for all URIs is 20.

This configuration file entry replaces the functionality of the *HttpOutMaxConnection* registry key that was used in BizTalk 2004. If you have upgraded from BizTalk Server 2004 to BizTalk Server 2006 and you were using this registry key, you will need to apply this configuration file entry instead (Microsoft, 2006).[16]

CLR Tuning

Bottlenecks caused by contention for resources, misuse of threads, inefficient resource cleanup, or resource leaks can be rectified by tuning the CLR thread pool or memory thresholds. The use of memory thresholds will be discussed later in the "Throttling" section.

In situations with low CPU utilization or the CPU is fully saturated and yet the solution is not meeting the required throughput, increasing the maximum number of threads in the .NET thread pool by modifying the *maxIOThreads* and *maxWorkerThreads* registry keys might improve performance. Tuning the maximum number of threads in the thread pool down might

16. Copyright © 2004 by Microsoft Corporation. Reprinted with permission from Microsoft Corporation.

come in handy if the CPU utilization is pretty high, while the solution's overall throughput is still lower than expected. This could be because the system is spending more time context-switching between threads than processing.

If the solution is expected to handle load bursts, prepping the engine to maintain a minimum number of threads active to avoid the overhead of resources and thread allocation when those bursts occur is a good idea. This is done by setting the *minIOThreads* and *minWorkerThreads* registry keys to ensure that a minimum number of threads are always allocated in the thread pool. A value of the expected load during a spike + 10% is usually the recommended value for the *minIOThreads* and *minWorkerThreads* settings.

To modify the hosted CLR .NET thread pool for a particular BizTalk host, you have to create the following registry keys and set their values for that particular host.

- HKEY_LOCAL_MACHINE\SYSTEM\CurrentControlSet\Services\BTSSvc{$HostName}\CLR Hosting\MaxWorkerThreads (REG_DWORD)
- HKEY_LOCAL_MACHINE\SYSTEM\CurrentControlSet\Services\BTSSvc {$HostName}\CLR Hosting\MaxIOThreads (REG_DWORD)
- HKEY_LOCAL_MACHINE\SYSTEM\CurrentControlSet\Services\BTSSvc {$HostName}\CLR Hosting\MinWorkerThreads (REG_DWORD)
- HKEY_LOCAL_MACHINE\SYSTEM\CurrentControlSet\Services\BTSSvc {$HostName}\CLR Hosting\MinIOThreads (REG_DWORD)[17]

File Tuning

Several issues can occur with the file adapter. File adapter–related issues are usually the result of NetBIOS limitations or the polling agent. Microsoft's support articles recommend to increase the *MaxMpxCt* and the *MaxCmds* registry keys at HKEY_LOCAL_MACHINE\SYSTEM\CurrentControlSet\Services\lanmanworkstation\parameters to 2048 on the BizTalk Server as well as the file server holding the file share.[18]

BizTalk Server 2006 can encounter problems when a polling notification and a file change notification occur at the same time. This problem can be avoided by disabling FRF (File Receive Functions) polling through the File Receive Location property pages.

File Tuning: Batch Files

When dealing with large flat files that generate thousands of subdocuments in an envelope, isolate the File Receive Adapter in a separate host. Set the batch size to 1 and the thread-pool size for that host to 1. This will reduce the number of files you are processing in one transaction from 20 to 1 and single thread the host. The batch size property could be set on the

17. The {$HostName} in BTSSvc{$HostName} should be replaced by the actual host name. In BizTalk 2004 or BizTalk 2006 installations that are an upgrade from BizTalk 2004, the {$HostName} should be replaced with the GUID for that host. To get the GUID for a particular host, open the Services Console from the Administrative Tools, locate the host that requires the tuning, and get its ServiceName including the GUID.

18. The support article "'The Network BIOS Command Limit Has Been Reached' Error Message in Windows Server 2003, in Windows XP, and in Windows 2000 Server" can be found at http://support.microsoft.com/?id=810886.

receive location property page. To set the thread-pool size to 1, set the *MessagingThreadsPerCpu* property, which defines the number of threads per CPU for the thread pool, on the host's property pages and create the *MessagingThreadPoolSize* registry key, which defines the number of threads per CPU in the thread pool, under HKEY_LOCAL_MACHINE\SYSTEM\CurrentControlSet\Services\BTSSvc {$HostName }. The respective default values for both properties are 2 and 10. Setting those two values to 1 and dedicating a single thread in the host's thread pool to message processing ensures that multiple large flat files will not be competing for system resources within that host and that all the host's memory resources will be dedicated to processing the large message.

■ **Note** If you have multiple receive locations receiving large flat files as well as smaller ones, group them under different receive handlers running on different hosts. This ensures that the tuning performed on the host instances running the File Receive handler for large-flat-file processing does not affect the rest of the file receive functions processing smaller files. It is recommended to partition those receive handlers on different servers within the BizTalk Server Group by interleaving host instances on the different servers to ensure they are not competing for the same system resources.

When supporting large interchanges in BizTalk Server 2006, multiple smaller interchanges utilize the CPU processor more efficiently than fewer large interchanges. As a general guideline, use the following formula to determine the maximum size of an interchange for any given deployment (number of CPU processors):

Maximum number of messages per interchange <=
200,000 / (Number of CPUs × BatchSize × MessagingThreadPoolSize)

So, for example, a BizTalk host running on a four-CPU server tuned for large-flat-file processing, having a batch size of 1 and a single thread in its messaging thread pool, would be able to process an infinite number of interchanges as long as each interchange contains a maximum of 50,000 messages (200,000 divided by 4).Thus, *MessagingThreadPoolSize* is set to 1.

Parsing and Persistence

Persistence affects the overall system performance. Message parsing affects performance due to the incurred persistence points in the process. To tune the BizTalk solution and minimize the number of persistence points, change the Large Message Threshold and Fragment Size property of the BizTalk Server Group. The default value for this property is 1MB, meaning that each 1MB read from the message will result in a fragment being persisted to the Messagebox. To further elaborate, as stated in the white paper "BizTalk Server 2006 Runtime Improvements" (Microsoft, 2005):[19]

---

19. Copyright © 2005 by Microsoft Corporation. Reprinted with permission from Microsoft Corporation.

In previous releases of BizTalk Server, mapping of documents always occurred in-memory. While in-memory mapping provides the best performance, it can quickly eat up resources when large documents are mapped. For this reason, BizTalk Server 2006 introduced support for large message transformations. A different transformation engine is used when transforming large messages so that memory is utilized in an efficient manner. When dealing with large messages, the message data is buffered to the file system instead of being loaded into memory using the DOM (Document Object Model). This way the memory consumption remains flat as memory is used only to store the cashed data and indexes for the buffer. However, as the file system is used, there is expected performance degradation when comparing with in-memory transformation. Because of the potential performance impact, the two transformation engines will coexist in BizTalk Server 2006.

When message size is smaller than a specified threshold, the in-memory transformation will be used. If message size exceeds the threshold then the large message transformation engine is used. The threshold is configurable using the registry

- *DWORD 'TransformThreshold'*
- *'HKLM\\Software\\Microsoft\\BizTalk Server\\3.0\\Administration'.*

If the solution handles a low number of large messages, increase this value to a large value like 5MB. If the solution handles a high number of small/medium messages, set this value to 250K. You will need to experiment with this setting to find the optimum value for your solution and messages. Increasing the Large Message Threshold and Fragment Size property for the BizTalk Server Group results in fewer persistence points, in turn causing fewer round-trips to the database and faster message processing. The drawback of this approach is higher memory utilization, as fragments kept in memory now are much larger in size. To compensate for the expected higher memory utilization by the large message fragments, control the number of large message buffers that are created by the BizTalk host. You can do so by creating a *MessagingLMBufferCacheSize* (DWORD) registry key under System\CurrentControlSet\Services\BTSSvc<HostName> and setting its value to 5.

By controlling the number of large message buffers, you are hedging the risk of having the host run into low memory situations due to large message processing without incurring the penalty of constant round-trips to the Messagebox (Wasznicky, 2006).[20]

Latency

The time taken to process a message is dependent on how often the different BizTalk Server components pick up work items from the Messagebox. This interval affects the rate at which received messages are being published to the Messagebox as well as the rate at which they are being picked up from the Messagebox for processing or delivery. To deliver enterprise capabilities such as fault tolerance and scalability, the distributed BizTalk Server agents have to communicate asynchronously through the Messagebox. This asynchronous communication scheme means that the agents have to check the Messagebox for state updates to pick up new

20. Copyright © 2006 by Microsoft Corporation. Reprinted with permission from Microsoft Corporation.

items for processing and update the Messagebox at appropriate points in the process. This polling process contributes to the inherent latency of BizTalk solutions. If the end-to-end processing time per business transaction under low loads is unacceptable, you might want to look into tuning the interval at which the different agents check the Messagebox. By default, the *MaxReceiveInterval* is set to 500 msecs. You can reset this interval to a value as low as 100 msecs by modifying it in the adm_ServiceClass table for the XLANG/s, Messaging Isolated, and Messaging In-Process hosts. If the overall environment is experiencing high loads on the database while the overall end-to-end business transaction processing speed is acceptable, you can increase the *MaxReceiveInterval* and check whether that improves the overall environment's stability.

Throttling

Throttling is the mechanism by which the runtime engine prevents itself from thrashing and dropping dead when exposed to a high load. A properly throttled engine takes up only the amount of load that it can handle, and detects a stressed situation quickly and mitigates the situation accordingly.

Before BizTalk Server 2006

In BizTalk 2004, throttling BizTalk Server includes manipulating entries in the adm_ServiceClass table. Manipulating that table manually is now deprecated as it was troublesome and originally undocumented. Throttling BizTalk Server 2004 manually usually leads to more problems if inexperienced administrators start manipulating it, as it is mostly a trial-and-error exercise.

Manipulating the adm_ServiceClass table affects the entire BizTalk Server Group, not just a specific host instance. The configuration settings are not host specific and hence are not useful in any configuration with multiple hosts. If different servers in the BizTalk Server Group have different hardware configurations, having the same settings across different hardware is not the best approach. Other problem areas in BizTalk Server 2004 are as follows:

- The stress detection mechanism in BizTalk 2004 is grossly dependent on user input, namely the low and high watermark numbers in the adm_ServiceClass table.
- The configuration parameters are not exposed to the user through the UI.
- The inbound throttling heuristic (session count based) is not very effective because XLANG does not factor this at all, and all the sessions are shared across all the service classes.
- The agent's memory-based throttling policy has two major drawbacks:
    - First, it looks into the global memory and does not take into account the local memory usage. So if the server has more memory than 2GB, it might not be throttling properly, as the maximum amount of memory that a host instance can consume is 2GB on a Windows 32-bit platform. So, while the server could still have free memory that is not being consumed by other services, a particular host might be running out of the memory that it could consume without throttling.

- Second, while enforcing throttling due to low memory condition, the agent does not do anything to improve the memory usage situation, other than elevating the stress level. Once it enters a stress mode due to high memory condition, no measure is taken for it to come out of this stage, and hence it remains in this state for a long time. As the system starts again, it reloads all dehydrated orchestrations, resulting in an elevated rate of resource consumption leading to the same situation that caused the throttle in the first place (Wasznicky, 2006).[21]

Throttling Goals for BizTalk Server 2006

One of the Microsoft development team's objectives for BizTalk Server 2006 was to get around the nuances of throttling configuration. The target was a system that avoids using user-input parameters for detecting stress condition—a system with heuristics that include monitoring of resources (e.g., memory, threads, database sessions), utilization, and progress of work items against submitted work items. This would allow the system to function automatically without the administrator having to deal with the unknowns surrounding the various control knobs for the watermark numbers and other settings in the adm_ServiceClass table. Some parameters still have to be configured manually. The bright side is that they can be set and manipulated through the administration UI, and they have out-of-box valid settings. Those parameters are now at host level rather than group level.

The aim is to eventually communicate throttling actions to the system administrator through event logs and performance counters. Presently only the inbound throttling is communicated through the event log.

If the system is throttled due to lack of a particular resource, the engine proactively tries to mitigate the situation by releasing that particular resource so that it comes out of the stress situation. For example, under low memory, cache should be shrunk and MSMQT instances should be dehydrated.

Unlike BizTalk Server 2004, BizTalk Server 2006 throttling takes into account process memory, in addition to global memory. All components follow uniform throttling policies to ensure a fair distribution of resources.

Auto-Throttling in 2006

BizTalk Server 2006 auto-throttling consists of a set of load detection algorithms and mitigation plans. Table 11-4 highlights those algorithms.

---

21. Copyright © 2006 by Microsoft Corporation. Reprinted with permission from Microsoft Corporation.

Table 11-4. *BizTalk Server 2006 Auto-Throttling Mechanisms (Wasznicky, 2006)*[22]

Detection	Mitigation	Affected Components	Monitors
Compare Message Delivery Rate with the Message Completion Rate. When the latter falls short, it is an indication of the fact that messages are being pushed at higher rate than the service can handle	Throttle message delivery so that the delivery rate comes down and becomes at par with the completion rate.	XLANG All outbound transports	Need to monitor Message Delivery Rate and Message Completion Rate.
Compare the Publishing Request Rate with Publishing Completion Rate. When the latter falls short, it is an indication of the Messagebox being unable to cope with the load.	Block the publishing threads to slow down the publishing rate AND/OR indicate service class to slow down publishing	XLANG All inbound transports	Need to monitor entry and exit of Commit Batch call.
Process memory exceeds a threshold.	Throttle publishing if batch has steep memory requirement. Throttle delivery. Indicate service to dehydrate/shrink cache.	XLANG All transports	Monitor Private Bytes.
System memory exceeds a threshold.	Throttle publishing if batch has steep memory requirement. Throttle delivery.	XLANG All transports	Monitor physical memory.
Database sessions being used by the process exceed a threshold count.	Throttle publishing.	XLANG All inbound transports	Monitor average session usage per Messagebox.
Any host message queue size, the spool size, or the tracking data size exceeds a particular host-specific threshold in database.	Throttle publishing if batch is going to create more records in the database than delete.	XLANG All inbound transports	Monitor queue size against respective threshold.
Process thread count exceeds a particular threshold.	Throttle publishing. Throttle delivery. Indicate service to reduce thread-pool size.	XLANG All transports	Monitor threads per CPU.
Number of messages delivered to a service class exceeds a particular threshold count.	Throttle delivery.	XLANG All outbound transports	This is needed for send port throttling where the EPM expects only a limited number of messages at a time.

To perform this auto-throttling, the server uses the configurable parameters detailed in Table 11-5.

22. Copyright © 2006 by Microsoft Corporation. Reprinted with permission from Microsoft Corporation.

Table 11-5. *BizTalk Server 2006 Auto-Throttling Parameters (Wasznicky, 2006)*[23]

Name	Type	Description	Default Value	Min Value	Max Value
Message Delivery Throttling Configuration					
Sample-space size	Long	Number of samples that are used for determining the rate of the message delivery to all service classes of the host. This parameter is used to determine whether the samples collected for applying rate-based throttling are valid or not. If the number of samples collected is lower than the sample size, the samples are discarded because the system is running under a low load and hence no throttling may be required. Thus this value should be at par with a reasonable rate at which messages can be consumed under a medium load. For example, if the system is expected to process at 100 docs per second in a medium load, then this parameter should be set to (100 × sample window duration in seconds). If the value is set too low, the system may overthrottle on low load. If the value is too high, there may not be enough samples for this technique to be effective. **Zero indicates rate-based message delivery throttling is disabled**.	100	0	N/A
Sample-space window	Long	Duration of the sliding time window (in milliseconds) within which samples will be considered for calculation of rate. **Zero indicates rate-based message delivery throttling is disabled**.	15,000	1,000	N/A
Overdrive factor	Long	Percent factor by which the system will try to overdrive the input. That is, if the output rate is 200 per second and the overdrive factor is 125%, the system will allow up to 250 (200 × 125%) per second to be passed as input before applying rate-based throttling. A smaller value will cause a very conservative throttling and may lead to overthrottling when load is increased, whereas a higher value will try to adapt to the increase in load quickly, at the expense of slight underthrottling.	125	100	N/A
Maximum delay	Long	Maximum delay (in milliseconds) imposed for message delivery throttling. The actual delay imposed is a factor of how long the throttling condition persists and the severity of the particular throttling trigger. **Zero indicates message delivery throttling is completely disabled**.	300,000	0	N/A

Continued

Table 11-5. *Continued*

Name	Type	Description	Default Value	Min Value	Max Value
Message Publishing Throttling Configuration					
Sample-space size	Long	Number of samples that are used for determining the rate of the message publishing by the service classes. This parameter is used to determine whether the samples collected for applying rate-based throttling are valid or not. If the number of samples collected is lower than the sample size, the samples are discarded because the system is running under a low load, and hence no throttling may be required. Thus this value should be at par with a reasonable rate at which messages can be consumed under a medium load. For example, if the system is expected to publish 100 docs per second in a medium load, this parameter should be set to (100 × sample window duration in seconds). If the value is set too low, then the system may overthrottle on low load. If the value is too high, there may not be enough samples for this technique to be effective. **Zero indicates rate-based message publishing throttling is disabled.**	100	0	N/A
Sample-space window	Long	Duration of the sliding time window (in milliseconds) within which samples will be considered for calculation of rate. **Zero indicates rate-based message publishing throttling is disabled.**	15,000	1,000	N/A
Overdrive factor	Long	Percent factor by which the system will try to overdrive the input. That is, if the output rate is 200 per second and the overdrive factor is 125%, the system will allow up to 250 (200 × 125%) per second to be passed as input before applying rate-based throttling. A smaller value will cause a very conservative throttling and may lead to overthrottling when load is increased, whereas a higher value will try to adapt to the increase in load quickly, at the expense of slight underthrottling.	125	100	N/A
Maximum delay	Long	Maximum delay (in milliseconds) imposed for message publishing throttling. The actual delay imposed is a factor of how long the throttling condition persists and the severity of the particular throttling trigger. **Zero indicates message publishing throttling is completely disabled.**	300,000	0	N/A

Name	Type	Description	Default Value	Min Value	Max Value
Other Configuration and Thresholds					
Delivery queue size	Long	Size of the in-memory queue that the host maintains as a temporary placeholder for delivering messages. Messages for the host are dequeued and placed in this in-memory queue before finally delivering to the service classes. Setting a large value can improve low-latency scenarios since more messages will be proactively dequeued. However, if the messages are large, the messages in the delivery queue would consume memory and hence a low queue size would be desirable for large message scenarios to avoid excessive memory consumption. The host needs to be restarted for this change to take effect.	100	1	N/A
Database session threshold	Long	Maximum number of concurrent database sessions (per CPU) allowed before throttling begins. Note that the idle database sessions in the common per-host session pool do not add to this count, and this check is made strictly on the number of sessions actually being used by the host. This is disabled by default and may be enabled if the database server is low end compared to the host servers. **Zero indicates session-based throttling is disabled.**	0	0	N/A
System memory threshold	Long	Maximum system-wide physical memory usage allowed before throttling begins. This threshold can be presented either in absolute value in MB or in percent-available format. A value of less than 100 indicates a percent value. Throttling based on this factor is equivalent to yielding to other processes in the system that consume physical memory. **Zero indicates system memory-based throttling is disabled.**	0	0	N/A

Continued

Table 11-5. *Continued*

Name	Type	Description	Default Value	Min Value	Max Value
Process memory threshold	Long	Maximum process memory (in MB) allowed before throttling begins. This threshold can be presented either in absolute value in MB or in percent-available format. A value of less than 100 indicates a percent value, and when a percent value is specified, the actual MB limit is dynamically computed based on the total virtual memory that the host can grow to (limited by the amount of free physical memory and page file; and on 32-bit systems, this is further limited by the 2GB address space). The user-specified value is used as a guideline, and the host may dynamically self-tune this threshold value based on the memory usage pattern of the process. This value should be set to a low value for scenarios having large memory requirement per message. Setting a low value will kick in throttling early on and prevent a memory explosion within the process. **Zero indicates process-memory-based throttling is disabled.**	25%	0	
Thread threshold	Long	Maximum number of threads in the process (per CPU) allowed before throttling begins. The user-specified value is used as a guideline, and the host may dynamically self-tune this threshold value based on the memory usage pattern of the process. The thread-based throttling is disabled by default. In scenarios where excessive load can cause an unbounded thread growth (e.g., custom adapter creates a thread for each message), this should be enabled. **Zero indicates thread-count-based throttling is disabled.**	0	0	N/A
Message count in database threshold	Long	Maximum number of unprocessed messages in the database (aggregated over all Messageboxes). This factor essentially controls how many records will be allowed in the destination queue(s) before throttling begins. In addition to watching the destination queues, the host also checks the size of the spool table and the tracking-data tables and ensures they do not exceed a certain record count (by default, 10 times the message-count threshold). **Zero indicates database-size-based throttling is disabled.**	50,000	0	N/A

Name	Type	Description	Default Value	Min Value	Max Value
In-process message threshold	Long	Maximum number of in-memory in-flight messages (per CPU) allowed before message delivery is throttled. In-process messages are those that are handed off to the transport manager/XLANG engine, but not yet processed. The user-specified value is used as a guideline and the host may dynamically self-tune this threshold value based on the memory usage pattern of the process. In scenarios where the transport may work more efficiently with fewer messages at a time, this value should be set to a low value. **Zero indicates in-process message-count-based throttling is disabled.**	1,000	0	N/A

APPENDIX

■ ■ ■

Bibliography

Flanders, Jon. "Per-Instance pipeling—Tool for BizTalk Server 2004." Jon Flanders' Blog: BizTalk and Windows Workflow Foundation, 2005. www.masteringbiztalk.com/blogs/jon/PermaLink,guid,2f6500ae-d832-495f-92a3-f7032ef317ca.aspx.

Foreman, Angus and Andy Nash. "Developing Integration Solutions with BizTalk Server 2004." MSDN, 2004. http://msdn.microsoft.com/library/default.asp?url=/library/en-us/BTS_2004WP/html/ffda72df-5aec-4a1b-b97a-ac98635e81dc.asp.

GotDotNet.Com. "BizUnit Workspace Release Package Documentation." Microsoft Corporation, 2005. Downloaded from www.gotdotnet.com/workspaces/workspace.aspx?id=85ef830b-5903-4872-8071-4d4123a5553b.

GotDotNet.Com. "BizTalk Server Pipeline Component Wizard: Workspace Home." Microsoft Corporation, 2004. www.gotdotnet.com/Workspaces/Workspace.aspx?id=1d4f7d6b-7d27-4f05-a8ee-48cfcd5abf4a.

Hall, Matt. "BizTalk 2006—Introduction to Error Handling." Matt Hall's Blog, 2006. http://blogs.conchango.com/matthall/archive/2005/07/28/1894.aspx.

Hohpe, Gregor and Bobby Woolf. *Enterprise Integration Patterns.* Boston, MA: Addison-Wesley Publishing, 2004.

Meier, J.D., et al. "Improving .NET Application Performance and Scalability." MSDN, 2004. http://msdn.microsoft.com/library/default.asp?url=/library/en-us/dnpag/html/scalenet.asp.

Microsoft. "BizTalk Server Business Rules Framework." Microsoft Corporation, 2003. Downloaded from http://download.microsoft.com/download/e/6/f/e6fcf394-e03e-4e15-bd80-8c1c127e88e7/BTBusRul.doc.

Microsoft. "BizTalk Server Framework 2.0: Document and Message Specification." Microsoft Corporation, 2001. www.microsoft.com/biztalk/techinfo/whitepapers/2000/framwork20.mspx.

Microsoft. "BizTalk Server 2004, A Messaging Engine Overview." MSDN, 2004. http://msdn.microsoft.com/library/default.asp?url=/library/en-us/BTS_2004WP/html/1e2e50f7-6609-4eb2-a9a1-3a951700f840.asp.

Microsoft. "BizTalk Server 2006 Documentation." MSDN, 2006. Downloaded from http://msdn.microsoft.com/biztalk/ref/default.aspx.

Microsoft. "BizTalk Server 2006 Runtime Improvements." Microsoft Corporation, 2006. Downloaded from http://download.microsoft.com/download/1/a/6/1a67c784-8802-4e7e-a3bf-2772c34bb4ae/BizTalkServer2006_Runtime.doc.

Microsoft. "Integration Patterns." MSDN, 2004. http://msdn.microsoft.com/library/default.asp?url=/library/en-us/dnpag/html/intpatt.asp.

Microsoft. "Microsoft BizTalk Pricing and Licensing." Microsoft Corporation, 2006. www.microsoft.com/biztalk/howtobuy/default.mspx.

Microsoft. "Microsoft.BizTalk.Component.Interop Namespace." MSDN, 2004. http://msdn.microsoft.com/library/default.asp?url=/library/en-us/sdk/htm/frlrfmicrosoftbiztalkcomponentinteropipipelinecontextmemberstopic.asp.

Microsoft. "Microsoft.BizTalk.Component.Utilities Namespace." MSDN, 2004. http://msdn.microsoft.com/library/default.asp?url=/library/en-us/sdk/htm/frlrfmicrosoftbiztalkcomponentinteropipipelinecontextmemberstopic.asp.

Microsoft. "Microsoft.BizTalk.Message.Interop Namespace." MSDN, 2004. http://msdn.microsoft.com/library/default.asp?url=/library/en-us/sdk/htm/frlrfmicrosoftbiztalkmessageinteropibasemessagememberstopic.asp.

Microsoft. "Microsoft SQL Server Pricing and Licensing." Microsoft Corporation, 2005. www.microsoft.com/sql/howtobuy/default.mspx.

Microsoft. "Team Development with Visual Studio .NET and Visual SourceSafe." MSDN, 2004. http://msdn.microsoft.com/library/default.asp?url=/library/en-us/dnbda/html/tdlg_ch1.asp.

Microsoft. "Understanding BizTalk Server Performance, BizTalk Server Performance." MSDN blog, 2005. http://blogs.msdn.com/biztalkperformance/archive/2005/04/07/406343.aspx.

Moons, Jonathan. "BizTalk Business Rules Engine Quick Tips." Microsoft Corporation, 2005.

Moran, Chris. "Does Your Project Need a Rule Engine: Separating the Business Rules from the Application Logic." *Java Development Journal*, retrieved June 2, 2006. http://java.sys-con.com/read/45082.htm.

Northrup, Tony. "Performance Tuning a .NET Framework Deployment." MSDN, 2006. http://msdn.microsoft.com/netframework/technologyinfo/infrastructure/tuning/default.aspx.

Nyswonger, Luke. "The QuickStart Guide to Learning BizTalk Server 2004." MSDN blog, 2004. http://blogs.msdn.com/luke/articles/380519.aspx.

Summers, Jonathan. "Error Handling in BizTalk 2006." Jonathan Summers' Blog, 2005. http://dallas.sark.com/SarkBlog/jmsummers/archive/0001/01/01/2192.aspx.

Thomas, Steven W. "Property Schema and Promoted Properties Inside Custom Pipelines for BizTalk 2004." Steven W. Thomas BizTalk Blog, 2004. www.geekswithblogs.net/sthomas/archive/2004/08/27/10301.aspx.

Wasznicky, Marty. "BizTalk 2006 Deep Dive Workshop." Microsoft Corporation, 2006.

Woodgate, Scott, Stephen Mohr, and Brian Loesgen. *Microsoft BizTalk Server 2004 Unleashed.* Indianapolis, IN: SAMS, 2005.

Xi, William. "Implementation Guide of BizTalk's Business Rules." Microsoft Corporation, 2006.

Index

C

F

G

N

O

S

T

U

V

W